THE SEAGULL

Essays

Fourth Edition

edited by Joseph Kelly

College of Charleston

W. W. NORTON & COMPANY
Independent Publishers Since 1923

W. W. Norton & Company has been independent since its founding in 1923, when William Warder Norton and Mary D. Herter Norton first published lectures delivered at the People's Institute, the adult education division of New York City's Cooper Union. The firm soon expanded its program beyond the Institute, publishing books by celebrated academics from America and abroad. By midcentury, the two major pillars of Norton's publishing program—trade books and college texts—were firmly established. In the 1950s, the Norton family transferred control of the company to its employees, and today—with a staff of five hundred and hundreds of trade, college, and professional titles published each year—W. W. Norton & Company stands as the largest and oldest publishing house owned wholly by its employees.

Copyright © 2021, 2016, 2008, 2002 by W. W. Norton & Company, Inc.

All rights reserved.

Printed in the United States of America.

Since this page cannot legibly accommodate all the copyright notices, the Permissions Acknowledgments constitute an extension of the copyright page.

Manufacturing: LSC Communications, Crawfordsville.
Book design: Chris Welch.
Production manager: Jeremy Burton.

Names: Kelly, Joseph, 1962- editor.
Title: The seagull book of essays / edited by Joseph Kelly, College of Charleston.
Other titles: Seagull reader. Essays
Description: Fourth edition. | New York, N.Y. : W.W. Norton & Company, [2021] | Previous editions published under the title The seagull reader: Essays. | Includes bibliographical references.
Identifiers: LCCN 2020051054 | **ISBN 9780393428155 (paperback)** | ISBN 9780393538373 (epub)
Subjects: LCSH: American essays. | English essays. | College readers.
Classification: LCC PS682 .S43 2021 | DDC 808.84—dc23
LC record available at https://lccn.loc.gov/2020051054

W. W. Norton & Company, Inc., 500 Fifth Avenue, New York, N.Y. 10110
www.wwnorton.com
W. W. Norton & Company Ltd., 15 Carlisle Street, London W1D 3BS

1 2 3 4 5 6 7 8 9 0

✶

Contents

• New to this edition

• New to this edition

• New to this edition

• New to this edition

✶

Acknowledgments

I would like to credit the help of fellow teachers who have advised me either on my own essay courses or on this manuscript, especially Susan Farrell, Julia Eichelberger, and John Ruszkiewicz. I would also like to thank my colleagues at W. W. Norton, whose steady and careful work deserves much of the credit for the Seagull Books: Sarah Touborg, Emma Peters, Linda Feldman, Jeremy Burton, Joy Cranshaw, Katie Bolger, Cooper Wilhelm, Thomas Persano, and Elizabeth Trammell. Finally, I want to acknowledge the support of Hannah and Owen Kelly, and Spencer Jones.

Along with the publisher, I am happy to thank the following for their assistance as we prepared this book:

For the fourth edition: Linda Barro (East Central University), Lorraine Dubuisson (Middle Georgia State), Wendy Harrison (Abraham Baldwin Agricultural College), Susan Henderson (East Central University), Kara Lybarger-Monson (Moorpark College), Heather Marcovitch (Red Deer College), Rachel McWhorter (St. Charles Community College), Benjamin Railton (Fitchburg State), Laurie Rodrigues (University of La Verne), and Steve Yarborough (Bellevue College).

For the third edition: Troy Appling (Florida Gateway College), Jason Brown (Herkimer Community College), Patrick Callan (Monroe Community College), William Bedford Clark (Texas A&M University), Paul Cockeram (Harrisburg Area Community College), Linda DeFelice (Glouster Community College), James Donahue (SUNY Potsdam), Michael Given (Stephen F. Austin

State University), Anthony Holsten (Pitt Community College), Laura Howes (University of Tennessee), Betty LaFace (Bainbridge College), Alison Langdon (Western Kentucky University), Luke Leonard (Brevard Community College), Mary McKinlay (University of Dubuque), John Morillo (North Carolina State University), Roxanna Pisiak (SUNY Morrisville), Keri Sanburn Behr (Marylhurst University), Ritu Sharma (Lake Erie College), Amie Siedman (Bainbridge College), Kenneth Untiedt (Stephen F. Austin State University), and Deborah Zeringue (Florida Gateway College).

For the first and second editions: Judith Allen-Leventhal (College of Southern Maryland), Amy Amendt-Raduege (Marquette University), Sonja Andrus (Collin College), Michael Antonucci (Marquette University), Janet M. Atwill (University of Tennessee), Kathleen Baca (Dona Ana Branch Community College), Nancy Barendse (Charleston Southern University), William Beaumont (Collin County Community College), Linda Bennett (Collin County Community College), Brittain A. Blair (Southeastern Illinois College), D. Brickey (Charleston Southern University), John Briggs (University of California, Riverside), Gloria Brooks (Tyler Junior College), Stuart Brown (New Mexico State University), Sean A. Brumfield (Chattahoochee Technical College), Stephen Carroll (Santa Clara University), Michele Clingman (College of the Southwest), Elizabeth L. Cobb (Chapman University), Linda Connell (New Mexico Junior College), Kathleen Davies (Ohio University, Chillicothe) Carol Bunch Davis (Texas A&M Galveston), Debra Dew (University of Colorado, Colorado Springs), Shari Dinkins (University of Southern Indiana), Patrick A. Dolan Jr. (University of Iowa), James Drake (University of Southern Indiana), Thomas Durkin (Marquette University), Marilyn Edwards (Athens Technical College), John Farnsworth (Santa Clara University), Tyler Farrell (University of Dubuque), Susan Felch (Calvin College), Edward Geist (University of Bridgeport), Nate Gordon (Kishwaukee College), William Gorski (University of Southern California), Kathy Greenwood (New Mexico State University, Carlsbad), Susan Grimland (Collin County Community College), Bruce Gronbeck (University of Iowa), Loren Gruber (Missouri Valley College), Ann

H. Guess (Alvin Community College), Judy Harris (Tomball College), J. A. Hayden (University of Tampa), Judith Hebb (Atlanta Christian College), Audrey A. Herbrich (Blinn College), Lisa Hernandez (St. Edward's University), Sharon Hileman (Sul Ross State University), Lynda James (Collin County Community College), Robert Johnson (Midwestern State University), T. R. Johnson (Tulane University), Emily Schuering Jones (John Wood Community College), Maria Keaton (Marquette University), Robert Kinsley (Ohio University), Carol Klees-Starks (Marquette University), Janna Knittel (St. Cloud State University), Katheryn Laborde (Xavier University), John Larkin (Castleton State College), Todd Lieber (Simpson College), Trudy Fortun Lohr (Marquette University), Wendy Lym (St. Edwards/Independent Scholar), Giny Brown Machann (Blinn Junior College), George Manner (Santa Fe Community College), Terry Mathias (Southeastern Illinois College), Linda Matteson (Alvin Community College), Jill McCartney (Southwest Minnesota State University), Ruth McClain (Ohio University, Chillicothe), Ryan Meany (University of Tampa), Dominic Micer (University of Southern Indiana), Joyce M. Miller (Collin College), Claudia Milstead (Missouri Valley College), Laura Moe (Ohio University, Zanesville), Bridget Moore (Tyler Junior College), Jason Nado (Marquette University), John Netland (Calvin College), Stacy Oberle (Blinn College), Chris Partida (North Harris College), David Phillips (Charleston Southern University), Dee Preteau (Southwest Minnesota State University), Stella Price (Gordon College), Mary Reilly (St. Edward's University), Donald R. Riccomini (Santa Clara University), Pam Rittof (John Wood Community College), Ray Rotella (Ohio University, Zanesville), Beverly G. Six (Sul Ross State University), Audell Shelburne (University of Mary Hardin-Baylor), Beth Shelton (Paris Junior College), Bethany Sinnott (Catawba College), Andy Solomon (University of Tampa), Helen Strait (Southwest Texas Junior College), Jacob Stratman (Marquette University), Michael Suwak (College of Southern Maryland), Elizabeth Taylor (Brown University), David Urban (Calvin College), Martha Van Cise (Berry College), Robin Visel (Furman University), Kathleen Volk (Marquette University), Rebecca T. Watson (Midland College), Wendy Weaver (Marquette University), Jeanna White (East Texas Baptist University), Jennifer

Willacker (Marquette University), Joanne Williams (Olivet College), Linda Woodson (University of Texas, San Antonio), Scott Yarbrough (Charleston Southern University), Delores Zumwalt (Collin County Community College).

INTRODUCTION

How to Read Essays

We might begin with the basic question, *What is an essay?* This book calls itself an anthology of essays, but that's a loose use of the term. When essays were first invented by Michel de Montaigne in 1580, they were shortish, thoughtful, exploratory treatments of a single subject. Montaigne wrote essays on just about every subject you can imagine: cannibals, books, drunkenness, the education of children, liars, smells, and more. The writing was conversational and informal. Montaigne tried to purge his mind of preconceptions so he could look at each subject objectively and honestly. He wanted to draw his conclusions from reason alone. The earliest essayists were intelligent nonexperts who looked at their subjects afresh, trying not to be influenced by previous writers or by society's prejudices.

Some of the selections in this book follow that classic form of the essay pretty well. In "Evaluation" from *Nickel and Dimed*, for instance, Barbara Ehrenreich (see p. 546) sounds a lot like a modern version of Michel de Montaigne. She's writing about economics, but her academic training was in biology. Readers see a thoughtful, intelligent person trying to get to the bottom of a controversial subject. And, though she cites expert economists, Ehrenreich is not really poking her head into their specialized conversations; she's talking to other thoughtful nonexperts. About half of the selections in this book are like that—they're intended for a general audience. But the other half were written for particular groups of readers. A trade organization's resolution is meant for people within that trade; a government report is for people who design public policy; academic articles are for scholars in a particular field. For example, in her essay, "Sponsors of Literacy" (see p. 98), Deborah Brandt writes: "The field of writing studies has had much to say about individual literacy development. Especially in the last quarter of the twentieth century, we have theorized, researched, critiqued, debated . . . the literate potentials of ordinary citizens." The "we" she mentions is not the general reading public; it is a relatively small group of professionals in "the field of writing studies."

Whether it was written for general readers or a more specialized audience, each selection in this volume is an example of **rhetoric.** Almost 2,400 years ago, the philosopher Aristotle defined rhetoric as the art of persuasion. To **persuade** means to change someone's opinion or behavior. Dozens, if not hundreds, of the verbal messages we see each day are rhetorical: they are designed to influence us, to get us to buy Pepsi rather than Coke or to abandon soda altogether; to dislike some actor; to be proud of our country; to exercise more; to go to a party rather than study for an exam; to like a Twitter post; to click on this; to swipe right. You already know how to interpret and produce these types of messages, so, whether you're aware of it or not, you're a rhetorician. You've already internalized many of the elements of rhetoric. You might not know the names of those elements, just as you don't need to know the parts of speech to speak and understand English or your first language. But learning the rules of grammar will probably improve your speech and writing.

The next section, which explains the "rules" of argument, will teach you how to recognize, analyze, and evaluate arguments. Once you understand these elements, you'll be a much better judge of other people's arguments. You'll be less susceptible to manipulation. You'll learn how to test evidence. With practice, you'll be able to evaluate whether an argument is persuasive or unpersuasive, and why. And when you apply this knowledge to your own arguments, you will persuade people more effectively.

Some of the terminology will seem arcane and even a bit daunting. And, if you're like most people, you'll find it pretty hard to use this grammar at first. That can be frustrating. Stick with it.

Argument

Why do we argue?

Let me begin with a story.

On a dark winter night in the fragrant hills of Tuscany, Galileo peered at the stars, not with his bare eyes, as had every human being since before recorded history, but through a newly invented telescope. He discovered two shocking facts: that the moon has mountains, just like Earth, and that Jupiter has moons. Two months later, in March 1610, he published his famous book, *The Starry Messenger*, which revealed the telescope's evidence that Earth is not the center of the universe: that, in fact, Earth orbits the sun. The book made Galileo famous, and it is remembered today not only for its revolutionary ideas about astronomy but also because Galileo used a new way of thinking, what we call today the "scientific method," which ignored holy scripture and doctrine. In fact, *The Starry Messenger* contradicted orthodox interpretations of the Bible, which got Galileo in trouble with the Inquisition, the prosecuting arm of the Roman Catholic Church. Years later, in 1632, Galileo reasserted his opinion, and the Inquisition interrogated him again, threatened him with torture, censored his writing, and sentenced him to house arrest for the remainder of his life. He was forced to kneel, confess his heresy, and declare his wish that his books should convince no one to stop believing that the sun revolves around an immovable Earth. An apocryphal tale has Galileo, as he finished making his coerced confession, mumbling, "And yet it moves." In other words, no confession would change the scientific fact: Earth orbits the sun. That bit of the story is probably not true, but it captures the spirit of the affair. No matter what church doctrine said, the scientific truth was not altered.

1. Academic Discourse

In the long term, of course, Galileo's arguments were vindicated and church doctrine was proven false.[1] That's because he was part of a whole community of people attracted to the scientific way of thinking. Galileo exchanged letters with some of them, like astronomer Johannes Kepler in Prague, discussing their observations of nature—their data—and the conclusions they were drawing from what they observed. It was the beginning of what historians call a "republic of letters," an international group of intellectuals who talked to each other through letters, pamphlets, and books. Through these conversations, Galileo and others like him throughout Europe began developing the norms of modern scientific research—the rules of scientific discourse. **Discourse** simply refers to the network of all of these verbal communications. Arguments had to be based on observations of nature or data from experiments:

1. In 1992, the Catholic Church's Pontifical Academy of Sciences formally acknowledged that Galileo was right.

nothing from the Bible was allowed. When someone felt they'd discovered some law of nature—for instance, that in a vacuum all objects fall at the same rate—they wrote up their reasoning and sent it round to persuade their fellow scientists they were right. When Galileo wrote *The Starry Messenger*, he was trying to persuade people like Kepler, who used Galileo's findings to figure out that planets follow elliptical, not circular, orbits around the sun. That's how a discourse builds up knowledge collaboratively—people in a community write arguments to each other, and each persuasive argument forms the basis for further developments.

The republic of letters was one kind of community, one with no formal membership requirements. But there were some formal communities or "societies" in the seventeenth century. Galileo belonged to a formal group of mathematicians, physicists, physicians, etc., who called themselves the Lincean Academy. Founded in 1603, this group was one of the first "learned societies," like the Royal Society (founded in England in 1660) and the American Philosophical Society (founded by Benjamin Franklin in 1743), that sprang up like weeds in the seventeenth and eighteenth centuries. Members would meet to discuss their ideas, and the societies started collecting libraries so their members could read the newest scientific books. By the nineteenth century, so many people were doing this kind of work that science branched into specialized disciplines, each with its own society. Naturalists reported their observations of flora and fauna. Chemists exchanged papers with other chemists. Physicians shared their knowledge of the body. If a scientist's arguments were persuasive, their society might publish their findings so they could be recorded and distributed widely to other libraries. In this way, learned societies became the arbiter of what was and was not considered sound research. Members tailored their arguments to the society's expectations; that is, they wrote in a way to which other members of the society had become accustomed.

These societies were what linguist John Swales would much later call a **discourse community**,[2] a group of people who, because they share similar goals, have developed a way of communicating effectively with each other and a set of conventions that determines for them which

2. Composition experts began using the term "discourse community" in the 1980s. See John M. Swales, "The Concept of Discourse Community: Some Recent Personal History," *Composition Forum*, 37 (Fall 2017). Online. Accessed 12 April 2020. https://compositionforum.com/issue/37/swales-retrospective.php

arguments are and which are not persuasive. For example, here's a bit of text from the FAQ page of the American Kennel Club's website:

> **If I purchase/acquire a dog that is not from a litter produced by an FSS®-recorded sire and dam but the dog is from an acceptable registry, can I apply for FSS® recording?**
> Yes, you can apply to the FSS® by forwarding your application and fee to the AKC for review. Every application will be evaluated on its own merit. Applications for the FSS® can be downloaded from our website.

Kennel Club members will understand this bit of communication with no trouble, but if you're like me, this question and answer is a little bewildering. What does "FSS®" mean, and what's a "sire" and "dam"? I'm not a member of this discourse community, so its specialized vocabulary is foreign to me. I don't know what makes a registry "acceptable" or "unacceptable." Nevertheless, I know that "FAQ" means "Frequently Asked Questions," because I see that form of information all the time on websites I use, like that of the American Historical Association, which has its own FAQ page. So members of the American Kennel Club and I overlap in the much larger, unorganized community of website users. *That* community has developed the FAQ page as good way of communicating information.

Academic discourse communities are formal and well-regulated groups of scholars. Each discipline—history, say, or political science or electrical engineering or marketing—has its own "learned society," however formal or informal, and its own way of credentialing its members. Scholars in each different field talk to each other through scholarly journals and conference papers, and they've developed specialized vocabularies, methods of research, styles, and sometimes even their own rules of argument. The boards of editors of those journals come from the ranks of the scholars in those fields, and they act as gatekeepers: to get something published, the writer must convince those editors that the conclusions are trustworthy, given the discipline's standards of argument and evidence. That's what **peer review** means. It's a way of sifting good research from bad. Members of the writer's discourse community have examined the essay carefully and find its arguments plausible. Writing in an academic setting, then, is writing in the context of one of these specialized discourse communities, which correspond (more or less) to college majors: biology, sociology, literature, secondary education, women's studies, environmental studies, etc. The writer is trying to persuade readers in their community to believe the findings. When you pick up a scholarly essay, it's helpful to know which community of scholars produced it.

Deborah Brandt wrote her essay "Sponsors of Literacy" for members of the National Council of Teachers of English (NCTE). It was first published in the NCTE's journal, *College Composition and Communication* (*CCC*). And so, Brandt's writing mirrors the way that NCTE members talk to each other. She uses concepts and vocabulary familiar to those readers but unfamiliar to the uninitiated. What counts for evidence in *CCC* varies from what counts in a biology or philosophy journal. There are substantial differences, for instance, between how people argue in the humanities, in the social sciences, and in the physical sciences. Even within these broad divisions there will be some variation. A literary critic writes a different kind of essay than a historian, just as a marine biologist might find themselves at sea trying to follow an astrophysicist's argument.

The specialized forms of writing developed by discourse communities are called **genres**. You can think of genres as tools. They help members of a community effectively communicate with each other, which tends to mean that people outside the community, people not used to their specialized forms, can find their writing a little hard to understand. A genre defines the norms of writing: rules (both written and unwritten) that members of a discourse community use with each other. A Facebook post is a genre. If you're in the Facebook "community" you know how to read a post, but if you've never logged in, you might find the format a little difficult to interpret at first. A scholarly article is a genre, too. As you get deeper into your major in college, you'll become more and more familiar with the genre(s) that your discipline uses. It's almost like an apprenticeship. Semester by semester, you'll move from being a novice in your discipline toward membership in that community. Senior economics majors (to take one example) can read articles in economics journals that might baffle sophomores, because they've learned the vocabulary economists use to convey economic concepts, how to read and interpret statistical data, the tenets governing economic research, etc.

College writing has its own genres. Research papers, proposals, lab reports, literature reviews, profiles, blog posts, and reflection essays are all examples of genres you're likely to encounter in your college classes. Part of the hard work of being a college student is simply getting familiar with the genres of writing you're asked to produce.

Almost all academic writing—whether it's produced by students to be graded by an instructor or by scholars to be judged by editors—has a good deal of overlap. It all uses the same fundamentals of argument. In other words, all of the university disciplines together constitute one large discourse community, sometimes called "academia" or "the academy" or "higher education," and people in that community expect writing to follow certain rules of argument. Formally learning those rules will help you to understand essays written for academic readers, and it's also a critical skill that transfers to professional life outside of college.

In an academic setting, then, "argument" is not like having an argument with a friend over dinner or with a rival at a bar. Usually, it is not adversarial. One writer is not trying to defeat another. "Winning" an argument means getting other members of your community to think you're probably right. Normally, argument within academic disciplines is collaborative. Once an argument is approved by peer review, other members of the learned society tend to trust its findings—and use those findings in their own subsequent work. The result is a progressive accumulation of human knowledge. That's how we can go in a mere four centuries from Galileo's telescope, which was weaker than a pair of today's standard binoculars, to the Galileo spacecraft, which orbited Jupiter for eight years and surveyed its surface and moons up close. The answer to the question, *Why argue?* is this: virtually all human knowledge from African American studies to zoology has been generated in the forums of academic argument. The impulse to persuade other learned people that you are right is how we generate and share knowledge. We can conquer novel diseases, because researchers in the medical profession have developed ways of arguing about a vaccine's effectiveness. Schools are far better today than they were centuries ago, because professionals know how to argue about what does and does not help students learn. We might just solve climate change, because, as Elizabeth Kolbert reports in her essay, "Can Carbon-Dioxide Removal Save the World?" (p. 257), a scientist named Klaus Lackner began arguing in physics journals about removing carbon from the atmosphere.

2. Public Discourse

Have you heard of the "marketplace of ideas"? It's a concept popularized by Justice Oliver Wendell Holmes Jr. in a 1919 Supreme Court case about free speech. Holmes was an old Civil War veteran sporting a giant white, bushy, grandfatherly handlebar moustache, and he played the part of the wise elder very well. He warned people against suppressing ideas they disagree with. "[T]he best test of truth," he wrote, "is the power of the thought to get itself accepted in the competition of the market." Ideas about public affairs are not peer-reviewed by gate-keepers. They're tossed more or less indiscriminately into the marketplace of newspapers, magazines, books, television, and, increasingly, digital media. Who decides which ideas are good and which are bad? According to Holmes, you and I do. Where there's a "free trade in ideas," public opinion will tend, in the long run, to choose the good ideas and reject the bad.

The court of public opinion might be a lot bigger, less regulated, and more diverse than peer review in a learned society. But it is a forum for judgment just the same. More people will buy into the sound argument and divest from the weak argument. In a democracy, then, the entire public is itself a discourse community. In fact, some political scientists will tell you that you can only have a real "public" within a liberal democracy, where people can freely discuss policies and government. People living under a dictatorship, people who are afraid to criticize the government, people who are not free to argue about issues important to society, and people who read only a government-regulated press cannot really be called a "public," because they do not have this forum by which the people, in aggregate, can make up its mind. If the public is to form an opinion on any matter of importance, people must have their own free forum for argument. There has to be a space we call the public sphere. That's how democracy works.

We also argue, then, because that's how a free society thinks things out. Though it often looks adversarial, public argument can be seen as collaborative, like academic argument. Argument is how a community thinks. Many of the essays in this volume might have been written for a small discourse community, but they are also examples of speech in the market of ideas. Barbara Ehrenreich writing about the working class, Michelle Alexander talking about the War on Drugs, Ronald Reagan criticizing the federal government—all are trying to influence public opinion. They are all trying to pull the "mind of the country" (to borrow another phrase from Holmes) in one direction or another. Should we build a wall along the Rio Grande? What should we do about the climate disaster? Should we lower tuition for public colleges? Is decent health care a right? Should your local school district consolidate two middle schools? Should your city build a bike lane along Main Street? Should your hometown open a new landfill? Does a minimum wage help or hurt workers? We will find the best answers to those questions by listening to and judging arguments in the marketplace of ideas.

It might go without saying, then, that learning about the nuts and bolts of argument is pretty important to a democracy. "An educated, enlightened and informed population," Nelson Mandela explained, "is one of the surest ways of promoting the health of a democracy." He should know: Mandela spent twenty-seven years in prison for trying to transform South Africa into a democracy. If the people are going to reject bad ideas, if they are going to discern real news from fake news, if they are going to avoid being fooled by demagogues and fear-mongers, if they are going to see through false reasoning and resist dishonest appeals, they need to know about argument.

In the next sections, you'll begin learning the elements of argument. These skills lay the foundation of your academic reading and writing, no matter what discipline you pursue in college. Reading and writing arguments in college prepares you for your professional career. These skills also prepare you for the important role of citizenship in civil society. Not many people have the rhetorical powers you'll learn here, which makes your own responsibility greater.

Skeptical Reading

Most of the essays in this volume were written for the wide-ranging marketplace of ideas. Some of the essays were first written within a specialized discourse community, such as Brandt's essay, which was first and foremost written to be read by teachers of English composition. More than likely, you're not a member of that discourse community. But I haven't selected any essays that are so narrow in their original context that an intelligent, general reader is baffled. Even these more specialized essays, like Brandt's, circulate in the gigantic, diverse, wild and woolly market where ideas compete for public approval. This discourse community also includes you. You are a member of the jury in the court of public opinion. So, you can read every essay in this volume as if it were addressed to you. As a responsible member of the reading public, you should be **skeptical**. You should presume a writer is wrong until they convince you they are right. Don't be easily swayed. Be on guard against manipulations. Make the writer work to persuade you.

But being skeptical does not mean being closed-minded. It's all too easy in today's polarized political climate to stop listening to those who disagree with us. You can see this phenomenon in forums like Facebook, which uses algorithms to flood your "news" feed with opinions that already match your own. On social media, we usually encounter different points of view only when they're being mocked or put down. I invite you to read Emily Chamlee-Wright's essay, "The Need to Presume Good Faith" (p. 141), before you read anything else. Chamlee-Wright talks about a habit of mind that will counteract the Facebook phenomenon. You want to suspend your own prejudices so you can honestly evaluate the merits of someone else's argument.

Analyzing and Evaluating Arguments

I have spoken about the different ways the various academic disciplines argue. Each has its own genre. But all academic genres share the same fundamentals of argument. What you learn in this section applies to your own reading and writing, whether your major is in secondary education, public health, Latinx studies, or biochemistry.

When you **analyze** something, you break it down into its parts. Rhetorical analysis breaks down an instance of persuasion into its parts. Those parts divide into three categories. There's the target audience—what we'll call "readers" because we're dealing here with written rhetoric. There's the person who's doing the persuading—the speaker or writer. And there's the subject matter itself—the issue that is under discussion or debate. Each of these elements has its own rhetorical strategies—techniques that contribute to the overall success or failure to persuade. Rhetoricians call these strategies "arguments." **Pathos** or **pathetic arguments** are emotional appeals to readers. **Ethos** or **ethical arguments** are strategies related to the writer. **Logos** or **logical arguments** concern the subject or issue at hand. In an academic setting, logical arguments are by far the most important rhetorical arguments to master, so we'll spend most of our time on them. But the others should not be neglected.

1. Pathetic Arguments

Pathos refers to the emotional state of readers. They are not "arguments" in the normal sense, but rhetoricians use that term because they persuade people. Pathetic arguments can appeal to readers' pity or loathing, fear or delight, happiness, sadness, or any other emotion that words can excite. Most types of academic discourse frown on the use of pathetic arguments because emotions can so easily cloud logic. Even when discussing a volatile subject—say an essay on voter suppression in a political science journal or an article on debilitating childhood diseases in a medical journal—an emotional appeal could be a red flag. That's one reason a lot of academic writing can tend to be dry and boring. It purposely tries to avoid exciting readers' emotions. But pathetic arguments are normal in public discourse, and people writing for general readers use them all the time. When you read in the public sphere, you should be wary of your emotions. That's not to say you should suppress them or distrust them altogether. Rather, you should learn to recognize and evaluate pathetic arguments by asking your

- At what point will th and so forth?
- How did the writer e
- Are these emotional

You might wonder what I mean when I talk about "justified emotions." What makes one pathetic argument honest and another dishonest? Let's look at a passage from Martin Luther King Jr.'s "Letter from Birmingham Jail":

> [Y]ou suddenly find your tongue twisted and your speech stammering as you seek to explain to your six-year-old daughter why she can't go to the public amusement park that has just been advertised on television, and see tears welling up in her eyes when she is told that Funtown is closed to colored children, and see ominous

> clouds of inferiority beginning to form in her little mental sky, and see her beginning to distort her personality by developing an unconscious bitterness toward white people. (see pp. 551–52)

Imagine you're one of the white "moderates" who were Dr. King's primary readers. You don't agree with segregation, you sympathize with Dr. King's demand for equality, but you think there's no great hurry to act. You are afraid that events will move so quickly that they will upset society. You fear social upheaval. King's story triggers your emotions. You sympathize with the father, whose powerlessness is exposed to his child, and you feel for the young girl, who is hurt as she discovers what it means to be Black living under white supremacy. Eliciting emotion helped Dr. King convince his white moderate readers that America urgently needed to be integrated. He put a human face on the abstract concept of segregation.

But was it an honest emotional appeal? In this case, the pathetic argument is an **anecdote**—a single example meant to represent what segregation does to all people who suffer it. We might be unmoved by an abstraction like this: *segregation distorts the personalities of millions of people.* But when we see the suffering of one six-year-old girl, we're moved to tears and then, maybe, to action. Anecdotes are honest to the degree that the particular example accurately represents the general experience. Is this girl's case unusual, or have millions of African Americans experienced their own personal version of her dispiriting epiphany? Because Dr. King's emotional example does accurately represent the Black experience of segregation, we'd conclude that this is a responsible use of a pathetic argument. (I'll talk more about anecdotes in the section on inductive arguments.)

Be on your guard whenever an essay appeals to readers' emotions. Not all writers are as honorable as Dr. King. In fact, demagogues love to use pathetic arguments. That's what demagoguery does: incite strong emotion to compensate for a lack of logic. More often than not, demagogues elicit fear and anger, which are especially effective ways to distract readers from bad reasoning. In our times, demagogues are stirring up all sorts of fears, trying to get people to do things they wouldn't otherwise do. Caution is your watchword.

2. Ethical Arguments

Rhetorical strategies regarding the writer are called ethos or ethical arguments. Again, these are not "arguments" in the way that word is commonly used. Ethical arguments are the way writers present themselves to readers, especially the impression readers get of their moral character.

When someone gives a speech before a live audience, how she dresses, how she stands on the podium, the tenor of her voice, her gestures, what she says about herself, how she treats her opponents—all contribute to the audience's impression of her character. A high school student apply [illegible] basketball shorts and [illegible] interpret those cloth[illegible] probably think that t[illegible] county council who [illegible] not want to come dre[illegible] that his interests are those of bankers, not farmers. Dress, grooming, posture, voice, gestures, and the like all make their impressions, which in turn can help or hurt persuasion.

Writers don't have the visual or aural cues that a speaker uses because a reader cannot see or hear the writer. Even so, every essay paints a picture of its writer. Take, for example, Michelle Alexander's Introduction to *The New Jim Crow*. She says in her fourth paragraph, "I reached the conclusions presented in this book reluctantly." That single sentence tells readers that Alexander is not the kind of person who jumps to conclusions. She fits my description of the skeptical but open-minded thinker. She'll follow the evidence to its logical conclusion, even when it contradicts her own preconceptions. Those are always good characteristics to convey. But Alexander's ethical arguments go even further. Alexander tells readers that she was elated when Barack Obama was first elected president in 2008, that she worked for the Racial Justice Project of the American Civil Liberties Union, that she does not consider herself a radical, and that she is a lawyer. All of these details help persuade her readers that they can trust what she says: they lend her credibility with those she sees as her primary readers: liberals. She slips in another important detail: "I was rushing to catch the bus," she writes, when "[I] noticed a sign stapled to a telephone pole." She's talking about when she first encountered the concept of the "New" Jim Crow, but I'm interested now in that detail about the bus. I love that. It suggests a certain humility. Alexander might be a lawyer, the detail implies, but she's not some Mercedes-driving fancy suit who observes injustice through the window of her high-rise office.

How writers establish their credibility depends, of course, on the readers they are trying to reach. Telling readers that she once worked for the ACLU might give Alexander credit with liberals, but what if she were trying to persuade conservatives, who tend to view the ACLU with suspicion? In that case, she might talk a little more about how skeptical she was when she first heard these criticisms of police, prosecutors, and prisons. She would want to emphasize how hard she resisted those assertions, how she insisted on convincing logical arguments. If Alexander shares some common ground with conservatives, she might sneak that into her discussion. People are naturally more open-minded when they are listening to someone within their group, with whom they share common ground, so to speak, than when they are listening to someone who seems to be an outsider. (I'll discuss later how writers use **common ground** effectively in their deductive arguments.)

When you're evaluating someone's ethical arguments, you should answer questions like these:

- What authority does the writer claim? Are they an expert?
- Do they know more about the subject than their readers (or I) do?
- Why should readers (or why should I) listen to what they have to say?
- Is the writer trustworthy?
- Is the writer reasonable?
- Is the writer careful and precise when they cite their sources?
- Will readers (or do I) like the writer? Would readers (or I) be happy to meet and talk with them?

The headnotes to each essay might help you answer some of these questions, and some famous writers can count on their celebrity to supply an image of their moral character. Most people have preformed impressions of someone like James Baldwin, for instance, or the Dalai Lama. But even famous writers will use their essays to convince readers that they are reasonable, trustworthy, and likeable and that they belong to the readers' community.

Applying those criteria is not a precise science. It's very subjective, and judgments tend to fall somewhere on a spectrum. So rhetoricians do not say an inductive argument is true or false; we say it is **strong** or **weak**. My own assessment of Ehrenreich's argument is that it's pretty strong, but it could be even stronger if she told readers how they could verify the figures from the Economic Policy Institute. That would make me more confident that the data are accurate.

3b. Deductive Arguments

Deduction is top-down reasoning. You don't begin with facts: you begin with a presumption, then add facts, which leads to a conclusion. Every deductive argument has three parts: major premise(s), minor premise(s), and a conclusion.

Major premises tend to be categorical statements: a claim that is applied to everything within a category. The Declaration of Independence begins with the assertion that all men are created equal and that they possess the unalienable rights of life, liberty, and the pursuit of happiness. These claims apply to all humanity—a pretty large category. Major premises tend to look like what we might call "belief" statements or presumptions, and indeed, the Declaration says that these assertions are "truths" that "we hold" or believe.

By contrast, **minor premises** are statements that apply to a particular case within the category of the major premise. For example, ever since Congress adopted the Declaration in 1776, people from Benjamin Franklin to Martin Luther King Jr. to Michelle Alexander have pointed out that African Americans are part of "all men" or humanity. That's a statement of fact about a case within the category. Minor premises tend to look like statements of fact that can be pretty conclusively verified or disproven.

You can see where these particular premises are logically leading: to the conclusion that African Americans should enjoy rights equal to white Americans. Just as in inductive arguments, the **conclusion** is the payoff—what the writer wants to persuade readers to believe or do.

i. Analyzing deductive arguments To practice analyzing and evaluating deduction, let's look at an argument that's more complex. Here's my summary of Michelle Alexander's argument in her Introduction to *The New Jim Crow*:

> Racial caste systems should be illegal—they clearly violate the American ideal of equality expressed in the Declaration of Independence and later written into the Constitution. That's why the civil rights legislation and court decisions in the 1950s and 1960s struck down Jim Crow laws. Today's so-called legal War on Drugs is just another version of Jim Crow, a system of laws that turn African Americans into an inferior racial caste. So we need to do again what we did in the 1950s and 1960s: repeal the War on Drugs.

Usually, deductive arguments are harder to analyze than inductive arguments. How do we break this complex argument down to its parts? A helpful trick is to paraphrase the argument using "because" and "therefore":

> BECAUSE racial caste systems violate the Declaration of Independence and the U.S. Constitution, and
> BECAUSE the War on Drugs is a racial caste system,
> THEREFORE, we should repeal the War on Drugs.

The first "because" statement is a categorical statement about racial caste systems, so we'd call it a major premise. The second "because" statement asserts a fact about a specific case, the War on Drugs, so that's the minor premise. The "therefore" statement is the logical conclusion, almost as if the deductive argument were a mathematical formula: when you put the premises together they yield the conclusion.

Notice that my analysis did not include everything in the original argument. You want to strip a deductive argument down to its bare essentials this way. Then you can see that the other material—in this case, the mention of legislation and court decisions in the 1950s and 1960s—helps persuade readers that the major premise is true. Similarly, the comparison between Jim Crow and the War on Drugs supports the assertion that the latter is a caste system. In both cases, that material is support for the premises rather than an essential part of the argument.

ii. Evaluating deductive arguments The next step, evaluating the argument, is much easier. First you test **validity**. Philosophers have complex, technical ways of testing validity, but in rhetoric it's usually enough to trust your own common sense. I suggested above that the argument is like a mathematical equation, and that's a good way to think of it: ask yourself, *When I cross the major premise with the minor premise, do they equal the conclusion?* I've found with my own students that if they simply ask themselves, *Does the conclusion follow logically from the premises?* more often than not they judge correctly. Your inner sense of logic will steer you right most of the time. In this case, you'll probably say that the argument is valid: The two statements taken together—that caste systems violate the Declaration and Constitution, and that the War on Drugs institutes and maintains a caste system—lead logically to the conclusion that the War on Drugs violates the Declaration and the Constitution. Who readers are should not matter with validity. Everyone should judge validity the same way, and if one set of readers thinks an argument is valid and another thinks it is invalid, one of them is wrong.

Who is reading the argument is very important in the second test, the **truth** test. I'm using "truth" as a technical, rhetorical term: it means simply that the readers agree with the argument's premises. What's true for one group of readers might seem false to another. For example, most people will accept as true the major premise of Alexander's argument—that the Declaration and Constitution are incompatible with a racial caste system. The minor premise is more controversial. In fact, Alexander herself understands this: she explains that people who have been through the criminal justice system tend to believe the War on Drugs is designed to keep Black Americans in an inferior position in our society. But other readers—even liberal readers who are sympathetic to the convict's plight—will think that premise is false. And those are the people Alexander is targeting, so she needs to do a lot of work to persuade them to agree with the minor premise. This situation is not at all unusual: in fact, it's pretty typical that the premises in a deductive argument, especially minor premises, need to be supported by other arguments—sometimes by inductive arguments. In this case, Alexander spends several chapters of her book showing readers how the War on Drugs has been waged mostly against Black Americans. She knows her overarching argument cannot succeed unless she gets readers to agree with that point.

If at the end of an argument the reader does not agree with a premise, we say that premise is **false**. If that's the case, we say the argument is **unsound**. We use the same term for validity: an invalid argument is unsound, even if the reader agrees with the premises. For a deductive argument to be **sound**, it must be both valid and true.

iii. Enthymemes You need to know about an especially slippery form of deduction called the **enthymeme**. An enthymeme is a deductive argument that leaves out one of the premises. Usually, but not always, the missing premise is the major premise. You run into enthymemes all the time. In fact, writers might leave out premises more often than they state them all plainly. Take these for example:

- You better study tonight, because tomorrow's exam is going to be really hard.
- I wouldn't go to that restaurant. Jacob got sick after eating there last week.
- You should vote for the challenger, because she's a lot smarter than the incumbent.
- If you're lonely, you should get a pet.

Each of these arguments has a conclusion and a minor premise, but none has a major premise. Let's examine the last one. The conclusion is that *you should get a pet.* One premise is stated: *you are lonely.* The major premise that validly connects the statement of fact to the conclusion is implied rather than stated. If readers are going to evaluate this enthymeme, they have to figure out what that premise would be. So your analysis of this enthymeme would look like this:

(major premise, unstated) BECAUSE pets can provide human beings with satisfying companionship, and
(minor premise) BECAUSE you are lonely,
(conclusion) THEREFORE, you should get a pet.

When you evaluate an enthymeme, it's always going to pass the validity test, because you yourself have supplied the missing premise that will lead logically to the conclusion. So all that's left is the truth test: Do you believe the premises? If you believe that pets cure loneliness, and if you believe you're lonely, you'll agree that you ought to get a pet. The argument is sound.

Dishonest but clever rhetoricians will hide a premise to fool people into believing an unsound argument. If a major premise is somewhat sketchy, a writer might decide to just leave it unstated so they can hide the argument's flaw. For example, let's take this argument: *you should vote for the challenger, because she's smarter than the incumbent.* On the surface, the argument sounds pretty reasonable, and the unwary listeners might think to themselves, "Yeah, that makes sense." But let's break it down into its parts and then evaluate it. If the argument succeeds, readers will vote for the challenger: that's the conclusion. The only premise stated is the statement of fact (minor premise) that the challenger is smarter than the incumbent. As a trained rhetorician, you know you must figure out the unstated—and perhaps purposely suppressed—categorical statement that logically connects the minor premise to the conclusion. In this case, it will be something like this: *the best candidate is always the smartest candidate* or *the smarter elected official will always provide better government* or something similar. So the analysis might look like this:

> (major premise, unstated) BECAUSE the smarter candidate is always the better officeholder, and
> (minor premise) BECAUSE the challenger is smarter than the incumbent,
> (conclusion) THEREFORE, you should vote for the challenger.

Now you can see its defect very easily. Couldn't a really smart person be corrupt and thus be worse in office? Couldn't a less-smart officeholder rely on really smart advisors and thus provide better government? What if the challenger is only very slightly smarter than the incumbent? Would that matter? And what if the smarter candidate disagrees with my own political philosophy? Isn't it more important that the candidate's vision of government matches mine? When readers actually see the major premise in this enthymeme, they'll probably decide it's false and that the argument is unsound. Political rhetoric and especially campaign rhetoric is often purposely deceptive in this way.

4. Fallacies

Just as the right ways of constructing arguments have been around for more than 2,000 years, so have the wrong ways. Often people make these mistakes because they don't know what they're doing. Sometimes people use these fallacies to deliberately hide their weak or unsound logic. Learning to identify these common fallacies will help you identify bad arguments when you read and construct better arguments when you write.

ad hominem: literally, an argument *to the person.* When purportedly refuting someone's argument, the writer actually attacks their character. For example:

> The congresswoman has proposed that we lower the deficit by increasing taxes on the top 1 percent of income earners. When considering whether or not to vote for her proposal, you should bear in mind that she has described herself as a socialist.

In this case, people are asked to reject the congresswoman's argument not because of any defect in the proposal itself but because of who she is. A person's character should not affect your evaluation of their logic. Someone's poor ethos might make you suspect their evidence, but you should judge the accuracy of their argument based on your own research, not on a smeared reputation. An ad hominem attack is a red flag alerting you to a refutation's weakness.

bandwagon appeal: readers are enticed to accept a position on an issue because it is popular: *come along with us—jump on the bandwagon!* It is a pathetic fallacy—an emotional appeal—that will often hide a false major premise. For example:

> Every serious film buff agrees that musicals are entertaining schlock. So it's a travesty that *La La Land* was nominated for best picture.

The writer tries to get readers to accept a very shaky major premise ("musicals are entertaining schlock") by suggesting they would be shallow to disagree.

either/or fallacy: also called "false choice" or "false dilemma," this fallacy is often a defective form of enthymeme. It usually presents the conclusion as the only logical action to take because its alternative is extreme and obviously unacceptable to readers. For example:

> If this city wants to balance its budget, it's got to raise taxes. The only alternative is to cut services to the bone.

The argument breaks down like this:

> (major premise, unstated) BECAUSE there are only two ways to balance a city's budget—severely cut services or raise taxes—and
> (minor premise) BECAUSE we don't want to cut services to the bone,
> (conclusion) THEREFORE, we must raise taxes.

Once the major premise is stated openly, most readers will see that premise is false: there are other ways to increase revenue besides raising taxes (user fees, federal and state grants, etc.) and other ways to cut spending (hiring freezes, travel restrictions, reduced hours, the introduction of new efficiencies, etc.). Very few situations are so uncomplex as to come down to a simple choice between X or Y.

false analogy: conclusions based on comparing one case to another. For example:

> The best way to prevent flooding from climate change in the United States is to do what the Dutch have done: build massive seawalls and gates at the mouths of our rivers and harbors.

Someone refuting this argument need only cite the many differences between topography and climatic events in the Netherlands and the United States. For example, Hurricane Harvey flooded Houston with more than forty inches of rain—which sea walls could not have prevented. Analogies in themselves are almost always weak arguments, because it's so easy to find dissimilarities between cases. Analogies should always be accompanied by more inductive evidence.

hasty generalization: an inductive argument with too narrow or insufficient evidence. For example:

> I can just look out my window and see that this city is much more prosperous today than it was ten years ago. All my friends say the same thing: houses in their neighborhoods have been renovated, their streets are in better repair, and more expensive cars sit in the driveways.

The conclusion of this argument, *this city is more prosperous than it was ten years ago*, is based on anecdotal evidence: the writer's and the writer's friends' experiences. People tend to make friends within their own socioeconomic level, so this sample of evidence is so small that it probably does not represent all the neighborhoods in the city. Generalizing from too little or unrepresentative data makes for a very weak inductive argument.

straw man argument: refuting an exaggerated or false version of someone's argument. For example:

> Person A: We shouldn't have Christmas trees in public schools because it suggests Christianity is our state religion.
> Person B: Trying to ban Christmas is downright un-American; many of the Founding Fathers were Christians, and the majority of people of this nation have been celebrating Christmas every year since 1776.

In this example, Person B is refuting something Person A never argued: that we should "ban" Christmas. A real refutation would contest the idea that erecting a Christmas tree in school is a government endorsement of a particular religion.

★

How to Write Convincing Arguments

Everyone's a rhetorician. What I said about evaluating other people's arguments is true about constructing your own: you already do it. Every day. Probably ten times a day. You made an argument when you persuaded your friend to go to the Mexican restaurant for lunch rather than the cafeteria. You made an argument when you tried to persuade your professor to give you an extension. You used argument when you wrote that history paper about the causes of World War I or that lab report in chemistry. You argued with yourself when you decided to keep studying, despite how tired you were, after you got the baby to sleep. Almost instinctively, you already know the art of persuasion.

But like any art, you get better by learning about technique and then by practicing what you've learned. It's the same as playing piano or tennis or gardening or cooking. Everyone can swing a tennis racket. Even the clumsiest of us can hit the ball over the net sometimes. But to become a good tennis player you need to learn the proper setup and follow-through, how to maximize the torque of your hips, chest, arms, and hands. It's the same with rhetoric. You don't yet know how to maximize the powers of persuasion that you already have. You're the occasional cook who can whip up some eggs or a can of soup. Now you're going to learn to fix a gourmet dinner.

Remember: before you can be a great chef, you've got to be a bad cook. Before you can play Beethoven on the piano, you've got to master "Twinkle, Twinkle, Little Star." You're going to be relatively bad at arguing before you're good at it, and the only way to get better is to learn the techniques and then practice. Sure, some natural talent might be involved. Rhetoricians like Kwame Anthony Appiah and Barbara Ehrenreich might have been born with some natural facility for arguing. But natural talent accounts for less than you might think, and you can be sure that every writer in this book was bad at arguing before they were good. Martin Luther King Jr. honed his art in the pulpit of Ebenezer Baptist Church on Auburn Avenue in Atlanta. Elizabeth Warren learned to argue in law school. If you're a student, you'll polish your talents in the classroom.

The advice I give in this section applies specifically to the context of academia. It's useful advice in most rhetorical situations, but it is especially helpful if you're in a course that introduces you to academic writing. You should take two lessons to heart right away: know your readers and know your stuff.

Know Your Readers

We won't spend much time on pathetic arguments. Emotional appeals to readers can support and supplement effective logical arguments, but it's easy to overdo them in an academic setting. But that does not mean you should ignore readers: your ethical arguments and even key parts of your coolheaded logic do depend on knowing who your readers are. Examine the details of your assignment to see if you've been told to target specific readers. For example, you might have been instructed to write to fellow classmates; you might be asked to respond to an assigned reading as if you were conversing with its author; the assignment might tell you to think of your readers as the general public, as if you were writing a guest column in a newspaper; or you might be asked to address members of your own major discipline—other biologists or management scholars or computer scientists or what have you. Many writing assignments don't stipulate anything about readers. In that case, you should imagine that you're writing to well-educated, reasonable people who are used to looking at things as objectively as they can. In short, imagine they are people in the college or university community. College campuses constitute a discourse community, and members of that community expect writing to do certain things and to look a certain way. A big part of what you learn in a college writing course is how to produce writing that people at universities are used to reading. It's true, as I mentioned earlier, that each academic discipline constitutes its own specialized community and that each has its own genres. But nearly all academic writing, no matter the discipline, features dispassionate, logical reasoning; demonstrates the writer's knowledge of what others have said on the subject; includes careful citations of sources; and has a main point or thesis, etc. You probably already have some experience writing in the academic context. The discussion of the writing process will build on what you know already.

No matter who your target readers are, you should think of them as skeptical. Imagine people who disagree with you. They've been generous enough to give your arguments a hearing. They have opened themselves up to being persuaded to agree with your thesis. Nevertheless, they dispute your opinion—at least before they read your essay. You have to win them over.

Know Your Stuff

Everyone has the right to express an opinion, but not everyone has the right to a reader's attention. Your readers have opened themselves up to the possibility of changing their minds on your issue. That gesture is generous on their part, and it puts you under an obligation. You need to make your essay worthy of their trust. If you want people to extend you the courtesy of taking your opinion seriously, you better know what you're talking about. You must become something of an expert on your topic. You must be at least as informed as your audience, and in truth you really ought to make yourself better informed than your readers. That probably means you need to do research.

Your particular assignment will determine the kind of research you need to do. Is this piece of writing a 500-word blog post about your class's assigned reading for the day? In that case, knowing your stuff might mean reading the assignment carefully, taking marginal notes as you go, and skimming it a second time to test your first impressions. Have you been asked to write a formal research paper requiring ten or more scholarly sources? Or have you been asked to write something in between? In "Researching Your Topic" (p. 33) I'll discuss some rules of thumb about responsible, scholarly research. Right here I want to emphasize how important it is that you know what you're talking about.

If you have any doubts, you should read Michael Kinsley's essay (p. 93). Your readers will know pretty quickly if you're wasting their time, and they'll learn to distrust your opinions. That's especially true of teachers grading your essays: if they see that you are arguing from ignorance, they won't take your essay seriously. And conversely, if they see you've made a good-faith effort to inform yourself, they'll respect what you have to say.

The Writing Process

No one, not even the cleverest rhetoricians, can write effective persuasive essays completely off the top of their head. *Thinking* takes you only so far. It is by *writing* that we generate ideas, test those ideas with evidence, try out arguments, rethink our initial notions, and revise our strategies of persuasion. Writing a persuasive essay has steps or stages. If your assignment gives you a week or even longer to write the essay, you can be sure your instructor expects you to go through what composition specialists call the writing process. Shorter, overnight homework assignments will benefit from a shortened version of this process. Even essays you write in a timed exam should go through an abbreviated process.

The writing process is **recursive**. Textbooks like this one necessarily present the process as if it were a recipe, but don't think of it that way. Writers rarely follow step-by-step instructions the way a cook follows a recipe. When you're cooking, you might have to melt the butter before you toss the onions in the pan, and you might have to sauté the onions before you put them in the soup. Steps go in a necessary order. Writing doesn't work that way. You'll find yourself constantly circling back to earlier steps. Don't worry if it seems more natural for you to do step 4 before you've finished step 2, and don't worry about going back to step 3 after you've finished step 5. Follow your instincts. The writing process is not linear. It spirals back on itself all the time.

Nor should you worry about completing each and every step in the first place. The process of writing is impossible to pin down in a recipe. You should ignore these instructions whenever they impede your progress. If you're more productive by going your own way, skipping a step, adding your own, then do it. Writing is very individual; no two people go through the process exactly the same way. One of the most important things you can do in a writing class is to figure out what's the most productive process for you personally. You might find that you can't generate your ideas unless you're already writing a rough draft of your paper, so you might begin with drafting before you outline. You'll see later that I advise you to forget about your audience when you're first composing your logical arguments, and only start thinking about readers in revision. But you might find it helpful to keep readers in mind from the get-go. Then do it, and ignore my advice. All writers use their own personalized process, and you've got to figure out what's most productive for you.

But the one universal is this: writing is a *process*. It takes several stages to produce an effective paper, and each of those stages takes time and energy.

1. Researching Your Topic

You might have a strong opinion on your topic right from the start, but you should adopt a flexible attitude toward that opinion. Be open to modifying, qualifying, or even reversing your opinion once you learn more about the topic. In the previous section, I insisted that before you start writing, before you presume to express and defend your opinion, you need to *know your stuff.* That means finding evidence and using that evidence to test and generate ideas. Of course you won't be starting from scratch. You already know *something* about your issue just by having gone through your life this far. You might know quite a bit if you happen to have lots of experience in that area. But be humble about your prior knowledge. For instance, say you're writing about the influence of popular media on youth. You might have your own YouTube channel and through personal experience might know a lot about the medium and its effects on viewers, but until you study it you'll still be fairly ignorant. How do you get to that point of intelligence? Through research.

Research is a pretty broad term. Talking to your friends at lunch can be research, if you're writing about the popularity of cafeteria food. A social scientist might research by conducting surveys of random people. A chemist conducting an experiment is engaging in research, just as a paleontologist digging for fossils in the desert is doing research. We might call these efforts direct, primary, or field research. I'll focus here on what's sometimes called secondary research: finding and using the work of other people.

1a. Background Research
You can begin most research projects with an internet search engine like Google, Bing, or Yahoo!, which might bring up some useful websites—newspapers, blogs, government sites, nonprofit websites, etc. For instance, my Google search for the term *pandemic prevention* turned up websites hosted by WebMD (a for-profit medical information service), the Centers for Disease Control (a federal agency), the *New York Times*, the World Health Organization (which is a branch of the United Nations), and *Science* magazine (which is a peer-reviewed journal of a learned society, the American Association for the Advancement of Science). Most of these are reliable sources of information. You might view WebMD a little more critically: as one might expect of a for-profit organization, it has been accused of steering readers toward sponsored products. In general, you need to be cautious with Google or Bing searches, because less reliable sources will try to mimic the look of these more authoritative websites. My Google search also turned up PhRMA.org, which is the public page of the Pharmaceutical Research and Manufacturers of America. That's a consortium of for-profit drug companies, and, while the information on their page is probably accurate, it will definitely be slanted to benefit the bottom lines of those companies. In fact, a second glance indicated to me that the webpage came up in the search because it's an ad: PhRMA paid Google so its webpage would appear near the top of a search.

You always need to question a website's credibility. Who is responsible for the content? Who owns the website? Is the owner a respected news agency? Is the owner someone with a political or profit motive? For example, you can trust the facts that appear in a mainstream media outlet like the *New York Times.* The editorial staff at the *Times* might be more liberal than the staff of (say) the *Wall Street Journal*, which is fairly conservative, but you can trust the reporting at both newspapers to be accurate. You should be very suspicious of alternative media like *Breitbart News*: do not accept as fact anything published on such partisan sites without corroborating it in the mainstream media.

My Google search also turned up Wikipedia. Your instructor might have a general rule against using wikis, but if they don't, Wikipedia is a great place to start your research. It usually gives you a helpful, if brief, overview of a topic. But you should just use it for background. Do not quote Wikipedia in your paper. If you find a helpful fact or idea in

Wikipedia, follow it to the source, and make sure that source is a proper authority. And if you cannot find the original source of something you find on Wikipedia, *don't use it*! It might be accurate, but there's too high a possibility that it's inaccurate. You will probably find that the best use you can make of general information sites like Wikipedia is to use them to find other, more authoritative sources of information.

The chart at the end of this section gives you a sense of the various sources you might consult in your research, where to find them, and how trustworthy the sources can be. It also alerts you to potential problems.

1b. Researching the Scholarship on an Issue

If you're a college student, your library probably subscribes to dozens, if not hundreds, of databases, many of which will lead you to full-text articles written by experts in all fields. These are not available to the general public; you will have access via your student library or computing account. Databases are specialized collections of scholarship or other material. Some databases cater exclusively to one discipline (history, biology, economics, public administration, education, etc.), cataloging articles published in journals devoted to only one field. The ACM Digital Library, for instance, catalogs dozens of journals dealing with computer science, while publications regarding veterinary medicine are gathered in the Zoological Record. Some databases are more general. JSTOR is a pretty comprehensive database of humanities and social science scholarly journals. Google Scholar is a gigantic database that searches all disciplines and is available to the general public. Your instructor or your librarian will be able to help you find databases related to your topic.

You search databases the same way you search with a Web browser, by entering key terms. You might be able to arrange the results by date of publication (generally speaking, you want sources that are more recent) or by relevance. If your search turns up too many hits, look for an "advanced search" option to narrow them down. You might limit results to articles available to you in full-text online versions or in hard copy in your library. You might add search terms to filter the results of an initial search. Experiment. Each database has its own search interface, but they're all similar, and while they tend to be more complex than Google or Bing searches, you can learn to navigate them with a little trial and error.

3. COVID-19 **pandemic**; **prevention**, treatment, and mental health.

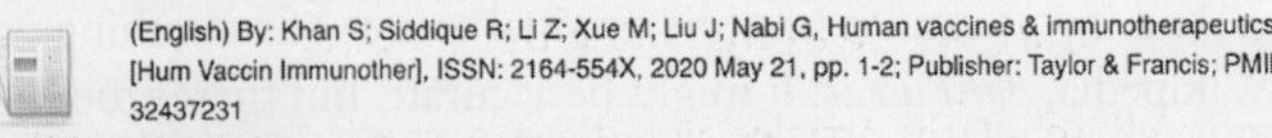

(English) By: Khan S; Siddique R; Li Z; Xue M; Liu J; Nabi G, Human vaccines & immunotherapeutics [Hum Vaccin Immunother], ISSN: 2164-554X, 2020 May 21, pp. 1-2; Publisher: Taylor & Francis; PMID: 32437231

Academic Journal

Find It At CofC ***

4. Psychopathological problems related to the COVID-19 **pandemic** and possible **prevention** with music therapy.

(English) ; Abstract available. By: Mastnak W, Acta paediatrica (Oslo, Norway : 1992) [Acta Paediatr], ISSN: 1651-2227, 2020 May 12; Publisher: Wiley-Blackwell; PMID: 32395840

Editorial & Opinion

COVID-19 is having a profound effect on societies worldwide and the impact that it is having on children cannot be underestimated. Although Brodin (1) stated that the disease tends to be mild in ...

Find It At CofC *** PlumX Metrics

Results of a search in the MEDLINE database using the term *pandemic prevention.* A similar search in your library's database might be formatted slightly differently, but the essential information will be the same.

These searches will find scholarly articles. For example, using the term *pandemic prevention* in the MEDLINE database, I found articles in several journals, including *Human Vaccines & Immunotherapeutics* and *Acta Paediatrica* (see figure above). Scholarly articles are written for other scholars in a particular discipline. (Most scholars work at colleges and universities, while others are employed by the government or private industry.) As I discussed in the section "How to Read Essays," scholars use specialized language and forms when they talk to each other. Part of your research is learning how to read genres of academic writing that seem strange and even forbidding. It's hard. Even though I have a PhD and have conducted my own research for over thirty years, I'm a fish out of water in the pages of *Human Vaccines & Immunotherapeutics.* That's because my training is in literature and composition. You, too, might feel in over your head when you first start reading in scholarly journals. You might be tempted to throw your hands up in frustration.

Don't. Frustration is normal. It's a necessary stage in the process of joining a discourse community. Every beginner feels overwhelmed. As you gradually become a scholar, you'll find it easier to navigate academic journals. As you get further into your own chosen discipline, almost like an apprentice learning a trade you'll get used to reading the genres used by your particular community of scholars. Here are a few strategies that might ease the process:

- Nearly all scholarly articles will have a thesis—a controversial assertion the writer is trying to persuade other scholars to believe. Begin by looking for that statement. Sometimes, the article might come with an **abstract**, which will state the thesis and summarize the arguments and evidence proving that thesis. Otherwise, the thesis should appear within the first few paragraphs.
- Many scholarly articles also include a **review of literature** somewhere near the beginning: that's a summary of what other scholars have said on the subject.
- Long articles can be broken down into sections. Try to tackle sections one at a time, identifying what you don't understand and what you do. Each of those sections—indeed, sometimes each paragraph—will have a main assertion or main point the writer is trying to prove. Try to identify those assertions and mark them.
- Look for the types of evidence the writer uses. In general, all of the lessons in the "How to Read Essays" section will apply to scholarly articles.
- You will have to read the article or at least the important sections of it several times before you understand. Be ready to reread and reread again.
- Take notes. That might mean highlighting parts of the article, writing in the margins of a hard copy or commenting on an electronic version, or taking notes.

Use one scholarly article to lead you to others. If you find a good article that addresses your issue, that single article might lead you to better sources than any number of searches in a database. Look for the writer's review of literature. Read through the article's bibliography, item by item. You'll probably find a title that promises useful information, and *that* article will probably lead you to others in a chain of references.

Get into the habit of keeping good records of your research. I recommend that you open a folder on your computer in which you deposit all online, full-text sources; if you have hard copies of journal articles, keep them all in a physical folder. The more carefully you keep records of your research, the easier it will be to cite your source. Later in this section you'll find a short guide to proper citations.

Source	Trustworthiness	Why You Can Trust It	Why You Should Be Careful	Where to Find It
Books from academic presses	Very trustworthy	Thoroughly vetted by peer review and often written by experts in the field	Often written by experts for other experts, so read closely to make sure you understand this source fully	Available at your school's library or as etexts available through your library's website
Articles in scholarly journals	Very trustworthy	Thoroughly vetted by peer review and often written by experts in the field	Often written by experts for other experts, so read closely to make sure you understand this source fully	Available through subscription databases at your school's library
Newspapers and magazines (*Time, Washington Post, National Journal*)	Mostly trustworthy	Committed to high standard of accuracy and often a balance between different opinions	Many newspapers and magazines also feature opinion content that is not held to as high a standard	Online and at your school's library
University websites	Mostly trustworthy	Official or department-sponsored pages are generally accurate and unbiased	Individual webpages are largely unvetted and may or may not be accurate, depending on the authors	.edu websites
Government information	Mostly trustworthy	Most government releases tend to be strictly about the facts gathered	Can be influenced by political opinion	.gov websites

Commercial websites	Not necessarily reliable	Well-established corporations need to protect their reputations	Most commercial websites will reveal nothing that threatens their bottom line	.com, .net, and .org websites
Nonprofit organization websites	Mostly trustworthy	Most nonprofits serve the public good	Some nonprofits might have a political agenda; look for a mission statement	.org and .net websites
Personal websites	Not necessarily reliable	Can offer specific information about a topic	Reliability determined completely by the author, who may or may not be accurate or biased	.com, .net, .org, and even some .edu websites
Wikipedia	Mostly trustworthy*	Sources at the end of a Wikipedia article can offer a reliable overview of research on a topic	Many Wikipedia articles can be poorly sourced or inaccurately reported	wikipedia.org

*A special note on Wikipedia because it is often the first website found on any internet search: avoid citing Wikipedia articles, but use that encyclopedia to lead you to sources that have genuine authority. In fact, one good way of judging the reliability of a Wikipedia article is to look at its sources. Does the article rely on dubious webpages? Or does it cite scholarly articles and books, government studies, and other identifiable experts in the field? If it cites sources that are themselves clearly reliable, then you should go to those sources.

2. Outlining Your Arguments

Write your **thesis** at the top of a blank piece of paper or word processing document. A thesis encapsulates your main point in one or two sentences. That point must be a matter of opinion. For example, "Many people today are concerned about global warming" is not a thesis. That statement does little more than announce an essay's topic, as if to say, "I'm going to be writing about global warming." Nor is this statement a thesis: "The Earth is in the midst of a warming trend that is changing climates across the globe." Virtually no one anywhere disputes that fact. But this statement could be the thesis of a persuasive essay: "Carbon emissions from coal-fired power plants contribute significantly to global warming, and reducing them will help stabilize climates." As of right now, in 2021, many groups dispute just how much of global warming should be blamed on coal, and whether switching to other means of generating energy will have any effect on climate change. Proving that statement will require you to compose some persuasive arguments.

When I say "persuasive" arguments, I mean arguments that persuade any reasonable person. Maybe the best way to think about that is to think of arguments that persuade *you*. Later, during revision, you'll think very carefully about exactly who you are targeting and how to best shape your arguments with those readers in mind. At this early stage, it's better to just try to imagine what you think are the best arguments supporting your position. Your outline will map those arguments. Of course you'll be influenced by the research you've done, but at this point, it's better to work from your memory rather than from your notes. What are the logical steps of argument that will lead a skeptical reader to conclude that we ought to reduce the amount of energy we generate from coal? Your list might look something like this:

1. Demonstrate that burning coal produces carbon dioxide, which contributes to global warming.
2. Demonstrate how large of a share of the world's energy comes from coal.
3. Compare coal's emissions to those of other energy sources.
4. Establish how much we must lower carbon dioxide emissions to slow global warming.
5. Demonstrate that reductions in burned coal will help reach those lower levels of carbon dioxide emissions.
6. Prove that the energy now generated by coal could be generated in the future by alternative sources.

Someone else's list might be different from my outline, but whatever it looks like, you'll have a number of different points you must prove on the way to proving your thesis. Each of these points represents a stage in your essay—a paragraph or a small group of paragraphs. Put them in a logical order, numbering each.

The outline must map out a logical series of arguments that will lead readers to agree with the thesis. This idea of a map is a useful metaphor. Before getting to point 3, readers must first pass through 1 and 2. The only way to get to point 5 is through 4. Your arguments should have this kind of necessary order.

3. Drafting Your Arguments

In the drafting stage, you actually write what resembles a paper. Consequently, students often find this point the most challenging: the words don't come; you stare at a blank screen; the fingers on the keyboard are uninspired. The advice here will help you generate that first draft.

Skip the introduction. Most writers find that to write an effective introduction, they have to wait until the very last stage of the process. Fretting about an introduction at this early stage is probably wasted energy. All you need at the head of your paper right now is your first version of your thesis.

Then use your outline. You don't have to write from beginning to end. Pick a section that you feel most confident about. Maybe it's your third point. Maybe a lot of your research provides information regarding that point. Maybe you've thought more about that particular part of the argument. Begin where you're most sure of yourself. Then, once the ball is rolling, go back to the other parts.

Many writers try too hard on their first draft. They'll work on one paragraph, realize that it's not quite right, and so they'll tinker with it, rewrite it, improve it. Resist the temptation to perfect one paragraph before you move on to the next. Your main goal in drafting is to get all of your ideas and evidence down for the first time in paragraph format. You're in conversation with yourself, so there's no need for perfection. Your readers are not going to see what you've written at this stage in the process. If you tend to try to write the perfect paper on your first draft, you should train yourself to be comfortable with a poorly argued train of thought or an awkwardly stated complex idea. You'll have plenty of time to improve things later, so just keep moving on from one point in your outline to another.

You might even time yourself: allow fifteen minutes to prove your second point. After the minutes are up, move on to the next section, no matter what shape point 2 is in—even if you've got nothing on paper but a couple of broken sentences. When I assign a rough draft for homework, I tell my students to give themselves a strict limit of time: an hour perhaps, and no more than two hours at any one sitting. If it's a long paper, break these sessions apart. Don't try to write eight pages in one evening. And this above all: don't waste time polishing anything. Just write. Compose those arguments.

You'll find later, in the revision stage, that your arguments are using induction and deduction to prove your points. But don't worry about that right now. Don't try to analyze your own arguments in the way I describe in "How to Read Essays." That will probably get you bogged down in one narrow point, while at this stage of the process you want to get through all of your points, no matter how ineffectively you may argue them.

When you're done writing your arguments, you should draft a full conclusion. Sum up your arguments and restate your thesis. Now that you've drafted your first version of your arguments, ask yourself again, *What is it that I want my readers to agree with?* You might discover that your answer to that question is different—maybe not totally different but different in some details—from the thesis you composed for your outline. That's OK. In fact, it's a good sign. As composition scholars have discovered, writing an essay does not just express your opinion. It helps you to form your opinion. This is one of the reasons why you must produce at least two versions of your essay: a first rough draft and a revision.

4. Revising Your Arguments

Revising is a lot more important than many writers realize. If you used two hours in one evening to write your rough draft, you could easily find yourself devoting eight hours over several days to revising. If writing the entire paper, from research to proofreading, takes thirty hours of work, you could easily spend fifteen hours on this stage.

It's best to let your rough draft sit for a day or so before you start revising, so you can come to it cold, so to speak, reading it with a more objective eye. "Rough" draft is probably the wrong metaphor, because it implies that your draft is a gemstone that just needs a little judicious cutting and polish before you turn it in. Instead, think of drafts like mountains that you're going to mine to find veins or seams of argument embedded within. I really think of that first draft as a type of what rhetoricians call discovery or invention: by writing the rough draft, you discover your arguments.

Because the rough draft is so provisional, you should treat your revision as an entirely new document. Open a blank document in your word processor and title it Draft 2. This way, you'll really write a second draft rather than merely tinker with your rough draft. You're not going to discard the rough draft. You're going find what's usable in it and reproduce those arguments in the revision, rearranging, improving, and expanding as you go.

4a. Revising Inductive Arguments

Now, in revision, you need to think about your readers, and you need to analyze and evaluate your own arguments with those readers in mind. Essentially, you've got to read your draft with the skills I discussed in the previous chapter, treating your own work as if it were written by someone else. What's the rhetorical context for your essay? What is your purpose and who is your audience? Are you trying to persuade other students in your class? Are you trying to influence public opinion? Are you writing in the general context of academia—for scholars devoted to logical argument and on guard against emotional appeals? Does your assignment designate some other community of readers? Before you go any further, get a clear picture in your mind of who your readers are. Then start analyzing and evaluating your arguments, paragraph by paragraph.

Let's say you're revising a paragraph that tries to prove its point with an inductive argument. To continue with our example, imagine you've drafted a paragraph trying to prove that a large share of the world's electricity is generated by burning coal, which was the second point in the outline I sketched previously. In your research, you found that the website of the U.S. Energy Information Administration (EIA) indicates that 39 percent of U.S. electricity comes from coal-powered plants. That statistic carries the weight of the argument in your draft. So now you have to evaluate your evidence: apply the tests for accuracy, relevance, sufficiency, and representativeness. Clearly, the evidence is relevant. But is it accurate? Will your readers believe it? Remember: whoever they are, your readers are skeptical. If the essay you're writing is going to be read by scholars in the field of energy, you don't need to explain why the EIA is a reliable source of information. But if your readers are your fellow students, who probably have never heard of the agency, you should explain to them what the EIA is and why they can trust that agency's data. Make sure your readers *believe* your data. Part of earning trust is citing sources correctly. Your readers will only trust data they can double-check for themselves. (Hint: if your citations are clear and precise, most readers will be satisfied and won't bother to double-check, just as they'll distrust your evidence if your citations are sloppy or incomplete.) You might also note that the point the essay was trying to prove is that a big share of the *world's* electricity comes from burning coal. The EIA data only attests to U.S. energy. What about Europe, China, and other big energy consumers? You should realize, then, that your evidence does not yet represent all the data you should sample. You need to do more research to find data on other economies, or you need to revise the point you're proving in this paragraph so it refers only to the United States. This is how you can strengthen a weak inductive argument by fleshing it out in revision. The key to revising inductive arguments is thinking about your readers: will your target audience think the evidence is accurate, sufficient, and representative?

You should also consider including **anecdotal evidence**. Remember, an anecdote is a single example that represents a larger data set (see p. 44). If your inductive data consists of dry statistics, it will help convince readers if you can put a face on those abstract figures. Anecdotes give life and color to abstract ideas and convey to readers the context and perspective that a plain statement of facts may not.

4b. Revising Deductive Arguments

You need to scrutinize your deductive arguments just as skeptically. And, again, it's important to know who you want to persuade. Take this example from the recent coronavirus outbreak.

It's an actual argument made by U.S. president Donald Trump in late March 2020:

> [The lockdown has] been very painful for our country, and very destabilizing for our country. . . . We're going back to work much sooner than people thought.

If we analyzed this argument, again filling in the missing parts, it would look like this:

> (major premise) BECAUSE economic stability is our number one priority, and
> (minor premise) BECAUSE the lockdown destabilizes the economy,
> (conclusion) THEREFORE we need to reopen the economy sooner rather than later.

The argument seems to have convinced one audience: conservative Republicans. For example, Dan Patrick, the lieutenant governor of Texas, famously announced that, as a senior citizen, he was willing to risk his own health to keep the economy healthy. Not many would put their position in such blunt terms, but numerous conservatives around the country began clamoring to "liberate" their states from strict lockdown measures. But the argument fell flat in other areas. It did not convince other governors, especially Democrats, like Governor Andrew Cuomo of New York, who said,

> If you ask the American people to choose between public health and the economy, then it's no contest. . . . No American is going to say, 'accelerate the economy at the cost of human life.' My mother is not expendable. Your mother is not expendable. . . . We are not going to accept a premise that human life is disposable.

Cuomo did not contradict the validity of Trump's argument. The president's conclusion follows logically enough on his premises. But Cuomo pointed out that one of those premises—that the economy is our number one priority—was false. Now if we analyzed Governor Cuomo's argument, we'd end up with something like this:

(major premise) BECAUSE our number one priority is saving lives,
(minor premise) BECAUSE reopening the economy prematurely will revive the coronavirus, and
(minor premise) BECAUSE the coronavirus endangers lives,
(conclusion) THEREFORE we should delay reopening the economy.

That argument did not go far with Trump, not because it was invalid but because it began with a premise that the president did not share. Cuomo was not too effective in convincing Republicans, and Trump did not persuade many Democrats because neither argued from common ground.

A deductive argument is based on **common ground** when the writer uses major premises that readers already believe. The argument begins with values shared by both the writer and the readers. For example, when Thomas Jefferson said, "We hold these truths to be self-evident," he was saying that he presumed his readers believed his major premises. Those principles were common ground. Saying they are "self-evident" was an admission that his argument will not persuade anyone who disagrees with those principles. Jefferson was not going to bother trying to convince anyone of the major premises. If some group of readers believed (for instance) in the divine right of kings, they just wouldn't be convinced by the Declaration of Independence, and there's not much Jefferson could do to change their minds. This point is important to remember when you're revising your deductive arguments: it's really hard to get someone to change their beliefs, so it helps if you can reason from common ground, from principles shared by you and your readers.

To come back to our example, let's look at how both sides began to revise their arguments about the pandemic as they became more sensitive to the other's values. Proponents of restoring normal economic activity more quickly made this argument (and here I'm paraphrasing their logic):

> It is true that we've got to save lives. No human life is disposable. That's why we need to reopen the economy quickly. An extended economic shutdown risks triggering a long-term recession, and recessions are bad for public health—maybe even worse than a spike in coronavirus outbreaks.

This argument has a better chance of working with Democrats, because it begins with the value voiced by Governor Cuomo: that public health is our top priority; no life should be sacrificed for financial gain. Readers might be skeptical about the claim that a recession could be worse for public health than a pandemic, but at least they're open to being persuaded of that point. The writer might support the claim with an inductive argument drawing on evidence about public health during the Great Recession of 2007–2009.

Likewise, people arguing to delay reopening the economy revised their strategies. Many of those arguments went something like this:

> We should protect the economy. No one wants to trigger a long-term economic catastrophe. That's why we need to keep the country locked down longer. Opening the economy too soon risks losing control of the disease, and out-of-control pandemics cause deep and long-lasting economic damage.

This argument has a much better chance at succeeding with Republicans, because it reasons from their own stated value: the economy's health is the highest priority. Skeptical readers might question how much damage an out-of-control coronavirus could actually do to the economy, but they're open to being persuaded on that point because it doesn't challenge their own political philosophy. The writer might use inductive evidence drawn from similar crises to prove how harmful pandemics can be to economies.

4c. Handling Quotations and Paraphrases

Your research provides evidence for your essay, and you'll probably also borrow other writers' ideas and claims. You should incorporate such material as seamlessly as possible into your own prose, which means you'll use a mixture of quotations and paraphrase.

Quotation means you're borrowing someone else's exact wording. For example, here are a couple of sentences from a journal article about violent video games, written by Craig A. Anderson and Brad J. Bushman and published in *Psychological Science*:

> Is there a reliable association between exposure to violent video games and aggression? Across 33 independent tests of the relation between video-game violence and aggressions, involving 3,033 participants, the average effect was positive and significant. . . . High video-game violence was definitely associated with heightened aggression.[1]
>
> 1. "Effects of Violent Video Games on Aggressive Behavior, Aggressive Cognition, Aggressive Affect, Physiological Arousal, and Prosocial Behavior: A Meta-Analytic Review of the Scientific Literature." *Psychological Science* 12.5 (2001): 357. *JSTOR*, Web. 12 Dec. 2014.

What I've just done is inserted a long quotation into my paragraph. Long quotations are indicated not by quotation marks but by larger margins, and usually they do not blend with the grammar of your own sentences. Nor do you use different spacing for long quotations. If your paper is double-spaced, your long quotation should be double-spaced also. Often writers introduce long quotations a bit formally, as I did here, with a colon. If you're quoting more than one complete sentence or if you're quoting three or more lines of text, you should present the quotation in the long form, using larger margins to set it off from your own words.

Short quotations convey other writers' meaning using only some of their exact words. Here's another way to handle the same material, this time using short quotations:

> Scientists Anderson and Bushman studied "3,033 participants" in "33 independent tests of the relation between video-game violence and aggression." They found that "[h]igh video-game violence was definitely associated with heightened aggression."

There's no definite rule about how many words you need to be borrowing before you need to use quotation marks. But you should err on the side of caution: whenever you use at least two words in a row by another author, put them in quotation marks. For example, I put quotation marks around a two-word combination: "33 participants." Sometimes you would put even one word in quotation marks, if the word expresses some particular claim of the writer you're quoting. For example, you might write:

> There is little doubt about the effect of violent video games. One team of researchers found that they "definitely" caused aggressive behavior.

In this case, you want your readers to know that *definitely* is Anderson and Bushman's exact interpretation of the data. The quotation marks tell readers that the emphatic *definitely* is their word, not yours, and so it helps support your claim about there being little doubt.

When you borrow a few words, as I've done in the examples of short quotations, you must incorporate those words into the grammar of your own sentence. If you took out the quotation marks, the sentence would have to be perfectly grammatical. This may mean changing the punctuation of the quotation, altering the tense of a verb, or replacing a capital letter with a lowercase one. When making such adjustments, be sure to indicate the change you've made with brackets, and note deletions with ellipses. Perhaps the best way to explain this is to show you what not to do. For example, here's an ungrammatical use of a short quotation:

> Anderson and Bushman reviewed "Across 33 independent tests of the relation between video-game violence and aggressions, involving 3,033 participants."

If you read that sentence aloud, you'll hear the awkwardness at the beginning of the quotation. One does not "review across tests." You might not be able to identify the grammatical error, but you can hear that the sentence sounds wrong. A good trick is to read your short-quotation sentences aloud this way because your ear will not be tricked by the quotation marks, as the eye often is. If a short-quotation sentence does not sound right, you probably have not incorporated the quoted material into the grammar of your sentence. Try again. In this case, you might simply drop the word *Across:*

> Anderson and Bushman reviewed "33 independent tests of the relation between video-game violence and aggressions, involving 3,033 participants."

If you read that sentence aloud, you should hear the improvement over the first attempt.

Punctuating short quotations is a little trickier. You might have noted that in an earlier example I changed a capital letter to lowercase in this sentence: They found that "[h]igh video-game violence was definitely associated with heightened aggression." The word *high* began one of Anderson and Bushman's sentences, so they capitalized it, but in the grammar of my sentence the word should not be capitalized, so I changed it. I alerted my readers to the change by inserting the brackets. Similarly, you could add your own words into a short quotation to fix the grammar. For example, you might write:

> Anderson and Bushman ask if "there [is] a reliable association between exposure to violent video games and aggression."

The original sentence read, "Is there a reliable association between exposure to violent video games and aggression?" The meaning of the two constructions is the same, so I am justified in changing the wording to suit the grammar of your sentence. But to do so, I had to move the verb *is*. By using brackets, I am telling my readers that I have changed the grammar of the original sentence. But a word of caution: if you change the grammar of someone's words by inserting your own words, be absolutely sure you have not changed their meaning.

So long as you're being faithful to the meaning of the original, you can add and omit words, as convenient to your purposes. You might write:

> According to two researchers, "the average effect [of video-game violence] was positive and significant."

The words *of video-game violence* are not Anderson and Bushman's, but they faithfully convey their meaning, and inserting the words helps you incorporate the quotation smoothly into your sentence. Similarly, you can omit words that are not needed for your purposes, if you indicate the omission with ellipses:

> According to two researchers, "the average effect was . . . significant."

Generally speaking, you should prefer short quotations to long quotations. If you find yourself using a lot of long quotations, you should try to rewrite several using a combination of your own words and short quotations. An effective research paper might not use any long quotations. But every paper should include at least some short quotations. They are like seasoning—the salt and pepper of an essay. Used judiciously, they improve the flavor of your arguments; used too much, they'll overwhelm your argument. As a rule of thumb, most of your borrowed material will be most effective if you present it in paraphrase.

A **paraphrase** uses your own words to convey the meaning of someone else's words. A paraphrase of our long quotation might read like this:

> According to scientists Anderson and Bushman, violent games significantly increased aggression in over 3,000 participants in more than thirty different studies.

This sentence uses Anderson and Bushman's main point (that playing violent video games makes people aggressive) and mentions the inductive evidence backing up that claim (the studies of 3,033 people). But it does not use the writers' words.

By putting someone else's evidence and claims into your own words, you demonstrate your comprehension of their text. Sometimes, student writers rely on quotations, especially long quotations, because they do not quite understand what the experts are talking about. Paraphrase will avoid that problem because it forces you to master the meaning of the original text.

This section is a general guide. There are more particulars, especially regarding how to punctuate quotations, that would require a lot more explanation. Additional resources for this book are available online at Norton/Write.

5. Writing Refutations, Conclusions, and Introductions

After you've revised your arguments, you can turn your attention to special paragraphs. These are not part of your chain of arguments; nevertheless, they are important to your readers' experience of the essay.

5a. Refutations

Not all essays have a refutation, but if you handle them right they can be powerfully persuasive. In a **refutation**, you state what you think would be a skeptical reader's main objection to your argument, and then you refute it. Skeptical readers might point out some supposed weakness in your argument. Or, more likely, they will offer their own argument supporting the opposing side of the controversy. For instance, if you're arguing that we ought to shut down coal-fired power plants, hostile readers might concede the dangers such plants pose for the climate, but they might argue that other ways of generating power are even more hazardous. They might point to the meltdowns at the Chernobyl and Fukushima power plants as examples of the dangers of nuclear reactors. In a refutation, you'd acknowledge this counter argument and explain to readers why you think it is wrong.

Be respectful, even generous to your readers. You might begin, for example, by saying, "An intelligent objection to my argument might be. . ." A refutation is an opportunity not only to undermine your readers' main objections but to demonstrate to them how open minded you are, that you've considered the opposing point of view, and that you respect those who hold the opposing point of view.

Traditionally, refutations come after your arguments but before your conclusion. But you might find that your refutation logically fits somewhere else in your paper. Follow your own best judgment.

5b. Conclusions

The main task of your conclusion is to restate your thesis. That's why I recommended that you write a conclusion in the drafting stage. Often it's only after drafting arguments that a writer really figures out what they want to prove to readers. Now that you've finished revising your arguments, you need to assert the claim that they prove. This assertion might have changed a lot since you first wrote a thesis in the outlining stage of the writing process.

An essay is like a journey. Your arguments are the necessary stages of that journey. Your conclusion is the actual destination: be sure to inform your readers that they've arrived there.

If your paper is so long that the stages of the journey might only be dimly recalled when readers get to the end, you might remind them of the main points in your arguments. In other words, you might summarize your arguments. But in shorter papers, when only a few minutes of reading separate the conclusion from the early arguments, summarizing what you've just said might seem awkward and formulaic. You might use the conclusion to speculate about the future. You might return to the concrete image you used in your introduction, describing the consequences your argument might have for that particular case. However you handle the conclusion, you want to give your readers a sense of closure: you want to make them feel like you've covered the bases you need to cover.

5c. Introductions

An introduction serves several purposes. It introduces readers to the controversial topic you're writing about. It draws them into that controversy and compels them to read your essay. And it delivers your thesis, so they'll know exactly what you're trying to prove in the essay. There's no single strategy that you have to use, but often you'll find that some sort of anecdote or vivid description in which you paint a situation or scene can introduce readers to the controversy and grab their interest at the same time. For instance, imagine that your topic is global warming and the pollution that comes from burning coal. You might begin with a description of the smoke coming from a coal-fired generating plant: not a general description, but a very specific description of a particular plant, like Georgia's Plant Scherer, a large-scale polluter. Or you might begin with a powerful example of the effects of global warming—a description of the disappearance of glaciers in Montana's Glacier National Park, for example. A specific case that illustrates the controversy works better than a general statement in abstract terms.

Your introduction must also explain to readers why the issue is controversial. For instance, no one is in favor of melting the glaciers in Glacier National Park, but many people don't think what's happening in Montana should determine our policy about a power plant in Georgia. So your introduction should give some indication of why this issue is controversial, how there are at least two legitimate sides to the issue. Don't treat the issue as a no-brainer. If the proper position to take is that obvious to everyone, then there would be no need for you to write your paper and no need for anyone to read it. Presenting the issue as a controversy will highlight the significance of your thesis.

Your introduction should also convey to readers the particular urgency of your issue. Rhetoricians call this **exigence.** In a sense, this means answering the questions, *Why are you writing your paper? What is compelling you to produce this piece of rhetoric?* Another way of thinking of exigence is this: *Why is it important that your audience should read your paper?* In the example on the previous page, the exigence is an impending climate disaster. An introduction that paints a picture of glaciers melting at an alarming rate or a coal-fired power plant spewing tons of carbon dioxide into the atmosphere might be enough to convey exigence. But in most rhetorical situations, exigence is not so obviously addressed. You need to figure out how to convey to readers a sense that it is important for them to read your paper.

Presenting your thesis is the most important thing that your introduction accomplishes. This is your main claim, your position on the controversy, and you must tell readers what that position is before you begin trying to persuade them to adopt it as their own opinion. One of the reasons I advise you to write your introduction *after* you've revised your arguments is because your thesis often changes in the process of writing and revising those arguments. So don't just repeat the thesis you used when you first outlined your arguments. Look at the conclusion that follows your revised arguments. That's where you'll find the assertion your essay is actually proving. Usually, writers put the thesis at the end of the introduction, just before they start their arguments.

6. Citation

You use citations to tell your reader where your borrowed information came from. Strictly speaking, all of the information in your paper is "borrowed," because none of us is born with knowledge. We learn things along the way through life. But speaking practically, you're not expected to trace some things back to their source. Things that are common knowledge, for example, do not need to be cited. What constitutes common knowledge, though, can be a bit murky. It depends on your audience. If you're speaking to a group of scientists, you wouldn't need to tell them where you learned that burning coal produces carbon dioxide or that carbon dioxide is a greenhouse gas. Such things are common knowledge to that group of readers. But if your readers are your classmates, you might want to let them know that you learned burning coal emits carbon dioxide from the Environmental Protection

Agency website or from a chemistry textbook. When to cite and when not to cite can be hard to determine. If you're going to err, err on the side of caution, and cite when you might not have to. If you err on the other side, you might be accused of plagiarism.

Whenever you quote, and just about whenever you paraphrase, you should cite your source. The citation has two purposes. The first is to give readers a quick idea of where your information came from. The other is to give them enough information to find your sources and look for themselves. How do you do this?

Citations have two parts. Whenever you're citing material, you need to refer to the source in the text of your essay. That might mean an in-text citation, referring readers to a works cited list, or it might mean a superscript number pointing readers to a footnote or endnote. So every citation includes both a reference (at the place in your essay where the borrowed material appears) and the full bibliographic information about the sources (somewhere else in your paper, either at the bottom of the page or at the end of the essay).

Academic disciplines have developed conventions—rules, basically—that tell you how to handle your citations. For example, the Modern Language Association (MLA), which is the professional organization for college English teachers, publishes its rules in a book-length style guide. The American Psychological Association (APA) publishes a different style guide for its members, and some other social scientists use it as well. The *Chicago Manual of Style*, which in its seventeenth edition is over 1,000 pages long, is popular with several disciplines. Each discipline uses a style guide that tailors the rules to its particular needs. As you progress further into your own discipline, you will become familiar with the rules of that discipline's professional organization. Perhaps you'll even memorize the most commonly applied citation rules as you accustom yourself to research in your area of specialization. But your goal should not be to memorize the rules of the MLA or APA or any other style guide your instructor has chosen. You just need to demonstrate your ability to follow the rules in the style guide assigned to you.

Following such arcane rules to the letter can feel like drudgery. In fact, there is a lot of drudgery to it. But correct citations have a very powerful persuasive effect. First of all, they help persuade readers that your evidence is accurate. If you tell readers exactly where they themselves can find your information, they're more likely to trust it; if your citations are sloppy and it's hard to follow your evidence to the source, readers will be suspicious. That's just human nature. So citations have an important role in demonstrating the accuracy of inductive evidence, and they help minor premises in deductive arguments pass the truth test.

You need to correctly cite your sources to avoid **plagiarism**. Plagiarism is intellectual theft. You present someone else's research or ideas as your own. The most obvious and prosecutable form of plagiarism is when you use someone else's exact words without using quotation marks or larger margins. That kind of deliberate theft of intellectual property is easy to avoid. Don't do it. On the internet, websites steal words from other websites all the time. But that does not mean it's okay. You might see the exact same text in Wikipedia repeated in several other websites. That doesn't mean those words are public property that anyone can use as their own. It just means some anonymous webmaster has stolen someone else's intellectual property. The consequences for the owner of some website are negligible. The consequences for you are enormous. Never cut and paste any electronic source—text from a website, for instance—into your paper. Always type your quotations. If you are caught trying to pretend you wrote something you did not write, even a short string of words, you might be expelled. Don't ever do it.

But if it's easy to avoid that kind of plagiarism, it's all too easy to fall into plagiarism by keeping sloppy records of your research or through lazy or last-minute essay writing. You might have come across a good argument somewhere, but your research records are so messy that you can't remember where you read it. It's too important to the train of your arguments to leave out, so you include it without a citation. Or you might draft your arguments without slowing down to cite your sources, thinking you'll add them later. But later, when you're editing your paper, you can't find where some particular information came from. So you leave it in, uncited. Or perhaps there's a particularly complex paragraph in which you borrowed material from several sources, but you forgot to cite one of them. All of these are examples of plagiarism, and they might earn you an F on the assignment or as a final grade for your course. As I mentioned earlier, they can even get you expelled.

Citations also play a gigantic part in ethical arguments. Ethos, remember, is the presentation of self. For a speaker, this includes how you dress, how you modulate your voice, your posture, and what you say about yourself. It might seem that these have no counterparts in written arguments, especially in academic essays, which leave little room for personal anecdotes. But they do. Even if you submit your essay electronically, it has a physical dimension every bit as important as a public speaker's dress and posture and voice. The grammar, punctuation, consistency of margins, headers and footers, proper handling of quotations, and especially proper use of citations all contribute to a reader's sense of who you are. This impression is, perhaps, even more important to your instructor than to the typical reader. Someone who takes the care to do the drudge work of citations correctly seems more like an expert than someone who has done the exact same research but cites her sources in a slapdash way. You will look smart if you cite sources accurately.

The rules governing how to refer to your sources are easy to master. But getting the bibliographic information correct is pretty complex because there are so many different types of sources, especially now that we get so much information off the internet. Most style guides, like those from the MLA and *Chicago*, run to the length of full books. But you can find reliable, convenient condensed versions online that will probably give you all of the information you need for a research essay. Consult a site like Norton/Write or Purdue OWL (owl.purdue.edu/owl).

7. Editing

If revision is a complete rewriting of an earlier draft, editing is closer to tinkering. You're not going to open a new blank document to produce a new draft. You edit a close-to-finished draft by making changes to the revised essay itself. Go through your revision, assessing whether your arguments flow from paragraph to paragraph, one leading logically into the next. And examine the internal workings of the paragraphs to make sure your arguments are as clear and persuasive as they can be. You might do a little rearranging of paragraphs at this stage, but more likely you'll be working on smaller problems. You might add a little evidence to an inductive argument. You might make the conclusion of a deductive argument clearer to your reader. Think of editing as fine-tuning. You're trying to experience your arguments as your readers will experience them. Identify any places that could use improvement and address them.

8. Proofreading

Your essay is almost ready to turn in, but not quite. In the editing stage, you were fine-tuning your arguments. You're not concerned with arguments when you proofread. You're improving the clarity of your sentences. Read through the entire paper. I often tell my students to read the paper backward, sentence by sentence. That way, you get out of the flow of your arguments, and you can see each sentence *as a sentence.* You're looking for sentences that sound confusing or even ungrammatical. You're looking for spelling and punctuation errors. Have you documented your quotations and paraphrases correctly? Mark anything that's suspicious. If it sounds slightly unclear to you, you can be sure the sentence is very unclear to your readers. Go through the entire paper, pausing only long enough to mark where there's a problem. Only when you've read through the entire paper and identified problem sentences should you go on to the next step of fixing the problems.

Some of those problems will be easy to fix because they're mere typos, either mistyped words or simple errors that derive from haste or inattention, like an *it's* for an *its*. But some problems might take more work, especially those sentences that sound confusing to you. If you've got a sentence that seems tangled, whose sense is not clear and you're not quite sure why, try this easy trick of the trade: ask yourself, *What was I trying to say here?* Then write down the answer as it comes to you. Probably, your answer will be clearer, the grammar will be correct, and you can just plug it into your paper, replacing the problem sentence. I've found that when students use this trick, their corrections are almost always longer than the original problem sentences, and sometimes they use two or three sentences to explain what they were trying to say. That's not surprising. Often the problem with tangled sentences is that you're trying to do too much all at once. When you explain what you were trying to say, you slow down and write more expansively.

Once each of the problems you noted in your proofreading has been corrected, you're ready to turn in your essay.

CHAPTER 1

✶

Literacy, Language, Argument

Literacy, Language, Argument

Frederick Douglass

c. 1817–1895

Douglass escaped from slavery in Maryland when he was about twenty-one. Three years later, at a meeting of abolitionists in Nantucket, Massachusetts, he rose from the audience to speak of his experiences. William Garrison, the most prominent abolitionist in America, was so moved that he hired Douglass to lecture for the Anti-Slavery Society, which he did very effectively for four years. When he was accused of being an imposter in 1845, he wrote the Narrative of the Life of Frederick Douglass. *It was published by the Anti-Slavery Society and was an instant success. Within two years, 30,000 copies had been printed in America, Ireland, England, France, and Holland. Its reach extended even further: one reviewer in 1846 estimated that the book influenced more than a million people in Great Britain and Ireland alone. This essay is a short excerpt from the* Narrative, *which Douglass hoped would "do something toward throwing light on the American slave system, and hastening the glad day of deliverance to the millions of my brethren in bonds." Douglass wrote to affect broad public opinion, which, in a democracy, can influence public policy. He knew that state-sponsored censorship would prevent even sympathetic Southerners from seeing the book, so Douglass took aim at Northerners. Garrison declared in his preface that the* Narrative *would strike "a stunning blow . . . on northern prejudice against [Black people]." The* Narrative *did not expose just the material degradations of slavery—like the brutal punishments some masters inflicted on the bodies of the people they enslaved—it also exposed the psychological and spiritual effects, what Garrison called "the outrage which is inflicted by [slavery] on the godlike nature of its victims."*

Learning to Read

I lived in Master Hugh's family about seven years. During this time, I succeeded in learning to read and write. In accomplishing this, I was compelled to resort to various stratagems. I had no regular teacher. My mistress, who had kindly commenced to instruct me, had, in compliance with the advice and direction of her husband, not only ceased to instruct, but had set her face against my being instructed by any one else. It is due, however, to my mistress to say of her, that she did not adopt this course of treatment immediately. She at first lacked the depravity indispensable to shutting me up in mental darkness. It was at least necessary for her to have some training in the exercise of irresponsible power, to make her equal to the task of treating me as though I were a brute.

My mistress was, as I have said, a kind and tender-hearted woman; and in the simplicity of her soul she commenced, when I first went to live with her, to treat me as she supposed one human being ought to treat another. In entering upon the duties of a slaveholder, she did not seem to perceive that I sustained to her the relation of a mere chattel, and that for her to treat me as a human being was not only wrong, but dangerously so. Slavery proved as injurious to her as it did to me. When I went there, she was a pious, warm, and tender-hearted woman. There was no sorrow or suffering for which she had not a tear. She had bread for the hungry, clothes for the naked, and comfort for every mourner that came within her reach. Slavery soon proved its ability to divest her of these heavenly qualities. Under its influence, the tender heart became stone, and the lamblike disposition gave way to one of tiger-like fierceness. The first step in her downward course was in her ceasing to instruct me. She now commenced to practise her husband's precepts. She finally became even more violent in her opposition than her husband himself. She was not satisfied with simply doing as well as he had commanded; she seemed anxious to do better. Nothing seemed to make her more angry than to see me with a newspaper. She seemed to think that here lay the danger. I have had her rush at me with a face made all up of fury, and snatch from me a newspaper, in a manner that fully revealed her apprehension. She was an apt woman; and a little experience soon demonstrated, to her satisfaction, that education and slavery were incompatible with each other.

From this time I was most narrowly watched. If I was in a separate room any considerable length of time, I was sure to be suspected of having a book, and was at once called to give an account of myself. All this, however, was too late. The first step had been taken.

Mistress, in teaching me the alphabet, had given me the *inch*, and no precaution could prevent me from taking the *ell.*[1]

The plan which I adopted, and the one by which I was most successful, was that of making friends of all the little white boys whom I met in the street. As many of these as I could, I converted into teachers. With their kindly aid, obtained at different times and in different places, I finally succeeded in learning to read. When I was sent of errands, I always took my book with me, and by going one part of my errand quickly, I found time to get a lesson before my return. I used also to carry bread with me, enough of which was always in the house, and to which I was always welcome; for I was much better off in this regard than many of the poor white children in our neighborhood. This bread I used to bestow upon the hungry little urchins, who, in return, would give me that more valuable bread of knowledge. I am strongly tempted to give the names of two or three of those little boys, as a testimonial of the gratitude and affection I bear them; but prudence forbids;—not that it would injure me, but it might embarrass them; for it is almost an unpardonable offence to teach slaves to read in this Christian country. It is enough to say of the dear little fellows, that they lived on Philpot Street, very near Durgin and Bailey's ship-yard. I used to talk this matter of slavery over with them. I would sometimes say to them, I wished I could be as free as they would be when they got to be men. "You will be free as soon as you are twenty-one, *but I am a slave for life!* Have not I as good a right to be free as you have?" These words used to trouble them; they would express for me the liveliest sympathy, and console me with the hope that something would occur by which I might be free.

I was now about twelve years old, and the thought of being *a slave for life* began to bear heavily upon my heart. Just about this time, I got hold of a book entitled "The Columbian Orator."[2] Every opportunity I got, I used to read this book. Among much of other interesting matter, I found in it a dialogue between a master and his slave. The slave was represented as having run away from his master three times. The dialogue represented the conversation which took place

1. A unit of measurement equal to forty-five inches.

2. A collection of poems, dialogues, plays, and speeches popular in the period.

between them, when the slave was retaken the third time. In this dialogue, the whole argument in behalf of slavery was brought forward by the master, all of which was disposed of by the slave. The slave was made to say some very smart as well as impressive things in reply to his master—things which had the desired though unexpected effect; for the conversation resulted in the voluntary emancipation of the slave on the part of the master.

In the same book, I met with one of Sheridan's mighty speeches on and in behalf of Catholic emancipation.[3] These were choice documents to me. I read them over and over again with unabated interest. They gave tongue to interesting thoughts of my own soul, which had frequently flashed through my mind, and died away for want of utterance. The moral which I gained from the dialogue was the power of truth over the conscience of even a slaveholder. What I got from Sheridan was a bold denunciation of slavery, and a powerful vindication of human rights. The reading of these documents enabled me to utter my thoughts, and to meet the arguments brought forward to sustain slavery; but while they relieved me of one difficulty, they brought on another even more painful than the one of which I was relieved. The more I read, the more I was led to abhor and detest my enslavers. I could regard them in no other light than a band of successful robbers, who had left their homes, and gone to Africa, and stolen us from our homes, and in a strange land reduced us to slavery. I loathed them as being the meanest as well as the most wicked of men. As I read and contemplated the subject, behold! that very discontentment which Master Hugh had predicted would follow my learning to read had already come, to torment and sting my soul to unutterable anguish. As I writhed under it, I would at times feel that learning to read had been a curse rather than a blessing. It had given me a view of my wretched condition, without the remedy. It opened my eyes to the horrible pit, but to no ladder upon which to get out. In moments of agony, I envied my fellow-slaves for their stupidity. I have often wished myself a beast. I preferred the condition of the meanest reptile to my own. Any thing, no matter what, to get

3. Richard Brinsley Sheridan (1751–1816), an Irish-born playwright and politician favoring Catholic emancipation. The speech arguing for civil and political rights for Catholics in England and Ireland was actually made by Arthur O'Connor, an Irish patriot.

rid of thinking! It was this everlasting thinking of my condition that tormented me. There was no getting rid of it. It was pressed upon me by every object within sight or hearing, animate or inanimate. The silver trump of freedom had roused my soul to eternal wakefulness. Freedom now appeared, to disappear no more forever. It was heard in every sound, and seen in every thing. It was ever present to torment me with a sense of my wretched condition. I saw nothing without seeing it, I heard nothing without hearing it, and felt nothing without feeling it. It looked from every star, it smiled in every calm, breathed in every wind, and moved in every storm.

I often found myself regretting my own existence, and wishing myself dead; and but for the hope of being free, I have no doubt but that I should have killed myself, or done something for which I should have been killed. While in this state of mind, I was eager to hear any one speak of slavery. I was a ready listener. Every little while, I could hear something about the abolitionists. It was some time before I found what the word meant. It was always used in such connections as to make it an interesting word to me. If a slave ran away and succeeded in getting clear, or if a slave killed his master, set fire to a barn, or did any thing very wrong in the mind of a slaveholder, it was spoken of as the fruit of *abolition*. Hearing the word in this connection very often, I set about learning what it meant. The dictionary afforded me little or no help. I found it was "the act of abolishing"; but then I did not know what was to be abolished. Here I was perplexed. I did not dare to ask any one about its meaning, for I was satisfied that it was something they wanted me to know very little about. After a patient waiting, I got one of our city papers, containing an account of the number of petitions from the north, praying for the abolition of slavery in the District of Columbia, and of the slave trade between the States. From this time I understood the words *abolition* and *abolitionist*, and always drew near when that word was spoken, expecting to hear something of importance to myself and fellow-slaves. The light broke in upon me by degrees. I went one day down on the wharf of Mr. Waters; and seeing two Irishmen unloading a scow of stone, I went, unasked, and helped them. When we had finished, one of them came to me and asked me if I were a slave. I told him I was. He asked, "Are ye a slave for life?" I told him that I was. The good Irishman seemed to be deeply affected by the statement. He said to the other that it was a pity so fine a little fellow as myself should be a slave for life. He said it was a shame to hold me. They both advised me to run away to the north; that I should find friends there, and that I should be free. I pretended not to be interested in what they said, and treated them as if I did not understand them; for I feared they might be treacherous. White men have been known to encourage slaves to escape, and then, to get the reward, catch them and return them to their masters. I was afraid that these seemingly good men might use me so; but I nevertheless remembered their advice, and from that time I resolved to run away. I looked forward to a time at which it would be safe for me to escape. I was too young to think of doing so immediately; besides, I wished to learn how to write, as I might have occasion to write my own pass. I consoled myself with the hope that I should one day find a good chance. Meanwhile, I would learn to write.

The idea as to how I might learn to write was suggested to me by being in Durgin and Bailey's ship-yard, and frequently seeing the ship carpenters, after hewing, and getting a piece of timber ready for use, write on the timber the name of that part of the ship for which it was intended. When a piece of timber was intended for the larboard side, it would be marked thus—"L." When a piece was for the starboard side, it would be marked thus—"S." A piece for the larboard side forward, would be marked thus—"L. F." When a piece was for starboard side forward, it would be marked thus—"S. F." For larboard aft, it would be marked thus—"L. A." For starboard aft, it would be marked thus—"S. A." I soon learned the names of these letters, and for what they were intended when placed upon a piece of timber in the ship-yard. I immediately commenced copying them, and in a short time was able to make the four letters named. After that, when I met with any boy who I knew could write, I would tell him I could write as well as he. The next word would be, "I don't believe you. Let me see you try it." I would then make the letters which I had been so fortunate as to learn, and ask him to beat that. In this way I got a good many lessons in writing, which it is quite possible I should never have gotten in any other way. During this time, my copy-book was the board fence, brick wall, and pavement; my pen and ink was a lump of chalk. With these, I learned mainly how to write. I then commenced and continued copying the Italics in Webster's Spelling Book,[4] until I could make them all without looking on the book. By this time, my little Master Thomas had gone to school, and learned how to write, and had written over a number of copy-books. These had been brought home, and shown to some of our near neighbors, and then laid aside. My mistress used to go to class meeting at the Wilk Street meetinghouse every Monday afternoon, and leave me to take care of the house. When left thus, I used to spend the time in writing in the spaces left in Master Thomas's copy-book, copying what he had written. I continued to do this until I could write a hand very similar to that of Master Thomas. Thus, after a long, tedious effort for years, I finally succeeded in learning how to write.

1845

4. Italics were used to make type resemble handwriting in *The American Spelling Book* (1783), by the American lexicographer Noah Webster (1758–1843).

George Orwell

1903–1950

Orwell is probably best known for his two novels, Animal Farm *and* 1984, *which were published just after World War II. Both warned the liberal democracies of the West against the dangers of modern mass politics. In particular,* 1984 *diagnosed the manipulative power of political propaganda as it was practiced by totalitarian regimes on the far left (Stalinist Russia) and far right (Nazi Germany). "Newspeak," as he calls this linguistic practice, limits vocabulary and dumbs down complex thought to simple, catchy phrases: ultimately, it prevents complex thought and renders the public incapable of critical reasoning. In this essay, it's not the general public that is threatened, but thinkers and writers—those we might call intellectuals—who produce public discourse: magazine writers, historians, critics, lawyers, government bureaucrats, and policy wonks. (The essay first appeared in 1946 in a British magazine,* Horizon, *which, though small, was read by many writers.) Intellectuals are not endangered by the stripping down of language to primitive grunts. Their danger consists of the bad tendency to emit a mist of empty verbiage, which clouds a subject the way a fog blurs your vision. The ability to judge something validly fades in the murk of rhythmic, somnolent, meaningless phrases. The rules for precision that Orwell offers here have defined the style of good rhetoric for more than seventy years.*

Politics and the English Language

Most people who bother with the matter at all would admit that the English language is in a bad way, but it is generally assumed that we cannot by conscious action do anything about it. Our civilization is decadent and our language—so the argument runs—must inevitably share in the general collapse. It follows that any struggle against the abuse of language is a sentimental archaism, like preferring candles to electric light or hansom cabs to aeroplanes. Underneath this lies the half-conscious belief that language is a natural growth and not an instrument which we shape for our own purposes.

Now, it is clear that the decline of a language must ultimately have political and economic causes: it is not due simply to the bad influence of this or that individual writer. But an effect can become a cause, reinforcing the original cause and producing the same effect in an intensified form, and so on indefinitely. A man may take to drink because he feels himself to be a failure, and then fail all the more completely because he drinks. It is rather the same thing that is happening to the English language. It becomes ugly and inaccurate because our thoughts are foolish, but the slovenliness of our language makes it easier for us to have foolish thoughts. The point is that the process is reversible. Modern English, especially written English, is full of bad habits which spread by imitation and which can be avoided if one is willing to take the necessary trouble. If one gets rid of these habits one can think more clearly, and to think clearly is a necessary first step toward political regeneration: so that the fight against bad English is not frivolous and is not the exclusive concern of professional writers. I will come back to this presently, and I hope that by that time the meaning of what I have said here will have become clearer. Meanwhile, here are five specimens of the English language as it is now habitually written.

These five passages have not been picked out because they are especially bad—I could have quoted far worse if I had chosen—but because they illustrate various of the mental vices from which we now suffer. They are a little below the average, but are fairly representative examples. I number them so that I can refer back to them when necessary:

1. I am not, indeed, sure whether it is not true to say that the Milton who once seemed not unlike a seventeenth-century Shelley had not become, out of an experience ever more bitter in each year, more alien (*sic*) to the founder of that Jesuit sect which nothing could induce him to tolerate.

   Professor Harold Laski (*Essay in Freedom of Expression*).

2. Above all, we cannot play ducks and drakes with a native battery of idioms which prescribes egregious collocations of vocables as the Basic *put up with* for *tolerate*, or *put at a loss* for *bewilder*.

   Professor Lancelot Hogben (*Interglossia*).

3. On the one side we have the free personality: by definition it is not neurotic, for it has neither conflict nor dream. Its desires, such as they are, are transparent, for they are just what institutional approval keeps in the forefront of consciousness; another institutional pattern would alter their number and intensity, there is little in them that is natural, irreducible, or culturally dangerous. But on the other side, the social bond itself is nothing but the mutual reflection of these self-secure integrities. Recall the definition of love. Is not this the very picture of a small academic? Where is there a place in this hall of mirrors for either personality or fraternity?

   Essay on psychology in *Politics* (New York).

4. All the "best people" from the gentlemen's clubs, and all the frantic Fascist captains, united in common hatred of Socialism and bestial horror at the rising tide of the mass revolutionary movement, have turned to acts of provocation, to foul incendiarism, to medieval legends of poisoned wells, to legalize their own destruction of proletarian organizations, and rouse the agitated petty-bourgeoise to chauvinistic fervor on behalf of the fight against the revolutionary way out of the crisis.

   Communist pamphlet.

5. If a new spirit is to be infused into this old country, there is one thorny and contentious reform which must be tackled, and that is the humanization and galvanization of the B.B.C. Timidity here will bespeak canker and atrophy of the soul. The heart of Britain may be sound and of strong beat, for instance, but the British lion's roar at present is like that of Bottom in Shakespeare's *A Midsummer Night's Dream*—as gentle as any sucking dove. A virile new Britain cannot continue indefinitely to be traduced in the eyes or rather ears, of the world by the effete languors of Langham Place, brazenly masquerading as "standard English," When the Voice of Britain is heard at nine o'clock, better far and infinitely less ludicrous to hear aitches honestly dropped than the present priggish, inflated, inhibited, school-ma'amish arch braying of blameless bashful mewing maidens!

   Letter in *Tribune*.

Each of these passages has faults of its own, but, quite apart from avoidable ugliness, two qualities are common to all of them. The first is staleness of imagery; the other is lack of precision. The writer either has a meaning and cannot express it, or he inadvertently says something else, or he is almost indifferent as to whether his words mean anything or not. This mixture of vagueness and sheer incompetence is the most marked characteristic of modern English prose, and especially of any kind of political writing. As soon as certain topics are raised, the concrete melts into the abstract and no one seems able to think of turns of speech that are not hackneyed: prose consists less and less of words chosen for the sake of their meaning, and more and more of phrases tacked together like the sections of a prefabricated hen-house. I list below, with notes and examples, various of the tricks by means of which the work of prose-construction is habitually dodged.

Dying metaphors. A newly invented metaphor assists thought by evoking a visual image, while on the other hand a metaphor which is technically "dead" (e.g. *iron resolution*) has in effect reverted to being an ordinary word and can generally be used without loss of vividness. But in between these two classes there is a huge dump of worn-out metaphors which have lost all evocative power and are merely used because they save people the trouble of inventing phrases for themselves. Examples are: *Ring the changes on, take up the cudgels for, toe the line, ride roughshod over, stand shoulder to shoulder with, play into the hands of, no axe to grind, grist to the mill, fishing in troubled waters, on the order of the day, Achilles' heel, swan song, hotbed.* Many of these are used without knowledge of their meaning (what is a "rift," for instance?), and incompatible metaphors are frequently mixed, a sure sign that the writer is not interested in what he is saying. Some metaphors now current have been twisted out of their original meaning without those who use them even being aware of the fact. For example, *toe the line* is sometimes written as *tow the line.* Another example is *the hammer and the anvil,* now always used with the implication that the anvil gets the worst of it. In real life it is always the anvil that breaks the hammer, never the other way about: a writer who stopped to think what he was saying would avoid perverting the original phrase.

Operators, or *verbal false limbs.* These save the trouble of picking out appropriate verbs and nouns, and at the same time pad each sentence with extra syllables which give it an appearance of symmetry. Characteristic phrases are: *render inoperative, militate against, prove unacceptable, make contact with, be subject to, give rise to, give grounds for, have the effect of, play a leading part (role) in, make itself felt, take effect, exhibit a tendency to, serve the purpose of,* etc. The keynote is the elimination of simple verbs. Instead of being a single word, such as *break, stop, spoil, mend, kill,* a verb becomes a *phrase,* made up of a noun or adjective tacked on to some general-purposes verb such as *prove, serve, form, play, render.* In addition, the passive voice is wherever possible used in preference to the active, and noun constructions are used instead of gerunds (*by examination of* instead of *by examining*). The range of verbs is further cut down by means of the *-ize* and *de-* formations, and banal statements are given an appearance of profundity by means of the *not un-* formation. Simple conjunctions and prepositions are replaced by such phrases as *with respect to, having regard to, the fact that, by dint of, in view of, in the interests of, on the hypothesis that;* and the ends of sentences are saved from anticlimax by such resounding commonplaces as *greatly to be desired, cannot be left out of account, a development to be expected in the near future, deserving of serious consideration, brought to a satisfactory conclusion,* and so on and so forth.

Pretentious diction. Words like *phenomenon, element, individual* (as noun), *objective, categorical, effective, virtual, basic, primary, promote, constitute, exhibit, exploit, utilize, eliminate, liquidate,* are used to dress up simple statements and give an air of scientific impartiality to biassed judgements Adjectives like *epoch-making, epic, historic, unforgettable, triumphant, age-old, inevitable, inexorable, veritable,* are used to dignify the sordid processes of international politics, while writing that aims at glorifying war usually takes on an archaic colour, its characteristic words being: *realm, throne, chariot, mailed fist, trident, sword, shield, buckler, banner, jackboot, clarion.* Foreign words and expressions such as *cul de sac, ancien régime, deus ex machina, mutatis mutandis, status quo, Gleichschaltung, Weltanschauung,* are used to give an air of culture and elegance. Except for the useful abbreviations *i.e., e.g.,* and *etc.,* there is no real need for any of the hundreds of foreign phrases now current in English. Bad writers, and especially scientific, political and sociological writers, are nearly always haunted by the notion that Latin or Greek words are grander

In our time it is broadly true that political writing is bad writing. Where it is not true, it will generally be found that the writer is some kind of rebel, expressing his private opinions, and not a "party line." Orthodoxy, of whatever colour, seems to demand a lifeless, imitative style. The political dialects to be found in pamphlets, leading articles, manifestos, White Papers and the speeches of Under-Secretaries do, of course, vary from party to party, but they are all alike in that one almost never finds in them a fresh, vivid, home-made turn of speech. When one watches some tired hack on the platform mechanically repeating the familiar phrases—*bestial atrocities, iron heel, blood-stained tyranny, free peoples of the world, stand shoulder to shoulder*—one often has a curious feeling that one is not watching a live human being but some kind of dummy: a feeling which suddenly becomes stronger at moments when the light catches the speaker's spectacles and turns them into blank discs which seem to have no eyes behind them. And this is not altogether fanciful. A speaker who uses that kind of phraseology has gone some distance toward turning himself into a machine. The appropriate noises are coming out of his larynx, but his brain is not involved as it would be if he were choosing his words for himself. If the speech he is making is one that he is accustomed to make over and over again, he may be almost unconscious of what he is saying, as one is when one utters the responses in church. And this reduced state of consciousness, if not indispensable, is at any rate favourable to political conformity.

In our time, political speech and writing are largely the defence of the indefensible. Things like the continuance of British rule in India, the Russian purges and deportations, the dropping of the atom bombs on Japan, can indeed be defended, but only by arguments which are too brutal for most people to face, and which do not square with the professed aims of political parties.[3] Thus political language has to consist largely of euphemism, question-begging and

3. The British East India Company began ruling the subcontinent in 1757; India did not gain political independence until 1948, two years after this essay was written. "Russian purges" probably refers to the atrocities committed by Joseph Stalin's regime on citizens of the USSR; somewhere in the neighborhood of a million people died in the "Great Purge" of 1937–1938. "Atom bombs": in 1945, the United States dropped atom bombs on two cities, Hiroshima and Nagasaki, forcing the Japanese finally to surrender and end World War II; historians estimate the bombs killed between 130,000 and 226,000 people, many if not most of them women, children, and the aged [editor's note].

sheer cloudy vagueness. Defenceless villages are bombarded from the air, the inhabitants driven out into the countryside, the cattle machine-gunned, the huts set on fire with incendiary bullets: this is called *pacification.* Millions of peasants are robbed of their farms and sent trudging along the roads with no more than they can carry: this is called *transfer of population* or *rectification of frontiers.* People are imprisoned for years without trial, or shot in the back of the neck or sent to die of scurvy in Arctic lumber camps: this is called *elimination of unreliable elements.* Such phraseology is needed if one wants to name things without calling up mental pictures of them. Consider for instance some comfortable English professor defending Russian totalitarianism. He cannot say outright, "I believe in killing off your opponents when you can get good results by doing so." Probably, therefore, he will say something like this:

> While freely conceding that the Soviet régime exhibits certain features which the humanitarian may be inclined to deplore, we must, I think, agree that a certain curtailment of the right to political opposition is an unavoidable concomitant of transitional periods, and that the rigours which the Russian people have been called upon to undergo have been amply justified in the sphere of concrete achievement.

The inflated style is itself a kind of euphemism. A mass of Latin words falls upon the facts like soft snow, blurring the outlines and covering up all the details. The great enemy of clear language is insincerity. When there is a gap between one's real and one's declared aims, one turns as it were instinctively to long words and exhausted idioms, like a cuttlefish spurting out ink. In our age there is no such thing as "keeping out of politics." All issues are political issues, and politics itself is a mass of lies, evasions, folly, hatred and schizophrenia. When the general atmosphere is bad, language must suffer. I should expect to find—this is a guess which I have not sufficient knowledge to verify—that the German, Russian and Italian languages have all deteriorated in the last ten or fifteen years, as a result of dictatorship.

But if thought corrupts language, language can also corrupt thought. A bad usage can spread by tradition and imitation, even among people who should and do know better. The debased language that I have been discussing is in some ways very convenient. Phrases like *a not unjustifiable assumption, leaves much to be desired, would serve no good purpose, a consideration which we should do well to bear in mind,* are a continuous temptation, a packet of aspirins always at one's elbow. Look back through this essay, and for certain you will find that I have again and again committed the very faults I am protesting against. By this morning's post I have received a pamphlet dealing with conditions in Germany.[4] The author tells me that he "felt impelled" to write it. I open it at random, and here is almost the first sentence that I see: "(The Allies) have an opportunity not only of achieving a radical transformation of Germany's social and political structure in such a way as to avoid a nationalistic reaction in Germany itself, but at the same time of laying the foundations of a co-operative and unified Europe." You see, he "feels impelled" to write—feels, presumably, that he has something new to say—and yet his words, like cavalry horses answering the bugle, group themselves automatically into the familiar dreary pattern. This invasion of one's mind by ready-made phrases (*lay the foundations, achieve a radical transformation*) can only be prevented if one is constantly on guard against them, and every such phrase anaesthetizes a portion of one's brain.

I said earlier that the decadence of our language is probably curable. Those who deny this would argue, if they produced an argument at all, that language merely reflects existing social conditions, and that we cannot influence its development by any direct tinkering with words and constructions. So far as the general tone or spirit of a language goes, this may be true, but it is not true in detail. Silly words and expressions have often disappeared, not through any evolutionary process but owing to the conscious action of a minority. Two recent examples were *explore every avenue* and *leave no stone unturned,* which were killed by the jeers of a few journalists. There is a long list of fly-blown metaphors which could similarly be got rid of if enough people would interest themselves in the job; and it should

4. After Germany surrendered in May 1945, the major allied nations (the United States, the UK, and the USSR) had to decide how to rule and rebuild the defeated, shattered nation [editor's note].

also be possible to laugh the *not un-* formation out of existence,[5] to reduce the amount of Latin and Greek in the average sentence, to drive out foreign phrases and strayed scientific words, and, in general, to make pretentiousness unfashionable. But all these are minor points. The defence of the English language implies more than this, and perhaps it is best to start by saying what it does *not* imply.

To begin with it has nothing to do with archaism, with the salvaging of obsolete words and turns of speech, or with the setting up of a "standard English" which must never be departed from. On the contrary, it is especially concerned with the scrapping of every word or idiom which has outworn its usefulness. It has nothing to do with correct grammar and syntax, which are of no importance so long as one makes one's meaning clear or with the avoidance of Americanisms, or with having what is called a "good prose style." On the other hand it is not concerned with fake simplicity and the attempt to make written English colloquial. Nor does it even imply in every case preferring the Saxon word to the Latin one, though it does imply using the fewest and shortest words that will cover one's meaning. What is above all needed is to let the meaning choose the word, and not the other way about. In prose, the worst thing one can do with words is to surrender them. When you think of a concrete object, you think wordlessly, and then, if you want to describe the thing you have been visualising, you probably hunt about till you find the exact words that seem to fit it. When you think of something abstract you are more inclined to use words from the start, and unless you make a conscious effort to prevent it, the existing dialect will come rushing in and do the job for you, at the expense of blurring or even changing your meaning. Probably it is better to put off using words as long as possible and get one's meanings as clear as one can through pictures and sensations. Afterward one can choose—not simply *accept*—the phrases that will best cover the meaning, and then switch round and decide what impression one's words are likely to make on another person. This last effort of the mind cuts out all stale or mixed images, all prefabricated phrases, needless repetitions, and humbug and vagueness generally. But one can often be in doubt about the effect

5. One can cure oneself of the *not un-* formation by memorizing this sentence: *A not unblack dog was chasing a not unsmall rabbit across a not ungreen field.*

of a word or a phrase, and one needs rules that one can rely on when instinct fails. I think the following rules will cover most cases:

i. Never use a metaphor, simile or other figure of speech which you are used to seeing in print.
ii. Never use a long word where a short one will do.
iii. If it is possible to cut a word out, always cut it out.
iv. Never use the passive where you can use the active.
v. Never use a foreign phrase, a scientific word or a jargon word if you can think of an everyday English equivalent.
vi. Break any of these rules sooner than say anything outright barbarous.

These rules sound elementary, and so they are, but they demand a deep change of attitude in anyone who has grown used to writing in the style now fashionable. One could keep all of them and still write bad English, but one could not write the kind of stuff that I quoted in those five specimens at the beginning of this article.

I have not here been considering the literary use of language, but merely language as an instrument for expressing and not for concealing or preventing thought. Stuart Chase and others have come near to claiming that all abstract words are meaningless, and have used this as a pretext for advocating a kind of political quietism. Since you don't know what Fascism is, how can you struggle against Fascism? One need not swallow such absurdities as this, but one ought to recognize that the present political chaos is connected with the decay of language, and that one can probably bring about some improvement by starting at the verbal end. If you simplify your English, you are freed from the worst follies of orthodoxy. You cannot speak any of the necessary dialects, and when you make a stupid remark its stupidity will be obvious, even to yourself. Political language—and with variations this is true of all political parties, from Conservatives to Anarchists—is designed to make lies sound truthful and murder respectable, and to give an appearance of solidity to pure wind. One cannot change this all in a moment, but one can at least change one's own habits, and from time to time one can even, if one jeers loudly enough, send some worn-out and useless phrase—some *jackboot, Achilles' heel, hotbed, melting pot, acid test, veritable inferno* or other lump of verbal refuse—into the dustbin where it belongs.

1946

Margaret Chase Smith
1897–1995

In February 1950, Senator Joseph McCarthy began the now-infamous "McCarthy era" of public accusations, prosecutions, and persecutions of suspected communists and gay people. On successive occasions, McCarthy exposed hundreds of supposed subversives in the State Department, U.S. Army, and other places of public trust, usually without any credible evidence. As a member of Congress he was immune from the laws that protect citizens from libel and slander, so he did not have to substantiate his claims. Few of the accused were ever tried, let alone convicted, but many reputations and lives were ruined in the witch-hunt atmosphere McCarthy stirred up. When Senator Lester Hunt from Wyoming introduced a bill removing those congressional privileges, McCarthy threatened (and followed through on) the prosecution of Hunt's son for being gay. In 1954, with his son in jail and under severe stress, Hunt committed suicide. Not long after that, the Senate censured McCarthy, fully discrediting him and his tactics. This essay, which was delivered near the beginning of McCarthy's campaign, is considered today to be a hallmark defense of reason in times of political hysteria.

Declaration of Conscience[1]

Mr. President, I would like to speak briefly and simply about a serious national condition. It is a national feeling of fear and frustration that could result in national suicide and the end of everything that we Americans hold dear. It is a condition that comes from the lack of effective leadership either in the legislative branch or the executive branch of our government.

That leadership is so lacking that serious and responsible proposals are being made that national advisory commissions be appointed to provide such critically needed leadership.

I speak as briefly as possible because too much harm has already been done with irresponsible words of bitterness and selfish political

1. U.S., Congress, Senate, *Congressional Record*, 81st Congress, 2d sess., pp. 7894–95.

opportunism. I speak as simply as possible because the issue is too great to be obscured by eloquence. I speak simply and briefly in the hope that my words will be taken to heart.

Mr. President, I speak as a Republican. I speak as a woman. I speak as a United States senator. I speak as an American.

"A Forum of Hate and Character Assassination"

The United States Senate has long enjoyed worldwide respect as the greatest deliberative body in the world. But recently that deliberative character has too often been debased to the level of a forum of hate and character assassination sheltered by the shield of congressional immunity.

It is ironical that we senators can in debate in the Senate, directly or indirectly, by any form of words, impute to any American who is not a senator any conduct or motive unworthy or unbecoming an American—and without that non-senator American having any legal redress against us—yet if we say the same thing in the Senate about our colleagues we can be stopped on the grounds of being out of order.

It is strange that we can verbally attack anyone else without restraint and with full protection, and yet we hold ourselves above the same type of criticism here on the Senate floor. Surely the United States Senate is big enough to take self-criticism and self-appraisal. Surely we should be able to take the same kind of character attacks that we "dish out" to outsiders.

I think that it is high time for the United States Senate and its members to do some real soul searching and to weigh our consciences as to the manner in which we are performing our duty to the people of America and the manner in which we are using or abusing our individual powers and privileges.

I think that it is high time that we remembered that we have sworn to uphold and defend the Constitution. I think that it is high time that we remembered that the Constitution, as amended, speaks not only of the freedom of speech but also of trial by jury instead of trial by accusation.

Whether it be a criminal prosecution in court or a character prosecution in the Senate, there is little practical distinction when the life of a person has been ruined.

"The Basic Principles of Americanism"

Those of us who shout the loudest about Americanism in making character assassinations are all too frequently those who, by our own words and acts, ignore some of the basic principles of Americanism—

The right to criticize.

The right to hold unpopular beliefs.

The right to protest.

The right of independent thought.

The exercise of these rights should not cost one single American citizen his reputation or his right to a livelihood nor should he be in danger of losing his reputation or livelihood merely because he happens to know someone who holds unpopular beliefs. Who of us does not? Otherwise none of us could call our souls our own. Otherwise thought control would have set in.

The American people are sick and tired of being afraid to speak their minds lest they be politically smeared as "Communists" or "Fascists" by their opponents. Freedom of speech is not what it used to be in America. It has been so abused by some that it is not exercised by others.

The American people are sick and tired of seeing innocent people smeared and guilty people whitewashed. But there have been enough proved cases, such as the *Amerasia*[2] case, the Hiss case,[3] the Coplon case,[4] the Gold case,[5] to cause nationwide distrust and strong suspicion that there may be something to the unproved, sensational accusations.

A Challenge to the Republican Party

As a Republican, I say to my colleagues on this side of the aisle that the Republican party faces a challenge today that is not unlike the

2. *Amerasia* was a pro-Communist publication in whose New York office a number of classified government documents were found. The editor and two foreign service officers were arrested but never brought to trial.

3. Alger Hiss (1904–1996) was an adviser to the State Department who was accused of spying for Russia. After appearing before the House Committee on Un-American Activities in 1948, he was convicted of perjury in 1950. He served four years in prison, although he continued to maintain that he was innocent.

4. In March 1950 Judith Coplon was found guilty of attempted espionage against the United States.

5. In 1950, with a number of others, Harry Gold was arrested and convicted of passing American atomic secrets to the USSR.

challenge which it faced back in Lincoln's day. The Republican party so successfully met that challenge that it emerged from the Civil War as the champion of a united nation—in addition to being a party which unrelentingly fought loose spending and loose programs.

Today our country is being psychologically divided by the confusion and the suspicions that are bred in the United States Senate to spread like cancerous tentacles of "know nothing, suspect everything" attitudes. Today we have a Democratic administration which has developed a mania for loose spending and loose programs.[6] History is repeating itself—and the Republican party again has the opportunity to emerge as the champion of unity and prudence. The record of the present Democratic administration has provided us with sufficient campaign issues without the necessity of resorting to political smears. America is rapidly losing its position as leader of the world simply because the Democratic administration has pitifully failed to provide effective leadership.

The Democratic administration has completely confused the American people by its daily contradictory grave warnings and optimistic assurances, which show the people that our Democratic administration has no idea of where it is going.

The Democratic administration has greatly lost the confidence of the American people by its complacency to the threat of communism here at home and the leak of vital secrets to Russia through key officials of the Democratic administration. There are enough proved cases to make this point without diluting our criticism with unproved charges.

Surely these are sufficient reasons to make it clear to the American people that it is time for a change and that a Republican victory is necessary to the security of the country. Surely it is clear that this nation will continue to suffer so long as it is governed by the present ineffective Democratic administration.

"The Four Horsemen of Calumny"

Yet to displace it with a Republican regime embracing a philosophy that lacks political integrity or intellectual honesty would prove

6. Harry S Truman, a Democrat, was president from 1945 to 1953, when the Republican Dwight D. Eisenhower entered the White House. In 1950, the Democrats held significant majorities in both the U.S. House and Senate [editor's note].

equally disastrous to the nation. The nation sorely needs a Republican victory. But I do not want to see the Republican party ride to political victory on the Four Horsemen of Calumny—Fear, Ignorance, Bigotry, and Smear.

I doubt if the Republican party could do so, simply because I do not believe the American people will uphold any political party that puts political exploitation above national interest. Surely we Republicans are not that desperate for victory.

I do not want to see the Republican party win that way. While it might be a fleeting victory for the Republican party, it would be a more lasting defeat for the American people. Surely it would ultimately be suicide for the Republican party and the two-party system that has protected our American liberties from the dictatorship of a one-party system.

As members of the minority party, we do not have the primary authority to formulate the policy of our government. But we do have the responsibility of rendering constructive criticism, of clarifying issues, of allaying fears by acting as responsible citizens.

As a woman, I wonder how the mothers, wives, sisters, and daughters feel about the way in which members of their families have been politically mangled in Senate debate—and I use the word "debate" advisedly.

"Irresponsible Sensationalism"

As a United States senator, I am not proud of the way in which the Senate has been made a publicity platform for irresponsible sensationalism. I am not proud of the reckless abandon in which unproved charges have been hurled from this side of the aisle. I am not proud of the obviously staged, undignified countercharges which have been attempted in retaliation from the other side of the aisle.

I do not like the way the Senate has been made a rendezvous for vilification, for selfish political gain at the sacrifice of individual reputations and national unity. I am not proud of the way we smear outsiders from the floor of the Senate and hide behind the cloak of congressional immunity and still place ourselves beyond criticism on the floor of the Senate.

As an American, I am shocked at the way Republicans and Democrats alike are playing directly into the Communist design of "confuse, divide, and conquer." As an American, I do not want a Democratic administration "whitewash" or "coverup" any more than I want a Republican smear or witch hunt.

As an American, I condemn a Republican Fascist just as much as I condemn a Democrat Communist. I condemn a Democrat Fascist just as much as I condemn a Republican Communist. They are equally dangerous to you and me and to our country. As an American, I want to see our nation recapture the strength and unity it once had when we fought the enemy instead of ourselves.

It is with these thoughts that I have drafted what I call a Declaration of Conscience. I am gratified that the senator from New Hampshire [Mr. TOBEY], the senator from Vermont [Mr. AIKEN], the senator from Oregon [Mr. MORSE], the senator from New York [Mr. IVES], the senator from Minnesota [Mr. THYE], and the senator from New Jersey [Mr. HENDRICKSON] have concurred in that declaration and have authorized me to announce their concurrence.

The declaration reads as follows:

Statement of Seven Republican Senators

1. We are Republicans. But we are Americans first. It is as Americans that we express our concern with the growing confusion that threatens the security and stability of our country. Democrats and Republicans alike have contributed to that confusion.
2. The Democratic administration has initially created the confusion by its lack of effective leadership, by its contradictory grave warnings and optimistic assurances, by its complacency to the threat of communism here at home, by its oversensitiveness to rightful criticism, by its petty bitterness against its critics.
3. Certain elements of the Republican party have materially added to this confusion in the hopes of riding the Republican party to victory through the selfish political exploitation of fear, bigotry, ignorance, and intolerance. There are enough mistakes of the Democrats for Republicans to criticize constructively without resorting to political smears.

4. To this extent, Democrats and Republicans alike have unwittingly, but undeniably, played directly into the Communist design of "confuse, divide, and conquer."
5. It is high time that we stopped thinking politically as Republicans and Democrats about elections and started thinking patriotically as Americans about national security based on individual freedom. It is high time that we all stopped being tools and victims of totalitarian techniques—techniques that, if continued here unchecked, will surely end what we have come to cherish as the American way of life.

Margaret Chase Smith, Maine
Charles W. Tobey, New Hampshire
George D. Aiken, Vermont
Wayne L. Morse, Oregon
Irving M. Ives, New York
Edward J. Thye, Minnesota
Robert C. Hendrickson, New Jersey[7]

1950

7. Charles W. Tobey (1880–1953) served in the Senate, 1939–1953; George D. Aiken (1892–1984) served in the Senate, 1941–1975; Wayne L. Morse (1900–1974) served in the Senate, 1945–1969 (he became an Independent in 1953 and then a Democrat in 1955); Irving M. Ives (1896–1962) served in the Senate, 1947–1959; Edward J. Thye (1896–1969) served in the Senate, 1947–1959; Robert C. Hendrickson (1898–1964) served in the Senate, 1949–1955.

Deborah Tannen

b. 1945

Tannen is a linguist who has published several books about conversational styles: for instance, the difference between the way men and women communicate verbally, and the different conventions between speakers of various geographic regions. Many of her studies explore miscommunications—how differing styles of speech might confuse rather than convey meaning. For example, saying "It's hot in here" might be an indirect way of saying "Open the window," and indirect styles of conversation, Tannen argues, are typically misinterpreted (especially in American workplaces) as weakness. Over the last generation, Tannen believes, Americans have been using an increasingly adversarial style of communication, which she calls "agonism." Agonism, she explains, is our knee-jerk habit of relying on combative, military metaphors in so many realms of discourse. "War metaphors come so easily," she writes, "and are so catchy, that we hardly notice them." The battle lines are drawn *between debating politicians; we* fight wars *on crime, on poverty, on drugs, on just about anything we want public policy to alleviate. The ubiquity of such metaphors closes off our access to collaborative styles of discourse and solutions. In this essay, Tannen suggests that a related phenomenon occurs in academic settings. In fact, though this essay first appeared in the* New York Times, *twenty years later she expanded it for the MIT journal* Daedalus, *which targets an audience of scholars. The character of the academic enterprise is imagined as a contest of ideas, where a new notion must establish itself by insistently disputing someone's previous notion. The phrase "marketplace of ideas," for instance, which is often used to describe academic discourse, is a metaphor about* competition, *not collaboration. Pay particular attention to what Tannen says about the way we seek truth in college classrooms—does your own experience support her assertions?*

The Triumph of the Yell

I put the question to a journalist who had written a vitriolic attack on a leading feminist researcher: "Why do you need to make others wrong for you to be right?" Her response: "It's an argument!"

Several years ago I was on a television talk show with a representative of the men's movement. I didn't foresee any problem, since there is nothing in my work that is anti-male. But in the room where guests gather before the show I found a man wearing a shirt and tie and a floor-length skirt, with waist-length red hair. He politely introduced himself and told me he liked my book. Then he added: "When I get out there, I'm going to attack you. But don't take it personally. That's why they invite me on, so that's what I'm going to do."

When the show began, I spoke only a sentence or two before this man nearly jumped out of his chair, threw his arms before him in gestures of anger and began shrieking—first attacking me, but soon moving on to rail against woman. The most disturbing thing about his hysterical ranting was what it sparked in the studio audience: they too became vicious, attacking not me (I hadn't had a chance to say anything) and not him (who wants to tangle with someone who will scream at you?) but the other guests: unsuspecting women who had agreed to come on the show to talk about their problems communicating with their spouses.

This is the most dangerous aspect of modeling intellectual interchange as a fight: it contributes to an atmosphere of animosity that spreads like a fever. In a society where people express their anger by shooting, the result of demonizing those with whom we disagree can be truly demonic.

I am not suggesting that journalists stop asking tough questions necessary to get at the facts, even if those questions may appear challenging. And of course it is the responsibility of the media to represent serious opposition when it exists, and of intellectuals everywhere to explore potential weaknesses in others' arguments. But when opposition becomes the overwhelming avenue of inquiry, when the lust for opposition exalts extreme views and obscures complexity, when our eagerness to find weaknesses blinds us to strengths, when the atmosphere of animosity precludes respect and poisons our relations with one another, then the culture of critique is stifling us. If we could move beyond it, we would move closer to the truth.

1994

Michael Kinsley
b. 1951

This essay argues that we should respect the opinion of "the people" only when they know what they're talking about. Kinsley was writing in 1995, just about the same time that the internet was becoming commonly available and years before the appearance of convenient information clearinghouses such as Wikipedia, which was launched in 2001. Today it is comparatively easy to inform oneself of the facts, and yet, as the Washington Post *reported in 2013, the typical American still thinks that about 28 percent of the federal budget went to foreign aid, while the real figure was about 1 percent (and about a third of that 1 percent was military aid). As a student of rhetoric, you have a great obligation to know your facts before you assert your opinion. Because you are training in the arts of persuasion, you can do more damage than the typical citizen. More than 2,000 years ago, Plato and Aristotle warned against rhetoricians who practiced their art in the service of power rather than truth. These they called "Sophists," and our common term* sophistry, *meaning "fallacious or deceptive arguments," derives from these Greeks. At the dawn of the scientific revolution, Sir Francis Bacon decried such reasoning as the Idol of the Theater: ignorant acceptance of traditional, popular notions inculcated by religious or political ideologies. Plato, Aristotle, Bacon, and Kinsley all impose a special obligation on rhetoricians, such as yourself, to look at the evidence before drawing conclusions.*

The Intellectual Free Lunch

The weekend before President Clinton's State of the Union Address, the *Wall Street Journal* assembled a focus group of middle-class white males—the demographic group *du jour*—to plumb the depth of their proverbial anger. The results were highly satisfactory. These guys are mad as hell. They're mad at welfare, they're mad at special-interest lobbyists. "But perhaps the subject that produces the most agreement among the group," the *Journal* reports, "is the view that Washington should stop sending money abroad and instead zero in on the domestic front."

A poll released last week by the Program on International Policy Attitudes at the University of Maryland contains similar findings. According to this survey, seventy-five per cent of Americans believe that the United States spends "too much" on foreign aid, and sixty-four per cent want foreign-aid spending cut. Apparently, a cavalier eleven per cent of Americans think it's fine to spend "too much" on foreign aid. But there is no denying the poll's larger finding that big majorities say they think the tab is too high.

Respondents were also asked, though, how big a share of the federal budget currently goes to foreign aid. The median answer was fifteen per cent; the average answer was eighteen per cent. The correct answer is less than one per cent: the United States government spends about fourteen billion dollars a year on foreign aid (including military assistance), out of a total budget of a trillion and a half. To a question about how much foreign-aid spending would be "appropriate," the median answer was five per cent of the budget. A question about how much would be "too little" produced a median answer of three per cent—more than three times the current level of foreign-aid spending.

To the International Policy folks at the University of Maryland, these results demonstrate "strong support for maintaining foreign aid at current spending levels or higher." That's just their liberal-internationalist spin, of course. You might say with equal justice that the results demonstrate a national wish to see foreign aid cut by two-thirds. It's true that after the pollsters humiliated their subjects with the correct answer to the question about how much (or, rather, how little) the United States spends on foreign aid, only thirty-five per cent of the respondents had the fortitude to say they still wanted to see it cut. But what people will say after being corrected by an authority figure with a clipboard hardly constitutes "strong support."

This poll is less interesting for what it shows about foreign aid than for what it shows about American democracy. It's not just that Americans are scandalously ignorant. It's that they seem to believe they have a democratic right to their ignorance. All over the country—at dinner tables, in focus groups, on call-in radio shows, and, no doubt, occasionally on the floor of Congress—citizens are expressing outrage about how much we spend on foreign aid, without having the faintest idea what that amount is. This is not, surely, a question of being misinformed. No one—not even Rush Limbaugh[1]—is out there spreading the falsehood that we spend fifteen percent of the federal budget (two hundred and twenty-five billion dollars) on foreign aid. People are forming and expressing passionate views about foreign aid on the basis of no information at all. Or perhaps they think that the amount being spent on foreign aid is a matter of opinion, like everything else.

Populism, in its latest manifestation, celebrates ignorant opinion and undifferentiated rage. As long as you're mad as hell and aren't going to take it anymore, no one will inquire very closely into what, exactly, "it" is and whether you really ought to feel that way. Pandering politicians are partly to blame, to be sure. So is the development christened "hyper-democracy" by last week's *Time*: the way the communications revolution is eroding representative government by providing instant feedback between voters' whims and politicians' actions.[2] But ubiquitous opinion polls are part of the problem, too.

The typical opinion poll about, say, foreign aid doesn't trouble to ask whether the respondent knows the first thing about the topic being opined upon, and no conventional poll disqualifies an answer on the ground of mere total ignorance. The premise of opinion polling is that people are, and of right ought to be, omni-opinionated—that they should have views on all subjects at all times—and that all such views are equally valid. It's always remarkable how few people say they "aren't sure" about or "don't know" the answer to some pollster's question. ("Never thought about it," "Couldn't care less," and "Let me get back to you on that after I've done some reading" aren't even options.) So, given the prominence of polls in our political culture, it's no surprise that people have come to believe that their opinions on the issues of the day need not be fettered by either facts or reflection.

Add opinions to the list of symptoms of the free-lunch disease that blights American politics. First, in the early nineteen-eighties, came the fiscal free lunch: taxes can be cut without cutting middle-class

1. Rush Limbaugh (b. 1951), conservative radio personality. [All notes are the editor's.]

2. On January 23, 1995, Robert Wright published a cover story in *Time* ("Hyper-democracy: Washington isn't dangerously disconnected from the people; the trouble may be it's too plugged in") that argued that electronic media were forcing lawmakers to become too responsive to the uncritical whims of the people.

government benefits. Then, with the end of the Cold War, came the foreign-policy free lunch: America can strut as the world's superpower without putting blood or treasure at risk. Now there's the intellectual free lunch: I'm entitled to vociferous opinions on any subject, without having to know, or even think, about it.

All this may sound horribly snooty. But it isn't. It is not the argument that Walter Lippmann made in "Public Opinion," where he advocated relying on élite "bureaus" of wise men to make crucial policy decisions.[3] Lippmann's belief was that modern life had rendered public policy too complex for the average voter. But there is nothing especially complex about the factual question of how much the country spends on foreign aid. It may be too heavy a burden of civic responsibility to expect every citizen—what with work and family and life outside politics—to carry this number around in his or her head. But it is not asking too much to expect a citizen to recognize that he or she needs to know that number, at least roughly, in order to have a valid opinion about whether it is too large or too small. Americans are capable of making informed, reflective decisions on policy questions. But they often seem to be under the impression that they needn't bother.

We need a new form of democratic piety. It shows respect, not contempt, for "the people" to hold them to something approaching the intellectual standard you would apply to yourself or a friend. By contrast, it is contemptuous, not respectful, to excuse "the people" from all demands of intellectual rigor or honesty on the ground that their judgments are wise by definition. We honor our friends by challenging them when we think they're wrong. It shows that we take them seriously. Believers in democracy owe "the people" no less.

1995

3. Walter Lippmann (1889–1974), journalist whose 1922 book *Public Opinion* argued for mechanisms that would distance the masses from the direct exercise power.

Deborah Brandt
b. 1951

If you're using this book as part of a course in academic writing, this essay might be the most important in the whole volume. It discusses how people acquire "literacy," which, broadly speaking, means more than the ability to read and write. It means the ability to use language, especially written language, in any number of different rhetorical situations. Learning to write in an academic context, for example, is like learning a new language. Similarly, when you learn how to write for a specialized internet media—let's say Facebook—you have to figure out what's appropriate in that setting and what is not, what tone to use, how to phrase things for this particular community of readers. The stakes are much higher, of course, when the community of readers is in the workplace, not in our leisure spaces. As this essay demonstrates, the acquisition of literacies is a lifelong process, as we continuously encounter new communities of writers and readers and as the rules governing old communities evolve. Brandt first published this article in the journal, College Composition and Communication (CCC), *which is the main trade publication of college writing teachers. (As a consequence of the essay's having been written for a specialized audience, you might find the vocabulary and sentence-style a bit difficult on your first read: Brandt was not talking to you but to people who study and teach writing. You might also note how much this community relies on personal testimony for evidence.) After this essay was published, many college writing instructors redesigned their courses to educate students about how important these literacies are in the modern information age and to teach students to analyze new writing contexts and adapt to them. Many courses include a "literacy narrative" assignment to facilitate this learning. You might pay particular attention to how success or failure in acquiring new literacies translates into how much economic and political power one has.*

Sponsors of Literacy

In his sweeping history of adult learning in the United States, Joseph Kett describes the intellectual atmosphere available to young apprentices who worked in the small, decentralized print shops of antebellum America. Because printers also were the solicitors and editors of what they published, their workshops served as lively incubators for literacy and political discourse. By the mid-nineteenth century, however, this learning space was disrupted when the invention of the steam press reorganized the economy of the print industry. Steam presses were so expensive that they required capital outlays beyond the means of many printers. As a result, print jobs were outsourced, the processes of editing and printing were split, and, in tight competition, print apprentices became low-paid mechanics with no more access to the multi-skilled environment of the craft-shop (Kett 67–70). While this shift in working conditions may be evidence of the deskilling of workers induced by the Industrial Revolution (Nicholas and Nicholas), it also offers a site for reflecting upon the dynamic sources of literacy and literacy learning. The reading and writing skills of print apprentices in this period were the achievements not simply of teachers and learners nor of the discourse practices of the printer community. Rather, these skills existed fragilely, contingently within an economic moment. The pre-steam press economy enabled some of the most basic aspects of the apprentices' literacy, especially their access to material production and the public meaning or worth of their skills Paradoxically, even as the steam-powered penny press made print more accessible (by making publishing more profitable), it brought an end to a particular form of literacy sponsorship and a drop in literate potential.

The apprentices' experience invites rumination upon literacy learning and teaching today. Literacy looms as one of the great engines of profit and competitive advantage in the 20th century: a lubricant for consumer desire; a means for integrating corporate markets; a foundation for the deployment of weapons and other technology; a raw material in the mass production of information. As ordinary citizens have been compelled into these economies, their reading and writing skills have grown sharply more central to the everyday trade of information and goods as well as to the pursuit of education, employment, civil rights, status. At the same time, people's literate skills have grown vulnerable to unprecedented turbulence in their economic value, as conditions, forms, and standards of literacy achievement seem to shift with almost every new generation of learners. How are we to understand the vicissitudes of individual literacy development in relationship to the large-scale economic forces that set the routes and determine the wordly worth of that literacy?

The field of writing studies has had much to say about individual literacy development. Especially in the last quarter of the 20th century, we have theorized, researched, critiqued, debated, and sometimes even managed to enhance the literate potentials of ordinary citizens as they have tried to cope with life as they find it. Less easily and certainly less steadily have we been able to relate what we see, study, and do to these larger contexts of profit making and competition. This even as we recognize that the most pressing issues we deal with—tightening associations between literate skill and social viability, the breakneck pace of change in communications technology, persistent inequities in access and reward—all relate to structural conditions in literacy's bigger picture. When economic forces are addressed in our work, they appear primarily as generalities: contexts, determinants, motivators, barriers, touchstones. But rarely are they systematically related to the local conditions and embodied moments of literacy learning that occupy so many of us on a daily basis.[1]

This essay does not presume to overcome the analytical failure completely. But it does offer a conceptual approach that begins to connect literacy as an individual development to literacy as an economic development, at least as the two have played out over the last ninety years or so. The approach is through what I call sponsors of literacy. Sponsors, as I have come to think of them, are any agents, local or distant, concrete or abstract, who enable, support, teach, model, as well as recruit, regulate, suppress, or withhold literacy—and gain advantage by it in some way. Just as the ages of radio and television accustom us to having programs *brought* to us by various commercial sponsors, it is useful to think about who or what underwrites occasions of literacy learning and use. Although the interests of the sponsor and the sponsored do not have to converge (and, in

1. Three of the keenest and most eloquent observers of economic impacts on writing teaching and learning have been Lester Faigley, Susan Miller, and Kurt Spellmeyer.

fact, may conflict), sponsors nevertheless set the terms for access to literacy and wield powerful incentives for compliance and loyalty. Sponsors are a tangible reminder that literacy learning throughout history has always required permission, sanction, assistance, coercion, or, at minimum, contact with existing trade routes. Sponsors are delivery systems for the economies of literacy, the means by which these forces present themselves to—and through—individual learners. They also represent the causes into which people's literacy usually gets recruited.[2]

For the last five years I have been tracing sponsors of literacy across the 20th century as they appear in the accounts of ordinary Americans recalling how they learned to write and read. The investigation is grounded in more than 100 in-depth interviews that I collected from a diverse group of people born roughly between 1900 and 1980. In the interviews, people explored in great detail their memories of learning to read and write across their lifetimes, focusing especially on the people, institutions, materials, and motivations involved in the process. The more I worked with these accounts, the more I came to realize that they were filled with references to sponsors, both explicit and latent, who appeared in formative roles at the scenes of literacy learning. Patterns of sponsorship became an illuminating site through which to track the different cultural attitudes people developed toward writing vs. reading as well as the ideological congestion faced by late-century literacy learners as their sponsors proliferated and diversified (see my essays on "Remembering Reading" and "Accumulating Literacy"). In this essay I set out a case for why the concept of sponsorship is so richly suggestive for exploring economies of literacy and their effects. Then, through use of extended case examples, I demonstrate the practical application of this approach for interpreting current conditions of literacy teaching and learning, including persistent stratification of opportunity and escalating standards for literacy achievement. A final section addresses implications for the teaching of writing.

2. My debt to the writings of Pierre Bourdieu will be evident throughout this essay. Here and throughout I invoke his expansive notion of "economy," which is not restricted to literal and ostensible systems of money making but to the many spheres where people labor, invest, and exploit energies—their own and others'—to maximize advantage. See Bourdieu and Wacquant, especially 117–120 and Bourdieu, Chapter 7.

Sponsorship

Intuitively, *sponsors* seemed a fitting term for the figures who turned up most typically in people's memories of literacy learning: older relatives, teachers, priests, supervisors, military officers, editors, influential authors. Sponsors, as we ordinarily think of them, are powerful figures who bankroll events or smooth the way for initiates. Usually richer, more knowledgeable, and more entrenched than the sponsored, sponsors nevertheless enter a reciprocal relationship with those they underwrite. They lend their resources or credibility to the sponsored but also stand to gain benefits from their success, whether by direct repayment or, indirectly, by credit of association. *Sponsors* also proved an appealing term in my analysis because of all the commercial references that appeared in these 20th-century accounts—the magazines, peddled encyclopedias, essay contests, radio and television programs, toys, fan clubs, writing tools, and so on, from which so much experience with literacy was derived. As the 20th century turned the abilities to read and write into widely exploitable resources, commercial sponsorship abounded.

In whatever form, sponsors deliver the ideological freight that must be borne for access to what they have. Of course, the sponsored can be oblivious to or innovative with this ideological burden. Like Little Leaguers who wear the logo of a local insurance agency on their uniforms, not out of a concern for enhancing the agency's image but as a means for getting to play ball, people throughout history have acquired literacy pragmatically under the banner of others' causes. In the days before free, public schooling in England, Protestant Sunday Schools warily offered basic reading instruction to working-class families as part of evangelical duty. To the horror of many in the church sponsorship, these families insistently, sometimes riotously demanded of their Sunday Schools more instruction, including in writing and math, because it provided means for upward mobility.[3] Through the sponsorship of Baptist and Methodist ministries,

3. Thomas Laqueur (124) provides a vivid account of a street demonstration in Bolton, England, in 1834 by a "pro-writing" faction of Sunday School students and their teachers. This faction demanded that writing instruction continue to be provided on Sundays, something that opponents of secular instruction on the Sabbath were trying to reverse.

African Americans in slavery taught each other to understand the Bible in subversively liberatory ways. Under a conservative regime, they developed forms of critical literacy that sustained religious, educational, and political movements both before and after emancipation (Cornelius). Most of the time, however, literacy takes its shape from the interests of its sponsors And, as we will see below, obligations toward one's sponsors run deep, affecting what, why, and how people write and read.

The concept of sponsors helps to explain, then, a range of human relationships and ideological pressures that turn up at the scenes of literacy learning—from benign sharing between adults and youths, to euphemized coercions in schools and workplaces, to the most notorious impositions and deprivations by church or state. It also is a concept useful for tracking literacy's materiel: the things that accompany writing and reading and the ways they are manufactured and distributed. Sponsorship as a sociological term is even more broadly suggestive for thinking about economies of literacy development. Studies of patronage in Europe and *compradrazgo* in the Americas show how patron-client relationships in the past grew up around the need to manage scarce resources and promote political stability (Bourne; Lynch; Horstman and Kurtz). Pragmatic, instrumental, ambivalent, patron-client relationships integrated otherwise antagonistic social classes into relationships of mutual, albeit unequal dependencies. Loaning land, money, protection, and other favors allowed the politically powerful to extend their influence and justify their exploitation of clients. Clients traded their labor and deference for access to opportunities for themselves or their children and for leverage needed to improve their social standing. Especially under conquest in Latin America, *compradrazgo* reintegrated native societies badly fragmented by the diseases and other disruptions that followed foreign invasions. At the same time, this system was susceptible to its own stresses, especially when patrons became clients themselves of still more centralized or distant overlords, with all the shifts in loyalty and perspective that entailed (Horstman and Kurtz 13–14).

In raising this association with formal systems of patronage, I do not wish to overlook the very different economic, political, and educational systems within which U.S. literacy has developed. But where we find the sponsoring of literacy, it will be useful to look for its function within larger political and economic arenas. Literacy, like land, is a valued commodity in this economy, a key resource in gaining profit and edge. This value helps to explain, of course, the lengths people will go to secure literacy for themselves or their children. But it also explains why the powerful work so persistently to conscript and ration the powers of literacy. The competition to harness literacy, to manage, measure, teach, and exploit it, has intensified throughout the century. It is vital to pay attention to this development because it largely sets the terms for individuals' encounters with literacy. This competition shapes the incentives and barriers (including uneven distributions of opportunity) that greet literacy learners in any particular time and place. It is this competition that has made access to the right kinds of literacy sponsors so crucial for political and economic well being. And it also has spurred the rapid, complex changes that now make the pursuit of literacy feel so turbulent and precarious for so many.

In the next three sections, I trace the dynamics of literacy sponsorship through the life experiences of several individuals, showing how their opportunities for literacy learning emerge out of the jockeying and skirmishing for economic and political advantage going on among sponsors of literacy. Along the way, the analysis addresses three key issues: (1) how, despite ostensible democracy in educational chances, stratification of opportunity continues to organize access and reward in literacy learning; (2) how sponsors contribute to what is called "the literacy crisis," that is, the perceived gap between rising standards for achievement and people's ability to meet them; and (3) how encounters with literacy sponsors, especially as they are configured at the end of the 20th century, can be sites for the innovative rerouting of resources into projects of self-development and social change.

Sponsorship and Access

A focus on sponsorship can force a more explicit and substantive link between literacy learning and systems of opportunity and access. A statistical correlation between high literacy achievement and high socioeconomic, majority-race status routinely shows up in results of national tests of reading and writing performance.[4] These findings capture yet, in their shorthand way, obscure the unequal conditions of literacy sponsorship that lie behind differential outcomes in academic performance. Throughout their lives, affluent people from high-caste racial groups have multiple and redundant contacts with powerful literacy sponsors as a routine part of their economic and political privileges. Poor people and those from low-caste racial groups have less consistent, less politically secured access to literacy sponsors—especially to the ones that can grease their way to academic and economic success. Differences in their performances are often attributed to family background (namely education and income of parents) or to particular norms and values operating within different ethnic groups or social classes. But in either case, much more is usually at work.

As a study in contrasts in sponsorship patterns and access to literacy, consider the parallel experiences of Raymond Branch and Dora Lopez, both of whom were born in 1969 and, as young children, moved with their parents to the same, mid-sized university town in the midwest.[5] Both were still residing in this town at the time of our interviews in 1995. Raymond Branch, a European American, had been born in southern California, the son of a professor father and a real estate executive mother. He recalled that his first grade classroom in 1975 was hooked up to a mainframe computer at Stanford University and that, as a youngster, he enjoyed fooling around with computer programming in the company of "real users" at his father's science lab. This process was not interrupted much when, in the late 1970s, his family moved to the midwest. Raymond received his first personal computer as a Christmas present from his parents when he was twelve years old, and a modem the year after that. In the 1980s, computer hardware and software stores began popping up within a bicycle-ride's distance from where he lived. The stores were serving the university community and, increasingly, the high-tech industries that were becoming established in that vicinity. As an adolescent, Raymond spent his summers roaming these stores, sampling new

4. See, for instance, National Assessments of Educational Progress in reading and writing (Applebee et al.; and "Looking").

5. All names used in this essay are pseudonyms.

computer games, making contact with founders of some of the first electronic bulletin boards in the nation, and continuing, through reading and other informal means, to develop his programming techniques. At the time of our interview he had graduated from the local university and was a successful freelance writer of software and software documentation, with clients in both the private sector and the university community.

Dora Lopez, a Mexican American, was born in the same year as Raymond Branch, 1969, in a Texas border town, where her grandparents, who worked as farm laborers, lived most of the year. When Dora was still a baby her family moved to the same midwest university town as had the family of Raymond Branch. Her father pursued an accounting degree at a local technical college and found work as a shipping and receiving clerk at the university. Her mother, who also attended technical college briefly, worked part-time in a bookstore. In the early 1970s, when the Lopez family made its move to the midwest, the Mexican-American population in the university town was barely one per cent. Dora recalled that the family had to drive seventy miles to a big city to find not only suitable groceries but also Spanish-language newspapers and magazines that carried information of concern and interest to them. (Only when reception was good could they catch Spanish-language radio programs coming from Chicago, 150 miles away.) During her adolescence, Dora Lopez undertook to teach herself how to read and write in Spanish, something, she said, that neither her brother nor her U.S.-born cousins knew how to do. Sometimes, with the help of her mother's employee discount at the bookstore, she sought out novels by South American and Mexican writers, and she practiced her written Spanish by corresponding with relatives in Colombia. She was exposed to computers for the first time at the age of thirteen when she worked as a teacher's aide in a federally funded summer school program for the children of migrant workers. The computers were being used to help the children to be brought up to grade level in their reading and writing skills. When Dora was admitted to the same university that Raymond Branch attended, her father bought her a used word processing machine that a student had advertised for sale on a bulletin board in the building where Mr. Lopez worked. At the time of our interview, Dora Lopez had transferred from the university to a technical college. She was working for a cleaning company, where she performed extra duties as a translator, communicating on her supervisor's behalf with the largely Latina cleaning staff. "I write in Spanish for him, what he needs to be translated, like job duties, what he expects them to do, and I write lists for him in English and Spanish," she explained.

In Raymond Branch's account of his early literacy learning we are able to see behind the scenes of his majority-race membership, male gender, and high-end socioeconomic family profile. There lies a thick and, to him, relatively accessible economy of institutional and commercial supports that cultivated and subsidized his acquisition of a powerful form of literacy. One might be tempted to say that Raymond Branch was born at the right time and lived in the right place—except that the experience of Dora Lopez troubles that thought. For Raymond Branch, a university town in the 1970s and 1980s provided an information-rich, resource-rich learning environment in which to pursue his literacy development, but for Dora Lopez, a female member of a culturally unsubsidized ethnic minority, the same town at the same time was information- and resource-poor. Interestingly, both young people were pursuing projects of self-initiated learning, Raymond Branch in computer programming and Dora Lopez in biliteracy. But she had to reach much further afield for the material and communicative systems needed to support her learning. Also, while Raymond Branch, as the son of an academic, was sponsored by some of the most powerful agents of the university (its laboratories, newest technologies, and most educated personnel), Dora Lopez was being sponsored by what her parents could pull from the peripheral service systems of the university (the mail room, the bookstore, the second-hand technology market). In these accounts we also can see how the development and eventual economic worth of Raymond Branch's literacy skills were underwritten by late-century transformations in communication technology that created a boomtown need for programmers and software writers. Dora Lopez's biliterate skills developed and paid off much further down the economic-reward ladder, in government-sponsored youth programs and commercial enterprises, that, in the 1990s, were absorbing surplus migrant workers into a low-wage, urban service economy.[6] Tracking patterns of literacy sponsorship, then, gets beyond SES shorthand to expose more fully how unequal literacy chances relate to systems of unequal subsidy and reward for literacy. These are the systems that deliver large-scale economic, historical, and political conditions to the scenes of small-scale literacy use and development.

This analysis of sponsorship forces us to consider not merely how one social group's literacy practices may differ from another's, but how everybody's literacy practices are operating in differential economies, which supply different access routes, different degrees of sponsoring power, and different scales of monetary worth to the practices in use. In fact, the interviews I conducted are filled with examples of how economic and political forces, some of them originating in quite distant corporate and government policies, affect people's day-to-day ability to seek out and practice literacy. As a telephone company employee, Janelle Hampton enjoyed a brief period in the early 1980s as a fraud investigator, pursuing inquiries and writing up reports of her efforts. But when the breakup of the telephone utility reorganized its workforce, the fraud division was moved two states away and she was returned to less interesting work as a data processor. When, as a seven-year-old in the mid-1970s, Yi Vong made his way with his family from Laos to rural Wisconsin as part of the first resettlement group of Hmong refugees after the Vietnam War, his school district—which had no ESL programming—placed him in a school for the blind and deaf, where he learned English on audio and visual language machines. When a meager retirement pension forced Peter Hardaway and his wife out of their house and into a trailer, the couple stopped receiving newspapers and magazines in order to avoid cluttering up the small space they had to share. An analysis of sponsorship systems of literacy would help educators everywhere to think through the effects that economic and political changes in their regions are having on various people's ability to write and read,

6. I am not suggesting that literacy that does not "pay off" in terms of prestige or monetary reward is less valuable. Dora Lopez's ability to read and write in Spanish was a source of great strength and pride, especially when she was able to teach it to her young child. The resource of Spanish literacy carried much of what Bourdieu calls cultural capital in her social and family circles. But I want to point out here how people who labor equally to acquire literacy do so under systems of unequal subsidy and unequal reward.

their chances to sustain that ability, and their capacities to pass it along to others. Recession, relocation, immigration, technological change, government retreat all can—and do—condition the course by which literate potential develops.

Sponsorship and the Rise in Literacy Standards

As I have been attempting to argue, literacy as a resource becomes available to ordinary people largely through the mediations of more powerful sponsors. These sponsors are engaged in ceaseless processes of positioning and repositioning, seizing and relinquishing control over meanings and materials of literacy as part of their participation in economic and political competition. In the give and take of these struggles, forms of literacy and literacy learning take shape. This section examines more closely how forms of literacy are created out of competitions between institutions. It especially considers how this process relates to the rapid rise in literacy standards since World War II. Resnick and Resnick lay out the process by which the demand for literacy achievement has been escalating, from basic, largely rote competence to more complex analytical and interpretive skills. More and more people are now being expected to accomplish more and more things with reading and writing. As print and its spinoffs have entered virtually every sphere of life, people have grown increasingly dependent on their literacy skills for earning a living and exercising and protecting their civil rights. This section uses one extended case example to trace the role of institutional sponsorship in raising the literacy stakes. It also considers how one man used available forms of sponsorship to cope with this escalation in literacy demands.

The focus is on Dwayne Lowery, whose transition in the early 1970s from line worker in an automobile manufacturing plant to field representative for a major public employees union exemplified the major transition of the post–World War II economy—from a thing-making, thing-swapping society to an information-making, service-swapping society. In the process, Dwayne Lowery had to learn to read and write in ways that he had never done before. How his experiences with writing developed and how they were sponsored—and distressed—by institutional struggle will unfold in the following narrative.

A man of Eastern European ancestry, Dwayne Lowery was born in 1938 and raised in a semi-rural area in the upper midwest, the third of five children of a rubber worker father and a homemaker mother. Lowery recalled how, in his childhood home, his father's feisty union publications and left-leaning newspapers and radio shows helped to create a political climate in his household. "I was sixteen years old before I knew that goddamn Republicans was two words," he said. Despite this influence, Lowery said he shunned politics and newspaper reading as a young person, except to read the sports page. A diffident student, he graduated near the bottom of his class from a small high school in 1956 and, after a stint in the Army, went to work on the assembly line of a major automobile manufacturer. In the late 1960s, bored with the repetition of spraying primer paint on the right door checks of 57 cars an hour, Lowery traded in his night shift at the auto plant for a day job reading water meters in a municipal utility department. It was at that time, Lowery recalled, that he rediscovered newspapers, reading them in the early morning in his, department's break room. He said:

> At the time I guess I got a little more interested in the state of things within the state. I started to get a little political at that time and got a little more information about local people. So I would buy [a metropolitan paper] and I would read that paper in the morning. It was a pretty conservative paper but I got some information.

At about the same time Lowery became active in a rapidly growing public employees union, and, in the early 1970s, he applied for and received a union-sponsored grant that allowed him to take off four months of work and travel to Washington, D.C. for training in union activity. Here is his extended account of that experience.

> When I got to school, then there was a lot of reading. I often felt bad. If I had read more [as a high-school student] it wouldn't have been so tough. But they pumped a lot of stuff at us to read. We lived in a hotel and we had to some extent homework we had to do and reading we had to do and not make written reports but make some presentation on our part of it. What they were trying

> to teach us, I believe, was regulations, systems, laws. In case anything in court came up along the way, we would know that. We did a lot of work on organizing, you know, learning how to negotiate contracts, contractual language, how to write it. Gross National Product, how that affected the Consumer Price Index. It was pretty much a crash course. It was pretty much crammed in. And I'm not sure we were all that well prepared when we got done, but it was interesting.

After a hands-on experience organizing sanitation workers in the west, Lowery returned home and was offered a full-time job as a field staff representative for the union, handling worker grievances and contract negotiations for a large, active local near his state capital. His initial writing and rhetorical activities corresponded with the heady days of the early 1970s when the union was growing in strength and influence, reflecting in part the exponential expansion in information workers and service providers within all branches of government. With practice, Lowery said he became "good at talking," "good at presenting the union side," "good at slicing chunks off the employer's case." Lowery observed that, in those years, the elected officials with whom he was negotiating often lacked the sophistication of their Washington-trained union counterparts. "They were part-time people," he said. "And they didn't know how to calculate. We got things in contracts that didn't cost them much at the time but were going to cost them a ton down the road." In time, though, even small municipal and county governments responded to the public employees' growing power by hiring specialized attorneys to represent them in grievance and contract negotiations. "Pretty soon," Lowery observed, "ninety percent of the people I was dealing with across the table were attorneys."

This move brought dramatic changes in the writing practices of union reps, and, in Lowery's estimation, a simultaneous waning of the power of workers and the power of his own literacy. "It used to be we got our way through muscle or through political connections," he said. "Now we had to get it through legalistic stuff. It was no longer just sit down and talk about it. Can we make a deal?" Instead, all activity became rendered in writing: the exhibit, the brief, the transcript, the letter, the appeal. Because briefs took longer to write, the wheels of justice took longer to turn. Delays in grievance hearings became routine, as lawyers and union reps alike asked hearing judges for extensions on their briefs. Things went, in Lowery's words, "from quick competent justice to expensive and long term justice."

In the meantime, Lowery began spending up to 70 hours a week at work, sweating over the writing of briefs, which are typically fifteen to thirty-page documents laying out precedents, arguments, and evidence for a grievant's case. These documents were being forced by the new political economy in which Lowery's union was operating. He explained:

> When employers were represented by an attorney, you were going to have a written brief because the attorney needs to get paid. Well, what do you think if you were a union grievant and the attorney says, well, I'm going to write a brief and Dwayne Lowery says, well, I'm not going to. Does the worker somehow feel that their representation is less now?

To keep up with the new demands, Lowery occasionally traveled to major cities for two or three-day union-sponsored workshops on arbitration, new legislation, and communication skills. He also took short courses at a historic School for Workers at a nearby university. His writing instruction consisted mainly of reading the briefs of other field reps, especially those done by the college graduates who increasingly were being assigned to his district from union headquarters. Lowery said he kept a file drawer filled with other people's briefs from which he would borrow formats and phrasings. At the time of our interview in 1995, Dwayne Lowery had just taken an early and somewhat bitter retirement from the union, replaced by a recent graduate from a master's degree program in Industrial Relations. As a retiree, he was engaged in local Democratic party politics and was getting informal lessons in word processing at home from his wife.

Over a 20-year period, Lowery's adult writing took its character from a particular juncture in labor relations, when even small units of government began wielding (and, as a consequence, began spreading) a "legalistic" form of literacy in order to restore political dominance over public workers. This struggle for dominance shaped the kinds of literacy skills required of Lowery, the kinds of genres he learned and used, and the kinds of literate identity he developed. Lowery's rank-and-file experience and his talent tor representing that experience around a bargaining table became increasingly peripheral to his ability to prepare documents that could compete in kind with those written by his formally educated, professional adversaries. Face-to-face meetings became occasions mostly for a ritualistic exchange of texts, as arbitrators generally deferred decisions, reaching them in private, after solitary deliberation over complex sets of documents. What Dwayne Lowery was up against as a working adult in the second half of the 20th century was more than just living through a rising standard in literacy expectations or a generalized growth in professionalization, specialization, or documentary power—although certainly all of those things are, generically, true. Rather, these developments should be seen more specifically, as outcomes of ongoing transformations in the history of literacy as it has been wielded as part of economic and political conflict. These transformations become the arenas in which new standards of literacy develop. And for Dwayne Lowery—as well as many like him over the last 25 years—these are the arenas in which the worth of existing literate skills become degraded. A consummate debater and deal maker, Lowery saw his value to the union bureaucracy subside, as power shifted to younger, university-trained staffers whose literacy credentials better matched the specialized forms of escalating pressure coming from the other side.

In the broadest sense, the sponsorship of Dwayne Lowery's literacy experiences lies deep within the historical conditions of industrial relations in the 20th century and, more particularly, within the changing nature of work and labor struggle over the last several decades. Edward Stevens Jr. has observed the rise in this century of an "advanced contractarian society" (25) by which formal relationships of all kinds have come to rely on "a jungle of rules and regulations" (139). For labor, these conditions only intensified in the 1960s and 1970s when a flurry of federal and state civil rights legislation curtailed the previously unregulated hiring and firing power of management. These developments made the appeal to law as central as collective bargaining for extending employee rights (Heckscher 9). I mention this broader picture, first, because it relates to the forms of employer backlash that Lowery began experiencing by the early

1980s and, more important, because a history of unionism serves as a guide for a closer look at the sponsors of Lowery's literacy.

These resources begin with the influence of his father, whose membership in the United Rubber Workers during the ideologically potent 1930s and 1940s grounded Lowery in class-conscious progressivism and its favorite literate form: the newspaper. On top of that, though, was a pragmatic philosophy of worker education that developed in the U.S. after the Depression as an anti-communist antidote to left-wing intellectual influences in unions. Lowery's parent union, in fact, had been a central force in refocusing worker education away from an earlier emphasis on broad critical study and toward discrete techniques for organizing and bargaining. Workers began to be trained in the discrete bodies of knowledge, written formats, and idioms associated with those strategies. Characteristic of this legacy, Lowery's crash course at the Washington-based training center in the early 1970s emphasized technical information, problem solving, and union-building skills and methods. The transformation in worker education from critical, humanistic study to problem-solving skills was also lived out at the school for workers where Lowery rook short courses in the 1980s. Once a place where factory workers came to write and read about economics, sociology, and labor history, the school is now part of a university extension service offering workshops—often requested by management—on such topics as work restructuring, new technology, health and safety regulations, and joint labor-management cooperation.[7] Finally, in this inventory of Dwayne Lowery's literacy sponsors, we must add the latest incarnations shaping union practices: the attorneys and college-educated co-workers who carried into Lowery's workplace forms of legal discourse and "essayist literacy."[8]

What should we notice about this pattern of sponsorship? First, we can see from yet another angle how the course of an ordinary person's literacy learning—its occasions, materials, applications, potentials—follows the transformations going on within sponsoring institutions as those institutions fight for economic and ideological position. As

7. For useful accounts of this period in union history, see Heckscher; Nelson.

8. Marcia Farr associates "essayist literacy" with written genres esteemed in the academy and noted for their explicitness, exactness, reliance on reasons and evidence, and impersonal voice.

a result of wins, losses, or compromises, institutions undergo change, affecting the kinds of literacy they promulgate and the status that such literacy has in the larger society. So where, how, why, and what Lowery practiced as a writer—and what he didn't practice—took shape as part of the post-industrial jockeying going on over the last thirty years by labor, government, and industry. Yet there is more to be seen in this inventory of literacy sponsors. It exposes the deeply textured history that lies within the literacy practices of institutions and within any individual's literacy experiences. Accumulated layers of sponsoring influences—in families, workplaces, schools, memory—carry forms of literacy that have been shaped out of ideological and economic struggles of the past. This history, on the one hand, is a sustaining resource in the quest for literacy. It enables an older generation to pass its literacy resources onto another. Lowery's exposure to his father's newspaper-reading and supper-table political talk kindled his adult passion tor news, debate, and for language that rendered relief and justice. This history also helps to create infrastructures of opportunity. Lowery found crucial supports for extending his adult literacy in the educational networks that unions established during the first half of the 20th century as they were consolidating into national powers. On the other hand, this layered history of sponsorship is also deeply conservative and can be maladaptive because it teaches forms of literacy that oftentimes are in the process of being overtaken by new political realities and by ascendent forms of literacy. The decision to focus worker education on practical strategies of recruiting and bargaining—devised in the thick of Cold War patriotism and galloping expansion in union memberships—became, by the Reagan years, a fertile ground for new forms of management aggression and cooptation.

It is actually this lag or gap in sponsoring forms that we call the rising standard of literacy. The pace of change and the place of literacy in economic competition have both intensified enormously in the last half of the 20th century. It is as if the history of literacy is in fast forward. Where once the same sponsoring arrangements could maintain value across a generation or more, forms of literacy and their sponsors can now rise and recede many times within a single life span. Dwayne Lowery experienced profound changes in forms of union-based literacy not only between his father's time and his but between the time he joined the union and the time he left it, twenty-odd years later. This phenomenon is what makes today's literacy feel so advanced and, at the same time, so destabilized.

Sponsorship and Appropriation in Literacy Learning

We have seen how literacy sponsors affect literacy learning in two powerful ways. They help to organize and administer stratified systems of opportunity and access, and they raise the literacy stakes in struggles for competitive advantage. Sponsors enable and hinder literacy activity, often forcing the formation of new literacy requirements while decertifying older ones. A somewhat different dynamic of literacy sponsorship is treated here. It pertains to the potential of the sponsored to divert sponsors' resources toward ulterior projects, often projects of self-interest or self-development. Earlier I mentioned how Sunday School parishioners in England and African Americans in slavery appropriated church-sponsored literacy for economic and psychic survival. "Misappropriation" is always possible at the scene of literacy transmission, a reason for the tight ideological control that usually surrounds reading and writing instruction. The accounts that appear below are meant to shed light on the dynamics of appropriation, including the role of sponsoring agents in that process. They are also meant to suggest that diversionary tactics in literacy learning may be invited now by the sheer proliferation of literacy activity in contemporary life. The uses and networks of literacy crisscross through many domains, exposing people to multiple, often amalgamated sources of sponsoring powers, secular, religious, bureaucratic, commercial, technological. In other words, what is so destabilized about contemporary literacy today also makes it so available and potentially innovative, ripe for picking, one might say, for people suitably positioned. The rising level of schooling in the general population is also an inviting factor in this process. Almost everyone now has some sort of contact, for instance, with college educated people, whose movements through workplaces, justice systems, social service organizations, houses of worship, local government, extended families, or circles of friends spread dominant forms of literacy (whether wanted or not, helpful or not) into public and private spheres. Another condition favorable for appropriation is the deep hybridity of literacy practices extant in many settings. As we saw in Dwayne Lowery's case, workplaces, schools, families bring together multiple strands of the history of literacy in complex and influential forms. We need models of literacy that more astutely account for these kinds of multiple contacts, both in and out of school and across a lifetime. Such models could begin to grasp the significance of re-appropriation, which, for a number of reasons, is becoming a key requirement for literacy learning at the end of the 20th century.

The following discussion will consider two brief cases of literacy diversion. Both involve women working in subordinate positions as secretaries, in print-rich settings where better-educated male supervisors were teaching them to read and write in certain ways to perform their clerical duties. However, as we will see shortly, strong loyalties outside the workplace prompted these two secretaries to lift these literate resources for use in other spheres. For one, Carol White, it was on behalf of her work as a Jehovah's Witness. For the other, Sarah Steele, it was on behalf of upward mobility for her lower middle-class family.

Before turning to their narratives, though, it will be wise to pay some attention to the economic moment in which they occur. Clerical work was the largest and fastest growing occupation for women in the 20th century. Like so much employment for women, it offered a mix of gender-defined constraints as well as avenues for economic independence and mobility. As a new information economy created an acute need for typists, stenographers, bookkeepers and other office workers, white, American-born women and, later, immigrant and minority women saw reason to pursue high school and business-college educations. Unlike male clerks of the 19th century, female secretaries in this century had little chance for advancement. However, office work represented a step up from the farm or the factory for women of the working class and served as a respectable occupation from which educated, middle-class women could await or avoid marriage (Anderson, Strom). In a study of clerical work through the first half of the 20th century, Christine Anderson estimated that secretaries might encounter up to 97 different genres in the course of doing dictation or transcription. They routinely had contact with an array of professionals, including lawyers, auditors, tax examiners, and other government overseers (52–53). By 1930, 30% of women office workers used machines other than typewriters (Anderson 76) and, in contemporary offices, clerical workers have often been the first employees to learn to operate CRTs[9] and personal computers and to teach others how to use them. Overall, the daily duties of 20th-century secretaries could serve handily as an index to the rise of complex administrative and accounting procedures, standardization of information, expanding communication, and developments in technological systems.

With that background, consider the experiences of Carol White and Sarah Steele. An Oneida, Carol White was born into a poor, single-parent household in 1940. She graduated from high school in 1960 and, between five maternity leaves and a divorce, worked continuously in a series of clerical positions in both the private and public sectors. One of her first secretarial jobs was with an urban firm that produced and disseminated Catholic missionary films. The vice-president with whom she worked most closely also spent much of his time producing a magazine for a national civic organization that he headed. She discussed how typing letters and magazine articles and occasionally proofreading for this man taught her rhetorical strategies in which she was keenly interested. She described the scene of transfer this way:

> [My boss] didn't just write to write. He wrote in a way to make his letters appealing. I would have to write what he was writing in this magazine too. I was completely enthralled. He would write about the people who were in this [organization] and the different works they were undertaking and people that died and people who were sick and about their personalities. And he wrote little anecdotes. Once in a while I made some suggestions too. He was a man who would listen to you.

The appealing and persuasive power of the anecdote became especially important to Carol White when she began doing door-to-door missionary work for the Jehovah's Witnesses, a pan-racial,

9. Cathode ray tubes: the stand-alone monitors used with the earliest versions of personal computers; CRTs, like old televisions, were big, bulky devices with their own set of controls [editor's note].

millenialist religious faith. She now uses colorful anecdotes to prepare demonstrations that she performs with other women at weekly service meetings at their Kingdom Hall. These demonstrations, done in front of the congregation, take the form of skits designed to explore daily problems through Bible principles. Further, at the time of our interview, Carol White was working as a municipal revenue clerk and had recently enrolled in an on-the-job training seminar called Persuasive Communication, a two-day class offered free to public employees. Her motivation for taking the course stemmed from her desire to improve her evangelical work. She said she wanted to continue to develop speaking and writing skills that would be "appealing," "motivating," and "encouraging" to people she hoped to convert.

Sarah Steele, a woman of Welsh and German descent, was born in 1920 into a large, working-class family in a coal mining community in eastern Pennsylvania. In 1940, she graduated from a two-year commercial college. Married soon after, she worked as a secretary in a glass factory until becoming pregnant with the first of four children. In the 1960s, in part to help pay for her children's college educations, she returned to the labor force as a receptionist and bookkeeper in a law firm, where she stayed until her retirement in the late 1970s.

Sarah Steele described how, after joining the law firm, she began to model her household management on principles of budgeting that she was picking up from one of the attorneys with whom she worked most closely. "I learned cash flow from Mr. B_____," she said. "I would get all the bills and put a tape in the adding machine and he and I would sit down together to be sure there was going to be money ahead." She said that she began to replicate that process at home with household bills. Before that," she observed, "I would just cook beans when I had to instead of meat." Sarah Steele also said she encountered the genre of the credit report during routine reading and typing on the job. She figured out what constituted a top rating, making sure her husband followed these steps in preparation for their financing a new car. She also remembered typing up documents connected to civil suits being brought against local businesses, teaching her, she said, which firms never to hire for home repairs. "It just changes the way you think," she observed about the reading and writing she did on her job. "You're not a pushover after you learn how business operates."

The dynamics of sponsorship alive in these narratives expose important elements of literacy appropriation, at least as it is practiced at the end of the 20th century. In a pattern now familiar from the earlier sections, we see how opportunities for literacy learning—this time for diversions of resources—open up in the clash between long-standing, residual forms of sponsorship and the new: between the lingering presence of literacy's conservative history and its pressure for change. So, here, two women—one Native American and both working-class—filch contemporary literacy resources (public relations techniques and accounting practices) from more educated, higher-status men. The women are emboldened in these acts by ulterior identities beyond the workplace: Carol White with faith and Sarah Steele with family. These affiliations hark back to the first sponsoring arrangements through which American women were gradually allowed to acquire literacy and education. Duties associated with religious faith and child rearing helped literacy to become, in Gloria Main's words, "a permissible feminine activity" (579). Interestingly, these roles, deeply sanctioned within the history of women's literacy—and operating beneath the newer permissible feminine activity of clerical work—become grounds for covert, innovative appropriation even as they reinforce traditional female identities.

Just as multiple identities contribute to the ideologically hybrid character of these literacy formations, so do institutional and material conditions. Carol White's account speaks to such hybridity. The missionary film company with the civic club vice president is a residual site for two of literacy's oldest campaigns—Christian conversion and civic participation—enhanced here by 20th-century advances in film and public relations techniques. This ideological reservoir proved a pleasing instructional site for Carol White, whose interests in literacy, throughout her life, have been primarily spiritual. So literacy appropriation draws upon, perhaps even depends upon, conservative forces in the history of literacy sponsorship that are always hovering at the scene of acts of learning. This history serves as both a sanctioning force and a reserve of ideological and material support.

At the same time, however, we see in these accounts how individual acts of appropriation can divert and subvert the course of literacy's history, how changes in individual literacy experiences relate to larger scale transformations. Carol White's redirection of personnel management techniques to the cause of the Jehovah's Witnesses is an almost ironic transformation in this regard. Once a principal sponsor in the initial spread of mass literacy, evangelism is here rejuvenated through late-literate corporate sciences of secular persuasion, fund-raising, and bureaucratic management that Carol White finds circulating in her contemporary workplaces. By the same token, through Sarah Steele, accounting practices associated with corporations are, in a sense, tracked into the house, rationalizing and standardizing even domestic practices. (Even though Sarah Steele did not own an adding machine, she penciled her budget figures onto adding-machine tape that she kept for that purpose.) Sarah Steele's act of appropriation in some sense explains how dominant forms of literacy migrate and penetrate into private spheres, including private consciousness. At the same time, though, she accomplishes a subversive diversion of literate power. Her efforts to move her family up in the middle class involved not merely contributing a second income but also, from her desk as a bookkeeper, reading her way into an understanding of middle-class economic power.

Teaching and the Dynamics of Sponsorship

It hardly seems necessary to point out to the readers of *College Composition and Communication (CCC)* that we haul a lot of freight for the opportunity to teach writing. Neither rich nor powerful enough to sponsor literacy on our own terms, we serve instead as conflicted brokers between literacy's buyers and sellers. At our most worthy, perhaps, we show the sellers how to beware and try to make sure these exchanges will be a little fairer, maybe, potentially, a little more mutually rewarding. This essay has offered a few working case studies that link patterns of sponsorship to processes of stratification, competition, and reappropriation. How much these dynamics can be generalized to classrooms is an ongoing empirical question.

I am sure that sponsors play even more influential roles at the scenes of literacy learning and use than this essay has explored. I have focused on some of the most tangible aspects—material supply, explicit teaching, institutional aegis. But the ideological pressure of sponsors affects many private aspects of writing processes as well as public aspects of finished texts. Where one's sponsors are multiple or even at odds, they can make writing maddening. Where they are absent, they make writing unlikely. Many of the cultural formations we associate with writing development—community practices, disciplinary traditions, technological potentials—can be appreciated as make-do responses to the economics of literacy, past and present. The history of literacy is a catalogue of obligatory relations. That this catalogue is so deeply conservative and, at the same time, so ruthlessly demanding of change is what fills contemporary literacy learning and teaching with their most paradoxical choices and outcomes.[1]

In bringing attention to economies of literacy learning I am not advocating that we prepare students more efficiently for the job markets they must enter. What I have tried to suggest is that as we assist and study individuals in pursuit of literacy, we also recognize how literacy is in pursuit of them. When this process stirs ambivalence, on their part or on ours, we need to be understanding.

Acknowledgments. This research was sponsored by the NCTE Research Foundation and the Center on English Learning and Achievement. The Center is supported by the U.S. Department of Education's Office of Educational Research and Improvement, whose views do not necessarily coincide with the author's. A version of this essay was given as a lecture in the Department of English, University of Louisville, in April 1997. Thanks to Anna Syvertsen and Julie Nelson for their help with archival research. Thanks, too, to colleagues who lent an ear along the way: Nelson Graff, Jonna Gjevre, Anne Gere, Kurt Spellmeyer, Tom Fox, and Bob Gundlach.

1. Lawrence Cremin makes similar points about education in general in his essay "The Cacophony of Teaching." He suggests that complex economic and social changes since World War Two, including the popularization of schooling and the penetration of mass media, have created "a far greater range and diversity of languages, competencies, values, personalities, and approaches to the world and to its educational opportunities" than at one time existed. The diversity most of interest to him (and me) resides not so much in the range of different ethnic groups there are in society but in the different cultural formulas by which people assemble their educational—or, I would say, literate—experience.

Komysha Hassan
b. 1988

This essay is housed in the Digital Archive of Literacy Narratives (DALN), a website open to the public and maintained by The Ohio State University and Georgia State University. The site is used mostly by academics, especially researchers and college composition teachers. Rather than trying to persuade readers to adopt some point of view or take some action, the "literacy narratives" record writers' memories of how they became readers and writers in various contexts (see Deborah Brandt's essay). College first-year writing courses often require students to write a literacy narrative, and the assignment is often designed to help students discover their relationship to the written word and to various discourse communities. "Literacy" here means more than the ability to read and write. It means being able to understand and communicate using the written conventions that are habitually used within a particular group of people. For example, academic writing is pretty specialized. Producing a text within the context of school demands that writers do certain things not expected in other contexts, like social media or creative writing. A literacy narrative might recount how you figured out how to write for academic readers, your early failures and successes, and who helped and who hindered the process of learning. As an exercise of self-discovery, literacy narratives usually are written for the writer's own edification. Though often read (and graded!) by an instructor, and sometimes made available to the public through depositories like DALN, writers do not generally select and shape their stories for any audience besides themselves. Hassan, a student of Egyptian, Norwegian, and American heritage, described this essay as a story about "how [she] rediscovered writing."

Komysha Hassan
Prof. Steffen Guenzel
ENC 1101-0011
19 September 2013

Righting History

20th of August, 2013. . . . 12:00 P.M.
Rm. 217
Visual Arts Building, University of Central Florida

Here I am in a classroom along with 20-some other students, mostly freshmen like myself, some not. Not so much confused but intrigued, even beguiled by this new experience. Being home-schooled, I had never been in a traditional class setting, and was now in the second largest university in the U.S. English composition is hardly an exciting topic, more reminiscent of tedium than inspiration though I was excited nonetheless, not so much by the subject but by the entirety of the experience. An hour and a half passed quickly, the instruction was simple, the required reading would be at the campus bookstore and we were handed each a copy of the course syllabus. Surprisingly, this was not an overview of grammatical proficiency or an expansive punctuation drill, hardly. I read through the course objectives and subject and ideas started to percolate. Going to the bookstore, I leafed through the first chapter of the book and still more ideas bubbled forth. I am no stranger to the raging cauldron of ideas that my head often becomes at the simplest coaxing, but articulating them in writing was a lost ability I needed to remember.

Johnny Cochran: Literacy Sponsor

The year was 1994. I was six years old. Hardly ancient history, but it might as well be. There it was, the unfolding of one of the most famous, or perhaps, infamous, trials in recent American history at the time: The O.J. Simpson murder trial.[1] All of what we see today of incessant television coverage for criminal trials, started with that

1. Orenthal James Simpson (b. 1947), celebrated running back in the National Football League. Apprehended after a "low speed" chase on California highways, which was covered live by national media and witnessed by as many as 95 million people, Simpson was charged in 1994 with murdering his ex-wife, Nicole Simpson Brown, and Ronald Goldman. The subsequent trial was a national sensation. [All notes are the editor's.]

case. For me, the case marked a turning point in my literacy. An avid reader already, and not so occasional writer, this case was a goldmine of literary stimulation with its dizzying display of articulated arguments and flamboyant oratory flourishes; my perspective was permanently changed as a writer and reader. Words were not simply recordings of observations or expressions of feelings but they were statements about events, conclusions and arguments, powerful enough to send a man to the gallows or set him free.

Johnny Cochran, the lead defense attorney for Simpson in the case, stole the headlines as an articulate and animated talker, who through his oral arguments, witnesses were built or destroyed and cases were made or dissolved.[2] But even more compelling a figure to me was Barry Scheck.[3] Though less flamboyant, his arguments were irrefutable, supported by evidence, bolstered by precedent and testimony. In this medium I saw the power of good, articulate presentations, whether written or orated, and the consequence and effect that it can have. I wanted to be like that.

Love, at First Write

I cannot remember when or what were the first words I had put to paper, but writing was always something I loved from as far as I can remember. My father would tell me I would be a lawyer and I was proud of that distinction. I wanted to meet that goal. I started out by writing "legal letters" to my family, around the age of five. My parents' support was indispensable in cultivating my love of writing from the beginning. They were always very receptive to it, encouraging me to continue and challenging me to be better. Communication was critical at home with a multi-lingual, multi-cultural family. In the same way that I played the role of translator to friends (and family, on occasion), I saw the greater need to play that role in society. Even at this early age, young children my age had inquisitive

2. Johnnie Lee Cochran (1937–2005), a leader of the Simpson defense team. Cochran used a riveting, theatrical style of oratory in the courtroom. Referencing Simpson's attempt to put on one of the bloody gloves found at the crime scene, Cochran famously rhymed, "If it doesn't fit, you must acquit."

3. Barry Scheck (b. 1949), part of O. J. Simpson's legal defense team. Scheck specialized in DNA evidence and successfully challenged the reliability of such evidence in the murder trial. He is the director of the Innocence Project, which reexamines the DNA evidence in cold cases, often liberating people jailed for crimes they did not commit.

questions for which pertinent answers were needed and they had to be communicated effectively. I tried to express that in my writing, always concerned with creating a compelling story.

Father Knows Best

My parents always stressed the importance of education in our household. Reading and writing were akin to eating and drinking—it was not a matter of choice but necessity. They took their role in our education seriously—so seriously that they taught us themselves. Homeschooling was nothing like public school; the latter I know less from experience but from the telling of others' experience of it. The world was my classroom, everything and everyone was a study subject. Our textbooks and study material ranged from the daily newspaper and news magazines to substantive television programming and religious texts. Everything was accorded due scrutiny by the prying, questioning eyes of young children. My family, to their credit, held nothing too sacred for that.

The biggest contribution of homeschooling to my learning was the number of ways things could be studied, and thus necessarily were. Field study and investigation were an integral part of the home-school experience. The library was a great resource for guides and materials on any subject. My sister's collection of Audubon field guides was an example. They were rich with detail and data that could be and were part of any body of work related to nature. I was always envious of my sister's ability to identify almost every species of insect, reptile, amphibian, bird and even plant that we passed by. She was not stingy with her knowledge, but I never became proficient in that area.

There were never limitations on the subjects I could write about, or my papers' word counts. You had to work hard to perfect everything you did, because we were always held to a higher standard of work. Parents of home-schooled children who submitted their paperwork for school board or teacher review and took voluntary term tests, took pains to make sure that the body of work superseded that required by the public school system; and therefore it always did by lengths (case in point: a 56-page fictional story for my 11th grade English). It was hard work sometimes. I cannot say schooling was always fun, but it never was dull because you always owned the curriculum—more often than not your assignment was about something you chose, you wanted to write about or study.

Not All Sibling Rivalry Is Bad

As things inevitably do, the O.J. Simpson trial came to an end (about which I wrote a 10-page report), but it was just the beginning of my writing "career." News was the daily occurrence that always had a back story, and I was determined to find out what it was and investigate it, presenting my conclusions in print. For every story I had a report, multiple ones even, which my parents would have me read aloud to the family, and they were always accorded generous praise. We held family discussions where commentary would be exchanged about news events, political happenings, scientific discoveries, anything that piqued our individual interests—and the discussions never ended there. They started other heated sub-discussions between my siblings with strong arguments being made from every which side. I was determined to validate my opinions not just to my parents but to my siblings as well. I needed to make an argument and bolster that argument with evidence, precedent. Make it irrefutable, unarguable. This was how I could compete and prove myself. This was how to win a case.

Devolving

As I grew older my perspective on life had changed. My brother was born and I was now an older sister, with the responsibilities I felt towards that role. I was still just a kid, nine or ten, but felt much more mature. Reading reports aloud to my family was the stuff of childhood to which I clearly did not belong. Computers began to become more mainstream and available to consumers, shifting my focus from the way I wrote traditionally, to using words and writing in a different medium, for different purposes.

Thinking back on how the Internet was being used and considered at the time, it is hard to believe that just a little over ten years have elapsed. Nonetheless, I took to this newfound tool with excited pursuit, immediately starting to build websites and discussion board pages. On the limited time I was given to use the computer weekly, I had soon built two websites, a business model and a non-profit model, as well as a political webpage—really an early precursor to the blog. I wrote a lot of content for them, trying to produce text that was appropriate for the genre (business, politics). I soon discovered pigeon discussion boards, too; being an avid pigeon breeder,

I immediately joined them, exchanging information and finding myself to be a knowledgeable resource for others.

Moral: Take Notes, Keep Writing

Soon, my debates had left the page and occupied the air. Oration was how I communicated my ideas, made arguments, debated and commentated. I still wrote a lot, but not the kind of writing I had always written. Commenting on message boards or writing content for webpages or eventually, as I became part of the family business, drafting contracts and the like, was not creative writing to argue a point or present a case. When I did put pen to paper to write a story, real or fictional, my mind would race and my hand was too slow to catch up to it. Writing felt stifling, messy and limited. It lacked the dramatic flourishes of oration, the emotional punctuation and presence. I never gave up on it, but I might as well have. It was no longer an exciting pursuit, but an occasionally necessary chore. Close to a decade would elapse before I re-discovered that passion in a classroom 500 miles from home.

Leonard Pitts

b. 1957

Fox News aired the specific program discussed here in January 2015. Launched as a 24/7 news channel by Rupert Murdoch in 1996, Fox News, despite its "fair and balanced" motto, has made no secret of its ideological bias, airing such personalities as the highly conservative Bill O'Reilly and Sean Hannity, consistently supporting Republican agendas, and opposing Democrats. Critics often charge that the network sensationalizes the events it covers, fanning the flames of controversy to increase viewership and advance Murdoch's personal ideology. In other words, the channel has been accused of abrogating the ethics of journalism. Fox's defenders dismiss such charges as the accusations of those blinded by their own political biases. They accuse the so-called mainstream media—such as NBC, ABC, CBS, and CNN—of having a built-in liberal bias. Today's purveyors of news, especially as disseminated in new media, often deliberately blur the line between journalism and entertainment. The intelligent citizen today must regard their news with more caution and even skepticism than was required a generation ago. That does not mean we must throw up our hands in futility, distrusting all news. Many journalists still adhere to professional ethical standards. The lessons about argument in the opening of this book will help skeptics judge what to trust and what to dismiss as propaganda.

Fox Faux News Forces Rare Apology

Tucker Carlson said on Fox that more children die of bathtub drownings than of accidental shootings. They don't.

Steve Doocy said on Fox that NASA scientists faked data to make the case for global warming. They didn't.

Rudy Giuliani said on Fox that President Obama has issued propaganda asking everybody to "hate the police." He hasn't.

John Stossel said on Fox that there is "no good data" proving secondhand cigarette smoke kills non-smokers. There is.

So maybe you can see why serious people—a category excluding those who rely upon it for news and information—do not take Fox, well . . . seriously, why they dub it Pox News and Fakes News, to name two of the printable variations. Fox is, after all, the network of death panels, terrorist fist jabs, birtherism, anchor babies, victory mosques, wars on Christmas and Benghazi, Benghazi, Benghazi.[1] It's not just that it is the chief global distributor of unfact and untruth but that it distributes unfact and untruth with a bluster, an arrogance, a gonad-grabbing swagger, that implicitly and intentionally dares you to believe fact and truth matter.

Many of us have gotten used to this. We don't even bother to protest Fox being Fox. Might as well protest a sewer for stinking.

But the French and the British, being French and British, see it differently. And that's what produced the scenario that recently floored many of us.

1. A reference to the persistent attempt to find evidence of a conspiracy and cover-up regarding the terrorist attack on the U.S. diplomatic compound in Benghazi, Libya, which killed U.S. Ambassador J. Christopher Stephens and another American on September 11, 2012. "Death panels": term coined by Sarah Palin referring to the way Fox News characterized a provision in Obamacare that allowed for end-of-life counseling (debated in Congress in 2009). "Terrorist fist jabs": the way Fox News anchor E. D. Hill questioned a fist bump President Obama shared with his wife in June 2008. "Birtherism": the belief, persistent among conspiracy theorists and encouraged by Fox News, that Barack Obama was born outside the United States. "Wars on Christmas": a reference to, among other things, Fox News commentator Megyn Kelly's December 2013 insistence, in the face of people wanting to represent his race differently, that Santa Claus is white.

There was Fox, doing what Fox does, in this case hosting one Steve Emerson, a supposed expert on Islamic extremist terrorism, who spoke about so-called "no go" zones in Europe—i.e., areas of Germany, Sweden, France and Great Britain—where non-Muslims are banned, the government has no control and sharia law is in effect. Naturally, Fox did not question this outrageous assertion—in fact, it repeated it throughout the week—and most of us, long ago benumbed by the network's serial mendacities, did not challenge Fox.

Then, there erupted from Europe the jarring sound of a continent laughing. British Prime Minister David Cameron called Emerson an "idiot." A French program in the mold of *The Daily Show* sent correspondents—in helmets!—to interview people peaceably sipping coffee in the no-go zones. Twitter went medieval on Fox's backside. And the mayor of Paris threatened to sue.

Last week, Fox did something Fox almost never does. It apologized. Indeed, it apologized profusely, multiple times, on air.

The most important takeaway here is not the admittedly startling news that Fox, contrary to all indications, is capable of shame. Rather, it is what the European response tells us about ourselves and our waning capacity for moral indignation with this sort of garbage.

It's amazing, the things you can get used to, that can come to seem normal. In America, it has come to seem normal that a major news organization functions as the propaganda arm of an extremist political ideology, that it spews a constant stream of racism, sexism, homophobia, Islamophobia, paranoia and manufactured outrage, and that it does so with brazen disregard for what is factual, what is right, what is fair, what is balanced—virtues that are supposed to be the sine qua non of anything calling itself a newsroom.

If you live with aberrance long enough, you can forget it's aberrance. You can forget that facts matter, that logic is important, that science is critical, that he who speaks claptrap loudly still speaks claptrap—and that claptrap has no place in reasoned and informed debate. Sometimes, it takes someone from outside to hold up a mirror and allow you to see more clearly what you have grown accustomed to.

This is what the French and the British did for America last week.

For that, Fox owed them an apology. But serious people owe them thanks.

2015

ACLU

Est. 1957

The American Civil Liberties Union (ACLU) published this document on its webpage. It's one of dozens of position papers meant to guide Americans as they confront challenges to liberties—from free speech to voting rights to privacy issues to reproductive rights. The ACLU has been protecting rights since World War I, when new Espionage and Sedition Acts empowered the government to suppress speech critical of the government and to deport with little due process immigrants considered undesirable. An alarmed group of lawyers, activists, and philanthropists, most of them in New York City, formed the ACLU to more effectively oppose these and other violations of the Bill of Rights. They gathered like-minded people, and today it is a very large nonprofit organization employing hundreds of lawyers. We tend to associate political liberals with the ACLU, but that's not necessarily always the case. Many conservatives approve of the ACLU's resistance to leviathan-like government, so it is difficult to pin down a target readership here other than anyone who might do a web search using the terms "free speech" and "college." The question and answer portion of this piece is meant to help students, faculty, and administrators determine whether or not a particular instance of speech on their college campus is protected by the Constitution. It's not really an argument. It is not meant to persuade *people to believe something. It summarizes Supreme Court interpretations of free speech, which gives people reliable major premises from which to reason through individual cases on their own campuses. Constitutional arguments tend to unfold deductively: Supreme Court decisions or the Constitution itself provide major premises, and minor premises assert something about a particular instance of speech. For example, an argument might unfold this way:*

> ***Major premise:*** *The Supreme Court has said harassment in schools is unconstitutional.*
> ***Major premise:*** *Painting a swastika on someone's dorm door is harassment.*

Minor premise: *Student X painted a swastika on student Y's door.*
Therefore: *Student X violated the Constitution.*

So this selection is not included here as a model *for your own arguments. It is meant to help you construct your own deductive arguments about free speech in the context of college life.*

Speech on Campus

The First Amendment to the Constitution protects speech no matter how offensive its content. Restrictions on speech by public colleges and universities amount to government censorship, in violation of the Constitution. Such restrictions deprive students of their right to invite speech they wish to hear, debate speech with which they disagree, and protest speech they find bigoted or offensive. An open society depends on liberal education, and the whole enterprise of liberal education is founded on the principle of free speech.

How much we value the right of free speech is put to its severest test when the speaker is someone we disagree with most. Speech that deeply offends our morality or is hostile to our way of life warrants the same constitutional protection as other speech because the right of free speech is indivisible: When we grant the government the power to suppress controversial ideas, we are all subject to censorship by the state. Since its founding in 1920, the ACLU has fought for the free expression of all ideas, popular or unpopular. Where racist, misogynist, homophobic, and transphobic speech is concerned, the ACLU believes that more speech—not less—is the answer most consistent with our constitutional values.

But the right to free speech is not just about the law; it's also a vital part of our civic education. As Supreme Court Justice Robert Jackson wrote in 1943 about the role of schools in our society: "That they are educating the young for citizenship is reason for scrupulous protection of Constitutional freedoms of the individual, if we are not to strangle the free mind at its source and teach youth to discount important principles of our government as mere platitudes."

Remarkably, Justice Jackson was referring to grade school students. Inculcating constitutional values—in particular, the value of free expression—should be nothing less than a core mission of any college or university.

To be clear, the First Amendment does not protect behavior on campus that crosses the line into targeted harassment or threats, or that creates a pervasively hostile environment for vulnerable students. But merely offensive or bigoted speech does not rise to that level, and determining when conduct crosses that line is a legal question that requires examination on a case-by-case basis. Restricting such speech may be attractive to college administrators as a quick fix to address campus tensions. But real social change comes from hard work to address the underlying causes of inequality and bigotry, not from purified discourse. The ACLU believes that instead of symbolic gestures to silence ugly viewpoints, colleges and universities have to step up their efforts to recruit diverse faculty, students, and administrators; increase resources for student counseling; and raise awareness about bigotry and its history.

Questions

Q: The First Amendment prevents the government from arresting people for what they say, but who says the Constitution guarantees speakers a platform on campus?

A: The First Amendment does not require the government to provide a platform to anyone, but it does prohibit the government from discriminating against speech on the basis of the speaker's viewpoint. For example, public colleges and universities have no obligation to fund student publications; however, the Supreme Court has held that if a public university voluntarily provides these funds, it cannot selectively withhold them from particular student publications simply because they advocate a controversial point of view.

Of course, public colleges and universities are free to invite whomever they like to speak at commencement ceremonies or other events, just as students are free to protest speakers they find offensive. College administrators cannot, however, dictate which speakers students may invite to campus on their own initiative. If a college or university usually allows students to use campus resources (such as auditoriums) to entertain guests, the school cannot withdraw those resources simply because students have invited a controversial speaker to campus.

Q: Does the First Amendment protect speech that invites violence against members of the campus community?

A: In *Brandenburg v. Ohio*,[1] the Supreme Court held that the government cannot punish inflammatory speech unless it **intentionally** and **effectively** provokes a crowd to **immediately** carry out violent and unlawful action. This is a very high bar, and for good reason.

The incitement standard has been used to protect all kinds of political speech, including speech that at least tacitly endorses violence, no matter how righteous or vile the cause. For example, in *NAACP v. Clairborne Hardware*, the court held that civil rights icon Charles Evans could not be held liable for the statement, "if we catch any of you going in any of them racist stores, we're going to break your damn neck." In *Hess v. Indiana*, the court held that an anti-war protestor could not be arrested for telling a crowd of protestors, "We'll take the fucking street later." And in *Brandenburg* itself, the court held that a Ku Klux Klan leader could not be jailed for a speech stating "that there might have to be some revengeance [sic] taken" for the "continued suppression of the white, Caucasian race."

The First Amendment's robust protections in this context reflect two fundamentally important values. First, political advocacy—rhetoric meant to inspire action against unjust laws or policies—is essential to democracy. Second, people should be held accountable for their own conduct, regardless of what someone else may have said. To protect these values, the First Amendment allows lots of breathing room for the messy, chaotic, ad hominem, passionate, and even bigoted speech that is part and parcel of American politics. It's the price we pay to keep bullhorns in the hands of political activists.

Q: But isn't it true you can't shout "fire" in a crowded theater?

People often associate the limits of First Amendment protection with the phrase "shouting 'fire' in a crowded theater." But that phrase is just

1. In the online version of this piece, each of these court cases was a live link to respective Wikipedia articles, which summarize the facts, arguments, and decisions. [All notes are the editor's.]

(slightly inaccurate) shorthand for the legal concept of "incitement." (Although, if you think there's a fire—even if you're wrong—you'd better yell!) The phrase, an incomplete reference to the concept of incitement, comes from the Supreme Court's 1919 decision in *Schenck v. United States.* Charles Schenck and Elizabeth Baer were members of the Executive Committee of the Socialist Party in Philadelphia, which authorized the publication of more than 15,000 fliers urging people not to submit to the draft for the First World War. The fliers said things like: "Do not submit to intimidation," and "Assert your rights." As a result of their advocacy, Schenck and Baer were convicted for violating the Espionage Act, which prohibits interference with military operations or recruitment, insubordination in the military, and support for enemies of the United States during wartime.

Writing for the Supreme Court, Justice Oliver Wendell Holmes Jr. held that Schenck's and Baer's convictions did not violate the First Amendment. Observing that the "most stringent protection of free speech would not protect a man in falsely shouting 'fire' in a theater and causing a panic," Holmes reasoned by analogy that speech urging people to resist the draft posed a "clear and present danger" to the United States and therefore did not deserve protection under the First Amendment. This is the problem with the line about shouting "fire" in a crowded theater—it can be used to justify suppressing any disapproved speech, no matter how tenuous the analogy. Justice Holmes later advocated for much more robust free speech protections, and *Schenck* was ultimately overruled. It is now emphatically clear that the First Amendment protects the right to urge resistance to a military draft, and much else.

Q: But what about campus safety? Doesn't the First Amendment have an exception for "fighting words" that are likely to provoke violence?

A: The Supreme Court ruled in 1942 that the First Amendment does not protect "fighting words," but this is an extremely limited exception. It applies only to intimidating speech directed at a specific individual in a face-to-face confrontation that is likely to provoke a violent reaction. For example, if a white student confronts a student of color on campus and starts shouting racial slurs in a one-on-one confrontation, that student may be subject to discipline.

Over the past 50 years, the Supreme Court hasn't found the "fighting words" doctrine applicable in any of the cases that have come before it, because the circumstances did not meet the narrow criteria outlined above. The "fighting words" doctrine does not apply to speakers addressing a large crowd on campus, no matter how much discomfort, offense, or emotional pain their speech may cause.

In fact, the Supreme Court has made clear that the government cannot prevent speech on the ground that it is likely to provoke a hostile response—this is called the rule against a "heckler's veto." Without this vital protection, government officials could use safety concerns as a smokescreen to justify shutting down speech they don't like, including speech that challenges the status quo. Instead, the First Amendment requires the government to provide protection to all speakers, no matter how provocative their speech might be. This includes taking reasonable measures to ensure that speakers are able to safely and effectively address their audience, free from violence or censorship. It's how our society ensures that the free exchange of ideas is uninhibited, robust, and wide-open.

Q: What about nonverbal symbols, like swastikas and burning crosses? Are they constitutionally protected?

A: Symbols of hate are constitutionally protected if they're worn or displayed before a general audience in a public place—say, in a march or at a rally in a public park. The Supreme Court has ruled that the First Amendment protects symbolic expression, such as swastikas, burning crosses, and peace signs because it's "closely akin to 'pure speech.'" The Supreme Court has accordingly upheld the rights of students to wear black armbands in school to protest the Vietnam War, as well as the right to burn the American flag in public as a symbolic expression of disagreement with government policies.[2]

But the First Amendment does not protect the use of nonverbal symbols to directly threaten an individual, such as by hanging a noose over their dorm room or office door. Nor does the First Amendment

2. The armband protest was adjudicated in *Tinker v. Des Moines Independent Community School District*; flag-burning was the issue in *Texas v. Johnson*. Both were cases before the U.S. Supreme Court.

protect the use of a nonverbal symbol to encroach upon or desecrate private property, such as by burning a cross on someone's lawn or spray-painting a swastika on the wall of a synagogue or dorm. In *R.A.V. v. City of St. Paul*, for example, the Supreme Court struck down as unconstitutional a city ordinance that prohibited cross-burnings based solely on their symbolism. But the Court's decision makes clear that the government may prosecute cross-burners under criminal trespass and/or anti-harassment laws.

Q: Isn't there a difference between free speech and dangerous conduct?

A: Yes. Speech does not merit constitutional protection when it targets a particular individual for harm, such as a true threat of physical violence. And schools must take action to remedy behavior that interferes with a particular student's ability to exercise their right to participate fully in the life of the university, such as targeted harassment.

The ACLU isn't opposed to regulations that penalize acts of violence, harassment, or threats. To the contrary, we believe that these kinds of conduct can and should be proscribed. Furthermore, we recognize that the mere use of words as one element in an act of violence, harassment, intimidation, or invasion of privacy does not immunize that act from punishment.

Q: Aren't restrictions on speech an effective and appropriate way to combat white supremacy, misogyny, and discrimination against LGBT people?

A: Historically, restrictions on speech have proven at best ineffective, and at worst counter-productive, in the fight against bigotry. Although drafted with the best intentions, these restrictions are often interpreted and enforced to oppose social change. Why? Because they place the power to decide whether speech is offensive and should be restrained with authority figures—the government or a college administration—rather than with those seeking to question or dismantle existing power structures.

For example, under a speech code in effect at the University of Michigan for 18 months, there were 20 cases in which white students charged Black students with offensive speech. One of the cases resulted in the punishment of a Black student for using the term "white trash" in conversation with a white student. The code was struck down as unconstitutional in 1989.[3]

To take another example, public schools throughout the country have attempted to censor pro-LGBT messages because the government thought they were controversial, inappropriate for minors, or just wrong. Heather Gillman's school district banned her from wearing a shirt that said "I Support My Gay Cousin." The principal maintained that her T-shirt and other speech supporting LGBT equality, such as "I Support Marriage Equality," were divisive and inappropriate for impressionable students. The ACLU sued the school district and won, because the First Amendment prevents the government from making LGBT people and LGBT-related issues disappear.

These examples demonstrate that restrictions on speech don't really serve the interests of marginalized groups. The First Amendment does.

Q: But don't restrictions on speech send a strong message against bigotry on campus?

A: Bigoted speech is symptomatic of a huge problem in our country. Our schools, colleges, and universities must prepare students to combat this problem. That means being an advocate: speaking out and convincing others. Confronting, hearing, and countering offensive speech is an important skill, and it should be considered a core requirement at any school worth its salt. When schools shut down speakers who espouse bigoted views, they deprive their students of the opportunity to confront those views themselves. Such incidents do not shut down a single bad idea, nor do they protect students from the harsh realities of an often unjust world. Silencing a bigot accomplishes nothing except turning them into a martyr for the principle of free expression. The better approach, and the one more consistent with our constitutional tradition, is to respond to ideas we hate with the ideals we cherish.

3. See *Doe v. University of Michigan*, heard in the U.S. District Court for the Eastern District of Michigan.

Q: Why does the ACLU use its resources to defend the free speech rights of white supremacists, misogynists, homophobes, transphobes, and other bigots?

A: Free speech rights are indivisible. Restricting the speech of one group or individual jeopardizes everyone's rights because the same laws or regulations used to silence bigots can be used to silence you. Conversely, laws that defend free speech for bigots can be used to defend civil rights workers, anti-war protestors, LGBT activists, and others fighting for justice. For example, in the 1949 case of *Terminiello v. City of Chicago*, the ACLU successfully defended an ex-Catholic priest who had delivered a racist and anti-Semitic speech. The precedent set in that case became the basis for the ACLU's defense of civil rights demonstrators in the 1960s and 1970s.

Q: How does the ACLU propose to ensure equal opportunity in education?

A: Universities are obligated to create an environment that fosters tolerance and mutual respect among members of the campus community, an environment in which all students can exercise their right to participate meaningfully in campus life without being subject to discrimination. To advance these values, campus administrators should:

- speak out loudly and clearly against expressions of racist, sexist, homophobic, and transphobic speech, as well as other instances of discrimination against marginalized individuals or groups;
- react promptly and firmly to counter acts of discriminatory harassment, intimidation, or invasion of privacy;
- create forums and workshops to raise awareness and promote dialogue on issues of race, sex, sexual orientation, and gender identity;
- intensify their efforts to ensure broad diversity among the student body, throughout the faculty, and within the college administration;
- vigilantly defend the equal rights of all speakers and all ideas to be heard, and promote a climate of robust and uninhibited dialogue and debate open to all views, no matter how controversial.

2017

Emily Chamlee-Wright
b. 1966

This essay was first published by Inside HigherEd, *which is an online magazine read mostly by college professors. Much of* Inside HigherEd's *content consists of "views" or opinion pieces, like this one. Emily Chamlee-Wright suggests that Adam Smith's "impartial spectator" is a good tool writers can use to judge their own arguments, which we naturally tend to regard too fondly. But what about the more contentious speech in public squares today? What are the rules of free speech on college campuses? How should we conduct civil discourse? Where do we draw the line between unpopular speech and oppressive speech? These difficult questions have been raising passions across college campuses in our increasingly partisan nation, and Chamlee-Wright's readers (college professors) might very well have to play referee for these debates: in their classrooms, in public lecture halls, and in writing university policies. Chamlee-Wright does not necessarily present a logical argument here. She lays down an important ground rule for civil discourse—a rule this textbook advocates. If Chamlee-Wright persuades her readers, she does so through ethos. She establishes herself not only as an authority but as a moral, humane person. Pay careful attention to how Chamlee-Wright presents her "self" in this essay.*

The Need to Presume Good Faith in Campus Conversations and Debates (Opinion)

I recently returned to Beloit College, where I taught for nearly 20 years before moving on to Washington College and the Institute for Humane Studies. Slated to speak on the topic of campus speech at an institution still wrestling with its own speech-related controversy, I was somewhat nervous.

I needn't have been.

Perhaps it was the bookish title of my talk—"Conversational Ethics: What Would Adam Smith Have Us Do?"[1] Perhaps I still had

1. Adam Smith (1723–1790), English philosopher considered the father of modern economics. He is best known for writing *The Wealth of Nations* (1776). *The Theory of Moral Sentiments* (1759) provides a psychological explanation for why human beings develop a conscience. [All notes are the editor's.]

some street cred on campus. Or perhaps folks were simply worn out. But no one came loaded for bear.

Smith has a lot to teach us about the ethics of conversation, particularly when public discourse becomes acrimonious. In *The Theory of Moral Sentiments*, he observed that the "violence and injustice of faction" tests us in ways that the ordinary "bustle of business in the world" does not. He writes, "The violence and loudness with which blame is sometimes poured out upon us seems to stupify and benumb our natural sense of praise-worthiness and blame-worthiness." In other words, the clamor of the crowd can make it hard to tell right from wrong.

Smith counsels that to prepare ourselves for the prospect of unjust condemnation, we must gain practice at viewing our beliefs and conduct not from the vantage point of the crowd but from the perspective of a well-informed impartial judge. If this imagined "impartial spectator" approves of our stance, then we are justified in ignoring the clamor. With practice, we become wiser and more accustomed to summoning the "self-command" we need to stand tall in the face of injustice.

But a sophomore in the audience recognized that this advice only helps the speaker. It doesn't stop us from being part of the unjust crowd. He asked, "What can we do, in practical terms, to keep the conversation positive?"

It was one of those moments when a dozen possible answers come to mind, but the voice in your head says, "Pick one!" The words that came out of my mouth were, "We could all do a better job of assuming good faith." Then the voice said, "Why did you pick *that* one?"

As soon as I said it, I realized that the 19-year-old asking the question might not know what I meant by such an old-fashioned phrase. I realized too late that though I use the phrase frequently, I had not thought through a full explanation of its meaning. As I started to unpack it in the moment, I realized what a potent concept it is and how far we have drifted from it.

Assuming good faith means that we expect that our conversation partner is interested in learning from us and is seeking to understand our point of view. It means that we should assume, unless we have good evidence to the contrary, that their intent is not to deceive or to offend. We can certainly point out when an error has been made or why offense has been taken, but it should be with the intent of making the conversation better, not closing it down.

A presumption of good faith demands a lot from us. It requires that we suspend judgment long enough to ask questions in a spirit of openness and curiosity. If the student in the audience and I disagree, I should focus first on figuring out why it is that he and I draw different conclusions even though we are looking at the same world. Perhaps there's something in his history, or mine, that led us to different places.

Good faith means that I should take my time to thoughtfully consider his perspective before I decide to praise it or condemn it. But time for thoughtful confederation seems to have fallen out of fashion. As we saw in the Covington Catholic story[2]—in which a viral video clip inspired many to signal their disgust for a group of teenage boys accused of racism and disrespect, only to learn later that the story was far more complicated—we feel pressure to be the first to signal our moral commitments to the world. We fear that if we take our time we will be seen as being complicit with wrongdoing. So, we take shortcuts. We bypass the hard work of moral reasoning, and instead praise or condemn based on factional affiliation.

But through the cracks of the political divide we are also seeing positive examples emerge. University of Michigan students Kate Westa and Brett Zaslavsky, for example, lead WeListen, a bipartisan club dedicated to civil cross-ideological debate. At the national level, StoryCorps' One Small Step is facilitating one-on-one conversations in which people who disagree listen and respond to one another with respect. This is good faith in practice.[3]

2. Students from Covington Catholic High School attended the annual March for Life event near the Lincoln Memorial in Washington, DC, in January 2019. Some students got into a testy encounter with other activists, including a Native American man. Brief videos of the event seemed to indicate the students engaged in racist behavior, and they were roundly condemned across the country when those videos were circulated through social media and broadcast by news organizations. Later, longer video of the incident seemed to contradict the initial impressions of the students' conduct.

3. StoryCorps is an independent nonprofit agency dedicated to recording the stories ordinary people tell about their own lives. Some of their recordings are regularly broadcast on National Public Radio, and StoryCorps publishes books consisting of transcripts of recordings. Their first book, published in 2007, is *Listening Is an Act of Love.*

Arguably, there are exceptions to when we are expected to assume good faith. If we extend this and other conversational courtesies to incendiary speakers who gain prominence by violating those same courtesies, it is out of grace, not entitlement. We are obliged to respect their First Amendment rights but nothing more.

Incendiary speakers, however, are the exception. And we shouldn't base our ethical standards on the exception. Our default should be the presumption of good faith.

The practice of good faith is not an obvious remedy. It's a difficult discipline. It offers none of the psychic rewards that moral outrage delivers. But it's a practice that keeps the conversation going. And it's a practice that allows everyone in the conversation to teach and to learn.

2019

CHAPTER 2

✶

Cultural Criticism

Jonathan Swift

1667–1745

Swift, the dean of St. Patrick's Cathedral in Dublin, was a minister of the Anglican Church and a member of the English ruling class of Ireland. He thought it his responsibility "to tell the People what is their Duty; and then to convince them that it is so." "A Modest Proposal," which Swift published anonymously in 1729, is written in the style typical of eighteenth-century "projectors," writers (usually economists) who project what will happen if their proposed reforms are put into practice. This pamphlet crowned ten years of Swift's own determined effort to persuade all classes—Catholic peasants, middle-class shopkeepers, and Protestant landlords—to adopt higher morals and patriotism. (The projector's list of the other "expedients" for solving Ireland's ills is a fair summary of these efforts.) No particular event precipitated "A Modest Proposal," but Swift wrote it in the midst of intense, ineffectual parliamentary debate over how to end a famine and economic depression in Ireland that had been worsening for years. He criticizes the landowning ruling class, the shopkeepers, the peasants, Protestants and Catholics alike who feel greed more keenly than kinship to their fellow countrymen. The essay's argument is a famous example of irony, of saying the opposite of what you mean. Obviously, Swift does not really *believe that the Irish poor should fatten their babies for the tables of the Irish rich. Rather, Swift's point is that the Irish* already *act as if they are beasts: The poor are idle, thieving, and promiscuous; the middle class is greedy and cheating; while the rich, uninspired by patriotism, are content. The irony establishes common ground with readers who have been unmoved by Swift's earlier, more direct appeals. Recoiling from the projector's rational but inhumane solution and uneasy with the suspicion that they already are (at least metaphorically) cannibalizing their nation, readers will view the other "expedients" as all the more attractive, urgent, and right.*

A Modest Proposal

For Preventing the Children of Poor People in Ireland from Being a Burden to Their Parents or Country, and for Making Them Beneficial to the Public

It is a melancholy object to those who walk through this great town[1] or travel in the country, when they see the streets, the roads, and cabin doors, crowded with beggars of the female-sex, followed by three, four, or six children, all in rags and importuning every passenger for an alms. These mothers, instead of being able to work for their honest livelihood, are forced to employ all their time in strolling to beg sustenance for their helpless infants, who, as they grow up, either turn thieves for want of work, or leave their dear native country to fight for the Pretender in Spain, or sell themselves to the Barbadoes.[2]

I think it is agreed by all parties that this prodigious number of children in the arms, or on the backs, or at the heels of their mothers, and frequently of their fathers, is in the present deplorable state of the kingdom a very great additional grievance; and therefore whoever could find out a fair, cheap, and easy method of making these children sound, useful members of the commonwealth would deserve so well of the public as to have his statue set up for a preserver of the nation.

But my intention is very far from being confined to provide only for the children of professed beggars; it is of a much greater extent, and shall take in the whole number of infants at a certain age who are born of parents in effect as little able to support them as those who demand our charity in the streets.

As to my own part, having turned my thoughts for many years upon this important subject, and maturely weighed the several schemes of other projectors, I have always found them grossly mistaken in their computation. It is true, a child just dropped from its dam may be supported by her milk for a solar year, with little other nourishment; at most not above the value of two shillings,[3] which the mother may certainly get, or the value in scraps, by her lawful occupation of begging; and it is exactly at one year old

1. Dublin. [All notes are the editor's.]

2. Many of the poor in Ireland emigrated as indentured servants, for they were unable to pay for their own passage. Such bargains made them virtual slaves for a fixed period of time, usually about seven years. The Pretender, son of King James II, was dethroned in a Protestant revolution, and barred from succeeding to the British crown. Many Irish Catholics supported his claim as rightful heir, joined him in exile, and tried to further his unsuccessful efforts at counterrevolution.

3. There were twelve shillings to the British pound, and a pound in 1729 would have bought approximately one hundred fifty dollars worth of goods in today's money.

that I propose to provide for them in such a manner as instead of being a charge upon their parents or the parish, or wanting food and raiment for the rest of their lives, they shall on the contrary contribute to the feeding, and partly to the clothing, of many thousands.

There is likewise another great advantage in my scheme, that it will prevent those voluntary abortions, and that horrid practice of women murdering their bastard children, alas, too frequent among us, sacrificing the poor innocent babes, I doubt,[4] more to avoid the expense than the shame, which would move tears and pity in the most savage and inhuman breast.

The number of souls in this kingdom being usually reckoned one million and a half, of these I calculate there may be about two hundred thousand couple whose wives are breeders; from which number I subtract thirty thousand couples who are able to maintain their own children, although I apprehend there cannot be so many under the present distresses of the kingdom; but this being granted, there will remain an hundred and seventy thousand breeders. I again subtract fifty thousand for those women who miscarry, or whose children die by accident or disease within the year. There only remain an hundred and twenty thousand children of poor parents annually born. The question therefore is, how this number shall be reared and provided for, which, as I have already said, under the present situation of affairs, is utterly impossible by all the methods hitherto proposed. For we can neither employ them in handicraft or agriculture; we neither build houses (I mean in the country) nor cultivate land. They can very seldom pick up a livelihood by stealing till they arrive at six years old, except where they are of towardly parts;[5] although I confess they learn the rudiments much earlier, during which time they can however be looked upon only as probationers, as I have been informed by a principal gentleman in the county of Cavan, who protested to me that he never knew above one or two instances under the age of six, even in a part of the kingdom so renowned for the quickest proficiency in that art.

I am assured by our merchants that a boy or a girl before twelve years old is no salable commodity; and even when they come to this

4. "Expect" or "believe."

5. Show talent.

age they will not yield above three pounds, or three pounds and half a crown[6] at most on the Exchange; which cannot turn to account either to the parents or the kingdom, the charge of nutriment and rags having been at least four times that value.

I shall now therefore humbly propose my own thoughts, which I hope will not be liable to the least objection.

I have been assured by a very knowing American of my acquaintance in London, that a young healthy child well nursed is at a year old a most delicious, nourishing, and wholesome food, whether stewed, roasted, baked, or boiled; and I make no doubt that it will equally serve in a fricassee or a ragout.

I do therefore humbly offer it to public consideration that of the hundred and twenty thousand children, already computed, twenty thousand may be reserved for breed, whereof only one fourth part to be males, which is more than we allow to sheep, black cattle, or swine; and my reason is that these children are seldom the fruits of marriage, a circumstance not much regarded by our savages, therefore one male will be sufficient to serve four females. That the remaining hundred thousand may at a year old be offered in sale to the persons of quality and fortune through the kingdom, always advising the mother to let them suck plentifully in the last month, so as to render them plump and fat for a good table. A child will make two dishes at an entertainment for friends; and when the family dines alone, the fore or hind quarter will make a reasonable dish, and seasoned with a little pepper or salt will be very good boiled on the fourth day, especially in winter.

I have reckoned upon a medium that a child just born will weigh twelve pounds, and in a solar year if tolerably nursed increaseth to twenty-eight pounds.

I grant this food will be somewhat dear, and therefore very proper for landlords, who, as they have already devoured most of the parents, seem to have the best title to the children.

Infant's flesh will be in season throughout the year, but more plentiful in March, and a little before and after. For we are told by a grave author, an eminent French physician,[7] that fish being a prolific diet, there are more children born in Roman Catholic countries

6. A crown was one-fourth of a pound.

7. François Rabelais (1483–1553), a comic writer.

about nine months after Lent than at any other season; therefore, reckoning a year after Lent, the markets will be more glutted than usual, because the number of popish infants is at least three to one in this kingdom; and therefore it will have one other collateral advantage, by lessening the number of Papists among us.[8]

I have already computed the charge of nursing a beggar's child (in which list I reckon all cottagers, laborers, and four fifths of the farmers) to be about two shillings per annum, rags included; and I believe no gentleman would repine to give ten shillings for the carcass of a good fat child, which, as I have said, will make four dishes of excellent nutritive meat, when he hath only some particular friend or his own family to dine with him. Thus the squire will learn to be a good landlord, and grow popular among the tenants; the mother will have eight shillings net profit, and be fit for work till she produces another child.

Those who are more thrifty (as I must confess the times require) may flay the carcass; the skin of which artificially[9] dressed will make admirable gloves for ladies, and summer boots for fine gentlemen.

As to our city of Dublin, shambles[1] may be appointed for this purpose in the most convenient parts of it, and butchers we may be assured will not be wanting; although I rather recommend buying the children alive, and dressing them hot from the knife as we do roasting pigs.

A very worthy person, a true lover of his country, and whose virtues I highly esteem, was lately pleased in discoursing on this matter to offer a refinement upon my scheme. He said that many gentlemen of this kingdom, having of late destroyed their deer, he conceived that the want of venison might be well supplied by the bodies of young lads and maidens, not exceeding fourteen years of age nor under twelve, so great a number of both sexes in every county being now ready to starve for want of work and service; and these to be disposed of by their parents, if alive, or otherwise by their nearest relations. But with due deference to so excellent a friend and so deserving a patriot, I cannot be altogether in his sentiments; for as to the males, my American acquaintance assured me from frequent experience that their flesh was generally tough and lean, like that of our schoolboys,

8. Swift's audience would have been Anglo-Irish Protestants. Papists are Roman Catholics.

9. Skillfully.

1. Slaughterhouses.

by continual exercise, and their taste disagreeable; and to fatten them would not answer the charge. Then as to the females, it would, I think with humble submission, be a loss to the public, because they soon would become breeders themselves: and besides, it is not improbable that some scrupulous people might be apt to censure such a practice (although indeed very unjustly) as a little bordering upon cruelty; which, I confess, hath always been with me the strongest objection against any project, how well soever intended.

But in order to justify my friend, he confessed that this expedient was put into his head by the famous Psalmanazar,[2] a native of the island Formosa, who came from thence to London above twenty years ago, and in conversation told my friend that in his country when any young person happened to be put to death, the executioner sold the carcass to persons of quality as a prime dainty; and that in his time the body of a plump girl of fifteen, who was crucified for an attempt to poison the emperor, was sold to his Imperial Majesty's prime minister of state, and other great mandarins of the court, in joints from the gibbet, at four hundred crowns. Neither indeed can I deny that if the same use were made of several plump young girls in this town, who without one single groat to their fortunes cannot stir abroad without a chair,[3] and appear at the playhouse and assemblies in foreign fineries which they never will pay for, the kingdom would not be the worse.

Some persons of a desponding spirit are in great concern about that vast number of poor people who are aged, diseased, or maimed, and I have been desired to employ my thoughts what course may be taken to ease the nation of so grievous an encumbrance. But I am not in the least pain upon that matter, because it is very well known that they are every day dying and rotting by cold and famine, and filth and vermin, as fast as can be reasonably expected. And as to the younger laborers, they are now in almost as hopeful a condition. They cannot get work, and consequently pine away for want of nourishment to a degree that if at any time they are accidentally hired to common labor, they have not strength to perform

2. George Psalmanazar, a Frenchman who pretended to be from Formosa (now Taiwan), had written a book about his supposed homeland that described human sacrifice and cannibalism.

3. A chair, often covered, carried on poles by two people; akin to a taxi. "Groat": Worth about four English pence; there were 240 pence to the pound in 1729.

it; and thus the country and themselves are happily delivered from the evils to come.

I have too long digressed, and therefore shall return to my subject. I think the advantages by the proposal which I have made are obvious and many, as well as of the highest importance.

For first, as I have already observed, it would greatly lessen the number of Papists, with whom we are yearly overrun, being the principal breeders of the nation as well as our most dangerous enemies; and who stay at home on purpose to deliver the kingdom to the Pretender, hoping to take their advantage by the absence of so many good Protestants, who have chosen rather to leave their country than to stay at home and pay tithes against their conscience to an Episcopal curate.

Secondly, the poorer tenants will have something valuable of their own, which by law may be made liable to distress,[4] and help to pay their landlord's rent, their corn and cattle being already seized and money a thing unknown.

Thirdly, whereas the maintenance of an hundred thousand children, from two years old and upwards, cannot be computed at less than ten shillings a piece per annum, the nation's stock will be thereby increased fifty thousand pounds per annum, besides the profit of a new dish introduced to the tables of all gentlemen of fortune in the kingdom who have any refinement in taste. And the money will circulate among ourselves, the goods being entirely of our own growth and manufacture.

Fourthly, the constant breeders, besides the gain of eight shillings sterling per annum by the sale of their children, will be rid of the charge of maintaining them after the first year.

Fifthly, this food would likewise bring great custom to taverns, where the vintners will certainly be so prudent as to procure the best receipts[5] for dressing it to perfection, and consequently have their houses frequented by all the fine gentlemen, who justly value themselves upon their knowledge in good eating; and a skillful cook, who understands how to oblige his guests, will contrive to make it as expensive as they please.

Sixthly, this would be a great inducement to marriage, which all wise nations have either encouraged by rewards or enforced by laws

4. Seizure in payment of debts.

5. Recipes.

and penalties. It would increase the care and tenderness of mothers toward their children, when they were sure of a settlement for life to the poor babes, provided in some sort by the public, to their annual profit instead of expense. We should see an honest emulation among the married women, which of them could bring the fattest child to the market. Men would become as fond of their wives during the time of their pregnancy as they are now of their mares in foal, their cows in calf, or sows when they are ready to farrow; nor offer to beat or kick them (as is too frequent a practice) for fear of a miscarriage.

Many other advantages might be enumerated. For instance, the addition of some thousand carcasses in our exportation of barreled beef, the propagation of swine's flesh, and improvement in the art of making good bacon, so much wanted among us by the great destruction of pigs, too frequent at our tables, which are no way comparable in taste or magnificence to a well-grown, fat, yearling child, which roasted whole will make a considerable figure at a lord mayor's feast or any other public entertainment. But this and many others I omit, being studious of brevity.

Supposing that one thousand families in this city would be constant customers for infants' flesh, besides others who might have it at merry meetings, particularly weddings and christenings, I compute that Dublin would take off annually about twenty thousand carcasses, and the rest of the kingdom (where probably they will be sold somewhat cheaper) the remaining eighty thousand.

I can think of no one objection that will possibly be raised against this proposal, unless it should be urged that the number of people will be thereby much lessened in the kingdom. This I freely own, and it was indeed one principal design in offering it to the world. I desire the reader will observe, that I calculate my remedy for this one individual kingdom of Ireland and for no other that ever was, is, or I think ever can be upon earth. Therefore let no man talk to me of other expedients: of taxing our absentees at five shillings a pound: of using neither clothes nor household furniture except what is of our own growth and manufacture: of utterly rejecting the materials and instruments that promote foreign luxury: of curing the expensiveness of pride, vanity, idleness, and gaming in our women: of introducing a vein of parsimony, prudence, and temperance: of learning to love our country, in the want of which we differ even from Laplanders and the inhabitants of Topinamboo:[6] of quitting our animosities and factions, nor acting any longer like the Jews, who were murdering one another at the very moment their city was taken: of being a little cautious not to sell our country and conscience for nothing: of teaching landlords to have at least one degree of mercy toward their tenants: lastly, of putting a spirit of honesty, industry, and skill into our shopkeepers; who, if a resolution could now be taken to buy only our native goods, would immediately unite to cheat and exact upon us in the price, the measure, and the goodness, nor could ever yet be brought to make one fair proposal of just dealing, though often and earnestly invited to it.

Therefore I repeat, let no man talk to me of these and the like expedients, till he hath at least some glimpse of hope that there will ever be some hearty and sincere attempt to put them in practice.

But as to myself, having been wearied out for many years with offering vain, idle, visionary thoughts, and at length utterly despairing of success, I fortunately fell upon this proposal, which, as it is wholly new, so it hath something solid and real, of no expense and little trouble, full in our own power, and whereby we can incur no danger in disobliging England. For this kind of commodity will not bear exportation, the flesh being of too tender a consistence to admit a long continuance in salt, although perhaps I could name a country[7] which would be glad to eat up our whole nation without it.

After all, I am not so violently bent upon my own opinion as to reject any offer proposed by wise men, which shall be found equally innocent, cheap, easy, and effectual. But before something of that kind shall be advanced in contradiction to my scheme, and offering a better, I desire the author or authors will be pleased maturely to consider two points. First, as things now stand, how they will be able to find food and raiment for an hundred thousand useless mouths and backs. And secondly, there being a round million of creatures in human figure throughout this kingdom, whose sole subsistence put into a common stock would leave them in debt two millions of pounds sterling, adding those who are beggars by profession to the bulk of farmers, cottagers, and laborers, with their wives and children who are beggars in effect; I desire those politicians who dislike my overture, and may

6. In Brazil.

7. England.

perhaps be so bold to attempt an answer, that they will first ask the parents of these mortals whether they would not at this day think it a great happiness to h[…] for food at a year old in the manner I prescribe, […] misfortunes as th[…]dlords, the imposs[…]want of common […]r them from the […]le prospect of en[…]forever.

I profe[…]east personal int[…], having no other[…]dvancing our trad[…]ng some pleasure[…]ose to get a single[…] wife past childbe[…]

1729

***Amy C*[…]**

b. 1962

This short essay is the first chapter of Chua's memoir […]e Hymn of the Tiger Mom, *which touched off an explosive public debate about parenting, education, and race. Some people praised it for advocating a disciplined road to success for children in any family; others vilified it for reinforcing racial stereotypes; still others for promoting a family culture that could damage children's psyche. Because it is the introduction to a book—and that book a personal memoir—we should not expect a thorough, airtight argument. Chua's purpose here is to intrigue the reader to read more, not to present a complete argument. Nevertheless, if she is to get people to read more, they have to find the beginnings of her argument plausible, and Chua deploys some rhetorical maneuvers quite deftly. Note, for instance, how her construction of a definition ("Chinese mother") contributes to her ethos and anticipates the charge that she's promoting a racist ideology. Note also how she uses induction to support the notion that "cultural stereotypes" about parenting are true. In essence, her whole memoir provides a piece of anecdotal evidence (the experience of one family) that illustrates the data collected in those studies.*

Introduction to *Battle Hymn of the Tiger Mother*

A lot of people wonder how Chinese parents raise such stereotypically successful kids. They wonder what these parents do to produce so many math whizzes and music prodigies, what it's like inside the family, and whether they could do it too. Well, I can tell them, because I've done it. Here are some things my daughters, Sophia and Louisa, were never allowed to do:

- attend a sleepover
- have a playdate
- be in a school play
- complain about not being in a school play
- watch TV or play computer games
- choose their own extracurricular activities
- get any grade less than an A
- not be the #1 student in every subject except gym and drama
- play any instrument other than the piano or violin
- not play the piano or violin.

I'm using the term "Chinese mother" loosely. I recently met a supersuccessful white guy from South Dakota (you've seen him on television), and after comparing notes we decided that his working-class father had definitely been a Chinese mother. I know some Korean, Indian, Jamaican, Irish, and Ghanaian parents who qualify too. Conversely, I know some mothers of Chinese heritage, almost always born in the West, who are *not* Chinese mothers, by choice or otherwise.

I'm also using the term "Western parents" loosely. Western parents come in all varieties. In fact, I'll go out on a limb and say that Westerners are far more diverse in their parenting styles than the Chinese. Some Western parents are strict; others are lax. There are same-sex parents, Orthodox Jewish parents, single parents, ex-hippie parents, investment banker parents, and military parents. None of these "Western" parents necessarily sees eye to eye, so when I use the term "Western parents," of course I'm not referring to all Western parents just as "Chinese mother" doesn't refer to all Chinese mothers.

All the same, even when Western parents think they're being strict, they usually don't come close to being Chinese mothers. For example, my Western friends who consider themselves strict make their children practice their instruments thirty minutes every day. An hour at most. For a Chinese mother, the first hour is the easy part. It's hours two and three that get tough.

Despite our squeamishness about cultural stereotypes, there are tons of studies out there showing marked and quantifiable differences between Chinese and Westerners when it comes to parenting. In one study of 50 Western American mothers and 48 Chinese immigrant mothers, almost 70 percent of the Western mothers said either that "stressing academic success is not good for children" or that "parents need to foster the idea that learning is fun." By contrast, roughly 0 percent of the Chinese mothers felt the same way. Instead, the vast majority of the Chinese mothers said that they believe their children can be "the best" students, that "academic achievement reflects successful parenting," and that if children did not excel at school then there was "a problem" and parents "were not doing their job." Other studies indicate that compared to Western parents, Chinese parents spend approximately ten times as long every day drilling academic activities with their children. By contrast, Western kids are more likely to participate in sports teams.

This brings me to my final point. Some might think that the American sports parent is an analog to the Chinese mother. This is so wrong. Unlike your typical Western overscheduling soccer mom, the Chinese mother believes that (1) schoolwork always comes first; (2) an A-minus is a bad grade; (3) your children must be two years ahead of their classmates in math; (4) you must never compliment your children in public; (5) if your child ever disagrees with a teacher or coach, you must always take the side of the teacher or coach; (6) the only activities your children should be permitted to do are those in which they can eventually win a medal; and (7) that medal must be gold.

Author's Note

The statistics I cite are from the following studies: Ruth K. Chao, "Chinese and European American Mothers' Beliefs About the Role of Parenting in Children's School Success," *Journal of Cross-Cultural*

Psychology 27 (1996): 403–23; Paul E. Jose, Carol S. Huntsinger, Phillip R. Huntsinger, and Fong-Rucy Liaw, "Parental Values and Practices Relevant to Young Children's Social Development in Taiwan and the United States," *Journal of Cross-Cultural Psychology* 31 (2000): 677–702; and Parminder Parmar, "Teacher or Playmate? Asian Immigrant and Euro-American Parents' Participation in Their Young Children's Daily Activities," *Social Behavior and Personality* 36(2) (2008): 163–76.

2011

Ta-Nehisi Coates

b. 1975

Your class will probably find it difficult to discuss this essay frankly, for the very reason that Coates explains: it is almost impossible for someone who is not Black to utter the N-word without committing an act of psychological violence. It's important to remember that one can commit such acts by accident, without intending to. I have encountered this issue myself when teaching literature like Huckleberry Finn *and* Heart of Darkness. *Even reading the N-word aloud, in quotation, exhibits a potency that almost defies explanation. Nevertheless, as a student of rhetoric, you should not let this difficulty prevent you from examining this potency and learning how to explain it. In his 1955 book* How to Do Things with Words, *British linguist J. L. Austin explained that many of the things people say are "speech acts"—that is, rather than asserting something that is true or false, they attempt to do something the way you might try to bake bread or drive a car. An obvious example consists of the words* I do. *Given the right context, saying those words actually* does *something: it transforms you from a single person to a married person. In a different context, the words do not accomplish this feat. A marriage ceremony might be a comparatively rare set of circumstances; nevertheless, as Austin discovered, the things we say in our normal, everyday lives exhibit this kind of* doing *far more often than we realize. In other words, given certain contexts, words perform deeds. Their "meaning" is not so much something one might look up in a dictionary, a description of what the word refers to, as it is an act one performs. Whether the N-word does violence or enacts a degree of camaraderie depends entirely on the context of its utterance, which, in this case, depends in part upon the race of the person using it. Coates refers to Black "nationhood and community." There has always been a tension in the civil rights movement about whether integration can ever fully, or even ought to, bring us to a completely color-blind society that dissolves the boundaries between racial ethnicities.*

In Defense of a Loaded Word

My father's name is William Paul Coates. I, like my six brothers and sisters, have always addressed him as Dad. Strangers often call him Mr. Coates. His friends call him Paul. If a stranger or one of my father's friends called him Dad, my father might have a conversation. When I was a child, relatives of my paternal grandmother would call my father Billy. Were I to ever call my father Billy, we would probably have a different conversation.

I understand, like most people, that words take on meaning within a context. It might be true that you refer to your spouse as Baby. But were I to take this as license to do the same, you would most likely protest. Right names depend on right relationships, a fact so basic to human speech that without it, human language might well collapse. But as with so much of what we take as human, we seem to be in need of an African-American exception.

Three weeks ago the Miami Dolphins guard Richie Incognito, who is white, was reported to have addressed his fellow Dolphin as a "half-nigger." About a week later, after being ejected from a game, the Los Angeles Clippers forward Matt Barnes, who is black, tweeted that he was "done standing up for these niggas" after being ejected for defending his teammate. This came after the Philadelphia Eagles wide receiver Riley Cooper, who is white, angrily called a black security guard a "nigger" in July.

What followed was a fairly regular ritual debate over who gets to say "nigger" and who does not. On his popular show "Pardon the

Interruption," Tony Kornheiser called on the commissioners of the National Football League, the National Basketball Association and Major League Baseball to ban their players from publicly using the word. The ESPN host Skip Bayless went further, calling "nigger" "the most despicable word in the English language—verbal evil" and wishing that it could "die the death it deserves."

Mr. Bayless and Mr. Kornheiser are white, but many African-Americans have reached the same conclusion. On Thursday, the Fritz Pollard Alliance Foundation, a group promoting diversity in coaching and in the front offices of the N.F.L., called on players to stop using "the worst and most derogatory word ever spoken in our country" in the locker rooms.[1] In 2007 the N.A.A.C.P. organized a "funeral" in Detroit for the word "nigger." "Good riddance. Die, n-word," said Kwame Kilpatrick, then the mayor. "We don't want to see you around here no more."[2] But "nigger" endures—in our most popular music, in our most provocative films and on the lips of more black people (like me) than would like to admit it. Black critics, not unjustly, note the specific trauma that accompanies the word. For some the mere mention of "nigger" conjures up memories of lynchings and bombings. But there's more here—a deep fear of what our use of the word "nigger" communicates to white people. "If you call yourself the n-word," said the Rev. Al Sharpton, "you can't get mad when someone treats you like that."

This is the politics of respectability—an attempt to raise black people to a superhuman standard. In this case it means exempting black people from a basic rule of communication—that words take on meaning from context and relationship. But as in all cases of respectability politics, what we are really saying to black people is, "Be less human." This is not a fight over civil rights; it's an attempt to raise a double standard. It is no different from charging "ladies" with being ornamental and prim while allowing for the great wisdom of boys being boys. To prevent enabling oppression, we demand that black people be twice as good. To prevent verifying stereotypes, we pledge to never eat a slice a watermelon in front of white people.

But white racism needs no verification from black people. And a scientific poll of right-thinking humans will always conclude that

1. "Group wants end of N-word in NFL," ESPN NFL. ESPN.com. 2015. Online. 10 February 2015.

2. "The 'N' Word Is Laid to Rest by the NAACP," NAACP. 9 July 2007. Online. 10 February 2015.

watermelon is awesome. That is because its taste and texture appeal to certain attributes that humans tend to find pleasurable. Humans also tend to find community to be pleasurable, and within the boundaries of community relationships, words—often ironic and self-deprecating—are always spoken that take on other meanings when uttered by others.

A few summers ago one of my best friends invited me up to what he affectionately called his "white-trash cabin" in the Adirondacks. This was not how I described the outing to my family. Two of my Jewish acquaintances once joked that I'd "make a good Jew." My retort was not, "Yeah, I certainly am good with money." Gay men sometimes laughingly refer to one another as "faggots." My wife and her friends sometimes, when having a good time, will refer to one another with the word "bitch." I am certain that should I decide to join in, I would invite the same hard conversation that would greet me, should I ever call my father Billy.

A separate and unequal standard for black people is always wrong. And the desire to ban the word "nigger" is not anti-racism, it is finishing school. When Matt Barnes used the word "niggas" he was being inappropriate. When Richie Incognito and Riley Cooper used "nigger," they were being violent and offensive. That we have trouble distinguishing the two evidences our discomfort with the great chasm between black and white America. If you could choose one word to represent the centuries of bondage, the decades of terrorism, the long days of mass rape, the totality of white violence that birthed the black race in America, it would be "nigger."

But though we were born in violence, we did not die there. That such a seemingly hateful word should return as a marker of nationhood and community confounds our very notions of power. "Nigger" is different because it is attached to one of the most vibrant cultures in the Western world. And yet the culture is inextricably linked to the violence that birthed us. "Nigger" is the border, the signpost that reminds us that the old crimes don't disappear. It tells white people that, for all their guns and all their gold, there will always be places they can never go.

2013

The American Psychological Association

Est. 1892

The American Psychological Association (APA) is the main trade organization of psychologists in America. Most professions have such an organization that governs the knowledge and conduct of practitioners within the profession, sometimes even licensing people to practice. They also provide the public with expert guidance based on the most advanced research in the field. For example, the American Dental Association (ADA) grants its seal of approval to products, like toothpaste, that meet its own rigorous, up-to-date standards; the ADA seal informs consumers; and the need to please consumers drives manufacturers to comply with ADA guidelines.

This "Resolution" works in a similar way: the APA is hoping to influence regulations and channel public research money in certain directions. An important audience, then, are nonexpert officials who draft public policy. The APA is establishing ethos when it asserts that its resolutions are "informed by the best science currently available and that it accurately represents the research findings directly related to the topic." Scientists who research human beings tend to use large samples of people from whom they can generalize: in other words, inductive reasoning. Often, this process requires two groups, one in which people are exposed to some variable and another "control" group that is not. The difference between the groups can indicate a correlation between the variable and an outcome, but it does not necessarily indicate an effect's direct cause. A large part of the work of a social scientist is to figure out what all the inductive data tells us. Working with human behaviors and motivations is not like physical sciences, where causes and effects are more easily demonstrated. So it is important to note where there is consensus among psychologists who study violent video games and where they disagree about "the interpretation of the effect."

The resolution format at the end of the essay, "WHEREAS" and "THEREFORE," follows the formula of a deductive argument. WHEREAS clauses present premises that are based on the inductive data collected in various studies. And the "BE IT RESOLVED" clauses are conclusions that logically derive from those premises.

Resolution on Violent Video Games

Video game use has become pervasive in the American child's life: more than 90% of U.S. children play some kind of video games; when considering only adolescents ages 12–17, that figure rises to 97% (Lenhart et al., 2008; NPD Group, 2011). Although high levels of video game use are often popularly associated with adolescence, children younger than age 8 who play video games spend a daily average of 69 minutes on handheld console games, 57 minutes on computer games, and 45 minutes on mobile games, including tablets (Rideout, 2013). Considering the vast number of children and youth who use video games and that more than 85% of video games on the market contain some form of violence, the public has understandably been concerned about the effects that using violent video games may have on individuals, especially children and adolescents.

News commentators often turn to violent video game use as a potential causal contributor to acts of mass homicide. The media point to perpetrators' gaming habits as either a reason that they have chosen to commit their crimes, or as a method of training. This practice extends at least as far back as the Columbine massacre (1999) and has more recently figured prominently in the investigation into and reporting of the Aurora, CO, theatre shootings (2012), Sandy Hook massacre (2012), and Washington Navy Yard massacre (2013). This coverage has contributed to significant public discussion of the impacts of violent video game use. As a consequence of this popular perception, several efforts have been made to limit children's consumption of violent video games, to better educate parents about the effects of the content to which their children are being exposed, or both. Several jurisdictions have attempted to enact laws limiting the sale of violent video games to minors, and in 2011 the US Supreme Court considered the issue in *Brown v. Entertainment Merchants Association*, concluding that the First Amendment fully protects violent speech, even for minors.

In keeping with the American Psychological Association's (APA) mission to advance the development, communication, and application of psychological knowledge to benefit society, the Task Force on Violent Media was formed to review the APA Resolution on Violence in Video Games and Interactive Media adopted in 2005 and the related literature in order to ensure that the APA's resolution on the topic continues to be informed by the best science currently available and that it accurately represents the research findings directly related to the topic. This Resolution is based on the Task Force's review and is an update of the 2005 Resolution.

Scientists have investigated the effects of violent video game use for more than two decades. Multiple meta-analyses[1] of the research have been conducted. Quantitative reviews since APA's 2005 Resolution that have focused on the effects of violent video game use have found a direct association between violent video game use and aggressive outcomes (Anderson et al., 2010; Ferguson, 2007a; Ferguson, 2007b; Ferguson & Kilburn, 2009). Although the effect sizes reported are all similar (0.19, 0.15, 0.08, and 0.16, respectively), the interpretations of these effects have varied dramatically, contributing to the public debate about the effects of violent video games.

The link between violent video game exposure and aggressive behavior is one of the most studied and best established. Since the earlier meta-analyses, this link continues to be a reliable finding and shows good multi-method consistency across various representations of both violent video game exposure and aggressive behavior (e.g., Moller & Krahe, 2009; Saleem, Anderson & Gentile, 2012). Aggressive behavior examined in this research included experimental proxy paradigms, such as the administration of a noise blast to a confederate, and self-report questionnaires, peer nominations and teacher ratings of aggressiveness focused on behaviors including insults, threats, hitting, pushing, hair pulling, biting and other forms of verbal and physical aggression. The findings have also been seen over a range of samples, including those with older children, adolescent, and young adult participants. There is also consistency over time, in that the new findings are similar in effect size to those from past meta-analyses.

Similarly, the research conducted since the 2005 APA Resolution using aggressive cognitions and aggressive affect as outcomes also shows a direct effect of violent video game use (e.g., Hasan, Begue, Scharkow & Bushman, 2013; Shafer, 2012). Researchers have

1. meta-analysis: an analysis of various studies on the same or a similar issue to reach a general conclusion. a meta-analysis does not produce its own data from new experimentation or direct investigation; it relies on data collected in other studies [editor's note].

also continued to find that violent video game use is associated with decreases in socially desirable behavior such as prosocial behavior, empathy, and moral engagement (e.g., Arriaga, Monteiro & Esteves, 2011; Happ, Melzer & Steffgen, 2013).

The violent video game literature uses a variety of terms and definitions in considering aggression and aggressive outcomes, sometimes using "violence" and "aggression" interchangeably, or using "aggression" to represent the full range of aggressive outcomes studied, including multiple types and severity levels of associated behavior, cognitions, emotions, and neural processes. This breadth of coverage but lack of precision in terminology has contributed to some debate about the effects of violent video game use. In part, the numerous ways that violence and aggression have been considered stem from the multidisciplinary nature of the field. Epidemiologists, criminologists, physicians and others approach the phenomena of aggression and violence from different perspectives than do psychologists, and emphasize different definitions of the phenomena accordingly. Some disciplines are interested only in violence, and not other dimensions of aggression. In psychological research, aggression is usually conceptualized as behavior that is intended to harm another (see Baron & Richardson, 1994; Coie & Dodge, 1998; Huesmann & Taylor, 2006; VandenBos, 2007). Violence can be defined as an extreme form of aggression (see Encyclopedia of Psychology, 2000) or the intentional use of physical force or power, that either results in or has a high likelihood of resulting in harm (Krug, Dahlberg, Mercy, Zwi & Lozano, 2002).

Thus, all violence, including lethal violence, is aggression, but not all aggression is violence. This distinction is important for understanding this research literature, which has not focused on lethal violence as an outcome. Insufficient research has examined whether violent video game use causes lethal violence. The distinction is also important for considering the implications of the research and for interpreting popular press accounts of the research and its applicability to societal events.

Resolution

Consistent with the APA's mission to advance the development, communication and application of psychological knowledge to benefit society and improve people's lives, this Resolution on Violent Video Games finds:

WHEREAS scientific research has demonstrated an association between violent video game use and both increases in aggressive behavior, aggressive affect, aggressive cognitions and decreases in prosocial behavior, empathy, and moral engagement;

WHEREAS there is convergence of research findings across multiple methods and multiple samples with multiple types of measurements demonstrating the association between violent video game use and both increases in aggressive behavior, aggressive affect, aggressive cognitions and decreases in prosocial behavior, empathy, and moral engagement;

WHEREAS all existing quantitative reviews of the violent video game literature have found a direct association between violent video game use and aggressive outcomes;

WHEREAS this body of research, including laboratory experiments that examine effects over short time spans following experimental manipulations and observational longitudinal studies lasting more than 2 years, has demonstrated that these effects persist over at least some time spans;

WHEREAS research suggests that the relation between violent video game use and increased aggressive outcomes remains after considering other known risk factors associated with aggressive outcomes;

WHEREAS although the number of studies directly examining the association between the amount of violent video game use and amount of change in adverse outcomes is still limited, existing research suggests that higher amounts of exposure are associated with higher levels of aggression and other adverse outcomes;

WHEREAS research demonstrates these effects for children older than 10 years, adolescents, and young adults, but very little research has included children younger than 10 years;

WHEREAS research has not adequately examined whether the association between violent video game use and aggressive outcomes differs for males and females;

WHEREAS research has not adequately included samples representative of the current population demographics;

WHEREAS research has not sufficiently examined the potential moderator effects of ethnicity, socioeconomic status, or culture;

WHEREAS many factors are known to be risk factors for increased aggressive behavior, aggressive cognition and aggressive affect, and reduced prosocial behavior, empathy and moral engagement, and violent video game use is one such risk factor;

Therefore,

BE IT RESOLVED that the APA engage in public education and awareness activities disseminating these findings to children, parents, teachers, judges and other professionals working with children in schools and communities;

BE IT FURTHER RESOLVED that APA support funding of basic and intervention research by the federal government and philanthropic organizations to address the following gaps in knowledge about the effects of violent video game use:

The association between violent video game use and negative outcomes for understudied ethnic and sociocultural populations who may be at increased risk for negative outcomes because of increased violent video game exposure or the presence of other risk factors for aggressive outcomes;

The nature of the association between violent video game use and negative outcomes for males and females separately;

The association between violent video game use and negative outcomes for school age and preschool age children;

The relation between degree of exposure to violent video games and negative outcomes;

The persistence of negative outcomes over time;

The relation between game ratings and types, amounts, and degrees of violence present in violent video games;

The relation between negative outcomes and game characteristics such as properties of the game, including type and degree of violence, how the game is played, and how the game is perceived by the player;

The intersection of variables related to negative outcomes of violent video game use and the broader context of violence within the games, including choices about targets of violence, game themes, and the development and marketing of games;

The impact of rapidly changing game technology and formats on users' experience and outcomes;

The role of competition and cooperation in the association between violent video game use and negative outcomes; and

The role of media literacy in mediating negative effects associated with violent video game use;

BE IT FURTHER RESOLVED that APA endorses the development and implementation of rigorously tested interventions that educate children, youth and families about the effects of violent video game use; and

BE IT FURTHER RESOLVED that APA strongly encourages the Entertainment Software Rating Board (ESRB) to refine the ESRB rating system specifically to reflect the levels and characteristics of violence in games in addition to the current global ratings.

References

American Psychological Association, Task Force on Violent Media. (2015). *Technical report on the review of the violent video game literature.* Washington, DC: Author.

Anderson, C. A., Shibuya, A., Ihori, N., Swing, E. L., Bushman, B. J., Sakamoto, A., Rothstein, H. R., & Saleem, M. (2010). Violent video game effects on aggression, empathy, and prosocial behavior in eastern and western countries: A meta-analytic review. *Psychological Bulletin, 136(2)*, 151–173.

Arriaga, P., Monteiro, M. B., & Esteves, F. (2011). Effects of playing violent computer games on emotional desensitization and aggressive behavior. *Journal of Applied Social Psychology, 41(8)*, 1900–1925.

Baron, R. A., & Richardson, D. R. (Eds.) (1994). *Human Aggression: Perspectives in Social Psychology.* New York, NY: Springer.

Coie, J. D., & Dodge, K. A. (1988). Multiple sources of data on social behavior and social status in the school: A cross-age comparison. *Child Development, 59(3)*, 815–829.

Ferguson, C. J., & Kilburn, J. (2009). The public health risks of media violence: A meta-analytic review. *The Journal of Pediatrics*, 1–5. 10.1016/j.jpeds.2008.11.033.

Ferguson, C. J. (2007a). Evidence for publication bias in video game violence effects literature: A meta analytic review. *Aggression and Violent Behavior, 12,* 470–482.

Ferguson, C. J. (2007b). The good, the bad and the ugly: A meta-analytic review of positive and negative effects of violent video games. *Psychiatric Quarterly, 78*, 309–316. DOI 10.1007/s11126-007-9056-9.

Happ, C., Melzer, A., & Steffgen, G. (2013). Superman v. BAD man? The effects of empathy and game character in violent video games. Cyberpsychology, behavior, and social networking. 1–7.

Hasan, Y., Begue, L., Scharkow, M., & Bushman, B. J. (2013). The more you play, the more aggressive you become: A long-term experimental study of cumulative violent video game effects on hostile expectations and aggressive behavior. *Journal of Experimental Social Psychology, 49*, 224–227.

Huesmann, R. L., & Taylor, L. D. (2006). The role of media violence in violent behavior. *Annual Review of Public Health, 27*, 393–415. DOI:10.1146/annurev.publhealth.26.021304.144640.

Krug, E. G., Dahlberg, L. L., Mercy, J. A., Zwi, A. B., & Lozano, R. (2002). *World report on violence and health.* Geneva: World Health Organization.

Lenhart, A., Kahne, J., Middaugh, E., MacGill, A., Evans, C., & Vitak, J. (2008). *Teens, videogames and civics.* Washington, DC: Pew Internet & American Life Project. files.eric.ed.gov/fulltext/ED525058

Moller, I., & Krahe, B. (2009). Exposure to violent video games and aggression in German adolescents: A longitudinal analysis. *Aggressive Behavior, 35*, 75–89.

NPD Group. (2011). *Kids and gaming, 2011.* Port Washington, NY: The NPD Group, Inc.

Rideout, V. (2013). *Zero to eight: Children's media use in America 2013.* San Francisco, CA: Common Sense Media.

In her 1979 review of a Norman Mailer novel, Joan Didion wrote that the authentic Western voice is "heard often in life but only rarely in literature, the reason being that to truly know the West is to lack all will to write it down."[3] The lack of good words is part of the deal: "Infinity" means you've stopped watching yourself, or watching others as if you don't belong with them, and maybe being that inside of it means limited access to the picture frame, Joseph Cornell box,[4] Polly Pocket dream house that you get to hold firmly once you've turned something into a story.

I guess "Infinity" is like what psychologists call "flow,"[5] when you get so focused on something that everything else kind of falls away. Psychoanalyst D. W. Winnicott used "transitional space"[6] to describe the unquantifiable dimension that opens up in play, sex, and other feeling-not-thinking activities. Polymath Michael Polanyi coined the term "tacit knowledge"[7] in opposition to explicit knowledge, so that we at least have an articulatable distinction between what can and cannot be articulated.

In Donna Tartt's *The Secret History*, the students in a cult-like classics course conduct an ancient Dionysian ritual in the woods at night, in order to fully lose any sense of self, and achieve what their passionate professor calls "the fire of pure being." In Maggie Nelson's

3. Didion, Joan. "I Want To Go Ahead and Do It." *New York Times*, October 7, 1979. Review of Norman Mailer's *The Executioner's Song*.

4. The Joseph Cornell Box. https://www.josephcornellbox.com/boxes.htm.

5. "In positive psychology, a flow state, also known colloquially as being in the zone, is the mental state in which a person performing an activity is fully immersed in a feeling of energized focus, full involvement, and enjoyment in the process of the activity." "Flow (Psychology)." Wikipedia. Wikimedia Foundation, June 8, 2020. https://en.wikipedia.org/wiki/Flow_(psychology).

6. Laura Praglin, "The Nature of the 'In-Between' in D. W. Winnicott's Concept of Transitional Space and in Martin Buber's *das Zwischenmenschliche*." *Universitas* 2.2 (Fall 2006). https://universitas.uni.edu/archive/fall06/pdf/art_praglin.pdf.

7. "Tacit knowledge (as opposed to formal, codified or explicit knowledge) is the kind of knowledge that is difficult to transfer to another person by means of writing it down or verbalizing it. For example, that London is in the United Kingdom is a piece of explicit knowledge that can be written down, transmitted, and understood by a recipient. However, the ability to speak a language, ride a bicycle, knead dough, play a musical instrument, or design and use complex equipment requires all sorts of knowledge which is not always known explicitly, even by expert practitioners, and which is difficult or impossible to explicitly transfer to other people." "Tacit Knowledge." Wikipedia. Wikimedia Foundation, April 26, 2020. https://en.wikipedia.org/wiki/Tacit_knowledge.

Bluets, a different Dionysius—Dionysius the Areopagite, a Syrian monk—is cited as one of the first Christian advocates for the idea of a Divine Darkness, an experience which attests that "by not-seeing and unknowing, we attain true vision and knowledge."

Theater is one of the last things on the planet that can't be recorded with any semblance to the live experience, making every show a disappearing act. In the 1977 film *Opening Night*, the immediacy of stage acting ushers its protagonist, Myrtle Gordon, out of her own head and into a performance so real and funny that I rewatch it all the time like a reward for whatever shit I had to do that day and also get curmudgeonly and frustrated about everything that's gotten to be called "real" or "funny" in the years of filmmaking since. The movie starts with Myrtle, an aging theater star, witnessing the death of a pretty young fan just as she was trying to get her autograph. She's haunted for months by visions of the girl, and by the latest role she's agreed to play: a woman her own age. She repeatedly makes her case to the playwright and director as to why she can't be seen being good at playing an older woman, and they have to chase her down—drunk and far away from the theater, minutes before her entrance—for the opening night performance.

She doesn't succeed in the end by escaping into the part, undergoing some huge transformation, or any of those self-annihilating acting stereotypes: she continues to grapple with the fear of becoming old and unlovable, but instead of monologuing, looks past herself, to her scene partner, so that the two of them can joke about it together. The self-sabotaging tendencies that terrorized every rehearsal are overpowered by her desire to give the audience something human. From the Criterion edition's essay by Dennis Lim:[8] "Myrtle's triumph has less to do with reaffirmed public adoration than with her revitalized faith in art as a way of life. Onstage, she defiantly reanimates the self-help cliché of existing 'in the moment' and, however briefly, entertains the possibility of pure experience."

Some of my favorite fictional characters have experienced such a sensation when they've found themselves in love, or at least having

8. Lim, Dennis. "Opening Night: The Play's the Thing." The Criterion Collection. Accessed October 25, 2013. https://www.criterion.com/current/posts/341-opening-night-the-play-s-the-thing.

sex, or something in-between. From Miranda July's *The First Bad Man*: "Was all this real to her? Did she think it was temporary? Or maybe that was the point of love: not to think." From Emma Cline's *The Girls*: "There was nothing to figure out, no complicated puzzles—just the obvious fact of the moment, the only place where love really existed." From James Baldwin's *Giovanni's Room*:

> "I told her that I had loved her once and I made myself believe it. But I wonder if I had. I was thinking, no doubt, of our nights in bed, of the peculiar innocence and confidence, which will never come again, which had made those nights so delightful, so unrelated to past, present, or anything to come, so unrelated, finally, to my life since it was not necessary for me to take any but the most mechanical responsibility for them. And these nights were being acted out under a foreign sky, with no one to watch, no penalties attached . . ."

And Marguerite Duras's *The Lover*:

> "He calls me a whore, a slut, he says I'm his only love, and that's what he ought to say, and what you do say when you just let things say themselves, when you let the body alone, to seek and find and take what it likes. . . ."

And my diary from last year. I started my blog when I was 11 and began keeping handwritten diaries regularly at 15. (I now have about 70 of them, in a fireproof safe the size of a mini-fridge.) Once I graduated from high school, moved to New York, and started performing on Broadway in the play *This Is Our Youth*, I experimented with letting everything about this mind-blowing transition disappear into the ether. There were a few panicked catch-ups that would trail off into "this is pointless": staring at my laptop screen in the Bryant Park Library and feeling so weighed down by the history of the carvings on the walls that *why even try*; talking into a recorder on my bed late at night before asking myself who it was really for, if you can really live for the memories you'll have to look back on when you're older if you could also get hit by a bus tomorrow, if your legacy makes any difference to you when you finally lose all consciousness, if commodifying everyone I meet into a fictive character diminishes the potential for love. What was I closing myself off from by trying to decide what everything meant as soon as it happened? *While* it was happening? Sometimes, even, beforehand?

Every night that fall and winter, with *Groundhog Day*–like repetition, I performed a play as a young woman in New York set up on a kind-of date with a weird guy in his friend's apartment. After a series of false starts, it ends up going remarkably well and offers a glimmer of hope to each of them as to what kind of human connection is possible in the awful expanse of adulthood before them. In the morning, they have a bad misunderstanding that's no one's fault until they both return to their defenses and become strangers again. After the show, I'd go straight to the apartment of a new guy I was kind-of seeing, each of us so skilled at remaining unknowable that it was like a one-night stand, every night. Then I'd wake up in his bed, maybe go out into the world for a few hours before the next show and maybe not, and repeat it all again.

I started keeping a diary again the day after we broke up, scrambling to save what I could, but all my efforts felt futile. On the right night, after hearing the right song, or rereading any of my favorite parts of *The Secret History*—a devastating lesson on the impossibility of perfection, let alone a kind that can last—it makes me crumble all over again. When I started writing this thing about Infinity, I talked to my therapist about how hopeful it was making me, as if, through the powers of my storytelling, I could rearrange the past and dictate the future, and then how stupid I feel every time I recognize the hubris there. Sarah Manguso in her book *Ongoingness*: "How ridiculous to believe myself powerful enough to stop time just by thinking."

"Give yourself a break," she said. "You had a secret world together. Sex and watching movies and giggling. Sex and secret worlds are the symbolic, and they're way more powerful than the narrative; than 'we went for a walk, then we did this, then we did this.' It's play. You guys played together like little kids. And that's not something you can really articulate without sounding mushy."

"But it feels like bad writing to just say something is indescribable. Though I guess some things really just are." (Scary thought: What would it mean if they weren't? If you really could describe everything? The world would be . . . underwhelming?)

She brought up the debate at the beginning of Maggie Nelson's *The Argonauts*, about whether language is precise or fallible. I wrote down the exchange you just read. So here I am again, sad and alone and without any words. Also there's a spider bite *on my toe.*

Drawing on a memory can also mean defacing it, adding another subconscious layer of commentary with every recollection. Things get even more unwieldy once they sprawl out across the imaginations of the strangers reading it, should one choose to share. Unfortunately, the thing itself is over as soon as it's over; dead whether you choose to "kill it with the word" (Goethe, via *Bluets*) or not. I do think there's a way to approach writing about one's own life that cultivates acceptance instead of clinging, and unearths discoveries which simple event-recording, with no real digging or reflecting, can't offer. This alleged act of murder is also a way of giving birth to something new: there's an Infinity on the other side of words, too; on what can become possible when you *do* try to gather up your engrams of an event and let them guide you through writing to a previously unrealized truth.

This is enough. Not in the grand scheme of what remains a million years from now when the earth is dust and holograms of dead future-celebrities are political leaders on Mars, but what'll I care by then anyways? Picking up the piles of dirty laundry in my brain makes room for new experiences, new partners, new plays. Weirdly, by starting up the diary again and sticking with it, it got easier to surrender to the impact of an event, live in it without immediate reflection, and charge forth like the speck that I am. It's gotten shockingly effortless to live in Infinity, and trust that I'll retain what I need to later, and if not, accept the price of a life fully lived.

Over the course of this month, I'll share on Rookie some of the diary entries which made up that transition. We also want to know what Infinity looks and feels like for you, so head over to our Submit page for more ideas from our editors, and information on sending in your work.[9] Doesn't have to be made up of words, like mine: send your photography, illustration, collage, playlists, all of it!

9. *Rookie* is now only an archived page, so the submit link does not work; I have left this reference unchanged to maintain some genre features of the blog post [editor's note].

We will definitely be celebrating five years of Rookie all month, as well, so stay tuned for some very not-casual joy and reflection in that regard!

Onward like a speck,
With love,
Tavi

2016

Dana Stevens
b. 1966

Most readers will be familiar with the genre of movie review. Above all else, reviewers report on the film so readers can decide if they want to pay to go see it. But reviewers also try to influence the public's opinion about a film—is it good or bad? What films are similar to it? How should it be interpreted? Is it worthy of an Oscar? In this case, Stevens enters into a public debate about the whole genre of movies based on comic books. For example, the award-winning film director Martin Scorsese published a scathing op-ed in the New York Times *in response to comic book movies, arguing that cinema ought to be "an art form." Films should reveal beauty, emotion, and spirit; they need to present to viewers "the complexity of people and their contradictory and sometimes paradoxical nature"; above all else films must make people "confront the unexpected." Movies in the Marvel Cinematic Universe, Scorsese asserts, don't do these things. There's no "revelation, mystery, or genuine emotional danger. Nothing is at risk." Therefore, he concludes deductively, they are not "cinema."*

Stevens's review came before Scorsese's op-ed, so it is not a direct response, but Scorsese's scorn for movies made from comic books was out there long before he articulated it, and we might take Stevens's review as a defense of the whole genre against the naysayers. Published in Slate *online magazine, this review compares* Avengers: Endgame *to a play written by Nobel Prize laureate Samuel Beckett. Whether or not the film's title consciously alludes to Beckett is a debatable point, but to make the comparison at all suggests that we need to take the movie—and perhaps the whole genre of comic book films—more seriously than Scorsese does. If you agree with Stevens, you might consider how you would refute Scorsese's argument—would you undermine the major or the minor premises? Does Stevens's review help you do so?*

Waiting for Thanos

"The end is in the beginning, and yet you go on," observes one of the four characters in Samuel Beckett's play *Endgame*, a starkly minimalist meditation on the inevitability of death and the necessity of maintaining human connections, however imperfect and infuriating the humans we're stuck with may be.[1] The *Avengers* installment of the same title, the conclusion of an 11-year, 22-movie cycle of Marvel Cinematic Universe (MCU) adventures[2]—is the precise opposite of minimalist: It's three hours long, stuffed with dozens of characters, and takes place not in a bare room with a chair and two windows but across multiple galaxies, time spans, and alternate universes. But in its own sentimental, fan-servicing, spaceship-exploding way, *Avengers: Endgame*, directed by brothers Joe and Anthony Russo, takes on some of the same hard questions as its existentialist namesake. Whether you're a bickering old couple stuck in a pair of garbage cans or a gang of bickering superheroes trying yet again to save the cosmos, how are you supposed to confront loss, the ineluctably sad fact that the people and institutions and, yes, even movie franchises you care about are always in the process of changing, disappearing, and dying?

1. *Endgame* by Samuel Beckett is a play that was first performed in 1957. The play uses minimal staging, and it expresses (not without humor) Beckett's existentialist view of the universe. The play's four characters are not quite realistic, though they might be described as "smaller than life" in contrast to the "larger than life" characters in the film discussed here. Two of those characters appear in garbage cans, which Stevens alludes to later in the review. The play's title alludes to the strategy used in the final stage in a game of chess, which concludes either with a checkmate or a draw. [All notes are the editor's.]

2. The "Marvel Cinematic Universe" is a group of sometimes loosely connected films based on characters and storylines first developed in comic books. The individual films share the same "universe," presenting to viewers a coherent world and consistent characters, which sometimes cross over (in cameos or larger roles) from one film to another. Their complex, disparate storylines converge and conclude in *Avengers: Endgame.*

Lest that analogy—Beckett in space!—sound too somber, take heart that (like the play *Endgame*, actually) *Avengers: Endgame* throws in plenty of laughs along the way. In fact, in the long stretch between its appropriately somber opening chapter and an emotionally grueling finale, it may be the most lighthearted and character-driven Marvel movie since the giddy comic entry *Thor: Ragnarok*.[3] *Endgame* consists almost entirely of the downtime scenes that were always secretly everyone's favorite parts of these movies anyway—the Avengers hanging out, dunking on each other's outsized egos, indulging in passive-aggressive dominance displays disguised as banter, or casually offering each other their uneaten peanut butter sandwiches. But this epic installment (scripted by MCU veterans Christopher Markus and Stephen McFeely) is still capacious enough to fit in ample time—more than ample, I'd say—for spectacular if cacophonous action scenes, serious dramatic storytelling, some touches of light romance, and a surprising amount of what you might call well-earned brooding, not just on the parts of the heroes but of the villain too.

That would be Thanos, the hulking, purple-skinned bad guy (voiced by Josh Brolin) whose utilitarian moral principles had him halving the universe's population of living things with a single finger snap in the shockingly bleak ending of the last chapter, *Avengers: Infinity War*. When we revisit our heroes, even those who haven't been dissolved into mulch have been transformed by the event—sometimes literally. (A huge prosthetic stomach worn by one of these super-specimens veers cringily near fat-joke territory, but the hero's insistent self-confidence makes the transformation more endearing than pitiable.) It takes a character who's only briefly crisscrossed with this now-downtrodden group in the past—Paul Rudd's size-shifting Ant-Man—to propose a plan: Why not hop back in time, reconstruct the all-powerful glove before Thanos can, and snap the missing 50 percent back into being again? That will of course require the construction of a time machine, but with a reluctant Tony Stark (Robert Downey Jr.) dragged back into the game, such a device is only one epiphany away.[4] (Pro tip: Just reverse the rotating Möbius strip that

3. Released in 2017; the seventeenth film in the Marvel Cinematic Universe and the direct sequel of two earlier *Thor* movies in the MCU series.

4. Tony Stark is the alter ego of Iron Man. The first film in the MCU is the 2008 *Iron Man*.

floats in holographic form above your super-advanced home computing system!)

Storywise, the middle stretch of the movie consists of crosscutting among various interplanetary timelines as our heroes split up, Scooby Doo–style, to recover the scattered jewels.[5] By this point in the series, there are so many plot threads to tie up, old friends to mourn (or reanimate), and intra-Avengers scores to settle that in its relatively swift-moving three hours, *Avengers: Endgame* scarcely spends a minute with a single character who *isn't* super. Sure, the task at hand is to bring back 50 percent of the universe's living beings—according to one character's estimate, the number of disappeared creatures belongs in the trillions—but the world of this movie is curiously intimate, focused all but completely on the history and relationships of the dozen or so super-beings at its center. I won't tell you who makes it back to the world of the living—nor who leaves it, sometimes in ways too absolute to be reversible.

But as I got caught up in, say, the gruff resolution of the *Civil War*–era beef between Iron Man and Captain America (Chris Evans), or accompanied Hawkeye (Jeremy Renner) and Black Widow (Scarlett Johansson) through a wrenching turning point in their too-long-neglected platonic friendship, I realized grudgingly that these movies—which have taken me in the past 11 years on an emotional journey from charmed (*Iron Man*) to bored (*Iron Man 2* and *3*, most of the *Thor* movies) to pleasantly amused (*Guardians of the Galaxy*, the aforementioned *Ragnarok*) to legitimately moved (*Black Panther*, *Captain America: Winter Soldier*, *Infinity War*, and now *Endgame*)—no longer feel only like products rolled off the Marvel factory line, engineered for maximum global box office and product tie-in possibilities. Though not every outing has escaped the constraints placed on it by formula and the marketplace, this motley crew of super-friends has become a part of our shared popular culture, largely thanks to the charisma and interpersonal chemistry of the actors playing them. You can curse the stranglehold comic book blockbusters have on the film industry and still resist the idea of a world with *no one* super in it.

5. *Scooby-Doo* is a cartoon multimedia franchise that began with the children's television show, *Scooby-Doo, Where Are You!* in 1969. It features an ensemble cast (including the eponymous dog, Scooby-Doo) who split up during each episode to solve some mystery.

For the first time since the Bush administration, the final credit sequence for a Marvel adventure contains no midroll or ending "stinger," no sly, enigmatic glimpse of what new villain or hero awaits us in the movie to come. That's not to say there won't be new Marvel products rolling out in the near future; if this is indeed the twilight of the gods, a well-funded and globally marketed dawn (and a welcomely diversified new pantheon) is around the corner. But there was something peaceful, almost soothing, about getting up midway through the credit roll—I admit I did stick around for one last image of all the major characters, some accompanied, in good fan-service style, by the autographs of the actors playing them—and leaving the theater without looking back. Given that time in our own universe keeps on stubbornly moving in the same direction, sometimes things—movie franchises, actors' contracts, even the lives of long-beloved characters—come to an end, and there's just time to take a breath and look up at the sky before the building of the next universe begins.

2019

CHAPTER 3

✶

Education

What does flight signify in Black literature?

Language

trembled
epidemic
release
anxious
tradition-bound
Strutted
exerting
pressure
authority
overpoked
play sister
Bubba
spirit
shared (understanding)

How does "Graduation" reflect poem?

↳ Paper Idea

Poem: primary

Grad: secondary

Labor vs. Intellect

p. 186; 192-193

How does suspense function in text?

what lang; what outside sources, images; POV; experiences; observations; used to support arg in text?

↓

multiple

Auto bio's have purpose for most part

Maya Angelou
1928–2014

"Graduation" is an excerpt from Angelou's autobiography, I Know Why the Caged Bird Sings *(1970). The title of that book is a quotation from the 1899 poem "Sympathy" by African American poet Paul Laurence Dunbar, which concludes with these lines:*

I know why the caged bird sings, ah me,
When his wing is bruised and his bosom sore,—
When he beats his bars and he would be free;
It is not a carol of joy or glee,
But a prayer that he sends from his heart's deep core,
But a plea, that upward to Heaven he flings—
I know why the caged bird sings!

At least one of Angelou's intentions was to expose the bars constraining Black Americans (and in particular Black women). She also means to number herself among the poets, preachers, musicians, and blues singers of "the wonderful, beautiful Negro race."

Graduation

The children in Stamps[1] trembled visibly with anticipation. Some adults were excited too, but to be certain the whole young population had come down with graduation epidemic. Large classes were graduating from both the grammar school and the high school. Even those who were years removed from their own day of glorious release were anxious to help with preparations as a kind of dry run. The junior students who were moving into the vacating classes' chairs were tradition-bound to show their talents for leadership and management. They strutted through the school and around the campus exerting pressure on the lower grades. Their authority was so new that occasionally if they pressed a little too hard it had to be overlooked. After all, next term was coming, and it never hurt a sixth grader to have a play sister in the eighth grade,

1. A small, rural town in Arkansas. [All notes are the editor's.]

or a tenth-year student to be able to call a twelfth grader Bubba.[2] So all was endured in a spirit of shared understanding. But the graduating classes themselves were the nobility. Like travelers with exotic destinations on their minds, the graduates were remarkably forgetful. They came to school without their books, or tablets or even pencils. Volunteers fell over themselves to secure replacements for the missing equipment. When accepted, the willing workers might or might not be thanked, and it was of no importance to the pregraduation rites. Even teachers were respectful of the now quiet and aging seniors, and tended to speak to them, if not as equals, as beings only slightly lower than themselves. After tests were returned and grades given, the student body, which acted like an extended family, knew who did well, who excelled, and what piteous ones had failed.

Unlike the white high school,[3] Lafayette County Training School distinguished itself by having neither lawn, nor hedges, nor tennis court, nor climbing ivy. Its two buildings (main classrooms, the grade school and home economics) were set on a dirt hill with no fence to limit either its boundaries or those of bordering farms. There was a large expanse to the left of the school which was used alternately as a baseball diamond or a basketball court. Rusty hoops on the swaying poles represented the permanent recreational equipment, although bats and balls could be borrowed from the P. E. teacher if the borrower was qualified and if the diamond wasn't occupied.

Over this rocky area relieved by a few shady tall persimmon trees the graduating class walked. The girls often held hands and no longer bothered to speak to the lower students. There was a sadness about them, as if this old world was not their home and they were bound for higher ground. The boys, on the other hand, had become more friendly, more outgoing. A decided change from the closed attitude they projected while studying for finals. Now they seemed not ready to give up the old school, the familiar paths and classrooms. Only a small percentage would be continuing on to college—one of the South's A & M (agricultural and mechanical) schools, which trained Negro youths to be carpenters, farmers, handymen, masons, maids, cooks and baby nurses. Their future rode heavily on their shoulders, and blinded them

2. Slang for *Brother*.

3. Before the 1954 Supreme Court decision *Brown v. Board of Education of Topeka, Kansas*, many public schools in America were racially segregated.

to the collective joy that had pervaded the lives of the boys and girls in the grammar school graduating class.

Parents who could afford it had ordered new shoes and ready-made clothes for themselves from Sears and Roebuck or Montgomery Ward. They also engaged the best seamstresses to make the floating graduating dresses and to cut down second-hand pants which would be pressed to a military slickness for the important event.

Oh, it was important, all right. Whitefolks would attend the ceremony, and two or three would speak of God and home, and the Southern way of life, and Mrs. Parsons, the principal's wife, would play the graduation march while the lower-grade graduates paraded down the aisles and took their seats below the platform. The high school seniors would wait in empty classrooms to make their dramatic entrance.

In the Store I was the person of the moment. The birthday girl. The center. Bailey[4] had graduated the year before, although to do so he had had to forfeit all pleasures to make up for his time lost in Baton Rouge.

My class was wearing butter-yellow piqué dresses, and Momma launched out on mine. She smocked the yoke into tiny crisscrossing puckers, then shirred the rest of the bodice. Her dark fingers ducked in and out of the lemony cloth as she embroidered raised daisies around the hem. Before she considered herself finished she had added a crocheted cuff on the puff sleeves, and a pointy crocheted collar.

I was going to be lovely. A walking model of all the various styles of fine hand sewing and it didn't worry me that I was only twelve years old and merely graduating from the eighth grade. Besides, many teachers in Arkansas Negro schools had only that diploma and were licensed to impart wisdom.

The days had become longer and more noticeable. The faded beige of former times had been replaced with strong and sure colors. I began to see my classmates' clothes, their skin tones, and the dust that waved off pussy willows. Clouds that lazed across the sky were objects of great concern to me. Their shiftier shapes might have held a message that in my new happiness and with a little bit of time I'd soon decipher. During that period I looked at the arch of heaven so religiously my neck kept a steady ache. I had taken to smiling more

4. Angelou's brother.

often, and my jaws hurt from the unaccustomed activity. Between the two physical sore spots, I suppose I could have been uncomfortable, but that was not the case. As a member of the winning team (the graduating class of 1940) I had outdistanced unpleasant sensations by miles. I was headed for the freedom of open fields.

Youth and social approval allied themselves with me and we trammeled memories of slights and insults. The wind of our swift passage remodeled my features. Lost tears were pounded to mud and then to dust. Years of withdrawal were brushed aside and left behind, as hanging ropes of parasitic moss.

My work alone had awarded me a top place and I was going to be one of the first called in the graduating ceremonies. On the classroom blackboard, as well as on the bulletin board in the auditorium, there were blue stars and white stars and red stars. No absences, no tardinesses, and my academic work was among the best of the year. I could say the preamble to the Constitution even faster than Bailey. We timed ourselves often: "WethepeopleoftheUnitedStatesinordertoformamoreperfectunion . . ." I had memorized the Presidents of the United States from Washington to Roosevelt in chronological as well as alphabetical order.

My hair pleased me too. Gradually the black mass had lengthened and thickened, so that it kept at last to its braided pattern, and I didn't have to yank my scalp off when I tried to comb it.

Louise and I had rehearsed the exercises until we tired out ourselves. Henry Reed was class valedictorian. He was a small, very black boy with hooded eyes, and long, broad nose and an oddly shaped head. I had admired him for years because each term he and I vied for the best grades in our class. Most often he bested me, but instead of being disappointed I was pleased that we shared top places between us. Like many Southern Black children, he lived with his grandmother, who was as strict as Momma and as kind as she knew how to be. He was courteous, respectful and soft-spoken to elders, but on the playground he chose to play the roughest games. I admired him. Anyone, I reckoned, sufficiently afraid or sufficiently dull could be polite. But to be able to operate at a top level with both adults and children was admirable.

His valedictory speech was entitled "To Be or Not to Be." The rigid tenth-grade teacher had helped him write it. He'd been working on the dramatic stresses for months.

The weeks until graduation were filled with heady activities. A group of small children were to be presented in a play about buttercups and daisies and bunny rabbits. They could be heard throughout the building practicing their hops and their little songs that sounded like silver bells. The older girls (nongraduates, of course) were assigned the task of making refreshments for the night's festivities. A tangy scent of ginger, cinnamon, nutmeg and chocolate wafted around the home economics building as the budding cooks made samples for themselves and their teachers.

In every corner of the workshop, axes and saws split fresh timber as the woodshop boys made sets and stage scenery. Only the graduates were left out of the general bustle. We were free to sit in the library at the back of the building or look in quite detachedly, naturally, on the measures being taken for our event.

Even the minister preached on graduation the Sunday before. His subject was, "Let your light so shine that men will see your good works and praise your Father, Who is in Heaven." Although the sermon was purported to be addressed to us, he used the occasion to speak to backsliders, gamblers and general ne'er-do-wells. But since he had called our names at the beginning of the service we were mollified.

Among Negroes the tradition was to give presents to children going only from one grade to another. How much more important this was when the person was graduating at the top of the class. Uncle Willie and Momma had sent away for a Mickey Mouse watch like Bailey's. Louise gave me four embroidered handkerchiefs. (I gave her three crocheted doilies.) Mrs. Sneed, the minister's wife, made me an underskirt to wear for graduation, and nearly every customer gave me a nickel or maybe even a dime with the instruction "Keep on moving to higher ground," or some such encouragement.

Amazingly the great day finally dawned and I was out of bed before I knew it. I threw open the back door to see it more clearly, but Momma said, "Sister, come away from that door and put your robe on."

I hoped the memory of that morning would never leave me. Sunlight was itself still young, and the day had none of the insistence maturity would bring it in a few hours. In my robe and barefoot in the backyard, under cover of going to see about my new beans, I gave myself up to the gentle warmth and thanked God that no matter what evil I had done in my life He had allowed me to live to see this day. Somewhere in my fatalism I had expected to die, accidentally, and never have the chance to walk up the stairs in the auditorium and gracefully receive my hard-earned diploma. Out of God's merciful bosom I had won reprieve.

Bailey came out in his robe and gave me a box wrapped in Christmas paper. He said he had saved his money for months to pay for it. It felt like a box of chocolates, but I knew Bailey wouldn't save money to buy candy when we had all we could want under our noses.

He was as proud of the gift as I. It was a soft-leather-bound copy of a collection of poems by Edgar Allan Poe, or, as Bailey and I called him, "Eap." I turned to "Annabel Lee" and we walked up and down the garden rows, the cool dirt between our toes, reciting the beautifully sad lines.

Momma made a Sunday breakfast although it was only Friday. After we finished the blessing, I opened my eyes to find the watch on my plate. It was a dream of a day. Everything went smoothly and to my credit. I didn't have to be reminded or scolded for anything. Near evening I was too jittery to attend to chores, so Bailey volunteered to do all before his bath.

Days before, we had made a sign for the Store, and as we turned out the lights Momma hung the cardboard over the doorknob. It read clearly: CLOSED. GRADUATION.

My dress fitted perfectly and everyone said that I looked like a sunbeam in it. On the hill, going toward the school, Bailey walked behind with Uncle Willie, who muttered, "Go on, Ju." He wanted him to walk ahead with us because it embarrassed him to have to walk so slowly. Bailey said he'd let the ladies walk together, and the men would bring up the rear. We all laughed, nicely.

Little children dashed by out of the dark like fireflies. Their crepe-paper dresses and butterfly wings were not made for running and we heard more than one rip, dryly, and the regretful "uh uh" that followed.

The school blazed without gaiety. The windows seemed cold and unfriendly from the lower hill. A sense of ill-fated timing crept over me, and if Momma hadn't reached for my hand I would have drifted back to Bailey and Uncle Willie, and possibly beyond. She made a few slow jokes about my feet getting cold, and tugged me along to the now-strange building.

Around the front steps, assurance came back. There were my fellow "greats," the graduating class. Hair brushed back, legs oiled, new dresses and pressed pleats, fresh pocket handkerchiefs and little handbags, all homesewn. Oh, we were up to snuff, all right. I joined my comrades and didn't even see my family go in to find seats in the crowded auditorium.

The school band struck up a march and all classes filed in as had been rehearsed. We stood in front of our seats, as assigned, and on a signal from the choir director, we sat. No sooner had this been accomplished than the band started to play the national anthem. We rose again and sang the song, after which we recited the pledge of allegiance. We remained standing for a brief minute before the choir director and the principal signaled to us, rather desperately I thought, to take our seats. The command was so unusual that our carefully rehearsed and smooth-running machine was thrown off. For a full minute we fumbled for our chairs and bumped into each other awkwardly. Habits change or solidify under pressure, so in our state of nervous tension we had been ready to follow our usual assembly pattern: the American national anthem, then the pledge of allegiance, then the song every Black person I knew called the Negro National Anthem. All done in the same key, with the same passion and most often standing on the same foot.

Finding my seat at last, I was overcome with a presentiment of worse things to come. Something unrehearsed, unplanned, was going to happen, and we were going to be made to look bad. I distinctly remember being explicit in the choice of pronoun. It was "we," the graduating class, the unit, that concerned me then.

The principal welcomed "parents and friends" and asked the Baptist minister to lead us in prayer. His invocation was brief and punchy, and for a second I thought we were getting back on the high road to right action. When the principal came back to the dais, however, his voice had changed. Sounds always affected me profoundly and the principal's voice was one of my favorites. During assembly it melted and lowed weakly into the audience. It had not been in my plan to listen to him, but my curiosity was piqued and I straightened up to give him my attention.

He was talking about Booker T. Washington, our "late great leader," who said we can be as close as the fingers on the hand,[5] etc. . . . Then he said a few vague things about friendship and the

5. From Washington's Atlanta Compromise speech (September 18, 1895), in which he accepted racial segregation in exchange for economic advancement: "In all things that are purely social we can be as separate as the fingers, yet one as the hand in all things essential to mutual progress."

friendship of kindly people to those less fortunate than themselves. With that his voice nearly faded, thin, away. Like a river diminishing to a stream and then to a trickle. But he cleared his throat and said, "Our speaker tonight, who is also our friend, came from Texarkana to deliver the commencement address, but due to the irregularity of the train schedule, he's going to, as they say, 'speak and run.'" He said that we understood and wanted the man to know that we were most grateful for the time he was able to give us and then something about how we were willing always to adjust to another's program, and without more ado—"I give you Mr. Edward Donleavy."

Not one but two white men came through the door off-stage. The shorter one walked to the speaker's platform, and the tall one moved over to the center seat and sat down. But that was our principal's seat, and already occupied. The dislodged gentleman bounced around for a long breath or two before the Baptist minister gave him his chair, then with more dignity than the situation deserved, the minister walked off the stage.

Donleavy looked at the audience once (on reflection, I'm sure that he wanted only to reassure himself that we were really there), adjusted his glasses and began to read from a sheaf of papers.

He was glad "to be here and to see the work going on just as it was in the other schools."

At the first "Amen" from the audience I willed the offender to immediate death by choking on the word. But Amens and Yes, sir's began to fall around the room like rain through a ragged umbrella.

He told us of the wonderful changes we children in Stamps had in store. The Central School (naturally, the white school was Central) had already been granted improvements that would be in use in the fall. A well-known artist was coming from Little Rock to teach art to them. They were going to have the newest microscopes and chemistry equipment for their laboratory. Mr. Donleavy didn't leave us long in the dark over who made these improvements available to Central High. Nor were we to be ignored in the general betterment scheme he had in mind.

He said that he had pointed out to people at a very high level that one of the first-line football tacklers at Arkansas Agricultural and Mechanical College had graduated from good old Lafayette County Training School. Here fewer Amen's were heard. Those few that did break through lay dully in the air with the heaviness of habit.

He went on to praise us. He went on to say how he had bragged that "one of the best basketball players at Fisk sank his first ball right here at Lafayette County Training School."

The white kids were going to have a chance to become Galileos and Madame Curies and Edisons and Gauguins, and our boys (the girls weren't even in on it) would try to be Jesse Owenses and Joe Louises.

Owens and the Brown Bomber were great heroes in our world, but what school official in the white-goddom of Little Rock had the right to decide that those two men must be our only heroes? Who decided that for Henry Reed to become a scientist he had to work like George Washington Carver, as a bootblack, to buy a lousy microscope? Bailey was obviously always going to be too small to be an athlete, so which concrete angel glued to what county seat had decided that if my brother wanted to become a lawyer he had to first pay penance for his skin by picking cotton and hoeing corn and studying correspondence books at night for twenty years?

The man's dead words fell like bricks around the auditorium and too many settled in my belly. Constrained by hard-learned manners I couldn't look behind me, but to my left and right the proud graduating class of 1940 had dropped their heads. Every girl in my row had found something new to do with her handkerchief. Some folded the tiny squares into love knots, some into triangles, but most were wadding them, then pressing them flat on their yellow laps.

On the dais, the ancient tragedy was being replayed. Professor Parsons sat, a sculptor's reject, rigid. His large, heavy body seemed devoid of will or willingness, and his eyes said he was no longer with us. The other teachers examined the flag (which was draped stage right) or their notes, or the windows which opened on our now-famous playing diamond.

Graduation, the hush-hush magic time of frills and gifts and congratulations and diplomas, was finished for me before my name was called. The accomplishment was nothing. The meticulous maps, drawn in three colors of ink, learning and spelling decasyllabic words, memorizing the whole of *The Rape of Lucrece*[6]—it was for nothing. Donleavy had exposed us.

We were maids and farmers, handymen and washerwomen, and anything higher that we aspired to was farcical and presumptuous.

6. A long narrative poem by William Shakespeare.

Then I wished that Gabriel Prosser and Nat Turner had killed all whitefolks in their beds[7] and that Abraham Lincoln had been assassinated before the signing of the Emancipation Proclamation, and that Harriet Tubman[8] had been killed by that blow on her head and Christopher Columbus had drowned in the *Santa María.*

It was awful to be Negro and have no control over my life. It was brutal to be young and already trained to sit quietly and listen to charges brought against my color with no chance of defense. We should all be dead. I thought I should like to see us all dead, one on top of the other. A pyramid of flesh with the whitefolks on the bottom, as the broad base, then the Indians with their silly tomahawks and teepees and wigwams and treaties, the Negroes with their mops and recipes and cotton sacks and spirituals sticking out of their mouths. The Dutch children should all stumble in their wooden shoes and break their necks. The French should choke to death on the Louisiana Purchase (1803) while silkworms ate all the Chinese with their stupid pigtails. As a species, we were an abomination. All of us.

Donleavy was running for election, and assured our parents that if he won we could count on having the only colored paved playing field in that part of Arkansas. Also—he never looked up to acknowledge the grunts of acceptance—also, we were bound to get some new equipment for the home economics building and the workshop.

He finished, and since there was no need to give any more than the most perfunctory thank-you's, he nodded to the men on the stage, and the tall white man who was never introduced joined him at the door. They left with the attitude that now they were off to something really important. (The graduation ceremonies at Lafayette County Training School had been a mere preliminary.)

The ugliness they left was palpable. An uninvited guest who wouldn't leave. The choir was summoned and sang a modern arrangement of "Onward, Christian Soldiers," with new words pertaining to graduates seeking their place in the world. But it didn't work. Elouise, the daughter of the Baptist minister, recited "Invictus,"[9] and I

7. Prosser and Turner both led rebellions in which the slaves killed their "masters."

8. African American abolitionist (c. 1820–1913) who led slaves to freedom on the Underground Railroad.

9. An inspirational poem by William Ernst Henley (1849–1903).

could have cried at the impertinence of "I am the master of my fate, I am the captain of my soul."

My name had lost its ring of familiarity and I had to be nudged to go and receive my diploma. All my preparations had fled. I neither marched up to the stage like a conquering Amazon, nor did I look in the audience for Bailey's nod of approval. Marguerite Johnson,[1] I heard the name again, my honors were read, there were noises in the audience of appreciation, and I took my place on the stage as rehearsed.

I thought about colors I hated: ecru, puce, lavender, beige and black.

There was shuffling and rustling around me, then Henry Reed was giving his valedictory address, "To Be or Not to Be." Hadn't he heard the whitefolks? We couldn't *be*, so the question was a waste of time. Henry's voice came out clear and strong. I feared to look at him. Hadn't he got the message? There was no "nobler in the mind" for Negroes because the world didn't think we had minds, and they let us know it. "Outrageous fortune"? Now, that was a joke. When the ceremony was over I had to tell Henry Reed some things. That is, if I still cared. Not "rub," Henry, "erase." "Ah, there's the erase." Us.

Henry had been a good student in elocution. His voice rose on tides of promise and fell on waves of warnings. The English teacher had helped him to create a sermon winging through Hamlet's soliloquy. To be a man, a doer, a builder, a leader, or to be a tool, an unfunny joke, a crusher of funky toadstools. I marveled that Henry could go through with the speech as if we had a choice.

I had been listening and silently rebutting each sentence with my eyes closed; then there was a hush, which in an audience warns that something unplanned is happening. I looked up and saw Henry Reed, the conservative, the proper, the A student, turn his back to the audience and turn to us (the proud graduating class of 1940) and sing, nearly speaking,

"Lift ev'ry voice and sing
Till earth and heaven ring
Ring with the harmonies of Liberty . . ."

1. Angelou's given name. Bailey nicknamed her "Maya," and "Angelou" is a variation of her first husband's last name—"Angelo."

It was the poem written by James Weldon Johnson. It was the music composed by J. Rosamond Johnson. It was the Negro national anthem. Out of habit we were singing it.

Our mothers and fathers stood in the dark hall and joined the hymn of encouragement. A kindergarten teacher led the small children onto the stage and the buttercups and daisies and bunny rabbits marked time and tried to follow:

"Stony the road we trod
Bitter the chastening rod
Felt in the days when hope, unborn, had died.
Yet with a steady beat
Have not our weary feet
Come to the place for which our fathers sighed?"

Every child I knew had learned that song with his ABC's and along with "Jesus Loves Me This I Know." But I personally had never heard it before. Never heard the words, despite the thousands of times I had sung them. Never thought they had anything to do with me.

On the other hand, the words of Patrick Henry had made such an impression on me that I had been able to stretch myself tall and trembling and say, "I know not what course others may take, but as for me, give me liberty or give me death."

And now I heard, really for the first time:

"We have come over a way that with tears
has been watered,
We have come, treading our path through
the blood of the slaughtered."

While echoes of the song shivered in the air, Henry Reed bowed his head, said "Thank you," and returned to his place in the line. The tears that slipped down many faces were not wiped away in shame.

We were on top again. As always, again. We survived. The depths had been icy and dark, but now a bright sun spoke to our souls. I was no longer simply a member of the proud graduating class of 1940; I was a proud member of the wonderful, beautiful Negro race.

Oh, Black known and unknown poets, how often have your auctioned pains sustained us? Who will compute the lonely nights made less lonely by your songs, or by the empty pots made less tragic by your tales?

If we were a people much given to revealing secrets, we might raise monuments and sacrifice to the memories of our poets, but slavery cured us of that weakness. It may be enough, however, to have it said that we survive in exact relationship to the dedication of our poets (include preachers, musicians and blues singers).

1970

Louis Menand

b. 1952

This essay entered into a controversial public debate about the role of higher education in American society (see also Malloy Owen's essay below). With the decline in tax revenue during the Great Recession of 2007–2009, state legislatures across the country slashed their higher education budgets. Ten years after the start of the recession and long after the national economy recovered, the vast majority of states still spend less per college pupil than they spent before the recession. One reason for this retreat from public education might be the perception of many Republican legislators that college faculties have drifted away from the free and open inquiry that is the hallmark of the American university system; that they discourage conservative professors and indoctrinate students in liberal ideology. Menand tries to rise above partisanship to look at the issue from a social scientific point of view. Menand, who was a professor of English at Harvard University, regularly contributes essays to several left-leaning national magazines, including the New Yorker. *Though he is himself a part of the system he's describing, Menand doesn't rely on anecdotal evidence. Instead, he develops an inductive argument based on statistics drawn from several studies. Menand's footnotes give readers a lot of information with which they can evaluate his data. Take a close look at those studies to determine whether you think his argument is strong or weak.*

Why Do Professors All Think Alike?

1.

The politics of professors has been an issue in higher education since the end of the nineteenth century. And why shouldn't it be? Professors enjoy social authority, they virtually monopolize the business of knowledge production in many areas, and they have intimate and largely unsupervised access to developing minds. Their political views are important. At the same time, it is a custom in the modern university to segregate those views from the professional identities of professors—that is, to treat views extraneous to the subject matter of teaching and scholarship as somehow "out of bounds" to the evaluation of job performance. We don't approve when the chemistry professor gives anti-war speeches (or pro-war speeches, for that matter) in chemistry class, and we may intervene, because we feel that the professor has impermissibly mixed her politics and her job. But we choose to not make it a problem when she gives such speeches out in the quad or on the street.

Professors have the protection of this firewall as part of a deal more or less tacitly worked out at the time of the establishment of the American Association of University Professors in 1915.[1] The AAUP was founded to articulate and defend the principle of academic freedom in the wake of several notorious cases in which professors were fired for expressing political views that trustees or administrators considered obnoxious. The principle of academic freedom was designed to allow professors to pursue inquiry wherever it leads, without fear of damaging their careers if they reach results other people find offensive. It is, in effect, a pact with the rest of society: the results of academic inquiry will be worthwhile if professors are held immune from sanctions for the political implications of their work and for their personal political views. But another reason for the principle of academic freedom is that it helped to define academic inquiry as, by its nature, a value-neutral enterprise. Protecting

1. The classic history is Richard Hofstadter and Walter P. Metzger, *The Development of Academic Freedom in the United States* (New York: Columbia University Press, 1955).

professors' political and religious views was a way of underscoring their irrelevance to research and teaching. The modern university was about knowledge, not ideology. It was about facts, not values. It should have been obvious that patrolling this distinction was going to be a never-ending task.

It did not seem so at first, at least to John Dewey,[2] the Columbia philosopher who (with Arthur Lovejoy) was the founder of the AAUP and who became its first president. When he took office, Dewey said that he imagined that within a few years, cases involving violations of professors' academic freedom would be rare—a comment that gives an idea of the irenic nature of Dewey's mind. Characteristically, he was too optimistic, and by the end of the year, he had to admit that he had been mistaken.[3] Professors' politics are usually a low-level issue in higher education. They become a high-level, and sometimes inflammatory, issue during times of public anxiety: during turn-of-the-century debates over immigration, for example, or when the United States entered the First World War. The politics of professors was an issue during the McCarthy period in the early Cold War, and at the time of the protests against the war in Vietnam. They became an issue in the so-called culture wars in the late 1980s, and again after the attacks of September 11, 2001.

Almost all professors subscribe to the principle of academic freedom under a fairly non-restrictive interpretation, and they are right to do so. Faculty members are by nature contentious and inefficient self-governors, but faculties must govern themselves. Simply as a practical matter, experience shows that you cannot dictate to tenured professors, or put their feet to the fire of public opinion, with much hope of success. Administrators come and go, but tenure is forever. But the importance of the principle goes

2. John Dewey (1859–1952), philosopher, psychologist, and very influential educator. Dewey argued that education ought to emphasize critical thinking, experiential learning, and problem solving as opposed to memorization and drill. His ideas revolutionized pedagogy and still form the basis of modern curricula [editor's note].

3. John Dewey, "Introductory Address to the American Association of University Professors," January 1, 1915, and "Annual Address of the President to the American Association of University Professors," December 15, 1915, both in *The Middle Works, 1899–1924*, ed. Jo Ann Boydston (Carbondale, IL: Southern Illinois University Press, 1976–83), Vol. 8, pp. 98–108.

beyond that. Academic freedom is not just a nice job perk. It is the philosophical key to the whole enterprise of higher education.[4] It informs more than the odd case of the professor who writes articles that can be read as promoting man-boy love or as condoning terrorism.[5] It includes practices and customs such as the inability of the football coach to influence the quarterback's grade in math class. It gives academics a (circumscribed) zone of autonomy in which to work.

The claim by conservatives that the academy is under the control of a left-wing professoriate is an old one, and studies since the fifties have tended to confirm the general suspicion that professors, as a group, are more liberal than the general public. In 1952, for example, social science professors voted for Adlai Stevenson over Dwight Eisenhower in the presidential election by a margin of 58 percent to 30 percent, even though Eisenhower (who, when he ran for office, was the president of Columbia University) won the election by almost 11 percentage points.[6] Stevenson was not exactly Ho Chi Minh, though. He was, by the standards of only a decade later, quite conservative on issues like race relations and women's rights. It was after the campus protests of the sixties—over free speech, civil rights, the draft, and the war in Vietnam—that the notion of the professoriate as a group of tenured radicals became dominant in the discourse of the culture wars.[7] That charge was revived after September 11 by critics outside the academy, such as David Horowitz (who was once an untenured radical himself, but by 2001 had become an activist against academic leftism),[8] and there have been

4. I discuss the role of the principle of academic freedom in "The Limits of Academic Freedom," in Louis Menand, ed., *The Future of Academic Freedom* (Chicago: University of Chicago Press, 1996), pp. 3–20.

5. These are references to actual cases, at the University of Missouri–Kansas City, involving Harris Mirkin, in 2002, and at the University of Colorado at Boulder, involving Ward Churchill, in 2005.

6. Paul F. Lazersfeld and Wagner Thielens Jr., *The Academic Mind: Social Scientists in a Time of Crisis* (Glencoe, IL: The Free Press, 1958), p. 14.

7. Roger Kimball, *Tenured Radicals: How Politics Has Corrupted Our Higher Education* (New York: Harper & Row, 1990). A similar, bestselling account from the same period is Dinesh D'Souza, *Illiberal Education: The Politics of Race and Sex on Campus* (New York: The Free Press, 1991).

8. David Horowitz and Eli Lehrer, "Political Bias in the Administrations and Faculties of 32 Elite Colleges and Universities" (San Francisco: Center for the Study of Popular Culture, 2002). Horowitz sponsors a related Web site, www.studentsforacademicfreedom.org.

a few surveys—from a social scientific point of view rather sketchy ones—done to support it.[9]

In 2007, two sociologists working at Harvard and George Mason, Neil Gross and Solon Simmons, conducted a national survey of the political views of the professoriate that observed all the protocols of scientific research and that has a good claim to being an accurate statistical picture of the views of the 630,000 full-time professors, at every level of institution, from research universities to community colleges, in the United States at the time.[1] (Gross and Simmons did not include part-time faculty in their survey, although they note that about 47 percent of college instruction in the United States is done by part-timers. Assessing the views of part-time faculty presents methodological challenges, but of course those views are relevant to an understanding of politics in academic life.) The results of the survey are quite stunning.[2]

2.

Gross and Simmons argue that the significant finding in their survey is that professors are not as radical as some critics have charged: 9.4 percent of American professors identify themselves as "extremely

9. Daniel Klein and Andrew Western, "Voter Registration of Berkeley and Stanford Faculty," *Academic Questions*, 18 (2004–05): 53–65; Klein and Charlotta Stern, "Political Diversity in Six Disciplines," *Academic Questions*, 18 (2004–05): 40–52; Stanley Rothman, S. Robert Lichter, and Neil Nevitte, "Politics and Professional Advancement Among College Faculty," *The Forum*, vol. 3, no. 1 (2005), article 2; Gary A. Tobin and Aryeh K. Weinberg, "A Profile of American College Faculty: Political Beliefs and Behavior" (San Francisco: Institute for Jewish and Community Research, 2006); and John F. Zipp and Rudy Fenwick, "Is the Academy a Liberal Hegemony? The Political Orientations and Educational Values of Professors," *Public Opinion Quarterly*, 70 (2006): 304–26. The methodologies of these surveys are critiqued in Gross and Simmons, cited in note 1 below.

1. Neil Gross and Solon Simmons, "The Social and Political Views of American Professors" (2007), working paper, at https://www.conservativecriminology.com/uploads/5/6/1/7/56173731/lounsbery_9-25.pdf. The survey was supported by a grant from the Richard Lounsbery Foundation and was the subject of a conference, "The Politics of the Professors," at Harvard University in 2007. I was a principal investigator on the grant and involved in the construction of the questionnaire; I was not involved in the administration of the survey or the analysis of the results. The data I draw on are from the working paper and are still subject to review.

2. The final, peer-reviewed version of Neil Gross and Solon Simmons's working paper was published as Neil Gross and Solon Simmons, "The Social and Political Views of American College and University Professors," in *Professors and Their Politics,* Neil Gross and Solon Simmons, eds. (Baltimore: Johns Hopkins University Press, 2014): 17–49. The final figures are nearly but not precisely identical to the preliminary results of the working paper Menand cites [editor's note].

liberal" (only 3 percent of professors say they are Marxists) and 13.5 percent of faculty describe themselves as "liberal activists." These self-reports are meaningful because professors demonstrate a much greater degree of ideological constraint in their views than most people do. That is, if professors say that they are liberals, their views on specific issues will be coherently and consistently liberal views.[3] In the general population, most people do not know what it means to identify themselves as liberals or conservatives. People will report themselves to be liberals in an opinion poll and then answer specific questions with views normally thought of as conservative. People also give inconsistent answers to the same questions over time. This is because most people are not ideologues—they don't have coherent political belief systems—and their views on the issues do not hang together. Their reporting is not terribly accurate.[4] But academics do tend to be ideologues, in this social science sense, so if less than 10 percent of them identify themselves as "extremely liberal," that is a relatively reliable finding. If more than 90 percent of full-time faculty are not "extremely liberal," then academia is not dominated by people with radical political views.

Gross and Simmons also found that, contrary to some assumptions, the more elite the institution, the less likely the professors there are to be left-wing. Professors at liberal arts colleges are much more to the left than professors at PhD-granting institutions. This is interesting, since the education and socialization of professors at liberal arts colleges and professors at research universities is usually identical: they are trained in the same graduate programs and are hired from the same pool. It suggests some institutional treatment effects in a realm where most of the results suggest selection effects (as we will discuss later). Gross and Simmons found that younger professors today tend to be more moderate in their political views than older professors, supporting the theory that the generation that entered the professoriate in the sixties was a spike on the chart ideologically. They also found, however, that

3. Gross and Simmons used a number of measures to confirm the self-reporting: for example, they correlated answers to survey questions about political persuasion and political party with views on specific issues, such as the war in Iraq, abortion, homosexual relations, and so on.

4. The classic study, whose results have been much confirmed, is Philip Converse, "The Nature of Belief Systems in Mass Publics," in David Apter, ed., *Ideology and Discontent* (Glencoe, IL: The Free Press, 1964), pp. 206–61.

younger professors are more liberal in their social views. But the most important finding of the survey, they say, is that a large plurality of professors holds a center-left politics. Most professors are not Ralph Naderites or socialists; they are mainstream liberal Democrats—at the time of the survey, John Kerry supporters.[5]

What is striking about these results is not the finding that professors tend to be mainstream liberals. It is the finding that they are so *overwhelmingly* mainstream liberals. These are the data:

Political Orientation	Percentage
Extremely liberal	9.4
Liberal	34.7
Slightly liberal	18.1
Middle-of-the-road	18.0
Slightly conservative	10.5
Conservative	8.0
Very conservative	1.2[6]

This means that 62.2 percent of the professoriate is some kind of liberal; only 19.7 percent is some kind of conservative. Collapsing this to a three-point scale—merging the slightly liberal and the slightly conservative with the middle-of-the-roads—we get: 44.1 percent of professors are liberal and 9.2 percent are conservative. By contrast, in the public opinion poll closest to the time of the survey, the American public as a whole reported itself to be 23.3 percent liberal and 31.9 percent conservative.[7]

There are differences in the distribution of political views as one moves up and down the higher education hierarchy, but the distribution is surprisingly consistent across the liberal arts divisions. (Gross and Simmons did not include professors at professional schools in their study.)

5. John Kerry (b. 1943), Democratic U.S. senator from Massachusetts, ran for president against George W. Bush in 2004. Ralph Nader (b. 1934) rose to fame as a consumer advocate; he ran for president several times. In 2000, Nader ran as the Green Party candidate, and his appeal to some liberal voters is credited with sinking Al Gore's chances in battleground states, like Florida, in the tight race against Republican George W. Bush [editor's note].

6. These and subsequent data are from Gross and Simmons's working paper. When the numbers do not add up to 100, it is due to rounding.

7. Data from 2004. Liberal-Conservative self-identification 1972–2004, *ANES Guide to Public Opinion and Electoral Behavior*, at http://www.electionstudies.org/nesguide/toptable/tab3_1.htm.

Field	Liberal (%)	Moderate (%)	Conservative (%)
Natural sciences	45.2	47.0	7.8
Social sciences	58.2	36.9	4.9
Humanities	52.5	44.3	3.6

Outside the liberal arts fields—in health, business, and computer science and engineering—liberals and conservatives are about equally distributed, with more professors identifying themselves as moderates than as either liberal or conservative. Overall, professors skew Democratic: 51 percent call themselves Democrats and 35.3 percent say they are independents, with most of these leaning Democratic. Only 13.7 percent of professors identify themselves as Republicans. In the public at large, in 2006, 34.3 percent of the population identified themselves as Democrats and 30.4 percent as Republicans.[8] In the 2004 presidential election, George Bush won 50.7 percent of the vote and John Kerry won 48.2 percent; 77.6 percent of professors voted for Kerry, 20.4 percent for Bush.

These statistics reflect the views of large samples of the professoriate—all natural scientists at every type of institution, for example. When you begin to crunch the data more finely, you find more extreme skewing: 51 percent of English professors are Democrats, for example, and 2 percent are Republicans. In history departments, 3.8 percent of professors are Republicans; 79.2 percent are Democrats. Only 5.5 percent of sociologists and 6.3 percent of political scientists are Republicans. At elite institutions, only 9.5 percent of professors in all fields are Republicans; over 60 percent are Democrats. The statistical breakdown of faculty voting patterns in the 2004 presidential election is fairly striking. At elite colleges and universities, 95 percent of social science professors voted for Kerry; the rest voted for third-party candidates. Zero percent (statistically) voted for Bush. More than 95 percent of humanities professors at elite institutions voted for Kerry, 0 percent for Bush.

There are a number of explanations for why academics are significantly more liberal than the rest of the population. There is a high correlation between education and liberal social and political views, for one thing. For another, professors are trained to question the status quo, so they are less likely to be conservative to the extent that conservatism means resistance to change. (Of course, for this explanation

8. Gallup poll cited in Gross and Simmons.

to be consistent, one would expect that in an environment in which liberalism *is* the status quo, many professors might choose not to identify themselves as liberals. This does not seem to be the case.) There may be fewer institutional havens for left-wing intellectuals than there are for right-wing intellectuals, so liberals tend to congregate in universities, conservatives elsewhere—in foundations or, during the years of the Bush administration, in Washington.

It also may be the case that people with conservative views generally find work in the for-profit sector more congenial than people with liberal views do. A recent survey done by two political scientists suggests that young people with conservative views are more likely to seek careers outside academia because they value making money and/or having a family more highly than liberal young people do.[9] And there are possible demographic explanations: as Gross and Simmons point out, younger cohorts in the professoriate are significantly more moderate politically than the baby boom cohort. So the left-wing skewing may continue to moderate as baby boomers move out of the system. What this means, though, is that the professoriate will become even *less* ideologically diverse than it is today, since there will be shrinkage on the far left of the political spectrum. The radicals will die or retire and opinion will regress toward the mean—which is to say, the ideology of the center-liberal Democrat.

Possibly more pressing is the question whether holding liberal views has become a tacit requirement for entry and promotion in the academic profession. This issue has a number of aspects. One has to do with the way in which class cuts across the distribution of political and social views among the professoriate. Gross and Simmons note that "preliminary regression analysis suggests that it is the lower average levels of educational attainment and lower social class origins of conservative and Republican academics that may do the most to account for their underrepresentation in elite research institutions." In other words, a conservative who goes into academic life is likely to start lower down in the educational hierarchy than a liberal, and may therefore have a harder time reaching elite ranks. (One might wonder whether this factor, starting at a lower level of socioeconomic status, operates similarly for white and non-white academics, though.)

9. See Robin Wilson, "Conservatives Just Aren't into Academe, Study Finds," *Chronicle of Higher Education*, 54 (February 22, 2007): A1–A8 (reporting on a paper by Matthew Woessner and Elizabeth Kelly-Woessner, "Left Pipeline: Why Conservatives Don't Get Doctorates").

Another possible aspect of the issue has to do with the decline in adherence to the standard of scientific neutrality, or disinterestedness, in the American higher education system—the very standard that once made it possible to argue that a professor's political views were irrelevant to his or her research. Of the respondents in Gross and Simmons's survey, 70.9 percent said that it was all right for a professor's research to be guided by his or her political or religious beliefs; only 5.1 percent of liberal professors described themselves as "ardent advocates of neutrality." These data might be useful to anyone claiming that colleges and universities discriminate against people with conservative views. The data certainly don't prove discrimination, but they suggest the emergence of an ethos in which there is less aversion to weighing political views in evaluating merit than might have been the case thirty or forty years ago. If so, this would affect the career of someone whose views were outside the mainstream of the profession.

Still, the important lesson of the survey is not that the politics of the professoriate is liberal. The important lesson is that the politics of the professoriate is homogeneous. Is this because of treatment effects? Are professors trained in a way that converts them to liberal opinions? Or is it a question of selection? Do people become professors because they are already liberal when they enter into their training? More significantly, is there a code, which would include opinions on political and social matters but would also include views on matters of intellectual, pedagogical, and collegial decorum, that entrants are required to demonstrate for admission to the profession? Does the profession select for attitudes about how the academic system works, about standards for performance, even about personal manner and appearance? The higher the barriers to entry in an occupation, the more likely there are to be implicit codes that need to be mastered in addition to the explicit entrance requirements. And the profession of college professor has a pretty high threshold. In fact, the height of the threshold may explain a lot of what we see in these studies of professors' politics.[1]

* * *

1. In the cut section, Menand discusses how the number of liberal arts majors has declined since 1970; how the length of time required to earn a PhD in liberal arts fields has increased; and how fewer than half the people who earn doctorates in the liberal arts ever find satisfactory teaching jobs in colleges and universities [editor's note].

4.

It may be that the increased time to degree, combined with the weakening job market for liberal arts PhDs, is what is responsible for squeezing the profession into a single ideological box. It takes three years to become a lawyer. It takes four years to become a doctor. But it takes from six to nine years, and sometimes longer, to be eligible to teach poetry to college students for a living. Tightening up the oversight on student progress might reduce the time to degree by a little, but as long as the requirements remain, as long as students in most disciplines have general exams, field (or oral) exams, and monograph-length dissertations, it is not easy to see how the reduction will be significant. What is clear is that students who spend eight or nine years in graduate school are being seriously overtrained for the jobs that are available. The argument that they need the training to be qualified to teach undergraduates is belied by the fact that they are already teaching undergraduates. Undergraduate teaching is part of doctoral education; at many institutions, graduate students begin teaching classes the year they arrive. And the idea that the doctoral thesis is a rigorous requirement is belied by the quality of most doctoral theses. If every graduate student were required to publish a single peer-reviewed article instead of writing a thesis, the net result would probably be a plus for scholarship.

One pressure on universities to reduce radically the time to degree is simple humanitarianism. Lives are warped because of the length and uncertainty of the doctoral education process. Many people drop in and drop out and then drop in again; a large proportion of students never finish; and some people have to retool at relatively advanced ages. Put in less personal terms, there is a huge social inefficiency in taking people of high intelligence and devoting resources to training them in programs that half will never complete and for jobs that most will not get. Unfortunately, there is an institutional efficiency, which is that graduate students constitute a cheap labor force. There are not even search costs involved in appointing a graduate student to teach. The system works well from the institutional point of view not when it is producing PhDs, but when it is producing

ABDs.[2] It is mainly ABDs who run sections for lecture courses and they often offer courses of their own. The longer students remain in graduate school, the more people are available to staff undergraduate classes. Of course, overproduction of PhDs also creates a buyer's advantage in the market for academic labor. These circumstances explain the graduate student union movement that has been going on in higher education since the mid-1990s.[3]

But the main reason for academics to be concerned about the time it takes to get a degree has to do with the barrier this represents to admission to the profession. The obstacles to entering the academic profession are now so well known that the students who brave them are already self-sorted before they apply to graduate school. A college student who has some interest in further education, but who is unsure whether she wants a career as a professor, is not going to risk investing eight or more years finding out. The result is a narrowing of the intellectual range and diversity of those entering the field, and a widening of the philosophical and attitudinal gap that separates academic from non-academic intellectuals. Students who go to graduate school already talk the talk, and they learn to walk the walk as well. There is less ferment from the bottom than is healthy in a field of intellectual inquiry. Liberalism needs conservatism, and orthodoxy needs heterodoxy, if only in order to keep on its toes.

And the obstacles at the other end of the process, the anxieties over placement and tenure, do not encourage iconoclasm either. The academic profession in some areas is not reproducing itself so much as cloning itself. If it were easier and cheaper to get in and out of the doctoral motel, the disciplines would have a chance to get oxygenated by people who are much less invested in their paradigms. And the gap between inside and outside academia, which is partly created

2. ABD: "all but dissertation." These letters are a slang designation for PhD candidates who have finished their coursework but have not written the dissertation required for graduation. Such people teach many lower-level courses at large universities, but they are paid a small fraction of the salaries paid to tenure-track faculty [editor's note].

3. For responses and analysis, see Cary Nelson, ed., *Will Teach for Food: Academic Labor in Crisis* (Minneapolis: University of Minnesota Press, 1997), on the graduate student unionization movement, and Marc Bousquet, *How the University Works: Higher Education and the Low-Wage Nation* (New York: New York University Press, 2008), on the rise of "contingent faculty."

by the self-sorting, increases the hostility of the non-academic world toward what goes on in university departments, especially in the humanities. The hostility makes some disciplines less attractive to college students, and the cycle continues.

The moral of the story that the numbers tell once seemed straightforward: if there are fewer jobs for people with PhDs, then universities should stop giving so many PhDs—by making it harder to get into a PhD program (reducing the number of entrants) or harder to get through (reducing the number of graduates). But this has not worked. Possibly the story has a different moral, which is that there should be a lot *more* PhDs, and they should be much easier to get. The non-academic world would be enriched if more people in it had exposure to academic modes of thought, and had thereby acquired a little understanding of the issues that scare terms like "deconstruction" and "postmodernism" are attempts to deal with. And the academic world would be livelier if it conceived of its purpose as something larger and more various than professional reproduction—and also if it had to deal with students who were not so neurotically invested in the academic intellectual status quo. If PhD programs were determinate in length—if getting a PhD were like getting a law degree—then graduate education might acquire additional focus and efficiency. It might also attract more of the many students who, after completing college, yearn for deeper immersion in academic inquiry, but who cannot envision spending six years or more struggling through a graduate program and then finding themselves virtually disqualified for anything but a teaching career that they cannot count on having.

It is unlikely that the opinions of the professoriate will ever be a true reflection of the opinions of the public, and, in any case, that would be in itself an unworthy goal. Fostering a greater diversity of views within the professoriate is a worthy goal, however. The evidence suggests that American higher education is going in the opposite direction. Professors tend increasingly to think alike because the profession is increasingly self-selected. The university may not explicitly require conformity on more than scholarly matters, but the existing system implicitly demands and constructs it.

2010

Debra Humphreys
Patrick Kelly

This selection is part of a longer report commissioned by the American Association of Colleges and Universities (AAC&U), which is an organization devoted to promoting the liberal arts. As the president of the AAC&U declares in her foreword, the report responds to a suspicion among lawmakers, intensified during and after the Great Recession, that the liberal arts are obsolete. In the last ten years or so, many states have sharply reduced their funding of public colleges. In 1998, for instance, public colleges and universities accounted for 13 percent of state budgets, while in 2011 that figure was down to 10.1 percent. Even with these reductions, lots of public money is at stake: $170 billion, as of 2011.[1] *Dollar-conscious state legislatures have expressed their suspicion that nonprofessional programs do not have much social value, and they have increasingly called on public schools to justify their curricula. Federal politicians are part of the debate also. In November 2013, President Obama proposed a federal reporting system that would rank schools according to their "graduates' median salary levels." Such proposals greatly worried the AAC&U, which holds that "concerns that graduates who majored in humanities or social science fields are unemployed and unemployable . . . are unfounded." This report is meant to "put [those concerns] to rest." It provides some of the clearest examples of inductive arguments in this volume, so you should determine if you think the evidence is accurate, sufficiently large, and representative.*

How Liberal Arts and Sciences Majors Fare in Employment: A Report on Earnings and Long-Term Career Paths

1. Is a College Degree Still a Good Investment?

Prior to examining data about employment outcomes for those majoring in specific fields, it is essential to note that a college degree of any kind remains a good investment of time and money (see fig. 1), This has remained true even in the wake of a crippling recession (see fig. 2) and in light of a highly competitive

1. "Higher Education," National Association of State Budget Officers, 2012. Online.

Figure 1. The earnings premium for college study and degree attainment

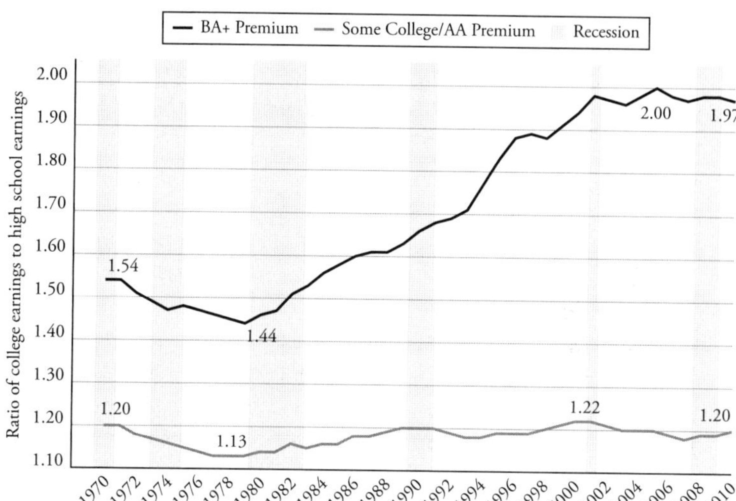

Source: Reprinted by permission from Carnevale, Jayasundera, and Cheah (2012, fig. 7); authors' estimate using Current Population Survey data (1970–2011).

Note: The estimates are the three-month moving averages of mean earnings of full-time, full-year wage and salary workers ages 25 to 54. The four-year college earnings premium is the mean earnings of workers with bachelor's degrees or better relative to the mean earnings of workers with only a high school diploma. The AA premium is the earnings of workers with associate's degrees or some college relative to mean earnings of their high school–only counterparts. The shaded bars indicate periods of recession as reported by the National Bureau of Economic Research.

BA+ Premium: wage premium for workers with bachelor's degrees or better over workers with high school diplomas or less

Some College/AA Premium: wage premium for workers with associate's degrees or some college over workers with high school diplomas or less

global employment market. As Anthony Carnevale and his colleagues at the Georgetown University Center on Education and the Workforce make clear in their 2012 report, *The College Advantage: Weathering the Economic Storm*, "the average earnings of a bachelor's degree-holder remain nearly twice as much as those of a worker with only a high school diploma" (Carnevale, Jayasundera, and Cheah 2012, 12). Moreover, the report continues, "the recession hit those with less schooling disproportionately hard—nearly four out of five jobs lost were held by those with no formal education beyond high school." Those with a four-year degree, on the other hand, were "largely protected

Figure 2. Impact of the 2008–10 recession on employment

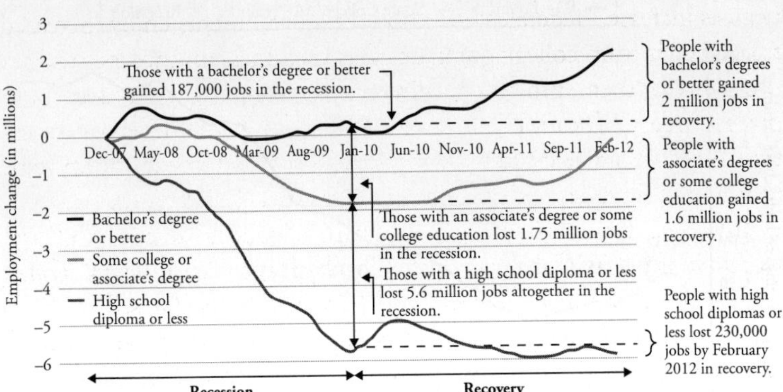

Source: Reprinted by permission from Carnevale, Jayasundera, and Cheah (2012, fig. 1); authors' estimate of the Current Population Survey data (2007–2012). Employment includes all workers aged 18 and older.

Note: The monthly employment numbers are seasonally adjusted using the US Census Bureau X–12 procedure and smoothed using four-month moving averages. The graph represents the total employment losses by education since the beginning of the recession in December 2007 to January 2010 and employment gains in recovery from January 2010 to February 2012.

against job losses during the recession and some had job gains" (3). As the authors of the report themselves put it, "college degrees have served as protection for Americans seeking shelter during a tough economic storm" (Georgetown University Center on Education and the Workforce 2012). According to an earlier report from the center, over the course of their lifetimes, workers with a baccalaureate degree earn 84 percent more than workers who complete high school only (Carnevale, Rose, and Cheah 2011, 1).

These trends are confirmed by the findings of a more recent study by the College Board. The study's authors observe in their report, *Education Pays 2013*, that "the financial return associated with college credentials and the gaps in earnings by education level have increased over time." Moreover, they note that "the 2012 unemployment rate for four year college graduates ages 25–34 was 7.1 percentage points *below* that for high school graduates" (Baum, Ma, and Payea 2013, 5; emphasis added). It is clear that investment in a college degree pays off for individuals.

There also is persuasive evidence that public investments designed to increase the number of college graduates in a particular region "pay off" for entire communities, and that such investments are essential to future economic growth (Carnevale, Smith, and Strohl 2010). As Baum, Ma, and Payea point out, when regional percentages of residents with college degrees increase, "federal, state, and local governments enjoy increased tax revenues from college graduates and spend less on income support programs for them, providing a direct financial return on investment in postsecondary education." Further, "adults with higher levels of education are more active citizens than others," and "college education leads to healthier lifestyles, reducing health care costs" (2013, 5–6).

Investing time and money to attain a college degree is clearly worth it. But, as Carnevale and Cheah point out in *Hard Times: College Majors, Unemployment and Earnings*, while "it still pays to earn a college degree . . . not all college degrees are created equal" (2013, 3). Some graduates are prepared for and enter professions that pay significantly more than others. This is the result of several factors, including the relative supply and demand of workers in certain fields who possess specific skill sets and differences in how particular professions are "valued" in our society.

2. How Important Is the Choice of Undergraduate Major?

The focus of several recent reports—including this one—on relationships between college graduates' major field of study and their employment outcomes may give the impression that the choice of undergraduate major is the most important factor in workplace success. But this is not necessarily the case. In fact, about 40 percent of baccalaureate degree holders in the paid labor force are working in a profession that is *unrelated* to their major field of study (Georgetown University Center on Education and the Workforce 2013). Moreover, the view that the choice of undergraduate major is the determining factor for success in the labor market is not one that is held by most employers.

In 2013, the Association of American Colleges and Universities commissioned a survey of employers in order to probe their views on college learning and workforce preparation. When asked about what they look for in job candidates, the vast majority of the employers surveyed (93 percent) agreed that "a candidate's demonstrated capacity to think critically, communicate clearly, and solve complex problems is *more important* than their undergraduate major" (see table 1). In addition, more than three in four employers urged colleges and universities to

Table 1. Employer priorities for new hires

Percentage of employers who agree "somewhat" or "strongly" with each statement	
Our company puts a priority on hiring people with the intellectual and interpersonal skills that will help them contribute to innovation in the workplace.	95%
Candidates' demonstrated capacity to think critically, communicate clearly, and solve complex problems is more important than their undergraduate major.	93%
Whatever their major, all students should have experience in solving problems with colleagues whose views are different from their own.	91%

Source: Data from Hart Research Associates (2013).

"place more emphasis" on five key learning outcomes: critical thinking, complex problem solving, written and oral communication, and applied knowledge in real-world settings (Hart Research Associates 2013, 1). While undergraduate programs in many fields excel at helping students develop these cross-cutting capacities, liberal arts majors tend to be *more focused* than others on these kinds of highly transferable skills (Arum and Roksa 2010). Accordingly, graduates with liberal arts majors are especially well prepared to succeed in volatile job market conditions and in environments that put a premium on flexibility and creativity.

Especially when considered together with findings from AAC&U's previous employer surveys (Peter D. Hart Research Associates 2006, 2008; Hart Research Associates 2010), the findings from the 2013 survey strongly suggest that, in today's competitive, fast-moving economic environment, those seeking well-paying and rewarding jobs will require both specific knowledge in a field of study and a broad range of skills that extend across fields—some of which are particularly well developed through study in the liberal arts. As figure 3 shows, a majority of employers (55 percent) believe that, in order to advance and achieve long-term success in their companies, it is most important for college graduates to possess both field-specific knowledge and skills, on the one hand, and a broad range of knowledge and skills, on the other. These employer surveys provide clear evidence of the high value employers place on broad learning, or what educators call "general education," one of the hallmark features of higher education in the United States. Across all parts of the US higher education system, general education consists primarily of studies in the liberal arts and sciences. Finally, employers across a

Figure 3. Employer views on requirements for advancement and long-term career success

Which of the following ranges of knowledge and skills are more important for recent graduates who want to pursue advancement and long-term career success at your company?

- Knowledge and skills that apply to a specific field or position
- A range of knowledge and skills that apply to a range of fields or positions
- Both field-specific knowledge and skills *and* a broad range of knowledge and skills

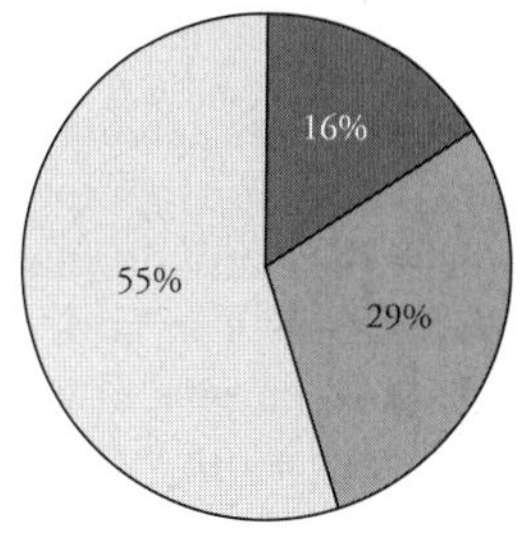

Source: Data from Hart Research Associates (2013).

range of fields understand that all college students—whatever their chosen major—should have educational experiences that teach them about building civic capacity, broad knowledge about the liberal arts and sciences, and cultures outside the United States (see table 2).

When examining data about the earnings and employment status of college graduates, it is not entirely unhelpful to disaggregate by undergraduate major. But ultimately, the success of both individuals and companies alike may be more dependent on the availability of a diverse group of well-educated workers who hold degrees in a wide array of fields and who possess broad capacities and diverse skill sets.

Table 2. Employer views on the liberal arts and sciences and selected learning outcomes

Percentage of employers who agree "somewhat" or "strongly" with each statement	
All students should have educational experiences that teach them how to solve problems with people whose views are different from their own.	91%
All students should learn about ethical issues and public debates important in their field.	87%
All students should have direct learning experiences working with others to solve problems important in their communities.	86%
All students should take courses that build knowledge, judgment, commitment to communities, ensure integrity/vitality of democracy.	82%
All students should acquire broad knowledge in liberal arts and sciences.	80%
All students should learn about societies and cultures outside the United States and about global issues and developments.	78%

Source: Data from Hart Research Associates (2013).

3. What Are the Median Earnings and Employment Rates for Graduates in Different Fields?

When college graduates are grouped according to area of undergraduate major, comparison of their median annual earnings over the course of their working lives reveals, not surprisingly, some differences (see fig. 4). The annual earnings of graduates with a baccalaureate degree in engineering, in particular, are consistently higher than the earnings of those with a degree in a humanities or social science field, a professional or preprofessional field, one of the physical or natural sciences, or mathematics. However, not all students are interested in or prepared to pursue an engineering degree. While there is a shortage right now of qualified workers in engineering fields, the median annual earnings of those employed in those fields would be likely to decrease in relation to the size of any future influx of graduates with baccalaureate degrees in engineering. Currently, only about 9 percent of college graduates in the labor force hold engineering degrees. Therefore, for the purposes of this study, we have chosen to focus primarily on the 91 percent of graduates who hold degrees in liberal arts and sciences fields and in professional or preprofessional fields.

Figure 4. Median annual earnings for college graduates, by age-group and area of undergraduate major (2010–11)

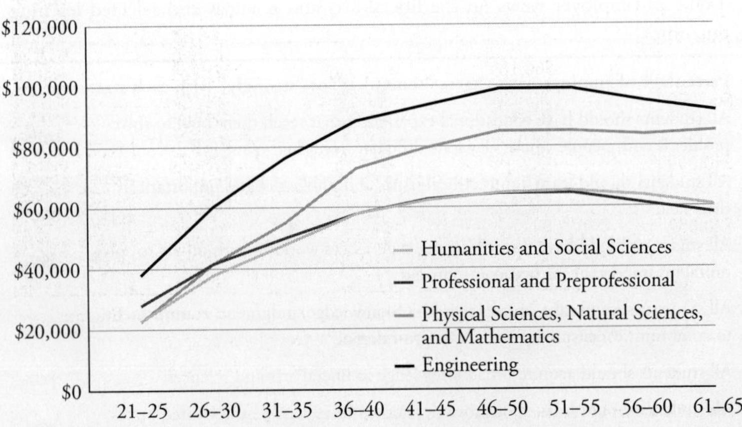

Source: Data from US Census Bureau, 2012 American Community Survey.

Note: The figure depicts median earnings for those employed full time (35+ hours per week).

Figure 4 shows that median annual earnings are roughly the same for those between the ages of twenty-one and twenty-five with an undergraduate major in a humanities or social science field, a professional or preprofessional field, one of the physical or natural sciences, or mathematics. Over time, however, as college graduates gain more experience, the annual earnings of those with a baccalaureate degree in engineering, science, or mathematics increase significantly compared to the annual earnings of those with a baccalaureate degree in a humanities, social science, professional, or preprofessional field. The difference in earnings between those with a baccalaureate degree in science or mathematics and those with a baccalaureate degree in engineering decreases over time.

As figure 5 shows, the median annual earnings for *recent* college graduates with a baccalaureate degree in a humanities or social science field are slightly lower than those for recent graduates with a baccalaureate degree in a professional or preprofessional field. The median annual earnings for humanities and social science degree holders between

Figure 5. Short-term vs. long-term earnings: Median annual earnings for graduates directly out of college compared with peak, by area of undergraduate major (2010–11)

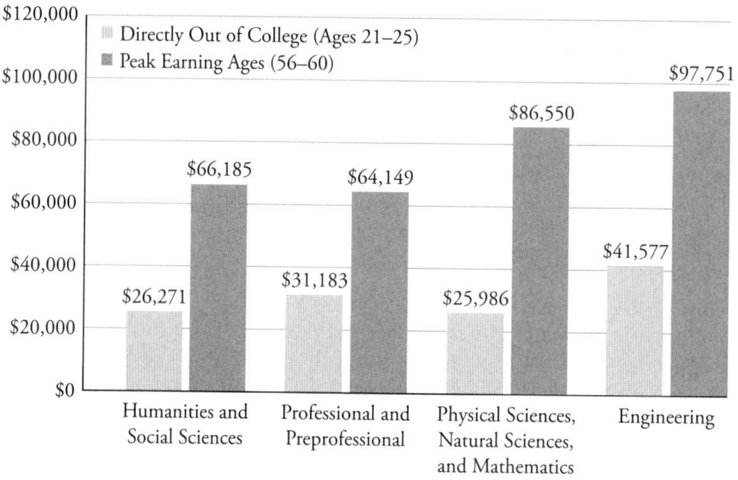

Source: Data from US Census Bureau, 2012 American Community Survey.

Note: This chart depicts median annual earnings for college graduates employed full time (35+ hours per week) by area of undergraduate major, regardless of whether or not they also attained an advanced degree in the same or a different field of study. The American Community Survey does not identify fields of postgraduate study.

the ages of twenty-one and twenty-five are about $4,900 lower than those for professional or preprofessional degree holders. However, as individuals age and gain more work experience, the gap in earnings between these two groups closes. In fact, the median annual earnings for those between the ages of fifty-six and sixty with a baccalaureate degree in a humanities or social science field *exceeds* the median annual earnings for those with a baccalaureate degree in a professional or pre-professional field. Mature workers who majored in a humanities or social science field earn on average about $2,000 *more* than those who majored in a professional or preprofessional field.

Figure 5 also shows that median earnings increase substantially over time, with the biggest increase from early postgraduation to peak earning ages occurring among those with a baccalaureate degree in science or mathematics. At peak earning ages, those with a baccalaureate degree in a humanities or social science field earn nearly $40,000 more annually than they earned in the early years after graduation. For those with a baccalaureate degree in science or mathematics, annual earnings are more than $60,000 higher at peak ages than in the early years after graduation. Notably, and contrary to widespread assumptions, the earnings gap between those with a baccalaureate degree in a humanities or social science field and those with a baccalaureate degree in a professional or preprofessional field closes over time (see fig. 5). In fact, while those with humanities or social science degrees earn nearly $5,000 less than those with professional or preprofessional degrees employed directly out of college, they earn more than $2,000 more at peak ages.

In this context, it is important to note the effect that earning a graduate or professional degree, in addition to the baccalaureate, has on median earnings overall and on gaps between groups of degree holders—an effect that is especially pronounced for those who majored in a liberal arts and sciences field. Figure 6 shows that, for those who do not earn an advanced degree, the earnings gap between those with a baccalaureate degree in a humanities or social science field and those with a baccalaureate degree in a professional or preprofessional field persists over time. (The effects of earning an advanced degree are examined in greater depth in chapter 4.)

Apart from the earnings trajectories associated with different areas of undergraduate major, how well do particular baccalaure

Figure 6. Median annual earnings for college graduates with a baccalaureate degree only, by age group and area of undergraduate major (2010–11)

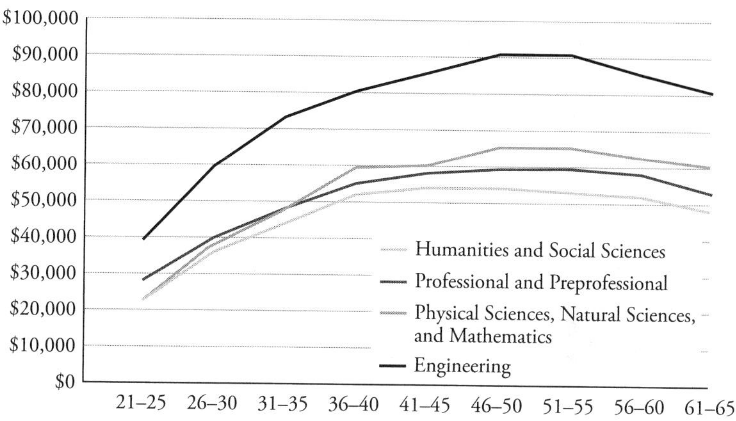

Source: Data from US Census Bureau, 2012 American Community Survey.

Note: This chart depicts median annual earnings only for graduates employed full time (35+ hours per week) for whom the baccalaureate degree was the highest degree earned.

ate degrees protect against unemployment over time? As noted in chapter 1, the unemployment rates for college graduates are substantially lower than for those who do not graduate from college. However, there are differences across areas of undergraduate major. The unemployment rates for those who major either in a humanities or social science field or in science or mathematics decline over time, while the unemployment rates for those who major either in a professional or preprofessional field or in engineering initially decline and then rise slightly (see fig. 7).

In addition, differences in unemployment rates vary between areas of undergraduate major and over time. For example, the unemployment rate for those between the ages of twenty-one and thirty who hold a baccalaureate degree in a humanities or social science field is 5.2 percent—a full percentage point higher than for those with a degree in a professional or preprofessional field and more than 2 percentage points higher than for those with a degree in engineering, science, or mathematics. However, for those between the ages of forty-one and fifty who hold a baccalaureate degree in a humanities or social science field, the unemployment rate is only 3.5 percent—

FIGURE 7. Unemployment rates for college graduates by age group and area of undergraduate major (2010–11)

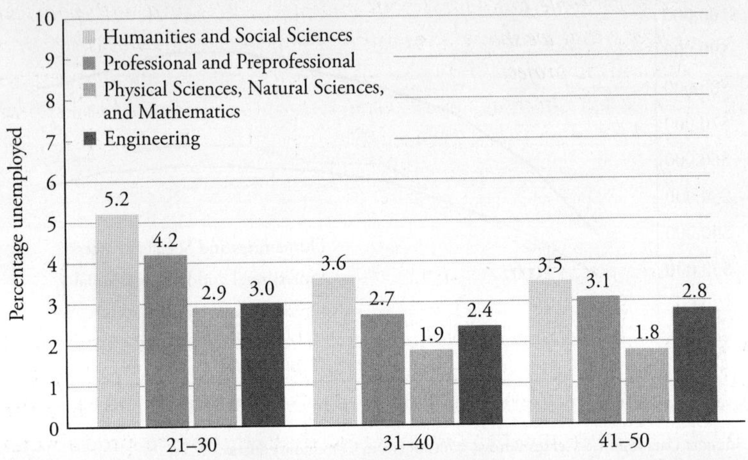

SOURCE: Data from US Census Bureau, 2012 American Community Survey.

NOTE: This chart depicts unemployment rates for college graduates by area of undergraduate major, regardless of whether or not they also attained an advanced degree in the same or a different field of study. The American Community Survey does not identify fields of postgraduate study.

just 0.4 percentage points higher than the rate for those with a professional or preprofessional degree.

2014

Malloy Owen

b. 1996

Malloy Owen admits that it is difficult to calculate the personal and social value of the liberal arts. It cannot be measured in dollars added to a graduate's wealth; in fact, he seems to suggest that that kind of inductive evidence will never prove the value of the humanities. Instead, he argues deductively, taking as his major premises several assertions that he claims are conservative principles. That strategy makes sense, because he published this essay in the American Conservative, *a print magazine and blog that promotes what it calls "Main Street" conservatism and "opposes unchecked power in government and business." He's trying to persuade like-minded people to adopt a policy normally associated with political liberals: that we should spend some of our tax dollars on artistic and humanistic projects. The essay includes a clear example of a refutation, when Owen argues inductively that the National Endowment for the Arts and the National Endowment for the Humanities are not anti-conservative organizations.*

Funding the Humanities

In the mid-19th century, literary circles in Russia were embroiled in a controversy over the relative value of boots and poetry. On one side, an influential group of leftists, led by figures like the nihilist Zaytsev and the radical critic Pisarev, took to proclaiming that cultural productions were worthless in a world where material suffering was still possible. Zaytsev announced that "every tradesman has a value that much greater than any poet, just as any number, no matter how small, has a value greater than zero." Pisarev wrote a series of articles attacking Alexander Pushkin—who was widely honored at the time as Russia's greatest artist—for worshiping beauty and neglecting real life.[1]

Conservative elements in the Russian intelligentsia were outraged. Fyodor Dostoyevsky was particularly disturbed by the Russian left's attempts to make art commensurable with material goods. He offered an impassioned rebuttal of the left's nihilist anti-aesthetics in his 1872 novel *Demons*, in which a middle-aged intellectual who has become disillusioned with the radical materialism of the younger generation delivers a confused but fervent defense of art and beauty to an audience of young radicals:

> "Shakespeare and Raphael are higher than the liberation of the peasants, higher than nationality, higher than socialism, higher than the

1. Alexander Pushkin (1799–1837), playwright and novelist who was exiled by Tsar Alexander I for his liberal views; though a proponent of Enlightenment views, Pushkin was himself an aristocrat. Varfolomey Zaytsev (1842–1882), Russian journalist and critic; Dmitry Pisarev (1840–1868), Russian writer and critic. [All notes are the editor's.]

younger generation, higher than chemistry, higher than almost the whole of humanity. . . . Mankind . . . cannot live without beauty, for then there would be nothing at all to do in the world! Science itself would not stand for a minute without beauty—it would turn into boorishness, you couldn't invent the nail!"

Dostoyevsky's defense of beauty as the ground of every human endeavor still resonates today when American elites make practical arguments against funding for the humanities. In 1860s Russia, it was the radical socialists who believed that culture and humanistic education were a waste of time in a world of material want; in 21st-century America, the same arguments tend to be made by conservatives. Marco Rubio tells philosophy students that the job market would be kinder to them if they were welders. Rick Scott argues that the state has no vital interest in anthropology.[2] Like Russia's radical materialists, our conservatives argue that people should put off the pursuit of culture until they have satisfied their material needs. They understand the arts and humanities as luxury goods—pleasures for people who have already made their mark in the world of hard facts, but certainly not directed at fundamental human needs.

It seems to be in this spirit that Donald Trump has proposed to eliminate the National Endowment for the Arts and the National Endowment for the Humanities—a move that the White House described as a simple cost-cutting measure. The NEA and NEH are relatively small and inexpensive programs, but they are important sources of funds for artists and researchers whose work might otherwise fall by the wayside. They are also difficult to defend in an age in which government policy is invariably justified with statistics and empirical evidence. The goods the humanities produce and secure can't always be represented on charts and graphs. In fact, studying the humanities may worsen people's *economic* prospects by inducing them to pursue virtue—which doesn't always pay well—rather than profit.

If we believe that poetry can give us something that boots cannot, we should be suspicious of the materialist impulse to judge culture by economic standards or reduce it to a mere luxury. This suspicion is essentially conservative: while a great deal of left-liberal public policy

2. Marco Rubio (b. 1971), Republican U.S. senator from Florida; Rick Scott (b. 1952), Republican governor of Florida (2010–2018) and U.S. senator (first elected in 2018).

is based on the doctrine that health, safety, and pleasure are the highest goods, conservatives would deny that the best and most beautiful aspects of human existence are secured through money or force.

Conservatism also allows us to claim that living well is an art cultivated over many generations and not something that each person figures out for herself by herself. The humanities are a living body of reasoning—some ancient and some quite recent—on how to live well. Life without culture is deeply solitary because it forces us to do this sort of reasoning without any help from outside ourselves. The sorts of projects that the NEH and NEA support—from research in the humanities to museum exhibitions to programs that bring Shakespeare plays to rural schoolchildren—give ordinary people access to the history of serious thought about the good. Funding from the two endowments ensures that the old books are still read and talked about; it also supports the production of new works that may find a place in the canon someday.

Many conservatives accept these arguments while arguing that free markets are the best means to spread artistic masterworks across the country. But although markets may be useful for producing and distributing material goods, they are not especially good at regulating cultural production. Good and ennobling art is not always lucrative, and government subsidies are precisely meant to secure goods that society is not wholly capable of securing on its own.

Conservatives are also understandably reluctant to give the state the power to determine what constitutes worthy cultural work. Their arguments are all the more forceful because they can point to numerous cases in which federal grants have supported projects in the arts and humanities that were uninteresting, obscene, or both. As a 1997 Heritage Foundation report calling for the abolition of the NEH and NEA documented in gruesome detail,[3] some funding from these programs goes to genuinely offensive projects.

But the two endowments also support work that conservatives are more likely to consider worthwhile. The NEH funds projects on Marlowe, Machiavelli, and Boccaccio. It has supported invaluable websites like hymnary.org and the Stanford Encyclopedia of

3. Lawrence Jarvik, "Ten Good Reasons to Eliminate Funding for the National Endowment for the Arts," *The Heritage Foundation Backgrounder*, no. 1110, April 29, 1997.

Philosophy. It provided a great deal of the funding for Ken Burns's magisterial documentary series on the Civil War, and it recently helped to pay for the publication of the 13-volume journals of the Lewis and Clark expedition. For its part, the NEA has backed programs like *Live From Lincoln Center*, which broadcasts serious music across the country, and Shakespeare in American Communities, which has allowed two million American students to watch Shakespeare plays performed live. An NEA grant helped the Louisiana State University Press publish the then-unknown writer John Kennedy Toole's novel *A Confederacy of Dunces*, which has become a conservative favorite. In recent years NEA money has supported new translations of Euripides, Aeschylus, and Homer, among many others.

The range of projects that the NEH and NEA support—from revisionist and progressive work to explorations of tradition—should please conservatives who do not want the government circumscribing the human good within politically narrow definitions. By assigning grants on the basis of artistic seriousness, the NEH and NEA demonstrate their commitment to ideological pluralism.

The National Foundation on the Arts and Humanities Act of 1965, which established the NEH and NEA, gave eleven reasons justifying government support for the arts and humanities. Some of these reasons were almost Dostoyevskian. "Democracy demands wisdom and vision in its citizens," the act declared. "It must therefore foster and support a form of education, and access to the arts and the humanities, designed to make people of all backgrounds and wherever located *masters of their technology and not its unthinking servants*" (emphasis mine).

It is the duty of conservatives to stand against thoughtless progress in every form. In 19th-century Russia, thoughtless progress was mostly driven by the socialist left. Today in the United States, both political parties seem equally eager to rush into whatever brave new world technology and market forces generate. The arts and humanities give us the resources to step back from continual progress and consider the meaning of human life. They may even be able to prevent us from destroying ourselves.

2017

David Brooks
b. 1961

David Brooks is one of the most famous conservative voices in the United States today, but you typically find his arguments in venues we associate with liberals. He publishes a regular opinion column in the New York Times, *for example. If you've seen him on the* PBS NewsHour, *you'll know that he never parrots the conservative party line. His independent line of thinking often brings him into conflict with prominent Republicans, like Donald Trump. On his PBS segment,* Shields and Brooks, *he champions the conservative view in frequent debate with the liberal commentator, Mark Shields, but the two disputants always demonstrate how to talk to people who disagree with you. In today's often abrasive style of argument, Brooks is considered a model practitioner of civil discourse, one who always strives to argue from common ground. You might study this essay to see how Brooks establishes common ground with "hostile" readers. Several disparate threads in contemporary politics come together in this piece, such as public policy regarding gun violence, the permanence of (apparently) ephemeral media, racism, the consequences attached to public speech, and, of course, college admission practices. But it touches also on the wide issue of how society deals with transgression and repentance.*

Harvard's False Path to Wisdom

Over the past year and a half, the students from Marjory Stoneman Douglas High School in Parkland, Fla., have handled themselves with a fervor and commitment that has, most of the time, inspired the nation.

One of those students was Kyle Kashuv. Despite the trauma of the shootings and a busy impromptu career as a school safety advocate, Kashuv was able to graduate second in his class, with a weighted G.P.A. of 5.345, according to the *Daily Wire* (how is that even possible?). Along with his classmate David Hogg, he was admitted into Harvard.

Most of the famous Parkland students lean progressive and support gun control laws. Kashuv leans conservative. He's appeared on conservative media, got to meet Donald Trump and lobbied for the

STOP School Violence Act, which would create an annual $50 million grant to schools for training programs and reporting systems. He became a student face for the gun rights crowd.

He's handled himself with an earnest sincerity. When *Vox* asked if he'd worked through what happened on the day of the shootings, he said, "Honestly, I don't think we'll ever have it all worked through."

The *Miami Herald* asked if he should be spared criticism on account of his youth. He responded: "When you're pushing policy, the protections as a kid are gone. I'm rightfully not granted that. I think even David and Emma truly . . . want to stop gun deaths and school shootings, and that shouldn't be delegitimized, ever. They want the same end result that I do, they just do it through different means."

A few weeks ago, documents leaked showing that about two years ago, when he was 16, some months before the shootings, Kashuv wrote racist comments in text messages and on a collaborative Google doc.

He was studying for the A.P. U.S. History exam with some classmates online. Around midnight they began posting childish things. Kashuv's comments were repulsive—blatantly racist and anti-Semitic. He wrote the N-word 12 times and then explained that he was good at typing that word. "[P]ractice uhhhhhh makes perfect."

When the comments became public last month, Kashuv immediately apologized. "We were 16-year-olds making idiotic comments, using callous and inflammatory language in an effort to be as extreme and shocking as possible," he noted.

On May 24, Harvard's admissions dean, William Fitzsimmons, wrote to him explaining that Harvard was considering revoking his admission. Harvard reserves the right to revoke admissions for behavior "that brings into question your honesty, maturity or moral character."

Kashuv wrote back unequivocally apologizing for his comments. His letter is contrite and ashamed: "I am no longer the same person, especially in the aftermath of the Parkland shooting and all that has transpired since." He also wrote to the Harvard diversity office, apologizing and asking what he could do to be a better person.

Harvard decided to revoke Kashuv's admission. He asked for a face-to-face meeting but was told the matter was closed. Conservative Twitter erupted Monday, arguing that this was another case of liberal elite Harvard bashing conservatives, shutting down free speech, etc. Is there no such thing as privacy? or being underage?

This case has nothing to do with free speech. Harvard clearly has a right to disinvite students who violate its standards. I'd say, rather, that the decision, which Harvard is not commenting on, may reflect a misunderstanding of how moral character develops.

The Harvard admissions committee is the epicenter of the meritocracy. In the meritocracy, winners win. If you get a straight-A average, that proves you have mastered the art of learning math (or at least mastered the tests that are supposed to measure these things). If you get a D in math, that piece of information is a problem to the committee.

Moral formation is not like learning math. It's not cumulative; it's inverse. In a sin-drenched world it's precisely through the sins and the ensuing repentance that moral formation happens. That's why we try not to judge people by what they did in their worst moment, but rather by how they respond to their worst moment. That's why we are forgiving of 16-year-olds, because they haven't disgraced themselves enough to have earned maturity.

Knowledge comes by memorizing information and is measurable by G.P.A. Wisdom comes through a renovation of the heart, the way Aeschylus centuries ago famously said it did: "Even in our sleep pain that cannot forget falls drop by drop upon the heart, and in our own despair, against our will, comes wisdom to us by the awful grace of God."[1]

These days many people seem to think that the way to prove virtue is by denouncing and shunning, not through mercy and rigorous forgiveness. Harvard could have but didn't take the truth-and-reconciliation approach—confronting the outrage, but trying to use it to get to a deeper eventual embrace.[2]

It's hard to know if Kashuv has learned from his repulsive comments, but if he has, wouldn't Harvard want a kid who is intellectually rigorous and morally humble? Wouldn't it want a student who could lend a hand to all the perfect résumé children who may not have yet committed a disgrace, but who will?

2019

1. Aeschylus (c. 525–456 BCE), playwright considered the father of tragedy. These lines are from *Agamemnon*, the first play in the *Oresteia* trilogy. [All notes are the editor's.]

2. The phrase originated with the Truth and Reconciliation Commission of South Africa, which was established to help deal with what happened under apartheid in that nation. The commission hears testimony about crimes—including state-sponsored crimes—against humanity, but it emphasizes acknowledgment and forgiveness over punishment. It has been become a global model for how a newly established, more just state addresses historical injustices while also satisfying victims' desire for retribution.

CHAPTER 4

Environment

Rachel Carson

1907–1964

Carson, a marine biologist, published her book Silent Spring *in 1962. She wanted to tell her readers that modern chemical pesticides, especially DDT, were destroying the environment. Ultimately, she hoped to change the way we think about our relationship to nature—to stop us from imagining humans as nature's conquerer and to prompt us to see ourselves as but one member in a delicate collaboration. It is notoriously difficult to measure the effect any single work has on a culture, but* Silent Spring *is generally credited with sparking the public debate about the environment that led to a sea change in the American consciousness. The immediate purpose of "A Fable for Tomorrow," the first chapter in* Silent Spring, *is to get people to read the following chapters, in which she presents and analyzes the dangers of pesticides. In and of itself, then, this short excerpt does not offer an argument. The evidence that supports Carson's position comes later in the book. As you read the description of what has befallen the small town described in this piece, you might think of this tale not as a realistic depiction of life in the United States in 1962, but rather as the fruit of Carson's "fabulous" imagination. Carson expects that reaction. In fact, the power of the final two paragraphs presumes it.*

A Fable for Tomorrow

There was once a town in the heart of America where all life seemed to live in harmony with its surroundings. The town lay in the midst of a checkerboard of prosperous farms, with fields of grain and hillsides of orchards where, in spring, white clouds of bloom drifted above the green fields. In autumn, oak and maple and birch set up a blaze of color that flamed and flickered across a backdrop of pines. Then foxes barked in the hills and deer silently crossed the fields, half hidden in the mists of the fall mornings.

Along the roads, laurel, viburnum and alder, great ferns and wildflowers delighted the traveler's eye through much of the year. Even in winter the roadsides were places of beauty, where countless birds came to feed on the berries and on the seed heads of the dried weeds rising above the snow. The countryside was, in fact, famous for the abundance and variety of its bird life, and when the flood of migrants was pouring through in spring and fall people traveled from great distances to observe them. Others came to fish the streams, which flowed clear and cold out of the hills and contained shady pools where trout lay. So it had been from the days many years ago when the first settlers raised their houses, sank their wells, and built their barns.

Then a strange blight crept over the area and everything began to change. Some evil spell had settled on the community: mysterious maladies swept the flocks of chickens; the cattle and sheep sickened and died. Everywhere was a shadow of death. The farmers spoke of much illness among their families. In the town the doctors had become more and more puzzled by new kinds of sickness appearing among their patients. There had been several sudden and unexplained deaths, not only among adults but even among children, who would be stricken suddenly while at play and die within a few hours.

There was a strange stillness. The birds, for example—where had they gone? Many people spoke of them, puzzled and disturbed. The feeding stations in the backyards were deserted. The few birds seen anywhere were moribund; they trembled violently and could not fly. It was a spring without voices. On the mornings that had once throbbed with the dawn chorus of robins, catbirds, doves, jays, wrens, and scores of other bird voices there was now no sound; only silence lay over the fields and woods and marsh.

On the farms the hens brooded, but no chicks hatched. The farmers complained that they were unable to raise any pigs—the litters were small and the young survived only a few days. The apple trees were coming into bloom but no bees droned among the blossoms, so there was no pollination and there would be no fruit.

The roadsides, once so attractive, were now lined with browned and withered vegetation as though swept by fire. These, too, were silent, deserted by all living things. Even the streams were now lifeless. Anglers no longer visited them, for all the fish had died.

In the gutters under the eaves and between the shingles of the roofs, a white granular powder still showed a few patches; some weeks before it had fallen like snow upon the roofs and the lawns, the fields and streams.

No witchcraft, no enemy action had silenced the rebirth of new life in this stricken world. The people had done it themselves.

This town does not actually exist, but it might easily have a thousand counterparts in America or elsewhere in the world. I know of no community that has experienced all the misfortunes I describe. Yet every one of these disasters has actually happened somewhere, and many real communities have already suffered a substantial number of them. A grim specter has crept upon us almost unnoticed, and this imagined tragedy may easily become a stark reality we all shall know.

What has already silenced the voices of spring in countless towns in America? This book is an attempt to explain.

1962

N. Scott Momaday

b. 1934

In this essay, Momaday provides an example of a land ethic, and this is meant to persuade readers of the truth of his conclusion: "We Americans must come again to a moral comprehension of the earth and air." The essay first appeared in the 1970 Ecotactics: The Sierra Club Handbook for Environmental Activists. *Like Chief Seattle's letter, it helped express the philosophical foundation of the modern environmental movement. Throughout the essay, Momaday refers to his book* The Way to Rainy Mountain, *which is an amalgam of Kiowa mythology, history, and Momaday's personal recollections. Rainy Mountain is in Kiowa County, Oklahoma, not far from Momaday's birthplace, and was a natural landmark and gathering spot for Plains Indians; later, it was within the reservations that constituted most of Oklahoma before the tribal lands were settled by whites. In Momaday's view, it has a deep and mysterious racial connection to the Kiowa.*

An American Land Ethic

I

One night a strange thing happened. I had written the greater part of *The Way to Rainy Mountain*—all of it, in fact, except the epilogue. I had set down the last of the old Kiowa[1] tales, and I had composed both the historical and the autobiographical commentaries for it. I had the sense of being out of breath, of having said what it was in me to say on that subject. The manuscript lay before me in the bright light, small, to be sure, but complete; or nearly so. I had written the second of the two poems in which that book is framed. I had uttered the last word, as it were. And yet a whole, penultimate piece was missing. I began once again to write:

> During the first hours after midnight on the morning of November 13, 1833, it seemed that the world was coming to an end. Suddenly the stillness of the night was broken; there were brilliant flashes of light in the sky, light of such intensity that people were awakened by it. With the speed and density of a driving rain, stars were falling in the universe. Some were brighter than Venus; one was said to be as large as the moon.

I went on to say that that event, the falling of the stars on North America, that explosion of Leonid meteors which occurred 137 years ago, is among the earliest entries in the Kiowa calendars. So deeply impressed upon the imagination of the Kiowas is that old phenomenon that it is remembered still; it has become a part of the racial memory.

"The living memory," I wrote, "and the verbal tradition which transcends it, were brought together for me once and for all in the person of Ko-sahn." It seemed eminently right for me to deal, after all, with that old woman. Ko-sahn is among the most venerable people I have ever known. She spoke and sang to me one summer afternoon in

1. The Kiowa are a large tribe of Native Americans who originated in Montana but eventually moved south over the Great Plains, finally allying themselves with the Comanche of Texas and Oklahoma. [All notes are the editor's.]

Oklahoma. It was like a dream. When I was born she was already old; she was a grown woman when my grandparents came into the world. She sat perfectly still, folded over on herself. It did not seem possible that so many years—a century of years—could be so compacted and distilled. Her voice shuddered, but it did not fail. Her songs were sad. An old whimsy, a delight in language and in remembrance, shone in her one good eye. She conjured up the past, imagining perfectly the long continuity of her being. She imagined the lovely young girl, wild and vital, she had been. She imagined the Sun Dance:

> There was an old, old woman. She had something on her back. The boys went out to see. The old woman had a bag full of earth on her back. It was a certain kind of sandy earth. That is what they must have in the lodge. The dancers must dance upon the sandy earth. The old woman held a digging tool in her hand. She turned towards the south and pointed with her lips. It was like a kiss, and she began to sing:
>
> *We have brought the earth.*
> *Now it is time to play;*
> *As old as I am, I still have the feeling of play.*
>
> That was the beginning of the Sun Dance.

By this time I was back into the book, caught up completely in the act of writing. I had projected myself—imagined myself—out of the room and out of time. I was there with Ko-sahn in the Oklahoma July. We laughed easily together; I felt that I had known her all of my life—all of hers. I did not want to let her go. But I had come to the end. I set down, almost grudgingly, the last sentences:

> It was—all of this and more—a quest, a going forth upon the way to Rainy Mountain. Probably Ko-sahn too is dead now. At times, in the quiet of evening, I think she must have wondered, dreaming, who she was. Was she become in her sleep that old purveyor of the sacred earth, perhaps, that ancient one who, old as she was, still had the feeling of play? And in her mind, at times, did she see the falling stars?

For some time I sat looking down at these words on the page, trying to deal with the emptiness that had come about inside of me. The words did not seem real. The longer I looked at them, the more unfamiliar they became. At last I could scarcely believe that they made sense, that they had anything whatsoever to do with meaning. In desperation almost, I went back over the final paragraphs, backward and forward, hurriedly. My eyes fell upon the name Ko-sahn. And all at once everything seemed suddenly to refer to that name. The name seemed to humanize the whole complexity of language. All at once, absolutely, I had the sense of the magic of words and of names. Ko-sahn, I said. And I said again, KO-SAHN.

Then it was that that ancient, one-eyed woman stepped out of the language and stood before me on the page. I was amazed, of course, and yet it seemed to me entirely appropriate that this should happen.

"Yes, grandson," she said. "What is it? What do you want?"

"I was just now writing about you," I replied, stammering. "I thought—forgive me—I thought that perhaps you were . . . That you had . . ."

"No," she said. And she cackled. And she went on. "You have imagined me well, and so I am. You have imagined that I dream, and so I do. I have seen the falling stars."

"But all of this, this *imagining*," I protested, "this has taken place—is taking place in my mind. You are not actually here, not here in this room." It occurred to me that I was being extremely rude, but I could not help myself. She seemed to understand.

"Be careful of your pronouncements, grandson," she answered. "You imagine that I am here in this room, do you not? This is worth something. You see, I have existence, whole being, in your imagination. It is but one kind of being, to be sure, but it is perhaps the best of all kinds. If I am not here in this room, grandson, then surely neither are you."

"I think I see what you mean," I said. I felt justly rebuked. "Tell me grandmother, how old are you?"

"I do not know," she replied. "There are times when I think that I am the oldest woman on earth. You know, the Kiowas came into the world through a hollow log. In my mind's eye I have seen them emerge, one by one, from the mouth of the log. I have seen them so clearly, how they were dressed, how delighted they were to see the world around them. I *must* have been there. And I must have taken part in that old migration of the Kiowas from the Yellowstone to the southern plains, for I have seen antelope bounding in the tall grass near the Big Horn River, and I have seen the ghost forests in the Black Hills.[2] Once I saw the red cliffs of Palo Duro Canyon. I was with those who were camped in the Wichita Mountains[3] when the stars fell."

"You are indeed very old," I said, "and you have seen many things."

"Yes, I imagine that I have," she replied. Then she turned slowly around, nodding once, and receded into the language I had made. And then I imagined I was alone in the room.

II

Once in his life a man ought to concentrate his mind upon the remembered earth, I believe. He ought to give himself up to a particular landscape in his experience, to look at it from as many angles as he can, to wonder about it, to dwell upon it. He ought to imagine that he touches it with his hands at every season and listens to the sounds that are made upon it. He ought to imagine the creatures there and all the faintest motions of the wind. He ought to recollect the glare of noon and all the colors of the dawn and dusk.

The Wichita Mountains rise out of the southern plains in a long crooked line that runs from east to west. The mountains are made of red earth, and of rock that is neither red nor blue but some very rare admixture of the two, like the feathers of certain birds. They are not so high and mighty as the mountains of the Far West, and they bear a different relationship to the land around them. One does not imagine that they are distinctive in themselves, or indeed that they exist apart from the plain in any sense. If you try to think of them in the abstract, they lose the look of mountains. They are preeminently an expression of the larger landscape, more perfectly organic than one can easily imagine. To behold these mountains from the plain

2. In South Dakota, the grounds of the Kiowa before the Sioux drove them farther south around 1800. The Big Horn River is in Montana and was also in traditional Kiowa lands. A tributary of it was the site of Custer's Last Stand, the massacre of the 7th Cavalry by the Sioux.

3. In Oklahoma, part of the ancestral Kiowa and Comanche lands and later part of their reservation. Palo Duro Canyon is in Texas and was the site of one of the last battles between the U.S. Army and the Kiowa and Comanche tribes.

is one thing; to see the plain from the mountains is something else. I have stood on the top of Mount Scott and seen the earth below, bending out into the whole circle of the sky. The wind runs always close upon the slopes, and there are times when you hear the rush of it like water in the ravines.

Here is the hub of an old commerce. More than a hundred years ago the Kiowas and Comanches[4] journeyed outward from the Wichitas in every direction, seeking after mischief and medicine, horses and hostages. Sometimes they went away for years, but they always returned, for the land had got hold of them. It is a consecrated place, and even now there is something of the wilderness about it. There is a game preserve in the hills. Animals graze away in the open meadows or, closer by, keep to the shadows of the groves: antelope and deer, longhorns and buffalo. It was here, the Kiowas say, that the first buffalo came into the world.

The yellow grassy knoll that is called Rainy Mountain lies a short distance to the north and west. There, on the west side, is the ruin of an old school where my grandmother went as a wild girl in blanket and braids to learn of numbers and of names in English. And there she is buried.

Most is your name the name of this dark stone.
Deranged in death, the mind to be inheres
Forever in the nominal unknown,
The wake of nothing audible he hears
Who listens here and now to hear your name.
The early sun, red as a hunter's moon,
Runs in the plain. The mountain burns and shines;
And silence is the long approach of noon
Upon the shadow that your name defines—
And death this cold, black density of stone.

III

I am interested in the way that a man looks at a given landscape and takes possession of it in his blood and brain. For this happens, I am certain, in the ordinary motion of life. None of us lives apart from the land entirely; such an isolation is unimaginable. We have sooner

4. The Comanche Indians were a South Plains tribe closely allied with the Kiowas.

or later to come to terms with the world around us—and I mean especially the physical world, not only as it is revealed to us immediately through our senses, but also as it is perceived more truly in the long turn of seasons and of years. And we must come to moral terms. There is no alternative, I believe, if we are to realize and maintain our humanity, for our humanity must consist in part in the ethical as well as in the practical ideal of preservation. And particularly here and now is that true. We Americans need now more than ever before—and indeed more than we know—to imagine who and what we are with respect to the earth and sky. I am talking about an act of the imagination, essentially, and the concept of an American land ethic.

It is no doubt more difficult to imagine the landscape of America now, than it was in, say, 1900. Our whole experience as a nation in this century has been a repudiation of the pastoral ideal which informs so much of the art and literature of the nineteenth century. One effect of the technological revolution has been to uproot us from the soil. We have become disoriented, I believe; we have suffered a kind of psychic dislocation of ourselves in time and space. We may be perfectly sure of where we are in relation to the supermarket and the next coffee break, but I doubt that any of us knows where he is in relation to the stars and to the solstices. Our sense of the natural order has become dull and unreliable. Like the wilderness itself, our sphere of instinct has diminished in proportion as we have failed to imagine truly what it is. And yet I believe that it is possible to formulate an ethical idea of the land—a notion of what it is and must be in our daily lives—and I believe moreover that it is absolutely necessary to do so.

It would seem on the surface of things that a land ethic is something that is alien to, or at least dormant in, most Americans. Most of us have developed an attitude of indifference toward the land. In terms of my own experience, it is difficult to see how such an attitude could ever have come about.

IV

Ko-sahn could remember where my grandmother was born. "It was just there," she said, pointing to a tree, and the tree was like a hundred others that grew up in the broad depression of the

Washita River. I could see nothing to indicate that anyone had ever been there, spoken so much as a word, or touched the tips of his fingers to the tree. But in her memory Ko-sahn could see the child. I think she must have remembered my grandmother's voice, for she seemed for a long moment to listen and to hear. There was a still, heavy heat upon that place; I had the sense that ghosts were gathering there.

And in the racial memory, Ko-sahn had seen the falling stars. For her there was no distinction between the individual and the racial experience, even as there was none between the mythical and the historical. Both were realized for her in the one memory, and that was of the land. This landscape, in which she had lived for a hundred years, was the common denominator of everything that she knew and would ever know—and her knowledge was profound. Her roots ran deep into the earth, and from those depths she drew strength enough to hold still against all the forces of chance and disorder. And she drew therefrom the sustenance of meaning and of mystery as well. The falling stars were not for Ko-sahn an isolated or accidental phenomenon. She had a great personal investment in that awful commotion of light in the night sky. For it remained to be imagined. She must at last deal with it in words; she must appropriate it to her understanding of the whole universe. And, again, when she spoke of the Sun Dance, it was an essential expression of her relationship to the life of the earth and to the sun and moon.

In Ko-sahn and in her people we have always had the example of a deep, ethical regard for the land. We had better learn from it. Surely that ethic is merely latent in ourselves. It must now be activated, I believe. We Americans must come again to a moral comprehension of the earth and air. We must live according to the principle of a land ethic. The alternative is that we shall not live at all.

1970

NASA

Est. 1958

You probably know NASA for its space missions, such as the Apollo moon missions and the International Space Station. But in partnership with the scientific community, NASA also works "to achieve . . . a deep understanding of our planet." It is one of the most trusted scientific agencies in the world, employing thousands of scientists and educators. This website, produced by the Jet Propulsion Laboratory's Earth Science Communications Team, is meant to settle the public debate about anthropogenic global warming (AGW), or human-caused climate change. U.S. president Donald Trump has called AGW a "hoax," has recommitted the nation to carbon-polluting fossil fuels like coal and oil, and in 2017 withdrew the United States from the Paris Climate Agreement, an international cooperative effort designed to slow global warming. According to the New York Times, *"every member of the elected Republican leadership" in Congress was "united in their praise."*

Global Climate Change: Evidence and Scientific Consensus

Climate Change: How Do We Know?

The Earth's climate has changed throughout history. Just in the last 650,000 years there have been seven cycles of glacial advance and retreat, with the abrupt end of the last ice age about 11,700 years ago marking the beginning of the modern climate era—and of human civilization. Most of these climate changes are attributed to very small variations in Earth's orbit that change the amount of solar energy our planet receives.

Scientific Consensus

Ninety-seven percent of climate scientists agree that climate-warming trends over the past century are extremely likely due to human activities, and most of the leading scientific organizations worldwide have issued public statements endorsing this position.

Click here for a partial list of these public statements and related resources.[1]

1. This box appeared on the NASA website as a clickable link, which brought readers to the information included below the heading, "Scientific Consensus: Earth's Climate is Warming" [editor's note].

This graph, based on the comparison of atmospheric samples contained in ice cores and more recent direct measurements, provides evidence that atmospheric CO_2 has increased since the Industrial Revolution. (Credit: Luthi, D., et al. 2008; Etheridge, D.M., et al. 2010; Vostok ice core data/J.R. Petit et al.; NOAA Mauna Loa CO_2 record.) Find out more about ice cores (external site).

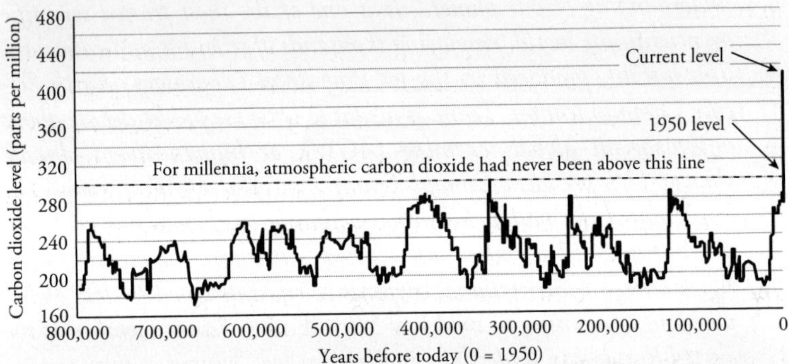

The current warming trend is of particular significance because most of it is extremely likely (greater than 95 percent probability) to be the result of human activity since the mid-20th century and proceeding at a rate that is unprecedented over decades to millennia.[2]

Earth-orbiting satellites and other technological advances have enabled scientists to see the big picture, collecting many different types of information about our planet and its climate on a global scale. This body of data, collected over many years, reveals the signals of a changing climate.

2. IPCC Fifth Assessment Report, Summary for Policymakers.

B.D. Santer et al., "A search for human influences on the thermal structure of the atmosphere," Nature vol. 382, 4 July 1996, 39–46; Gabriele C. Hegerl, "Detecting Greenhouse-Gas-Induced Climate Change with an Optimal Fingerprint Method," Journal of Climate, v. 9, October 1996, 2281–2306; V. Ramaswamy et al., "Anthropogenic and Natural Influences in the Evolution of Lower Stratospheric Cooling," Science 311 (24 February 2006), 1138–1141; B.D. Santer et al., "Contributions of Anthropogenic and Natural Forcing to Recent Tropopause Height Changes," Science vol. 301 (25 July 2003), 479–483.

The heat-trapping nature of carbon dioxide and other gases was demonstrated in the mid-19th century.[3] Their ability to affect the transfer of infrared energy through the atmosphere is the scientific basis of many instruments flown by NASA. There is no question that increased levels of greenhouse gases must cause the Earth to warm in response.

Ice cores drawn from Greenland, Antarctica, and tropical mountain glaciers show that the Earth's climate responds to changes in greenhouse gas levels. Ancient evidence can also be found in tree rings, ocean sediments, coral reefs, and layers of sedimentary rocks. This ancient, or paleoclimate, evidence reveals that current warming is occurring roughly ten times faster than the average rate of ice-age-recovery warming.[4]

The Evidence for Rapid Climate Change is Compelling:

Global Temperature Rise

The planet's average surface temperature has risen about 1.62 degrees Fahrenheit (0.9 degrees Celsius) since the late 19th century, a change

3. In the 1860s, physicist John Tyndall recognized the Earth's natural greenhouse effect and suggested that slight changes in the atmospheric composition could bring about climatic variations. In 1896, a seminal paper by Swedish scientist Svante Arrhenius first predicted that changes in the levels of carbon dioxide in the atmosphere could substantially alter the surface temperature through the greenhouse effect.

4. National Research Council (NRC), 2006. Surface Temperature Reconstructions For the Last 2,000 Years. National Academy Press, Washington, D.C. http://earthobservatory.nasa.gov/Features/GlobalWarming/page3.php

driven largely by increased carbon dioxide and other human-made emissions into the atmosphere.[5] Most of the warming occurred in the past 35 years, with the five warmest years on record taking place since 2010. Not only was 2016 the warmest year on record, but eight of the 12 months that make up the year—from January through September, with the exception of June—were the warmest on record for those respective months.[6]

Warming Oceans

The oceans have absorbed much of this increased heat, with the top 700 meters (about 2,300 feet) of ocean showing warming of more than 0.4 degrees Fahrenheit since 1969.[7]

5. https://www.ncdc.noaa.gov/monitoring-references/faq/indicators.php; http://www.cru.uea.ac.uk/cru/data/temperature; http://data.giss.nasa.gov/gistemp

6. https://www.giss.nasa.gov/research/news/20170118/

7. Levitus, S.; Antonov, J.; Boyer, T.; Baranova, O.; Garcia, H.; Locarnini, R.; Mishonov, A.; Reagan, J.; Seidov, D.; Yarosh, E.; Zweng, M. (2017). NCEI ocean heat content, temperature anomalies, salinity anomalies, thermosteric sea level anomalies, halosteric sea level anomalies, and total steric sea level anomalies from 1955 to present calculated from in situ oceanographic subsurface profile data (NCEI Accession 0164586). Version 4.4. NOAA National Centers for Environmental Information. Dataset. doi:10.7289/V53F4MVP

Shrinking Ice Sheets

The Greenland and Antarctic ice sheets have decreased in mass. Data from NASA's Gravity Recovery and Climate Experiment show Greenland lost an average of 286 billion tons of ice per year between 1993 and 2016, while Antarctica lost about 127 billion tons of ice per year during the same time period. The rate of Antarctica ice mass loss has tripled in the last decade.[8]

Flowing meltwater from the Greenland ice sheet.

Glacial Retreat

Glaciers are retreating almost everywhere around the world—including in the Alps, Himalayas, Andes, Rockies, Alaska and Africa.[9]

The disappearing snowcap of Mount Kilimanjaro, from space.

8. https://www.jpl.nasa.gov/news/news.php?feature=7159

9. National Snow and Ice Data Center; World Glacier Monitoring Service

Decreased Snow Cover

Satellite observations reveal that the amount of spring snow cover in the Northern Hemisphere has decreased over the past five decades and that the snow is melting earlier.[1]

Sea Level Rise

Global sea level rose about 8 inches in the last century. The rate in the last two decades, however, is nearly double that of the last century and is accelerating slightly every year.[2]

Republic of Maldives: Vulnerable to sea level rise.

1. National Snow and Ice Data Center; Robinson, D. A., D. K. Hall, and T. L. Mote. 2014. *MEaSUREs Northern Hemisphere Terrestrial Snow Cover Extent Daily 25 km EASE-Grid 2.0, Version 1.* [Indicate subset used]. Boulder, Colorado USA. NASA National Snow and Ice Data Center Distributed Active Archive Center. doi: https://doi.org/10.5067/MEASURES/CRYOSPHERE/nsidc-0530.001. [Accessed 9/21/18]; http://nsidc.org/cryosphere/sotc/snow_extent.html; Rutgers University Global Snow Lab, Data History [accessed September 21, 2018].

2. R. S. Nerem, B. D. Beckley, J. T. Fasullo, B. D. Hamlington, D. Masters and G. T. Mitchum. Climate-change–driven accelerated sea-level rise detected in the altimeter era. *PNAS*, 2018 DOI: 10.1073/pnas.1717312115

Declining Arctic Sea Ice

Both the extent and thickness of Arctic sea ice has declined rapidly over the last several decades.[3]

Visualization of the 2012 Arctic sea ice minimum, the lowest on record.

Extreme Events

The number of record high temperature events in the United States has been increasing, while the number of record low temperature events has been decreasing, since 1950. The United States has also witnessed increasing numbers of intense rainfall events.[4]

3. https://nsidc.org/cryosphere/sotc/sea_ice.html

4. USGCRP, 2017: *Climate Science Special Report: Fourth National Climate Assessment, Volume I* [Wuebbles, D.J., D.W. Fahey, K.A. Hibbard, D.J. Dokken, B.C. Stewart, and T.K. Maycock (eds.)]. U.S. Global Change Research Program, Washington, DC, USA, 470 pp, doi: 10.7930/J0J964J6

Ocean Acidification

Since the beginning of the Industrial Revolution, the acidity of surface ocean waters has increased by about 30 percent.[5, 6] This increase is the result of humans emitting more carbon dioxide into the atmosphere and hence more being absorbed into the oceans. The amount of carbon dioxide absorbed by the upper layer of the oceans is increasing by about 2 billion tons per year.[7, 8]

5. http://www.pmel.noaa.gov/co2/story/What+is+Ocean+ Acidification%3F

6. http://www.pmel.noaa.gov/co2/story/Ocean+Acidification

7. C. L. Sabine et.al., "The Oceanic Sink for Anthropogenic CO_2," Science vol. 305 (16 July 2004), 367–371

8. Copenhagen Diagnosis, p. 36.

Scientific Consensus: Earth's Climate Is Warming

Multiple studies published in peer-reviewed scientific journals[9] show that 97 percent or more of actively publishing climate scientists agree[1]: Climate-warming trends over the past century are extremely likely due to human activities. In addition, most of the leading scientific organizations worldwide have issued public statements endorsing this position. The following is a partial list of these organizations, along with links to their published statements and a selection of related resources.

9. J. Cook, et al, "Consensus on consensus: a synthesis of consensus estimates on human-caused global warming," *Environmental Research Letters* Vol. 11 No. 4, (13 April 2016); DOI:10.1088/1748-9326/11/4/048002; Quotation from page 6: "The number of papers rejecting AGW [Anthropogenic, or human-caused, Global Warming] is a miniscule proportion of the published research, with the percentage slightly decreasing over time. Among papers expressing a position on AGW, an overwhelming percentage (97.2 percent based on self-ratings, 97.1 percent based on abstract ratings) endorses the scientific consensus on AGW." J. Cook, et al, "Quantifying the consensus on anthropogenic global warming in the scientific literature," *Environmental Research Letters* Vol. 8 No. 2, (15 May 2013); DOI:10.1088/1748-9326/8/2/024024; Quotation from page 3: "Among abstracts that expressed a position on AGW, 97.1 percent endorsed the scientific consensus. Among scientists who expressed a position on AGW in their abstract, 98.4 percent endorsed the consensus." W. R. L. Anderegg, "Expert Credibility in Climate Change," *Proceedings of the National Academy of Sciences* Vol. 107 No. 27, 12107–12109 (21 June 2010); DOI: 10.1073/pnas.1003187107; P. T. Doran & M. K. Zimmerman, "Examining the Scientific Consensus on Climate Change," *Eos Transactions American Geophysical Union* Vol. 90 Issue 3 (2009), 22; DOI: 10.1029/2009EO030002; N. Oreskes, "Beyond the Ivory Tower: The Scientific Consensus on Climate Change," *Science* Vol. 306 no. 5702, p. 1686 (3 December 2004); DOI: 10.1126/science.1103618.

1. Technically, a "consensus" is a general agreement of opinion, but the scientific method steers us away from this to an objective framework. In science, facts or observations are explained by a hypothesis (a statement of a possible explanation for some natural phenomenon), which can then be tested and retested until it is refuted (or disproved).

As scientists gather more observations, they will build off one explanation and add details to complete the picture. Eventually, a group of hypotheses might be integrated and generalized into a scientific theory, a scientifically acceptable general principle or body of principles offered to explain phenomena.

A World of Agreement: Temperatures are Rising

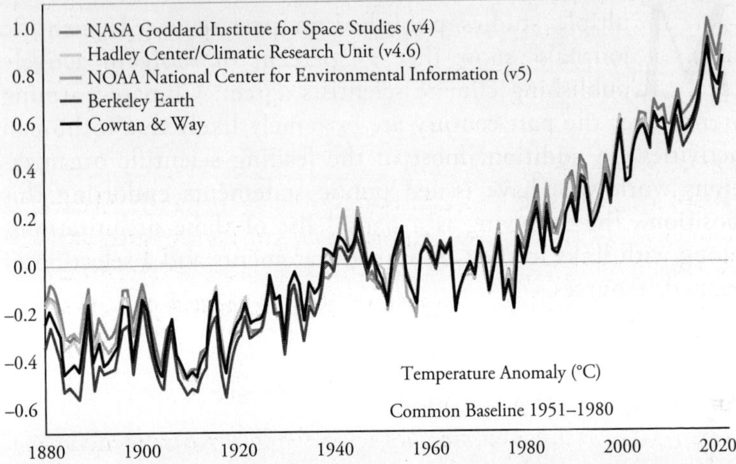

Temperature data showing rapid warming in the past few decades, the latest data going up to 2018. According to NASA data, 2016 was the warmest year since 1880, continuing a long-term trend of rising global temperatures. The 10 warmest years in the 139-year record all have occurred since 2005, with the five warmest years being the five most recent years. Credit: NASA's Earth Observatory.

American Scientific Societies

Statement on Climate Change from 18 Scientific Associations
"Observations throughout the world make it clear that climate change is occurring, and rigorous scientific research demonstrates that the greenhouse gases emitted by human activities are the primary driver." (2009)[2]

American Association for the Advancement of Science
"Based on well-established evidence, about 97 percent of climate scientists have concluded that human-caused climate change is happening." (2014)[3]

2. Statement on climate change from 18 scientific associations (2009)

3. AAAS Board Statement on Climate Change (2014)

American Chemical Society
"The Earth's climate is changing in response to increasing concentrations of greenhouse gases (GHGs) and particulate matter in the atmosphere, largely as the result of human activities." (2016–2019)[4]

American Geophysical Union
"Based on extensive scientific evidence, it is extremely likely that human activities, especially emissions of greenhouse gases, are the dominant cause of the observed warming since the mid-twentieth century. There is no alterative explanation supported by convincing evidence." (2019)[5]

American Medical Association
"Our AMA . . . supports the findings of the Intergovernmental Panel on Climate Change's fourth assessment report and concurs with the scientific consensus that the Earth is undergoing adverse global climate change and that anthropogenic contributions are significant." (2019)[6]

American Meteorological Society
"Research has found a human influence on the climate of the past several decades . . . The IPCC (2013), USGCRP (2017), and USGCRP (2018) indicate that it is extremely likely that human influence has been the dominant cause of the observed warming since the mid-twentieth century." (2019)[7]

American Physical Society
"Earth's changing climate is a critical issue and poses the risk of significant environmental, social and economic disruptions around the globe. While natural sources of climate variability are significant, multiple lines of evidence indicate that human influences have had

4. ACS Public Policy Statement: Climate Change (2016–2019)

5. Society Must Address the Growing Climate Crisis Now (2019)

6. Global Climate Change and Human Health (2019)

7. Climate Change: An Information Statement of the American Meteorological Society (2019)

an increasingly dominant effect on global climate warming observed since the mid-twentieth century." (2015)[8]

The Geological Society of America

"The Geological Society of America (GSA) concurs with assessments by the National Academies of Science (2005), the National Research Council (2011), the Intergovernmental Panel on Climate Change (IPCC, 2013) and the U.S. Global Change Research Program (Melillo et al., 2014) that global climate has warmed in response to increasing concentrations of carbon dioxide (CO_2) and other greenhouse gases. . . . Human activities (mainly greenhouse-gas emissions) are the dominant cause of the rapid warming since the middle 1900s (IPCC, 2013)." (2015)[9]

Science Academies

International Academies: Joint Statement

"Climate change is real. There will always be uncertainty in understanding a system as complex as the world's climate. However, there is now strong evidence that significant global warming is occurring. The evidence comes from direct measurements of rising surface air temperatures and subsurface ocean temperatures and from phenomena such as increases in average global sea levels, retreating glaciers, and changes to many physical and biological systems. It is likely that most of the warming in recent decades can be attributed to human activities (IPCC 2001)." (2005, 11 international science academies)[1]

U.S. National Academy of Sciences

"Scientists have known for some time, from multiple lines of evidence, that humans are changing Earth's climate, primarily through greenhouse gas emissions."[2]

8. APS National Policy 07.1 Climate Change (2015)

9. GSA Position Statement on Climate Change (2015)

1. Joint science academies' statement: Global response to climate change (2005)

2. Climate at the National Academies

U.S. Government Agencies

U.S. Global Change Research Program
"Earth's climate is now changing faster than at any point in the history of modern civilization, primarily as a result of human activities." (2018, 13 U.S. government departments and agencies)[3]

Intergovernmental Bodies

Intergovernmental Panel on Climate Change
"Warming of the climate system is unequivocal and, since the 1950s, many of the observed changes are unprecedented over decades to millennia. The atmosphere and ocean have warmed, the amounts of snow and ice have diminished, and sea level has risen."[4]

"Human influence on the climate system is clear, and recent anthropogenic emissions of greenhouse gases are the highest in history. Recent climate changes have had widespread impacts on human and natural systems."[5]

Other Resources

List of Worldwide Scientific Organizations
The following page lists the nearly 200 worldwide scientific organizations that hold the position that climate change has been caused by human action. http://www.opr.ca.gov/facts/list-of-scientific-organizations.html

U.S. Agencies
The following page contains information on what federal agencies are doing to adapt to climate change. https://www.c2es.org/site/assets/uploads/2012/02/climate-change-adaptation-what-federal-agencies-are-doing.pdf

Site last updated 15 January 2020.

3. Fourth National Climate Assessment: Volume II (2018)

4. IPCC Fifth Assessment Report, Summary for Policymakers (2014)

5. IPCC Fifth Assessment Report, Summary for Policymakers (2014)

William D. Ruckelshaus
1932–2019
Lee M. Thomas
b. 1944
William K. Reilly
b. 1940
Christine Todd Whitman
b. 1946

Vice presidential candidate Sarah Palin's memorable phrase, "Drill, baby, drill," during the 2008 campaign succinctly expresses the Republican Party's commitment to fossil fuels as a cheap source of energy. As scientists and environmentalists call for the United States to reduce its carbon footprint, several Republican members of Congress continue to deny that human activity causes global warming, and the 2012 Republican platform required Congress to "take quick action to prohibit the [Environmental Protection Agency] from moving forward with new greenhouse gas regulations." This op-ed piece, which appeared in the New York Times *in July 2013, presents a powerful ethical argument for changing the party's position. It persuades not because of its logic (which hundreds of scientists have voiced before) but because of the reputations of those making the assertions. Ruckelshaus was the EPA's first director when Republican president Richard Nixon created the agency. Congress passed the Clean Water Act of 1972 during his tenure. While Thomas directed the EPA, Republican president Ronald Reagan signed the 1987 Montreal Protocol, which phased out the use of ozone-depleting chemicals. Reilly headed the EPA in 1990, when Republican president George H. W. Bush signed an amendment to the Clean Air Act that created a cap-and-trade program, which has successfully reduced the sulfur dioxide emissions from coal-fired power plants, a leading cause of acid rain. Whitman directed the EPA during the Republican presidential administration of George W. Bush. (The authors' footnotes appeared as hyperlinks in the original online version of this essay.)*

A Republican Case for Climate Action

Each of us took turns over the past 43 years running the Environmental Protection Agency. We served Republican presidents, but we have a message that transcends political affiliation: the United States must move now on substantive steps to curb climate change, at home and internationally.

There is no longer any credible scientific debate about the basic facts: our world continues to warm, with the last decade the hottest in modern records, and the deep ocean warming faster than the earth's atmosphere. Sea level is rising. Arctic Sea ice is melting years faster than projected.

The costs of inaction are undeniable. The lines of scientific evidence grow only stronger and more numerous. And the window of time remaining to act is growing smaller: delay could mean that warming becomes "locked in."

A market-based approach, like a carbon tax, would be the best path to reducing greenhouse-gas emissions, but that is unachievable in the current political gridlock in Washington. Dealing with this political reality, President Obama's June climate action plan lays out achievable actions that would deliver real progress.[1] He will use his executive powers to require reductions in the amount of carbon dioxide emitted by the nation's power plants and spur increased investment in clean energy technology, which is inarguably the path we must follow to ensure a strong economy along with a livable climate.

The president also plans to use his regulatory power to limit the powerful warming chemicals known as hydrofluorocarbons and encourage the United States to join with other nations to amend the Montreal Protocol to phase out these chemicals.[2] The landmark international treaty, which took effect in 1989, already has been hugely successful in solving the ozone problem.

Rather than argue against his proposals, our leaders in Congress should endorse them and start the overdue debate about what bigger steps are needed and how to achieve them—domestically and internationally.

1. "President Obama's Plan to Fight Climate Change," The White House, June 25, 2013.

2. "The Montreal Protocol on Substances That Deplete the Ozone Layer," United Nations Environment Programme, Ozone Secretariat, 2010–2011.

As administrators of the EPA under Presidents Richard M. Nixon, Ronald Reagan, George Bush and George W. Bush, we held fast to common-sense conservative principles—protecting the health of the American people, working with the best technology available and trusting in the innovation of American business and in the market to find the best solutions for the least cost. That approach helped us tackle major environmental challenges to our nation and the world: the pollution of our rivers, dramatized when the Cuyahoga River in Cleveland caught fire in 1969; the hole in the ozone layer; and the devastation wrought by acid rain.[3]

The solutions we supported worked, although more must be done. Our rivers no longer burn, and their health continues to improve. The United States led the world when nations came together to phase out ozone-depleting chemicals. Acid rain diminishes each year, thanks to a pioneering, market-based emissions-trading system adopted under the first President Bush in 1990. And despite critics' warnings, our economy has continued to grow.

Climate change puts all our progress and our successes at risk. If we could articulate one framework for successful governance, perhaps it should be this: When confronted by a problem, deal with it. Look at the facts, cut through the extraneous, devise a workable solution and get it done.

We can have both a strong economy and a livable climate. All parties know that we need both. The rest of the discussion is either detail, which we can resolve, or purposeful delay, which we should not tolerate.

Mr. Obama's plan is just a start. More will be required. But we must continue efforts to reduce the climate-altering pollutants that threaten our planet. The only uncertainty about our warming world is how bad the changes will get, and how soon. What is most clear is that there is no time to waste.

2013

3. Occurs when sulfur dioxide and nitrogen oxides, common pollutants from coal-fired electric plants, dissolve in raindrops and fall back to the earth, killing plants and animals. "Cuyahoga River": toxic waste dumped into the river caught fire in 1969, spurring President Richard Nixon to create the Environmental Protection Agency. "Ozone": a gas in the upper atmosphere that blocks harmful solar radiation. In the 1970s, scientists discovered that the emission of chemicals in common items such as spray deodorants and air conditioners had poked a hole in the ozone layer [editor's note].

Elizabeth Kolbert

b. 1961

Kolbert is a journalist who regularly publishes articles on environmental issues in the New Yorker *weekly magazine, where this essay was first published on November 20, 2017. The* New Yorker *targets well-educated, middle- and upper-middle-class readers not just in New York City but across the nation. Many of its articles, like this one, are midway between a traditional opinion column and straight reportage. Kolbert uses the techniques of a reporter's feature article—for instance, she gathers much of her information from interviews. And the thesis may be implicit rather than explicit. But this piece is not reportage, because Kolbert definitely means to persuade readers to adopt an opinion: in this case, that we must quickly develop large-scale carbon removal systems. Other than its lack of an overt thesis, the essay comes close to the form of a speech in classical rhetoric as defined by Aristotle. After the introductory sketch and interview of Adrian Corless, Kolbert defines "carbon removal." She follows with the background history and an explanation of why action is now urgent. Her interviews with experts in the field and her reportage on their efforts provide the arguments about how carbon removal might be done. She also refutes an important opposing view near the end of the essay. Readers of the* New Yorker *expect articles to really engage their interest, if not entertain them—a demand not made of academic writing targeting a narrow audience of experts. And so Kolbert provides, for instance, vivid physical sketches of people and landscapes, which don't obviously advance her argument. But even these help persuade: consider, for instance, what those sketches of scientists do for their ethos and thus for their authority in the eyes of readers.*

Can Carbon-Dioxide Removal Save the World?

Carbon Engineering, a company owned in part by Bill Gates, has its headquarters on a spit of land that juts into Howe Sound, an hour north of Vancouver. Until recently, the land was a toxic-waste site, and the company's equipment occupies a long, barnlike building that, for many years, was used to process contaminated water. The offices, inherited from the business that poisoned the site, provide a spectacular view of Mt. Garibaldi, which rises to a snow-covered point, and of the Chief, a granite monolith that's British Columbia's answer to El Capitan. To protect the spit against rising sea levels, the local government is planning to cover it with a layer of fill six feet deep. When that's done, it's hoping to sell the site for luxury condos.

Adrian Corless, Carbon Engineering's chief executive, who is fifty-one, is a compact man with dark hair, a square jaw, and a concerned expression. "Do you wear contacts?" he asked, as we were suiting up to enter the barnlike building. If so, I'd have to take extra precautions, because some of the chemicals used in the building could cause the lenses to liquefy and fuse to my eyes.

Inside, pipes snaked along the walls and overhead. The thrum of machinery made it hard to hear. In one corner, what looked like oversized beach bags were filled with what looked like white sand. This, Corless explained over the noise, was limestone—pellets of pure calcium carbonate.

Corless and his team are engaged in a project that falls somewhere between toxic-waste cleanup and alchemy. They've devised a process that allows them, in effect, to suck carbon dioxide out of the air. Every day at the plant, roughly a ton of CO_2 that had previously floated over Mt. Garibaldi or the Chief is converted into calcium carbonate. The pellets are subsequently heated, and the gas is forced off, to be stored in cannisters. The calcium can then be recovered, and the process run through all over again.

"If we're successful at building a business around carbon removal, these are trillion-dollar markets," Corless told me.

This past April, the concentration of carbon dioxide in the atmosphere reached a record four hundred and ten parts per million. The amount of CO_2 in the air now is probably greater than it's been at any time since the mid-Pliocene, three and a half million years ago, when there was a lot less ice at the poles and sea levels were sixty feet higher. This year's record will be surpassed next year, and next year's the year after that. Even if every country fulfills the pledges made in the Paris climate accord—and the United States has said that it doesn't intend to—carbon dioxide could soon reach levels that, it's widely agreed, will lead to catastrophe, assuming it hasn't already done so.

Carbon-dioxide removal is, potentially, a trillion-dollar enterprise because it offers a way not just to slow the rise in CO_2 but to reverse it. The process is sometimes referred to as "negative emissions": instead of adding carbon to the air, it subtracts it. Carbon-removal plants could be built anywhere, or everywhere. Construct enough of them and, in theory at least, CO_2 emissions could continue unabated and still we could avert calamity. Depending on how you look at things, the technology represents either the ultimate insurance policy or the ultimate moral hazard.

Carbon Engineering is one of a half-dozen companies vying to prove that carbon removal is feasible. Others include Global Thermostat, which is based in New York, and Climeworks, based near Zurich. Most of these owe their origins to the ideas of a physicist named Klaus Lackner, who now works at Arizona State University, in Tempe, so on my way home from British Columbia I took a detour to visit him. It was July, and on the day I arrived the temperature in the city reached a hundred and twelve degrees. When I got to my hotel, one of the first things I noticed was a dead starling lying, feet up, in the parking lot. I wondered if it had died from heat exhaustion.

Lackner, who is sixty-five, grew up in Germany. He is tall and lanky, with a fringe of gray hair and a prominent forehead. I met him in his office at an institute he runs, the Center for Negative Carbon Emissions. The office was bare, except for a few *New Yorker* cartoons on the theme of nerd-dom, which, Lackner told me, his wife had cut out for him. In one, a couple of scientists stand in front of an enormous whiteboard covered in equations. "The math is right," one of them says. "It's just in poor taste."

In the late nineteen-seventies, Lackner moved from Germany to California to study with George Zweig, one of the discoverers of quarks. A few years later, he got a job at Los Alamos National Laboratory. There, he worked on fusion. "Some of the work was classified," he said, "some of it not."

Fusion is the process that powers the stars and, closer to home, thermonuclear bombs. When Lackner was at Los Alamos, it was being touted as a solution to the world's energy problem; if fusion could be harnessed, it could generate vast amounts of carbon-free power using isotopes of hydrogen. Lackner became convinced that a fusion reactor was, at a minimum, decades away. (Decades later, it's generally agreed that a workable reactor is still decades away.) Meanwhile, the globe's growing population would demand more and more energy, and this demand would be met, for the most part, with fossil fuels.

"I realized, probably earlier than most, that the claims of the demise of fossil fuels were greatly exaggerated," Lackner told me. (In fact, fossil fuels currently provide about eighty per cent of the world's energy. Proportionally, this figure hasn't changed much since the mid-eighties, but, because global energy use has nearly doubled, the amount of coal, oil, and natural gas being burned today is almost two times greater.)

One evening in the early nineties, Lackner was having a beer with a friend, Christopher Wendt, also a physicist. The two got to wondering why, as Lackner put it to me, "nobody's doing these really crazy, big things anymore." This led to more questions and more conversations (and possibly more beers).

Eventually, the two produced an equation-dense paper in which they argued that self-replicating machines could solve the world's energy problem and, more or less at the same time, clean up the mess humans have made by burning fossil fuels. The machines would be powered by solar panels, and as they multiplied they'd produce more solar panels, which they'd assemble using elements, like silicon and aluminum, extracted from ordinary dirt. The expanding collection of panels would produce ever more power, at a rate that would increase exponentially. An array covering three hundred and eighty-six thousand square miles—an area larger than Nigeria but, as Lackner and Wendt noted, "smaller than many deserts"—could supply all the world's electricity many times over.

This same array could be put to use scrubbing carbon dioxide from the atmosphere. According to Lackner and Wendt, the power generated by a Nigeria-size solar farm would be enough to remove all the CO_2 emitted by humans up to that point within five years. Ideally, the CO_2 would be converted to rock, similar to the white sand produced by Carbon Engineering; enough would be created to cover

Venezuela in a layer a foot and a half deep. (Where this rock would go the two did not specify.)

Lackner let the idea of the self-replicating machine slide, but he became more and more intrigued by carbon-dioxide removal, particularly by what's become known as "direct air capture."

"Sometimes by thinking through this extreme end point you learn a lot," he said. He began giving talks and writing papers on the subject. Some scientists decided he was nuts, others that he was a visionary. "Klaus is, in fact, a genius," Julio Friedmann, a former Principal Deputy Assistant Secretary of Energy and an expert on carbon management, told me.

In 2000, Lackner received a job offer from Columbia University. Once in New York, he pitched a plan for developing a carbon-sucking technology to Gary Comer, a founder of Lands' End. Comer brought to the meeting his investment adviser, who quipped that Lackner wasn't looking for venture capital so much as "adventure capital." Nevertheless, Comer offered to put up five million dollars. The new company was called Global Research Technologies, or G.R.T. It got as far as building a small prototype, but just as it was looking for new investors the [2008] financial crisis hit.

"Our timing was exquisite," Lackner told me. Unable to raise more funds, the company ceased operations. As the planet continued to warm, and carbon-dioxide levels continued to climb, Lackner came to believe that, unwittingly, humanity had already committed itself to negative emissions.

"I think that we're in a very uncomfortable situation," he said. "I would argue that if technologies to pull CO_2 out of the environment fail then we're in deep trouble."

Lackner founded the Center for Negative Carbon Emissions at A.S.U. in 2014. Most of the equipment he dreams up is put together in a workshop a few blocks from his office. The day I was there, it was so hot outside that even the five-minute walk to the workshop required staging. Lackner delivered a short lecture on the dangers of dehydration and handed me a bottle of water.

In the workshop, an engineer was tinkering with what looked like the guts of a foldout couch. Where, in the living-room version, there would have been a mattress, in this one was an elaborate array of plastic ribbons. Embedded in each ribbon was a powder made from thousands upon thousands of tiny amber-colored beads. The beads, Lackner explained, could be purchased by the truckload; they were composed of a resin normally used in water treatment to remove chemicals like nitrates. More or less by accident, Lackner had discovered that the beads could be repurposed. Dry, they'd absorb carbon dioxide. Wet, they'd release it. The idea was to expose the ribbons to Arizona's thirsty air, and then fold the device into a sealed container filled with water. The CO_2 that had been captured by the powder in the dry phase would be released in the wet phase; it could then be piped out of the container, and the whole process re-started, the couch folding and unfolding over and over again.

Lackner has calculated that an apparatus the size of a semi trailer could remove a ton of carbon dioxide per day, or three hundred and sixty-five tons a year. The world's cars, planes, refineries, and power plants now produce about thirty-six billion tons of CO_2 annually, so, he told me, "if you built a hundred million trailer-size units you could actually keep up with current emissions." He acknowledged that the figure sounded daunting. But, he noted, the iPhone has been around for only a decade or so, and there are now seven hundred million in use. "We are still very early in this game," he said.

The way Lackner sees things, the key to avoiding "deep trouble" is thinking differently. "We need to change the paradigm," he told me. Carbon dioxide should be regarded the same way we view other waste products, like sewage or garbage. We don't expect people to stop producing waste. ("Rewarding people for going to the bathroom less would be nonsensical," Lackner has observed.) At the same time, we don't let them shit on the sidewalk or toss their empty yogurt containers into the street.

"If I were to tell you that the garbage I'm dumping in front of your house is twenty per cent less this year than it was last year, you would still think I'm doing something intolerable," Lackner said.

One of the reasons we've made so little progress on climate change, he contends, is that the issue has acquired an ethical charge, which has polarized people. To the extent that emissions are seen as bad, emitters become guilty. "Such a moral stance makes virtually everyone a sinner, and makes hypocrites out of many who are concerned about climate change but still partake in the benefits of modernity," he has written. Changing the paradigm, Lackner believes, will change the conversation. If CO_2 is treated as just another form of waste, which has to be disposed of, then people can stop arguing about whether it's a problem and finally start doing something.

Carbon dioxide was "discovered," by a Scottish physician named Joseph Black, in 1754. A decade later, another Scotsman, James Watt, invented a more efficient steam engine, ushering in what is now called the age of industrialization but which future generations may dub the age of emissions. It is likely that by the end of the nineteenth century human activity had raised the average temperature of the earth by a tenth of a degree Celsius (or nearly two-tenths of a degree Fahrenheit).

As the world warmed, it started to change, first gradually and then suddenly. By now, the globe is at least one degree Celsius (1.8 degrees Fahrenheit) warmer than it was in Black's day, and the consequences are becoming ever more apparent. Heat waves are hotter, rainstorms more intense, and droughts drier. The wildfire season is growing longer, and fires, like the ones that recently ravaged Northern California, more numerous. Sea levels are rising, and the rate of rise is accelerating. Higher sea levels exacerbated the damage from Hurricanes Harvey, Irma, and Maria, and higher water temperatures probably also made the storms more ferocious. "Harvey is what climate change looks like," Eric Holthaus, a meteorologist turned columnist, recently wrote.

Meanwhile, still more warming is locked in. There's so much inertia in the climate system, which is as vast as the earth itself, that the globe has yet to fully adjust to the hundreds of billions of tons of carbon dioxide that have been added to the atmosphere in the past few decades. It's been calculated that to equilibrate to current CO_2 levels the planet still needs to warm by half a degree. And every ten days another billion tons of carbon dioxide are released. Last month, the World Meteorological Organization announced that the concentration of carbon dioxide in the atmosphere jumped by a record amount in 2016.

No one can say exactly how warm the world can get before disaster—the inundation of low-lying cities, say, or the collapse of crucial ecosystems, like coral reefs—becomes inevitable. Officially, the threshold is two degrees Celsius (3.6 degrees Fahrenheit) above preindustrial levels. Virtually every nation signed on to this figure at a round of climate negotiations held in Cancún in 2010.

Meeting in Paris in 2015, world leaders decided that the two-degree threshold was too high; the stated aim of the climate accord is to hold "the increase in the global average temperature to well below 2°C" and to try to limit it to 1.5°C. Since the planet has already warmed by one degree and, for all practical purposes, is committed to another half a degree, it would seem impossible to meet the latter goal and nearly impossible to meet the former. And it *is* nearly impossible, unless the world switches course and instead of just adding CO_2 to the atmosphere also starts to remove it.

The extent to which the world is counting on negative emissions is documented by the latest report of the Intergovernmental Panel on Climate Change (IPCC), which was published the year before Paris. To peer into the future, the IPCC relies on computer models that represent the world's energy and climate systems as a tangle of equations, and which can be programmed to play out different "scenarios." Most of the scenarios involve temperature increases of two, three, or even four degrees Celsius—up to just over seven degrees Fahrenheit—by the end of this century. (In a recent paper in the *Proceedings of the National Academy of Sciences*, two climate scientists—Yangyang Xu, of Texas A&M, and Veerabhadran Ramanathan, of the Scripps Institution of Oceanography—proposed that warming greater than three degrees Celsius be designated as "catastrophic" and warming greater than five degrees as "unknown??" The "unknown??" designation, they wrote, comes "with the understanding that changes of this magnitude, not experienced in the last 20+ million years, pose existential threats to a majority of the population.")

When the IPCC went looking for ways to hold the temperature increase under two degrees Celsius, it found the math punishing. Global emissions would have to fall rapidly and dramatically—pretty much down to zero by the middle of this century. (This would entail, among other things, replacing most of the world's power plants, revamping its agricultural systems, and eliminating gasoline-powered vehicles, all within the next few decades.) Alternatively, humanity could, in effect, go into hock. It could allow CO_2 levels temporarily to exceed the two-degree threshold—a situation that's become known as "overshoot"—and then, via negative emissions, pull the excess CO_2 out of the air.

The IPCC considered more than a thousand possible scenarios. Of these, only a hundred and sixteen limit warming to below two degrees, and of these a hundred and eight involve negative emissions. In many below-two-degree scenarios, the quantity of negative emissions called for reaches the same order of magnitude as the "positive" emissions being produced today.

"The volumes are outright crazy," Oliver Geden, the head of the EU research division of the German Institute for International and Security Affairs, told me. Lackner said, "I think what the IPCC really is saying is 'We tried lots and lots of scenarios, and, of the scenarios which stayed safe, virtually every one needed some magic touch of a negative emissions. If we didn't do that, we ran into a brick wall.'"

Pursued on the scale envisioned by the IPCC, carbon-dioxide removal would yield at first tens of billions and soon hundreds of billions of tons of CO_2, all of which would have to be dealt with. This represents its own supersized challenge. CO_2 can be combined with calcium to produce limestone, as it is in the process at Carbon Engineering (and in Lackner's self-replicating-machine scheme). But the necessary form of calcium isn't readily available, and producing it generally yields CO_2, a self-defeating prospect. An alternative is to shove the carbon back where it came from, deep underground.

"If you are storing CO_2 and your only purpose is storage, then you're looking for a package of certain types of rock," Sallie Greenberg, the associate director for energy, research, and development at the Illinois State Geological Survey, told me. It was a bright summer day, and we were driving through the cornfields of Illinois's midsection. A mile below us was a rock formation known as the Eau Claire Shale, and below that a formation known as the Mt. Simon Sandstone. Together with a team of drillers, engineers, and geoscientists, Greenberg has spent the past decade injecting carbon dioxide into this rock "package" and studying the outcome. When I'd proposed over the phone that she show me the project, in Decatur, she'd agreed, though not without hesitation.

"It isn't sexy," she'd warned me. "It's a wellhead."

Our first stop was a building shaped like a ski chalet. This was the National Sequestration Education Center, a joint venture of the Illinois geological survey, the U.S. Department of Energy, and Richland Community College. Inside were classrooms, occupied that morning by kids making lanyards, and displays aimed at illuminating the very dark world of carbon storage. One display was a sort of oversized barber pole, nine feet tall and decorated in bands of tan and brown, representing the various rock layers beneath us. A long arrow on the side of the pole indicated how many had been drilled through for Greenberg's carbon-storage project; it pointed down, through the New Albany Shale, the Maquoketa Shale, and so on, all the way to the floor.

The center's director, David Larrick, was on hand to serve as a guide. In addition to schoolkids, he said, the center hosted lots of community groups, like Kiwanis clubs. "This is very effective as a visual," he told me, gesturing toward the pole. Sometimes farmers were concerned about the impact that the project could have on their water supply. The pole showed that the CO_2 was being injected more than a mile below their wells.

"We have had overwhelmingly positive support," he said. While Greenberg and Larrick chatted, I wandered off to play an educational video game. A cartoon figure in a hard hat appeared on the screen to offer factoids such as "The most efficient method of transport of CO_2 is by pipeline."

"Transport CO_2 to earn points!" the cartoon man exhorted.

After touring the center's garden, which featured grasses, like big bluestem, that would have been found in the area before it was plowed into cornfields, Greenberg and I drove on. Soon we passed through the gates of an enormous Archer Daniels Midland (ADM) plant, which rose up out of the fields like a small city.

Greenberg explained that the project we were visiting was one of seven funded by the Department of Energy to learn whether carbon injected underground would stay there. In the earliest stage of the project, initiated under President George W. Bush, Greenberg and her colleagues sifted through geological records to find an appropriate test site. What they were seeking was similar to what oil drillers look for—porous stone capped by a layer of impermeable rock—only they were looking not to extract fossil fuels but, in a manner of speaking, to stuff them back in. The next step was locating a ready source of carbon dioxide. This is where ADM came in; the plant converts corn into ethanol, and one of the by-products of this process is almost pure CO_2. In a later stage of the project, during the Obama Administration, a million tons of carbon dioxide from the plant were pumped underground. Rigorous monitoring has shown that, so far, the CO_2 has stayed put.

We stopped to pick up hard hats and went to see some of the monitoring equipment, which was being serviced by two engineers, Nick Malkewicz and Jim Kirksey. It was now lunchtime, so we made another detour, to a local barbecue place. Finally, Greenberg and I and the two men got to the injection site. It was, indeed, not sexy—just a bunch of pipes and valves sticking out of the dirt. I asked about the future of carbon storage.

"I think the technology's there and it's absolutely viable," Malkewicz said. "It's just a question of whether people want to do it or not. It's kind of an obvious thing."

"We know we can meet the objective of storing CO_2," Greenberg added. "Like Nick said, it's just a matter of whether or not as a society we're going to do it."

When work began on the Decatur project, in 2003, few people besides Klaus Lackner were thinking about sucking CO_2 from the air. Instead, the goal was to demonstrate the feasibility of an only slightly less revolutionary technology—carbon capture and storage (or, as it is sometimes referred to, carbon capture and sequestration [CCS]).

With CCS, the CO_2 produced at a power station or a steel mill or a cement plant is drawn off before it has a chance to disperse into the atmosphere. (This is called "post-combustion capture.") The gas, under very high pressure, is then injected into the appropriate package of rock, where it is supposed to remain permanently. The process has become popularly—and euphemistically—known as "clean coal," because, if all goes according to plan, a plant equipped with CCS produces only a fraction of the emissions of a conventional coal-fired plant.

Over the years, both Republicans and Democrats have touted clean coal as a way to save mining jobs and protect the environment. The coal industry has also, nominally at least, embraced the technology; one industry-sponsored group calls itself the American Coalition for Clean Coal Electricity. Donald Trump, too, has talked up clean coal, even if he doesn't seem to quite understand what the term means. "We're going to have clean coal, really clean coal," he said in March.

Currently, only one power plant in the United States, the Petra Nova plant, near Houston, uses post-combustion carbon capture on a large scale. Plans for other plants to showcase the technology have been scrapped, including, most recently, the Kemper County plant, in Mississippi. This past June, the plant's owner, Southern Company, announced that it was changing tacks. Instead of burning coal and capturing the carbon, the plant would burn natural gas and release the CO_2.

Experts I spoke to said that the main reason CCS hasn't caught on is that there's no inducement to use it. Capturing the CO_2 from a smokestack consumes a lot of power—up to twenty-five per cent of the total produced at a typical coal-burning plant. And this, of course, translates into costs. What company is going to assume such costs when it can dump CO_2 into the air for free?

"If you're running a steel mill or a power plant and you're putting the CO_2 into the atmosphere, people might say, 'Why aren't you using carbon capture and storage?'" Howard Herzog, an engineer at M.I.T. who for many years ran a research program on CCS, told me. "And you say, 'What's my financial incentive? No one's saying I *can't* put it in the atmosphere.' In fact, we've gone backwards in terms of sending signals that you're going to have to restrict it."

But, although CCS has stalled in practice, it has become ever more essential on paper. Practically all below-two-degree warming scenarios assume that it will be widely deployed. And even this isn't enough. To avoid catastrophe, most models rely on a yet to be realized variation of CCS, known as BECCS.

BECCS, which stands for "bio-energy with carbon capture and storage," takes advantage of the original form of carbon engineering: photosynthesis. Trees and grasses and shrubs, as they grow, soak up CO_2 from the air. (Replanting forests is a low-tech form of carbon removal.) Later, when the plants rot or are combusted, the carbon they have absorbed is released back into the atmosphere. If a power station were to burn wood, say, or cornstalks, and use

CCS to sequester the resulting CO_2, this cycle would be broken. Carbon would be sucked from the air by the green plants and then forced underground. BECCS represents a way to generate negative emissions and, at the same time, electricity. The arrangement, at least as far as the models are concerned, could hardly be more convenient.

"BECCS is unique in that it removes carbon *and* produces energy," Glen Peters, a senior researcher at the Center for International Climate Research, in Oslo, told me. "So the more you consume the more you remove." He went on, "In a sense, it's a dream technology. It's solving one problem while solving the other problem. What more could you want?"

The Center for Carbon Removal doesn't really have an office; it operates out of a co-working space in downtown Oakland. On the day I visited, not long after my trip to Decatur, someone had recently stopped at Trader Joe's, and much of the center's limited real estate was taken up by tubs of treats.

"Open anything you want," the center's executive director, Noah Deich, urged me, with a wave of his hand.

Deich, who is thirty-one, has a broad face, a brown beard, and a knowing sort of earnestness. After graduating from the University of Virginia, in 2009, he went to work for a consulting firm in Washington, D.C., that was advising power companies about how to prepare for a time when they'd no longer be able to release carbon into the atmosphere cost-free. It was the start of the Obama Administration, and that time seemed imminent. The House of Representatives had recently approved legislation to limit emissions. But the bill later died in the Senate, and, as Deich put it, "It's no fun to model the impacts of climate policies nobody believes are going to happen." He switched consulting firms, then headed to business school, at the University of California, Berkeley.

"I came into school with this vision of working for a clean-tech startup," he told me. "But I also had this idea floating around in the back of my head that we're moving too slowly to actually stop emissions in time. So what do we do with all the carbon that's in the air?" He started talking to scientists and policy experts at Berkeley. What he learned shocked him.

"People told me, 'The models show this major need for negative emissions,'" he recalled. "'But we don't really know how to do that, nor is anyone really thinking about it.' I was someone who'd been in the business and policy world, and I was, like, wait a minute—*what*?"

Business school taught Deich to think in terms of case studies. One that seemed to him relevant was solar power. Photovoltaic cells have been around since the nineteen-fifties, but for decades they were prohibitively expensive. Then the price started to drop, which increased demand, which led to further price drops, to the point where today, in many parts of the world, the cost of solar power is competitive with the cost of power from new coal plants.

"And the reason that it's now competitive is that governments decided to do lots and lots of research," Deich said. "And some countries, like Germany, decided to pay a lot for solar, to create a first market. And China paid a lot to manufacture the stuff, and states in the U.S. said, 'You must consume renewable energy,' and then consumers said, 'Hey, how can I buy renewable energy?'"

As far as he could see, none of this—neither the research nor the creation of first markets nor the spurring of consumer demand—was being done for carbon removal, so he decided to try to change that. Together with a Berkeley undergraduate, Giana Amador, he founded the center in 2015, with a hundred-and-fifty-thousand-dollar grant from the university. It now has an annual budget of about a million dollars, raised from private donors and foundations, and a staff of seven. Deich described it as a "think-and-do tank."

"We're trying to figure out: how do we actually get this on the agenda?" he said.

A compelling reason for putting carbon removal on "the agenda" is that we are already counting on it. Negative emissions are built into the IPCC scenarios and the climate agreements that rest on them.

But everyone I spoke with, including the most fervent advocates for carbon removal, stressed the huge challenges of the work, some of them technological, others political and economic. Done on a scale significant enough to make a difference, direct air capture of the sort pursued by Carbon Engineering, in British Columbia, would require an enormous infrastructure, as well as huge supplies of power. (Because CO_2 is more dilute in the air than it is in the exhaust of a power plant, direct air capture demands even more energy than

CCS.) The power would have to be generated emissions-free, or the whole enterprise wouldn't make much sense.

"You might say it's against my self-interest to say it, but I think that, in the near term, talking about carbon removal is silly," David Keith, the founder of Carbon Engineering, who teaches energy and public policy at Harvard, told me. "Because it almost certainly is cheaper to cut emissions now than to do large-scale carbon removal."

BECCS doesn't make big energy demands; instead, it requires vast tracts of arable land. Much of this land would, presumably, have to be diverted from food production, and at a time when the global population—and therefore global food demand—is projected to be growing. (It's estimated that to do BECCS on the scale envisioned by some below-two-degrees scenarios would require an area larger than India.) Two researchers in Britain, Naomi Vaughan and Clair Gough, who recently conducted a workshop on BECCS, concluded that "assumptions regarding the extent of bioenergy deployment that is possible" are generally "unrealistic."

For these reasons, many experts argue that even talking (or writing articles) about negative emissions is dangerous. Such talk fosters the impression that it's possible to put off action and still avoid a crisis, when it is far more likely that continued inaction will just produce a larger crisis. In "The Trouble with Negative Emissions," an essay that ran last year in *Science*, Kevin Anderson, of the Tyndall Centre for Climate Change Research, in England, and Glen Peters, of the climate-research center in Oslo, described negative-emissions technologies as a "high-stakes gamble" and relying on them as a "moral hazard par excellence."

We should, they wrote, "proceed on the premise that they will not work at scale."

Others counter that the moment for fretting about the hazards of negative emissions—moral or otherwise—has passed.

"The punch line is, it doesn't matter," Julio Friedmann, the former Principal Deputy Assistant Energy Secretary, told me. "We actually need to do direct air capture, so we need to create technologies that do that. Whether it's smart or not, whether it's optimized or not, whether it's the lowest-cost pathway or not, we know we need to do it."

"If you tell me that we don't know whether our stuff will work, I will admit that is true," Klaus Lackner said. "But I also would argue that nobody else has a good option."

One of the peculiarities of climate discussions is that the strongest argument for any given strategy is usually based on the hopelessness of the alternatives: this approach *must* work, because clearly the others aren't going to. This sort of reasoning rests on a fragile premise—what might be called solution bias. There has to be an answer out there somewhere, since the contrary is too horrible to contemplate.

[In early October 2017], the Trump Administration announced its intention to repeal the Clean Power Plan, a set of rules aimed at cutting power plants' emissions. The plan, which had been approved by the Obama Administration, was eminently achievable. Still, according to the current Administration, the cuts were too onerous. The repeal of the plan is likely to result in hundreds of millions of tons of additional emissions.

A few weeks later, the United Nations Environment Programme released its annual Emissions Gap Report. The report labelled the difference between the emissions reductions needed to avoid dangerous climate change and those which countries have pledged to achieve as "alarmingly high." For the first time, this year's report contains a chapter on negative emissions. "In order to achieve the goals of the Paris Agreement," it notes, "carbon dioxide removal is likely a necessary step."

As a technology of last resort, carbon removal is, almost by its nature, paradoxical. It has become vital without necessarily being viable. It may be impossible to manage and it may also be impossible to manage without.

2017

Greta Thunberg

b. 2003

There is scarcely any debate now about how industrial emissions, especially of carbon dioxide, are warming the Earth's climate (see NASA's "Climate Change: How Do We Know?"). The UN's own International Panel on Climate Change (IPCC), which consists of hundreds of scientists from dozens of countries, sifted through thousands of scientific papers. In 2018, they issued a report predicting calamity if the Earth warms 1.5 degrees Celsius and projected that we are currently headed for an increase of more than 3 degrees Celsius. On September 23, 2019, the United Nations sponsored a "Climate Action Summit" at its headquarters in New York City and invited Greta Thunberg, a young activist from Sweden, to speak. Thunberg first rose to fame when she began picketing the Swedish parliament in August 2018; she urged students go on strike to force politicians to reduce global warming. Her one-woman protest went viral, amplifying Thunberg's message of anger and defiance. In this speech, Thunberg addresses the older generations who make public policy, such as U.S. president Donald Trump, who refuses to believe humans are responsible for global warming. (With great fanfare, President Trump withdrew the United States from its commitment to reduce carbon emissions expressed in the 2015 Paris Climate Agreement.) Trump attended the 2019 Summit, listened to speeches by Angela Merkel (of Germany) and Narendra Modi (of India), but did not stay to hear Thunberg. Asked what she would say to President Trump if they sat down together, Thunberg replied, "Honestly, I don't think I would have said anything because obviously he's not listening to scientists and experts, so why would he listen to me?" Many students have been listening: millions staged supportive strikes during the summit. World leaders also listen to Thunberg, who seems to emit a special ethos of moral clarity and authority, which media have dubbed "the Thunberg effect."

The World Is Waking Up

UN General Assembly
New York City, September 23, 2019

This is all wrong. I shouldn't be standing here.

I should be back in school on the other side of the ocean. Yet you all come to us young people for hope? How dare you!

You have taken away my dreams and my childhood with your empty words. And yet I'm one of the lucky ones.

People are suffering. People are dying. Entire ecosystems are collapsing. We are in the beginning of a mass extinction. And all you can talk about is money and fairy tales of eternal economic growth. How dare you!

For more than thirty years the science has been crystal clear. How dare you continue to look away, and come here saying that you are doing enough.

When the politics and solutions needed are still nowhere in sight.

You say you "hear" us and that you understand the urgency. But no matter how sad and angry I am, I don't want to believe that. Because if you fully understood the situation and still kept on failing to act, then you would be evil.

And I refuse to believe that.

The popular idea of cutting our emissions in half in ten years only gives us a 50 per cent chance of staying below 1.5°C and the risk of setting off irreversible chain reactions beyond human control.

Fifty per cent may be acceptable to you.

But since those numbers don't include tipping points, most feedback loops, additional warming hidden by toxic air pollution, nor the aspect of equity, then a 50 per cent risk is simply not acceptable to us, we who have to live with the consequences. We do not accept these odds.

To have a 67 per cent chance of staying below a 1.5°C global temperature rise, the best odds given by the IPCC, the world had 420 gigatons of CO_2 left to emit back on 1 January 2018.

Today, as you can see, that figure is already down to less than 350 gigatons. How dare you pretend that this can be solved with business as usual and some technical solutions!

With today's emission levels, that remaining CO_2 budget will be entirely gone within less than 8.5 years.

There will not be any solutions or plans presented in line with these figures today. Because these numbers are too uncomfortable. And you are still not mature enough to tell it like it is.

Your generation is failing us. But the young people are starting to understand your betrayal. The eyes of all future generations are upon you.

And if you choose to fail us I say we will never forgive you.

We will not let you get away with this. Right here, right now is where we draw the line.

The world is waking up.

And change is coming, whether you like it or not.

2019

With today's emission levels, that remaining CO_2 budget will be entirely gone within less than 8.5 years.

There will not be any solutions or plans presented in line with these figures today. Because these numbers are too uncomfortable. And you are still not mature enough to tell it like it is.

Your generation is failing us. But the young people are starting to understand your betrayal. The eyes of all future generations are upon you.

And if you choose to fail us then we will never forgive you.

We will not let you get away with this. Right here, right now is where we draw the line.

The world is waking up.

And change is coming, whether you like it or not.

CHAPTER 5

Democracy

Thomas Jefferson

1743–1826

In June 1776, the American colonies had been at war with England for a year. Congress had raised an army, put it in the field, and even published a declaration (also drafted by Jefferson) explaining the reasons for these drastic steps. The escalating conflict persuaded Congress to instruct Jefferson, John Adams, Benjamin Franklin, and two others to draft a second declaration, the Declaration of Independence, explaining why Americans felt compelled to separate themselves permanently from the king's jurisdiction. Harried by the more pressing business of running the new government and supplying the army, the other committee members left the job to Jefferson, who drafted this document. Adams and Franklin revised it slightly, and it was submitted to Congress, where it was again revised before being adopted on July 4, 1776. Loyalists attacked the argument by disputing the truth or importance of many of the grievances, but Congress didn't expect to persuade hostile readers to the cause of independence. The target audience was sympathetic Americans: Congress instructed that the document be published domestically, distributed to each state's legislature, and (perhaps most significantly) read publicly to the army. The opening paragraph must have been especially calculated to hearten dispirited soldiers by persuading them that they fought for a just cause and a place in history. Another important audience was Europe—the English, French, and Dutch, who might aid the cause, especially King Louis of France. Congress sent a copy to its ambassador in France and instructed him to present it to the French court and distribute it to other European governments. The Declaration of Independence has inspired many similar documents by peoples around the world struggling to win their right of self-rule from foreign, imperial governments.

The Declaration of Independence

IN CONGRESS, JULY 4, 1776
THE UNANIMOUS DECLARATION OF THE
THIRTEEN UNITED STATES OF AMERICA

When in the Course of human events it becomes necessary for one people to dissolve the political bands which have connected them with another, and to assume among the powers of the earth, the separate and equal station to which the Laws of Nature and of Nature's God entitle them, a decent respect to the opinions of mankind requires that they should declare the causes which impel them to the separation.

We hold these truths to be self-evident, that all men are created equal, that they are endowed by their Creator with certain unalienable Rights, that among these are Life, Liberty and the pursuit of Happiness. That to secure these rights, Governments are instituted among Men, deriving their just powers from the consent of the governed. That whenever any Form of Government becomes destructive of these ends, it is the Right of the People to alter or to abolish it, and to institute new Government, laying its foundation on such principles and organizing its powers in such form, as to them shall seem most likely to effect their Safety and Happiness. Prudence, indeed, will dictate that Governments long established should not be changed for light and transient causes; and accordingly all experience hath shewn that mankind are more disposed to suffer, while evils are sufferable, than to right themselves by abolishing the forms to which they are accustomed. But when a long train of abuses and usurpations, pursuing invariably the same Object evinces a design to reduce them under absolute Despotism, it is their right, it is their duty, to throw off such Government, and to provide new Guards for their future security. Such has been the patient sufferance of these Colonies; and such is now the necessity which constrains them to alter their former Systems of Government. The history of the present King of Great Britain is a history of repeated injuries and usurpations, all having in direct object the establishment of an absolute Tyranny over these States. To prove this, let Facts be submitted to a candid world.

He has refused his Assent to Laws, the most wholesome and necessary for the public good.

He has forbidden his Government to pass laws of immediate and pressing importance, unless suspended in their operation till his Assent should be obtained; and when so suspended, he has utterly neglected to attend to them.

He has refused to pass other Laws for the accommodation of large districts of people, unless those people would relinquish the right of Representation in the Legislature, a right inestimable to them and formidable to tyrants only.

He has called together legislative bodies at places unusual, uncomfortable, and distant from the depository of their Public Records, for the sole purpose of fatiguing them into compliance with his measures.

He has dissolved Representative Houses repeatedly, for opposing with manly firmness his invasions on the rights of the people.

He has refused for a long time, after such dissolutions, to cause others to be elected; whereby the Legislative Powers, incapable of Annihilation, have returned to the People at large for their exercise; the State remaining in the mean time exposed to all the dangers of invasion from without, and convulsions within.

He has endeavored to prevent the population of these States; for that purpose obstructing the Laws for Naturalization of Foreigners; refusing to pass others to encourage their migration hither, and raising the conditions of new Appropriations of Lands.

He has obstructed the Administration of Justice, by refusing his Assent to Laws for establishing Judiciary Powers.

He has made Judges dependent on his Will alone, for the tenure of their offices, and the amount and payment of their salaries.

He has erected a multitude of New Offices, and sent hither swarms of Officers to harass our people, and eat out their substance.

He has kept among us, in times of peace, Standing Armies without the Consent of our legislatures.

He has affected to render the Military independent of and superior to the Civil Power.

He has combined with others to subject us to a jurisdiction foreign to our constitution, and unacknowledged by our laws; giving his Assent to their Acts of pretended Legislation:

For quartering large bodies of armed troops among us:

For protecting them, by a mock Trial, from punishment for any Murders which they should commit on the Inhabitants of these States:

For cutting off our Trade with all parts of the world:

For imposing Taxes on us without our Consent:

For depriving us in many cases, of the benefits of Trial by Jury;

For transporting us beyond Seas to be tried for pretended offenses:

For abolishing the free System of English Laws in a neighboring Province, establishing therein an Arbitrary government, and enlarging its Boundaries so as to render it at once an example and fit instrument for introducing the same absolute rule into these Colonies:

For taking away our Charters, abolishing our most valuable Laws and altering fundamentally the Forms of our Governments:

For suspending our own Legislatures, and declaring themselves invested with power to legislate for us in all cases whatsoever.

He has abdicated Government here, by declaring us out of his Protection and waging War against us.

He has plundered our seas, ravaged our Coasts, burnt our towns, and destroyed the lives of our people.

He is at this time transporting large Armies of foreign Mercenaries to complete the works of death, desolation and tyranny, already begun with circumstances of Cruelty & Perfidy scarcely paralleled in the most barbarous ages, and totally unworthy of the Head of a civilized nation.

He has constrained our fellow Citizens taken Captive on the high Seas to bear Arms against their Country, to become the executioners of their friends and Brethren, or to fall themselves by their Hands.

He has excited domestic insurrections amongst us, and has endeavored to bring on the inhabitants of our frontiers, the merciless Indian Savages, whose known rule of warfare, is an undistinguished destruction of all ages, sexes, and conditions.

In every stage of these Oppressions We have Petitioned for Redress in the most humble terms: Our repeated Petitions have been answered only by repeated injury. A Prince, whose character is thus marked by every act which may define a Tyrant, is unfit to be the ruler of a free people.

Nor have We been wanting in attention to our British brethren. We have warned them from time to time of attempts by their legislature to extend an unwarrantable jurisdiction over us. We have reminded them of the circumstances of our emigration and settlement here. We have appealed to their native justice and magnanimity, and we have conjured them by the ties of our common kindred to disavow these usurpations, which would inevitably interrupt our connections and correspondence. They too have been deaf to the voice of justice and of consanguinity. We must, therefore, acquiesce in the necessity, which denounces our Separation, and hold them, as we hold the rest of mankind, Enemies in War, in Peace Friends.

We, THEREFORE the Representatives of the UNITED STATES OF AMERICA, in General Congress, Assembled, appealing to the Supreme Judge of the world for the rectitude of our intentions, do, in the Name, and by Authority of the good People of these Colonies, solemnly publish and declare, That these United Colonies are, and of Right ought to be FREE AND INDEPENDENT STATES; that they are Absolved from all Allegiance to the British Crown, and that all political connection between them and the State of Great Britain, is and ought to be totally dissolved; and that as Free and Independent States, they have full Power to levy War, conclude Peace, contract Alliances, establish Commerce, and to do all other Acts and Things which Independent States may of right do. And for the support of this Declaration, with a firm reliance on the protection of Divine Providence, we mutually pledge to each other our Lives, our Fortunes, and our sacred Honor.

1776

Elizabeth Cady Stanton
1815–1902

In 1848, Stanton, Lucretia Mott, and three other women organized the first woman's rights convention in the small, upstate New York town of Seneca Falls, where Stanton lived. They announced it only in a local newspaper, but over three hundred people attended, many of whom were already leaders in the abolitionist movement, such as Frederick Douglass and Mott's husband, James. The five organizers drafted this declaration, paraphrasing Jefferson's Declaration of Independence, and Stanton read it aloud. The convention adopted the declaration. Each of the resolutions passed unanimously, except for the claim to a woman's right to vote, which passed by only a small margin. A hundred attendees signed the document (thirty-two of these were men). The declaration, like its model, addresses a "candid world," but its main target was women discontented with their second-class status in American society. Stanton indicated her purpose when she addressed the convention: "I should feel exceedingly diffident to appear before you at this time, having never before spoken in public, were I not nerved by a sense of right and duty, did I not feel that the time had come for the question of woman's wrongs to be laid before the public, did I not believe that woman herself must do this work." The Seneca Falls convention and the declaration that came from it served as the rallying cry for the nascent women's movement.

Declaration of Sentiments and Resolutions

When, in the course of human events, it becomes necessary for one portion of the family of man to assume among the people of the earth a position different from that which they have hitherto occupied, but one to which the laws of nature and of nature's God entitle them, a decent respect to the opinions of mankind requires that they should declare the causes that impel them to such a course.

We hold these truths to be self-evident: that all men and women are created equal; that they are endowed by their Creator with certain inalienable rights; that among these are life, liberty, and the pursuit of happiness; that to secure these rights governments are instituted, deriving their just powers from the consent of the governed. Whenever any form of government becomes destructive of these ends, it is the right of those who suffer from it to refuse allegiance to it, and to insist upon the institution of a new government, laying its foundation on such principles, and organizing its powers in such form, as to them shall seem most likely to effect their safety and happiness. Prudence indeed, will dictate that governments long established should not be changed for light and transient causes; and accordingly all experience hath shown that mankind are more disposed to suffer, while evils are sufferable, than to right themselves by abolishing the forms to which they were accustomed. But when a long train of abuses and usurpations, pursuing invariably the same object evinces a design to reduce them under absolute despotism, it is their duty to throw off such government, and to provide new guards for their future security. Such has been the patient sufferance of the women under this government, and such is now the necessity which constrains them to demand the equal station to which they are entitled.

The history of mankind is a history of repeated injuries and usurpations on the part of man toward woman, having in direct object the establishment of an absolute tyranny over her. To prove this, let facts be submitted to a candid world.

He has never permitted her to exercise her inalienable right to the elective franchise.

He has compelled her to submit to laws, in the formation of which she had no voice.

He has withheld from her rights which are given to the most ignorant and degraded men—both natives and foreigners.

Having deprived her of this first right of a citizen, the elective franchise, thereby leaving her without representation in the halls of legislation, he has oppressed her on all sides.

He has made her, if married, in the eye of the law, civilly dead.

He has taken from her all right in property, even to the wages she earns.

He has made her, morally, an irresponsible being, as she can commit many crimes with impunity, provided they be done in the presence of her husband. In the covenant of marriage, she is compelled to promise obedience to her husband, he becoming, to all intents and purposes, her master—the law giving him power to deprive her of her liberty, and to administer chastisement.

He has so framed the laws of divorce, as to what shall be the proper causes, and in case of separation, to whom the guardianship of the children shall be given, as to be wholly regardless of the happiness of women—the law, in all cases, going upon a false supposition of the supremacy of man, and giving all power into his hands.

After depriving her of all rights as a married woman, if single, and the owner of property, he has taxed her to support a government which recognizes her only when her property can be made profitable to it.

He has monopolized nearly all the profitable employments, and from those she is permitted to follow, she receives but a scanty remuneration. He closes against her all the avenues to wealth and distinction which he considers most honorable to himself. As a teacher of theology, medicine, or law, she is not known.

He has denied her the facilities for obtaining a thorough education, all colleges being closed against her.

He allows her in Church, as well as State, but a subordinate position, claiming Apostolic authority for her exclusion from the ministry, and, with some exceptions, from any public participation in the affairs of the Church.

He has created a false public sentiment by giving to the world a different code of morals for men and women, by which moral delinquencies which exclude women from society, are not only tolerated, but deemed of little account in man.

He has usurped the prerogative of Jehovah himself, claiming it as his right to assign for her a sphere of action, when that belongs to her conscience and to her God.

He has endeavored, in every way that he could, to destroy her confidence in her own powers, to lessen her self-respect, and to make her willing to lead a dependent and abject life.

Now, in view of this entire disfranchisement of one-half the people of this country, their social and religious degradation—in view of the unjust laws above mentioned, and because women do feel themselves aggrieved, oppressed, and fraudulently deprived of their most sacred rights, we insist that they have immediate admission to all the rights and privileges which belong to them as citizens of the United States.

In entering upon the great work before us, we anticipate no small amount of misconception, misrepresentation, and ridicule; but we shall use every instrumentality within our power to effect our object. We shall employ agents, circulate tracts, petition the State and National legislatures, and endeavor to enlist the pulpit and the press in our behalf. We hope this Convention will be followed by a series of Conventions embracing every part of the country.

1848

Abraham Lincoln

1809–1865

Lincoln was elected to the presidency in November 1860, and in the four months between the election and his inauguration, on March 4, 1861, six of the states that eventually made up the Confederacy followed South Carolina's lead into secession. Lame-duck president Buchanan did little to stop these states from taking over federal property—including forts, weapons, and the like. On the first day of the new administration, the entire nation—North and South—eagerly awaited Lincoln's inaugural address, for no one knew whether the new president would determinedly resist secession or resignedly accept it. When newspapers printed it, Lincoln's address was (in the words of his biographer, Carl Sandburg) "the most widely read and closely scrutinized utterance that had ever come from an American president." His speech had two distinct purposes: to persuade moderate Southerners that he would not threaten their constitutional right to own slaves and to persuade moderate Northerners that they should, if need be, preserve the Union by force of arms. Die-hard secessionists he could persuade of nothing; and he had no need to persuade militant Unionists. Lincoln's resolve probably helped persuade hundreds of thousands of Northerners to join the army when South Carolina bombarded Fort Sumter (April 14, 1861). Some border states—Missouri, Delaware, and Kentucky—never seceded. But Lincoln's first inaugural address was not enough to persuade North Carolina, Arkansas, Virginia, and Tennessee against joining the Confederacy.

The ensuing war was far more terrible than anyone had expected. (Eventually, more Americans would die in the Civil War than all other American wars combined.) After two years of disappointing battles, the Union won a decisive victory at Gettysburg, Pennsylvania. The Confederate army that had invaded the North was turned back. Even so, the outcome of the war was still in doubt, largely because it was not clear whether the North had the resolve to see it through to its bloody conclusion. In the 1864 election, for example, Lincoln would face considerable opposition from General George McClellan, who essentially promised to end the war by allowing the South to secede. Lincoln delivered his Gettysburg Address during a ceremony dedicating a cemetery at the Gettysburg battlefield. It was widely distributed by newspapers throughout the North.

First Inaugural Address

Fellow-citizens of the United States:

In compliance with a custom as old as the government itself, I appear before you to address you briefly, and to take, in your presence, the oath prescribed by the Constitution of the United States, to be taken by the President "before he enters on the execution of his office."

I do not consider it necessary at present for me to discuss those matters of administration about which there is no special anxiety or excitement.

Apprehension seems to exist among the people of the Southern States, that by the accession of a Republican Administration, their property, and their peace, and personal security, are to be endangered. There has never been any reasonable cause for such apprehension. Indeed, the most ample evidence to the contrary has all the while existed, and been open to their inspection. It is found in nearly all the published speeches of him who now addresses you. I do but quote from one of those speeches when I declare that "I have no purpose, directly or indirectly, to interfere with the institution of slavery in the States where it exists. I believe I have no lawful right to do so, and I have no inclination to do so." Those who nominated and elected me did so with full knowledge that I had made this, and many similar declarations, and had never recanted them. And more than this, they placed in the platform, for my acceptance, and as a law to themselves, and to me, the clear and emphatic resolution which I now read:

"*Resolved*, That the maintenance inviolate of the rights of the States, and especially the right of each State to order and control its own domestic institutions according to its own judgment exclusively, is essential to that balance of power on which the perfection and endurance of our political fabric depend; and we denounce the lawless invasion by armed force of the soil of any State or Territory, no matter under what pretext, as among the gravest of crimes."

I now reiterate these sentiments: and in doing so, I only press upon the public attention the most conclusive evidence of which the case is susceptible, that the property, peace and security of no section are to be in any wise endangered by the now incoming Administration. I add too, that all the protection which, consistently with the Constitution and the laws, can be given, will be cheerfully given to all the States when lawfully demanded, for whatever cause—as cheerfully to one section as to another.

There is much controversy about the delivering up of fugitives from service or labor.[1] The clause I now read is as plainly written in the Constitution as any other of its provisions:

"No person held to service or labor in one State, under the laws thereof, escaping into another, shall, in consequence of any law or regulation therein, be discharged from such service or labor, but shall be delivered up on claim of the party to whom such service or labor may be due."

It is scarcely questioned that this provision was intended by those who made it, for the reclaiming of what we call fugitive slaves; and the intention of the law-giver is the law. All members of Congress swear their support to the whole Constitution—to this provision as

1. Northerners refused openly or contrived to violate the clause of the Constitution Lincoln quotes here. [All notes are the editor's.]

much as to any other. To the proposition, then, that slaves whose cases come within the terms of this clause, "shall be delivered up," their oaths are unanimous. Now, if they would make the effort in good temper, could they not, with nearly equal unanimity, frame and pass a law, by means of which to keep good that unanimous oath?

There is some difference of opinion whether this clause should be enforced by national or by state authority; but surely that difference is not a very material one. If the slave is to be surrendered, it can be of but little consequence to him, or to others, by which authority it is done. And should any one, in any case, be content that his oath shall go unkept, on a merely unsubstantial controversy as to *how* it shall be kept?

Again, in any law upon this subject, ought not all the safeguards of liberty known in civilized and humane jurisprudence to be introduced, so that a free man be not, in any case, surrendered as a slave?[2] And might it not be well, at the same time to provide by law for the enforcement of that clause in the Constitution which guarantees that "the citizens of each State shall be entitled to all privileges and immunities of citizens in the several States"?

I take the official oath to-day, with no mental reservations, and with no purpose to construe the Constitution or laws, by any hypercritical rules. And while I do not choose now to specify particular acts of Congress as proper to be enforced, I do suggest that it will be much safer for all, both in official and private stations, to conform to, and abide by, all those acts which stand unrepealed, than to violate any of them, trusting to find impunity in having them held to be unconstitutional.

It is seventy-two years since the first inauguration of a President under our national Constitution. During that period fifteen different and greatly distinguished citizens, have, in succession, administered the executive branch of the government. They have conducted it through many perils; and, generally, with great success. Yet, with all this scope for precedent, I now enter upon the same task for the brief constitutional term of four years, under great and peculiar difficulty.

2. Free Black people living in the North were often kidnapped and sold into slavery by Southern bounty hunters. Southern states refused to treat such people as citizens.

A disruption of the Federal Union, heretofore only menaced, is now formidably attempted.

I hold, that in contemplation of universal law, and of the Constitution, the Union of these States is perpetual. Perpetuity is implied, if not expressed, in the fundamental law of all national governments. It is safe to assert that no government proper, ever had a provision in its organic law for its own termination. Continue to execute all the express provisions of our national Constitution, and the Union will endure forever—it being impossible to destroy it, except by some action not provided for in the instrument itself.

Again, if the United States be not a government proper, but an association of States in the nature of contract merely, can it, as a contract, be peaceably unmade, by less than all the parties who made it? One party to a contract may violate it—break it, so to speak; but does it not require all to lawfully rescind it?

Descending from these general principles, we find the proposition that, in legal contemplation, the Union is perpetual, confirmed by the history of the Union itself. The Union is much older than the Constitution. It was formed in fact, by the Articles of Association in 1774. It was matured and continued by the Declaration of Independence in 1776. It was further matured and the faith of all the then thirteen States expressly plighted and engaged that it should be perpetual, by the Articles of Confederation in 1778. And finally, in 1787, one of the declared objects for ordaining and establishing the Constitution, was "*to form a more perfect Union.*"

But if destruction of the Union, by one, or by a part only, of the States, be lawfully possible, the Union is *less* perfect than before the Constitution, having lost the vital element of perpetuity.

It follows from these views that no State, upon its own mere motion, can lawfully get out of the Union,—that *resolves* and *ordinances* to that effect are legally void, and that acts of violence, within any State or States, against the authority of the United States, are insurrectionary or revolutionary, according to circumstances.

I therefore consider that in view of the Constitution and the laws, the Union is unbroken; and to the extent of my ability I shall take care, as the Constitution itself expressly enjoins upon me, that the laws of the Union be faithfully executed in all the States. Doing this

I deem to be only a simple duty on my part; and I shall perform it, so far as practicable, unless my rightful masters, the American people, shall withhold the requisite means, or, in some authoritative manner, direct the contrary. I trust this will not be regarded as a menace, but only as the declared purpose of the Union that it will constitutionally defend and maintain itself.

In doing this there needs to be no bloodshed or violence; and there shall be none, unless it be forced upon the national authority. The power confided to me will be used to hold, occupy, and possess the property and places belonging to the government, and to collect the duties and imposts; but beyond what may be necessary for these objects, there will be no invasion—no using of force against or among the people anywhere. Where hostility to the United States, in any interior locality, shall be so great and so universal, as to prevent competent resident citizens from holding the Federal offices, there will be no attempt to force obnoxious strangers among the people for that object. While the strict legal right may exist in the government to enforce the exercise of these offices, the attempt to do so would be so irritating, and so nearly impracticable with all, that I deem it better to forego, for the time, the uses of such offices.

The mails, unless repelled, will continue to be furnished in all parts of the Union. So far as possible, the people everywhere shall have that sense of perfect security which is most favorable to calm thought and reflection. The course here indicated will be followed, unless current events and experience shall show a modification or change to be proper; and in every case and exigency my best discretion will be exercised according to circumstances actually existing, and with a view and a hope of a peaceful solution of the national troubles, and the restoration of fraternal sympathies and affections.

That there are persons in one section or another who seek to destroy the Union at all events, and are glad of any pretext to do it, I will neither affirm or deny; but if there be such, I need address no word to them. To those, however, who really love the Union, may I not speak?

Before entering upon so grave a matter as the destruction of our national fabric, with all its benefits, its memories and its hopes, would it not be wise to ascertain precisely why we do it? Will you hazard so desperate a step, while there is any possibility that any portion of the ills you fly from have no real existence? Will you, while the certain ills you fly to, are greater than all the real ones you fly from? Will you risk the commission of so fearful a mistake?

All profess to be content in the Union, if all constitutional rights can be maintained. Is it true, then, that any right, plainly written in the Constitution, has been denied? I think not. Happily the human mind is so constituted, that no party can reach to the audacity of doing this. Think, if you can, of a single instance in which a plainly written provision of the Constitution has ever been denied. If, by the mere force of numbers, a majority should deprive a minority of any clearly written constitutional right, it might, in a moral point of view, justify revolution—certainly would, if such a right were a vital one. But such is not our case. All the vital rights of minorities, and of individuals, are so plainly assured to them, by affirmations and negations, guarantees and prohibitions, in the Constitution, that controversies never arise concerning them. But no organic law can ever be framed with a provision specifically applicable to every question which may occur in practical administration. No foresight can anticipate, nor any document of reasonable length contain express provisions for all possible questions. Shall fugitives from labor be surrendered by national or by State authority? The Constitution does not expressly say. *May* Congress prohibit slavery in the territories? The Constitution does not expressly say. *Must* Congress protect slavery in the territories? The Constitution does not expressly say.[3]

From questions of this class spring all our constitutional controversies, and we divide upon them into majorities and minorities. If the minority will not acquiesce, the majority must, or the government must cease. There is no other alternative; for continuing the government, is acquiescence on one side or the other. If a minority, in such case, will secede rather than acquiesce, they make a precedent which, in turn, will divide and ruin them; for a minority of their own will secede from them whenever a majority refuses to be controlled

3. Whether to expand or prohibit slavery in the western territories was debated by Northern and Southern Congressmen.

by such minority. For instance, why may not any portion of a new confederacy, a year or two hence, arbitrarily secede again, precisely as portions of the present Union now claim to secede from it? All who cherish disunion sentiments, are now being educated to the exact temper of doing this.

Is there such perfect identity of interests among the States to compose a new Union, as to produce harmony only, and prevent renewed secession?

Plainly, the central idea of secession, is the essence of anarchy. A majority, held in restraint by constitutional checks and limitations, and always changing easily with deliberate changes of popular opinions and sentiments is the only true sovereign of a free people. Whoever rejects it, does, of necessity, fly to anarchy or to despotism. Unanimity is impossible; the rule of a minority, as a permanent arrangement, is wholly inadmissible; so that, rejecting the majority principle, anarchy or despotism in some form is all that is left.

I do not forget the position assumed by some, that constitutional questions are to be decided by the Supreme Court; nor do I deny that such decisions must be binding in any case, upon the parties to a suit, as to the object of that suit, while they are also entitled to very high respect and consideration in all parallel cases by all other departments of the government. And while it is obviously possible that such decision may be erroneous in any given case, still the evil effect following it, being limited to that particular case, with the chance that it may be over-ruled, and never become a precedent for other cases, can better be borne than could the evils of a different practice. At the same time, the candid citizen must confess that if the policy of the government upon vital questions, affecting the whole people, is to be irrevocably fixed by decisions of the Supreme Court, the instant they are made, in ordinary litigation between parties, in personal actions, the people will have ceased to be their own rulers, having to that extent practically resigned their government into the hands of that eminent tribunal. Nor is there in this view any assault upon the court or the judges. It is a duty from which they may not shrink, to decide cases properly brought before them; and it is no fault of theirs if others seek to turn their decisions to political purposes.

One section of our country believes slavery is *right*, and ought to be extended, while the other believes it is *wrong*, and ought not to be extended. This is the only substantial dispute. The fugitive slave clause of the Constitution, and the law for the suppression of the foreign slave trade, are each as well enforced, perhaps, as any law can ever be in a community where the moral sense of the people imperfectly supports the law itself. The great body of the people abide by the dry legal obligation in both cases, and a few break over in each. This, I think, cannot be perfectly cured; and it would be worse in both cases *after* the separation of the sections, than before. The foreign slave trade, now imperfectly suppressed, would be ultimately revived without restriction, in one section;[4] while fugitive slaves, now only partially surrendered, would not be surrendered at all, by the other.

Physically speaking, we cannot separate. We cannot remove our respective sections from each other, nor build an impassable wall between them. A husband and wife may be divorced, and go out of the presence, and beyond the reach of each other; but the different parts of our country cannot do this. They cannot but remain face to face; and intercourse, either amicable or hostile, must continue between them. Is it possible, then, to make that intercourse more advantageous or more satisfactory, *after* separation than *before*? Can aliens make treaties easier than friends can make laws? Can treaties be more faithfully enforced between aliens than laws can among friends? Suppose you go to war, you cannot fight always; and when, after much loss on both sides, and no gain on either, you cease fighting, the identical old questions, as to terms of intercourse, are again upon you.

This country, with its institutions, belongs to the people who inhabit it. Whenever they shall grow weary of the existing government, they can exercise their *constitutional* right of amending it, or their *revolutionary* right to dismember or overthrow it. I cannot be ignorant of the fact that many worthy and patriotic citizens are desirous of having the national Constitution amended. While I make no recommendation of amendments, I fully recognize the rightful

4. In 1808, as sanctioned by the Constitution, Congress banned the foreign slave trade.

authority of the people over the whole subject to be exercised in either of the modes prescribed in the instrument itself; and I should under existing circumstances favor rather than oppose a fair opportunity being afforded the people to act upon it.

I will venture to add that to me the Convention mode seems preferable, in that it allows amendments to originate with the people themselves, instead of only permitting them to take or reject propositions, originated by others, not especially chosen for the purpose, and which might not be precisely such as they would wish to either accept or refuse. I understand a proposed amendment to the Constitution, which amendment, however, I have not seen, has passed Congress, to the effect that the federal government shall never interfere with the domestic institutions of the States, including that of persons held to service. To avoid misconstruction of what I have said, I depart from my purpose not to speak of particular amendments, so far as to say that holding such a provision to now be implied constitutional law, I have no objection to its being made express and irrevocable.

The Chief Magistrate derives all his authority from the people, and they have conferred none upon him to fix terms for the separation of the States. The people themselves can do this also if they choose; but the executive, as such, has nothing to do with it. His duty is to administer the present government, as it came to his hands, and to transmit it, unimpaired by him, to his successor.

Why should there not be a patient confidence in the ultimate justice of the people? Is there any better or equal hope, in the world? In our present differences, is either party without faith of being in the right? If the Almighty Ruler of nations, with his eternal truth and justice, be on your side of the North or on yours of the South, that truth, and that justice, will surely prevail, by the judgment of this great tribunal, the American people.

By the frame of the government under which we live, this same people have wisely given their public servants but little power for mischief; and have, with equal wisdom, provided for the return of that little to their own hands at very short intervals.

While the people retain their virtue and vigilance, no administration, by any extreme of wickedness or folly, can very seriously injure the government in the short space of four years.

My countrymen, one and all, think calmly and *well*, upon this whole subject. Nothing valuable can be lost by taking time. If there be an object to *hurry* any of you, in hot haste, to a step which you would never take *deliberately*, that object will be frustrated by taking time; but no good object can be frustrated by it. Such of you as are now dissatisfied, still have the old Constitution unimpaired, and, on the sensitive point, the laws of your own framing under it; while the new administration will have no immediate power, if it would, to change either. If it were admitted that you who are dissatisfied, hold the right side in the dispute, there still is no single good reason for precipitate action. Intelligence, patriotism, Christianity, and a firm reliance on Him, who has never yet forsaken this favored land, are still competent to adjust, in the best way, all our present difficulty.

In *your* hands, my dissatisfied fellow countrymen, and not in *mine*, is the momentous issue of civil war. The government will not assail *you*. You can have no conflict, without being yourselves the aggressors. *You* have no oath registered in Heaven to destroy the government, while *I* shall have the most solemn one to "preserve, protect and defend" it.

I am loth to close. We are not enemies, but friends. We must not be enemies. Though passion may have strained, it must not break our bonds of affection. The mystic chords of memory, stretching from every battle-field, and patriot grave, to every living heart and hearth-stone, all over this broad land, will yet swell the chorus of the Union, when again touched, as surely they will be, by the better angels of our nature.

1861

Malcolm X

1925–1965

The career of Malcolm X paralleled Martin Luther King Jr.'s. Both sought racial justice but by different means. King, leader of the Southern Christian Leadership Conference, advocated nonviolent civil disobedience (see "Letter from Birmingham Jail"), which asked its practitioners to meet violence by following Jesus' instructions to "turn the other cheek." By contrast, the Nation of Islam taught its members to meet violence with violence. Less than a month before he gave this speech, Malcolm X split from Elijah Muhammad and the Nation of Islam, and parts of this speech address the evolution of his thinking about Black nationalism.

Malcolm X's fame for oratory rivaled King's, though the two men approached ethos very differently. Malcolm X was an ex-convict; he was educated—and converted to Islam—in prison. Do not be fooled by the humble and colloquial style of language in this speech. The arguments presented here develop along classical lines, and you can trace the valid logic of several deductive arguments—including constitutional arguments—and evaluate their premises as you would Thomas Jefferson's. As you think about those premises, remember that Malcolm X cared little about white people eavesdropping on his speeches. He spoke as a Black man to Black audiences, which allowed for common ground unavailable to someone, like King, who was trying to persuade white people, too.

This essay could go in the chapter on Social Justice alongside King's "Letter," but I put it here because it addresses the nuts and bolts of American democracy—voter suppression, how political parties work, the filibuster, etc. You should read it alongside Doris Kearns Goodwin's essay on how Lyndon Baines Johnson got the Civil Rights Act through Congress in 1964. In retrospect, we know that Congressmen from Southern states (the so-called Dixiecrats) failed to derail that bill; but in April 1964, when Malcolm X delivered this speech in many cities around the country, its fate was hardly assured. In fact, practically no one thought it would pass. Eighteen Southern senators began their filibuster to prevent the bill from coming to a vote just four days before Malcolm X gave this version of his speech in Cleveland.

Less than a year after Malcolm X delivered this speech, three members of the Nation of Islam assassinated him in New York City.

The Ballot or the Bullet

Mr. Moderator, Brother Lomax,[1] brothers and sisters, friends and enemies: I just can't believe everyone in here is a friend and I don't want to leave anybody out. The question tonight, as I understand it, is "The Negro Revolt, and Where Do We Go From Here?" or "What Next?" In my little humble way of understanding it, it points toward either the ballot or the bullet.

Before we try and explain what is meant by the ballot or the bullet, I would like to clarify something concerning myself. I'm still a Muslim, my religion is still Islam. That's my personal belief. Just as Adam Clayton Powell is a Christian minister who heads the Abyssinian Baptist Church in New York, but at the same time takes part in the political struggles to try and bring about rights to the black people in this country; and Dr. Martin Luther King is a Christian minister down in Atlanta, Georgia, who heads another organization fighting for the civil rights of black people in this country; and Rev. Galamison, I guess you've heard of him, is another Christian minister in New York who has been deeply involved in the school boycotts to eliminate segregated education; well, I myself am a minister, not a Christian minister, but a Muslim minister; and I believe in action on all fronts by whatever means necessary.

Although I'm still a Muslim, I'm not here tonight to discuss my religion. I'm not here to try and change your religion. I'm not here to argue or discuss anything that we differ about, because it's time for us to submerge our differences and realize that it is best for us to first see that we have the same problem, a common problem—a problem

1. Louis Lomax (1922–1970) was a journalist and supporter of the Congress of Racial Equality (CORE), the Southern Christian Leadership Conference (SCLC), and the Student Nonviolent Coordinating Committee (SNCC). In 1961, Lomax teamed up with Mike Wallace to produce a five-part exposé of the Nation of Islam, which aired on *60 Minutes* under the title, "The Hate that Hate Produced." His speech preceded Malcolm X's at this event, praising the nonviolent approach to civil rights activism. [All notes are the editor's.]

that will make you catch hell whether you're a Baptist, or a Methodist, or a Muslim, or a nationalist. Whether you're educated or illiterate, whether you live on the boulevard or in the alley, you're going to catch hell just like I am. We're all in the same boat and we all are going to catch the same hell from the same man. He just happens to be a white man. All of us have suffered here, in this country, political oppression at the hands of the white man, economic exploitation at the hands of the white man, and social degradation at the hands of the white man.

Now in speaking like this, it doesn't mean that we're anti-white, but it does mean we're anti-exploitation, we're anti-degradation, we're anti-oppression. And if the white man doesn't want us to be anti-him, let him stop oppressing and exploiting and degrading us. Whether we are Christians or Muslims or nationalists or agnostics or atheists, we must first learn to forget our differences. If we have differences, let us differ in the closet; when we come out in front, let us not have anything to argue about until we get finished arguing with the man. If the late President Kennedy could get together with Khrushchev and exchange some wheat, we certainly have more in common with each other than Kennedy and Khrushchev had with each other.[2]

If we don't do something real soon, I think you'll have to agree that we're going to be forced either to use the ballot or the bullet. It's one or the other in 1964. It isn't that time is running out—time has run out! [The year] 1964 threatens to be the most explosive year America has ever witnessed. The most explosive year. Why? It's also a political year. It's the year when all of the white politicians will be back in the so-called Negro community jiving you and me for some votes. The year when all of the white political crooks will be right back in your and my community with their false promises, building up our hopes for a letdown, with their trickery and their treachery, with their false promises which they don't intend to keep. As they nourish these dissatisfactions, it can only lead to one thing, an explosion; and now we have the type of black man on the scene in America today—I'm sorry, Brother Lomax—who just doesn't intend to turn the other cheek any longer.

2. On October 9, 1963, President John F. Kennedy announced that Nikita Khrushchev, premier of the USSR, had agreed to buy millions of tons of U.S. wheat, a gesture regarded by both sides as mitigating the rival nations' enmity.

Don't let anybody tell you anything about the odds are against you. If they draft you, they send you to Korea and make you face 800 million Chinese. If you can be brave over there, you can be brave right here. These odds aren't as great as those odds. And if you fight here, you will at least know what you're fighting for.[3]

I'm not a politician, not even a student of politics; in fact, I'm not a student of much of anything. I'm not a Democrat, I'm not a Republican, and I don't even consider myself an American. If you and I were Americans, there'd be no problem. Those Hunkies[4] that just got off the boat, they're already Americans; Polacks are already Americans; the Italian refugees are already Americans. Everything that came out of Europe, every blue-eyed thing, is already an American. And as long as you and I have been over here, we aren't Americans yet.

Well, I am one who doesn't believe in deluding myself. I'm not going to sit at your table and watch you eat, with nothing on my plate, and call myself a diner. Sitting at the table doesn't make you a diner, unless you eat some of what's on that plate. Being here in America doesn't make you an American. Being born here in America doesn't make you an American. Why, if birth made you American, you wouldn't need any legislation, you wouldn't need any amendments to the Constitution, you wouldn't be faced with civil-rights filibustering in Washington, D.C., right now. They don't have to pass civil-rights legislation to make a Polack an American.

No, I'm not an American. I'm one of the 22 million black people who are the victims of Americanism. One of the 22 million black people who are the victims of democracy, nothing but disguised hypocrisy. So, I'm not standing here speaking to you as an American, or a patriot, or a flag-saluter, or a flag-waver—no, not I. I'm speaking as a victim of this American system. And I see America through the eyes of the victim. I don't see any American dream; I see an American nightmare.

3. The Korean War (1950–1953) began when the communist northern part of the country invaded the capitalist southern part. The United Nations (led by the United States) intervened for the South, while the Chinese helped the North. More than 3 million people died in the war, including at least 36,000 American soldiers; more than 600,000 African Americans fought in the war.

4. Hunkies: a derogatory term for immigrants from central European countries like Hungary and Slovakia who settled especially in the coal country of western Pennsylvania and West Virginia.

These 22 million victims are waking up. Their eyes are coming open. They're beginning to see what they used to only look at. They're becoming politically mature. They are realizing that there are new political trends from coast to coast. As they see these new political trends, it's possible for them to see that every time there's an election, the races are so close that they have to have a recount. They had to recount in Massachusetts to see who was going to be governor, it was so close. It was the same way in Rhode Island, in Minnesota, and in many other parts of the country. And the same with Kennedy and Nixon when they ran for president. It was so close they had to count all over again. Well, what does this mean? It means that when white people are evenly divided, and black people have a bloc of votes of their own, it is left up to them to determine who's going to sit in the White House and who's going to be in the dog house.

It was the black man's vote that put the present administration in Washington, D.C. Your vote, your dumb vote, your ignorant vote, your wasted vote put in an administration in Washington, D.C., that has seen fit to pass every kind of legislation imaginable, saving you until last, then filibustering on top of that. And your and my leaders have the audacity to run around clapping their hands and talk about how much progress we're making. And what a good president we have. If he wasn't good in Texas, he sure can't be good in Washington, D.C. Because Texas is a lynch state. It is in the same breath as Mississippi, no different; only they lynch you in Texas with a Texas accent and lynch you in Mississippi with a Mississippi accent. And these Negro leaders have the audacity to go and have some coffee in the White House with a Texan, a Southern cracker—that's all he is—and then come out and tell you and me that he's going to be better for us because, since he's from the South, he knows how to deal with the Southerners. What kind of logic is that? Let Eastland be president, he's from the South too. He should be better able to deal with them than Johnson.[5]

5. Lyndon Baines Johnson (1908–1973), Texas congressman and vice president who became president of the United States when John F. Kennedy was assassinated on November 22, 1963. James Oliver Eastland (1904–1986) was a senator from Mississippi and chair of the Senate Judiciary Committee, where he killed all civil rights bills. He had to be bypassed via arcane parliamentary procedure to get the 1964 Civil Rights Act to the Senate floor. Richard Russell (1897–1971) was a U.S. senator from Georgia who coauthored (with Senator Strom Thurmond of South Carolina) the notorious 1954 Declaration of Constitutional Principles (or Southern Manifesto), which argued against the racial integration of public places, including schools.

In this present administration they have in the House of Representatives 257 Democrats to only 177 Republicans. They control two-thirds of the House vote. Why can't they pass something that will help you and me? In the Senate, there are 67 senators who are of the Democratic Party. Only 33 of them are Republicans. Why, the Democrats have got the government sewed up, and you're the one who sewed it up for them. And what have they given you for it? Four years in office, and just now getting around to some civil-rights legislation. Just now, after everything else is gone, out of the way, they're going to sit down now and play with you all summer long—the same old giant con game that they call filibuster. All those are in cahoots together. Don't you ever think they're not in cahoots together, for the man that is heading the civil-rights filibuster is a man from Georgia named Richard Russell. When Johnson became president, the first man he asked for when he got back to Washington, D.C., was "Dicky"—that's how tight they are. That's his boy, that's his pal, that's his buddy. But they're playing that old con game. One of them makes believe he's for you, and he's got it fixed where the other one is so tight against you, he never has to keep his promise.

So it's time in 1964 to wake up. And when you see them coming up with that kind of conspiracy, let them know your eyes are open. And let them know you got something else that's wide open too. It's got to be the ballot or the bullet. The ballot or the bullet. If you're afraid to use an expression like that, you should get on out of the country, you should get back in the cotton patch, you should get back in the alley. They get all the Negro vote, and after they get it, the Negro gets nothing in return. All they did when they got to Washington was give a few big Negroes big jobs. Those big Negroes didn't need big jobs, they already had jobs. That's camouflage, that's trickery, that's treachery, window dressing. I'm not trying to knock out the Democrats for the Republicans, we'll get to them in a minute. But it is true—you put the Democrats first and the Democrats put you last.

Look at it the way it is. What alibis do they use, since they control Congress and the Senate? What alibi do they use when you and I ask, "Well, when are you going to keep your promise?" They blame the Dixiecrats. What is a Dixiecrat? A Democrat. A Dixiecrat is nothing but a Democrat in disguise. The titular head of the Democrats is also the head of the Dixiecrats, because the Dixiecrats are a part of the Democratic Party. The Democrats have never kicked the Dixiecrats out of the party. The Dixiecrats bolted themselves once, but the Democrats didn't put them out. Imagine, these lowdown Southern segregationists put the Northern Democrats down. But the Northern Democrats have never put the Dixiecrats down. No, look at that thing the way it is. They have got a con game going on, a political con game, and you and I are in the middle. It's time for you and me to wake up and start looking at it like it is, and trying to understand it like it is; and then we can deal with it like it is.[6]

The Dixiecrats in Washington, D.C., control the key committees that run the government. The only reason the Dixiecrats control these committees is because they have seniority. The only reason they have seniority is because they come from states where Negroes can't vote. This is not even a government that's based on democracy. It is not a government that is made up of representatives of the people. Half of the people in the South can't even vote. Eastland is not even supposed to be in Washington. Half of the senators and congressmen who occupy these key positions in Washington, D.C., are there illegally, are there unconstitutionally.

I was in Washington, D.C., a week ago Thursday, when they were debating whether or not they should let the bill come onto the floor. And in the back of the room where the Senate meets, there's a huge map of the United States, and on that map it shows the location of Negroes throughout the country. And it shows that the Southern section of the country, the states that are most heavily concentrated with Negroes, are the ones that have senators and congressmen standing up filibustering and doing all other kinds of trickery to keep the Negro from being able to vote. This is pitiful. But it's not pitiful for us any longer; it's actually pitiful for the white man, because soon now, as the Negro awakens a little more and sees the vise that he's

6. Dixiecrat: a loose association of Democratic, segregationist congressmen from Southern states. In 1948, protesting the Democratic Party's commitment to civil rights, the Dixiecrats formed their own party and nominated Strom Thurmond for president. Destroyed in the election, the Dixiecrats rejoined the Democratic Party. When the Democratic Party continued its advocacy of racial justice in the 1960s, many Dixiecrats (like Strom Thurmond) switched to the Republican Party.

in, sees the bag that he's in, sees the real game that he's in, then the Negro's going to develop a new tactic.

These senators and congressmen actually violate the constitutional amendments that guarantee the people of that particular state or county the right to vote. And the Constitution itself has within it the machinery to expel any representative from a state where the voting rights of the people are violated. You don't even need new legislation. Any person in Congress right now, who is there from a state or a district where the voting rights of the people are violated, that particular person should be expelled from Congress. And when you expel him, you've removed one of the obstacles in the path of any real meaningful legislation in this country. In fact, when you expel them, you don't need new legislation, because they will be replaced by black representatives from counties and districts where the black man is in the majority, not in the minority.

If the black man in these Southern states had his full voting rights, the key Dixiecrats in Washington, D.C., which means the key Democrats in Washington, D.C., would lose their seats. The Democratic Party itself would lose its power. It would cease to be powerful as a party. When you see the amount of power that would be lost by the Democratic Party if it were to lose the Dixiecrat wing, or branch, or element, you can see where it's against the interests of the Democrats to give voting rights to Negroes in states where the Democrats have been in complete power and authority ever since the Civil War. You just can't belong to that party without analyzing it.

I say again, I'm not anti-Democrat, I'm not anti-Republican, I'm not anti-anything. I'm just questioning their sincerity, and some of the strategy that they've been using on our people by promising them promises that they don't intend to keep. When you keep the Democrats in power, you're keeping the Dixiecrats in power. I doubt that my good Brother Lomax will deny that. A vote for a Democrat is a vote for a Dixiecrat. That's why, in 1964, it's time now for you and me to become more politically mature and realize what the ballot is for; what we're supposed to get when we cast a ballot; and that if we don't cast a ballot, it's going to end up in a situation where we're going to have to cast a bullet. It's either a ballot or a bullet.

In the North, they do it a different way. They have a system that's known as gerrymandering, whatever that means. It means when Negroes become too heavily concentrated in a certain area, and begin to gain too much political power, the white man comes along and changes the district lines. You may say, "Why do you keep saying white man?" Because it's the white man who does it. I haven't ever seen any Negro changing any lines. They don't let him get near the line. It's the white man who does this. And usually, it's the white man who grins at you the most, and pats you on the back, and is supposed to be your friend. He may be friendly, but he's not your friend.

So, what I'm trying to impress upon you, in essence, is this: You and I in America are faced not with a segregationist conspiracy, we're faced with a government conspiracy. Everyone who's filibustering is a senator—that's the government. Everyone who's finagling in Washington, D.C., is a congressman—that's the government. You don't have anybody putting blocks in your path but people who are a part of the government. The same government that you go abroad to fight for and die for is the government that is in a conspiracy to deprive you of your voting rights, deprive you of your economic opportunities, deprive you of decent housing, deprive you of decent education. You don't need to go to the employer alone, it is the government itself, the government of America, that is responsible for the oppression and exploitation and degradation of black people in this country. And you should drop it in their lap. This government has failed the Negro. This so-called democracy has failed the Negro. And all these white liberals have definitely failed the Negro.

So, where do we go from here? First, we need some friends. We need some new allies. The entire civil-rights struggle needs a new interpretation, a broader interpretation. We need to look at this civil-rights thing from another angle—from the inside as well as from the outside. To those of us whose philosophy is black nationalism, the only way you can get involved in the civil-rights struggle is give it a new interpretation. That old interpretation excluded us. It kept us out. So, we're giving a new interpretation to the civil-rights struggle, an interpretation that will enable us to come into it, take part in it. And these handkerchief-heads who have been dillydallying and pussyfooting and compromising—we don't intend to let them pussyfoot and dillydally and compromise any longer.

How can you thank a man for giving you what's already yours? How then can you thank him for giving you only part of what's already yours? You haven't even made progress, if what's being given to you, you should have had already. That's not progress. And I love my Brother Lomax, the way he pointed out we're right back where we were in 1954. We're not even as far up as we were in 1954. We're behind where we were in 1954. There's more segregation now than there was in 1954. There's more racial animosity, more racial hatred, more racial violence today in 1964, than there was in 1954. Where is the progress?

And now you're facing a situation where the young Negro's coming up. They don't want to hear that "turn-the-other-cheek" stuff, no. In Jacksonville, those were teenagers, they were throwing Molotov cocktails. Negroes have never done that before. But it shows you there's a new deal coming in. There's new thinking coming in. There's new strategy coming in. It'll be Molotov cocktails this month, hand grenades next month, and something else next month. It'll be ballots, or it'll be bullets. It'll be liberty, or it will be death. The only difference about this kind of death—it'll be reciprocal. You know what is meant by "reciprocal"? That's one of Brother Lomax's words, I stole it from him. I don't usually deal with those big words because I don't usually deal with big people. I deal with small people. I find you can get a whole lot of small people and whip hell out of a whole lot of big people. They haven't got anything to lose, and they've got everything to gain. And they'll let you know in a minute: "It takes two to tango; when I go, you go."

The black nationalists, those whose philosophy is black nationalism, in bringing about this new interpretation of the entire meaning of civil rights, look upon it as meaning, as Brother Lomax has pointed out, equality of opportunity. Well, we're justified in seeking civil rights, if it means equality of opportunity, because all we're doing there is trying to collect for our investment. Our mothers and fathers invested sweat and blood. Three hundred and ten years we worked in this country without a dime in return—I mean without a *dime* in return. You let the white man walk around here talking about how rich this country is, but you never stop to think how it got rich so quick. It got rich because you made it rich.

You take the people who are in this audience right now. They're poor, we're all poor as individuals. Our weekly salary individually amounts to hardly anything. But if you take the salary of everyone in here collectively it'll fill up a whole lot of baskets. It's a lot of wealth. If you can collect the wages of just these people right here for a year, you'll be rich—richer than rich. When you look at it like that, think how rich Uncle Sam had to become, not with this handful, but millions of black people. Your and my mother and father, who didn't work an eight-hour shift, but worked from "can't see" in the morning until "can't see" at night, and worked for nothing, making the white man rich, making Uncle Sam rich.

This is our investment. This is our contribution—our blood. Not only did we give of our free labor, we gave of our blood. Every time he had a call to arms, we were the first ones in uniform. We died on every battlefield the white man had. We have made a greater sacrifice than anybody who's standing up in America today. We have made a greater contribution and have collected less. Civil rights, for those of us whose philosophy is black nationalism, means: "Give it to us now. Don't wait for next year. Give it to us yesterday, and that's not fast enough."

I might stop right here to point out one thing. Whenever you're going after something that belongs to you, anyone who's depriving you of the right to have it is a criminal. Understand that. Whenever you are going after something that is yours, you are within your legal rights to lay claim to it. And anyone who puts forth any effort to deprive you of that which is yours, is breaking the law, is a criminal. And this was pointed out by the Supreme Court decision. It outlawed segregation. Which means segregation is against the law. Which means a segregationist is breaking the law. A segregationist is a criminal. You can't label him as anything other than that. And when you demonstrate against segregation, the law is on your side. The Supreme Court is on your side.

Now, who is it that opposes you in carrying out the law? The police department itself. With police dogs and clubs. Whenever you demonstrate against segregation, whether it is segregated education, segregated housing, or anything else, the law is on your side, and anyone who stands in the way is not the law any longer. They are breaking the law, they are not representatives of the law. Any time you demonstrate against segregation and a man has the audacity to put a police dog on you, kill that dog, kill him, I'm telling you, kill that dog. I say it, if they put me in jail tomorrow, kill—that—dog. Then you'll put a stop to it. Now, if these white people in here don't want to see that kind of action, get down and tell the mayor to tell the police department to pull the dogs in. That's all you have to do. If you don't do it, someone else will.

If you don't take this kind of stand, your little children will grow up and look at you and think "shame." If you don't take an uncompromising stand—I don't mean go out and get violent; but at the same time you should never be nonviolent unless you run into some nonviolence. I'm nonviolent with those who are nonviolent with me. But when you drop that violence on me, then you've made me go insane, and I'm not responsible for what I do. And that's the way every Negro should get. Any time you know you're within the law, within your legal rights, within your moral rights, in accord with justice, then die for what you believe in. But don't die alone. Let your dying be reciprocal. This is what is meant by equality. What's good for the goose is good for the gander.

When we begin to get in this area, we need new friends, we need new allies. We need to expand the civil-rights struggle to a higher level—to the level of human rights. Whenever you are in a civil-rights struggle, whether you know it or not, you are confining yourself to the jurisdiction of Uncle Sam. No one from the outside world can speak out in your behalf as long as your struggle is a civil-rights struggle. Civil rights comes within the domestic affairs of this country. All of our African brothers and our Asian brothers and our Latin-American brothers cannot open their mouths and interfere in the domestic affairs of the United States. And as long as it's civil rights, this comes under the jurisdiction of Uncle Sam.

But the United Nations has what's known as the charter of human rights, it has a committee that deals in human rights. You may wonder why all of the atrocities that have been committed in Africa and in Hungary and in Asia and in Latin America are brought before the UN, and the Negro problem is never brought before the UN. This is part of the conspiracy. This old, tricky, blue-eyed liberal who is supposed to be your and my friend, supposed to be in our corner, supposed to be subsidizing our struggle, and supposed to be acting in the capacity of an adviser, never tells you anything about human rights. They keep you wrapped up in civil rights. And you spend so much time barking up the civil-rights tree, you don't even know there's a human-rights tree on the same floor.[7]

When you expand the civil-rights struggle to the level of human rights, you can then take the case of the black man in this country before the nations in the UN. You can take it before the General Assembly. You can take Uncle Sam before a world court. But the only level you can do it on is the level of human rights. Civil rights keeps you under his restrictions, under his jurisdiction. Civil rights keeps you in his pocket. Civil rights means you're asking Uncle Sam to treat you right. Human rights are something you were born with. Human rights are your God-given rights. Human rights are the rights that are recognized by all nations of this earth. And any time any one violates your human rights, you can take them to the world court. Uncle Sam's hands are dripping with blood, dripping with the blood of the black man in this country. He's the earth's number-one hypocrite. He has the audacity—yes, he has—imagine him posing as the leader of the free world. The free world!—and you over here singing "We Shall Overcome." Expand the civil-rights struggle to the level of human rights, take it into the United Nations, where our African brothers can throw their weight on our side, where our Asian brothers can throw their weight on our side, where our Latin-American brothers can throw their weight on our side, and where 800 million Chinamen are sitting there waiting to throw their weight on our side.

Let the world know how bloody his hands are. Let the world know the hypocrisy that's practiced over here. Let it be the ballot or the bullet. Let him know that it must be the ballot or the bullet.

When you take your case to Washington, D.C., you're taking it to the criminal who's responsible; it's like running from the wolf to the fox. They're all in cahoots together. They all work political chicanery and make you look like a chump before the eyes of the world. Here you are walking around in America, getting ready to be drafted and sent abroad, like a tin soldier, and when you get over there, people ask you what are you fighting for, and you have to stick your tongue in your cheek. No, take Uncle Sam to court, take him before the world.

7. All member states of the United Nations passed the Universal Declaration of Human Rights on December 10, 1948, guaranteeing (among other things) racial equality before the law.

By ballot I only mean freedom. Don't you know—I disagree with Lomax on this issue—that the ballot is more important than the dollar? Can I prove it? Yes. Look in the UN. There are poor nations in the UN; yet those poor nations can get together with their voting power and keep the rich nations from making a move. They have one nation—one vote, everyone has an equal vote. And when those brothers from Asia and Africa and the darker parts of this earth get together, their voting power is sufficient to hold Sam in check. Or Russia in check. Or some other section of the earth in check. So, the ballot is most important.

Right now, in this country, if you and I, 22 million African-Americans—that's what we are—Africans who are in America. You're nothing but Africans. Nothing but Africans. In fact, you'd get farther calling yourself African instead of Negro. Africans don't catch hell. You're the only one catching hell. They don't have to pass civil-rights bills for Africans. An African can go anywhere he wants right now. All you've got to do is tie your head up. That's right, go anywhere you want. Just stop being a Negro. Change your name to Hoogagagooba. That'll show you how silly the white man is. You're dealing with a silly man. A friend of mine who's very dark put a turban on his head and went into a restaurant in Atlanta before they called themselves desegregated. He went into a white restaurant, he sat down, they served him, and he said, "What would happen if a Negro came in here?" And there he's sitting, black as night, but because he had his head wrapped up the waitress looked back at him and says, "Why, there wouldn't no nigger dare come in here."

So, you're dealing with a man whose bias and prejudice are making him lose his mind, his intelligence, every day. He's frightened. He looks around and sees what's taking place on this earth, and he sees that the pendulum of time is swinging in your direction. The dark people are waking up. They're losing their fear of the white man. No place where he's fighting right now is he winning. Everywhere he's fighting, he's fighting someone your and my complexion. And they're beating him. He can't win any more. He's won his last battle. He failed to win the Korean War. He couldn't win it. He had to sign a truce. That's a loss. Any time Uncle Sam, with all his machinery for warfare, is held to a draw by some rice-eaters, he's lost the battle. He had to sign a truce. America's not supposed to sign a truce. She's supposed to be bad. But she's not bad any more. She's bad as long as she can use her hydrogen bomb, but she can't use hers for fear Russia might use hers. Russia can't use hers, for fear that Sam might use his. So, both of them are weaponless. They can't use the weapon because each's weapon nullifies the other's. So the only place where action can take place is on the ground. And the white man can't win another war fighting on the ground. Those days are over. The black man knows it, the brown man knows it, the red man knows it, and the yellow man knows it. So they engage him in guerrilla warfare. That's not his style. You've got to have heart to be a guerrilla warrior, and he hasn't got any heart. I'm telling you now.

I just want to give you a little briefing on guerrilla warfare because, before you know it, before you know it—It takes heart to be a guerrilla warrior because you're on your own. In conventional warfare you have tanks and a whole lot of other people with you to back you up, planes over your head and all that kind of stuff. But a guerrilla is on his own. All you have is a rifle, some sneakers and a bowl of rice, and that's all you need—and a lot of heart. The Japanese on some of those islands in the Pacific, when the American soldiers landed, one Japanese sometimes could hold the whole army off. He'd just wait until the sun went down, and when the sun went down they were all equal. He would take his little blade and slip from bush to bush, and from American to American. The white soldiers couldn't cope with that. Whenever you see a white soldier that fought in the Pacific, he has the shakes, he has a nervous condition, because they scared him to death.

The same thing happened to the French up in French Indochina. People who just a few years previously were rice farmers got together and ran the heavily-mechanized French army out of Indochina.[8] You don't need it—modern warfare today won't work. This is the day of the guerrilla. They did the same thing in Algeria. Algerians, who were nothing but Bedouins, took a rifle and sneaked off to the hills, and de Gaulle and all of his highfalutin' war machinery couldn't defeat those guerrillas. Nowhere on this earth does the white man win in

8. French Indochina: Vietnam. Eleven months after this speech was delivered, the first U.S. combat troops arrived in Vietnam, as the United States replaced France as the defender of South Vietnam.

a guerrilla warfare. It's not his speed. Just as guerrilla warfare is prevailing in Asia and in parts of Africa and in parts of Latin America, you've got to be mighty naive, or you've got to play the black man cheap, if you don't think some day he's going to wake up and find that it's got to be the ballot or the bullet.

I would like to say, in closing, a few things concerning the Muslim Mosque, Inc., which we established recently in New York City. It's true we're Muslims and our religion is Islam, but we don't mix our religion with our politics and our economics and our social and civil activities—not any more. We keep our religion in our mosque. After our religious services are over, then as Muslims we become involved in political action, economic action and social and civic action. We become involved with anybody, anywhere, any time and in any manner that's designed to eliminate the evils, the political, economic and social evils that are afflicting the people of our community.

The political philosophy of black nationalism means that the black man should control the politics and the politicians in his own community; no more. The black man in the black community has to be re-educated into the science of politics so he will know what politics is supposed to bring him in return. Don't be throwing out any ballots. A ballot is like a bullet. You don't throw your ballots until you see a target, and if that target is not within your reach, keep your ballot in your pocket. The political philosophy of black nationalism is being taught in the Christian church. It's being taught in the NAACP. It's being taught in CORE meetings. It's being taught in SNCC [Student Nonviolent Coordinating Committee] meetings. It's being taught in Muslim meetings. It's being taught where nothing but atheists and agnostics come together. It's being taught everywhere. Black people are fed up with the dillydallying, pussyfooting, compromising approach that we've been using toward getting our freedom. We want freedom *now*, but we're not going to get it saying "We Shall Overcome." We've got to fight until we overcome.

The economic philosophy of black nationalism is pure and simple. It only means that we should control the economy of our community. Why should white people be running all the stores in our community? Why should white people be running the banks of our community? Why should the economy of our community be in the hands of the white man? Why? If a black man can't move his store into a white community, you tell me why a white man should move his store into a black community. The philosophy of black nationalism involves a re-education program in the black community in regards to economics. Our people have to be made to see that any time you take your dollar out of your community and spend it in a community where you don't live, the community where you live will get poorer and poorer, and the community where you spend your money will get richer and richer. Then you wonder why where you live is always a ghetto or a slum area. And where you and I are concerned, not only do we lose it when we spend it out of the community, but the white man has got all our stores in the community tied up; so that though we spend it in the community, at sundown the man who runs the store takes it over across town somewhere. He's got us in a vise.

So the economic philosophy of black nationalism means in every church, in every civic organization, in every fraternal order, it's time now for our people to become conscious of the importance of controlling the economy of our community. If we own the stores, if we operate the businesses, if we try and establish some industry in our own community, then we're developing to the position where we are creating employment for our own kind. Once you gain control of the economy of your own community, then you don't have to picket and boycott and beg some cracker downtown for a job in his business.

The social philosophy of black nationalism only means that we have to get together and remove the evils, the vices, alcoholism, drug addiction, and other evils that are destroying the moral fiber of our community. We ourselves have to lift the level of our community, the standard of our community to a higher level, make our own society beautiful so that we will be satisfied in our own social circles and won't be running around here trying to knock our way into a social circle where we're not wanted.

So I say, in spreading a gospel such as black nationalism, it is not designed to make the black man reevaluate the white man—you know him already—but to make the black man re-evaluate himself. Don't change the white man's mind—you can't change his mind, and that whole thing about appealing to the moral conscience of America—America's conscience is bankrupt. She lost all conscience a long time ago. Uncle Sam has no conscience. They don't know what morals are. They don't try and eliminate an evil because it's evil, or because it's illegal, or because it's immoral; they eliminate it only when it threatens their existence. So you're wasting your time appealing to the moral conscience of a bankrupt man like Uncle Sam. If he had a conscience, he'd straighten this thing out with no more pressure being put upon him. So it is not necessary to change the white man's mind. We have to change our own mind. You can't change his mind about us. We've got to change our own minds about each other. We have to see each other with new eyes. We have to see each other as brothers and sisters. We have to come together with warmth so we can develop unity and harmony that's necessary to get this problem solved ourselves. How can we do this? How can we avoid jealousy? How can we avoid the suspicion and the divisions that exist in the community? I'll tell you how.

I have watched how Billy Graham comes into a city, spreading what he calls the gospel of Christ, which is only white nationalism. That's what he is. Billy Graham is a white nationalist; I'm a black nationalist. But since it's the natural tendency for leaders to be jealous and look upon a powerful figure like Graham with suspicion and envy, how is it possible for him to come into a city and get all the cooperation of the church leaders? Don't think because they're church leaders that they don't have weaknesses that make them envious and jealous—no, everybody's got it. It's not an accident that when they want to choose a cardinal [as Pope] over there in Rome, they get in a closet so you can't hear them cussing and fighting and carrying on.

Billy Graham comes in preaching the gospel of Christ, he evangelizes the gospel, he stirs everybody up, but he never tries to start a church. If he came in trying to start a church, all the churches would be against him. So, he just comes in talking about Christ and tells everybody who gets Christ to go to any church where Christ is; and in this way the church cooperates with him. So we're going to take a page from his book.

Our gospel is black nationalism. We're not trying to threaten the existence of any organization, but we're spreading the gospel of black nationalism. Anywhere there's a church that is also preaching and practicing the gospel of black nationalism, join that church. If the NAACP is preaching and practicing the gospel of black nationalism, join the NAACP. If CORE is spreading and practicing the gospel of black nationalism, join CORE. Join any organization that has a gospel that's for the uplift of the black man. And when you get into it and see them pussyfooting or compromising, pull out of it because that's not black nationalism. We'll find another one.

And in this manner, the organizations will increase in number and in quantity and in quality, and by August, it is then our intention to have a black nationalist convention which will consist of delegates from all over the country who are interested in the political, economic and social philosophy of black nationalism. After these delegates convene, we will hold a seminar, we will hold discussions, we will listen to everyone. We want to hear new ideas and new solutions and new answers. And at that time, if we see fit then to form a black nationalist party, we'll form a black nationalist party. If it's necessary to form a black nationalist army, we'll form a black nationalist army. It'll be the ballot or the bullet. It'll be liberty or it'll be death.

It's time for you and me to stop sitting in this country, letting some cracker senators, Northern crackers and Southern crackers, sit there in Washington, D.C., and come to a conclusion in their mind that you and I are supposed to have civil rights. There's no white man going to tell me anything about *my* rights. Brothers and sisters, always remember, if it doesn't take senators and congressmen and presidential proclamations to give freedom to the white man, it is not necessary for legislation or proclamation or Supreme Court decisions to give freedom to the black man. You let that white man know, if this is a country of freedom, let it be a country of freedom; and if it's not a country of freedom, change it.

We will work with anybody, anywhere, at any time, who is genuinely interested in tackling the problem head-on, nonviolently as long as the enemy is nonviolent, but violent when the enemy gets violent. We'll work with you on the voter-registration drive, we'll work with you on rent strikes, we'll work with you on school boycotts—I don't believe in any kind of integration; I'm not even worried about it because I know you're not going to get it anyway; you're not going to get it because you're afraid to die; you've got to be ready to die if you try and force yourself on the white man, because he'll get just as violent as those crackers in Mississippi, right here in Cleveland. But we will still work with you on the school boycotts because we're against a segregated school system. A segregated school system produces children who, when they graduate, graduate with crippled minds. But this does not mean that a school is segregated because it's all black. A segregated school means a school that is controlled by people who have no real interest in it whatsoever.

Let me explain what I mean. A segregated district or community is a community in which people live, but outsiders control the politics and the economy of that community. They never refer to the white section as a segregated community. It's the all-Negro section that's a segregated community. Why? The white man controls his own school, his own bank, his own economy, his own politics, his own everything, his own community—but he also controls yours. When you're under someone else's control, you're segregated. They'll always give you the lowest or the worst that there is to offer, but it doesn't mean you're segregated just because you have your own. You've got to *control* your own. Just like the white man has control of his, you need to control yours.

You know the best way to get rid of segregation? The white man is more afraid of separation than he is of integration. Segregation means that he puts you away from him, but not far enough for you to be out of his jurisdiction; separation means you're gone. And the white man will integrate faster than he'll let you separate. So we will work with you against the segregated school system because it's criminal, because it is absolutely destructive, in every way imaginable, to the minds of the children who have to be exposed to that type of crippling education.

Last but not least, I must say this concerning the great controversy over rifles and shotguns. The only thing that I've ever said is that in areas where the government has proven itself either unwilling or unable to defend the lives and the property of Negroes, it's time for Negroes to defend themselves. Article number two of the constitutional amendments provides you and me the right to own a rifle or a shotgun.[9] It is constitutionally legal to own a shotgun or a

9. In *United States v. Miller* (1939), the U.S. Supreme Court ruled that the Second Amendment applied only to weapons that have "some reasonable relationship to the preservation or efficiency of a well-regulated militia." That did not include (for example) sawed-off shotguns but did allow rifles and full-barrel shotguns.

rifle. This doesn't mean you're going to get a rifle and form battalions and go out looking for white folks, although you'd be within your rights—I mean, you'd be justified; but that would be illegal and we don't do anything illegal. If the white man doesn't want the black man buying rifles and shotguns, then let the government do its job. That's all. And don't let the white man come to you and ask you what you think about what Malcolm says—why, you old Uncle Tom. He would never ask you if he thought you were going to say, "Amen!" No, he is making a Tom out of you.

So, this doesn't mean forming rifle clubs and going out looking for people, but it is time, in 1964, if you are a man, to let that man know. If he's not going to do his job in running the government and providing you and me with the protection that our taxes are supposed to be for, since he spends all those billions for his defense budget, he certainly can't begrudge you and me spending $12 or $15 for a single-shot, or double-action. I hope you understand. Don't go out shooting people, but any time, brothers and sisters, and especially the men in this audience—some of you wearing Congressional Medals of Honor, with shoulders this wide, chests this big, muscles that big—any time you and I sit around and read where they bomb a church and murder in cold blood, not some grownups, but four little girls while they were praying to the same god the white man taught them to pray to, and you and I see the government go down and can't find who did it.[1]

Why, this man—he can find Eichmann hiding down in Argentina somewhere. Let two or three American soldiers, who are minding somebody else's business way over in South Vietnam, get killed, and he'll send battleships, sticking his nose in their business. He wanted to send troops down to Cuba and make them have what he calls free elections—this old cracker who doesn't have free elections in his own

1. On September 15, 1963, white supremacists bombed the Sixteenth Street Baptist Church in Birmingham, Alabama, killing four girls aged 11 to 14. The FBI quickly identified four suspects, all members of the Ku Klux Klan, but failed to bring charges. For many white people, this event unequivocally demonstrated the injustice of the Jim Crow system of government in southern states. One of the perpetrators was tried and convicted in 1977. The case was reopened in 1995. The second suspect, who suffered dementia, was ruled incompetent to stand trial; the third was convicted in 2001; and the fourth was convicted in 2002.

country. No, if you never see me another time in your life, if I die in the morning, I'll die saying one thing: the ballot or the bullet, the ballot or the bullet.

If a Negro in 1964 has to sit around and wait for some cracker senator to filibuster when it comes to the rights of black people, why, you and I should hang our heads in shame. You talk about a march on Washington in 1963, you haven't seen anything. There's some more going down in '64. And this time they're not going like they went last year. They're not going singing "We Shall Overcome." They're not going with white friends. They're not going with placards already painted for them. They're not going with round-trip tickets. They're going with one-way tickets.[2]

And if they don't want that non-nonviolent army going down there, tell them to bring the filibuster to a halt. The black nationalists aren't going to wait. Lyndon B. Johnson is the head of the Democratic Party. If he's for civil rights, let him go into the Senate next week and declare himself. Let him go in there right now and declare himself. Let him go in there and denounce the Southern branch of his party. Let him go in there right now and take a moral stand—right now, not later. Tell him, don't wait until election time. If he waits too long, brothers and sisters, he will be responsible for letting a condition develop in this country which will create a climate that will bring seeds up out of the ground with vegetation on the end of them looking like something these people never dreamed of. In 1964, it's the ballot or the bullet. Thank you.

1964

2. The March on Washington occurred on August 28, 1963, and culminated with Martin Luther King Jr.'s "I Have a Dream" speech. Malcolm X criticized the docility of the protest, which exited the nation's capital as swiftly as it entered.

Ronald Reagan

1911–2004

Reagan began developing this speech as spokesman for General Electric in the late 1950s. By 1962, he was warning GE's employees against Soviet communists and American liberals. General Electric asked him to stop discussing politics; when he didn't, he was fired. Soon after, he joined the Republican Party and became co-chair of California Citizens for Goldwater. He spent 1964 campaigning for Barry Goldwater in his presidential race against Lyndon Johnson. "A Time for Choosing" was Reagan's stump speech, and Goldwater was so impressed with it that on the eve of the election, October 27, 1964, he broadcast it to a national audience. Reagan's immediate goal was to get Barry Goldwater elected president. He failed in that. But conservatives point to the national broadcast of this speech as the beginning of the "Reagan revolution," so in this wider context "A Time for Choosing" has been very influential. In fact, its attack on big government and communism became the centerpiece of contemporary conservative politics in America, so that conservatives affectionately refer to it simply as "The Speech."

A Time for Choosing

Thank you very much. Thank you, and good evening. The sponsor has been identified, but unlike most television programs, the performer hasn't been provided with a script. As a matter of fact, I have been permitted to choose my own words and discuss my own ideas regarding the choice that we face in the next few weeks.

I have spent most of my life as a Democrat. I recently have seen fit to follow another course. I believe that the issues confronting us cross party lines. Now, one side in this campaign has been telling us that the issues of this election are the maintenance of peace and prosperity. The line has been used "We've never had it so good!"

But I have an uncomfortable feeling that this prosperity isn't something upon which we can base our hopes for the future. No nation in history has ever survived a tax burden that reached a third of its national income. Today thirty-seven cents out of every dollar earned in this country is the tax collector's share, and yet our government continues to spend 17 million dollars a day more than the government takes in. We haven't balanced our budget twenty-eight out of the last thirty-four years. We have raised our debt limit three times in the last twelve months, and now our national debt is one and a half times bigger than all the combined debts of all the nations of the world. We have 15 billion dollars in gold in our treasury—we don't own an ounce. Foreign dollar claims are 27.3 billion dollars, and we have just had announced that the dollar of 1939 will now purchase forty-five cents in its total value.

As for the peace that we would preserve, I wonder who among us would like to approach the wife or mother whose husband or son has died in Vietnam and ask them if they think this is a peace that should be maintained indefinitely. Do they mean peace, or do they mean we just want to be left in peace? There can be no real peace while one American is dying someplace in the world for the rest of us. We are at war with the most dangerous enemy that has ever faced mankind in his long climb from the swamp to the stars, and it has been said if we lose that war, and in so doing lose this way of freedom of ours, history will record with the greatest astonishment that those who had the most to lose did the least to prevent its happening. Well, I think it's time we ask ourselves if we still know the freedoms that were intended for us by the Founding Fathers.

Not too long ago two friends of mine were talking to a Cuban refugee, a businessman who had escaped from Castro,[1] and in the midst of his story one of my friends turned to the other and said, "We don't know how lucky we are." And the Cuban stopped and said, "How lucky you are! I had someplace to escape to." In that sentence he told us the entire story. If we lose freedom here, there is no place to escape to. This is the last stand on earth.

And this idea that government is beholden to the people, that it has no other source of power except the sovereign people, is still the newest and most unique idea in all the long history of man's relation to man. This is the issue of this election. Whether we believe in our capacity for

1. Fidel Castro (1926–2016) led the Cuban revolution against the corrupt dictatorship of Fulgencio Batista in 1959. He established a communist dictatorship, and many well-to-do and middle-class Cubans fled, as their property was confiscated by the regime. [All notes are the editor's.]

self-government or whether we abandon the American Revolution and confess that a little intellectual elite in a far-distant capital can plan our lives for us better than we can plan them ourselves.

You and I are told increasingly that we have to choose between a left or right, but I would like to suggest that there is no such thing as a left or right. There is only an up or down—up to man's age-old dream—the ultimate in individual freedom consistent with law and order—or down to the ant heap of totalitarianism, and regardless of their sincerity, their humanitarian motives, those who would trade our freedom for security have embarked on this downward course.

In this vote-harvesting time they use terms like the "Great Society,"[2] or as we were told a few days ago by the President, we must accept a "greater government activity in the affairs of the people." But they have been a little more explicit in the past and among themselves—and all of the things that I now will quote have appeared in print. These are not Republican accusations. For example, they have voices that say "the cold war will end through our acceptance of a not undemocratic socialism." Another voice says that the profit motive has become outmoded, it must be replaced by the incentives of the welfare state; or our traditional system of individual freedom is incapable of solving the complex problems of the twentieth century.

Senator Fulbright[3] has said at Stanford University that the Constitution is outmoded. He referred to the president as our moral teacher and our leader, and he said he is hobbled in his task by the restrictions in power imposed on him by this antiquated document. He must be freed so that he can do for us what he knows is best.

And Senator Clark[4] of Pennsylvania, another articulate spokes-man, defines liberalism as "meeting the material needs of the masses through the full power of centralized government." Well, I for one resent it when a representative of the people refers to you and me—the free

2. Slogan adopted by President Lyndon Johnson to describe the nation that would result from his domestic policies. He aspired to create a prosperous nation that had overcome its racial divisions and poverty. In his first State of the Union address, in 1964, Johnson advocated expanding the federal government's role in domestic affairs to realize these aims.

3. J. William Fulbright, Democratic senator from Arkansas, 1945–1975, best known for the Fulbright Act (1946), which provides for the exchange of students and teachers between the United States and many other countries.

4. Joseph S. Clark Jr., Democratic senator from Pennsylvania, 1957–1969.

men and women of this country—as "the masses." This is a term we haven't applied to ourselves in America. But beyond that, "the full power of centralized government"—this was the very thing the Founding Fathers sought to minimize. They knew that governments don't control *things*. A government can't control the economy without controlling people. And they knew when a government sets out to do that, it must use force and coercion to achieve its purpose. They also knew, those Founding Fathers, that outside of its legitimate functions, government does nothing as well or as economically as the private sector of the economy.

Now, we have no better example of this than the government's involvement in the farm economy over the last thirty years. Since 1955 the cost of this program has nearly doubled. One-fourth of farming in America is responsible for 85 percent of the farm surplus. Three-fourths of farming is out on the free market and has known a 21 percent increase in the per capita consumption of all its produce. You see, that one-fourth of farming is regulated and controlled by the federal government. In the last three years we have spent forty-three dollars in the feed grain program for every dollar bushel of corn we don't grow.

Senator Humphrey[5] last week charged that Barry Goldwater as president would seek to eliminate farmers. He should do his homework a little better, because he will find out that we have had a decline of 5 million in the farm population under these government programs. He will also find that the Democratic administration has sought to get from Congress an extension of the farm program to include that three-fourths that is now free. He will find that they have also asked for the right to imprison farmers who wouldn't keep books as prescribed by the federal government. The secretary of agriculture asked for the right to seize farms through condemnation and resell them to other individuals. And contained in that same program was a provision that would have allowed the federal government to remove 2 million farmers from the soil.

At the same time there has been an increase in the Department of Agriculture employees. There is now one for every thirty farms in the United States, and still they can't tell us how sixty-six shiploads of

5. Hubert Humphrey was a senator from Minnesota, 1948–1965 and 1972–1978; Lyndon Johnson's running mate in 1964; and vice president, 1965–1969.

grain headed for Austria disappeared without a trace, and Billie Sol Estes never left shore![6]

Every responsible farmer and farm organization has repeatedly asked the government to free the farm economy, but who are farmers to know what is best for them? The wheat farmers voted against a wheat program. The government passed it anyway. Now the price of bread goes up; the price of wheat to the farmers goes down.

Meanwhile, back in the city, under urban renewal[7] the assault on freedom carries on. Private property rights are so diluted that public interest is almost anything that a few government planners decide it should be. In a program that takes from the needy and gives to the greedy, we see such spectacles as in Cleveland, Ohio, a million-and-a-half-dollar building completed only three years ago must be destroyed to make way for what government officials call a "more compatible use of the land." The President tells us he is now going to start building public housing units in the thousands where heretofore we have only built them in the hundreds. But FHA[8] and the Veterans Administration tell us that they have 120,000 housing units they've taken back through mortgage foreclosures.

For three decades we have sought to solve the problems of unemployment through government planning, and the more the plans fail, the more the planners plan. The latest is the Area Redevelopment Agency.[9] They have just declared Rice County, Kansas, a depressed area. Rice County, Kansas, has two hundred oil wells, and the 14,000 people there have over thirty million dollars on deposit in personal savings in their banks. When the government tells you you are depressed, lie down and be depressed!

We have so many people who can't see a fat man standing beside a thin one without coming to the conclusion that the fat man got that way by taking advantage of the thin one! So they are going to solve all the problems of human misery through government and government

6. A reference to the allegedly corrupt federal grain contracts issued during this period. Billie Sol Estes was a friend of Lyndon Johnson's, known for his dishonest practices. He was investigated for fraud and tax evasion and convicted of these crimes in 1963.

7. A program whereby impoverished urban neighborhoods were to be resuscitated by tearing down existing structures and replacing them with publicly owned buildings, such as housing projects for the poor.

8. The Federal Housing Administration insures mortgage loans to lower-income Americans, providing more people with the opportunity to buy their homes.

9. Established by the Employment Bureau in 1961 to use federal funds for vocational training programs.

planning. Well, now if government planning and welfare had the answer, and they've had almost thirty years of it, shouldn't we expect government to read the score to us once in a while? Shouldn't they be telling us about the decline each year in the number of people needing help? . . . the reduction in the need for public housing?

But the reverse is true. Each year the need grows greater, the program grows greater. We were told four years ago that seventeen million people went to bed hungry each night. Well, that was probably true. They were all on a diet! But now we are told that 9.3 million families in this country are poverty-stricken on the basis of earning less than $3,000 a year. Welfare spending is ten times greater than in the dark depths of the Depression. We are spending 45 billion dollars on welfare. Now do a little arithmetic, and you will find that if we divided the 45 billion dollars up equally among those 9 million poor families, we would be able to give each family $4,600 a year, and this added to their present income should eliminate poverty! Direct aid to the poor, however, is running only about $600 per family. It seems that someplace there must be some overhead.

So now we declare "war on poverty," or "you, too, can be a Bobby Baker!"[1] How do they honestly expect us to believe that if we add 1 billion dollars to the 45 billion we are spending . . . one more program to the thirty-odd we have—and remember, this new program doesn't replace any, it just duplicates existing programs . . . do they believe that poverty is suddenly going to disappear by magic? Well, in all fairness I should explain that there is one part of the new program that isn't duplicated. This is the youth feature. We are now going to solve the dropout problem, juvenile delinquency, by reinstituting something like the old CCC[2] camps, and we are going to put our young people in camps, but again we do some arithmetic, and we find that we are going to spend each year just on room and board for each young person that we help $4,700 a year! We can send them to Harvard for $2,700! Don't get me wrong. I'm not suggesting that Harvard is the answer to juvenile delinquency!

1. Robert Baker (1928–2017), longtime aide and political operative of Lyndon Johnson. "War on poverty": from President Johnson's 1964 State of the Union address.

2. The Civilian Conservation Corps, an organization established in 1933 by Franklin Delano Roosevelt to employ hundreds of thousands of young men during the Great Depression. Living in military-style camps, the men in the CCC worked on outdoor construction projects, including many of the improvements to the national parks.

But seriously, what are we doing to those we seek to help? Not too long ago, a judge called me here in Los Angeles. He told me of a young woman who had come before him for a divorce. She had six children, was pregnant with her seventh. Under his questioning, she revealed her husband was a laborer earning $250 a month. She wanted a divorce so that she could get an $80 raise. She is eligible for $330 a month in the Aid to Dependent Children Program. She got the idea from two women in her neighborhood who had already done that very thing.

Yet anytime you and I question the schemes of the do-gooders, we are denounced as being against their humanitarian goals. They say we are always "against" things, never "for" anything. Well, the trouble with our liberal friends is not that they are ignorant, but that they know so much that isn't so! We are for a provision that destitution should not follow unemployment by reason of old age, and to that end we have accepted social security as a step toward meeting the problem.

But we are against those entrusted with this program when they practice deception regarding its fiscal shortcomings, when they charge that any criticism of the program means that we want to end payments to those people who depend on them for a livelihood. They have called it insurance to us in a hundred million pieces of literature. But then they appeared before the Supreme Court and they testified that it was a welfare program. They only use the term "insurance" to sell it to the people. And they said social security dues are a tax for the general use of the government, and the government has used that tax. There is no fund, because Robert Byers, the actuarial head, appeared before a congressional committee and admitted that social security as of this moment is $298 billion in the hole! But he said there should be no cause for worry because as long as they have the power to tax, they could always take away from the people whatever they needed to bail them out of trouble! And they are doing just that.

A young man, twenty-one years of age, working at an average salary . . . his social security contribution would, in the open market, buy him an insurance policy that would guarantee $220 a month at age sixty-five. The government promises 127! He could live it up until he is thirty-one and then take out a policy that would pay more than social security. Now, are we so lacking in business sense that we can't put this program on a sound basis so that people who do require those payments will find that they can get them when they are due . . . that the cupboard isn't bare? Barry Goldwater thinks we can.

At the same time, can't we introduce voluntary features that would permit a citizen to do better on his own, to be excused upon presentation of evidence that he had made provisions for the nonearning years? Should we not allow a widow with children to work, and not lose the benefits supposedly paid for by her deceased husband? Shouldn't you and I be allowed to declare who our beneficiaries will be under these programs, which we cannot do? I think we are for telling our senior citizens that no one in this country should be denied medical care because of a lack of funds. But I think we are against forcing all citizens, regardless of need, into a compulsory government program, especially when we have such examples, as announced last week, when France admitted that their medicare program was now bankrupt. They've come to the end of the road.

In addition, was Barry Goldwater so irresponsible when he suggested that our government give up its program of deliberate planned inflation so that when you do get your social security pension, a dollar will buy a dollar's worth, and not forty-five cents' worth?

I think we are for the international organization,[3] where the nations of the world can seek peace. But I think we are against subordinating American interests to an organization that has become so structurally unsound that today you can muster a two-thirds vote on the floor of the General Assembly among nations that represent less than 10 percent of the world's population. I think we are against the hypocrisy of assailing our allies because here and there they cling to a colony, while we engage in a conspiracy of silence and never open our mouths about the millions of people enslaved in Soviet colonies in the satellite nations.

I think we are for aiding our allies by sharing of our material blessings with those nations which share in our fundamental beliefs, but we are against doling out money government to government, creating bureaucracy, if not socialism, all over the world. We set out to help 19 countries. We are helping 107. We spent $146 billion. With that money, we bought a 2-million-dollar yacht for Haile Selassie.[4] We bought dress suits for Greek undertakers, extra wives for Kenya government officials. We bought a thousand TV sets for a place where they

3. The United Nations.

4. Emperor of Ethiopia (1930–1974).

have no electricity. In the last six years, fifty-two nations have bought $7 billion of our gold, and all fifty-two are receiving foreign aid from us. No government ever voluntarily reduces itself in size. Government programs, once launched, never disappear. Actually, a government bureau is the nearest thing to eternal life we'll ever see on this earth!

Federal employees number 2.5 million, and federal, state, and local, one out of six of the nation's work force is employed by government. These proliferating bureaus with their thousands of regulations have cost us many of our constitutional safeguards. How many of us realize that today federal agents can invade a man's property without a warrant? They can impose a fine without a formal hearing, let alone a trial by jury, and they can seize and sell his property in auction to enforce the payment of that fine. In Chicot County, Arkansas, James Wier overplanted his rice allotment. The government obtained a $17,000 judgment, and a U.S. marshal sold his 950-acre farm at auction. The government said it was necessary as a warning to others to make the system work! Last February 19th, at the University of Minnesota, Norman Thomas, six times candidate for president on the Socialist Party ticket, said, "If Barry Goldwater became president, he would stop the advance of socialism in the United States." I think that's exactly what he will do!

As a former Democrat, I can tell you Norman Thomas isn't the only man who has drawn this parallel to socialism with the present administration. Back in 1936, Mr. Democrat himself, Al Smith,[5] the great American, came before the American people and charged that the leadership of his party was taking the party of Jefferson, Jackson, and Cleveland down the road under the banners of Marx, Lenin, and Stalin. And he walked away from his party, and he never returned to the day he died, because to this day, the leadership of that party has been taking that party, that honorable party, down the road in the image of the labor socialist party of England. Now it doesn't require expropriation or confiscation of private property or business to impose socialism upon a people. What does it mean whether you hold the deed or the title to your business or property if the government holds the

5. Governor of New York, 1919–1920, 1923–1928; Democratic presidential nominee, 1928. Smith's opposition to FDR's pro-Russian policy during World War II made him shift his allegiance; he voted for the Republican candidate for the presidency when Roosevelt was elected to a third term in office.

power of life and death over that business or property? Such machinery already exists. The government can find some charge to bring against any concern it chooses to prosecute. Every businessman has his own tale of harassment. Somewhere a perversion has taken place. Our natural, inalienable rights are now considered to be a dispensation from government, and freedom has never been so fragile, so close to slipping from our grasp as it is at this moment. Our Democratic opponents seem unwilling to debate these issues. They want to make you and I think that this is a contest between two men . . . that we are to choose just between two personalities. Well, what of this man they would destroy . . . and in destroying, they would destroy that which he represents, the ideas that you and I hold dear.

Is he the brash and shallow and trigger-happy man they say he is? Well, I have been privileged to know him "when." I knew him long before he ever dreamed of trying for high office, and I can tell you personally I have never known a man in my life I believe so incapable of doing a dishonest or dishonorable thing.

This is a man who in his own business, before he entered politics, instituted a profit-sharing plan, before unions had ever thought of it. He put in health and medical insurance for all his employees. He took 50 percent of the profits before taxes and set up a retirement plan, and a pension plan for all his employees. He sent monthly checks for life to an employee who was ill and couldn't work. He provided nursing care for the children of mothers who work in the stores. When Mexico was ravaged by the floods from the Rio Grande, he climbed in his airplane and flew medicine and supplies down there.

An ex-GI told me how he met him. It was the week before Christmas during the Korean War, and he was at the Los Angeles airport trying to get a ride home to Arizona, and he said that there were a lot of servicemen there and no seats available on the planes. Then a voice came over the loudspeaker and said, "Any men in uniform wanting a ride to Arizona, go to runway such-and-such," and they went down there, and there was a fellow named Barry Goldwater sitting in his plane. Every day in the weeks before Christmas, all day long, he would load up the plane, fly to Arizona, fly them to their homes, then fly back over to get another load.

During the hectic split-second timing of a campaign, this is a man who took time out to sit beside an old friend who was dying of cancer.

His campaign managers were understandably impatient, but he said, "There aren't many left who care what happens to her. I'd like her to know that I care." This is a man who said to his nineteen-year-old son, "There is no foundation like the rock of honesty and fairness, and when you begin to build your life upon that rock, with the cement of the faith in God that you have, then you have a real start!" This is not a man who could carelessly send other people's sons to war. And that is the issue of this campaign that makes all of the other problems I have discussed academic, unless we realize that we are in a war that must be won.

Those who would trade our freedom for the soup kitchen of the welfare state have told us that they have a utopian solution of peace without victory. They call their policy "accommodation." And they say if we only avoid any direct confrontation with the enemy, he will forget his evil ways and learn to love us. All who oppose them are indicted as warmongers. They say we offer simple answers to complex problems. Well, perhaps there is a simple answer . . . not an easy one . . . but a simple one, if you and I have the courage to tell our elected officials that we want our *national* policy based upon what we know in our hearts is morally right.

We cannot buy our security, our freedom from the threat of the bomb by committing an immorality so great as saying to a billion human beings now in slavery behind the Iron Curtain, "Give up your dreams of freedom because to save our own skin, we are willing to make a deal with your slave-masters." Alexander Hamilton[6] said, "A nation which can prefer disgrace to danger is prepared for a master, and deserves one!" Let's set the record straight. There is no argument over the choice between peace and war, but there is only one guaranteed way you can have peace . . . and you can have it in the next second . . . surrender!

Admittedly there is a risk in any course we follow other than this, but every lesson in history tells us that the greater risk lies in appeasement, and this is the specter our well-meaning liberal friends refuse to face . . . that their policy of accommodation is appeasement, and it gives no choice between peace and war, only between fight or surrender. If we continue to accommodate, continue to back and retreat, eventually

6. Among his many accomplishments, Hamilton (1757–1804) advocated the cause of revolution in pamphlets and speeches, was confidential secretary to George Washington during the Revolutionary War, contributed half of the essays collected in *The Federalist*, and was secretary of the treasury, 1789–1795.

we have to face the final demand—the ultimatum. And what then? When Nikita Khrushchev has told his people he knows what our answer will be? He has told them that we are retreating under the pressure of the cold war, and someday, when the time comes to deliver the ultimatum, our surrender will be voluntary because by that time we will have been weakened from within spiritually, morally, and economically. He believes this because from our side he has heard voices pleading for "peace at any price" or "better Red than dead," or as one commentator put it, he would rather "live on his knees than die on his feet." And therein lies the road to war, because those voices don't speak for the rest of us. You and I know and do not believe that life is so dear and peace so sweet as to be purchased at the price of chains and slavery. If nothing in life is worth dying for, when did this begin—just in the face of this enemy?—or should Moses have told the children of Israel to live in slavery under the pharaohs? Should Christ have refused the cross? Should the patriots at Concord Bridge have thrown down their guns and refused to fire the shot heard round the world?[7] The martyrs of history were not fools, and our honored dead who gave their lives to stop the advance of the Nazis didn't die in vain! Where, then, is the road to peace? Well, it's a simple answer after all.

You and I have the courage to say to our enemies, "There is a price we will not pay." There is a point beyond which they must not advance! This is the meaning in the phrase of Barry Goldwater's "peace through strength!" Winston Churchill said that "the destiny of man is not measured by material computation. When great forces are on the move in the world, we learn we are spirits—not animals." And he said, "There is something going on in time and space, and beyond time and space, which, whether we like it or not, spells duty." You and I have a rendezvous with destiny. We will preserve for our children this, the last best hope of man on earth, or we will sentence them to take the last step into a thousand years of darkness.

We will keep in mind and remember that Barry Goldwater has faith in us. He has faith that you and I have the ability and the dignity and the right to make our own decisions and determine our own destiny.

Thank you.

1964

7. On April 19, 1775, American militiamen opposed the British army in the villages of Lexington and Concord, Massachusetts. News of this battle sparked the American Revolution.

Doris Kearns Goodwin
b. 1943

Goodwin is a historian who writes best-selling histories of U.S. presidents. You might think of history as a recitation of facts: a story that simply recites what happened in a particular place at a particular time. But, really, history is rhetoric. History always interprets *the past, and historical facts are the evidence in the historian's argument. This piece is taken from a book titled* Leadership in Turbulent Times. *Goodwin uses four examples from her previous research (on Abraham Lincoln, Teddy Roosevelt, Franklin Delano Roosevelt, and Lyndon Baines Johnson) to prove what is good leadership. The whole book, then, is a big inductive argument, using examples to derive a generalized conclusion.*

I picked this example of history because it is about *rhetoric. Goodwin recounts the rhetorical techniques and maneuvers Johnson used to coax a reluctant Congress to pass the Civil Rights Act of 1964. Johnson was a Democrat, and Democrats held both houses of Congress, but most Democrats from Southern states (sometimes called "Dixiecrats") desperately protected white supremacy. Johnson himself, who for decades had been a congressman from Texas before he became vice president, was a rare exception. He had to overcome opposition in his own party as well as the opposition of Republicans. "Lyndon Johnson," Goodwin writes, "knew that people were 'more easily influenced' by stories 'than any other way,' that stories were remembered far longer than facts and figures." Goodwin and Johnson both talk here of the power of the anecdote: the example that puts a human face on statistical evidence. One might argue in the abstract that Jim Crow laws deprive millions of their basic rights, but the image of Zephyr Wright having "to go squat in the middle of the field to pee" is what sticks in the mind. Similarly, Martin Luther King Jr. uses the powers of the anecdote when he tells the story of his daughter discovering she's barred from Funtown in "Letter from Birmingham Jail."*

Visionary Leadership: Lyndon Johnson and Civil Rights

Everything was in chaos, Lyndon Johnson recalled of the hours and days following Kennedy's assassination. One shocking event cascaded into the next as the country watched in real time, aghast—the announcement that shots had been fired at Kennedy's motorcade, confirmation of the president's death, the arrest and subsequent murder of Lee Harvey Oswald, the identification of Dallas nightclub owner Jack Ruby as the murderer, the speculation that both murders were part of a larger conspiracy related to Russia, Cuba, or the Mafia. For four days, from the assassination to the funeral, Americans remained transfixed before television screens as the three networks canceled all regular programming to cover the news.

This unfolding tragedy presented Lyndon Johnson with extreme danger yet also an unprecedented opportunity for action and judgment. A successful transition called for both the establishment of immediate command and the symbolic assurance of continuity. "The times cried out for leadership," Johnson later said. "A nation stunned, shaken to its very heart had to be reassured that the government was not in a state of paralysis." And beyond the nation, "the whole world would be anxiously following every move I made—watching, judging, weighing." As such, "it was imperative that I grasp the reins of power and do so without delay. Any hesitation or wavering, any false step, any sign of self-doubt, could have been disastrous."

"We were all spinning around and around, trying to come to grips with what had happened, but the more we tried to understand it, the more confused we got. We were like a bunch of cattle caught in the swamp, unable to move in either direction, simply circling round and round." With this imagery, Johnson harked back to his childhood in the Texas Hill Country, to the stories his grandfather told. "I knew what had to be done," Johnson continued. "There is but one way to get the cattle out of the swamp. And that is for the man on the horse to take the lead, to assume command, to provide direction. In the period of confusion after the assassination, I was that man."

Even as he showed strength and assurance to the public at large, however, he exhibited modesty and deference to Kennedy's inner circle. In contrast to Theodore Roosevelt, who, in the wake of McKinley's assassination, had three years to gain his footing before facing the electorate in his own right, Johnson had less than a year before the next election. There was no time to build a new team from scratch. Furthermore, the retention of the important Kennedy men signaled respect and steadiness. In this contradictory role of beseeching power, as humble apprentice striving gradually to attain mastery, Johnson had long excelled.

Johnson approached each of the Kennedy men: "I know how much *he* needed you. I need you that much more and so does our country." Never once did he suggest that however things were done before, this was now *his* White House. "I knew how they felt," he later said. "Suddenly *they* were outsiders just as I had been for almost three years, outsiders on the inside." Checking his storied arrogance, softening his tone, he conveyed a deep humility, sharing his doubts, continuously requesting patience, advice, and assistance. "There is much I don't know," he would say. "You must teach me." That so many key figures of Kennedy's cabinet and White House staff remained during the transition testified to the perfect pitch he displayed during this fraught transition.

So faultless was Johnson's performance upon his assumption of leadership that it appeared as if he had long rehearsed what he would do if he held the power and the time were ripe. Suddenly, the time was right. He chanced to hold the power and he intended to use it.

Everyone agreed that Lyndon Johnson was a master mechanic of the legislative process. What became apparent from the first hours of his presidency, however, was that he meant to use these unparalleled skills in the service of a full-blown vision of the role government should play in the lives of the people. From the outset, he knew exactly where he wanted to take the country in domestic affairs and he had a working idea of how to get there.

After landing in the nation's capital at 6 p.m. of the day of the assassination, he reached out by phone to scores of people, including former presidents Harry Truman and Dwight Eisenhower, and met with a delegation of congressional leaders in his vice presidential office in the Executive Office Building. At 10 p.m., he returned to "The Elms," his three-story residence in Spring Valley, Washington, with a small group of advisers and friends. "Spend the night with me," he entreated three close aides, Jack Valenti, Cliff Carter, and Bill Moyers. More than ever, he did not want to be alone. After this cataclysmic day, he especially needed an intimate circle of listeners to sort out his thoughts and to get his bearings. An hour later, after Lady Bird went to sleep in her own bedroom, Johnson put on his pajamas, and with the three men propped beside him on his immense bed, held forth as they all watched the nonstop reportage of the world-riveting story on the television.

In the early morning hours, Valenti recalled, "the new president began to ruminate aloud about his plans, his objectives, the great goals he was bound to attain." In his mind's eye he could already envision a future in which all of Kennedy's progressive legislation, then deadlocked in Congress, had become law: "I'm going to get Kennedy's tax cut out of the Senate Finance Committee, and we're going to get this economy humming again. Then I'm going to pass Kennedy's civil rights bill, which has been hung up too long in the Congress. And I'm going to pass it without changing a single comma or a word. After that we'll pass legislation that allows everyone anywhere in the country to vote, with all the barriers down. And that's not all. We're going to get a law that says every boy and girl in this country, no matter how poor, or the color of their skin, or the region they come from, is going to be able to get all the education they can take by loan, scholarship, or grant, right from the federal government. And I aim to pass Harry Truman's medical insurance bill that got nowhere before."

The somnolent vice president seemed magically reawakened as he revealed a rudimentary sketch of what would become the Great Society. This might seem an apocryphal tale had not three aides been there until 3 a.m. to witness his fierce resolve not simply to dislodge Kennedy's stalled agenda but to realize a society built on racial and economic justice far beyond the dreams of the New Deal and the New Frontier.

The vision Johnson traced in those predawn hours had been incubating for many decades. From his populist father he had inherited the belief that the role of government was to look after those who needed help. "That's what we're here for," his father had repeatedly reminded his son. The seminal concept that government should use its power to better the lives of others had been consolidated during his work in Roosevelt's New Deal. It was further enumerated in his "call to arms" speech in the wake of his near fatal heart attack, and informed his maneuvers to pass the 1957 civil rights bill.

"That whole night," Moyers recalled of Johnson's musings at The Elms, "he seemed to have several chambers of his mind operating simultaneously. It was formidable, very formidable."

How was Johnson able to actualize this vision?

Make a Dramatic Start.

Lyndon Johnson's most important task, the necessary condition upon which all else hinged, was to convince his countrymen that he was capable of filling the brutally sudden vacuum of leadership. He had to dispel doubts, quell suspicions, and allay fears.

In this time of dark national emergency, the new president was inclined by temperament to act quickly. At each new position in his long career he had sought a quick, sure start, an attention-fastening moment. Now, the day after Kennedy's burial, he chose to make a major speech to the nation. This choice was not without risk, for, with few exceptions, Johnson had revealed an inability to speak persuasively in large, formal settings. The man who could exercise instant command over any small gathering had tended to stiffen when forced to stand behind a podium. And this address would be the most important he had ever delivered. "He knew," Moyers said, "that the people watching it were burning with questions, wondering, 'Who is that man?'" When he stepped off the podium, "they would either have confidence in him—or not."

Lead With Your Strengths.

From the start, Johnson made two important decisions. First, he would deliver his speech before a live audience at a Joint Session of Congress rather than before a television camera in the empty Oval Office. Congress had been his home for more than three decades, the source of his security, achievement, and power. Many in the audience would be longtime friends and colleagues. Also in attendance would be the Supreme Court justices and the members of the cabinet, the full panoply of legitimate succession.

Second, he would use the occasion to call upon his former colleagues to break the total legislative gridlock that had prevented every one of Kennedy's major domestic initiatives from becoming law. A month before the assassination, columnist Walter Lippmann had written that there was "reason to wonder whether the Congressional system as it now operates is not a grave danger to the Republic." Indeed, as an editorial in *Life* magazine had pointed out, this Congress had sat longer than any previous body "while accomplishing practically nothing." The inability of Congress to move legislation forward, Johnson agreed, was "developing into a national crisis," exposing America's democratic system to widespread criticism at home and abroad.

In choosing to focus on Kennedy's blocked domestic agenda, Johnson settled on the field where he felt most deeply involved, most confident of his knowledge, most comfortable in dealing with policy details. The arenas of foreign and military affairs, which had been the specialty and focus of the Kennedy administration, were uncongenial to him. And he was fortunate to come into office at an ostensibly tranquil moment in international affairs.

"If any sense were to come of the senseless events which had brought me to the office of the Presidency," he later said, "it would come only from my using my experience as a legislator to encourage the legislative process to function." Believing that Kennedy's death had created "a sympathetic atmosphere" for the passage of the stalled New Frontier agenda, Johnson planned to turn the "dead man's program into a martyr's cause." But the window of opportunity was very small. If he had any chance of succeeding, he had to move ahead at warp speed before the supportive mood began to dissipate.

Simplify the Agenda.

From the outset, Johnson decided to pare down Kennedy's domestic agenda to two essential items: the civil rights bill designed to end segregation in the South and the tax cut intended to stimulate the economy. Over many hours of conversation at The Elms, Johnson's advisers debated the wisdom of these choices. "At one point," attorney Abe Fortas recalled, one of the men spoke up forcefully against recommending "congressional action on civil rights," and most particularly against making it his "number one" priority. "The presidency has only a certain amount of coinage to expend," he warned Johnson, "and you oughtn't to expend it on this. It will never get through."

"Well," Johnson replied with an unambiguous answer, "what the hell's the presidency for?"

When Johnson entered the House chamber at noon of November 27, 1963, a hush came over the audience. "All that I have," he began, "I would have given gladly not to be standing here today." With simple eloquence, he set a tone of sorrowful humility that would blend a funeral oration with an inaugural call for action.

> On the 20th day of January, in 1961, John F. Kennedy told his countrymen that our national work would not be finished "in the first thousand days, nor in the life of this administration, nor even perhaps in our lifetime on this planet. But," he said, "let us begin." Today, in this moment of new resolve, I say to all my fellow Americans, let us continue.

In contrast to the Kennedy inaugural, however, which presaged a resurgent America in the world's eye with no mention of domestic affairs, Johnson outlined his hopes for domestic policy with hardly a nod to foreign policy.

> First, no memorial oration or eulogy could more eloquently honor President Kennedy's memory than the earliest possible passage of the civil rights bill for which he fought so long. We have talked long enough in this country about equal rights. We have talked for one hundred years or more. It is time now to write the next chapter and to write it in the books of law.
>
> And second, no act of ours could more fittingly continue the work of President Kennedy than the early passage of the tax bill for which he fought all this long year.

He firmly believed, Johnson said, "in the ability of the Congress, despite the divisions of opinions which characterize our Nation, to act—to act wisely, to act vigorously, to act speedily when the need arises. The need is here. The need is now. I ask your help."

In his call for action to fill the leadership vacuum, one journalist noted, Johnson appeared to have "modeled" himself "after the man he has most admired in his political career—Franklin D. Roosevelt."

Just as Roosevelt had called "for action, and action now" to carry the people through a "dark hour" in their national life, so Johnson had exhorted us to show the world that "we can and will act and act now." Both men addressed a volatile, depressed, and fearful nation. Both men countered despondency and confusion and sought to give hope, confidence, and renewed direction. And both men ministered to a stricken nation and uplifted the country's morale.

By the time Johnson finished, the applauding audience was on its feet, many in tears. "It was a remarkable performance," critics agreed, "perfectly suitable to the most difficult circumstances, directly calculated to get results." Equal to the words of the address, his demeanor, measured pace, solemnity, and determination all conveyed that a genuine transference of power and purpose from the slain president to his successor had taken place. Headlines told the story:

LEADERSHIP IN GOOD HANDS
JOHNSON EMERGES GRAVE AND STRONG
NEW CHIEF MET THE TEST

Through this single speech, delivered to a nation still in mourning, Lyndon Johnson bridged what had seemed an impossible span. He had seized the reins of power and established a shared sense of direction and purpose for his sudden presidency.[1]

* * *

To sweep away stagnation, to get things moving in this lethargic Congress, Lyndon Johnson had used every straw of the broom. Furthermore, he made it clear to Congress and his administration that he was now prepared to brush aside all other pending legislation to clear space for a single-minded focus on civil rights.

Master the Power of Narrative.

Lyndon Johnson, like Abraham Lincoln and Franklin Roosevelt, knew that people were "more easily influenced" by stories "than any other way," that stories were remembered far longer than facts and

1. In the next section, which is removed here for the sake of space, Goodwin discusses Johnson's successful campaign to get his tax bill through Congress. [All notes are the editor's.]

figures. So now, when talking with civil rights leaders and die-hard southerners, Johnson told variations of the same personal story to underscore his conviction that the ironclad system of segregation that had governed daily life in the South for three-quarters of a century—the Jim Crow laws that prevented blacks from entering white-only public restaurants, bathrooms, hotels, motels, lunch counters, movie theaters, sports arenas, and concert halls—must stand no longer.

Every year, Johnson related, his longtime black employees—his housemaid and butler, Helen and Gene Williams, and his cook, Zephyr Wright—would drive his extra car from Washington back to Texas. On one of these arduous three-day journeys, Johnson asked Gene if he would take along the family beagle. Johnson was surprised when Gene balked. "He shouldn't give you any trouble, Gene. You know Beagle loves you." Gene was reluctant.

"Well, Senator," Gene explained, "it's tough enough to get all the way from Washington to Texas. We drive for hours and hours. We get hungry. But there's no place on the road we can stop and go in and eat. We drive some more. It gets pretty hot. We want to wash up. But the only bathroom we're allowed in is usually miles off the main highway. We keep going 'til night comes—'til we get so tired we can't stay awake any more. We're ready to pull in. But it takes us another hour or so to find a place to sleep. You see, what I'm saying is that a colored man's got enough trouble getting across the South on his own, without having a dog along." At that juncture, Johnson had confessed, "there was nothing I could say to Gene."

He told another variant of this anecdote to segregationist John Stennis of Mississippi after the senator vehemently denounced the public accommodations section of the civil rights bill. "You know, John," Johnson said, "that's just bad. That's wrong. And there ought to be something to change that. And it seems to me if the people in Mississippi don't change it voluntarily, that it's just going to be necessary to change it by law."

Still another version of this story was told to civil rights advocates when asked why he was so passionate about ending Jim Crow. It was just plain wrong, he told James Farmer, leader of the Congress of Racial Equality, that Zephyr Wright, his college-educated cook, had to "go squat in the middle of the field to pee." It was humiliating. Something had to be done about it.

And now, for the first time, Johnson concluded, the country finally had the makings of a real answer for Gene and for all black Americans. If the civil rights bill currently stonewalled in Congress could become the law of the land, blacks would no longer have to suffer the indignities of an outmoded and cruelly unjust system of segregation.

Know for What and When to Risk It All.

The proposed bill surely contained the most flammable social, political, and moral issues—and the most deeply personal ones—Johnson had ever taken on. The chances of failure were large. "My strength as President was then tenuous—I had no strong mandate from the people. I had not been elected to that office." The next presidential election was only eleven months away. Nor was the decision taken without a tremendous sense of personal loss: "It was destined to set me apart forever from the South, where I had been born and reared. It seemed likely to alienate me from some of the Southerners in Congress who had been my loyal friends for years."

And yet, "there comes a time in every leader's career," Johnson said, quoting Franklin Roosevelt's poker-playing vice president, John Nance Garner, "when he has to put in all his stack. I decided to shove in all my stack on this vital measure." As a consequence of the civil rights movement, the country was changing and so was he. Johnson intended to use "every ounce of strength" he possessed to achieve passage of the civil rights bill. Civil rights leader Roy Wilkins was immediately "struck by the enormous difference between Kennedy and Johnson." Where Kennedy was "dry-eyed, realistic," Johnson was passionate. Both Martin Luther King and Whitney Young also came away from their first meetings with the new president profoundly impressed by his "deep convictions" and "the depth of his concern" for civil rights. Indeed, Martin Luther King told friends that "it just might be that he's going to go where John Kennedy couldn't."

Rally Support Around a Strategic Target.

In the House of Representatives, the civil rights bill was stuck in procedural limbo by Virginia's eighty-year-old autocrat, Judge Howard Smith. A defiant Smith had predictably used his authority as Rules

Committee chair to prevent his committee from holding hearings to establish the rules of debate—without which no bill could even proceed to the floor. Meanwhile, the frustration of civil rights leaders mounted, and in the streets tensions escalated.

As Johnson analyzed the situation, he concluded that only one option remained—a rarely used House procedure known as a discharge petition. If a majority of the members (218) signed the petition, a bill bottled up in committee would be blasted onto the floor. Since House members generally felt protective of seniority and the traditional committee system, however, only a handful of discharge petitions had ever become law.

Johnson acknowledged that it was "a mighty hard route," but at the same time he understood that the fight for 218 signatures would give civil rights supporters a specific target to consolidate what was otherwise an ill-organized campaign. And he knew that for Judge Smith, no charm offensive would work; without coercion, Smith would "piddle along," delaying hearings all through winter and spring until summer came and it was time for Congress to adjourn.

Johnson understood that direct presidential meddling on a question of internal House proceedings might compromise the chances for the discharge petition. So instead, he worked to pressure members from the outside in. During his first two weeks in office, he met with civil rights leaders, liberal groups, union leaders, church groups, and members of the Business Council. He reasoned, prodded, pleaded, and, in the end, inspired them to make the discharge petition their priority. Then, day after day, he followed up with dozens of phone calls, which, fortunately for history, he secretly taped. These recordings reveal the conversational dexterity of a master strategist at work, providing a far more complex portrait of leadership than the bullying transgression of others' personal space, the jabbing index finger, and the simple-minded quid pro quo generally described as the "Johnson treatment."

He began with civil rights leaders A. Philip Randolph, Martin Luther King, and Roy Wilkins. He didn't want to be quoted, he told them, but he suggested that they concentrate all their focus on getting "every friend to sign that petition the moment it's laid down." Call on your supporters in Congress. Go to see them. Create a sense of momentum. "This ought to be your-all's strategy. And I want you to be thinking about it." He reached out to liberal groups who had long been skeptical of his leadership. "If I've done anything wrong in the past," Johnson told Americans for Democratic Action founder Joe Rauh, "I want you to know that's nothing now—we're going to work together." He told David McDonald, head of the United Steelworkers of America, that "if there's ever a time when you really need to talk to every human being you could," this is the time. "They'll be saying they don't want to violate procedure," he warned everyone, and offered the talking point: "Just say that the humblest man anywhere has a right to a hearing."

The drive for Democratic signatures from the North and West quickly totaled 150, but to reach the magic number of 218, 50 or 60 Republicans would be needed. Talking with members of the Business Council and with former officials in Eisenhower's cabinet, Johnson disclosed a dramatic new line of argument.[2] He told them to tell their Republican friends there was no longer a place to hide behind procedure: "You're either for civil rights or you're not. You're either the party of Lincoln or you ain't—by God, put up or shut up!"

In private phone calls to prominent journalists and editors, he laid out an attack against those unwilling to sign. "Point them up," he told the *Washington Post*'s Katharine Graham, "and have their pictures, and have editorials." Ask them, "Why are you against a hearing?" Whatever man is against a hearing to bring the bill to the floor where it can be voted on its merits, "is not a man that believes in giving humanity a fair shake." A few days later the *Washington Post* published an editorial, "Friend or Foe," which made the precise argument Johnson had outlined. "Let the members of the House make no mistake about it: the test is at hand. They will determine the fate of the civil rights bill by their willingness to sign the discharge petition before they go home for Christmas." This is no less than "a test of the capacity of Congress to meet an inescapable and historical challenge."

When, after two weeks, the number of signatures had climbed to 209 and was still rising, a ranking Republican member of the House Rules Committee approached Howard Smith. "I don't want to run over you, Judge, but . . ." Nothing more needed to be said. Smith

2. Dwight David Eisenhower, a Republican, was president from 1953 to 1961.

capitulated, avoiding "the indignity of being relieved of responsibility for the bill." On December 9, he promised to hold hearings as soon as Congress reconvened after Christmas. When the hearings concluded, the bill was finally brought before the floor on January 31. The majority succeeded in striking down every amendment that would have substantially weakened the bill.

Between the moral force of the civil rights movement and Johnson's skillful use of the bully pulpit, a consensus had been built. While "to some people," Johnson noted in his memoirs, the word *consensus* meant "a search for the lowest common denominator," that definition belied the "prime and indispensable obligation of the Presidency"—to decide first what needs "to be done regardless of the political implications" and then to "convince the Congress and the people to do it." For Johnson, a successful consensus was the consequence of effective persuasion.

On February 10, by a clear margin, the House of Representatives passed the strongest civil rights bill since Reconstruction. The wheels of democratic government were at last beginning to turn.

Draw a Clear Line of Battle.

As Johnson prepared for the Senate fight, he made it absolutely clear that this time, unlike 1957, he would allow no significant compromises. "I knew that the slightest wavering on my part would give hope to the opposition's strategy of amending the bill to death." Uncharacteristically, the master bargainer and wheeler-dealer had drawn a line in the sand. And upon that outcome Lyndon Johnson's relationship to his heritage, to his political career, and most of all to his vision for the country's future, hung in the balance.

To make his position transparent, he invited Richard Russell, leader of the southern opposition, to join him in the White House for a Sunday morning breakfast. In less august circumstances they had established this intimate tradition many years before. "Dick, I love you and I owe you," he began. "I wouldn't have been leader without you. I wouldn't have been vice-president, and I wouldn't have been president. So everything I am, I owe to you, and that's why I wanted to tell you face to face, because I love you: don't get in my way on this civil rights bill, or I'm going to run you down."

"Well, Mr. President, you may very well do that. But if you do, I promise, you'll not only lose the election, but you'll lose the South forever."[3]

"Dick, you may be right. But if that's the price I've got to pay, I'm going to gladly do it."

"These few words shaped the entire struggle," Johnson later wrote. The two old friends knew each other intimately. It would be a fight to the end. Russell would do everything in his power to hold on to his region's historic past, to prevent the federal government from forcibly changing the local laws and the customs that governed daily life. "It's too late in life for me to change," he said. For his part, Johnson saw beyond the present struggle to a time when the old South would be freed from "old hostilities" and "old hatreds," when a new South would rise, "growing every hour," joined "in single purpose" with "every section of this country."

Russell told a reporter in early January that he "would have beaten President Kennedy," or at least forced him to make substantial concessions, but now, with Johnson, it would be "three times harder." Kennedy "didn't have to pass a strong bill to prove anything on civil rights. President Johnson does." The moment a son of the South begins to compromise, Russell explained, his credibility among northerners would be shattered. Both men understood that "it would be a fight to total victory or total defeat without appeasement or attrition."

Impose Discipline in the Ranks.

So, even before the House bill reached the Senate, Russell had begun mobilizing his troops for what would become the longest filibuster in American history. He prepared a tag team of senators to talk for four or five hours at a time, reading the Constitution, reciting poetry, excoriating provisions of the bill. While Russell feared Johnson's mastery of the process, he knew that history was on his side. Never had advocates for a civil rights bill been able to

3. Russell refers here to what becomes the Republican Party's notorious "Southern" strategy: convince white voters in the South, who traditionally were Democrats, to start voting Republican by appealing to their racism.

achieve the two-thirds vote necessary to invoke cloture and bring debate to a close. Even senators who supported civil rights were reluctant to cut short a procedure that held an honored place in the Senate, especially among senators from smaller, less populous states who considered the filibuster a final defense against being bullied by the majority.

From the outset, Johnson understood that Russell's objective was "to talk the bill to death," or at least prolong its consideration until adjournment for the Republican convention in July, when public events might well change the configuration of things. Johnson also feared that the longer the bill was kept from reaching the floor, the greater the frustrations of the civil rights movement, the more likely the chance that any flaring violence in the cities might stoke white backlash against civil rights.

The battle thereby became a tug-of-war over time. Civil rights supporters aimed to compress time, opponents to extend it. Frequent quorum calls were a favorite southern tactic to prolong time. If fewer than fifty-one senators were on the floor, any member could request a quorum call. The day's activity would be interrupted while senators were rounded up. If a quorum could not be reached, the Senate would be compelled to adjourn. The current legislative day would cease, giving southerners a rest until the following morning. If these quorum calls resembled a child's game of musical chairs, it was deadly competition, providing the means for stretching time until the Senate adjourned without ever engaging the bill.

When only thirty-nine of the fifty-one senators showed up for a quorum call one Saturday in early April, Johnson angrily reacted, telling floor manager and civil rights champion Hubert Humphrey that liberals had to learn the rules, that they couldn't be "off making speeches when they ought to be in the Senate. I know you've got a great opportunity here but I'm afraid it's going to fall between the boards." At Johnson's insistence, Humphrey created "a corporal's guard," a team of ten civil rights supporters responsible for mustering five or six colleagues to answer the quorum call. The duty list changed daily, Humphrey recalled, "recognizing that some senators had to be away part of the time," especially those up for reelection.

That civil rights supporters never afterward missed a quorum call was theatrically apparent during the Washington Senators' opening day baseball game. President Johnson had invited dozens of senators to join him. A small group of southerners who had stayed behind to continue the filibuster took advantage of the absence and called for a quorum. "Attention please! Attention please!" the public address system blared, carrying the message through D.C. Stadium. "All senators must report back to the Senate for a quorum call!" A fleet of limousines pulled up to the park and carried the senators back to the Senate floor to meet the quorum call in twenty-three minutes. For the first time in the long struggle to pass meaningful civil rights legislation, the parliamentary skill and discipline of the southern contingent was met by the equally organized ranks of civil rights supporters.

Identify the Key to Success. Put Ego Aside.

A legendary nose-counter, Lyndon Johnson was certain "that without Republican support" (given the sectional split in the Democratic Party) "we'd have absolutely no chance of securing the two-thirds vote to defeat the filibuster. And I knew there was but one man who could secure us that support, the senator from Illinois, Everett Dirksen." Just as he had identified Senate finance chair Harry Byrd as the key to success in the tax struggle, so now he saw that Republican minority leader Dirksen was the one man able to corral the twenty-five or so Republicans needed to invoke cloture.

"The bill can't pass unless you get Ev Dirksen," Johnson instructed Humphrey. "You and I are going to get Ev. It's going to take time. But we're going to *get* him. You make up your mind now that you've got to spend time with Ev Dirksen. You've got to let him have a piece of the action. He's got to look good all the time. Don't let those bomb throwers talk you out of seeing Dirksen. Yet get in there to see Dirksen. You drink with Dirksen! You talk with Dirksen! You listen to Dirksen!"

Johnson told Humphrey that civil rights leaders, who might be chary of working with the conservative Dirksen, must understand that "unless we have the Republicans joining us," unless we "make this an American bill and not just a Democratic bill," there will be "mutiny in this goddamn country." Bipartisan unity was essential to placate the turbulence that would likely follow if the bill passed. To National Association for the Advancement of Colored People

(NAACP) leader Roy Wilkins, Johnson made a similar plea: "I think you're all going to have to sit down and persuade Dirksen this in the interest of the Republican Party and I think that he must know that if he helps you then you're going to help him." This issue at hand transcended party politics.

If letting Dirksen take center stage, even to the point of eclipsing both his own role and that of his Democratic colleagues, was essential to achieve effective harmony between the unfolding events in the political arena and in the volatile cities across the country, Johnson was more than ready to oblige.

Take the Measure of the Man.

Like a tailor stitching a bespoke suit, Lyndon Johnson took the measure of Everett Dirksen, just as he had of Harry Byrd, Judge Smith, and indeed, most of the other senators. A decade of experience with the Illinois Republican had taught Johnson that Dirksen had no hesitation asking for "a laundry list" of favors in return for his support on legislation. Now that pattern only accelerated as the filibuster droned on. Johnson would sit with Dirksen over drinks in the White House dispensing all manner of quid pro quos: a judgeship in the 5th District, a post office in Peoria, a promised presidential speech in Springfield, an ambassadorial appointment, a federal project in Chicago. A thick pile of memos in the Johnson Library attests to their copious swappings and dealings over the years.

But this time, Johnson offered Dirksen something far more important than tangible favors. Beneath the flamboyant minority leader's penchant for grandstanding, Johnson detected a genuine idealism and patriotism. He appealed to Dirksen's hunger to be remembered. "I saw your exhibit at the World's Fair, and it said, 'The Land of Lincoln,'" Johnson pointed out. "And the man from Lincoln is going to pass this bill and I'm going to see that he gets proper credit." With a gift for flattery equal to Dirksen's vanity, he assured the senator, "if you come with me on this bill, two hundred years from now there'll be only two people they'll remember from the state of Illinois: Abraham Lincoln and Everett Dirksen!"

As the filibuster dragged on week after week, Dirksen began to play what might have become a "dangerous game." Unless he could thumbprint the language of the final measure with some amendments of his own, Dirksen could not bring his fellow Republicans along. Although Johnson appreciated Dirksen's dilemma, he balked at any public discussion of amendments, relegating the process of negotiation with Dirksen to Humphrey, Attorney General Robert Kennedy, and the civil rights leaders. In the end, the civil rights coalition reached an agreement on several amendments that did not alter the fundamental integrity of the bill. "We've got a much better bill than anyone dreamed possible," Humphrey assured Johnson. Once that agreement was reached, Dirksen took to the floor to announce his support for the bill. Quoting Victor Hugo, Dirksen said: "Stronger than an Army is an idea whose time has come."[4] With the Senate minority leader fully on board, a cloture petition was filed, setting June 9 as the date for the vote. Dirksen's support notwithstanding, the civil rights forces appeared a half-dozen votes short.

The time had come for both the president and the civil rights coalition to shift into overdrive. In the waning hours, Johnson personally recruited several western senators, while clerics of all denominations reached out to their congregations. On June 9, after more than five hundred hours of talk stretched over seventy-five days, Humphrey was finally convinced he had secured the requisite sixty-seven votes. After a high-voltage, questioning phone call from Johnson, Humphrey stayed up all night to make sure.

When the Senate convened at 10 a.m. on June 10 for the final hour of debate before the cloture vote would be taken, every seat was filled and the walls of the Senate gallery were lined with people standing to witness the grand event. "I say to my colleagues of the Senate," Hubert Humphrey said, "that perhaps in your lives you will be able to tell your children's children that you were here for America to make the year 1964 our freedom year."

Tension rose as the clerk began the roll call. No sound was heard when California's senator Clair Engle's name was called. The fifty-two-year-old Engle had been hospitalized since April following surgery for a malignant brain tumor. The night before, after speaking

4. Victor Hugo (1802–1885) was a French novelist best known for his monumental historical tales, *Les Misérables* and *The Hunchback of Notre Dame.* This quotation is from an essay, "The History of Crime," about Napoleon III's rise to power in France.

with Engle's wife and doctor, Johnson had arranged for an ambulance to transport Engle to the Senate. Seated in a wheelchair, unable to speak, Engle slowly lifted his hand and pointed to his eye. "I guess that means 'aye,'" the clerk said, as the chamber erupted in applause. When the clerk reached the Ws, Delaware's John Williams recorded the 67th vote, shutting off the filibuster. Finally the majority could register its vote. There was nothing now to stop the passage of the sweeping bill that would vanquish legal segregation in the United States at last.

"Although I differ—and differ vigorously—with President Johnson on this so-called civil rights question," Russell said, "I expect to support the President just as strongly when I think he is right as I intend to oppose him when I think he is wrong." For his part, Johnson had approached Russell from the beginning with affection and sensitivity and without a trace of vindictiveness. Clearly, both men loved the South, but Russell clung to its past while Johnson nurtured a different economic and social vision for its future, a vision stillborn without the changes this bill promised to deliver.

On July 2, after the House accepted the Senate's version, Lyndon Johnson signed the Civil Rights Act of 1964 before members of Congress and the civil rights coalition at a memorable ceremony in the East Room of the White House. He gave the first of seventy-five signing pens to Everett Dirksen, followed by Hubert Humphrey, the House leaders, and leaders of the civil rights movement. During the reception, Johnson reminded Lady Bird that this was the ninth anniversary of his heart attack, the profound experience that had altered his outlook on power and purpose. "Happy anniversary," she told him with a laugh.

And a joyous day it was. After the signing, Johnson's thoughts returned "to that afternoon a decade before when there was absolutely nothing I could say to Gene Williams or to any black man, or to myself. That had been the day I first realized the sad truth that to the extent Negroes were imprisoned, so was I. On this day, July 2, 1964, I knew the positive side of that same truth: that to the extent Negroes were free, really free, so was I. And so was my country."

* * *

Know When to Hold Back, When to Move Forward.

After the long struggle to secure the Civil Rights Act of 1964, Johnson felt that the dust had to settle before pressing for the next item on the agenda of the civil rights coalition—a vastly strengthened voting rights bill. Congress, he adjudged, needed time to heal the wounds of division. On a practical level, federal agencies needed time to develop enforcement procedures to integrate public restaurants, bathrooms, and theaters. And the American people needed a period of calm without renewed discord in order to assimilate the vast political and social impact of the earlier bill.

Johnson's commitment to the objective of voting rights was never in question. He told Martin Luther King at the start of the 1965 congressional session that passage of a strong voting rights bill would be "the greatest breakthrough" for African Americans, more vital than the Civil Rights Act of 1964. "Once the black man's voice could be translated into ballots," he maintained, "many other breakthroughs would follow, and they would follow as a consequence of the black man's own legitimate power as an American citizen, not as a gift from the white man." For the present, he entreated King to work with him on the rest of the Great Society legislation. Both Medicare and aid to education were at critical stages, and both were vital to the quality of black as well as white lives. Queued behind these bills on the prospective assembly line awaited a public works bill for economically distressed communities, a nationwide job training act, a revitalization of inner cities, expanded poverty relief, and much more. Let this agenda get through to help all Americans, Johnson promised, and voting rights would be the absolute number one priority in 1966.

Events in Selma, Alabama, would alter the entire landscape. An added cog was driven into the orderly timetable of Lyndon Johnson's projected order of legislation. In early March 1965, King and civil rights activists had taken independent action to mobilize support for a voting rights bill that would eliminate the exclusionary and punitive tests southern officials required African Americans to pass before allowing registration. Such sham tests included quoting the first ten amendments, reciting sections of the Constitution, or explaining the Fourteenth Amendment. The discriminatory system worked precisely as southern officials planned: of fifteen thousand voting-age African Americans in Selma, only 335 were registered to vote.

On March 7, an infamous day that came to be known as "Bloody Sunday," more than six hundred civil rights activists gathered at Brown Chapel in Selma to begin a peaceful fifty-four-mile march to Montgomery, the state's capital. When they reached the narrow Edmund Pettus Bridge, they walked side by side, singing "We Shall Overcome," the anthem of the civil rights movement. At the top of the bridge, they were met by state troopers and Sheriff Jim Clark's mounted posse, armed with pistols, nightsticks, bullwhips, and billy clubs. As television cameras recorded the scene, "the mounted men charged. In minutes it was over, and more than sixty marchers lay injured, old women and young children among them. More than a score were taken to the hospital." As the marchers retreated toward Brown Chapel, the mounted posse pursued them. The carnage, which was witnessed by millions of television viewers, mobilized the conscience of the nation.

"It was important to move at once if we were to achieve anything permanent from this transitory mood," Johnson recalled. "It was equally important that we move in the right direction." As demonstrations across the country spread in size and intensity, massive pressure was brought to bear on Johnson to mobilize the National Guard to protect the marchers who planned to resume their walk to Montgomery. Pickets surrounded the White House carrying placards designed to shame the president into action: "LBJ, open your eyes, see the sickness of the South, see the horrors of your homeland." Despite the terrible pressure, Johnson deemed the moment had not yet come. He feared "that a hasty display of federal force at this time would destroy whatever possibilities existed for the passage of voting rights legislation." As a southerner, he knew well that the sending of federal troops would revive bitter memories of Reconstruction and risk transforming Alabama's governor George Wallace into a martyr for states' rights. "We had to have a real victory for the black people," he insisted, "not a psychological victory for the North."

As people from all over the country streamed into Selma to join the march, Johnson reached out to Governor Wallace. He understood that Wallace was caught in a bind. As governor, he was responsible for maintaining law and order. Continued bloodshed would damage his national standing and hopes for higher office. Yet if

Wallace deployed the Alabama State Guard to protect black citizens, his white political base would turn on him. "It's his ox that's in the ditch," Johnson figured. At a hastily arranged private meeting at the White House, Johnson suggested a deal. If Wallace *requested* help because the state could not properly protect the marchers with its own resources, Johnson would at once federalize the Alabama National Guard. Of utmost importance was at whose request federal force was brought to bear. When the troops went in, Johnson later explained, "they were not intruders forcing their way in," and "that made all the difference in the world."

With the immediate problem of law and order held in abeyance, Johnson focused on the major underlying issue—how best to utilize the Selma atrocity and the ensuing national humiliation to expedite passage of a voting rights bill. On Bloody Sunday, Johnson had directed Attorney General Nicholas Katzenbach to work nonstop to draft the strongest possible bill. By the following Sunday morning, the draft was completed. Through seven crisis-filled days, Johnson had outwaited critics and let the horrific events in Selma reverberate through the American people.

Now the time to push for voting rights had come. The question arose: how best to transmit the message and the bill to Congress. It had been nearly twenty years since a president appeared before Congress to deliver a legislative message. It was full of risk to bypass Congress and appeal directly to the people. Regardless, Johnson chose to seize this moment for executive advocacy with all the might of the bully pulpit. On Sunday evening, he summoned the leaders of Congress to the White House and asked to address a Joint Session at 9 p.m. on Monday night.

"I speak tonight for the dignity of man and the destiny of democracy," Johnson began, speaking with extreme deliberation. "At times history and fate meet at a single time in a single place to shape a turning point in man's unending search for freedom. So it was at Lexington and Concord. So it was a century ago at Appomattox. So it was last week in Selma, Alabama.

> There is no Negro problem. There is no Southern problem. There is only an American problem. And we are met here tonight as Americans—not as Democrats or Republicans—we are met here as Americans to solve that problem.

> There is no issue of States' rights or national rights. There is only the issue of human rights. But even if we pass this bill, the battle will not be over. What happened in Selma is part of a far larger movement which reaches into every section and State of America. It is the effort of American Negroes to secure for themselves the full blessings of American life.
>
> Their cause must be our cause too. Because it is not just Negroes, but really it is all of us, who must overcome the crippling legacy of bigotry and injustice.

Here Johnson stopped. He raised his arms and repeated the words of the old Baptist hymn. "And we . . . shall . . . overcome."

"There was an instant of silence," one White House staffer recalled, "the gradually apprehended realization that the president had proclaimed, adopted as his own rallying cry, the anthem of black protest, the hymn of a hundred embattled black marches." Then, in a matter of seconds, "almost the entire chamber—floor and gallery together—was standing, applauding, shouting, some stamping their feet."

The power of the speech was found not simply in its graceful rhetoric, but in its demonstration of consummate leadership at a critical juncture. Importantly, Johnson declared that "the real hero of this struggle is the American Negro," whose actions had "awakened the conscience of this Nation." Yet, he refused to scapegoat the South, making it clear that no part of the country was immune from responsibility for failing to accord justice to black citizens. "In Buffalo as well as Birmingham, in Philadelphia as well as Selma, Americans are struggling for the fruits of freedom." He reminded his countrymen that while the bill he was sending to Congress was designed for black Americans, civil rights was one part, albeit a keystone, of his vision for a Great Society in which *all* Americans would have "a decent home, and the chance to find a job, and the opportunity to escape from the clutches of poverty."

As he neared the close of his speech, Johnson returned to his own seminal experience as a teacher in the poor Mexican American community of Cotulla, Texas—the place where his ambitions for power were first joined with a deep sense of purpose.

> Somehow you never forget what poverty and hatred can do when you see its scars on the hopeful face of a young child. I never thought then, in 1928, that I would be standing here in 1965. It never occurred to me in my fondest dreams that I might have the chance to help the sons and daughters of those students and to help people like them all over this country.
>
> But now I do have that chance—and I'll let you in on a secret—I mean to use it. And I hope that you will use it with me.

The applause swelled to a crescendo, ignited by the manifest emotional conviction of this moment. "What convinces is conviction," Johnson liked to say. "You simply have to believe in the argument you are advancing." In this instance, Johnson spoke directly from the heart.

Even from his old friend and mentor Richard Russell came words that brought a gratifying smile to Johnson's face. While he couldn't vote for the bill, Russell told Johnson, "it was the best speech he ever heard any president give." More telling for the nation at large, there came a telegram from Martin Luther King: "Your speech to the Joint Session of Congress was the most moving, eloquent and passionate plea for human rights ever made by any President of the Nation."

2018

Notes

333 *"Everything was in chaos"*: Robert Caro, *The Years of Lyndon Johnson: The Path to Power* (New York: Vintage, 1990), p. 353.

333 *"The times cried . . . been disastrous"*: Lyndon Baines Johnson, *The Vantage Point: Perspectives of the Presidency, 1963–1969* (New York: Holt, Rinehart & Winston, 1971), pp. 12, 18.

333 *"We were all spinning . . . I was that man"*: Ibid., p. 172.

334 *"I know how much . . . does our country"*: Eric F. Goldman, *The Tragedy of Lyndon Johnson* (New York: Alfred A. Knopf, 1969), p. 26.

334 *"I knew how they felt . . . on the inside"*: Conversations between the author and LBJ, in the possession of the author.

334 *"There is much . . . teach me"*: Walter Heller, quoted in Rowland Evans and Robert Novak, *Lyndon B. Johnson: The Exercise of Power* (New York: New American Library, 1966), p. 360.

334 *"Spend the night with me"*: Discussion with Harry McPherson and Jack Valenti, "Achilles in the White House," *Wilson Quarterly* (Spring 2000), p. 90.

335 *"the new president . . . got nowhere before"*: Jack Valenti, "Lyndon Johnson: An Awesome Engine of a Man," in Thomas W. Cowger and Sherwin J. Markman, eds., *Lyndon Johnson Remembered: An Intimate Portrait of a Presidency* (Lanham, Md.: Rowman & Littlefield, 2003), p. 37.

335 *"That's what we're here for"*: Caro, *The Path to Power*, p. 82.

336 *"That whole night . . . very formidable"*: Merle Miller, *Lyndon: An Oral Biography* (New York: G. P. Putnam's Sons, 1980), p. 325.

336 *"He knew . . . him—or not"*: Caro, *The Passage of Power*, p. 426.

337 *"reason to wonder . . . to the Republic"*: LBJ, *VP*, p. 3.

337 *"while accomplishing practically nothing"*: *Life*, Dec. 13, 1963, p. 4.

337 *"developing into a national crisis"*: LBJ, *VP*, p. 21.

337 *"If any sense were . . . process to function"*: Ibid., p. 35.

337 *"a sympathetic atmosphere"*: Caro, *The Passage of Power*, p. 435.

337 *"dead man's program into a martyr's cause"*: DKG/LBJ Conversations.

337 *"At one point . . . hell's the presidency for?"*: Merle Miller, *Lyndon*, p. 337.

338 *"All that I have . . . I ask your help"*: Lyndon Baines Johnson, "Address before the Joint Session of Congress," Nov. 27, 1963, in *Public Papers of the President of the United States.* (Washington, D.C.: Government Printing Office, 1964–1970), 1:8–10.

338 *"modeled . . . Roosevelt"*: *San Antonio Express,* Dec. 1, 1963.

339 *"for action, and action now . . . dark hour"*: Franklin D. Roosevelt, Inaugural Address, March 4, 1933, in *The Public Papers and Addresses of Franklin D. Roosevelt*, Vols. 1–5. (New York: Random House, 1938), 2:12, 11.

339 *"we can . . . act now"*: LBJ, "Address before the Joint Session of Congress," Nov. 27, 1963, *PPP*, 1:9.

339 *"It was a remarkable performance . . . get results"*: *Anniston Star* (Ala.), Dec. 1, 1963.

339 *"LEADERSHIP IN GOOD HANDS"*: *Sheboygan Press* (Wisc.), Nov. 29, 1963.

339 *"JOHNSON EMERGES GRAVE AND STRONG"*: Caro, *The Passage of Power*, p. 433.

339 *"NEW CHIEF MET THE TEST"*: *Anniston Star* (Ala.), Dec. 1, 1963.

339 *"more easily influenced" . . . "than any other way"*: Donald Phillips, *Lincoln on Leadership* (New York: Warner Books, 1992), p. 158.

340 *"He shouldn't give . . . nothing I could say to Gene"*: LBJ, *VP*, pp. 153–54.

340 *"You know, John . . . change it by law"*: Merle Miller, *Lyndon*, p. 367.

340 *"go squat . . . the field to pee"*: Nick Kotz, *Judgment Days: Lyndon Baines Johnson, Martin Luther King Jr., and the Laws That Changed America* (New York: Houghton Mifflin, 2005), p. 22.

341 *"My strength as President . . . to that office"*: LBJ, *VP*, p. 157.

341 *"It was destined . . . friends for years"*: Ibid., p. 37.

341 *"there comes a time . . . this vital measure"*: Ibid., p. 38.

341 *"every ounce of strength"*: Ibid., p. 157.

341 *"struck by the enormous . . . deep convictions"*: Caro, *The Passage of Power*, p. 90.

341 *"the depth of his concern"*: *New York Times*, Dec. 3, 1963.

341 *"it just might . . . John Kennedy couldn't"*: Caro, *The Passage of Power*, p. 491.

342 *"a mighty hard route"*: Ibid., p. 490.

342 *"piddle along" . . . Congress to adjourn*: *The Presidential Recordings: Lyndon B. Johnson*, 7 vols. (New York: W. W. Norton, 2005), Vol. 1, p. 381.

342 *"Johnson treatment"*: Merle Miller, *Lyndon*, p. 411.

342 *"every friend to sign that . . . be thinking about it"*: *PRLBJ*, Vol. 1, p. 301.

343 *"If I've done anything wrong . . . to work together"*: Todd S. Purdum, *An Idea Whose Time Has Come: Two Presidents, Two Parties, and the Battle for the Civil Rights Act of 1964* (New York: Henry Holt, 2015), p. 176.

343 *"if there's ever a time" . . . is the time*: *PRLBJ*, Vol. 1, p. 263.

343 *"They'll be saying . . . violate procedure"*: Purdum, *An Idea Whose Time Has Come*, p. 164.

343 *"Just say that . . . a right to a hearing"*: *PRLBJ*, Vol. 1, p. 71.

343 *"You're either for . . . put up or shut up!"*: Ibid., p. 382.

343 *"Point them up . . . humanity a fair shake"*: *PRLBJ*, Vol. 2, p. 43.

343 *"Friend or Foe"*: *Washington Post*, Dec. 8, 1963, quoted in William C. Pool, Emmie Craddock, and David E. Conrad, *Lyndon Baines Johnson: The Formative Years* (San Marcos: Southwest Texas State College Press, 1965).

343 *"Let the members . . . and historical challenge"*: Ibid.

343 *"I don't want to run . . . but . . ."*: Purdum, *An Idea Whose Time Has Come*, p. 166.

344 *"the indignity . . . responsibility for the bill"*: *NYT*, Dec. 8, 1963.

344 *"to some people . . . the people to do it"*: LBJ, *VP*, p. 28.

344 *"I knew that the slightest . . . the bill to death"*: Ibid., p. 157.

344 *"Dick, I love you . . . to gladly do it"*: Discussion with Harry McPherson and Jack Valenti, "Achilles in the White House," *Wilson Quarterly* (Spring 2000), p. 94.

345 *"These few words . . . entire struggle"*: LBJ, *VP*, p. 157.

345 *"It's too late in life for me to change"*: William E. Leuchtenburg, *The White House Looks South: Franklin D. Roosevelt, Harry S. Truman, Lyndon B. Johnson* (Baton Rouge: Louisiana State University Press, 2005), p. 303.

345 *"old hostilities . . . every section of this country"*: LBJ, "Remarks in Atlanta at a Breakfast of the Georgia Legislature," May 8, 1964, *PPP*, 1:648.

345 *"would have beaten . . . Johnson does"*: *NYT*, Jan. 12, 1964.

345 *"it would be a fight . . . appeasement or attrition"*: LBJ, *VP*, p. 15.

346 *"to talk the bill to death"*: *Lake Charles American Press* [La.], April 7, 1964.

346 *"off making speeches . . . between the boards"*: Merle Miller, *Lyndon*, p. 368.

346 *"a corporal's guard"*: Kotz, *Judgment Days*, p. 122.

346 *"recognizing that . . . part of the time"*: Robert D. Loevy, ed., *The Civil Rights Act of 1964: The Passage of the Law That Ended Racial Segregation* (Albany: State University of New York Press, 1997), p. 82.

347 *"Attention please!" . . . quorum call in twenty-three minutes*: Ibid., p. 68.

347 *"that without Republican . . . Everett Dirksen"*: DKG/LBJ Conversations.

347 *"The bill can't pass . . . listen to Dirksen!"*: Kotz, *Judgment Days*, p. 115.

347 *"unless we have . . . this goddamn country"*: *PRLBJ*, Vol. 6, p. 696.

348 *"I think you're all going . . . going to help him"*: *PRLBJ*, Vol. 3, p. 192.

348 *"a laundry list"*: Kotz, *Judgment Days*, p. 117.

348 *"I saw your exhibit . . . proper credit"*: *PRLBJ*, Vol. 6, p. 662.

348 *"if you come with me . . . and Everett Dirksen!"*: Joseph A. Califano Jr., *The Triumph & Tragedy of Lyndon Johnson: The White House Years* (New York: Touchstone, 2015), p. xxvi.

348 *"dangerous game"*: Kotz, *Judgment Days*, p. 136.

349 *"We've got a much better bill . . . possible"*: *PRLBJ*, Vol. 6, p. 696.

349 *"Stronger than an Army . . . time has come"*: *Jefferson City Daily Capital News* (Missouri), May 20, 1964.

349 *"I say to my colleagues . . . 1964 our freedom year"*: Purdum, *An Idea Whose Time Has Come*, p. 316.

350 *"I guess that means 'aye'"*: Richard A. Arenberg and Robert B. Dove, *Defending the Filibuster: The Soul of the Senate* (Bloomington: Indiana University Press, 2012), p. 65.

350 *"Although I differ . . . I think he is wrong"*: Merle Miller, *Lyndon*, p. 369.

350 *"Happy anniversary"*: *NYT*, July 3, 1964.

350 *"to that afternoon . . . was my country"*: LBJ, *VP*, p. 160.

351 *"the greatest breakthrough"*: Michael Beschloss, ed., *Reaching for Glory: Lyndon Johnson's Secret White House Tapes, 1964–65* (New York: Touchstone, 2001), p. 159.

351 *"Once the black man's . . . from the white man"*: LBJ, *VP*, p. 161.

351 *The discriminatory system worked*: Califano, *The Triumph & Tragedy of Lyndon Johnson*, p. 44.

352 *"the mounted men . . . taken to the hospital"*: *Independent Press Telegram* (Long Beach, Calif.), March 14, 1965.

352 *"It was important to move . . . the right direction"*: LBJ, *VP*, p. 162.

352 *"LBJ, open your eyes . . . your homeland"*: Ibid., p. 228.

352 *"that a hasty display . . . victory for the North"*: Ibid., p. 161.

353 *"It's his ox that's in the ditch"*: Kotz, *Judgment Days*, p. 303.

353 *"they were not . . . difference in the world"*: LBJ, *VP*, p. 163.

353 *"I speak tonight . . . And we . . . shall . . . overcome"*: "Special Message to the Congress: The American Promise," March 15, 1965, *PPP*, 1965, 1:281, 284.

354 *"There was an instant . . . stamping their feet"*: Richard Goodwin, *Remembering America: A Voice from the Sixties* (New York: Little, Brown, 1988), p. 334.

354 *"the real hero . . . clutches of poverty"*: *PRLBJ*, Vol. 1, p. 285.

355 *"Somehow you never . . . will use it with me"*: Ibid., p. 286.

355 *"What convinces . . . you are advancing"*: DKG/LBJ Conversations.

355 *"it was the best . . . president give"*: Richard Goodwin, *Remembering America*, p. 237.

355 *"Your speech . . . President of the Nation"*: Daniel S. Lucks, *Selma to Saigon: The Civil Rights Movement and the Vietnam War* (Lexington: University Press of Kentucky, 2014), p. 142.

Abbreviations Used in Notes

DKG	Doris Kearns Goodwin
DKG/LBJ Conversations	Conversations between the author and LBJ, in the possession of the author.
FDR	Franklin D. Roosevelt
LBJ	Lyndon Baines Johnson
NYT	*New York Times*
PPA	Franklin D. Roosevelt. *The Public Papers and Addresses of Franklin D. Roosevelt.* Vols. 1–5. New York: Random House, 1938.
PPP	Lyndon Baines Johnson. *Public Papers of the Presidents of the United States.* Washington, D.C.: Government Printing Office, 1964–1970.
PRLBJ	*The Presidential Recordings: Lyndon B. Johnson.* 7 vols. New York: W. W. Norton, 2005.
VP	Lyndon Baines Johnson. *The Vantage Point: Perspectives of the Presidency, 1963–1969.* New York: Holt, Rinehart & Winston, 1971.

Elizabeth Warren

b. 1949

When she was running for the Democratic presidential nomination in 2019 and 2020, Senator Elizabeth Warren published several policy papers on her website—many more and in greater detail than the typical politician's published statements. Her propensity to be a policy "wonk" led to the ubiquitous phrase, "I've got a plan for that," which became almost a trademark for Warren's campaign. This policy paper is one of dozens of statements that Warren published in an attempt to let voters know what changes she'd make if elected president, but also to persuade them that these new policies would not balloon the federal deficit. She was trying to demonstrate to the general voter that she was a fiscal realist, especially compared to her rival progressive, Senator Bernie Sanders. But politicians tend to target certain classes of people—what we might call voting blocs—with their policy statements, and Warren is no different. Because primaries pit candidates from the same party against each other, campaigns tend to target the extremes: Republicans try to appeal to strongly conservative voters and Democrats try to sway progressives. Consequently, they generally do not need much evidence to persuade, because they know that their readers are like-minded rather than skeptical.

Even so, Warren was credited more than most politicians with backing up her claims. Do you find them convincing? You might consider who Warren imagines will be the main readers of this policy paper. Her arguments proceed from certain major premises, not all of them stated, which she takes as common ground with her audience: that we ought to prefer family farms to giant corporation-owned farming operations; that federal farm policy right now disfavors small farmers; that the federal government ought to encourage sustainable farming, etc. Certain conservative voters would tend to disagree with these positions. Do you think Warren's arguments would change if she won the Democratic nomination and had to appeal to less progressive voters?

A New Farm Economy

Consolidation in the agriculture sector is leaving America's family farmers with lower prices and fewer choices. Giant corporations use their market share to squeeze farmers from both sides. Farmers are pressured into taking on huge debts to pay the high prices that a small number of large suppliers charge them for inputs like seeds and fertilizer. Then, farmers are at the whim of a market that is controlled by meatpackers and grain traders that can pay them low prices for the commodities they produce—prices that often don't cover all the money farmers had to spend in the first place.

All of this causes tremendous overproduction of commodities. In the face of lower and lower prices in the market, farmers are left to produce more to try and break even. But this just causes prices to go down even further, benefiting the huge corporations looking to buy goods on the cheap and leaving farmers dependent on the government to backfill their costs.

As a consequence, the agriculture sector has become one of the largest polluters in our economy. As farmers are pressured to plant fence row to fence row and use more fertilizer in search of a higher yield, rural communities lose their soil and water, and the environment suffers.

Much of this situation is the direct result of government policy. Our current system of subsidies is supposed to make up the difference between the low prices farmers get on the market and what they have to pay to grow food. But instead it lets big corporations at the top of the supply chain get away with paying artificially low costs while farmers struggle and taxpayers make up the difference. It encourages overproduction by guaranteeing revenue regardless of prices or environmental conditions. And it feeds climate change.

Farmers and farmworkers are stewards of the land, and they know this system of overproduction is unsustainable—but without a change in incentives, they have no other choice.

To fix this problem, we need big, structural change. That's why I'm calling for a complete overhaul of our failed approach to the farm economy. **Instead of subsidizing industrial agriculture and starving farmers, farmworkers, and rural communities, my new approach will guarantee farmers a fair price, reduce overproduction, and pay farmers for environmental conservation.**

By making this shift, we can raise farm incomes and reduce taxpayer expenditures. We can break the stranglehold that giant agribusinesses have over our farm economy, and expand economic opportunities for small- and medium-sized farmers, family farmers, women farmers, farmers of color, and farmworkers. We can also provide consumers with affordable, high-quality, and often local food, while protecting our land and water and combating the existential threat of climate change.

Replacing Our Government's Failed Approach to the Farm Economy

Our agriculture markets are badly broken. American farmers spend their days toiling over their crops, but at sale time, more than half report negative income from their farming activity. In 2018, the median income farmers made from farming activity before federal subsidies was negative $1,316. Why? Because the market is paying farmers far less than what it costs them to produce their goods.

Farm subsidies that are necessary to keep farms afloat in this market do nothing to address the low prices and overproduction in our current environment. As it stands, our current system squeezes small farmers, undermines sustainable farming for the long-term, and damages our climate.

It hasn't always been this way. During the New Deal, FDR's administration recognized the critical role farmers would play in getting our country out of the Great Depression.[1] His administration set up a system that guaranteed farmers fair prices, tackled overproduction, and reversed environmental degradation. And it worked: for decades, this system gave farmers the security they needed to thrive, kept consumer prices stable, and helped restore our country's farmland.

But starting in the 1970s, giant agribusinesses convinced the Nixon Administration to change the system. Corporations called it "deregulating" the farm economy, but of course, this didn't actually

1. President Franklin Delano Roosevelt (1882–1945) funded massive federal programs to stimulate the American economy during the Great Depression, including the 1933 Agricultural Adjustment Act (AAA). By buying surplus and taking it off the market, the government successfully raised the prices that farmers got when selling their commodities. [All notes are the editor's.]

mean reducing government intervention. It just meant shifting that intervention from advancing the interests of farmers, consumers, and the environment to protecting the bottom line of giant agriculture corporations.

Now, the Department of Agriculture budgets over $10 billion each year on post-sale subsidies that are supposed to make up for the low prices that big corporations and livestock giants pay farmers on the market. Meanwhile, Big Ag pockets the profit: one study shows industrial livestock giants, for example, have saved $35 billion over twenty years from buying feed below the cost of production.

We need a new approach that uses taxpayer money more wisely, provides stable access to food, and accounts for the complexities of the agriculture markets. Just like workers need a living wage, farmers need a fair price—one that covers the costs they have to pay to produce their goods. We need to replace our failed system with a tried-and-true method that guarantees farmers that fair price and ends overproduction. **Building on the successful model of the New Deal, my plan calls for a new supply management program—which studies show would be billions cheaper for taxpayers than our current subsidy program, yet provide farm incomes that are higher.**

Here's how it will work. First, we guarantee farmers a price at their cost of production. To do that, the government would offer farmers a non-recourse loan that covers most of their costs of production—essentially, an offer to buy their products at cost if a farmer can't get a better price from a private purchaser on the market before the end of the loan period. Farmers can either repay the loan by selling their products or they can forfeit the products they used as collateral for the loan at the end of the loan period.

If the farmer does not sell those products to a private buyer during that time period, then the government will store the products in reserves. As supply comes off the market as a result, prices will rise. And if prices rise beyond a certain point, the government can release the supply from the reserves back onto the market, stabilizing prices once again. This mechanism guarantees farmers a fair price at a far lower cost than the current subsidy system.

In addition, to address overproduction, farmers will have the option of bidding acres of land currently used to produce commodities into conservation programs. The US Department of

Agriculture (USDA) will offer attractive prices based on the environmental benefit that repurposing the land towards conservation programs would provide. This will provide farmers with the choice—and revenue—to diversify their farms, rather than face mounting pressure to produce more and more of the same.

This approach has advantages beyond guaranteeing farmers a fair price for their goods. It gives us the tools to stabilize farm income where farmers aren't getting prices at the cost of production, like commodity crops and dairy. It enhances our food security by giving the government access to reserves if needed—a particularly important consideration as climate change continues to disrupt food production. It addresses our overproduction problem and helps reduce environmental damage. And it keeps consumer prices relatively stable.

It would also save taxpayers billions. Because a supply management program only pays for the amount of commodities that it takes off of the market, it would substantially reduce costs for taxpayers who, in the current subsidy approach, can end up paying for every single bushel and bale that farmers grow.

Paying Farmers to Fight Climate Change

To transition to a sustainable farm economy, we also need to diversify our agriculture sector. **As president, I will lead a full-out effort to decarbonize the agricultural sector by investing in our farmers and giving them the tools, research, and training they need to transform the sector—so that we can achieve the objectives of the Green New Deal to reach net-zero emissions by 2030.**

This begins with paying farmers for embracing techniques that promote a sustainable future for all of us. Farmers are already adopting climate-friendly practices—including proven and profitable techniques like cover crops. But today, there are far more farmers who want to join land conservation programs than there are funds available to support them. That's because we have continually underfunded a tried-and-true program—the Conservation Stewardship Program (CSP)—that provides funding for farmers eager to transition to sustainable practices, and that delivers substantial returns to taxpayers.

My plan will make it economically feasible for farmers to be part of the climate change solution by increasing CSP's payments

for sustainable farming practices from around $1 billion today to $15 billion annually—and expanding the types of practices eligible for compensation—so that every farmer who wants to use their land to fight climate change can do so. This will put our future investment in conservation above the level we currently fund commodity programs. And I will support staff at USDA to empower them in the fight against climate change, from scientists in Washington all the way down to the county-level offices tailoring solutions to challenges in their local communities.

Research and innovation are also essential in supporting a transition to sustainable farming. **I will dedicate resources from the $400 billion R&D commitment in my Green Manufacturing Plan towards innovations for decarbonizing the agriculture sector, including a farmer-led Innovation Fund that farmers can apply to use towards pioneering new methods of sustainable farming, like agroforestry.**

Our land grant universities also have a critical role to play—but first, we need to reclaim our land grant universities from Big Ag and restore them to their core purpose of supporting our family farmers. **My Administration will reinvest in our land grant universities and focus their agricultural efforts in part on evaluating farmers' ideas to decarbonize the agricultural sector and training a new generation of farmers.**

Take on Big Ag to Level the Playing Field for Family Farmers

We also must take on Big Ag head on if we want to create a new farm economy. When Nixon's Secretary of Agriculture told farmers to "get big or get out," he paved the way for the giant agribusinesses that have eroded America's rural communities and turned the agricultural sector into one of the largest polluters, all while making huge profits.

That ends now. I will use every tool at my disposal to level the playing field for family farmers and hold agribusinesses accountable for the damage they've wrought on our farmland.

- *Break up Big Agribusinesses.* Under my plan to level the playing field for America's farmers I'll use every tool I have to break up big agribusinesses, including by reviewing—and reversing—anti-competitive mergers.

- *Strengthen rules and enforcement under the Packers and Stockyards Act.* In 1921, Congress passed the Packers & Stockyards Act (P&S Act) to protect independent farmers. But Trump has eliminated Grain Inspection, Packers and Stockyards Administration (GIPSA)—the office responsible for upholding the P&S Act—as an independent office. My administration will restore GIPSA and make it easier for farmers to bring suits against unfair practices—including by clarifying that they do not have to prove harm across the entire sector to bring a claim.
- *Make sure programs benefit independent family farmers, not the rich and powerful.* Agribusinesses exploit loopholes to put taxpayer dollars that should be going towards family farmers into their own pockets instead. The Trump administration has handed over billions more into the pockets of the wealthiest through trade war bailouts. On average, the top 1 percent of recipients received over $180,000, and the bottom 80 percent received less than $5,000—all without Congressional authorization. I will prevent huge factory farms from accessing funds intended to benefit family farmers, like those for payment limitations and for programs like the Environmental Quality Incentives Program, and ban companies that violate labor and environmental standards from accessing funds, too.
- *Hold Big Ag accountable for environmental abuses.* Agribusinesses are the likely culprits for polluting hundreds of thousands of miles of rivers and streams and causing dead zones in our waters, including in the Chesapeake Bay and the Gulf of Mexico. I will make agribusinesses pay the full costs of the environmental damage they wreak by closing the loopholes that CAFOs use to get away with polluting and beefing up enforcement of the Clean Air and Clean Water Acts against them, including by working with state and local officials.[2]

Build Out Local and Regional Food Systems That Support Rural Farmers and Their Communities

Because giant agribusinesses control entire supply chains, many small farmers today must send their products to huge packaging

2. CAFOs: concentrated animal feeding operations. These are industrial-sized feed lots or sheds designed for one species of animal: chickens or pigs or cattle, e.g. These operations tend to hurt the environment more than smaller, diversified family farms, producing (for instance) gigantic streams of animal waste. They also tend to treat animals inhumanely.

and distribution centers that are hundreds of miles away from their farms and from the end consumer. This deprives rural communities from access to produce, contributing to food deserts and obesity.

I will provide farmers and rural communities with the resources they need to build thriving local and regional food systems so that every community has access to healthy food—and the billions in economic opportunities that come with it.

I will use the full power of federal and state procurement to ensure access to local, sustainable produce in all communities. **My administration will expand the "Farm-to-School" program a hundredfold and turn it into a billion-dollar "Farm to People" program in which all federally-supported public institutions—including military bases and hospitals—will partner with local, independent farmers to provide fresh, local food.**

To meet this additional demand, farmers will need access to local and regional supply chain infrastructure. USDA's Local Agriculture Market Program (LAMP) currently invests $50M a year in local infrastructure-building projects—which experts estimate falls far short of meeting the substantial demand. **I will increase LAMP's funding ten-fold, investing $500M a year over the next decade to fund food hubs, distribution centers, and points-of-sale that our rural and small town communities can use.**

Create Opportunities for Diverse and Beginning Farmers

Farmers of color have experienced a long history of discrimination, some of it at the hands of the federal government. This is especially true for Black farmers, who were stripped of 80 percent of their farmland over the past century. They received a mere fraction of the value of the land they lost—a staggering loss of wealth that is a major contributor to the racial wealth gap. It's time to tackle these problems head on. Black farmers, researchers, and advocates have spent decades calling out this history of discrimination and fighting for change, and I have been fortunate to learn from their experiences. I have updated and expanded on my plan to reflect their work.

✶ ✶ ✶

My plan will help create a new farm economy where family farmers have financial security and the freedom to do what they do best. Farmers and farmworkers of all backgrounds will finally have the economic freedom to pursue diverse, sustainable farming—and get paid up front for doing so. Americans will have a steady and affordable supply of food. Kids in rural communities will have healthy lunches grown in their backyards and packaged at local food hubs run by small town entrepreneurs. Taxpayers won't pay twice—once at the grocery store and once through their taxes—for overproduced commodities. We will replenish our soil and our water to chart a path towards a climate solution and achieve the goals of the Green New Deal.

2019

CHAPTER 6

Public Ethics

Henry David Thoreau

1817–1862

In the summer of 1846, when Thoreau was in the midst of his experimental hermitage on Walden Pond, the United States invaded Mexico. The Mexican War divided the nation. Southerners and empire-minded Northerners welcomed it, for it secured Texas (as a slave state) and won for the United States the spoils of Utah, New Mexico, Arizona, Nevada, and California, which Southerners expected to be admitted as slave states to balance the admittance of new states in the North. Abolitionists opposed it, as did anti-imperialists, for obvious reasons. Thoreau's opposition to the war and his opposition to slavery compelled him to protest by refusing to pay his annual poll tax, for which he was jailed in 1846. He was putting into practice the principle of nonviolent protest advocated by abolitionists for years. He described his night in jail and the principles behind his civil disobedience to the Concord Lyceum in 1848. Later, after the war was over, he published the lecture in the first and only issue of Aesthetic Papers. *That journal mustered only fifty subscribers and sold just as poorly in bookstores, so Thoreau's original audience was only the clique of radicals we have come to know as the Transcendentalists. In short, he was preaching to the choir: people who already regarded the Mexican War and slavery as evils. So he didn't need to persuade these like-minded people to reject slavery. Instead, he needed to persuade his readers to act on their beliefs. Although the Mexican War was over by the time this essay was published, an occasion to accept or reject Thoreau's advice would soon be pressed on the citizens of Massachusetts, for in 1850 Congress passed the second Fugitive Slave Act, which reinforced the Constitutional stipulation that Northern states return to their oppressors Black men and women who had escaped from slavery in the South and also penalized any individuals who helped slaves escape. "Civil Disobedience" was intended to challenge Thoreau's readers to defy this law and the Constitution.*

Civil Disobedience

I heartily accept the motto,—"That government is best which governs least;" and I should like to see it acted up to more rapidly and systematically. Carried out, it finally amounts to this, which also I believe,—"That government is best which governs not at all;" and when men are prepared for it, that will be the kind of government which they will have. Government is at best but an expedient; but most governments are usually, and all governments are sometimes, inexpedient. The objections which have been brought against a standing army, and they are many and weighty, and deserve to prevail, may also at last be brought against a standing government. The standing army is only an arm of the standing government. The government itself, which is only the mode which the people have chosen to execute their will, is equally liable to be abused and perverted before the people can act through it. Witness the present Mexican war, the work of comparatively a few individuals using the standing government as their tool; for, in the outset, the people would not have consented to this measure.

This American government,—what is it but a tradition, though a recent one, endeavoring to transmit itself unimpaired to posterity, but each instant losing some of its integrity? It has not the vitality and force of a single living man; for a single man can bend it to his will. It is a sort of wooden gun to the people themselves; and, if ever they should use it in earnest as a real one against each other, it will surely split. But it is not the less necessary for this; for the people must have some complicated machinery or other, and hear its din, to satisfy that idea of government which they have. Governments show thus how successfully men can be imposed on, even impose on themselves, for their own advantage. It is excellent, we must all allow; yet this government never of itself furthered any enterprise, but by the alacrity with which it got out of its way. *It* does not keep the country free. *It* does not settle the West. *It* does not educate. The character inherent in the American people has done all that has been accomplished; and it would have done somewhat more, if the government had not sometimes got in its way. For government is an expedient by which men would fain succeed in letting one another alone; and, as has been said, when it is most expedient, the governed are most let alone by it. Trade and commerce, if they were not made of India rubber, would never manage to bounce over the obstacles which legislators are continually putting in their way; and, if one were to judge these men wholly by the effects of their actions, and not partly by their intentions, they would deserve to be classed and punished with those mischievous persons who put obstructions on the railroads.

But, to speak practically and as a citizen, unlike those who call themselves no-government men, I ask for, not at once no government, but *at once* a better government. Let every man make known what kind of government would command his respect, and that will be one step toward obtaining it.

After all, the practical reason why, when the power is once in the hands of the people, a majority are permitted, and for a long period continue, to rule, is not because they are most likely to be in the right, nor because this seems fairest to the minority, but because they are physically the strongest. But a government in which the majority rule in all cases cannot be based on justice, even as far as men understand it. Can there not be a government in which majorities do not virtually decide right and wrong, but conscience?—in which majorities decide only those questions to which the rule of expediency is applicable? Must the citizen ever for a moment, or in the least degree, resign his conscience to the legislator? Why has every man a conscience, then? I think that we should be men first, and subjects afterward. It is not desirable to cultivate a respect for the law, so much as for the right. The only obligation which I have a right to assume, is to do at any time what I think right. It is truly enough said, that a corporation has no conscience; but a corporation of conscientious men is a corporation *with* a conscience. Law never made men a whit more just; and, by means of their respect for it, even the well-disposed are daily made the agents of injustice. A common and natural result of an undue respect for law is, that you may see a file of soldiers, colonel, captain, corporal, privates, powder-monkeys and all, marching in admirable order over hill and dale to the wars, against their wills, aye, against their common sense and consciences, which makes it very steep marching indeed, and produces a palpitation of the heart. They have no doubt that it is a damnable business in which they are concerned; they are all peaceably inclined. Now, what are they? Men at all? or small moveable forts and magazines, at the service of some unscrupulous man in power? Visit the Navy Yard, and behold a marine, such a man as an American government can make, or such as it can make a man with its black arts, a mere shadow and reminiscence of humanity, a man laid out alive and standing, and already, as one may say, buried under arms with funeral accompaniments, though it may be

"Not a drum was heard, nor a funeral note,
As his corse to the ramparts we hurried;
Not a soldier discharged his farewell shot
O'er the grave where our hero we buried."[1]

The mass of men serve the State thus, not as men mainly, but as machines, with their bodies. They are the standing army, and the militia, jailers, constables, *posse comitatus*, &c.[2] In most cases there is no free exercise whatever of the judgment or of the moral sense; but they put themselves on a level with wood and earth and stones; and wooden men can perhaps be manufactured that will serve the purpose as well. Such command no more respect than men of straw, or a lump of dirt. They have the same sort of worth only as horses and dogs. Yet such as these even are commonly esteemed good citizens. Others, as most legislators, politicians, lawyers, ministers, and office-holders, serve the State chiefly with their heads; and, as they rarely make any moral distinctions, they are as likely to serve the devil, without intending it, as God. A very few, as heroes, patriots, martyrs, reformers in the great sense, and *men*, serve the State with their consciences also, and so necessarily resist it for the most part; and they are commonly treated by it as enemies. A wise man will only be useful as a man, and will not submit to be "clay," and "stop a hole to keep the wind away," but leave that office to his dust at least:—

"I am too high-born to be propertied,
To be a secondary at control,

1. "The Burial of Sir John Moore at Corunna," lines 1–4, by Charles Wolfe. [All notes are the editor's unless otherwise specified.]

2. *Posse comitatus*: a group of citizens temporarily deputized by a sheriff to aid in law enforcement.

Or useful serving-man and instrument
To any sovereign state throughout the world."[3]

He who gives himself entirely to his fellow-men appears to them useless and selfish; but he who gives himself partially to them is pronounced a benefactor and philanthropist.

How does it become a man to behave toward this American government to-day? I answer that he cannot without disgrace be associated with it. I cannot for an instant recognize that political organization as *my* government which is the *slave's* government also.

All men recognize the right of revolution; that is, the right to refuse allegiance to and to resist the government, when its tyranny or its inefficiency are great and unendurable. But almost all say that such is not the case now. But such was the case, they think, in the Revolution of '75. If one were to tell me that this was a bad government because it taxed certain foreign commodities brought to its ports, it is most probable that I should not make an ado about it, for I can do without them: all machines have their friction; and possibly this does enough good to counterbalance the evil. At any rate, it is a great evil to make a stir about it. But when the friction comes to have its machine, and oppression and robbery are organized, I say, let us not have such a machine any longer. In other words, when a sixth of the population of a nation which has undertaken to be the refuge of liberty are slaves, and a whole country is unjustly overrun and conquered by a foreign army, and subjected to military law, I think that it is not too soon for honest men to rebel and revolutionize. What makes this duty the more urgent is the fact, that the country so overrun is not our own, but ours is the invading army.

Paley, a common authority with many on moral questions, in his chapter on the "Duty of Submission to Civil Government,"[4] resolves all civil obligation into expediency; and he proceeds to say, "that so long as the interest of the whole society requires it, that is, so long as the established government cannot be resisted or changed without public inconveniency, it is the will of God that the established government be obeyed, and no longer."—"This principle being admitted, the

3. *The Life and Death of King John*, Act V, Scene ii, lines 83–86, by William Shakespeare.

4. By William Paley (1743–1805), English theologian, appears in *Principles of Moral and Political Philosophy* (1785).

justice of every particular case of resistance is reduced to a computation of the quantity of the danger and grievance on the one side, and of the probability and expense of redressing it on the other." Of this, he says, every man shall judge for himself. But Paley appears never to have contemplated those cases to which the rule of expediency does not apply, in which a people, as well as an individual, must do justice, cost what it may. If I have unjustly wrested a plank from a drowning man, I must restore it to him though I drown myself. This, according to Paley, would be inconvenient. But he that would save his life, in such a case, shall lose it. This people must cease to hold slaves, and to make war on Mexico, though it cost them their existence as a people.

In their practice, nations agree with Paley; but does any one think that Massachusetts does exactly what is right at the present crisis?

"A drab of state, a cloth-o'-silver slut,
To have her train borne up, and her soul trail in the dirt."[5]

Practically speaking, the opponents to a reform in Massachusetts are not a hundred thousand politicians at the South, but a hundred thousand merchants and farmers here, who are more interested in commerce and agriculture than they are in humanity, and are not prepared to do justice to the slave and to Mexico, *cost what it may.* I quarrel not with far-off foes, but with those who, near at home, co-operate with, and do the bidding of those far away, and without whom the latter would be harmless. We are accustomed to say, that the mass of men are unprepared; but improvement is slow, because the few are not materially wiser or better than the many. It is not so important that many should be as good as you, as that there be some absolute goodness somewhere; for that will leaven the whole lump. There are thousands who are *in opinion* opposed to slavery and to the war, who yet in effect do nothing to put an end to them; who, esteeming themselves children of Washington and Franklin, sit down with their hands in their pockets, and say that they know not what to do, and do nothing; who even postpone the question of freedom to the question of free-trade, and quietly read the prices-current along with the latest advices from Mexico,

5. *The Revengers Tragadie*, Act IV, Scene iv, lines 77–78, by Cyril Tourneur.

after dinner, and, it may be, fall asleep over them both. What is the price-current of an honest man and patriot today? They hesitate, and they regret, and sometimes they petition; but they do nothing in earnest and with effect. They will wait, well disposed, for others to remedy the evil, that they may no longer have it to regret. At most, they give only a cheap vote, and a feeble countenance and Godspeed, to the right, as it goes by them. There are nine hundred and ninety-nine patrons of virtue to one virtuous man; but it is easier to deal with the real possessor of a thing than with the temporary guardian of it.

All voting is a sort of gaming, like chequers or backgammon, with a slight moral tinge to it, a playing with right and wrong, with moral questions; and betting naturally accompanies it. The character of the voters is not staked. I cast my vote, perchance, as I think right; but I am not vitally concerned that that right should prevail. I am willing to leave it to the majority. Its obligation, therefore, never exceeds that of expediency. Even voting *for the right* is *doing* nothing for it. It is only expressing to men feebly your desire that it should prevail. A wise man will not leave the right to the mercy of chance, nor wish it to prevail through the power of the majority. There is but little virtue in the action of masses of men. When the majority shall at length vote for the abolition of slavery, it will be because they are indifferent to slavery, or because there is but little slavery left to be abolished by their vote. *They* will then be the only slaves. Only *his* vote can hasten the abolition of slavery who asserts his own freedom by his vote.

I hear of a convention to be held at Baltimore, or elsewhere, for the selection of a candidate for the Presidency, made up chiefly of editors, and men who are politicians by profession; but I think, what is it to any independent, intelligent, and respectable man what decision they may come to, shall we not have the advantage of his wisdom and honesty, nevertheless? Can we not count upon some independent votes? Are there not many individuals in the country who do not attend conventions? But no: I find that the respectable man, so called, has immediately drifted from his position, and despairs of his country, when his country has more reason to despair of him. He forthwith adopts one of the candidates thus selected as the only *available* one, thus proving that he is himself *available* for any purposes of the demagogue. His vote is of no more worth than that of any unprincipled foreigner or hireling native, who may have been bought. Oh for a man who is a *man*, and, as my neighbor says, has a bone in his back which you cannot pass your hand through! Our statistics are at fault: the population has been returned too large. How many *men* are there to a square thousand miles in this country? Hardly one. Does not America offer any inducement for men to settle here? The American has dwindled into an Odd Fellow,[6]—one who may be known by the development of his organ of gregariousness, and a manifest lack of intellect and cheerful self-reliance; whose first and chief concern, on coming into the world, is to see that the alms-houses are in good repair; and, before yet he has lawfully donned the virile garb, to collect a fund for the support of the widows and orphans that may be; who, in short, ventures to live only by the aid of the mutual insurance company, which has promised to bury him decently.

It is not a man's duty, as a matter of course, to devote himself to the eradication of any, even the most enormous wrong; he may still properly have other concerns to engage him; but it is his duty, at least, to wash his hands of it, and, if he gives it no thought longer, not to give it practically his support. If I devote myself to other pursuits and contemplations, I must first see, at least, that I do not pursue them sitting upon another man's shoulders. I must get off him first, that he may pursue his contemplations too. See what gross inconsistency is tolerated: I have heard some of my townsmen say, "I should like to have them order me out to help put down an insurrection of the slaves, or to march to Mexico,—see if I would go;" and yet these very men have each, directly by their allegiance, and so indirectly, at least, by their money, furnished a substitute. The soldier is applauded who refuses to serve in an unjust war by those who do not refuse to sustain the unjust government which makes the war; is applauded by those whose own act and authority he disregards and sets at nought; as if the State were penitent to that degree that it hired one to scourge it while it sinned, but not to that degree that it left off sinning for a moment. Thus, under the name of order and civil government, we are all made at last to pay homage to and support our own meanness. After the first blush of sin, comes its indifference; and

6. A member of the Independent Order of Odd Fellows, a fraternal and benevolent secret society.

from immoral it becomes, as it were, *un*moral, and not quite unnecessary to that life which we have made.

The broadest and most prevalent error requires the most disinterested virtue to sustain it. The slight reproach to which the virtue of patriotism is commonly liable, the noble are most likely to incur. Those who, while they disapprove of the character and measures of a government, yield to it their allegiance and support, are undoubtedly its most conscientious supporters, and so frequently the most serious obstacles to reform. Some are petitioning the State to dissolve the Union, to disregard the requisitions of the President. Why do they not dissolve it themselves,—the union between themselves and the State,—and refuse to pay their quota into its treasury? Do not they stand in the same relation to the State, that the State does to the Union? And have not the same reasons prevented the State from resisting the Union, which have prevented them from resisting the State?

How can a man be satisfied to entertain an opinion merely, and enjoy *it*? Is there any enjoyment in it, if his opinion is that he is aggrieved? If you are cheated out of a single dollar by your neighbor, you do not rest satisfied with knowing that you are cheated, or with saying that you are cheated, or even with petitioning him to pay you your due; but you take effectual steps at once to obtain the full amount, and see that you are never cheated again. Action from principle,—the perception and the performance of right,—changes things and relations; it is essentially revolutionary, and does not consist wholly with any thing which was. It not only divides states and churches, it divides families; aye, it divides the *individual*, separating the diabolical in him from the divine.

Unjust laws exist: shall we be content to obey them, or shall we endeavor to amend them, and obey them until we have succeeded, or shall we transgress them at once? Men generally, under such a government as this, think that they ought to wait until they have persuaded the majority to alter them. They think that if they should resist, the remedy would be worse than the evil. But it is the fault of the government itself that the remedy *is* worse than the evil. *It* makes it worse. Why is it not more apt to anticipate and provide for reform? Why does it not cherish its wise minority? Why does it cry and resist before it is hurt? Why does it not encourage its citizens to be on the alert to point out its faults, and *do* better than it would have them? Why does it always crucify Christ, and excommunicate Copernicus and Luther, and pronounce Washington and Franklin rebels?[7]

One would think, that a deliberate and practical denial of its authority was the only offence never contemplated by government; else, why has it not assigned its definite, its suitable and proportionate penalty? If a man who has no property refuses but once to earn nine shillings for the State, he is put in prison for a period unlimited by any law that I know, and determined only by the discretion of those who placed him there; but if he should steal ninety times nine shillings from the State, he is soon permitted to go at large again.

If the injustice is part of the necessary friction of the machine of government, let it go, let it go: perchance it will wear smooth,—certainly the machine will wear out. If the injustice has a spring, or a pulley, or a rope, or a crank, exclusively for itself, then perhaps you may consider whether the remedy will not be worse than the evil; but if it is of such a nature that it requires you to be the agent of injustice to another, then, I say, break the law. Let your life be a counter friction to stop the machine. What I have to do is to see, at any rate, that I do not lend myself to the wrong which I condemn.

As for adopting the ways which the State has provided for remedying the evil, I know not of such ways. They take too much time, and a man's life will be gone. I have other affairs to attend to. I came into this world, not chiefly to make this a good place to live in, but to live in it, be it good or bad. A man has not every thing to do, but something; and because he cannot do *every thing*, it is not necessary that he should do *something* wrong. It is not my business to be petitioning the governor or the legislature any more than it is theirs to petition me; and, if they should not hear my petition, what should I do then? But in this case the State has provided no way: its very Constitution is the evil. This may seem to be harsh and stubborn and unconciliatory; but it is to treat with the utmost kindness and

7. Jesus (c. 2 B.C.E–33 A.D.) was executed by the Romans; Copernicus (1473–1543), famous for his revolutionary idea that the Earth and other planets orbited the sun, was never excommunicated; Martin Luther (1483–1546), religious reformer, was excommunicated in 1521.

consideration the only spirit that can appreciate or deserves it. So is all change for the better, like birth and death which convulse the body.

I do not hesitate to say, that those who call themselves abolitionists should at once effectually withdraw their support, both in person and property, from the government of Massachusetts, and not wait till they constitute a majority of one, before they suffer the right to prevail through them. I think that it is enough if they have God on their side, without waiting for that other one. Moreover, any man more right than his neighbors, constitutes a majority of one already.

I meet this American government, or its representative the State government, directly, and face to face, once a year, no more, in the person of its tax-gatherer; this is the only mode in which a man situated as I am necessarily meets it; and it then says distinctly, Recognize me; and the simplest, the most effectual, and, in the present posture of affairs, the indispensablest mode of treating with it on this head, of expressing your little satisfaction with and love for it, is to deny it then. My civil neighbor, the tax-gatherer, is the very man I have to deal with,—for it is, after all, with men and not with parchment that I quarrel,—and he has voluntarily chosen to be an agent of the government. How shall he ever know well what he is and does as an officer of the government, or as a man, until he is obliged to consider whether he shall treat me, his neighbor, for whom he has respect, as a neighbor and well-disposed man, or as a maniac and disturber of the peace, and see if he can get over this obstruction to his neighborliness without a ruder and more impetuous thought or speech corresponding with his action? I know this well, that if one thousand, if one hundred, if ten men whom I could name,—if ten *honest* men only,—aye, if *one* HONEST man, in this State of Massachusetts, *ceasing to hold slaves*, were actually to withdraw from this copartnership, and be locked up in the county jail therefore, it would be the abolition of slavery in America. For it matters not how small the beginning may seem to be: what is once well done is done for ever. But we love better to talk about it: that we say is our mission. Reform keeps many scores of newspapers in its service, but not one man. If my esteemed neighbor, the State's ambassador, who will devote his days to the settlement of the question of human rights in the Council Chamber, instead of being threatened with the prisons of Carolina, were to sit down the prisoner of Massachusetts, that State which is so anxious to foist the sin of slavery upon her sister,—though at present she can discover only an act of inhospitality to be the ground of a quarrel with her,—the Legislature would not wholly waive the subject the following winter.

Under a government which imprisons any unjustly, the true place for a just man is also a prison. The proper place to-day, the only place which Massachusetts has provided for her freer and less desponding spirits, is in her prisons, to be put out and locked out of the State by her own act, as they have already put themselves out by their principles. It is there that the fugitive slave, and the Mexican prisoner on parole, and the Indian come to plead the wrongs of his race, should find them; on that separate, but more free and honorable ground, where the State places those who are not *with* her but *against* her,—the only house in a slave-state in which a free man can abide with honor. If any think that their influence would be lost there, and their voices no longer afflict the ear of the State, that they would not be as an enemy within its walls, they do not know by how much truth is stronger than error, nor how much more eloquently and effectively he can combat injustice who has experienced a little in his own person. Cast your whole vote, not a strip of paper merely, but your whole influence. A minority is powerless while it conforms to the majority; it is not even a minority then; but it is irresistible when it clogs by its whole weight. If the alternative is to keep all just men in prison, or give up war and slavery, the State will not hesitate which to choose. If a thousand men were not to pay their tax-bills this year, that would not be a violent and bloody measure, as it would be to pay them, and enable the State to commit violence and shed innocent blood. This is, in fact, the definition of a peaceable revolution, if any such is possible. If the tax-gatherer, or any other public officer, asks me, as one has done, "But what shall I do?" my answer is, "If you really wish to do any thing, resign your office." When the subject has refused allegiance, and the officer has resigned his office, then the revolution is accomplished. But even suppose blood should flow. Is there not a sort of blood shed when the conscience is wounded? Through this wound a man's real manhood and immortality flow out, and he bleeds to an everlasting death. I see this blood flowing now.

I have contemplated the imprisonment of the offender, rather than the seizure of his goods,—though both will serve the same purpose,—because they who assert the purest right, and consequently are most dangerous to a corrupt State, commonly have not spent much time in accumulating property. To such the State renders comparatively small service, and a slight tax is wont to appear exorbitant, particularly if they are obliged to earn it by special labor with their hands. If there were one who lived wholly without the use of money, the State itself would hesitate to demand it of him. But the rich man—not to make any invidious comparison—is always sold to the institution which makes him rich. Absolutely speaking, the more money, the less virtue; for money comes between a man and his objects, and obtains them for him; and it was certainly no great virtue to obtain it. It puts to rest many questions which he would otherwise be taxed to answer; while the only new question which it puts is the hard but superfluous one, how to spend it. Thus his moral ground is taken from under his feet. The opportunities of living are diminished in proportion as what are called the "means" are increased. The best thing a man can do for his culture when he is rich is to endeavour to carry out those schemes which he entertained when he was poor. Christ answered the Herodians according to their condition. "Show me the tribute-money," said he;—and one took a penny out of his pocket;—If you use money which has the image of Cæsar on it, and which he has made current and valuable, that is, *if you are men of the State*, and gladly enjoy the advantages of Cæsar's government, then pay him back some of his own when he demands it; "Render therefore to Cæsar that which is Cæsar's, and to God those things which are God's,"[8]—leaving them no wiser than before as to which was which; for they did not wish to know.

When I converse with the freest of my neighbors, I perceive that, whatever they may say about the magnitude and seriousness of the question, and their regard for the public tranquillity, the long and the short of the matter is, that they cannot spare the protection of the existing government, and they dread the consequences of disobedience to it to their property and families. For my own part, I should not like to think that I ever rely on the protection of the State. But, if I deny the authority of the State when it presents its tax-bill, it will soon take and waste all my property, and so harass me and my children without end. This is hard. This makes it impossible for a man to live

8. Mark 12.17.

honestly and at the same time comfortably in outward respects. It will not be worth the while to accumulate property; that would be sure to go again. You must hire or squat somewhere, and raise but a small crop, and eat that soon. You must live within yourself, and depend upon yourself, always tucked up and ready for a start, and not have many affairs. A man may grow rich in Turkey even, if he will be in all respects a good subject of the Turkish government. Confucius said,—"If a State is governed by the principles of reason, poverty and misery are subjects of shame; if a State is not governed by the principles of reason, riches and honors are the subjects of shame." No: until I want the protection of Massachusetts to be extended to me in some distant southern port, where my liberty is endangered, or until I am bent solely on building up an estate at home by peaceful enterprise, I can afford to refuse allegiance to Massachusetts, and her right to my property and life. It costs me less in every sense to incur the penalty of disobedience to the State, than it would to obey. I should feel as if I were worth less in that case.

Some years ago, the State met me in behalf of the church, and commanded me to pay a certain sum toward the support of a clergyman whose preaching my father attended, but never I myself. "Pay it," it said, "or be locked up in the jail." I declined to pay. But, unfortunately, another man saw fit to pay it. I did not see why the schoolmaster should be taxed to support the priest, and not the priest the schoolmaster; for I was not the State's schoolmaster, but I supported myself by voluntary subscription. I did not see why the lyceum should not present its tax-bill, and have the State to back its demand, as well as the church. However, at the request of the selectmen, I condescended to make some such statement as this in writing:—"Know all men by these presents, that I, Henry Thoreau, do not wish to be regarded as a member of any incorporated society which I have not joined." This I gave to the town-clerk; and he has it. The State, having thus learned that I did not wish to be regarded as a member of that church, has never made a like demand on me since; though it said that it must adhere to its original presumption that time. If I had known how to name them, I should then have signed off in detail from all the societies which I never signed on to; but I did not know where to find a complete list.

I have paid no poll-tax for six years. I was put into a jail once on this account, for one night; and, as I stood considering the walls of solid stone, two or three feet thick, the door of wood and iron, a foot thick, and the iron grating which strained the light, I could not help being struck with the foolishness of that institution which treated me as if I were mere flesh and blood and bones, to be locked up. I wondered that it should have concluded at length that this was the best use it could put me to, and had never thought to avail itself of my services in some way. I saw that, if there was a wall of stone between me and my townsmen, there was a still more difficult one to climb or break through, before they could get to be as free as I was. I did not for a moment feel confined, and the walls seemed a great waste of stone and mortar. I felt as if I alone of all my townsmen had paid my tax. They plainly did not know how to treat me, but behaved like persons who are underbred. In every threat and in every compliment there was a blunder; for they thought that my chief desire was to stand the other side of that stone wall. I could not but smile to see how industriously they locked the door on my meditations, which followed them out again without let or hinderance, and *they* were really all that was dangerous. As they could not reach me, they had resolved to punish my body; just as boys, if they cannot come at some person against whom they have a spite, will abuse his dog. I saw that the State was half-witted, that it was timid as a lone woman with her silver spoons, and that it did not know its friends from its foes, and I lost all my remaining respect for it, and pitied it.

Thus the State never intentionally confronts a man's sense, intellectual or moral, but only his body, his senses. It is not armed with superior wit or honesty, but with superior physical strength. I was not born to be forced. I will breathe after my own fashion. Let us see who is the strongest. What force has a multitude? They only can force me who obey a higher law than I. They force me to become like themselves. I do not hear of *men* being *forced* to live this way or that by masses of men. What sort of life were that to live? When I meet a government which says to me, "Your money or your life," why should I be in haste to give it my money? It may be in a great strait, and not know what to do: I cannot help that. It must help itself; do as I do. It is not worth the while to snivel about it. I am not responsible for the successful working of the machinery of society. I am not the son of the engineer. I perceive that, when an acorn and a chestnut fall side by side, the one does not remain inert to make way for the other, but both obey their own laws, and spring and grow and flourish as best they can, till one, perchance, overshadows and destroys the other. If a plant cannot live according to its nature, it dies; and so a man.

The night in prison was novel and interesting enough. The prisoners in their shirt-sleeves were enjoying a chat and the evening air in the door-way, when I entered. But the jailer said, "Come, boys, it is time to lock up;" and so they dispersed, and I heard the sound of their steps returning into the hollow apartments. My room-mate was introduced to me by the jailer, as "a first-rate fellow and a clever man." When the door was locked, he showed me where to hang my hat, and how he managed matters there. The rooms were whitewashed once a month; and this one, at least, was the whitest, most simply furnished, and probably the neatest apartment in the town. He naturally wanted to know where I came from, and what brought me there; and, when I had told him, I asked him in my turn how he came there, presuming him to be an honest man, of course; and, as the world goes, I believe he was. "Why," said he, "they accuse me of burning a barn; but I never did it." As near as I could discover, he had probably gone to bed in a barn when drunk, and smoked his pipe there; and so a barn was burnt. He had the reputation of being a clever man, had been there some three months waiting for his trial to come on, and would have to wait as much longer; but he was quite domesticated and contented, since he got his board for nothing, and thought that he was well treated.

He occupied one window, and I the other; and I saw, that, if one stayed there long, his principal business would be to look out the window. I had soon read all the tracts that were left there, and examined where former prisoners had broken out, and where a grate had been sawed off, and heard the history of the various occupants of that room; for I found that even here there was a history and a gossip which never circulated beyond the walls of the jail. Probably this is the only house in the town where verses are composed, which are afterward printed in a circular form, but not published. I was shown quite a long list of verses which were composed by some young men who had been detected in an attempt to escape, who avenged themselves by singing them.

I pumped my fellow-prisoner as dry as I could, for fear I should never see him again; but at length he showed me which was my bed, and left me to blow out the lamp.

It was like travelling into a far country, such as I had never expected to behold, to lie there for one night. It seemed to me that I never had heard the town-clock strike before, nor the evening sounds of the village; for we slept with the windows open, which were inside the grating. It was to see my native village in the light of the middle ages, and our Concord was turned into a Rhine stream, and visions of knights and castles passed before me. They were the voices of old burghers that I heard in the streets. I was an involuntary spectator and auditor of whatever was done and said in the kitchen of the adjacent village-inn,—a wholly new and rare experience to me. It was a closer view of my native town. I was fairly inside of it. I never had seen its institutions before. This is one of its peculiar institutions; for it is a shire town.[9] I began to comprehend what its inhabitants were about.

In the morning, our breakfasts were put through the hole in the door, in small oblong-square tin pans, made to fit, and holding a pint of chocolate, with brown bread, and an iron spoon. When they called for the vessels again, I was green enough to return what bread I had left; but my comrade seized it, and said that I should lay that up for lunch or dinner. Soon after, he was let out to work at haying in a neighboring field, whither he went every day, and would not be back till noon; so he bade me good-day, saying that he doubted if he should see me again.

When I came out of prison,—for some one interfered, and paid the tax,—I did not perceive that great changes had taken place on the common, such as he observed who went in a youth, and emerged a tottering and gray-headed man; and yet a change had to my eyes come over the scene,—the town, and State, and country,—greater than any that mere time could effect. I saw yet more distinctly the State in which I lived. I saw to what extent the people among whom I lived could be trusted as good neighbors and friends; that their friendship was for summer weather only; that they did not greatly purpose to do right; that they were a distinct race from me by their prejudices and superstitions, as the Chinamen and Malays are; that, in their sacrifices to humanity, they ran no risks, not even to their property; that, after all, they were not so noble but they treated the thief as he had treated them, and hoped, by a certain outward observance and a few

9. County seat.

prayers, and by walking in a particular straight though useless path from time to time, to save their souls. This may be to judge my neighbors harshly; for I believe that most of them are not aware that they have such an institution as the jail in their village.

It was formerly the custom in our village, when a poor debtor came out of jail, for his acquaintances to salute him, looking through their fingers, which were crossed to represent the grating of a jail window, "How do ye do?" My neighbors did not thus salute me, but first looked at me, and then at one another, as if I had returned from a long journey. I was put into jail as I was going to the shoemaker's to get a shoe which was mended. When I was let out the next morning, I proceeded to finish my errand, and, having put on my mended shoe, joined a huckleberry party, who were impatient to put themselves under my conduct; and in half an hour,—for the horse was soon tackled[1]—was in the midst of a huckleberry field, on one of our highest hills, two miles off; and then the State was nowhere to be seen.

This is the whole history of "My Prisons."

I have never declined paying the highway tax, because I am as desirous of being a good neighbor as I am of being a bad subject; and, as for supporting schools, I am doing my part to educate my fellow-countrymen now. It is for no particular item in the tax-bill that I refuse to pay it. I simply wish to refuse allegiance to the State, to withdraw and stand aloof from it effectually. I do not care to trace the course of my dollar, if I could, till it buys a man, or a musket to shoot one with,—the dollar is innocent,—but I am concerned to trace the effects of my allegiance. In fact, I quietly declare war with the State, after my fashion, though I will still make what use and get what advantage of her I can, as is usual in such cases.

If others pay the tax which is demanded of me, from a sympathy with the State, they do but what they have already done in their own case, or rather they abet injustice to a greater extent than the State requires. If they pay the tax from a mistaken interest in the individual taxed, to save his property or prevent his going to jail, it is because they have not considered wisely how far they let their private feelings interfere with the public good.

1. In harness.

This, then, is my position at present. But one cannot be too much on his guard in such a case, lest his action be biassed by obstinacy, or an undue regard for the opinions of men. Let him see that he does only what belongs to himself and to the hour.

I think sometimes, Why, this people mean well; they are only ignorant; they would do better if they knew how: why give your neighbors this pain to treat you as they are not inclined to? But I think, again, this is no reason why I should do as they do, or permit others to suffer much greater pain of a different kind. Again, I sometimes say to myself, When many millions of men, without heat, without ill-will, without personal feeling of any kind, demand of you a few shillings only, without the possibility, such is their constitution, of retracting or altering their present demand, and without the possibility, on your side, of appeal to any other millions, why expose yourself to this overwhelming brute force? You do not resist cold and hunger, the winds and the waves, thus obstinately; you quietly submit to a thousand similar necessities. You do not put your head into the fire. But just in proportion as I regard this as not wholly a brute force, but partly a human force, and consider that I have relations to those millions as to so many millions of men, and not of mere brute or inanimate things, I see that appeal is possible, first and instantaneously, from them to the Maker of them, and, secondly, from them to themselves. But, if I put my head deliberately into the fire, there is no appeal to fire or to the Maker of fire, and I have only myself to blame. If I could convince myself that I have any right to be satisfied with men as they are, and to treat them accordingly, and not according, in some respects, to my requisitions and expectations of what they and I ought to be, then, like a good Mussulman[2] and fatalist, I should endeavor to be satisfied with things as they are, and say it is the will of God. And, above all, there is this difference between resisting this and a purely brute or natural force, that I can resist this with some effect; but I cannot expect, like Orpheus, to change the nature of the rocks and trees and beasts.[3]

I do not wish to quarrel with any man or nation. I do not wish to split hairs, to make fine distinctions, or set myself up as better than

2. Muslim.

3. In Greek mythology, the music of Orpheus's lyre was so beautiful that it charmed wild beasts, caused trees to dance and rivers to stand still.

my neighbors. I seek rather, I may say, even an excuse for conforming to the laws of the land. I am but too ready to conform to them. Indeed I have reason to suspect myself on this head; and each year, as the tax-gatherer comes round, I find myself disposed to review the acts and position of the general and state governments, and the spirit of the people, to discover a pretext for conformity. I believe that the State will soon be able to take all my work of this sort out of my hands, and then I shall be no better a patriot than my fellow-countrymen. Seen from a lower point of view, the Constitution, with all its faults, is very good; the law and the courts are very respectable; even this State and this American government are, in many respects, very admirable and rare things, to be thankful for, such as a great many have described them; but seen from a point of view a little higher, they are what I have described them; seen from a higher still, and the highest, who shall say what they are, or that they are worth looking at or thinking of at all?

However, the government does not concern me much, and I shall bestow the fewest possible thoughts on it. It is not many moments that I live under a government, even in this world. If a man is thought-free, fancy-free, imagination-free, that which *is not* never for a long time appearing *to be* to him, unwise rulers or reformers cannot fatally interrupt him.

I know that most men think differently from myself; but those whose lives are by profession devoted to the study of these or kindred subjects, content me as little as any. Statesmen and legislators, standing so completely within the institution, never distinctly and nakedly behold it. They speak of moving society, but have no resting-place without it. They may be men of a certain experience and discrimination, and have no doubt invented ingenious and even useful systems, for which we sincerely thank them; but all their wit and usefulness lie within certain not very wide limits. They are wont to forget that the world is not governed by policy and expediency. Webster never goes behind government, and so cannot speak with authority about it. His words are wisdom to those legislators who contemplate no essential reform in the existing government; but for thinkers, and those who legislate for all time, he never once glances at the subject. I know of those whose serene and wise speculations on this theme would soon reveal the limits of his mind's range and hospitality. Yet, compared with the cheap professions of most reformers, and the still cheaper wisdom and eloquence of politicians in general, his are almost the only sensible and valuable words, and we thank Heaven for him. Comparatively, he is always strong, original, and, above all, practical. Still his quality is not wisdom, but prudence. The lawyer's truth is not Truth, but consistency, or a consistent expediency. Truth is always in harmony with herself, and is not concerned chiefly to reveal the justice that may consist with wrong-doing. He well deserves to be called, as he has been called, the Defender of the Constitution. There are really no blows to be given by him but defensive ones. He is not a leader, but a follower. His leaders are the men of '87.[4] "I have never made an effort," he says, "and never propose to make an effort; I have never countenanced an effort, and never mean to countenance an effort, to disturb the arrangement as originally made, by which the various States came into the Union." Still thinking of the sanction which the Constitution gives to slavery, he says, "Because it was a part of the original compact,—let it stand." Notwithstanding his special acuteness and ability, he is unable to take a fact out of its merely political relations, and behold it as it lies absolutely to be disposed of by the intellect,—what, for instance, it behoves a man to do here in America to-day with regard to slavery, but ventures, or is driven, to make some such desperate answer as the following, while professing to speak absolutely, and as a private man,—from which what new and singular code of social duties might be inferred?—"The manner," says he, "in which the government of those States where slavery exists are to regulate it, is for their own consideration, under their responsibility to their constituents, to the general laws of priority, humanity, and justice, and to God. Associations formed elsewhere, springing from a feeling of humanity, or any other cause, have nothing whatever to do with it. They have never received any encouragement from me, and they never will."[5]

They who know of no purer sources of truth, who have traced up its stream no higher, stand, and wisely stand, by the Bible and the Constitution, and drink at it there with reverence and humility; but they who behold where it comes trickling into this lake or that pool,

4. Those who passed the Ordinance of 1787, frequently called the Northwest Ordinance, which created the Northwest Territory and prohibited the introduction of slavery there, but not the retention of those already enslaved.

5. These extracts have been inserted since the Lecture was read [Thoreau's note].

gird up their loins once more, and continue their pilgrimage toward its fountain-head.

No man with a genius for legislation has appeared in America. They are rare in the history of the world. There are orators, politicians, and eloquent men, by the thousand; but the speaker has not yet opened his mouth to speak, who is capable of settling the much-vexed questions of the day. We love eloquence for its own sake, and not for any truth which it may utter, or any heroism it may inspire. Our legislators have not yet learned the comparative value of free-trade and of freedom, of union, and of rectitude, to a nation. They have no genius or talent for comparatively humble questions of taxation and finance, commerce and manufactures and agriculture. If we were left solely to the wordy wit of legislators in Congress for our guidance, uncorrected by the seasonable experience and the effectual complaints of the people, America would not long retain her rank among the nations. For eighteen hundred years, though perchance I have no right to say it, the New Testament has been written; yet where is the legislator who has wisdom and practical talent enough to avail himself of the light which it sheds on the science of legislation?

The authority of government, even such as I am willing to submit to,—for I will cheerfully obey those who know and can do better than I, and in many things even those who neither know nor can do so well,—is still an impure one: to be strictly just, it must have the sanction and consent of the governed. It can have no pure right over my person and property but what I concede to it. The progress from an absolute to a limited monarchy, from a limited monarchy to a democracy, is a progress toward a true respect for the individual. Is a democracy, such as we know it, the last improvement possible in government? Is it not possible to take a step further towards recognizing and organizing the rights of man? There will never be a really free and enlightened State, until the State comes to recognize the individual as a higher and independent power, from which all its own power and authority are derived, and treats him accordingly. I please myself with imagining a State at last which can afford to be just to all men, and to treat the individual with respect as a neighbor; which even would not think it inconsistent with its own repose, if a few were to live aloof from it, not meddling with it, nor embraced by it, who fulfilled all the duties of neighbors and fellow-men. A State which bore this kind of fruit, and suffered it to drop off as fast as it ripened, would prepare the way for a still more perfect and glorious State, which also I have imagined, but not yet anywhere seen.

1848, 1849

Robert F. Kennedy

1925–1968

Robert F. Kennedy was running for president when he gave this speech in 1968. All campaigns are contentious, but in 1968 the United States was in extraordinary turmoil. President Lyndon Johnson, who ascended to that office when Robert's brother, John F. Kennedy, was assassinated, withdrew from the race because Eugene McCarthy, who vowed to remove American troops from Vietnam, nearly defeated him in the New Hampshire Democratic primary. Johnson was further discouraged when Robert Kennedy announced that he would seek the Democratic nomination. Also joining the race was George Wallace, governor of Alabama, who, running on a platform that advocated white supremacy, was popular in the South. Whoever was elected would have much to deal with. Civil rights for African Americans, made law by key victories in Congress, were being imposed on reluctant, sometimes militant Southern whites. Vietnam War protesters more and more defiantly opposed American foreign policy. College campuses were torn apart. Then, early in the primary season, Martin Luther King Jr. was assassinated in Memphis, threatening to provoke yet further conflict. Kennedy was scheduled to give a speech in a poor, African American section of Indianapolis when he learned that King was murdered. Rather than cancel the event, he gave this impromptu speech to a crowd of people who had not yet heard about the assassination. This speech is generally praised for the ethos Kennedy displays, and that ethos surely contributed to his victory, two months later, in the California primary. It looked like he was well on the way to being nominated by the Democratic Party, but within hours of his California victory, Kennedy himself was assassinated. That summer, at one of the most violent political conventions in American history, the Democrats nominated Hubert Humphrey, who lost the presidential election to Richard Nixon.

On the Death of the Reverend Dr. Martin Luther King, Jr.

I have bad news for you, for all of our fellow citizens, and people who love peace all over the world, and that is that Martin Luther King was shot and killed tonight.

Martin Luther King dedicated his life to love and to justice for his fellow human beings, and he died because of that effort.

In this difficult day, in this difficult time for the United States, it is perhaps well to ask what kind of a nation we are and what direction we want to move in. For those of you who are black—considering the evidence there evidently is that there were white people who were responsible—you can be filled with bitterness, with hatred, and a desire for revenge. We can move in that direction as a country, in great polarization—black people amongst black, white people amongst white, filled with hatred toward one another.

Or we can make an effort, as Martin Luther King did, to understand and to comprehend, and to replace that violence, that stain of bloodshed that has spread across our land, with an effort to understand with compassion and love.

For those of you who are black and are tempted to be filled with hatred and distrust at the injustice of such an act, against all white people, I can only say that I feel in my own heart the same kind of feeling. I had a member of my family killed, but he was killed by a white man. But we have to make an effort in the United States, we have to make an effort to understand, to go beyond these rather difficult times.

My favorite poet was Aeschylus.[1] He wrote: "In our sleep, pain which cannot forget falls drop by drop upon the heart until, in our own despair, against our will, comes wisdom through the awful grace of God."

What we need in the United States is not division; what we need in the United States is not hatred; what we need in the United States is not violence or lawlessness; but love and wisdom, and compassion toward one another, and a feeling of justice toward those who still suffer within our country, whether they be white or they be black.

So I shall ask you tonight to return home, to say a prayer for the family of Martin Luther King, that's true, but more importantly to

1. Aeschylus (c. 524–455 B.C.E.), Greek playwright, considered by many to be the father of tragedy. This quotation is from his play *Agamemnon*.

say a prayer for our own country, which all of us love—a prayer for understanding and that compassion of which I spoke.

We can do well in this country. We will have difficult times; we've had difficult times in the past; we will have difficult times in the future. It is not the end of violence; it is not the end of lawlessness; it is not the end of disorder.

But the vast majority of white people and the vast majority of black people in this country want to live together, want to improve the quality of our life, and want justice for all human beings who abide in our land.

Let us dedicate ourselves to what the Greeks wrote so many years ago: to tame the savageness of man and make gentle the life of this world.

Let us dedicate ourselves to that, and say a prayer for our country and for our people.

1968

Susan Moller Okin

1946–2004

In the 1960s and 1970s, liberal democracies began to recognize that the civil rights of minority groups were often legally *suppressed through systemic inequities. Take, for instance, the Jim Crow laws in the Southern United States. The injustice of racial discrimination was remedied by special treatment: for example, after the Civil Rights Acts of 1964 and 1965, states with a history of preventing African Americans from voting had to get the U.S. Department of Justice to approve changes to their election laws and policies. The DOJ would assure that the states were not designing clever ways to prevent African Americans from voting. Only by such special intervention was the equal treatment of minorities protected.*

This principle encouraged other groups, beginning in the 1970s, to seek special protections to allow their free exercise of constitutional rights, such as religious practice. This strategy is sometimes called "identity" politics, in which a member of a cultural group that is suffering discrimination is guaranteed justice by special laws enacted to protect that group. For example, Jewish or Islamic students might be allowed to miss school on days that are holy to their religion. The Native American Church might be allowed to use a controlled substance, peyote, in religious ceremonies. At the same time, multiculturalism was replacing the old "melting pot" metaphor of American life. While the melting pot suggests that new immigrant groups must assimilate into the mainstream of American culture, which itself is altered slightly by their addition, multiculturalism suggests that individual cultures have a right to retain their distinctiveness. Society should be a commingling of various and distinct cultures, a "salad bowl," not a melding of all into one homogeneous "American" culture.

This essay, first published in 1999, enters into this public debate about what society should look like in liberal democracies. Generally speaking, multiculturalism is more of a liberal than a conservative political value, but so is feminism, which holds that special treatment is needed if women are to secure equality in a society long-committed to their inequality. Susan Moller Okin published this piece in the Boston Review, *which is a somewhat iconoclastic, progressive magazine. In its own words, the* Boston Review *is "committed to equality" and believes "in the power of collective reasoning and imagination to create a more just world." In other words, while the general, educated, reading public might come across this essay, more specifically it was meant to influence a debate among liberals.*

Is Multiculturalism Bad for Women?

Until the past few decades, minority groups—immigrants as well as indigenous peoples—were typically expected to assimilate into majority cultures. This assimilationist expectation is now often considered oppressive, and many Western countries are seeking to devise new policies that are more responsive to persistent cultural differences. The appropriate policies vary with context: countries such as England with established churches or state-supported religious education find it hard to resist demands to extend state support to minority religious schools; countries such as France with traditions of strictly secular public education struggle over whether the clothing required by minority religions may be worn in the public schools. But one issue recurs across all contexts, though it has gone virtually unnoticed in current debate: What should be done when the claims of minority cultures or religions clash with the norm of gender equality that is at least formally endorsed by liberal states (however much they continue to violate it in their practice)?

In the late 1980s, for example, a sharp public controversy erupted in France about whether Magrbin girls could attend school wearing the traditional Muslim headscarves regarded as proper attire for post-pubescent young women. Staunch defenders of secular education lined up with some feminists and far-right nationalists against the practice; much of the old left supported the multiculturalist demands for flexibility and respect for diversity, accusing opponents of racism or cultural imperialism. At the very same time, however, the public was virtually silent about a problem of vastly greater importance to many French Arab and African immigrant women: polygamy.

During the 1980s, the French government quietly permitted immigrant men to bring multiple wives into the country, to the point where an estimated 200,000 families in Paris are now polygamous. Any suspicion that official concern over headscarves was motivated by an impulse toward gender equality is belied by the easy adoption of a permissive policy on polygamy, despite the burdens this practice imposes on women and the warnings issued by women from the relevant cultures.[1] On this issue, no politically effective opposition galvanized. But once reporters finally got around to interviewing the wives, they discovered what the government could have learned years earlier: that the women affected by polygamy regarded it as an inescapable and barely tolerable institution in their African countries of origin, and an unbearable imposition in the French context. Overcrowded apartments and the lack of each wife's private space lead to immense hostility, resentment, even violence both among the wives and against each other's children.

In part because of the strain on the welfare state caused by families with 20–30 members, the French government has recently decided to recognize only one wife and consider all the other marriages annulled. But what will happen to all the other wives and children? Having neglected women's view on polygamy for so long, the government now seems to be abdicating its responsibility for the vulnerability that women and children incurred because of its rash policy.

1. *International Herald Tribune*, 2 February 1996, News section.

The French accommodation of polygamy illustrates a deep and growing tension between feminism and multiculturalist concerns to protect cultural diversity. I think we—especially those of us who consider ourselves politically progressive and opposed to all forms of oppression—have been too quick to assume that feminism and multiculturalism are both good things that are easily reconciled. I shall argue instead that there is considerable likelihood of tension between them—more precisely, between feminism and a multiculturalist commitment to group rights for minority cultures.

A few words to explain the terms and focus of my argument. By "feminism," I mean the belief that women should not be disadvantaged by their sex, that they should be recognized as having human dignity equally with men, and the opportunity to live as fulfilling and as freely chosen lives as men can. "Multiculturalism" is harder to pin down, but the particular aspect that concerns me here is the claim, made in the context of basically liberal democracies, that minority cultures or ways of life are not sufficiently protected by ensuring the individual rights of their members and as a consequence should also be protected with special *group* rights or privileges. In the French case, for example, the right to contract polygamous marriages clearly constituted a group right, not available to the rest of the population. In other cases, groups claim rights to govern themselves, have guaranteed political representation, or be exempt from generally applicable law.

Demands for such group rights are growing—from indigenous native populations, minority ethnic or religious groups, and formerly colonized peoples (at least, when the latter immigrate to the former colonial state). These groups, it is argued, have their own "societal cultures" which—as Will Kymlicka, the foremost contemporary defender of cultural group rights, says—provide "members with meaningful ways of life across the full range of human activities, including social, educational, religious, recreational, and economic life, encompassing both public and private spheres."[2] Because societal cultures play so pervasive and fundamental a role

2. Will Kymlicka, *Multicultural Citizenship: A Liberal Theory of Minority Rights* (Oxford: Oxford University Press, 1995), 89, 76. See also Kymlicka, *Liberalism, Community, and Culture* (Oxford: The Clarendon Press, 1989). It should be noted that Kymlicka himself does not argue for extensive or permanent group rights for those who have voluntarily immigrated.

in the lives of members, and because such cultures are threatened with extinction, minority cultures should be protected by special rights: That, in essence, is the case for group rights.

Some proponents of group rights argue that even cultures that "flout the rights of [their individual members] in a liberal society"[3] should be accorded group rights or privileges if their minority status endangers the culture's continued existence. Others do not claim that all minority cultural groups should have special rights, but rather that such groups—even illiberal ones, that violate their individual members' rights, requiring them to conform to group beliefs or norms—have the right to be "let alone" in a liberal society.[4] Both claims seem clearly inconsistent with the basic liberal value of individual freedom, which entails that group rights should not trump the individual rights of their members; thus, I will not address the problems they present for feminists here.[5] But some defenders of multiculturalism largely confine their defense of group rights to groups that are internally liberal.[6] Even with these restrictions, feminists—anyone, that is, who endorses the moral equality of men and women—should remain skeptical. So I will argue.

Gender and Culture

Most cultures are suffused with practices and ideologies concerning gender. Suppose, then, that a culture endorses and facilitates the control of men over women in various ways (even if informally, in the private sphere of domestic life). Suppose, too, that there are fairly clear disparities of power between the sexes, such that the more powerful, male members are those who are generally in a position to determine and articulate the group's beliefs, practices, and interests. Under such conditions, group rights are potentially, and in many

3. Avishai Margalit and Moshe Halbertal, "Liberalism and the Right to Culture," *Social Research* 61, 3 (Fall, 1994): 491.

4. For example, Chandran Kukathas, "Are There any Cultural Rights?" *Political Theory* 20, 1 (1992): 105–39.

5. Okin, "Feminism and Multiculturalism: Some Tensions," *Ethics* (forthcoming 1998).

6. For example, Kymlicka, *Liberalism, Community, and Culture*, especially chap. 8. Kymlicka does not apply his requirement that groups be internally liberal to those he terms "national minorities," but I will not address this aspect of his theory here.

cases actually, antifeminist. They substantially limit the capacities of women and girls of that culture to live with human dignity equal to that of men and boys, and to live as freely chosen lives as they can.

Advocates of group rights for minorities within liberal states have not adequately addressed this simple critique of group rights, for at least two reasons. First, they tend to treat cultural groups as monoliths—to pay more attention to differences between and among groups than to differences within them. Specifically, they give little or no recognition to the fact that minority cultural groups, like the societies in which they exist (though to a greater or lesser extent), are themselves *gendered*, with substantial differences of power and advantage between men and women. Second, advocates of group rights pay no or little attention to the private sphere. Some of the best liberal defenses of group rights urge that individuals need "a culture of their own," and that only within such a culture can people develop a sense of self-esteem or self-respect, or the capacity to decide what kind of life is good for them. But such arguments typically neglect both the different roles that cultural groups require of their members and the context in which persons' senses of themselves and their capacities are first formed *and* in which culture is first transmitted—the realm of domestic or family life.

When we correct for these deficiencies by paying attention to internal differences and to the private arena, two particularly important connections between culture and gender come into sharp relief, both of which underscore the force of the simple critique. First, the sphere of personal, sexual, and reproductive life provides a central focus of most cultures, a dominant theme in cultural practices and rules. Religious or cultural groups are often particularly concerned with "personal law"—the laws of marriage, divorce, child custody, division and control of family property, and inheritance.[7] As a rule, then, the defense of "cultural practices" is likely to have much greater impact on the lives of women and girls than those of men and boys, since far more of women's time and energy goes into preserving and maintaining the personal, familial, and reproductive side of life.

7. See for example Krit Singh, "Obstacles to Women's Rights in India," in *Human Rights of Women: National and International Perspectives*, ed. Rebecca J. Cook (Philadephia: University of Pennsylvania Press, 1994), 375–96, especially 378–89.

Obviously culture is not only about domestic arrangements, but they do provide a major focus of most contemporary cultures. Home is, after all, where much of culture is practiced, preserved, and transmitted to the young. In turn, the distribution of responsibilities and power at home has a major impact on who can participate in and influence the more public parts of the cultural life, where rules and regulations about both public and private life are made.

Second, most cultures have as one of their principal aims the control of women by men.[8] Consider, for example, the founding myths of Greek and Roman antiquity, and of Judaism, Christianity, and Islam: they are rife with attempts to justify the control and subordination of women. These myths consist of a combination of denials of women's role in reproduction, appropriations by men of the power to reproduce themselves, characterizations of women as overly emotional, untrustworthy, evil, or sexually dangerous, and refusals to acknowledge mothers' rights over the disposition of their children. Think of Athena, sprung from the head of Zeus, and of Romulus and Remus, reared without a human mother. Or Adam, made by a male God, who then (at least according to one of the two biblical versions of the story) made Eve out of part of Adam. Consider Eve, whose weakness led Adam astray. Think of all those endless "begats" in Genesis, where women's primary role in reproduction is completely ignored, or of the textual justifications for polygamy, once practiced in Judaism, still practiced in many parts of the Islamic world, and (though illegally) by Mormons in some parts of the United States. Consider, too, the story of Abraham, a pivotal turning point in the development of monotheism.[9] God commands Abraham to sacrifice "his" greatly loved son. Abraham prepares to do exactly what God asks of him, without even telling,

8. I cannot discuss here the roots of this male preoccupation, except to say (following feminist theorists Dorothy Dinnerstein, Nancy Chodorow, Jessica Benjamin and, before them, Jesuit anthropologist Walter Ong) that it seems to have a lot to do with female primary parenting. It is also clearly related to the uncertainty of paternity, which technology has now changed. If these issues are at the root of it, then the cultural preoccupation with controlling women is not an inevitable fact of human life, but a contingent factor that feminists have a considerable interest in changing.

9. See Carol Delaney, *Abraham on Trial: Paternal Power and the Sacrifice of Children* (Princeton: Princeton University Press, forthcoming 1997). Note that in the Qur'anic version, it is not Isaac but Ishmael whom Abraham prepares to sacrifice.

much less asking, Isaac's mother, Sarah. Abraham's absolute obedience to God makes him the central, fundamental model of faith, for all three religions.

While the powerful drive to control women—and to blame and punish them for men's difficulty controlling their own sexual impulses—has been softened considerably in the more progressive, reformed versions of Judaism, Christianity, and Islam, it remains strong in their more orthodox or fundamentalist versions. Moreover, it is by no means confined to Western or monotheistic cultures. Many of the world's traditions and cultures, including those practiced within formerly conquered or colonized nation states—certainly including most of the peoples of Africa, the Middle East, Latin America and Asia—are quite distinctly patriarchal. They too have elaborate patterns of socialization, rituals, matrimonial customs, and other cultural practices (including systems of property ownership and control of resources) aimed at bringing women's sexuality and reproductive capabilities under men's control. Many such practices make it virtually impossible for women to choose to live independently of men, to be celibate or lesbian, or not to have children.

Those who practice some of the most controversial such customs—clitoridectomy, the marriage of children or marriages that are otherwise coerced, or polygamy—sometimes explicitly defend them as necessary for controlling women, and openly acknowledge that the customs persist at men's insistence. In an interview with *New York Times* reporter Celia Dugger, practitioners of clitoridectomy in Côte d'Ivoire and Togo explained that the practice "helps insure a girl's virginity before marriage and fidelity afterward by reducing sex to a marital obligation." As a female exciser said, "[a] woman's role in life is to care for her children, keep house and cook. If she has not been cut, [she] might think about her own sexual pleasure."[1] In Egypt, where a law banning female genital cutting was recently overturned by a court, supporters of the practice say it "curbs a girl's sexual appetite and makes her more marriageable."[2]

1. *New York Times*, 5 October 1996, A4. The role that older women in such cultures play in perpetuating them is important but complex, and cannot be addressed here.

2. *New York Times*, 26 June 1997, A9.

Moreover, in such contexts, many women have no economically viable alternative to marriage. Men in polygamous cultures, too, readily acknowledge that the practice accords with their self-interest and is a means of controlling women. As a French immigrant from Mali said in a recent interview: "When my wife is sick and I don't have another, who will care for me? . . . [O]ne wife on her own is trouble. When there are several, they are forced to be polite and well behaved. If they misbehave, you threaten that you'll take another wife." Women apparently see polygamy very differently. French African immigrant women deny that they like polygamy, and say not only that they are given "no choice" in the matter, but that their female forebears in Africa did not like it either.[3] As for child or otherwise coerced marriage: this practice is clearly a way not only of controlling whom the girls or young women marry, but also of ensuring that they are virgins at the time of marriage and, often, enhancing the husband's power by creating a significant age difference between husbands and wives.

Consider, too, the practice—common in much of Latin America, rural South East Asia and parts of West Africa—of encouraging or even requiring a rape victim to marry the rapist. In many such cultures—including fourteen countries of Latin America—rapists are legally exonerated if they marry or (in some cases) even offer to marry their victims. Clearly, rape is not seen in these cultures primarily as a violent assault on the girl or woman herself, but rather as a serious injury to her family and its honor. By marrying his victim, the rapist can help restore the family's honor and relieve it of a daughter who, as "damaged goods," has become unmarriageable. In Peru, this barbaric law was amended for the worse in 1991: the co-defendants in a gang rape are now all exonerated if one of them offers to marry the victim (feminists are fighting to get the law repealed). As a Peruvian taxi driver explained: "Marriage is the right and proper thing to do after a rape. A raped woman is a used item. No one wants her. At least with this law the woman will get a husband."[4] It is hard to imagine a worse fate for a woman than being pressured into marrying the man who has raped her. But worse fates do exist in some

3. *International Herald Tribune*, 2 February 1997, News section.

4. *New York Times*, 12 March 1997, A8.

cultures—notably in Pakistan and parts of the Arab Middle East, where women who bring rape charges are quite frequently charged with the serious Muslim offense of *zina*, or sex outside of marriage. Law allows for the whipping or imprisonment of such a woman, and culture condones the killing or pressuring into suicide of a raped woman by relatives concerned to restore the family's honor.[5]

Thus, many culturally based customs aim to control women and render them, especially sexually and reproductively, servile to men's desires and interests. Sometimes, moreover, "culture" or "traditions" are so closely linked with the control of women that they are virtually equated. In a recent news report about a small community of Orthodox Jews living in the mountains of Yemen—ironically, from a feminist point of view, the story was entitled "Yemen's small Jewish community thrives on mixed traditions"—the elderly leader of this small polygamous sect is quoted as saying: "We are Orthodox Jews, very keen on our traditions. If we go to Israel, we will lose hold over our daughters, our wives and our sisters." One of his sons added: "We are like Muslims, we do not allow our women to uncover their faces."[6] Thus the servitude of women is presented as virtually synonymous with "our traditions." (Only blindness to sexual servitude can explain the title; it is inconceivable that the article would have carried such a title if it were about a community that practiced any kind of slavery but sexual slavery.)

While virtually all of the world's cultures have distinctly patriarchal pasts, some—mostly, though by no means exclusively, Western liberal cultures—have departed far further from them than others. Western cultures, of course, still practice many forms of sex discrimination. They place far more stress on beauty, thinness, and youth in females and on intellectual accomplishment, skill, and strength in males; they expect women to perform for no economic reward far more than half of the unpaid work of their families, whether or not they also work for wages; partly as a consequence of this and partly because of workplace discrimination, women are far more likely than

5. This practice is discussed in Henry S. Richardson, *Practical Reasoning About Final Ends* (Cambridge: Cambridge University Press, 1994), especially 240–43, 262–63, 282–84.

6. *Agence France Presse*, 18 May 1997, International News section.

men to become poor; girls and women are also subjected by men to a great deal of (illegal) violence, including sexual violence. But women in more liberal cultures are, at the same time, legally guaranteed many of the same freedoms and opportunities as men. In addition, most families in such cultures, with the exception of some religious fundamentalists, do not communicate to their daughters that they are of less value than boys, that their lives are to be confined to domesticity and service to men and children, and that the only positive value of their sexuality is that it be strictly confined to marriage, the service of men, and reproductive ends. This, as we have seen, is quite different from women's situation in many of the world's other cultures, including many of those from which immigrants to Europe and Northern America come.

Group Rights?

Most cultures are patriarchal, then, and many (though not all) of the cultural minorities that claim group rights are more patriarchal than the surrounding cultures. So it is no surprise that the cultural importance of maintaining control over women shouts out to us in the examples given in the literature on cultural diversity and group rights within liberal states. Yet, though it shouts out, it is seldom explicitly addressed.[7]

A 1986 paper about the legal rights and culture-based claims of various immigrant groups and gypsies in contemporary Britain mentions the roles and status of women as "one very clear example" of the "clash of cultures."[8] In it, Sebastian Poulter discusses claims put forward by members of such groups for special legal treatment on account of their cultural differences. A few are non-gender-related claims: about a Muslim schoolteacher's being allowed to be absent part of Friday afternoons in order to pray, and gypsy children having less stringent schooling requirements than others on account of their

7. See, however, Bhikhu Parekh's "Minority Practices and Principles of Toleration," *International Migration Review* (April 1996): 251–84, in which he directly addresses and critiques a number of cultural practices that devalue the status of women.

8. Sebastian Poulter, "Ethnic Minority Customs, English Law, and Human Rights," *International and Comparative Law Quarterly* 36, 3 (1987): 589–615.

itinerant lifestyle. But the vast majority of the examples concern gender inequalities: child marriages, forced marriages, divorce systems biased against women, polygamy, and clitoridectomy. Almost all of the legal cases discussed stemmed from women's or girls' claims that their individual rights were being truncated or violated by the practices of their cultural groups.

Kymlicka regards cultures that discriminate overtly and formally against women—by denying them education, or the right to vote or to hold office—as not deserving special rights.[9] But sex discrimination is often far less overt. In many cultures, strict control of women is enforced in the private sphere by the authority of either actual or symbolic fathers, often acting through, or with the complicity of, the older women of the culture. In many cultures in which women's basic civil rights and liberties are formally assured, discrimination practiced against women and girls within the household not only severely constrains their choices, but seriously threatens their well-being and even their lives.[1] And such sex discrimination—whether severe or more mild—often has very powerful *cultural* roots.

Although Kymlicka rightly objects to the granting of group rights to minority cultures that practice overt sex discrimination, then, his arguments for multiculturalism fail to register what he acknowledges elsewhere: that the subordination of women is often informal and private, and that virtually no culture in the world today, minority or majority, could pass his "no sex discrimination" test if it were applied in the private sphere.[2] Those who defend group rights on liberal grounds need to address these very private, culturally reinforced kinds of discrimination. For surely self-respect and self-esteem require more than simple membership in a viable culture. Surely it is *not* enough, for one to be able to "question one's inherited social roles" and to have the capacity to make choices about the life one wants to lead, that one's culture be protected. At least

9. Kymlicka, *Multicultural Citizenship,* 153, 165.

1. See, for example, Amartya Sen, "More than One Hundred Million Women Are Missing," *New York Review of Books,* 20 December 1990.

2. Will Kymlicka, *Contemporary Political Philosophy: An Introduction* (Oxford: The Clarendon Press, 1990), 239–62.

as important to the development of self-respect and self-esteem is *our place within our culture*. And at least as important to our capacity to question our social roles is *whether our culture instills in and enforces particular social roles on us*. To the extent that their culture is patriarchal, in both these respects the healthy development of girls is endangered.

Part of the Solution?

It is by no means clear, then, from a feminist point of view, that minority group rights are "part of the solution." They may well exacerbate the problem. In the case of a more patriarchal minority culture in the context of a less patriarchal majority culture, no argument can be made on the basis of self-respect or freedom that the female members of the culture have a clear interest in its preservation. Indeed, they *may* be much better off if the culture into which they were born were either to become extinct (so that its members would become integrated into the less sexist surrounding culture) or, preferably, to be encouraged to alter itself so as to reinforce the equality of women—at least to the degree to which this is upheld in the majority culture. Other considerations would, of course, need to be taken into account, such as whether the minority group speaks a different language that requires protection, and whether the group suffers from prejudices such as racial discrimination. But it would take significant factors weighing in the other direction to counterbalance evidence that a culture severely constrained women's choices or otherwise undermined their well-being.

What some of the examples discussed above show us is how culturally endorsed practices that are oppressive to women can often remain hidden in the private or domestic sphere. And when Congress in 1996 passed a law criminalizing clitoridectomy, a number of US doctors objected to the law as unjustified, since it concerned a private matter which, as one said, "should be decided by a physician, the family, and the child."[3] It can take more or less extraordinary circumstances for such abuses of girls or women to become public or for the state to be able to intervene protectively.

3. *New York Times*, 12 October 1996, A6. Similar views were expressed on public radio.

Thus it is clear that many instances of private sphere discrimination against women on cultural grounds are never likely to emerge in public, where courts can enforce their rights and political theorists can label such practices as illiberal and therefore unjustified violations of women's physical or mental integrity. Establishing group rights to enable some minority cultures to preserve themselves may not be in the best interests of the girls and women of the culture, even if it benefits the men.

When liberal arguments are made for the rights of groups, then, special care must be taken to look at within-group inequalities. It is especially important to consider inequalities between the sexes, since they are likely to be less public, and less easily discernible. Moreover, policies aiming to respond to the needs and claims of cultural minority groups must take seriously the need for adequate representation of less powerful members of such groups. Since attention to the rights of minority cultural groups, if it is to be consistent with the fundamentals of liberalism, must be ultimately aimed at furthering the well-being of the members of these groups, there can be no justification for assuming that the groups' self-proclaimed leaders—invariably mainly composed of their older and their male members—represent the interests of all of the groups' members. Unless women—and, more specifically, young women, since older women often become co-opted into reinforcing gender inequality—are fully represented in negotiations about group rights, their interests may be harmed rather than promoted by the granting of such rights.

1999

Anne Applebaum
b. 1964

Shortly after 9/11, George W. Bush declared that the United States would wage a war against terrorism. Because terrorist groups like Al-Qaeda do not fight in uniforms or on battlefields, and because they generally operate underground, independent of any established nation, the United States determined that it had to pursue methods that violated accepted rules of war. For example, based on the advice of Alberto Gonzales, then a White House attorney, President Bush decided that the Geneva Conventions, which govern how nations must treat prisoners of war, did not apply to America's prisoners in the war on terrorism. Even more controversial were a series of legal opinions and tacit policy positions that sanctioned the torture of suspected terrorists. The debate became acute in November 2004, when Bush nominated Gonzales to replace John Ashcroft as the U.S. Attorney General. Such nominations require confirmation by the Senate, and many Democrats opposed Gonzales because, in the words of USA Today, *"while at the White House," Gonzales wrote legal memos arguing that "President Bush's wartime powers superseded anti-torture laws and treaties." Applebaum published this essay in the* Washington Post *shortly before the Senate began debating Gonzales's nomination. In February 2005, the Senate confirmed Gonzales in a vote of 60 to 36.*

The Torture Myth

Just for a moment, let's pretend that there is no moral, legal, or constitutional problem with torture. Let's also imagine a clear-cut case: a terrorist who knows where bombs are about to explode in Iraq. To stop him, it seems that a wide range of Americans would be prepared to endorse "cruel and unusual" methods. In advance of confirmation hearings for Attorney General–designate Alberto Gonzales last week, the *Wall Street Journal* argued that such scenarios must be debated, since "what's at stake in this controversy is nothing less than the ability of U.S. forces to interrogate enemies who want to murder innocent civilians." Alan Dershowitz, the liberal legal scholar, has argued in the past that interrogators in such a case should get a "torture warrant" from a judge.[1] Both of these arguments rest on an assumption: that torture—defined as physical pressure during interrogation—can be used to extract useful information.

But does torture work? The question has been asked many times since September 11, 2001. I'm repeating it, however, because the Gonzales hearings inspired more articles about our lax methods ("Too Nice

1. Alan Dershowitz (b. 1938), Harvard law professor, advocates many liberal ideas in court and has defended several celebrities accused of crimes, including O. J. Simpson. [All notes are the editor's.]

for Our Own Good" was one headline), because similar comments may follow this week's trial of Spec. Charles Graner, the alleged Abu Ghraib ringleader, and because I still cannot find a positive answer.[2] I've heard it said that the Syrians and the Egyptians "really know how to get these things done." I've heard the Israelis mentioned, without proof. I've heard Algeria mentioned, too, but Darius Rejali, an academic who recently trolled through French archives, found no clear examples of how torture helped the French in Algeria—and they lost that war anyway.[3] "Liberals," argued an article in the liberal online magazine *Slate* a few months ago, "have a tendency to accept, all too eagerly, the argument that torture is ineffective." But it's also true that "realists," whether liberal or conservative, have a tendency to accept, all too eagerly, fictitious accounts of effective torture carried out by someone else.

By contrast, it is easy to find experienced U.S. officers who argue precisely the opposite. Meet, for example, retired Air Force Col. John Rothrock, who, as a young captain, headed a combat interrogation team in Vietnam. More than once he was faced with a ticking time-bomb scenario: a captured Vietcong guerrilla who knew of plans to kill Americans. What was done in such cases was "not nice," he says. "But we did not physically abuse them." Rothrock used psychology, the shock of capture and of the unexpected. Once, he let a prisoner see a wounded comrade die. Yet—as he remembers saying to the "desperate and honorable officers" who wanted him to move faster—"if I take a Bunsen burner to the guy's genitals, he's going to tell you just about anything," which would be pointless. Rothrock, who is no squishy liberal, says that he doesn't know "any professional intelligence officers of my generation who would think this is a good idea."

Or listen to Army Col. Stuart Herrington, a military intelligence specialist who conducted interrogations in Vietnam, Panama, and Iraq during Desert Storm, and who was sent by the Pentagon in 2003—long before Abu Ghraib—to assess interrogations in Iraq. Aside from its immorality and its illegality, says Herrington, torture

2. Under Saddam Hussein, Abu Ghraib was a notorious prison where interrogators often tortured political prisoners. During its occupation, the United States used the prison to detain, interrogate, and in some instances humiliate and torture people captured during the invasion.

3. After an eight-year war for independence, which featured guerrilla tactics and terrorism, Algeria eventually won its independence from France in 1962. French enthusiasm for the war dissolved under the revelation of its own brutal tactics, including the torture of prisoners.

is simply "not a good way to get information." In his experience, nine out of ten people can be persuaded to talk with no "stress methods" at all, let alone cruel and unusual ones. Asked whether that would be true of religiously motivated fanatics, he says that the "batting average" might be lower: "perhaps six out of ten." And if you beat up the remaining four? "They'll just tell you anything to get you to stop."

Worse, you'll have the other side effects of torture. It "endangers our soldiers on the battlefield by encouraging reciprocity." It does "damage to our country's image" and undermines our credibility in Iraq. That, in the long run, outweighs any theoretical benefit. Herrington's confidential Pentagon report, which he won't discuss but which was leaked to *The Post* a month ago, goes farther.[4] In that document, he warned that members of an elite military and CIA task force were abusing detainees in Iraq, that their activities could be "making gratuitous enemies" and that prisoner abuse "is counterproductive to the Coalition's efforts to win the cooperation of the Iraqi citizenry."[5] Far from rescuing Americans, in other words, the use of "special methods" might help explain why the war is going so badly.

An up-to-date illustration of the colonel's point appeared in recently released FBI documents from the naval base at Guantánamo Bay, Cuba.[6] These show, among other things, that some military intelligence officers wanted to use harsher interrogation methods than the FBI did. As a result, complained one inspector, "every time the FBI established a rapport with a detainee, the military would step in and the detainee would stop being cooperative." So much for the utility of torture.

Given the overwhelmingly negative evidence, the really interesting question is not whether torture works but why so many people in our society want to believe that it works. At the moment, there is a myth in circulation, a fable that goes something like this: Radical terrorists will take advantage of our fussy legality, so we may have to suspend it to beat them. Radical terrorists mock our namby-pamby

4. Army generals received Herrington's report in December 2003; The *Washington Post* first published its summary of that report in December 2004.

5. Three other nations joined the U. S. invasion of Iraq in March 2003, and over thirty more joined this Coalition after the initial months of combat.

6. The United States has maintained a naval base at Guantánamo Bay in Cuba since 1903, and it established a detention camp there after the invasion of Afghanistan to imprison people captured in the War on Terror.

prisons, so we must make them tougher. Radical terrorists are nasty, so to defeat them we have to be nastier.

Perhaps it's reassuring to tell ourselves tales about the new forms of "toughness" we need, or to talk about the special rules we will create to defeat this special enemy. Unfortunately, that toughness is self-deceptive and self-destructive. Ultimately it will be self-defeating as well.

2005

Kwame Anthony Appiah
b. 1954

Appiah is a philosophy professor, and he wrote his early books, published by Cambridge and Oxford, for other philosophers to read. in the 1990s, he began writing for a general audience, as he does here. This essay is the first chapter in his book, Cosmopolitanism: Ethics in a World of Strangers. *Appiah is himself a cosmopolitan. He was born in London and educated at a boarding school in England and at Cambridge University, though he was raised, as he indicates in this essay, in the Ghanaian town of Kumasi. His father was a prominent Ghanaian lawyer and politician; his mother's family is English aristocracy; and, when he wrote this book in 2006, Appiah was living and teaching in New York City. People who live this kind of multinational life, who feel at home in various countries, who are more comfortable in cities than in small towns, who relish the heterogeneous hustle and bustle of multicultural crowds and restaurants and tongues, are often called "cosmopolitans." (Universities tend to be cosmopolitan because they are enclaves of diverse nationalities and cultures.) Typically, the cosmopolitans' opposites are imagined to be ardent patriots or nationalists, who, if not xenophobic, are much more comfortable in a homogeneous zone of cultural (and sometimes racial) solidarity. These two types also emblematize different ethics, the cosmopolitan outlook emphasizing human rights and obligations that transcend political boundaries, while the nationalist viewpoint is more tribal, looking to the good of one's own people and the privilege of kinship before any other considerations. These ethical systems often clash.*

Many historians, for example, blame World War II on the hyper-nationalism of Germany, Italy, and Japan. After that conflagration, several multinational associations seemed to swing the world toward a cosmopolitan way of thinking—not only the multinational, defensive Cold War alliances of "East" and "West," but the United Nations, World Bank, World Trade Organization, International Court of Justice, and European Union (EU), for example. After the demise of the communist Eastern bloc in the early 1990s, the twenty-seven member nations of the European Union and the three signatories of the North American Free Trade Agreement, among others groups of nations, developed free-trade zones that encouraged the "globalization" of business and industry, which intertwined national economies.

This essay was written during a flare-up between cosmopolitanism and nationalism. After 9/11, patriotism soared in America and led to the invasions of Afghanistan and Iraq. War tends to abuse universal human rights; you should note, for instance, that Cosmopolitanism *was written at about the same time that Anne Applebaum argued against torturing our prisoners ("The Torture Myth"). Even so, the essay is, perhaps, even more appropriate in today's world than it was in 2006. The unprecedented cross-border migration of peoples in recent years seems to have triggered a resurgence of nationalism. The United Kingdom's exit from the EU (Brexit), the proposed wall between the United States and Mexico, and the rise of illiberal democracies in Russia, the Philippines, Brazil, Hungary, and Poland, all seem to indicate the pendulum swinging away from cosmopolitanism. You might presume that Appiah writes not to gung-ho patriots but to university-educated, upper-middle-class readers whose families have benefited from globalization and most of whom lean toward the cosmopolitan outlook embodied by Appiah himself. If that is the case, you might ask, What is Appiah trying to do to these readers?*

Making Conversation

Our ancestors have been human for a very long time. If a normal baby girl born forty thousand years ago were kidnapped by a time traveler and raised in a normal family in New York, she would be ready for college in eighteen years.

She would learn English (along with—who knows?—Spanish or Chinese), understand trigonometry, follow baseball and pop music; she would probably want a pierced tongue and a couple of tattoos. And she would be unrecognizably different from the brothers and sisters she left behind. For most of human history, we were born into small societies of a few score people, bands of hunters and gatherers, and would see, on a typical day, only people we had known most of our lives. Everything our long-ago ancestors ate or wore, every tool they used, every shrine at which they worshipped, was made within that group. Their knowledge came from their ancestors or from their own experiences. That is the world that shaped us, the world in which our nature was formed.

Now, if I walk down New York's Fifth Avenue on an ordinary day, I will have within sight more human beings than most of those prehistoric hunter-gatherers saw in a lifetime. Between then and now some of our forebears settled down and learned agriculture; created villages, towns, and, in the end, cities; discovered the power of writing. But it was a slow process. The population of classical Athens when Socrates died, at the end of the fifth century BC, could have lived in a few large skyscrapers. Alexander set off from Macedon to conquer the world three-quarters of a century later with an army of between thirty and forty thousand, which is far fewer people than commute into Des Moines every Monday morning. When, in the first century, the population of Rome reached a million, it was the first city of its size. To keep it fed, the Romans had to build an empire that brought home grain from Africa. By then, they had already worked out how to live cheek by jowl in societies where most of those who spoke your language and shared your laws and grew the food on your table were people you would never know. It is, I think, little short of miraculous that brains shaped by our long history could have been turned to this new way of life.

Even once we started to build these larger societies, most people knew little about the ways of other tribes, and could affect just a few local lives. Only in the past couple of centuries, as every human community has gradually been drawn into a single web of trade and a global network of information, have we come to a point where each of us can realistically imagine contacting any other of our six billion conspecifics and sending that person something worth having:

a radio, an antibiotic, a good idea. Unfortunately, we could also send, through negligence as easily as malice, things that will cause harm: a virus, an airborne pollutant, a bad idea. And the possibilities of good and of ill are multiplied beyond all measure when it comes to policies carried out by governments in our name. Together, we can ruin poor farmers by dumping our subsidized grain into their markets, cripple industries by punitive tariffs, deliver weapons that will kill thousands upon thousands. Together, we can raise standards of living by adopting new policies on trade and aid, prevent or treat diseases with vaccines and pharmaceuticals, take measures against global climate change, encourage resistance to tyranny and a concern for the worth of each human life.

And, of course, the worldwide web of information—radio, television, telephones, the Internet—means not only that we can affect lives everywhere but that we can learn about life anywhere, too. Each person you know about and can affect is someone to whom you have responsibilities: to say this is just to affirm the very idea of morality. The challenge, then, is to take minds and hearts formed over the long millennia of living in local troops and equip them with ideas and institutions that will allow us to live together as the global tribe we have become.

Under what rubric to proceed? Not "globalization"—a term that once referred to a marketing strategy, and then came to designate a macroeconomic thesis, and now can seem to encompass everything, and nothing. Not "multiculturalism," another shape shifter, which so often designates the disease it purports to cure. With some ambivalence, I have settled on "cosmopolitanism." Its meaning is equally disputed, and celebrations of the "cosmopolitan" can suggest an unpleasant posture of superiority toward the putative provincial. You imagine a Comme des Garçons–clad sophisticate with a platinum frequent-flyer card regarding, with kindly condescension, a ruddy-faced farmer in workman's overalls. And you wince.

Maybe, though, the term can be rescued. It has certainly proved a survivor. Cosmopolitanism dates at least to the Cynics of the fourth century BC, who first coined the expression cosmopolitan, "citizen of the cosmos." The formulation was meant to be paradoxical, and reflected the general Cynic skepticism toward custom and tradition.

A citizen—a *politēs*—belonged to a particular *polis*, a city to which he or she owed loyalty. The cosmos referred to the world, not in the sense of the earth, but in the sense of the universe. Talk of cosmopolitanism originally signaled, then, a rejection of the conventional view that every civilized person belonged to a community among communities.

The creed was taken up and elaborated by the Stoics, beginning in the third century BC, and that fact proved of critical importance in its subsequent intellectual history. For the Stoicism of the Romans—Cicero, Seneca, Epictetus, and the emperor Marcus Aurelius—proved congenial to many Christian intellectuals, once Christianity became the religion of the Roman Empire. It is profoundly ironic that, though Marcus Aurelius sought to suppress the new Christian sect, his extraordinarily personal *Meditations*, a philosophical diary written in the second century AD as he battled to save the Roman Empire from barbarian invaders, has attracted Christian readers for nearly two millennia. Part of its appeal, I think, has always been the way the Stoic emperor's cosmopolitan conviction of the oneness of humanity echoes Saint Paul's insistence that "there is neither Jew nor Greek, there is neither bond nor free, there is neither male nor female: for ye are all one in Christ Jesus."[1]

Cosmopolitanism's later career wasn't without distinction. It underwrote some of the great moral achievements of the Enlightenment, including the 1789 "Declaration of the Rights of Man" and Immanuel Kant's work proposing a "league of nations." In a 1788 essay in his journal *Teutscher Merkur,* Christoph Martin Wieland—once called the German Voltaire—wrote, in a characteristic expression of the ideal, "Cosmopolitans . . . regard all the peoples of the earth as so many branches of a single family, and the universe as a state, of which they, with innumerable other rational beings, are citizens, promoting together under the general laws of nature the perfection of the whole, while each in his own fashion is busy about his own well-being."[2] And Voltaire himself—whom nobody, alas, ever called the French Wieland—spoke eloquently of the obligation to

1. Galatians 3:28. In quoting the Bible, I have used the King James version, except for the Pentateuch, where I have used Robert Alter's powerful modern translation, *The Five Books of Moses* (New York: Norton, 2004).

2. Cristoph Martin Wieland, "Das Geheimniβ des Kosmopolitenordens," *Teutscher Merkur* (August 1788), 107. (Where I give a reference only to a source that is not in English, the translation is mine.)

understand those with whom we share the planet, linking that need explicitly with our global economic interdependence. "Fed by the products of their soil, dressed in their fabrics, amused by games they invented, instructed even by their ancient moral fables, why would we neglect to understand the mind of these nations, among whom our European traders have traveled ever since they could find a way to get to them?"[3]

So there are two strands that intertwine in the notion of cosmopolitanism. One is the idea that we have obligations to others, obligations that stretch beyond those to whom we are related by the ties of kith and kind, or even the more formal ties of a shared citizenship. The other is that we take seriously the value not just of human life but of particular human lives, which means taking an interest in the practices and beliefs that lend them significance. People are different, the cosmopolitan knows, and there is much to learn from our differences. Because there are so many human possibilities worth exploring, we neither expect nor desire that every person or every society should converge on a single mode of life. Whatever our obligations are to others (or theirs to us) they often have the right to go their own way. As we'll see, there will be times when these two ideals—universal concern and respect for legitimate difference—clash. There's a sense in which cosmopolitanism is the name not of the solution but of the challenge.

A citizen of the world: how far can we take that idea? Are you really supposed to abjure all local allegiances and partialities in the name of this vast abstraction, humanity? Some proponents of cosmopolitanism were pleased to think so; and they often made easy targets of ridicule. "Friend of men, and enemy of almost every man he had to do with," Thomas Carlyle memorably said of the eighteenth-century physiocrat the Marquis de Mirabeau, who wrote the treatise *L'Ami des hommes* when he wasn't too busy jailing his own son. "A lover of his kind, but a hater of his kindred," Edmund Burke said of Jean-Jacques Rousseau, who handed each of the five children he fathered to an orphanage.

3. *Essai sur les mœurs et l'esprit des nations*, vol. 16 of *Oeuvres complètes de Voltaire* (Paris: L'Imprimerie de la Société Littéraire-Typographique, 1784), 241. Voltaire is speaking specifically here of "the Orient," and especially of China and India, but he would surely not have denied its more general application.

Yet the impartialist version of the cosmopolitan creed has continued to hold a steely fascination. Virginia Woolf once exhorted "freedom from unreal loyalties"—to nation, sex, school, neighborhood, and on and on. Leo Tolstoy, in the same spirit, inveighed against the "stupidity" of patriotism. "To destroy war, destroy patriotism," he wrote in an 1896 essay—a couple of decades before the tsar was swept away by a revolution in the name of the international working class. Some contemporary philosophers have similarly urged that the boundaries of nations are morally irrelevant—accidents of history with no rightful claim on our conscience.

But if there are friends of cosmopolitanism who make me nervous, I am happy to be opposed to cosmopolitanism's noisiest foes. Both Hitler and Stalin—who agreed about little else, save that murder was the first instrument of politics—launched regular invectives against "rootless cosmopolitans"; and while, for both, anti-cosmopolitanism was often just a euphemism for anti-Semitism, they were right to see cosmopolitanism as their enemy. For they both required a kind of loyalty to one portion of humanity—a nation, a class—that ruled out loyalty to all of humanity. And the one thought that cosmopolitans share is that no local loyalty can ever justify forgetting that each human being has responsibilities to every other. Fortunately, we need take sides neither with the nationalist who abandons all foreigners nor with the hard-core cosmopolitan who regards her friends and fellow citizens with icy impartiality. The position worth defending might be called (in both senses) a partial cosmopolitanism.

There's a striking passage, to this point, in George Eliot's *Daniel Deronda*, published in 1876, which was, as it happens, the year when England's first—and, so far, last—Jewish prime minister, Benjamin Disraeli, was elevated to the peerage as Earl of Beaconsfield. Disraeli, though baptized and brought up in the Church of England, always had a proud consciousness of his Jewish ancestry (given the family name, which his father spelled D'Israeli, it would have been hard to ignore). But Deronda, who has been raised in England as a Christian gentleman, discovers his Jewish ancestry only as an adult; and his response is to commit himself to the furtherance of his "hereditary people":

> It was as if he had found an added soul in finding his ancestry—his judgment no longer wandering in the mazes of impartial

> sympathy, but choosing, with the noble partiality which is man's best strength, the closer fellowship that makes sympathy practical—exchanging that bird's-eye reasonableness which soars to avoid preference and loses all sense of quality, for the generous reasonableness of drawing shoulder to shoulder with men of like inheritance.

Notice that in claiming a Jewish loyalty—an "added soul"—Deronda is not rejecting a human one. As he says to his mother, "I think it would have been right that I should have been brought up with the consciousness that I was a Jew, but it must always have been as good to me to have as wide an instruction and sympathy as possible." This is the same Deronda, after all, who has earlier explained his decision to study abroad in these eminently cosmopolitan terms: "I want to be an Englishman, but I want to understand other points of view. And I want to get rid of a merely English attitude in studies."[4] Loyalties and local allegiances determine more than what we want; they determine who we are. And Eliot's talk of the "closer fellowship that makes sympathy practical" echoes Cicero's claim that "society and human fellowship will be best served if we confer the most kindness on those with whom we are most closely associated."[5] A creed that disdains the partialities of kinfolk and community may have a past, but it has no future.

In the final message my father left for me and my sisters, he wrote, "Remember you are citizens of the world." But as a leader of the independence movement in what was then the Gold Coast, he never saw a conflict between local partialities and a universal morality—between being part of the place you were in and a part of a broader human community. Raised with this father and an English mother, who was both deeply connected to our family in England and fully rooted in Ghana, where she has now lived for half a century, I always had a sense of family and tribe that was multiple and overlapping: nothing could have seemed more commonplace.

Surely nothing *is* more commonplace. In geological terms, it has been a blink of an eye since human beings first left Africa, and there are few spots where we have not found habitation. The urge

4. George Eliot, *Daniel Deronda* (London: Penguin, 1995), 745, 661–62, 183.

5. Cicero, *De officiis* 1.50.

to migrate is no less "natural" than the urge to settle. At the same time, most of those who have learned the languages and customs of other places haven't done so out of mere curiosity. A few were looking for food for thought; most were looking for food. Thoroughgoing ignorance about the ways of others is largely a privilege of the powerful. The well-traveled polyglot is as likely to be among the worst off as among the best off—as likely to be found in a shantytown as at the Sorbonne. So cosmopolitanism shouldn't be seen as some exalted attainment: it begins with the simple idea that in the human community, as in national communities, we need to develop habits of coexistence: conversation in its older meaning, of living together, association.

And conversation in its modern sense, too. The town of Kumasi, where I grew up, is the capital of Ghana's Asante region, and, when I was a child, its main commercial thoroughfare was called Kingsway Street. In the 1950s, if you wandered down it toward the railway yards at the center of town, you'd first pass by Baboo's Bazaar, which sold imported foods and was run by the eponymous Mr. Baboo—a charming and courteous Indian—with the help of his growing family. Mr. Baboo was active in the Rotary and could always be counted on to make a contribution to the various charitable projects that are among the diversions of Kumasi's middle class, but the truth is that I remember Mr. Baboo mostly because he always had a good stock of candies and because he was always smiling. I can't reconstruct the tour down the rest of the street, for not every store had bonbons to anchor my memories. Still, I remember that we got rice from Irani Brothers; and that we often stopped in on various Lebanese and Syrian families, Muslim and Maronite, and even a philosophical Druze, named Mr. Hanni, who sold imported cloth and who was always ready, as I grew older, for a conversation about the troubles of his native Lebanon. There were other "strangers" among us, too: in the military barracks in the middle of town, you could find many northerners among the "other ranks," privates and NCOs, their faces etched in distinctive patterns of ethnic scarification. And then there was the occasional European—the Greek architect, the Hungarian artist, the Irish doctor, the Scots engineer, some English barristers and judges, and a wildly international assortment of professors at the university, many of whom, unlike the colonial officials, remained after independence. I never thought to wonder, as a child, why these people traveled so far to live and work in my hometown; still, I was glad they did. Conversations across boundaries can be fraught, all the more so as the world grows smaller and the stakes grow larger. It's therefore worth remembering that they can also be a pleasure. What academics sometimes dub "cultural otherness" should prompt neither piety nor consternation.

Cosmopolitanism is an adventure and an ideal: but you can't have any respect for human diversity and expect everyone to become cosmopolitan. The obligations of those who wish to exercise their legitimate freedom to associate with their own kind—to keep the rest of the world away as the Amish do in the United States—are only the same as the basic obligations we all have: to do for others what morality requires. Still, a world in which communities are neatly hived off from one another seems no longer a serious option, if it ever was. And the way of segregation and seclusion has always been anomalous in our perpetually voyaging species. Cosmopolitanism isn't hard work; repudiating it is.

In the wake of 9/11, there has been a lot of fretful discussion about the divide between "us" and "them." What's often taken for granted is a picture of a world in which conflicts arise, ultimately, from conflicts between values. This is what we take to be good; that is what they take to be good. That picture of the world has deep philosophical roots; it is thoughtful, well worked out, plausible. And, I think, wrong.

I should be clear: this book is not a book about policy, nor is it a contribution to the debates about the true face of globalization. I'm a philosopher by trade, and philosophers rarely write really useful books. All the same, I hope to persuade you that there are interesting conceptual questions that lie beneath the facts of globalization. The cluster of questions I want to take up can seem pretty abstract. How real are values? What do we talk about when we talk about difference? Is any form of relativism right? When do morals and manners clash? Can culture be "owned"? What do we owe strangers by virtue of our shared humanity? But the way these questions play out in our lives isn't so very abstract. By the end, I hope to have made it harder to think of the world as divided between the West and the Rest; between locals and moderns; between a bloodless ethic of profit and a bloody ethic of identity; between "us" and "them."

The foreignness of foreigners, the strangeness of strangers: these things are real enough. It's just that we've been encouraged, not least by well-meaning intellectuals, to exaggerate their significance by an order of magnitude.

As I'll be arguing, it is an error—to which we dwellers in a scientific age are peculiarly prone—to resist talk of "objective" values. In the absence of a natural science of right and wrong, someone whose model of knowledge is physics or biology will be inclined to conclude that values are not real; or, at any rate, not real like atoms and nebulae. In the face of this temptation, I want to hold on to at least one important aspect of the objectivity of values: that there are some values that are, and should be, universal, just as there are lots of values that are, and must be, local. We can't hope to reach a final consensus on how to rank and order such values. That's why the model I'll be returning to is that of conversation—and, in particular, conversation between people from different ways of life. The world is getting more crowded: in the next half a century the population of our once foraging species will approach nine billion. Depending on the circumstances, conversations across boundaries can be delightful, or just vexing: what they mainly are, though, is inevitable.

2006

Paul Krugman

b. 1953

In the years leading up to 2007, banks irresponsibly lent money to people buying real estate at inflated prices. Well-heeled financial brokers bought those mortgages, repackaged them to hide their fragility, and resold them to credulous speculators, who themselves often bought on credit issued to them by banks. When people began to default on the mortgages, and when foreclosures started eroding the value of real estate, big banks and insurance companies and brokerage firms collapsed, sending the national economy into the plunge we now call the Great Recession. The economy shrank from December 2007 to mid-summer 2009, but it took many more years to recover its original strength, and in the meantime millions of Americans suffered. The whole debacle exposed the growing gap between the richest 1 percent of Americans, many of whom were responsible for the economic meltdown, and the rest of us. One very visible grassroots movement—Occupy Wall Street—staged its protests under the motto, "We are the 99%!" When the French economist Thomas Piketty published his critique of the wealth gap in his 2013 Capital in the Twenty-First Century, *the world's economy was on the road to recovery, but the historic conditions underlying the financial market's collapse had not changed.*

As Krugman notes, Piketty writes very well for a learned economist; even so, as you can see from this summary, the argument is not too easy to follow for the nonexpert. Nevertheless, when Harvard University Press published its English translation in 2014, the book flew off the shelves, reaching far beyond the academic readers who typically buy such fare. Piketty topped the New York Times *bestseller list. Millions of regular people around the world read his book.*

The debate has not diminished. Whether or not the government should do something about the income gap divides Republicans from Democrats and constitutes one of the most important issues in contemporary American politics. Krugman, a Nobel-prize-winning economist who writes regularly for the New York Times, *is a well-known liberal intellectual. In 2007, he published a book called* The Conscience of a Liberal, *which argued that the government needed to intervene in the economy to diminish inequality.*

The New York Review of Books, *where this review was first published, might well be described as leaning to the left, but not too far from the center of American politics. It is somewhat unique in publishing: twice a month it presents readers with serious, often lengthy reviews of serious, often scholarly books. One might develop a pretty good sense of American intellectual thought by reading the* NYRB *regularly. Like many scholarly book reviews, its essays tend to have two functions: one is to summarize the scholar's argument, paying careful attention to its logic and evidence; the other is to evaluate, to pass expert judgment on how well or poorly the book persuades a well-informed audience. In essence, such reviews are a form of "peer review." This essay, then, exemplifies how the marketplace of ideas determines which arguments are convincing and which are not.*

Why We're in a New Gilded Age

Thomas Piketty, professor at the Paris School of Economics, isn't a household name, although that may change with the English-language publication of his magnificent, sweeping meditation on inequality, *Capital in the Twenty-First Century*. Yet his influence runs deep. It has become a commonplace to say that we are living in a second Gilded Age—or, as Piketty likes to put it, a second Belle Époque—defined by the incredible rise of the "one percent."[1] But it has only become a commonplace thanks to Piketty's work. In particular, he and a few colleagues (notably Anthony Atkinson at Oxford and Emmanuel Saez at Berkeley) have pioneered statistical techniques that make it possible to track the concentration of income and wealth deep into the past—back to the early twentieth century for America and Britain, and all the way to the late eighteenth century for France.

The result has been a revolution in our understanding of long-term trends in inequality. Before this revolution, most discussions of economic disparity more or less ignored the very rich. Some economists (not to mention politicians) tried to shout down any mention of inequality at all: "Of the tendencies that are harmful to sound economics, the most seductive, and in my opinion the most poisonous, is to focus on questions of distribution," declared Robert Lucas Jr. of the University of Chicago, the most influential macroeconomist of his generation, in 2004. But even those willing to discuss inequality generally focused on the gap between the poor or the working class and the merely well-off, not the truly rich—on college graduates whose wage gains outpaced those of less-educated workers, or on the comparative good fortune of the top fifth of the population compared with the bottom four-fifths, not on the rapidly rising incomes of executives and bankers.

1. The "Gilded Age" refers to late-nineteenth-century America, which saw the rapid expansion of large industries (like railroads) and corporations and a huge migration of immigrant workers (such as Irish, Italians, and Chinese), who constituted the lowest levels of the labor force. It was marked by ostentatious wealth displayed by a relatively few families (such as the Vanderbilts and Rockefellers) and demoralizing poverty among vast populations of workers. The "Belle Époque" designates similar economic conditions in Europe, especially France, in the same time period. Though the two terms describe nearly the same thing, Belle Époque carries fewer negative connotations, with its emphasis on fine arts and cultivated life, and is often invoked to contrast the horrors and destruction of the World Wars that succeeded it. [All notes are the editor's.]

It therefore came as a revelation when Piketty and his colleagues showed that incomes of the now famous "one percent," and of even narrower groups, are actually the big story in rising inequality. And this discovery came with a second revelation: talk of a second Gilded Age, which might have seemed like hyperbole, was nothing of the kind. In America in particular the share of national income going to the top one percent has followed a great U-shaped arc. Before World War I the one percent received around a fifth of total income in both Britain and the United States. By 1950 that share had been cut by more than half. But since 1980 the one percent has seen its income share surge again—and in the United States it's back to what it was a century ago.

Still, today's economic elite is very different from that of the nineteenth century, isn't it? Back then, great wealth tended to be inherited; aren't today's economic elite people who earned their position? Well, Piketty tells us that this isn't as true as you think, and that in any case this state of affairs may prove no more durable than the middle-class society that flourished for a generation after World War II. The big idea of *Capital in the Twenty-First Century* is that we haven't just gone back to nineteenth-century levels of income inequality, we're also on a path back to "patrimonial capitalism," in which the commanding heights of the economy are controlled not by talented individuals but by family dynasties.

It's a remarkable claim—and precisely because it's so remarkable, it needs to be examined carefully and critically. Before I get into that, however, let me say right away that Piketty has written a truly superb book. It's a work that melds grand historical sweep—when was the last time you heard an economist invoke Jane Austen and Balzac?—with painstaking data analysis. And even though Piketty mocks the economics profession for its "childish passion for mathematics," underlying his discussion is a tour de force of economic modeling, an approach that integrates the analysis of economic growth with that of the distribution of income and wealth. This is a book that will change both the way we think about society and the way we do economics.

1.

What do we know about economic inequality, and about when do we know it? Until the Piketty revolution swept through the field, most of what we knew about income and wealth inequality came from surveys, in which randomly chosen households are asked to fill in a questionnaire, and their answers are tallied up to produce a statistical portrait of the whole. The international gold standard for such surveys is the annual survey conducted once a year by the Census Bureau. The Federal Reserve also conducts a triennial survey of the distribution of wealth.

These two surveys are an essential guide to the changing shape of American society. Among other things, they have long pointed to a dramatic shift in the process of US economic growth, one that started around 1980. Before then, families at all levels saw their incomes grow more or less in tandem with the growth of the economy as a whole. After 1980, however, the lion's share of gains went to the top end of the income distribution, with families in the bottom half lagging far behind.

Historically, other countries haven't been equally good at keeping track of who gets what; but this situation has improved over time, in large part thanks to the efforts of the Luxembourg Income Study (with which I will soon be affiliated). And the growing availability of survey data that can be compared across nations has led to further important insights. In particular, we now know both that the United States has a much more unequal distribution of income than other advanced countries and that much of this difference in outcomes can be attributed directly to government action. European nations in general have highly unequal incomes from market activity, just like the United States, although possibly not to the same extent. But they do far more redistribution through taxes and transfers than America does, leading to much less inequality in disposable incomes.

Yet for all their usefulness, survey data have important limitations. They tend to undercount or miss entirely the income that accrues to the handful of individuals at the very top of the income scale. They also have limited historical depth. Even US survey data only take us to 1947.

Enter Piketty and his colleagues, who have turned to an entirely different source of information: tax records. This isn't a new idea. Indeed, early analyses of income distribution relied on tax data because they had little else to go on. Piketty et al. have, however, found ways to merge tax data with other sources to produce information that crucially complements survey evidence. In particular, tax data tell us a great deal about the elite. And tax-based estimates can reach much further into the past: the United States has had an income tax since 1913, Britain since 1909. France, thanks to elaborate estate tax collection and record-keeping, has wealth data reaching back to the late eighteenth century.

Exploiting these data isn't simple. But by using all the tricks of the trade, plus some educated guesswork, Piketty is able to produce a summary of the fall and rise of extreme inequality over the course of the past century. It looks like Table 1 on this page.

As I said, describing our current era as a new Gilded Age or Belle Époque isn't hyperbole; it's the simple truth. But how did this happen?

2.

Piketty throws down the intellectual gauntlet right away, with his book's very title: *Capital in the Twenty-First Century*. Are economists still allowed to talk like that?

It's not just the obvious allusion to Marx that makes this title so startling.[2] By invoking capital right from the beginning, Piketty breaks ranks with most modern discussions of inequality, and hearkens back to an older tradition.

TABLE 1

INCOME SHARES

	Low Inequality (Scandinavia 1970s/1980s)	*Medium Inequality (Europe 2010)*	*High Inequality (Europe 1910, US 2010)*
Top 1%	7%	10%	20%
Next 9%	18%	25%	30%
Next 40%	45%	40%	30%
Bottom 50%	30%	25%	20%

2. Karl Marx (1818–1883) was a German political and economic historian; his magnum opus, *Das Kapital*, published in three volumes between 1867 and 1883, predicts that income disparity under capitalism will eventually lead to a proletariat revolution across the industrialized world.

The general presumption of most inequality researchers has been that earned income, usually salaries, is where all the action is, and that income from capital is neither important nor interesting.[3] Piketty shows, however, that even today income from capital, not earnings, predominates at the top of the income distribution. He also shows that in the past—during Europe's Belle Époque and, to a lesser extent, America's Gilded Age—unequal ownership of assets, not unequal pay, was the prime driver of income disparities. And he argues that we're on our way back to that kind of society. Nor is this casual speculation on his part. For all that *Capital in the Twenty-First Century* is a work of principled empiricism, it is very much driven by a theoretical frame that attempts to unify discussion of economic growth and the distribution of both income and wealth. Basically, Piketty sees economic history as the story of a race between capital accumulation and other factors driving growth, mainly population growth and technological progress.

To be sure, this is a race that can have no permanent victor: over the very long run, the stock of capital and total income must grow at roughly the same rate. But one side or the other can pull ahead for decades at a time. On the eve of World War I, Europe had accumulated capital worth six or seven times national income. Over the next four decades, however, a combination of physical destruction and the diversion of savings into war efforts cut that ratio in half. Capital accumulation resumed after World War II, but this was a period of spectacular economic growth—the *Trente Glorieuses*, or "Glorious Thirty" years; so the ratio of capital to income remained low. Since the 1970s, however, slowing growth has meant a rising capital ratio, so capital and wealth have been trending steadily back toward Belle Époque levels. And this accumulation of capital, says Piketty, will eventually recreate Belle Époque–style inequality unless opposed by progressive taxation.

Why? It's all about *r* versus *g*—the rate of return on capital versus the rate of economic growth.

Just about all economic models tell us that if *g* falls—which it has since 1970, a decline that is likely to continue due to slower growth

3. Income earned by capital generally refers to profits made by investments, such as dividends from stocks and the appreciation of real estate.

in the working-age population and slower technological progress—*r* will fall too. But Piketty asserts that *r* will fall less than *g*. This doesn't have to be true. However, if it's sufficiently easy to replace workers with machines—if, to use the technical jargon, the elasticity of substitution between capital and labor is greater than one—slow growth, and the resulting rise in the ratio of capital to income, will indeed widen the gap between *r* and *g*. And Piketty argues that this is what the historical record shows will happen.

If he's right, one immediate consequence will be a redistribution of income away from labor and toward holders of capital. The conventional wisdom has long been that we needn't worry about that happening, that the shares of capital and labor respectively in total income are highly stable over time. Over the very long run, however, this hasn't been true. In Britain, for example, capital's share of income—whether in the form of corporate profits, dividends, rents, or sales of property, for example—fell from around 40 percent before World War I to barely 20 percent circa 1970, and has since bounced roughly halfway back. The historical arc is less clear-cut in the United States, but here, too, there is a redistribution in favor of capital underway. Notably, corporate profits have soared since the [2008] financial crisis began, while wages—including the wages of the highly educated—have stagnated.

A rising share of capital, in turn, directly increases inequality, because ownership of capital is always much more unequally distributed than labor income. But the effects don't stop there, because when the rate of return on capital greatly exceeds the rate of economic growth, "the past tends to devour the future": society inexorably tends toward dominance by inherited wealth.

Consider how this worked in Belle Époque Europe. At the time, owners of capital could expect to earn 4–5 percent on their investments, with minimal taxation; meanwhile economic growth was only around one percent. So wealthy individuals could easily reinvest enough of their income to ensure that their wealth and hence their incomes were growing faster than the economy, reinforcing their economic dominance, even while skimming enough off to live lives of great luxury.

And what happened when these wealthy individuals died? They passed their wealth on—again, with minimal taxation—to their heirs. Money passed on to the next generation accounted for 20 to 25 percent of annual income; the great bulk of wealth, around 90 percent, was inherited rather than saved out of earned income. And this inherited wealth was concentrated in the hands of a very small minority: in 1910 the richest one percent controlled 60 percent of the wealth in France; in Britain, 70 percent.[4]

No wonder, then, that nineteenth-century novelists were obsessed with inheritance. Piketty discusses at length the lecture that the scoundrel Vautrin gives to Rastignac in Balzac's *Père Goriot*, whose gist is that a most successful career could not possibly deliver more than a fraction of the wealth Rastignac could acquire at a stroke by marrying a rich man's daughter. And it turns out that Vautrin was right: being in the top one percent of nineteenth-century heirs and simply living off your inherited wealth gave you around two and a half times the standard of living you could achieve by clawing your way into the top one percent of paid workers.

You might be tempted to say that modern society is nothing like that. In fact, however, both capital income and inherited wealth, though less important than they were in the Belle Époque, are still powerful drivers of inequality—and their importance is growing. In France, Piketty shows, the inherited share of total wealth dropped sharply during the era of wars and postwar fast growth; circa 1970 it was less than 50 percent. But it's now back up to 70 percent, and rising. Correspondingly, there has been a fall and then a rise in the importance of inheritance in conferring elite status: the living standard of the top one percent of heirs fell below that of the top one percent of earners between 1910 and 1950, but began rising again after 1970. It's not all the way back to Rastignac levels, but once again it's generally more valuable to have the right parents (or to marry into having the right in-laws) than to have the right job.

And this may only be the beginning. Figure 1 on p. 434 shows Piketty's estimates of global *r* and *g* over the long haul, suggesting

4. Particularly conspicuous in the Belle Époque culture of Britain was a class of people known as the "rentier" class, which Krugman refers to later in this essay. The rentiers lived comfortable middle- or upper-middle-class lives without having to do work: their income came from dividends and interest on inherited investments. Virginia Woolf, for example, famously asserted that to be a writer a woman needed a room of her own and £500/year. In her calculation, the money would come not from work but from a portfolio of investments.

that the era of equalization now lies behind us, and that the conditions are now ripe for the reestablishment of patrimonial capitalism.

Given this picture, why does inherited wealth play as small a part in today's public discourse as it does? Piketty suggests that the very size of inherited fortunes in a way makes them invisible: "Wealth is so concentrated that a large segment of society is virtually unaware of its existence, so that some people imagine that it belongs to surreal or mysterious entities." This is a very good point. But it's surely not the whole explanation. For the fact is that the most conspicuous example of soaring inequality in today's world—the rise of the very rich one percent in the Anglo-Saxon world, especially the United States—doesn't have all that much to do with capital accumulation, at least so far. It has more to do with remarkably high compensation and incomes.

3.

Capital in the Twenty-First Century is, as I hope I've made clear, an awesome work. At a time when the concentration of wealth and income in the hands of a few has resurfaced as a central political issue, Piketty doesn't just offer invaluable documentation of what is happening, with unmatched historical depth. He also offers what amounts to a unified field theory of inequality, one that integrates economic growth, the distribution of income between capital and labor, and the distribution of wealth and income among individuals into a single frame.

And yet there is one thing that slightly detracts from the achievement—a sort of intellectual sleight of hand, albeit one that doesn't actually involve any deception or malfeasance on Piketty's part. Still, here it is: the main reason there has been a hankering for a book like this is the rise, not just of the one percent, but specifically of the American one percent. Yet that rise, it turns out, has happened for reasons that lie beyond the scope of Piketty's grand thesis.

Piketty is, of course, too good and too honest an economist to try to gloss over inconvenient facts. "US inequality in 2010," he declares, "is quantitatively as extreme as in old Europe in the first decade of the twentieth century, but the structure of that inequality is rather clearly different." Indeed, what we have seen in America and are starting to see elsewhere is something "radically new"—the rise of "supersalaries."

FIGURE 1

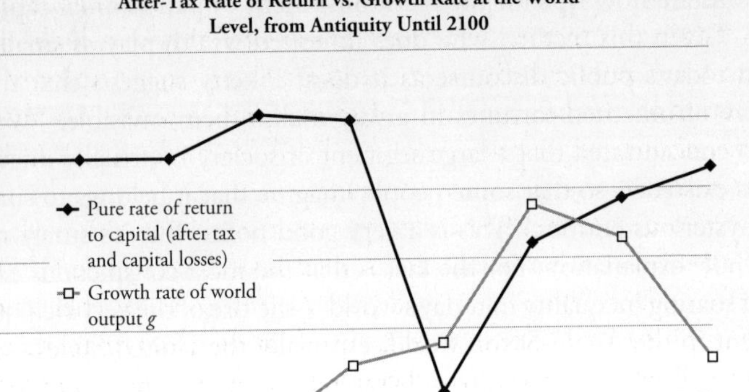

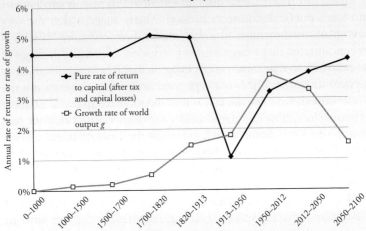

The rate of return to capital (after tax and capital losses) fell below the growth rate during the twentieth century, and may again surpass it in the twenty-first century.

SOURCES AND SERIES: See piketty.pse.ens.fr/capital21c

Capital still matters; at the very highest reaches of society, income from capital still exceeds income from wages, salaries, and bonuses. Piketty estimates that the increased inequality of capital income accounts for about a third of the overall rise in US inequality. But wage income at the top has also surged. Real wages for most US workers have increased little if at all since the early 1970s, but wages for the top one percent of earners have risen 165 percent, and wages for the top 0.1 percent have risen 362 percent. If Rastignac were alive today, Vautrin might concede that he could in fact do as well by becoming a hedge fund manager as he could by marrying wealth.

What explains this dramatic rise in earnings inequality, with the lion's share of the gains going to people at the very top? Some US economists suggest that it's driven by changes in technology. In a famous 1981 paper titled "The Economics of Superstars," the Chicago economist Sherwin Rosen argued that modern communications technology, by extending the reach of talented individuals, was creating winner-take-all markets in which a handful of exceptional individuals reap huge rewards, even if they're only modestly better at what they do than far less well-paid rivals.

Piketty is unconvinced. As he notes, conservative economists love to talk about the high pay of performers of one kind or another, such as movie and sports stars, as a way of suggesting that high incomes really are deserved. But such people actually make up only a tiny fraction of the earnings elite. What one finds instead is mainly executives of one sort or another—people whose performance is, in fact, quite hard to assess or give a monetary value to.

Who determines what a corporate CEO is worth? Well, there's normally a compensation committee, appointed by the CEO himself. In effect, Piketty argues, high-level executives set their own pay, constrained by social norms rather than any sort of market discipline. And he attributes skyrocketing pay at the top to an erosion of these norms. In effect, he attributes soaring wage incomes at the top to social and political rather than strictly economic forces.

Now, to be fair, he then advances a possible economic analysis of changing norms, arguing that falling tax rates for the rich have in effect emboldened the earnings elite. When a top manager could expect to keep only a small fraction of the income he might get by flouting social norms and extracting a very large salary, he might have decided that the opprobrium wasn't worth it. Cut his marginal tax rate drastically, and he may behave differently. And as more and more of the supersalaried flout the norms, the norms themselves will change.

There's a lot to be said for this diagnosis, but it clearly lacks the rigor and universality of Piketty's analysis of the distribution of and returns to wealth. Also, I don't think *Capital in the Twenty-First Century* adequately answers the most telling criticism of the executive power hypothesis: the concentration of very high incomes in finance, where performance actually can, after a fashion, be evaluated. I didn't mention hedge fund managers idly: such people are paid based on their ability to attract clients and achieve investment returns. You can question the social value of modern finance, but the Gordon Gekkos[5] out there are clearly good at something, and their

5. Gordon Gekko was the fictional lead in the 1987 film *Wall Street* and its sequel in 2010. Played by Michael Douglas, the character emblematizes the greed and unproductivity of the wheeler-dealer broker in the heady days of the bull market. He is famous for the line, "Greed is good."

rise can't be attributed solely to power relations, although I guess you could argue that willingness to engage in morally dubious wheeling and dealing, like willingness to flout pay norms, is encouraged by low marginal tax rates.

Overall, I'm more or less persuaded by Piketty's explanation of the surge in wage inequality, though his failure to include deregulation is a significant disappointment. But as I said, his analysis here lacks the rigor of his capital analysis, not to mention its sheer, exhilarating intellectual elegance.

Yet we shouldn't overreact to this. Even if the surge in US inequality to date has been driven mainly by wage income, capital has nonetheless been significant, too. And in any case, the story looking forward is likely to be quite different. The current generation of the very rich in America may consist largely of executives rather than rentiers, people who live off accumulated capital, but these executives have heirs. And America two decades from now could be a rentier-dominated society even more unequal than Belle Époque Europe.

But this doesn't have to happen.

4.

At times, Piketty almost seems to offer a deterministic view of history, in which everything flows from the rates of population growth and technological progress. In reality, however, *Capital in the Twenty-First Century* makes it clear that public policy can make an enormous difference, that even if the underlying economic conditions point toward extreme inequality, what Piketty calls "a drift toward oligarchy" can be halted and even reversed if the body politic so chooses.

The key point is that when we make the crucial comparison between the rate of return on wealth and the rate of economic growth, what matters is the *after-tax* return on wealth. So progressive taxation—in particular taxation of wealth and inheritance—can be a powerful force limiting inequality. Indeed, Piketty concludes his masterwork with a plea for just such a form of taxation. Unfortunately, the history covered in his own book does not encourage optimism.

It's true that during much of the twentieth century strongly progressive taxation did indeed help reduce the concentration of income and wealth, and you might imagine that high taxation at the top is the natural political outcome when democracy confronts high inequality. Piketty, however, rejects this conclusion; the triumph of progressive taxation during the twentieth century, he contends, was "an ephemeral product of chaos." Absent the wars and upheavals of Europe's modern Thirty Years' War, he suggests, nothing of the kind would have happened.

As evidence, he offers the example of France's Third Republic. The Republic's official ideology was highly egalitarian. Yet wealth and income were nearly as concentrated, economic privilege almost as dominated by inheritance, as they were in the aristocratic constitutional monarchy across the English Channel. And public policy did almost nothing to oppose the economic domination by rentiers: estate taxes, in particular, were almost laughably low.

Why didn't the universally enfranchised citizens of France vote in politicians who would take on the rentier class? Well, then as now great wealth purchased great influence—not just over policies, but over public discourse. Upton Sinclair famously declared that "it is difficult to get a man to understand something when his salary depends on his not understanding it." Piketty, looking at his own nation's history, arrives at a similar observation: "The experience of France in the Belle Époque proves, if proof were needed, that no hypocrisy is too great when economic and financial elites are obliged to defend their interest."

The same phenomenon is visible today. In fact, a curious aspect of the American scene is that the politics of inequality seem if anything to be running ahead of the reality. As we've seen, at this point the US economic elite owes its status mainly to wages rather than capital income. Nonetheless, conservative economic rhetoric already emphasizes and celebrates capital rather than labor—"job creators," not workers.

In 2012 Eric Cantor, the House majority leader, chose to mark Labor Day—Labor Day!—with a tweet honoring business owners:

> Today, we celebrate those who have taken a risk, worked hard, built a business and earned their own success.

Perhaps chastened by the reaction, he reportedly felt the need to remind his colleagues at a subsequent GOP retreat that most people don't own their own businesses—but this in itself shows how thoroughly the party identifies itself with capital to the virtual exclusion of labor.

Nor is this orientation toward capital just rhetorical. Tax burdens on high-income Americans have fallen across the board since the 1970s, but the biggest reductions have come on capital income—including a sharp fall in corporate taxes, which indirectly benefits stockholders—and inheritance. Sometimes it seems as if a substantial part of our political class is actively working to restore Piketty's patrimonial capitalism. And if you look at the sources of political donations, many of which come from wealthy families, this possibility is a lot less outlandish than it might seem.

Piketty ends *Capital in the Twenty-First Century* with a call to arms—a call, in particular, for wealth taxes, global if possible, to restrain the growing power of inherited wealth. It's easy to be cynical about the prospects for anything of the kind. But surely Piketty's masterly diagnosis of where we are and where we're heading makes such a thing considerably more likely. So *Capital in the Twenty-First Century* is an extremely important book on all fronts. Piketty has transformed our economic discourse; we'll never talk about wealth and inequality the same way we used to.

2014

The Dalai Lama

b. 1935

Very few people in the world can mount an ethical argument as effectively as the fourteenth Dalai Lama. When he was two years old, Tenzin Gyatso, the son of farmers, was recognized as the reincarnation of the thirteenth Dalai Lama, the spiritual leader of Buddhism in Tibet, who died the year Gyatso was born. Gyatso became the fourteenth Dalai Lama, and he was educated in a Buddhist monastery with the express purpose of preparing him for his holy office. Over his long life, the Dalai Lama has garnered a high reputation for humanity and wisdom, not only among Buddhists but among people of all beliefs. That reputation helps establish in readers' minds the truth of his major premises, which form the foundation of deductive arguments. For example, the Dalai Lama asserts that "our strong focus on material development and accumulating wealth has led us to neglect our basic human need for kindness and care." For many people, this would be common ground, but many of this essay's original readers were business leaders, whose bottom line is the literal bottom line: the soulless corporation's material profit. Rasmus Hougaard, who helped the Dalai Lama prepare this piece for publication, runs a company that advises businesses on how to better manage and organize their employees. And the selection was first published by the Harvard Business Review, *whose subscribers are executives who manage other people, in business and other types of organizations. An article written by the Dalai Lama would stand out as unusual in the discourse community of business executives, whom we might classify as skeptical, if not hostile readers. They might tend to dismiss out of hand a religious leader's advice about business—after all, what does the Dalai Lama or the Pope or some revered rabbi or imam know about running a company? The Dalai Lama anticipates this objection and is careful to note at the beginning that his wisdom comes not only from studying Buddhist philosophy but from long observation of real-life leaders.*

Why Leaders Should Be Mindful, Selfless, and Compassionate

Over the past nearly 60 years, I have engaged with many leaders of governments, companies, and other organizations, and I have observed how our societies have developed and changed. I am happy to share some of my observations in case others may benefit from what I have learned.

Leaders, whatever field they work in, have a strong impact on people's lives and on how the world develops. We should remember that we are visitors on this planet. We are here for 90 or 100 years at the most. During this time, we should work to leave the world a better place.

What might a better world look like? I believe the answer is straightforward: A better world is one where people are happier.

Why? Because all human beings want to be happy, and no one wants to suffer. Our desire for happiness is something we all have in common.

But today, the world seems to be facing an emotional crisis. Rates of stress, anxiety, and depression are higher than ever. The gap between rich and poor and between CEOs and employees is at a historic high. And the focus on turning a profit often overrules a commitment to people, the environment, or society.

I consider our tendency to see each other in terms of "us" and "them" as stemming from ignorance of our interdependence. As participants in the same global economy, we depend on each other, while changes in the climate and the global environment affect us all. What's more, as human beings, we are physically, mentally, and emotionally the same.

Look at bees. They have no constitution, police, or moral training, but they work together in order to survive. Though they may occasionally squabble, the colony survives on the basis of cooperation. Human beings, on the other hand, have constitutions, complex legal systems, and police forces; we have remarkable intelligence and a great capacity for love and affection. Yet, despite our many extraordinary qualities, we seem less able to cooperate.

In organizations, people work closely together every day. But despite working together, many feel lonely and stressed. Even though we are social animals, there is a lack of responsibility toward each other. We need to ask ourselves what's going wrong.

I believe that our strong focus on material development and accumulating wealth has led us to neglect our basic human need for kindness and care. Reinstating a commitment to the oneness of humanity and altruism toward our brothers and sisters is fundamental for societies and organizations and their individuals to thrive in the long run. Every one of us has a responsibility to make this happen.

What can leaders do?

Be Mindful

Cultivate peace of mind. As human beings, we have a remarkable intelligence that allows us to analyze and plan for the future. We have language that enables us to communicate what we have understood to others. Since destructive emotions like anger and attachment cloud our ability to use our intelligence clearly, we need to tackle them.

Fear and anxiety easily give way to anger and violence. The opposite of fear is trust, which, related to warmheartedness, boosts our self-confidence. Compassion also reduces fear, reflecting as it does a concern for others' well-being. This, not money and power, is what really attracts friends. When we're under the sway of anger or attachment, we're limited in our ability to take a full and realistic view of the situation. When the mind is compassionate, it is calm and we're able to use our sense of reason practically, realistically, and with determination.

Be Selfless

We are naturally driven by self-interest; it's necessary to survive. But we need wise self-interest that is generous and cooperative, taking others' interests into account. Cooperation comes from friendship, friendship comes from trust, and trust comes from kindheartedness. Once you have a genuine sense of concern for others, there's no room for cheating, bullying, or exploitation; instead, you can be honest, truthful, and transparent in your conduct.

Be Compassionate

The ultimate source of a happy life is warmheartedness. Even animals display some sense of compassion. When it comes to human beings, compassion can be combined with intelligence. Through the application of reason, compassion can be extended to all 7 billion human beings. Destructive emotions are related to ignorance, while compassion is a constructive emotion related to intelligence. Consequently, it can be taught and learned.

The source of a happy life is within us. Troublemakers in many parts of the world are often quite well educated, so it is not just education that we need. What we need is to pay attention to inner values.

The distinction between violence and nonviolence lies less in the nature of a particular action and more in the motivation behind the action. Actions motivated by anger and greed tend to be violent, whereas those motivated by compassion and concern for others are generally peaceful. We won't bring about peace in the world merely by praying for it; we have to take steps to tackle the violence and corruption that disrupt peace. We can't expect change if we don't take action.

Peace also means being undisturbed, free from danger. It relates to our mental attitude and whether we have a calm mind. What is crucial to realize is that, ultimately, peace of mind is within us; it requires that we develop a warm heart and use our intelligence. People often don't realize that warmheartedness, compassion, and love are actually factors for our survival.

Buddhist tradition describes three styles of compassionate leadership: the trailblazer, who leads from the front, takes risks, and sets an example; the ferryman, who accompanies those in his care and shapes the ups and downs of the crossing; and the shepherd, who sees every one of his flock into safety before himself. Three styles, three approaches, but what they have in common is an all-encompassing concern for the welfare of those they lead.

2019

CHAPTER 7

✶

Identity

Zora Neale Hurston
1903–1960

Hurston was a young member of the Harlem Renaissance, a movement of Black writers, musicians, artists, dancers, and scholars, when she published "How It Feels to Be Colored Me" in 1928. Her mentor, Alain Locke, who edited the influential journal The New Negro, *wanted his writers to win equal citizenship not by arguing for it but by producing art of equal greatness with any produced by whites. This was a departure from Frederick Douglass's writing, for example, which was overtly persuasive. Although Hurston later broke with Locke, she wrote this essay in the spirit Locke advocated. It was published in the journal* World Tomorrow, *which was read largely by whites who were already sympathetic to civil rights for African Americans. In this essay, Hurston is trying to explain the "New Negro" to this audience. Her patriotism would have reassured her readers, who would have been aware of the angrier speeches of Black nationalists like Marcus Garvey. But while Locke liked her essay, he believed it pandered to her audience. Hurston presumes that there are essential differences between Blacks and whites, a presumption that few intellectuals—white or Black—would accept today. In fact, in her 1979 edition of Hurston's work* I Love Myself When I'm Laughing, *the Black writer Alice Walker went so far as to say that this essay "makes one's flesh crawl" because it confirms white stereotypes of Blacks, including the belief that "the educated black person . . . is, underneath the thin veneer of civilization, still a 'heathen.'"*

How It Feels to Be Colored Me

I am colored but I offer nothing in the way of extenuating circumstances except the fact that I am the only Negro in the United States whose grandfather on the mother's side was *not* an Indian chief.

I remember the very day that I became colored. Up to my thirteenth year I lived in the little Negro town of Eatonville, Florida. It is exclusively a colored town. The only white people I knew passed through the town going to or coming from Orlando. The native whites rode dusty horses, the Northern tourists chugged down the sandy village road in automobiles. The town knew the Southerners and never stopped cane[1] chewing when they passed. But the Northerners were something else again. They were peered at cautiously from behind curtains by the timid. The more venturesome would come out on the porch to watch them go past and got just as much pleasure out of the tourists as the tourists got out of the village.

The front porch might seem a daring place for the rest of the town, but it was a gallery seat for me. My favorite place was atop the gate-post. Proscenium box for a born first-nighter. Not only did I enjoy the show, but I didn't mind the actors knowing that I liked it. I usually spoke to them in passing. I'd wave at them and when they returned my salute, I would say something like this: "Howdy-do-well-I-thank-you-where-you-goin'?" Usually automobile or the horse paused at this, and after a queer exchange of compliments, I would probably "go a piece of the way" with them, as we say in farthest Florida. If one of my family happened to come to the front in time to see me, of course negotiations would be rudely broken off. But even so, it is clear that I was the first "welcome-to-our-state" Floridian, and I hope the Miami Chamber of Commerce will please take notice.

During this period, white people differed from colored to me only in that they rode through town and never lived there. They liked to hear me "speak pieces" and sing and wanted to see me dance the parse-me-la, and gave me generously of their small silver for doing these things, which seemed strange to me for I wanted to do them so much that I needed bribing to stop. Only they didn't know it. The colored people gave no dimes. They deplored any joyful tendencies in me, but I was their Zora nevertheless. I belonged to them, to the nearby hotels, to the county—everybody's Zora.

But changes came in the family when I was thirteen, and I was sent to school in Jacksonville. I left Eatonville, the town of the oleanders,[2] as Zora. When I disembarked from the river-boat at Jacksonville, she was no more. It seemed that I had suffered a sea change. I was not Zora of Orange County any more, I was now a little colored girl. I found it out in certain ways. In my heart as well as in the mirror, I became a fast[3] brown—warranted not to rub nor run.

1. Sugarcane. [All notes are the editor's.]

2. A flowering tropical shrub.

3. Colorfast.

But I am not tragically colored. There is no great sorrow dammed up in my soul, nor lurking behind my eyes. I do not mind at all. I do not belong to the sobbing school of Negrohood who hold that nature somehow has given them a lowdown dirty deal and whose feelings are all hurt about it. Even in the helter-skelter skirmish that is my life, I have seen that the world is to the strong regardless of a little pigmentation more or less. No, I do not weep at the world—I am too busy sharpening my oyster knife.[4]

Someone is always at my elbow reminding me that I am the granddaughter of slaves. It fails to register depression with me. Slavery is sixty years in the past. The operation was successful and the patient is doing well, thank you. The terrible struggle[5] that made me an American out of a potential slave said "On the line!" The Reconstruction said "Get set!"; and the generation before said "Go!" I am off to a flying start and I must not halt in the stretch to look behind and weep. Slavery is the price I paid for civilization, and the choice was not with me. It is a bully adventure and worth all that I have paid through my ancestors for it. No one on earth ever had a greater chance for glory. The world to be won and nothing to be lost. It is thrilling to think—to know that for any act of mine, I shall get twice as much praise or twice as much blame. It is quite exciting to hold the center of the national stage, with the spectators not knowing whether to laugh or to weep.

The position of my white neighbor is much more difficult. No brown specter pulls up a chair beside me when I sit down to eat. No dark ghost thrusts its leg against mine in bed. The game of keeping what one has is never so exciting as the game of getting.

I do not always feel colored. Even now I often achieve the unconscious Zora of Eatonville before the Hegira.[6] I feel most colored when I am thrown against a sharp white background.

For instance at Barnard.[7] "Beside the waters of the Hudson" I feel my race. Among the thousand white persons, I am a dark rock surged upon, and overswept, but through it all, I remain myself. When covered by the waters, I am; and the ebb but reveals me again.

4. A reference to the expression "The world is my oyster."

5. The Civil War; the Reconstruction was the period immediately following the war.

6. Flight from a dangerous situation to a more desirable one; an exodus.

7. A women's college in New York City at which Hurston studied anthropology, 1925–1928.

Sometimes it is the other way around. A white person is set down in our midst, but the contrast is just as sharp for me. For instance, when I sit in the drafty basement that is The New World Cabaret with a white person, my color comes. We enter chatting about any little nothing that we have in common and are seated by the jazz waiters. In the abrupt way that jazz orchestras have, this one plunges into a number. It loses no time in circumlocutions, but gets right down to business. It constricts the thorax and splits the heart with its tempo and narcotic harmonies. This orchestra grows rambunctious, rears on its hind legs and attacks the tonal veil with primitive fury, rending it, clawing it until it breaks through to the jungle beyond. I follow those heathen—follow them exultingly. I dance wildly inside myself; I yell within, I whoop; I shake my assegai[8] above my head, I hurl it true to the mark *yeeeeooww!* I am in the jungle and living in the jungle way. My face is painted red and yellow and my body is painted blue. My pulse is throbbing like a war drum. I want to slaughter something—give pain, give death to what, I do not know. But the piece ends. The men of the orchestra wipe their lips and rest their fingers. I creep back slowly to the veneer we call civilization with the last tone and find the white friend sitting motionless in his seat, smoking calmly.

"Good music they have here," he remarks, drumming the table with his fingertips.

Music. The great blobs of purple and red emotion have not touched him. He has only heard what I felt. He is far away and I see him but dimly across the ocean and the continent that have fallen between us. He is so pale with his whiteness then and I am *so* colored.

At certain times I have no race, I am *me*. When I set my hat at a certain angle and saunter down Seventh Avenue, Harlem City, feeling as snooty as the lions in front of the Forty-Second Street Library, for instance. So far as my feelings are concerned, Peggy Hopkins Joyce on the Boule Mich[9] with her gorgeous raiment, stately carriage, knees knocking together in a most aristocratic manner, has

8. African spear.

9. Boulevard Saint-Michel, a fashionable street in Paris. Peggy Hopkins Joyce was a beautiful and fashionable white American in the 1920s.

nothing on me. The cosmic Zora emerges. I belong to no race nor time. I am the eternal feminine with its string of beads.

I have no separate feeling about being an American citizen and colored. I am merely a fragment of the Great Soul that surges within the boundaries. My country, right or wrong.

Sometimes, I feel discriminated against, but it does not make me angry. It merely astonishes me. How *can* any deny themselves the pleasure of my company? It's beyond me.

But in the main, I feel like a brown bag of miscellany propped against a wall. Against a wall in company with other bags, white, red and yellow. Pour out the contents, and there is discovered a jumble of small things priceless and worthless. A first-water diamond, an empty spool, bits of broken glass, lengths of string, a key to a door long since crumbled away, a rusty knife-blade, old shoes saved for a road that never was and never will be, a nail bent under the weight of things too heavy for any nail, a dried flower or two still a little fragrant. In your hand is the brown bag. On the ground before you is the jumble it held—so much like the jumble in the bags, could they be emptied, that all might be dumped in a single heap and the bags refilled without altering the content of any greatly. A bit of colored glass more or less would not matter. Perhaps that is how the Great Stuffer of Bags filled them in the first place—who knows?

1928

James Baldwin

1924–1987

Baldwin was writing his novel Go Tell It on the Mountain *(1953) in Paris when his lover, Lucien Happersberger, began to suspect that the writer was headed for a nervous breakdown. Happersberger took Baldwin to his family's chalet in Loèche-les-Bains, a remote mountain village in Switzerland. Baldwin spent two weeks there in the summer of 1951 and again that winter. His treatment in Switzerland led Baldwin to the insights he expresses in "Stranger in the Village" on the relation between Blacks and whites in America, an issue he'd been thinking about for a long time. He published this essay in* Harper's *magazine, whose readers would have been familiar, even as early as 1953, with the civil rights debate. They would have been mostly well-educated white men and women sympathetic to the difficulties faced by Blacks in America. Baldwin does not try to persuade these readers to any particular action or even to modify their political ideology. Instead, he tries to reveal to them certain aspects of their own character.*

Stranger in the Village

From all available evidence no black man had ever set foot in this tiny Swiss village before I came. I was told before arriving that I would probably be a "sight" for the village; I took this to mean that people of my complexion were rarely seen in Switzerland, and also that city people are always something of a "sight" outside of the city. It did not occur to me—possibly because I am an American—that there could be people anywhere who had never seen a Negro.

It is a fact that cannot be explained on the basis of the inaccessibility of the village. The village is very high, but it is only four hours from Milan and three hours from Lausanne. It is true that it is virtually unknown. Few people making plans for a holiday would elect to come here. On the other hand, the villagers are able, presumably, to come and go as they please—which they do: to another town at the foot of the mountain, with a population of approximately five thousand, the nearest place to see a movie or go to the bank. In the village there is no movie house, no bank, no library, no theater; very few radios, one jeep, one station wagon; and, at the moment, one typewriter, mine, an invention which the woman next door to me here had never seen. There are about six hundred people living here, all Catholic—I conclude this from the fact that the Catholic church is open all year round, whereas the Protestant chapel, set off on a hill a little removed from the village, is open only in the summertime when the tourists arrive. There are four or five hotels, all closed now, and four or five *bistros*, of which, however, only two do any business during the winter. These two do not do a great deal, for life in the village seems to end around nine or ten o'clock. There are a few stores, butcher, baker, *épicerie*,[1] a hardware store, and a money-changer—who cannot change travelers' checks, but must send them down to the bank, an operation which takes two or three days. There is something called the *Ballet Haus*, closed in the winter and used for God knows what, certainly not ballet, during the summer. There seems to be only one schoolhouse in the village, and this for the quite young children; I suppose this to mean that their older brothers and sisters at some point descend from these mountains in order to complete their education—possibly, again, to the town just below. The landscape is absolutely forbidding, mountains towering on all four sides, ice and snow as far as the eye can reach. In this white wilderness, men and women and children move all day, carrying washing, wood, buckets of milk or water, sometimes skiing on Sunday afternoons. All week long boys and young men are to be seen shoveling snow off the rooftops, or dragging wood down from the forest in sleds.

The village's only real attraction, which explains the tourist season, is the hot spring water. A disquietingly high proportion of these tourists are cripples, or semicripples, who come year after year—from other parts of Switzerland, usually—to take the waters. This lends the village, at the height of the season, a rather terrifying air of sanctity, as though it were a lesser Lourdes.[2] There is often something beautiful, there is always something awful, in the spectacle of a person who has lost one of his faculties, a faculty he never questioned until it was gone, and who struggles to recover it. Yet people remain people, on crutches or indeed on deathbeds; and wherever I passed, the first summer I was here, among the native villagers or among the lame, a wind passed with me—of astonishment, curiosity, amusement, and outrage. That first summer I stayed two weeks and never intended to return. But I did return in the winter, to work; the village offers, obviously, no distractions whatever and has the further advantage of being extremely cheap. Now it is winter again, a year later, and I am here again. Everyone in the village knows my name, though they scarcely ever use it, knows that I come from America—though, this, apparently, they will never really believe: black men

1. Grocery (French). [All notes are the editor's.]

2. Town in southwestern France famous for the miraculous cures attributed to its waters and for the purported appearances there of the Virgin Mary.

come from Africa—and everyone knows that I am the friend of the son of a woman who was born here, and that I am staying in their chalet. But I remain as much a stranger today as I was the first day I arrived, and the children shout *Neger! Neger!* as I walk along the streets.

It must be admitted that in the beginning I was far too shocked to have any real reaction. In so far as I reacted at all, I reacted by trying to be pleasant—it being a great part of the American Negro's education (long before he goes to school) that he must make people "like" him. This smile-and-the-world-smiles-with-you routine worked about as well in this situation as it had in the situation for which it was designed, which is to say that it did not work at all. No one, after all, can be liked whose human weight and complexity cannot be, or has not been, admitted. My smile was simply another unheard-of phenomenon which allowed them to see my teeth—they did not, really, see my smile and I began to think that, should I take to snarling, no one would notice any difference. All of the physical characteristics of the Negro which had caused me, in America, a very different and almost forgotten pain were nothing less than miraculous—or infernal—in the eyes of the village people. Some thought my hair was the color of tar, that it had the texture of wire, or the texture of cotton. It was jocularly suggested that I might let it all grow long and make myself a winter coat. If I sat in the sun for more than five minutes some daring creature was certain to come along and gingerly put his fingers on my hair, as though he were afraid of an electric shock, or put his hand on my hand, astonished that the color did not rub off. In all of this, in which it must be conceded there was the charm of genuine wonder and in which there was certainly no element of intentional unkindness, there was yet no suggestion that I was human: I was simply a living wonder.

I knew that they did not mean to be unkind, and I know it now; it is necessary, nevertheless, for me to repeat this to myself each time that I walk out of the chalet. The children who shout *Neger!* have no way of knowing the echoes this sound raises in me. They are brimming with good humor and the more daring swell with pride when I stop to speak with them. Just the same, there are days when I cannot pause and smile, when I have no heart to play with them; when, indeed, I mutter sourly to myself, exactly as I muttered on the streets of a city these children have never seen, when I was no bigger than these children are now: *Your* mother *was a nigger.* Joyce[3] is right about history being a nightmare—but it may be the nightmare from which no one *can* awaken. People are trapped in history and history is trapped in them.

There is a custom in the village—I am told it is repeated in many villages—of "buying" African natives for the purpose of converting them to Christianity. There stands in the church all year round a small box with a slot for money, decorated with a black figurine, and into this box the villagers drop their francs. During the *carnaval*[4] which precedes Lent, two village children have their faces blackened—out of which bloodless darkness their blue eyes shine like ice—and fantastic horsehair wigs are placed on their blond heads; thus disguised, they solicit among the villagers for money for the missionaries in Africa. Between the box in the church and the blackened children, the village "bought" last year six or eight African natives. This was reported to me with pride by the wife of one of the *bistro* owners and I was careful to express astonishment and pleasure at the solicitude shown by the village for the souls of black folk. The *bistro* owner's wife beamed with a pleasure far more genuine than my own and seemed to feel that I might now breathe more easily concerning the souls of at least six of my kinsmen.

I tried not to think of these so lately baptized kinsmen, of the price paid for them, or the peculiar price they themselves would pay, and said nothing about my father, who having taken his own conversion too literally never, at bottom, forgave the white world (which he described as heathen) for having saddled him with a Christ in whom, to judge at least from their treatment of him, they themselves no longer believed. I thought of white men arriving for the first time in an African village, strangers there, as I am a stranger here, and tried to imagine the astounded populace touching their hair and marveling at the color of their skin. But there is a great difference between being the first white man to be seen by Africans and being the first black man to be seen by whites. The white man takes the astonishment as tribute, for he arrives to conquer and to convert the natives,

3. James Joyce (1882–1941), Irish novelist. Baldwin is referring here to a line from Joyce's novel *Ulysses*: "History is a nightmare from which I am trying to awake."

4. A period of exuberance before Lent's abstinence; Mardi Gras.

whose inferiority in relation to himself is not even to be questioned; whereas I, without a thought of conquest, find myself among a people whose culture controls me, has even, in a sense, created me, people who have cost me more in anguish and rage than they will ever know, who yet do not even know of my existence. The astonishment with which I might have greeted them, should they have stumbled into my African village a few hundred years ago, might have rejoiced their hearts. But the astonishment with which they greet me today can only poison mine.

And this is so despite everything I may do to feel differently, despite my friendly conversations with the *bistro* owner's wife, despite their three-year-old son who has at last become my friend, despite the *saluts* and *bonsoirs* which I exchange with people as I walk, despite the fact that I know that no individual can be taken to task for what history is doing, or has done.[5] I say that the culture of these people controls me—but they can scarcely be held responsible for European culture. America comes out of Europe, but these people have never seen America, nor have most of them seen more of Europe than the hamlet at the foot of their mountain. Yet they move with an authority which I shall never have; and they regard me, quite rightly, not only as a stranger in their village but as a suspect latecomer, bearing no credentials, to everything they have—however unconsciously—inherited.

For this village, even were it incomparably more remote and incredibly more primitive, is the West, the West onto which I have been so strangely grafted. These people cannot be, from the point of view of power, strangers anywhere in the world; they have made the modern world, in effect, even if they do not know it. The most illiterate among them is related, in a way that I am not, to Dante, Shakespeare, Michelangelo, Aeschylus, Da Vinci, Rembrandt, and Racine; the cathedral at Chartres says something to them which it cannot say to me, as indeed would New York's Empire State Building, should anyone here ever see it.[6] Out of their hymns and dances come

5. French greetings equivalent to "hello" and "good day."

6. European writers and artists ranging from Greece in the 5th century B.C.E. (Aeschylus) to 18th-century France (Racine). Many consider the Chartres Cathedral in France, constructed over decades in the early thirteenth century, to be the finest example of Gothic architecture.

Beethoven and Bach.[7] Go back a few centuries and they are in their full glory—but I am in Africa, watching the conquerors arrive.

The rage of the disesteemed is personally fruitless, but it is also absolutely inevitable; this rage, so generally discounted, so little understood even among the people whose daily bread it is, is one of the things that makes history. Rage can only with difficulty, and never entirely, be brought under the domination of the intelligence and is therefore not susceptible to any arguments whatever. This is a fact which ordinary representatives of the *Herrenvolk*,[8] having never felt this rage and being unable to imagine it, quite fail to understand. Also, rage cannot be hidden, it can only be dissembled. This dissembling deludes the thoughtless, and strengthens rage and adds, to rage, contempt. There are, no doubt, as many ways of coping with the resulting complex of tensions as there are black men in the world, but no black man can hope ever to be entirely liberated from this internal warfare—rage, dissembling, and contempt having inevitably accompanied his first realization of the power of white men. What is crucial here is that, since white men represent in the black man's world so heavy a weight, white men have for black men a reality which is far from being reciprocal; and hence all black men have toward all white men an attitude which is designed, really, either to rob the white man of the jewel of his naïveté, or else to make it cost him dear.

The black man insists, by whatever means he finds at his disposal, that the white man cease to regard him as an exotic rarity and recognize him as a human being. This is a very charged and difficult moment, for there is a great deal of will power involved in the white man's naïveté. Most people are not naturally reflective any more than they are naturally malicious, and the white man prefers to keep the black man at a certain human remove because it is easier for him thus to preserve his simplicity and avoid being called to account for crimes committed by his forefathers, or his neighbors. He is inescapably aware, nevertheless, that he is in a better position in the world than black men are, nor can he quite put to death the suspicion that he is hated by black men therefore. He does not wish to be hated,

7. Ludwig van Beethoven (1779–1827) and Johann Sebastian Bach (1683–1750) were both classical composers.

8. Master race (German).

neither does he wish to change places, and at this point in his uneasiness he can scarcely avoid having recourse to those legends which white men have created about black men, the most usual effect of which is that the white man finds himself enmeshed, so to speak, in his own language which describes hell, as well as the attributes which lead one to hell, as being as black as night.

Every legend, moreover, contains its residuum of truth, and the root function of language is to control the universe by describing it. It is of quite considerable significance that black men remain, in the imagination, and in overwhelming numbers in fact, beyond the disciplines of salvation; and this despite the fact that the West has been "buying" African natives for centuries. There is, I should hazard, an instantaneous necessity to be divorced from this so visibly unsaved stranger, in whose heart, moreover, one cannot guess what dreams of vengeance are being nourished; and, at the same time, there are few things on earth more attractive than the idea of the unspeakable liberty which is allowed the unredeemed. When, beneath the black mask, a human being begins to make himself felt one cannot escape a certain awful wonder as to what kind of human being it is. What one's imagination makes of other people is dictated, of course, by the laws of one's own personality and it is one of the ironies of black-white relations that, by means of what the white man imagines the black man to be, the black man is enabled to know who the white man is.

I have said, for example, that I am as much a stranger in this village today as I was the first summer I arrived, but this is not quite true. The villagers wonder less about the texture of my hair than they did then, and wonder rather more about me. And the fact that their wonder now exists on another level is reflected in their attitudes and in their eyes. There are the children who make those delightful, hilarious, sometimes astonishingly grave overtures of friendship in the unpredictable fashion of children; other children, having been taught that the devil is a black man, scream in genuine anguish as I approach. Some of the older women never pass without a friendly greeting, never pass, indeed, if it seems that they will be able to engage me in conversation; other women look down or look away or rather contemptuously smirk. Some of the men drink with me and suggest that I learn how to ski—partly, I gather, because they cannot imagine what I would look like on skis—and want to know if I am married, and ask questions about my *métier*.[9] But some of the men have accused *le sale nègre*[1]—behind my back—of stealing wood and there is already in the eyes of some of them that peculiar, intent, paranoiac malevolence which one sometimes surprises in the eyes of American white men when, out walking with their Sunday girl, they see a Negro male approach.

There is a dreadful abyss between the streets of this village and the streets of the city in which I was born, between the children who shout *Neger!* today and those who shouted *Nigger!* yesterday—the abyss is experience, the American experience. The syllable hurled behind me today expresses, above all, wonder: I am a stranger here. But I am not a stranger in America and the same syllable riding on the American air expresses the war my presence has occasioned in the American soul.

For this village brings home to me this fact: that there was a day, and not really a very distant day, when Americans were scarcely Americans at all but discontented Europeans, facing a great unconquered continent and strolling, say, into a marketplace and seeing black men for the first time. The shock this spectacle afforded is suggested, surely, by the promptness with which they decided that these black men were not really men but cattle. It is true that the necessity on the part of the settlers of the New World of reconciling their moral assumptions with the fact—and the necessity—of slavery enhanced immensely the charm of this idea, and it is also true that this idea expresses, with a truly American bluntness, the attitude which to varying extents all masters have had toward all slaves.

But between all former slaves and slave-owners and the drama which begins for Americans over three hundred years ago at Jamestown, there are at least two differences to be observed. The American Negro slave could not suppose, for one thing, as slaves in past epochs had supposed and often done, that he would ever be able to wrest the power from his master's hands. This was a supposition which the modern era, which was to bring about such vast changes in the aims and dimensions of power, put to death; it only begins, in unprecedented fashion, and with dreadful implications, to be

9. Business (French).

1. Derogatory term, literally "dirty black" (French).

resurrected today. But even had this supposition persisted with undiminished force, the American Negro slave could not have used it to lend his condition dignity, for the reason that this supposition rests on another: that the slave in exile yet remains related to his past, has some means—if only in memory—of revering and sustaining the forms of his former life, is able, in short, to maintain his identity.

This was not the case with the American Negro slave. He is unique among the black men of the world in that his past was taken from him, almost literally, at one blow. One wonders what on earth the first slave found to say to the first dark child he bore. I am told that there are Haitians able to trace their ancestry back to African kings, but any American Negro wishing to go back so far will find his journey through time abruptly arrested by the signature on the bill of sale which served as the entrance paper for his ancestor. At the time—to say nothing of the circumstances—of the enslavement of the captive black man who was to become the American Negro, there was not the remotest possibility that he would ever take power from his master's hands. There was no reason to suppose that his situation would ever change, nor was there, shortly, anything to indicate that his situation had ever been different. It was his necessity, in the words of E. Franklin Frazier,[2] to find a "motive for living under American culture or die." The identity of the American Negro comes out of this extreme situation, and the evolution of this identity was a source of the most intolerable anxiety in the minds and the lives of his masters.

For the history of the American Negro is unique also in this: that the question of his humanity, and of his rights therefore as a human being, became a burning one for several generations of Americans, so burning a question that it ultimately became one of those used to divide the nation. It is out of this argument that the venom of the epithet *Nigger!* is derived. It is an argument which Europe has never had, and hence Europe quite sincerely fails to understand how or why the argument arose in the first place, why its effects are so frequently disastrous and always so unpredictable, why it refuses until today to be entirely settled. Europe's black possessions remained—and do remain—in Europe's colonies, at which remove they represented no threat whatever to European identity. If they posed any problem at all for the European

2. African American intellectual (1894–1962) and author of *Bourgeoisie noire* (1955) (The Black Bourgeoisie).

conscience, it was a problem which remained comfortingly abstract: in effect, the black man, *as a man*, did not exist for Europe. But in America, even as a slave, he was an inescapable part of the general social fabric and no American could escape having an attitude toward him. Americans attempt until today to make an abstraction of the Negro, but the very nature of these abstractions reveals the tremendous effects the presence of the Negro has had on the American character.

When one considers the history of the Negro in America it is of the greatest importance to recognize that the moral beliefs of a person, or a people, are never really as tenuous as life—which is not moral—very often causes them to appear; these create for them a frame of reference and a necessary hope, the hope being that when life has done its worst they will be enabled to rise above themselves and to triumph over life. Life would scarcely be bearable if this hope did not exist. Again, even when the worst has been said, to betray a belief is not by any means to have put oneself beyond its power; the betrayal of a belief is not the same thing as ceasing to believe. If this were not so there would be no moral standards in the world at all. Yet one must also recognize that morality is based on ideas and that all ideas are dangerous—dangerous because ideas can only lead to action and where the action leads no man can say. And dangerous in this respect: that confronted with the impossibility of remaining faithful to one's beliefs, and the equal impossibility of becoming free of them, one can be driven to the most inhuman excesses. The ideas on which American beliefs are based are not, though Americans often seem to think so, ideas which originated in America. They came out of Europe. And the establishment of democracy on the American continent was scarcely as radical a break with the past as was the necessity, which Americans faced, of broadening this concept to include black men.

This was, literally, a hard necessity. It was impossible, for one thing, for Americans to abandon their beliefs, not only because these beliefs alone seemed able to justify the sacrifices they had endured and the blood that they had spilled, but also because these beliefs afforded them their only bulwark against a moral chaos as absolute as the physical chaos of the continent it was their destiny to conquer. But in the situation in which Americans found themselves, these beliefs threatened an idea which, whether or not one likes to think so, is the very warp and woof of the heritage of the West, the idea of white supremacy.

Americans have made themselves notorious by the shrillness and the brutality with which they have insisted on this idea, but they did not invent it; and it has escaped the world's notice that those very excesses of which Americans have been guilty imply a certain, unprecedented uneasiness over the idea's life and power, if not, indeed, the idea's validity. The idea of white supremacy rests simply on the fact that white men are the creators of civilization (the present civilization, which is the only one that matters; all previous civilizations are simply "contributions" to our own) and are therefore civilization's guardians and defenders. Thus it was impossible for Americans to accept the black man as one of themselves, for to do so was to jeopardize their status as white men. But not so to accept him was to deny his human reality, his human weight and complexity, and the strain of denying the overwhelmingly undeniable forced Americans into rationalizations so fantastic that they approached the pathological.

At the root of the American Negro problem is the necessity of the American white man to find a way of living with the Negro in order to be able to live with himself. And the history of this problem can be reduced to the means used by Americans—lynch law and law, segregation and legal acceptance, terrorization and concession—either to come to terms with this necessity, or to find a way around it, or (most usually) to find a way of doing both these things at once. The resulting spectacle, at once foolish and dreadful, led someone to make the quite accurate observation that "the Negro-in-America is a form of insanity which overtakes white men."

In this long battle, a battle by no means finished, the unforeseeable effects of which will be felt by many future generations, the white man's motive was the protection of his identity; the black man was motivated by the need to establish an identity. And despite the terrorization which the Negro in America endured and endures sporadically until today, despite the cruel and totally inescapable ambivalence of his status in his country, the battle for his identity has long ago been won. He is not a visitor to the West, but a citizen there, an American; as American as the Americans who despise him, the Americans who fear him, the Americans who love him—the Americans who became less than themselves, or rose to be greater than themselves by virtue of the fact that the challenge he represented was inescapable. He is perhaps the only black man in the world whose relationship to white men is more terrible, more subtle, and more meaningful than the relationship of bitter possessed to uncertain possessor. His survival depended, and his development depends, on his ability to turn his peculiar status in the Western world to his own advantage and, it may be, to the very great advantage of that world. It remains for him to fashion out of his experience that which will give him sustenance, and a voice.

The cathedral at Chartres, I have said, says something to the people of this village which it cannot say to me; but it is important to understand that this cathedral says something to me which it cannot say to them. Perhaps they are struck by the power of the spires, the glory of the windows; but they have known God, after all, longer than I have known him, and in a different way, and I am terrified by the slippery bottomless well to be found in the crypt, down which heretics were hurled to death, and by the obscene, inescapable gargoyles jutting out of the stone and seeming to say that God and the devil can never be divorced. I doubt that the villagers think of the devil when they face a cathedral because they have never been identified with the devil. But I must accept the status which myth, if nothing else, gives me in the West before I can hope to change the myth.

Yet, if the American Negro has arrived at his identity by virtue of the absoluteness of his estrangement from his past, American white men still nourish the illusion that there is some means of recovering the European innocence, of returning to a state in which black men do not exist. This is one of the greatest errors Americans can make. The identity they fought so hard to protect has, by virtue of that battle, undergone a change: Americans are as unlike any other white people in the world as it is possible to be. I do not think, for example, that it is too much to suggest that the American vision of the world—which allows so little reality, generally speaking, for any of the darker forces in human life, which tends until today to paint moral issues in glaring black and white—owes a great deal to the battle waged by Americans to maintain between themselves and black men a human separation which could not be bridged. It is only now beginning to be borne in on us—very faintly, it must be admitted, very slowly, and very much against our will—that this vision of the world is dangerously inaccurate, and perfectly useless. For it protects our moral high-mindedness at the terrible expense of weakening our grasp of reality. People who shut their eyes to reality simply invite their own destruction, and anyone who insists on remaining in a state of innocence long after that innocence is dead turns himself into a monster.

The time has come to realize that the interracial drama acted out on the American continent has not only created a new black man, it has created a new white man, too. No road whatever will lead Americans back to the simplicity of this European village where white men still have the luxury of looking on me as a stranger. I am not, really, a stranger any longer for any American alive. One of the things that distinguishes Americans from other people is that no other people has ever been so deeply involved in the lives of black men, and vice versa. This fact faced, with all its implications, it can be seen that the history of the American Negro problem is not merely shameful, it is also something of an achievement. For even when the worst has been said, it must also be added that the perpetual challenge posed by this problem was always, somehow, perpetually met. It is precisely this black-white experience which may prove of indispensable value to us in the world we face today. This world is white no longer, and it will never be white again.

1953

Maxine Hong Kingston

b. 1940

"No Name Woman" is the first chapter in Kingston's award-winning book The Woman Warrior *(1976), which deals with a girl's experience growing up in a Chinese American family. Because it is a mixture of autobiography, imaginative fiction, and even Chinese myth and folklore, critics have a hard time classifying Kingston's memoir. It is, perhaps, the least rhetorical piece in this collection: certainly there is no overt persuasive agenda here. But Kingston does explore the problems of identity that confront all immigrants and, perhaps, everyone living in our multicultural society. It might be best to read "No Name Woman" as you would a short story. For example, examine the conflicting themes of individualism and community. Also consider point of view. Whom can we trust? How much of the story is the narrator making up? Can we believe even the little bit of information that her mother gives her? Does the narrator honor or dishonor her aunt by publishing her story?*

No Name Woman

"You must not tell anyone," my mother said, "what I am about to tell you. In China your father had a sister who killed herself. She jumped into the family well. We say that your father has all brothers because it is as if she had never been born.

"In 1924 just a few days after our village celebrated seventeen hurry-up weddings—to make sure that every young man who went 'out on the road' would responsibly come home—your father and his brothers and your grandfather and his brothers and your aunt's new husband sailed for America, the Gold Mountain. It was your grandfather's last trip. Those lucky enough to get contracts waved goodbye from the decks. They fed and guarded the stowaways and helped them off in Cuba, New York, Bali, Hawaii. 'We'll meet in California next year,' they said. All of them sent money home.

"I remember looking at your aunt one day when she and I were dressing; I had not noticed before that she had such a protruding melon of a stomach. But I did not think, 'She's pregnant,' until she began to look like other pregnant women, her shirt pulling and the white tops of her black pants showing. She could not have been pregnant, you see, because her husband had been gone for years. No one said anything. We did not discuss it. In early summer she was ready to have the child, long after the time when it could have been possible.

"The village had also been counting. On the night the baby was to be born the villagers raided our house. Some were crying. Like a great saw, teeth strung with lights, files of people walked zigzag across our land, tearing the rice. Their lanterns doubled in the disturbed black water, which drained away through the broken bunds. As the villagers closed in, we could see that some of them, probably men and women we knew well, wore white masks. The people with long hair hung it over their faces. Women with short hair made it stand up on end. Some had tied white bands around their foreheads, arms, and legs.

"At first they threw mud and rocks at the house. Then they threw eggs and began slaughtering our stock. We could hear the animals scream their deaths—the roosters, the pigs, a last great roar from the ox. Familiar wild heads flared in our night windows; the villagers encircled us. Some of the faces stopped to peer at us, their eyes rushing like searchlights. The hands flattened against the panes, framed heads, and left red prints.

"The villagers broke in the front and the back doors at the same time, even though we had not locked the doors against them. Their knives dripped with the blood of our animals. They smeared blood on the doors and walls. One woman swung a chicken, whose throat she had slit, splattering blood in red arcs about her. We stood together in the middle of our house, in the family hall with the pictures and tables of the ancestors around us, and looked straight ahead.

"At that time the house had only two wings. When the men came back, we would build two more to enclose our courtyard and a third one to begin a second courtyard. The villagers pushed through both wings, even your grandparents' rooms, to find your aunt's, which was also mine until the men returned. From this room a new wing for one of the younger families would grow. They ripped up her clothes and shoes and broke her combs, grinding them underfoot. They tore her work from the loom. They scattered the cooking fire and rolled the new weaving in it. We could hear them in the kitchen breaking our bowls and banging the pots. They overturned the great waist-high earthenware jugs; duck eggs, pickled fruits, vegetables burst out and mixed in acrid torrents. The old woman from the next field swept a broom through the air and loosed the spirits-of-the-broom over our heads. 'Pig.' 'Ghost.' 'Pig,' they sobbed and scolded while they ruined our house.

"When they left, they took sugar and oranges to bless themselves. They cut pieces from the dead animals. Some of them took bowls that were not broken and clothes that were not torn. Afterward we swept up the rice and sewed it back up into sacks. But the smells from the spilled preserves lasted. Your aunt gave birth in the pigsty that night. The next morning when I went for the water, I found her and the baby plugging up the family well.

"Don't let your father know that I told you. He denies her. Now that you have started to menstruate, what happened to her could happen to you. Don't humiliate us. You wouldn't like to be forgotten as if you had never been born. The villagers are watchful."

Whenever she had to warn us about life, my mother told stories that ran like this one, a story to grow up on. She tested our strength to establish realities. Those in the emigrant generations who could not reassert brute survival died young and far from home. Those of us in the first American generations have had to figure out how the invisible world the emigrants built around our childhoods fits in solid America.

The emigrants confused the gods by diverting their curses, misleading them with crooked streets and false names. They must try to confuse their offspring as well, who, I suppose, threaten them in similar ways—always trying to get things straight, always trying to name the unspeakable. The Chinese I know hide their names; sojourners take new names when their lives change and guard their real names with silence.

Chinese-Americans, when you try to understand what things in you are Chinese, how do you separate what is peculiar to childhood, to poverty, insanities, one family, your mother who marked your growing with stories, from what is Chinese? What is Chinese tradition and what is the movies?

If I want to learn what clothes my aunt wore, whether flashy or ordinary, I would have to begin, "Remember Father's drowned-in-the-well sister?" I cannot ask that. My mother has told me once and for all the useful parts. She will add nothing unless powered by Necessity, a riverbank that guides her life. She plants vegetable gardens rather than lawns; she carries the odd-shaped tomatoes home from the fields and eats food left for the gods.

Whenever we did frivolous things, we used up energy; we flew high kites. We children came up off the ground over the melting cones our parents brought home from work and the American movie on New Year's Day—*Oh, You Beautiful Doll* with Betty Grable one year, and *She Wore a Yellow Ribbon* with John Wayne another year.[1] After the one carnival ride each, we paid in guilt; our tired father counted his change on the dark walk home.

Adultery is extravagance. Could people who hatch their own chicks and eat the embryos and the heads for delicacies and boil the feet in vinegar for party food, leaving only the gravel, eating even the gizzard lining—could such people engender a prodigal aunt? To be a woman, to have a daughter in starvation time was a waste enough. My aunt could not have been the lone romantic who gave up everything for

1. *Oh, You Beautiful Doll*, popular 1949 film incorporating the 1911 song of the same title, starring Betty Grable (1916–1973), iconic actress famed for her beautiful legs. Also in 1949, John Wayne (1907–1979) starred in *She Wore a Yellow Ribbon*, now considered one of the classic Westerns. [All notes are the editor's.]

sex. Women in the old China did not choose. Some man had commanded her to lie with him and be his secret evil. I wonder whether he masked himself when he joined the raid on her family.

Perhaps she had encountered him in the fields or on the mountain where the daughters-in-law collected fuel. Or perhaps he first noticed her in the marketplace. He was not a stranger because the village housed no strangers. She had to have dealings with him other than sex. Perhaps he worked an adjoining field, or he sold her the cloth for the dress she sewed and wore. His demand must have surprised, then terrified her. She obeyed him; she always did as she was told.

When the family found a young man in the next village to be her husband, she had stood tractably beside the best rooster, his proxy, and promised before they met that she would be his forever. She was lucky that he was her age and she would be the first wife, an advantage secure now. The night she first saw him, he had sex with her. Then he left for America. She had almost forgotten what he looked like. When she tried to envision him, she only saw the black and white face in the group photograph the men had taken before leaving.

The other man was not, after all, much different from her husband. They both gave orders: she followed. "If you tell your family, I'll beat you. I'll kill you. Be here again next week." No one talked sex, ever. And she might have separated the rapes from the rest of living if only she did not have to buy her oil from him or gather wood in the same forest. I want her fear to have lasted just as long as rape lasted so that the fear could have been contained. No drawn-out fear. But women at sex hazarded birth and hence lifetimes. The fear did not stop but permeated everywhere. She told the man, "I think I'm pregnant." He organized the raid against her.

On nights when my mother and father talked about their life back home, sometimes they mentioned an "outcast table" whose business they still seemed to be settling, their voices tight. In a commensal tradition, where food is precious, the powerful older people made wrongdoers eat alone. Instead of letting them start separate new lives like the Japanese, who could become samurais and geishas, the Chinese family, faces averted but eyes glowering sideways, hung on to the offenders and fed them leftovers. My aunt must have lived in the same house as my parents and eaten at an outcast table. My mother spoke about the raid as if she had seen it, when she and my aunt, a daughter-in-law to a different household, should not have been living together at all. Daughters-in-law lived with their husbands' parents, not their own; a synonym for marriage in Chinese is "taking a daughter-in-law." Her husband's parents could have sold her, mortgaged her, stoned her. But they had sent her back to her own mother and father, a mysterious act hinting at disgraces not told me. Perhaps they had thrown her out to deflect the avengers.

She was the only daughter; her four brothers went with her father, husband, and uncles "out on the road" and for some years became western men. When the goods were divided among the family, three of the brothers took land, and the youngest, my father, chose an education. After my grandparents gave their daughter away to her husband's family, they had dispensed all the adventure and all the property. They expected her alone to keep the traditional ways, which her brothers, now among the barbarians, could fumble without detection. The heavy, deep-rooted women were to maintain the past against the flood, safe for returning. But the rare urge west had fixed upon our family, and so my aunt crossed boundaries not delineated in space.

The work of preservation demands that the feelings playing about in one's guts not be turned into action. Just watch their passing like cherry blossoms. But perhaps my aunt, my forerunner, caught in a slow life, let dreams grow and fade and after some months or years went toward what persisted. Fear at the enormities of the forbidden kept her desires delicate, wire and bone. She looked at a man because she liked the way the hair was tucked behind his ears, or she liked the question-mark line of a long torso curving at the shoulder and straight at the hip. For warm eyes or a soft voice or a slow walk—that's all—a few hairs, a line, a brightness, a sound, a pace, she gave up family. She offered us up for a charm that vanished with tiredness, a pigtail that didn't toss when the wind died. Why, the wrong lighting could erase the dearest thing about him.

It could very well have been, however, that my aunt did not take subtle enjoyment of her friend, but, a wild woman, kept rollicking company. Imagining her free with sex doesn't fit, though. I don't know any women like that, or men either. Unless I see her life branching into mine, she gives me no ancestral help.

To sustain her being in love, she often worked at herself in the mirror, guessing at the colors and shapes that would interest him, changing them frequently in order to hit on the right combination. She wanted him to look back.

On a farm near the sea, a woman who tended her appearance reaped a reputation for eccentricity. All the married women blunt-cut their hair in flaps about their ears or pulled it back in tight buns. No nonsense. Neither style blew easily into heart-catching tangles. And at their weddings they displayed themselves in their long hair for the last time. "It brushed the backs of my knees," my mother tells me. "It was braided, and even so, it brushed the backs of my knees."

At the mirror my aunt combed individuality into her bob. A bun could have been contrived to escape into black streamers blowing in the wind or in quiet wisps about her face, but only the older women in our picture album wear buns. She brushed her hair back from her forehead, tucking the flaps behind her ears. She looped a piece of thread, knotted into a circle between her index fingers and thumbs, and ran the double strand across her forehead. When she closed her fingers as if she were making a pair of shadow geese bite, the string twisted together catching the little hairs. Then she pulled the thread away from her skin, ripping the hairs out neatly, her eyes watering from the needles of pain. Opening her fingers, she cleaned the thread, then rolled it along her hairline and the tops of her eyebrows. My mother did the same to me and my sisters and herself. I used to believe that the expression "caught by the short hairs" meant a captive held with a depilatory string. It especially hurt at the temples, but my mother said we were lucky we didn't have to have our feet bound when we were seven. Sisters used to sit on their beds and cry together, she said, as their mothers or their slaves removed the bandages for a few minutes each night and let the blood gush back into their veins. I hope that the man my aunt loved appreciated a smooth brow, that he wasn't just a tits-and-ass man.

Once my aunt found a freckle on her chin, at a spot that the almanac said predestined her for unhappiness. She dug it out with a hot needle and washed the wound with peroxide.

More attention to her looks than these pullings of hairs and pickings at spots would have caused gossip among the villagers. They owned work clothes and good clothes, and they wore good clothes for feasting the new seasons. But since a woman combing her hair hexes beginnings, my aunt rarely found an occasion to look her best.

Women looked like great sea snails—the corded wood, babies, and laundry they carried were the whorls on their backs. The Chinese did not admire a bent back; goddesses and warriors stood straight. Still there must have been a marvelous freeing of beauty when a worker laid down her burden and stretched and arched.

Such commonplace loveliness, however, was not enough for my aunt. She dreamed of a lover for the fifteen days of New Year's, the time for families to exchange visits, money, and food. She plied her secret comb. And sure enough she cursed the year, the family, the village, and herself.

Even as her hair lured her imminent lover, many other men looked at her. Uncles, cousins, nephews, brothers would have looked, too, had they been home between journeys. Perhaps they had already been restraining their curiosity, and they left, fearful that their glances, like a field of nesting birds, might be startled and caught. Poverty hurt, and that was their first reason for leaving. But another, final reason for leaving the crowded house was the never-said.

She may have been unusually beloved, the precious only daughter, spoiled and mirror gazing because of the affection the family lavished on her. When her husband left, they welcomed the chance to take her back from the in-laws; she could live like the little daughter for just a while longer. There are stories that my grandfather was different from other people, "crazy ever since the little Jap bayoneted him in the head." He used to put his naked penis on the dinner table, laughing. And one day he brought home a baby girl, wrapped up inside his brown western-style greatcoat. He had traded one of his sons, probably my father, the youngest, for her. My grandmother made him trade back. When he finally got a daughter of his own, he doted on her. They must have all loved her, except perhaps my father, the only brother who never went back to China, having once been traded for a girl.

Brothers and sisters, newly men and women, had to efface their sexual color and present plain miens. Disturbing hair and eyes, a smile like no other, threatened the ideal of five generations living under one roof. To focus blurs, people shouted face to face and yelled from room to room. The immigrants I know have loud voices, unmodulated to American tones even after years away from the village where they called their friendships out across the fields. I have not been able to stop my mother's screams in public libraries or over telephones. Walking erect (knees straight, toes pointed forward, not pigeon-toed, which is Chinese-feminine) and speaking in an inaudible voice, I have tried to turn myself American-feminine. Chinese communication was loud, public. Only sick people had to whisper. But at the dinner table, where the family members came nearest one another, no one could talk, not the outcasts nor any eaters. Every word that falls from the mouth is a coin lost. Silently they gave and accepted food with both hands. A preoccupied child who took his bowl with one hand got a sideways glare. A complete moment of total attention is due everyone alike. Children and lovers have no singularity here, but my aunt used a secret voice, a separate attentiveness.

She kept the man's name to herself throughout her labor and dying; she did not accuse him that he be punished with her. To save her inseminator's name she gave silent birth.

He may have been somebody in her own household, but intercourse with a man outside the family would have been no less abhorrent. All the village were kinsmen, and the titles shouted in loud country voices never let kinship be forgotten. Any man within visiting distance would have been neutralized as a lover—"brother," "younger brother," "older brother"—one hundred and fifteen relationship titles. Parents researched birth charts probably not so much to assure good fortune as to circumvent incest in a population that has but one hundred surnames. Everybody has eight million relatives. How useless then sexual mannerisms, how dangerous.

As if it came from an atavism deeper than fear, I used to add "brother" silently to boys' names. It hexed the boys, who would or would not ask me to dance, and made them less scary and as familiar and deserving of benevolence as girls.

But, of course, I hexed myself also—no dates. I should have stood up, both arms waving, and shouted out across libraries, "Hey, you! Love me back." I had no idea, though, how to make attraction selective, how to control its direction and magnitude. If I made myself American-pretty so that the five or six Chinese boys in the class fell in love with me, everyone else—the Caucasian, Negro, and Japanese boys—would too. Sisterliness, dignified and honorable, made much more sense.

Attraction eludes control so stubbornly that whole societies designed to organize relationships among people cannot keep order, not even when they bind people to one another from childhood and raise them together. Among the very poor and the wealthy, brothers married their adopted sisters, like doves. Our family allowed some romance, paying adult brides' prices and providing dowries so that their sons and daughters could marry strangers. Marriage promises to turn strangers into friendly relatives—a nation of siblings.

In the village structure, spirits shimmered among the live creatures, balanced and held in equilibrium by time and land. But one human being flaring up into violence could open up a black hole, a maelstrom that pulled in the sky. The frightened villagers, who depended on one another to maintain the real, went to my aunt to show her a personal, physical representation of the break she had made in the "roundness." Misallying couples snapped off the future, which was to be embodied in true offspring. The villagers punished her for acting as if she could have a private life, secret and apart from them.

If my aunt had betrayed the family at a time of large grain yields and peace, when many boys were born, and wings were being built on many houses, perhaps she might have escaped such severe punishment. But the men—hungry, greedy, tired of planting in dry soil—had been forced to leave the village in order to send food-money home. There were ghost plagues, bandit plagues, wars with the Japanese, floods. My Chinese brother and sister had died of an unknown sickness. Adultery, perhaps only a mistake during good times, became a crime when the village needed food.

The round moon cakes and round doorways, the round tables of graduated sizes that fit one roundness inside another, round windows and rice bowls—these talismans had lost their power to warn this family of the law: a family must be whole, faithfully keeping the descent line by having sons to feed the old and the dead, who in turn look after the family. The villagers came to show my aunt and her lover-in-hiding a broken house. The villagers were speeding up the circling of events because she was too shortsighted to see that her infidelity had already harmed the village, that waves of consequences would return unpredictably, sometimes in disguise, as now, to hurt her. This roundness had to be made coin-sized so that she would see its circumference: punish her at the birth of her baby. Awaken her to the inexorable. People who refused fatalism because they could invent small resources insisted on culpability. Deny accidents and wrest fault from the stars.

After the villagers left, their lanterns now scattering in various directions toward home, the family broke their silence and cursed her. "Aiaa, we're going to die. Death is coming. Death is coming. Look what you've done. You've killed us. Ghost! Dead ghost! Ghost! You've never been born." She ran out into the fields, far enough from the house so that she could no longer hear their voices, and pressed herself against the earth, her own land no more. When she felt the birth coming, she thought that she had been hurt. Her body seized together. "They've hurt me too much," she thought. "This is gall, and it will kill me." With forehead and knees against the earth, her body convulsed and then relaxed. She turned on her back, lay on the ground. The black well of sky and stars went out and out and out forever; her body and her complexity seemed to disappear. She was one of the stars, a bright dot in blackness, without home, without a companion, in eternal cold and silence. An agoraphobia rose in her, speeding higher and higher, bigger and bigger; she would not be able to contain it; there would be no end to fear.

Flayed, unprotected against space, she felt pain return, focusing her body. This pain chilled her—a cold, steady kind of surface pain. Inside, spasmodically, the other pain, the pain of the child, heated her. For hours she lay on the ground, alternately body and space. Sometimes a vision of normal comfort obliterated reality: she saw the family in the evening gambling at the dinner table, the young people massaging their elders' backs. She saw them congratulating one another, high joy on the mornings the rice shoots came up. When these pictures burst, the stars drew yet further apart. Black space opened.

She got to her feet to fight better and remembered that old-fashioned women gave birth in their pigsties to fool the jealous, pain-dealing gods, who do not snatch piglets. Before the next spasms could stop her, she ran to the pigsty, each step a rushing out into emptiness. She climbed over the fence and knelt in the dirt. It was good to have a fence enclosing her, a tribal person alone.

Laboring, this woman who had carried her child as a foreign growth that sickened her every day, expelled it at last. She reached down to touch the hot, wet, moving mass, surely smaller than anything human, and could feel that it was human after all—fingers, toes, nails, nose. She pulled it up on to her belly, and it lay curled there, butt in the air, feet precisely tucked one under the other. She opened her loose shirt and buttoned the child inside. After resting, it squirmed and thrashed and she pushed it up to her breast. It turned its head this way and that until it found her nipple. There, it made little snuffling noises. She clenched her teeth at its preciousness, lovely as a young calf, a piglet, a little dog.

She may have gone to the pigsty as a last act of responsibility: she would protect this child as she had protected its father. It would look after her soul, leaving supplies on her grave. But how would this tiny child without family find her grave when there would be no marker for her anywhere, neither in the earth nor the family hall? No one would give her a family hall name. She had taken the child with her into the wastes. At its birth the two of them had felt the same raw pain of separation, a wound that only the family pressing tight could close. A child with no descent line would not soften her life but only trail after her, ghostlike, begging her to give it purpose. At dawn the villagers on their way to the fields would stand around the fence and look.

Full of milk, the little ghost slept. When it awoke, she hardened her breasts against the milk that crying loosens. Toward morning she picked up the baby and walked to the well.

Carrying the baby to the well shows loving. Otherwise abandon it. Turn its face into the mud. Mothers who love their children take them along. It was probably a girl; there is some hope of forgiveness for boys. "Don't tell anyone you had an aunt. Your father does not want to hear her name. She has never been born." I have believed that sex was unspeakable and words so strong and fathers so frail that "aunt" would do my father mysterious harm. I have thought that my family, having settled among immigrants who had also been their neighbors in the ancestral land, needed to clean their name, and a wrong word would incite the kinspeople even here. But there is more to this silence: they want me to participate in her punishment. And I have.

In the twenty years since I heard this story I have not asked for details nor said my aunt's name; I do not know it. People who can comfort the dead can also chase after them to hurt them further—a reverse ancestor worship. The real punishment was not the raid swiftly inflicted by the villagers, but the family's deliberately forgetting her. Her betrayal so maddened them, they saw to it that she would suffer forever, even after death. Always hungry, always needing, she would have to beg food from other ghosts, snatch and steal it from those whose living descendants give them gifts. She would have to fight the ghosts massed at crossroads for the buns a few thoughtful citizens leave to decoy her away from village and home so that the ancestral spirits could feast unharassed. At peace, they could act like gods, not ghosts, their descent lines providing them with paper suits and dresses, spirit money, paper houses, paper automobiles, chicken, meat, and rice into eternity—essences delivered up in smoke and flames, steam and incense rising from each rice bowl. In an attempt to make the Chinese care for people outside the family, Chairman Mao[2] encourages us now to give our paper replicas to the spirits of outstanding soldiers and workers, no matter whose ancestors they may be. My aunt remains forever hungry. Goods are not distributed evenly among the dead.

My aunt haunts me—her ghost drawn to me because now, after fifty years of neglect, I alone devote pages of paper to her, though not origamied into houses and clothes. I do not think she always means me well. I am telling on her, and she was a spite suicide, drowning herself in the drinking water. The Chinese are always very frightened of the drowned one, whose weeping ghost, wet hair hanging and skin bloated, waits silently by the water to pull down a substitute.

1976

Amy Tan

b. 1952

Tan wrote "Mother Tongue" for the Threepenny Review *in 1989, the same year that her best-selling novel* The Joy Luck Club *was published. Although the* Threepenny Review *is published in Berkeley, California, it has a national audience used to cosmopolitan fare. So Tan's intention is not to liberalize her readers' attitudes toward women like her mother: her readers are not like the hospital workers and the stockbroker in the essay. Her intent is more discursive and less persuasive. It concerns the influence her mother and her mother's language have had on Tan's writing. The point of the essay is wrapped up in the final anecdote.*

2. Mao Zedong (1893–1976), founder of the People's Republic of China; chief of state, 1949–1959; and chairman of the Communist Party until his death.

Mother Tongue

I am not a scholar of English or literature. I cannot give you much more than personal opinions on the English language and its variations in this country or others.

I am a writer. And by that definition, I am someone who has always loved language. I am fascinated by language in daily life. I spend a great deal of my time thinking about the power of language—the way it can evoke an emotion, a visual image, a complex idea, or a simple truth. Language is the tool of my trade. And I use them all—all the Englishes I grew up with.

Recently, I was made keenly aware of the different Englishes I do use. I was giving a talk to a large group of people, the same talk I had already given to half a dozen other groups. The nature of the talk was about my writing, my life, and my book, *The Joy Luck Club.* The talk was going along well enough, until I remembered one major difference that made the whole talk sound wrong. My mother was in the room. And it was perhaps the first time she had heard me give a lengthy speech—using the kind of English I have never used with her. I was saying things like, "The intersection of memory upon imagination" and "There is an aspect of my fiction that relates to thus-and-thus"—a speech filled with carefully wrought grammatical phrases, burdened, it suddenly seemed to me, with nominalized forms, past perfect tenses, conditional phrases—all the forms of standard English that I had learned in school and through books, the forms of English I did not use at home with my mother.

Just last week, I was walking down the street with my mother, and I again found myself conscious of the English I was using, the English I do use with her. We were talking about the price of new and used furniture and I heard myself saying this: "Not waste money that way." My husband was with us as well, and he didn't notice any switch in my English. And then I realized why. It's because over the twenty years we've been together I've often used that same kind of English with him, and sometimes he even uses it with me. It has become our language of intimacy, a different sort of English that relates to family talk, the language I grew up with.

So you'll have some idea of what this family talk I heard sounds like, I'll quote what my mother said during a recent conversation which I videotaped and then transcribed. During this conversation, my mother was talking about a political gangster in Shanghai who had the same last name as her family's, Du, and how the gangster in his early years wanted to be adopted by her family which was rich by comparison. Later, the gangster became more powerful, far richer than my mother's family, and one day showed up at my mother's wedding to pay his respects. Here's what she said in part:

"Du Yusong having business like fruit stand. Like off the street kind. He is Du like Du Zong—but not Tsung-ming Island people. The local people call putong, the river east side, he belong to that side local people. That man want to ask Du Zong father take him in like become own family. Du Zong father wasn't look down on him, but didn't take seriously, until that man big like become a mafia. Now important person, very hard to inviting him. Chinese way, came only to show respect, don't stay for dinner. Respect for making big celebration, he shows up. Mean gives lots of respect. Chinese custom. Chinese social life that way. If too important won't have to stay too long. He come to my wedding. I didn't see, I heard it. I gone to boy's side, they have YMCA dinner. Chinese age I was 19."

You should know that my mother's expressive command of English belies how much she actually understands. She reads the Forbes report, listens to Wall Street Week, converses daily with her stockbroker, reads all of Shirley MacLaine's books with ease—all kinds of things I can't begin to understand. Yet some of my friends tell me they understand fifty percent of what my mother says. Some say they understand eighty to ninety percent. Some say they understand none of it, as if she were speaking pure Chinese. But to me, my mother's English is perfectly clear, perfectly natural. It's my mother tongue. Her language, as I hear it, is vivid, direct, full of observation and imagery. That was the language that helped shape the way I saw things, expressed things, made sense of the world.

Lately, I've been giving more thought to the kind of English my mother speaks. Like others, I have described it to people as "broken" or "fractured" English. But I wince when I say that. It has always bothered me that I can think of no way to describe it other than "broken," as if it were damaged and needed to be fixed, as if it lacked a certain wholeness and soundness. I've heard other terms used, "limited

English," for example. But they seem just as bad, as if everything is limited, including people's perception of the limited English speaker.

I know this for a fact, because when I was growing up, my mother's "limited" English limited *my* perception of her. I was ashamed of her English. I believed that her English reflected the quality of what she had to say. That is, because she expressed them imperfectly her thoughts were imperfect. And I had plenty of empirical evidence to support me: the fact that people in department stores, at banks, and at restaurants did not take her seriously, did not give her good service, pretended not to understand her, or even acted as if they did not hear her.

My mother has long realized the limitations of her English as well. When I was fifteen, she used to have me call people on the phone to pretend I was she. In this guise, I was forced to ask for information or even to complain and yell at people who had been rude to her. One time it was a call to her stockbroker in New York. She had cashed out her small portfolio and it just so happened we were going to go to New York the next week, our very first trip outside California. I had to get on the phone and say in an adolescent voice that was not very convincing, "This is Mrs. Tan."

And my mother was standing in the back whispering loudly, "Why he don't send me check, already two weeks late. So mad he lie to me, losing me money."

And then I said in perfect English, "Yes, I'm getting rather concerned. You had agreed to send the check two weeks ago, but it hasn't arrived."

Then she began to talk more loudly, "What he want, I come to New York tell him front of his boss, you cheating me?" And I was trying to calm her down, make her be quiet, while telling the stockbroker, "I can't tolerate any more excuses. If I don't receive the check immediately, I am going to have to speak to your manager when I'm in New York next week." And sure enough, the following week there we were in front of this astonished stockbroker, and I was sitting there red-faced and quiet, and my mother, the real Mrs. Tan, was shouting at his boss in her impeccable broken English.

We used a similar routine just five days ago, for a situation that was far less humorous. My mother had gone to the hospital for an appointment, to find out about a benign brain tumor a CAT scan had revealed a month ago. She said she had spoken very good English, her best English, no mistakes. Still, she said, the hospital did not apologize when they said they had lost the CAT scan and she had come for nothing. She said they did not seem to have any sympathy when she told them she was anxious to know the exact diagnosis since her husband and son had both died of brain tumors. She said they would not give her any more information until the next time and she would have to make another appointment for that. So she said she would not leave until the doctor called her daughter. She wouldn't budge. And when the doctor finally called her daughter, me, who spoke in perfect English—lo and behold—we had assurances the CAT scan would be found, promises that a conference call on Monday would be held, and apologies for any suffering my mother had gone through for a most regrettable mistake.

I think my mother's English almost had an effect on limiting my possibilities in life as well. Sociologists and linguists probably will tell you that a person's developing language skills are more influenced by peers. But I do think that the language spoken in the family, especially in immigrant families which are more insular, plays a large role in shaping the language of the child. And I believe that it affected my results on achievement tests, IQ tests, and the SAT. While my English skills were never judged as poor, compared to math, English could not be considered my strong suit. In grade school, I did moderately well, getting perhaps Bs, sometimes B+s in English, and scoring perhaps in the sixtieth or seventieth percentile on achievement tests. But those scores were not good enough to override the opinion that my true abilities lay in math and science, because in those areas I achieved As and scored in the ninetieth percentile or higher.

This was understandable. Math is precise; there is only one correct answer. Whereas, for me at least, the answers on English tests were always a judgment call, a matter of opinion and personal experience. Those tests were constructed around items like fill-in-the-blank sentence completion, such as "Even though Tom was _____, Mary thought he was _____." And the correct answer always seemed to be the most bland combinations of thoughts, for example, "Even though Tom was shy, Mary thought he was charming," with the grammatical structure "even though" limiting the correct answer to some sort of semantic opposites, so you wouldn't get answers like "Even though Tom was foolish, Mary thought he was ridiculous." Well, according to my mother, there were very few limitations as to what Tom could have been, and what Mary might have thought of him. So I never did well on tests like that.

The same was true with word analogies, pairs of words, in which you were supposed to find some sort of logical, semantic relationship—for example, "sunset" is to "nightfall" as ____ is to ____." And here, you would be presented with a list of four possible pairs, one of which showed the same kind of relationship: "red" is to "stoplight," "bus" is to "arrival," "chills" is to "fever," "yawn" is to "boring." Well, I could never think that way. I knew what the tests were asking, but I could not block out of my mind the images already created by the first pair, "sunset is to nightfall"—and I would see a burst of colors against a darkening sky, the moon rising, the lowering of a curtain of stars. And all the other pairs of words—red, bus, stoplight, boring—just threw up a mass of confusing images, making it impossible for me to sort out something as logical as saying: "A sunset precedes nightfall" is the same as "a chill precedes a fever." The only way I would have gotten that answer right would have been to imagine an associative situation, for example, my being disobedient and staying out past sunset, catching a chill at night, which turns into feverish pneumonia as punishment, which indeed did happen to me.

I have been thinking about all this lately, about my mother's English, about achievement tests. Because lately I've been asked, as a writer, why there are not more Asian-Americans represented in American literature. Why are there few Asian-Americans enrolled in creative writing programs? Why do so many Chinese students go into engineering? Well, these are broad sociological questions I can't begin to answer. But I have noticed in surveys—in fact, just last week—that Asian students, as a whole, always do significantly better on math achievement tests than in English. And this makes me think that there are other Asian-American students whose English spoken in the home might also be described as "broken" or "limited." And perhaps they also have teachers who are steering them away from writing and into math and science, which is what happened to me.

Fortunately, I happen to be rebellious in nature, and enjoy the challenge of disproving assumptions made about me. I became an English major my first year in college after being enrolled as pre-med. I started writing non-fiction as a freelancer the week after I was told by my former boss that writing was my worst skill and I should hone my talents toward account management.

But it wasn't until 1985 that I finally began to write fiction. And at first I wrote using what I thought to be wittily crafted sentences, sentences that would finally prove I had mastery over the English language. Here's an example from the first draft of a story that later made its way into *The Joy Luck Club*, but without this line: "That was my mental quandary in its nascent state." A terrible line, which I can barely pronounce.

Fortunately, for reasons I won't get into today, I later decided I should envision a reader for the stories I would write. And the reader I decided upon was my mother, because these were stories about mothers. So with this reader in mind—and in fact, she did read my early drafts—I began to write stories using all the Englishes I grew up with: the English I spoke to my mother, which for lack of a better term, might be described as "simple"; the English she used with me, which for lack of a better term might be described as "broken"; my translation of her Chinese, which could certainly be described as "watered down"; and what I imagined to be her translation of her Chinese if she could speak in perfect English, her internal language, and for that I sought to preserve the essence, but not either an English or a Chinese structure. I wanted to capture what language ability tests can never reveal: her intent, her passion, her imagery, the rhythms of her speech and the nature of her thoughts.

Apart from what any critic had to say about my writing, I knew I had succeeded where it counted when my mother finished reading my book, and gave me her verdict: "So easy to read."

1989

Noel Ignatiev

1940–2019

When we talk about race in America, what it means to be "white" often goes without saying or figures merely as the position of privilege in contrast with which other identities are defined. This essay reminds us that "whiteness" does not exist in itself, but only in contrast to other, unprivileged identities; and also that privilege has gradations which become almost castes among the people we consider racially white. Ignatiev was a social historian from Harvard University, where he earned his PhD and where he taught for many years. The goal of a social historian is to reconstruct not the events we typically regard as "historic," the political upheavals and the advancing and retreating fortunes of armies, but the everyday experience of normal, unexalted people. What was it like to be Irish in America in 1840? in 1880? in 1900? What did Irish Americans do to fashion their own racial identity in polyglot America? To answer those kinds of questions, the historian gathers a range of inductive evidence—from newspapers, diaries, letters, popular culture, demographic data (baptismal, marriage, wills, death records, etc.). We don't see much of that evidence here, because this selection is the introduction to Ignatiev's book. Introductions do not intend to present readers with fully formed logical arguments, and they gesture toward rather than present convincing evidence. They explain to readers the overall argument of the book: hence, in the third to last paragraph, Ignatiev forecasts his strategy in each of the book's chapters. Introductions establish writers' credibility—that they are experts and that they are honest interpreters of historical data. And introductions tend to be provocative—they want to entice people to open up Chapter 1 and start reading.

"This book," Ignatiev declares, "asks how the Catholic Irish, an oppressed race in Ireland, became part of an oppressing race in America." To put that purpose more provocatively, Ignatiev proposes to examine "how one group of people became white." That particular phrase—how the Irish "became white"—certainly provoked public debate. On the one hand, some conservatives used the success of Irish Catholics to prove the supposed inferiority of Black Americans. The Irish and the African American occupied relatively similar positions in the nineteenth century, that argument goes, yet one group stagnated while the other flourished. If the Irish could "become white," why didn't African Americans also "become white" in the 130 years since the Civil War? "If only they worked as hard as the Irish . . ." Ignatiev himself does not make this argument—in fact, he would find it repugnant. Nevertheless, in reaction, many liberals assailed Ignatiev's book for suggesting an equivalence between African Americans and Irish Catholic immigrants. No matter what they suffered, such criticism goes, the Irish were never not "white" in America. Before the Civil War, they were never in danger of being enslaved; after the war, Jim Crow laws did not apply to them.

The first argument completely distorted—even reversed—the main point of Ignatiev's book; while the second disputed the provocative phrase rather than the detailed arguments of Ignatiev's book, which acknowledged and insisted that racial slavery was *a crucial difference between Blacks and the Irish.*

Besides this debate, Ignatiev also triggered a new interest in the complexity of being ethnically "white" in America, and several scholarly books developed his arguments: How Jews Became White Folks and What That Says about Race in America *(1998),* To Hell or Barbados: the Ethnic Cleansing of Ireland *(2001),* Working toward Whiteness: How America's Immigrants Became White *(2005),* White Cargo: the Forgotten History of Britain's White Slaves in America *(2007), and* White Identity Politics *(2019), among many others. This selection is presented here to address the complexity of what it means to identify—and be identified—as white in America. It is worth noting that three years before this selection was published, Ignatiev founded a magazine called* Race Traitor, *which advocated "treason to whiteness" as a means of establishing one's "loyalty to humanity." People "who have been brought up as white," he argued, should "become unwhite." He hoped to abolish whiteness as an identity.*

How the Irish Became White

The Irish, who, at home, readily sympathize with the oppressed everywhere, are instantly taught when they step upon our soil to hate and despise the Negro. . . . Sir, the Irish-American will one day find out his mistake.

—Frederick Douglass, May 10, 1853

Passage to the United States seems to produce the same effect upon the exile of Erin as the eating of the forbidden fruit did upon Adam and Eve. In the morning, they were pure, loving, and innocent; in the evening guilty.

—The Liberator, August 11, 1854

The Irish are the blacks of Europe. So say it loud—I'm black and I'm proud.

—The Commitments, 1991

No biologist has ever been able to provide a satisfactory definition of "race"—that is, a definition that includes all members of a given race and excludes all others. Attempts to give the term a biological foundation lead to absurdities: parents and children of different races, or the well-known phenomenon that a white woman can give birth to a black child, but a black woman can never give birth to a white child.[1] The only logical conclusion is that people are members of different races because they have been assigned to them.

Outside these labels and the racial oppression that accompanies them, the only race is the human. I'll be examining connections between concepts of race and acts of oppression. "By considering the notion of 'racial oppression' in terms of the substantive, the operative element, namely 'oppression,' it is possible to avoid the contradictions and howling absurdities that result from attempts to splice genetics and sociology. By examining racial oppression as a particular system of oppression—like gender oppression or class oppression or national oppression—we find further footing for analyzing . . . the peculiar function of the 'white race'. . . . The hallmark of racial oppression [is the reduction of] all members of the oppressed group to one undifferentiated social status, a status beneath that of any member of any social class" within the dominant group.[2] It follows, therefore, that the white race consists of those who partake of the privileges of the white skin in this society. Its most wretched members share a status higher, in certain respects, than that of the most exalted persons excluded from it.

This book looks at how one group of people became white. Put another way, it asks how the Catholic Irish, an oppressed race in Ireland, became part of an oppressing race in America. It is an attempt to reassess immigrant assimilation and the formation (or non-formation) of an American working class.

1. For a consideration of these and other absurdities, see Barbara J. Fields, "Ideology and Race in American History," in J. Morgan Kousser and James M. McPherson, *Region, Race and Reconstruction* (New York, 1982), 143–177.

2. Theodore W. Allen, *The Invention of the White Race, Volume One: Racial Oppression and Social Control* (New York, 1994), 28, 32.

The Irish who emigrated to America in the eighteenth and nineteenth centuries were fleeing caste oppression and a system of landlordism that made the material conditions of the Irish peasant comparable to those of an American slave. They came to a society in which color was important in determining social position. It was not a pattern they were familiar with and they bore no responsibility for it; nevertheless, they adapted to it in short order.

When they first began arriving here in large numbers they were, in the words of Mr. Dooley, given a shovel and told to start digging up the place as if they owned it. On the rail beds and canals they labored for low wages under dangerous conditions; in the South they were occasionally employed where it did not make sense to risk the life of a slave. As they came to the cities, they were crowded into districts that became centers of crime, vice, and disease.

There they commonly found themselves thrown together with free Negroes. Irish- and Afro-Americans fought each other and the police, socialized and occasionally intermarried, and developed a common culture of the lowly. They also both suffered the scorn of those better situated. Along with Jim Crow and Jim Dandy, the drunken, belligerent, and foolish Pat and Bridget were stock characters on the early stage. In antebellum America it was speculated that if racial amalgamation was ever to take place it would begin between those two groups.

As we know, things turned out otherwise. The outcome was not the inevitable consequence of blind historic forces, still less of biology, but the result of choices made, by the Irish and others, from among available alternatives. To enter the white race was a strategy to secure an advantage in a competitive society.

What did it mean to the Irish to become white in America? It did not mean that they all became rich, or even "middle-class" (however that is defined); to this day there are plenty of poor Irish. Nor did it mean that they all became the social equals of the Saltonstalls and van Rensselaers; even the marriage of Grace Kelly to the Prince of Monaco and the election of John F. Kennedy as president did not eliminate all barriers to Irish entry into certain exclusive circles. To Irish laborers, to become white meant at first that they could sell themselves piecemeal instead of being sold for life, and later that they could compete for jobs in all spheres instead of being confined to certain work; to Irish entrepreneurs, it meant that they could function outside of a segregated market. To both of these groups it meant that they were citizens of a democratic republic, with the right to elect and be elected, to be tried by a jury of their peers, to live wherever they could afford, and to spend, without racially imposed restrictions, whatever money they managed to acquire. In becoming white the Irish ceased to be Green.

Chapter One frames the study. It looks at the Irish-American response to the 1841 appeal by the "Liberator," Daniel O'Connell, to join with the abolitionists; Chapter Two turns back to the status of Catholics in Ireland and early contacts of Irish emigrants with American race patterns; Chapter Three uses the career of an early Irish immigrant to show how the party of Jefferson became the party of Van Buren, and the role it played in making the Irish white; Chapter Four looks at the labor market; Chapter Five examines the effect of anti-Negro rioting by the Irish and others, not on the direct victims but on those doing the rioting; Chapter Six recounts the Irish triumph over nativism, by tracing the career of a Philadelphia politician who played an important, if generally unknown, role in national politics in 1876; and the Afterword is a review of the literature, plus concluding remarks.

In viewing entry into the white race as something the Irish did "on" (though not by) themselves, this book seeks to make them the actors in their own history.

On one occasion many years ago, I was sitting on my front step when my neighbor came out of the house next door carrying her small child, whom she placed in her automobile. She turned away from him for a moment, and as she started to close the car door, I saw that the child had put his hand where it would be crushed when the door was closed. I shouted to the woman to stop. She halted in mid-motion, and when she realized what she had almost done, an amazing thing happened: she began laughing, then broke into tears and began hitting the child. It was the most intense and dramatic display of conflicting emotions I have ever beheld. My attitude toward the subjects of this study accommodates stresses similar to those I witnessed in that mother.

1995

Kwame Dawes
b. 1962

This essay was published in a 1997 book called Borrowed Power: Essays on Cultural Appropriation. *The editors of that volume admit that the term "cultural appropriation" is difficult to pin down—particularly because "culture" itself encompasses so much. A good part of Dawes' essay attempts to define exactly what appropriation is and how it differs from healthy cultural exchange.*

Dawes developed these reflections after participating in the 1992 "About Face/About Frame" conference he describes near the essay's end, a gathering of about forty artists from minority cultures in Canada. One purpose of the conference was to figure out how First Nations artists could better access public funding and grants from private foundations. (Canadians use the term "First Nations" in roughly the same way people in the United States use "Native American.") In the past, committee and board members making decisions about funding were virtually all white and had a bias toward "mainstream" culture. Sometimes, the attempts to correct that bias resulted in tokenism (in which an artist might be chosen merely to disrupt the across-the-board racial homogeneity of fund recipients); or, worse yet, artists from the dominant culture might be favored if they included elements in their art that derived from minority cultures.

This essay—and the volume it appeared in—is really addressed to people more or less sympathetic to the notion that some corrective measures are required. But what should those measures be? And might some "solutions" merely mask rather than solve the underlying problem? When Dawes references the "current debate surrounding the question of cultural appropriation," he's talking about these issues of public funding for the arts. Who should be on the boards that make those decisions? Whose art should represent minority cultures? The controversy about public and private grant funding for filmmakers in Canada is a particular instance that involves larger questions about how heterogeneous societies ought to handle diverse cultural identities. How can policy or even legislation discourage rather than encourage cultural appropriation?

Re-appropriating Cultural Appropriation

The current debate surrounding the question of cultural appropriation has provided the typically unimaginative instincts of top-heavy bureaucratic structures that participate in the funding business with another tool of exclusion and ghettoization which appears to wear the face of cultural tolerance and sensitivity. In fact, without an understanding of the role of power and its history in the context of colonialism and imperialism in determining what constitutes cultural appropriation, one is left with what can easily be another tool of fascist cultural exclusivity. Is Bob Marley's lyric "War" cultural appropriation because the text of the song is taken from a speech by Haile Selassie, an Ethiopian emperor? Is Marley, a Jamaican of Scottish and Jamaican descent, appropriating the culture of Ethiopia, and, if so, is this a bad thing? Is it the same as racist renditions of Native American culture or African culture seen in many Hollywood films? How is such difference defined and legislated without creating a situation in which simplistic criteria like "it's about Black people and he is white, thus we throw it out" become the operating rationale for funding policies?

Quite naturally, the greatest cry against cultural appropriation has come from people who are railing against the actions of exploitative white artists. Thus, it appears that support for legislation that seeks to end cultural appropriation would come from this group of individuals as well. And in many instances this is the case. However, it is also quite clear that the people who are designing and implementing policy to respond to these cries for change are not usually people of color or people of First Nations descent. Instead, white bureaucrats are formulating these policies and in many ways are merely replicating old racist and divisive models of government through an appropriation and misinterpretation of progressive political ideology. If legislation continues in the direction that it threatens to go, what will happen is that only Blacks will be able to write about Black experience, and only whites will be able to write about their experience. Cree people will not write about the Mohawk, nor will the Iroquois write about the Inuit. A straight woman will never include in her work a lesbian character, nor will a Mayan write about a Spanish-Mexican homosexual. The only artists who will be able to produce work of rich variety are those who have incredibly complex and mixed heritages, who are bisexual, who are androgynous, or those who don't need funding.

Can an Other person, a person different from myself because of sex, race, sexual orientation or history, effectively write about my experience in a way that I can connect with? As an artist, an avid reader and a viewer of films I must conclude that this is possible. It has to be. This does not mean that the picture will be perfect. But, by the same token, I would never presume to think that because someone is Black like myself, and male and heterosexual, that he automatically has the capacity and skill to represent my experience. However, I make a distinction between exploitative readings of my experience and readings that emerge out of dialogue and honest interaction founded on common humanity. To deny the possibility of art emerging out of such a context is to deny art its power—it is, in fact, to deny the very concept of learning.

But the issue is far more complex than that. One could quite easily declare on the basis of the above statements that legislation that seeks to uproot cultural appropriation is inherently absurd and unprogressive. Cultural appropriation—the argument goes—is not a bad thing all the time, and world cultures are already too intertwined to do anything about changing them. However, such thinking assumes that we are playing on an even playing field. This is not the case. Our society is marred by significant inequities which have, for years, led to the exclusion of "minorities" and communities not regarded as belonging to the "mainstream" of the society from telling their own stories. Riding on the back of a carefully designed and efficiently implemented system of the cultural oppression of colonialism and imperialism, much of Canada's cultural behavior merely reflects a privileging of white Eurocentric values. In this context, minorities have often been excluded from funding which would allow them to tell their stories—instead, white artists have had greater access to the money available, even when they are telling stories that have been taken from the cultures of the "minority" people. In light of this inequity, there is a strong and compelling case that can be made for a reassessment of the philosophical foundation upon which funding decisions are made. Such a reevaluation would be founded on the argument that since so many whites have told, for years, the stories of non-whites, and have, in the process, brutally misinterpreted them and established a discourse of inferiority in such portrayals, it is time to shift the emphasis and favor, instead, [to] the non-white artists who are willing and able to tell their own story and to tell it well. This is not to dismiss the noble and sincere sentiment that may have gone into the hundreds and thousands of pseudo-anthropological folk song and tale collections that have been produced by white writers over the past five hundred years, beginning in America with Columbus' quasi-anthropological evaluation of the Arawak people. However, as has been demonstrated in countless instances, many of these works are flawed by the heavy-handed application of Western values, prejudices and belief systems to the interpretation of the folkways of non-white people. This, coupled with exploitive absence of accountability to the people being written about, and the related lack of respect for their values, has generated work that is at best of poor and unreliable quality and at worst simply offensive and totally destructive.

In order to favor the non-white artist on the basis of this argument, certain assumptions about art have to be made. The first and most important is that art is essentially a commodity that exists within a political and ideological landscape. We must dismiss the notion that art exists outside of culture, or the idea that art somehow transcends culture and politics. It does not. This is the reality regardless of whether we like the idea or not. Art is money, art is power, art defines effectively. Art may be seen as a means by which we interpret and represent society in a fashion that is dictated by our discourse—our history, our culture, our social realities and our politics. If we grant, then, that white artists have essentially dominated the highest echelons of art for too long, and if we further accept that this is a product, not of artistic ability, but of political and cultural will, then there is a place for the redressing of what is essentially an injustice. There is a place for suggesting that non-white artists be allowed to tell their own story. In fact it must go further than that—non-white artists should be encouraged, aided, supported and funded such that they can tell their own stories. At the same time, white artists should be heavily scrutinized such that they can be discouraged from embarking on projects that essentially perpetuate the negative stereotyping of non-white cultures. For those who are quick to scream censorship, let it be understood that this has less to do with censorship than it has to do with copyright questions. As simplistic as this may seem, the rationale for such action is founded on the belief that white artists have been stealing from and misinterpreting non-white artists for too long. Now non-white artists are seeking to get back what is rightfully theirs.

The funding agencies and policy making structures should, as a consequence, so restructure themselves to allow non-white artists to feel and be included in the artistic mainstream. This means a redefinition of what constitutes mainstream—moving away from the notion that anything mainstream must be either white or acceptable to whites. These are political considerations and require political measures. But despite the compelling nature of the argument presented here, it is necessary to continue to bear in mind that political policy on such matters can easily shift from the liberal to the fascist. One must be wary, for instance, of the fact that legislation in such areas is often being carried out by individuals who are not necessarily sympathetic to the philosophy of change. In the context of this issue, this is a significant danger, for policies may be implemented in such a way as to aggravate the situation and perpetuate the ghettoization of non-white communities in the society. What I refer to here is the perpetuation of the concept of the existence of homogeneous and pure races and cultures and the hierarchical values that many racists over the years have attached to them: Hitler's attitude to jazz and Black culture in Nazi Germany, for instance. Would we applaud his passionate plea for his pure white people to not "appropriate" the music of Black America?

The fact is that we are dealing with a society that has still not fully internalized the need for systematic change when it comes to racism. Consequently, action that seeks to redress racist tendencies is being implemented by people who have not fully accepted the negative reality of racism. There are still many instances of racist policy of which the administrators who carry out legislation are blissfully unaware. They have not yet understood the pervasiveness and Hydra-like nature of racism. They just don't get it.

It is easy, then, for such ideological constructs to be redefined and misappropriated to suit the interests of a ruling class. The truth is that if, in fact, the legislation took the form of what I describe above, then we would have a situation that would simply ghettoize all communities, thus consolidating the domination of a "pure" white society and culture. Such politically rooted criteria would assume great importance so that questions of artistic quality would become redefined. This in itself may not be a bad thing except that this redefinition would be premised on the understanding that works produced by non-whites are defined and recommended purely on the basis of their politics and race-centeredness rather than on their vision and artistic credibility. Such thinking already exists today in the attitude that many Canadians have toward notions of affirmative action and employment equity Here, the non-white worker, it is assumed, is inherently weaker in skill and intelligence than the white worker but has managed to progress simply on the basis of his/her skin color. Translated into the art business, white artists are now dismissing the credibility of the work of non-white artists on the assumption that the only reason that such non-whites have been published, produced or displayed is that their works are a part of the privileged "minority backlash." So a white male academic is able to say to me, without the slightest acknowledgment of his racism and dismissal of my abilities, "You are lucky being Black—you will get a job easily. Now if you were a woman and maybe gay . . ." This is the kind of self-pitying cynicism that comes from people who have had it too easy in the past and who are now lamenting their loss of power without realizing that the power they once held was wrongly and unjustly acquired. They fail to recognize as well that their movement to positions of power at the time was not based on merit, but facilitated by their skin color. Such attitudes as described above are also becoming basic to the cultural arena, and it stems from the basic philosophy that is ingrained in the psyche of many white Canadians.

* * *

When cultural appropriation is counteracted by the qualities of respect, sensitivity and equal opportunity, the result is work that is wonderfully developed and filled with the richness of cultural interaction and dialogue. It is the difference between stealing and getting permission to take, borrow or share. The cry for measures against cultural appropriation emerged out of a sense of abuse and exploitation felt by disenfranchised minorities which characterized the work of many white artists dealing with subject matter that they did not respect or understand. It also involved the question of money. Many artists have stolen from other cultures without giving acknowledgment; they have misrepresented cultures and values with complete disdain and disregard for the values of the people that they have exploited, and, in the process, they have made significant amounts of money from such efforts. In many instances, our understanding of ourselves has been determined by the language and ideology of these exploitive artists whose sense of accountability is minimal largely because it is they who have the funding and power.

Thus it is possible for white documentary filmmakers to shoot Aztec people and yet state in the overdub that they are Mayans without these filmmakers feeling the least bit of anxiety about their credibility as cultural documenters. Quite simply, the audience they feel accountable to would not know the difference. It is this disrespect, this constant "dissing" of other cultures through exploitive artistic tendencies, that has driven many non-white artists to call for action against cultural appropriation. The truth is, what we are looking for, as non-white artists, is a chance to be able to determine how our stories are going to be told, and a chance to ensure that our values and culture are respected by those who seek to describe them. We, quite understandably, sometimes feel, in light of past practices of whites, that we are the only ones who can fairly treat our own experience. We are suspicious of the motives and practices of those who do not share our history of pain and abuse. Some of us take this thinking even further, suggesting that white artists do not have the capacity to tell our stories because they speak from a "comparatively superficial perspective," which does not allow them to share the pain and suffering that we have felt under their rule.[1] It is an understandable instinct, but it must be tempered by the awareness that it is an instinct born out of the demand for respect, accountability and dialogue.

For we concede, as well we must, that there are very few existing cultures that can be described as completely void of influence from other cultures. This may be, for many, a lamentable fact of imperial-

1. Janisse Browning, "Self-Determination and Cultural Appropriation," *Fuse Magazine* 15 (Spring 1992): 33.

ism and colonialism, but for me it is a compelling fact of industrialization and the instinct to explore and learn about other people. I suspect that this is a fact of the human condition. We are social creatures who have consistently shown a propensity to adapt our values, our sense of beauty and art, and our concepts of identity and place according to the cultures and civilizations that we encounter. This kind of interaction and sharing of culture—whether it be exploitive or that of mutual respect and sharing—is something that is arguably inherent in human behavior. To deny this, therefore, is to deny a fundamental human trait. Thus, any attempt to formulate policy that seeks to uphold a concept of culture as a homogeneous entity that is static and not subject to change through interaction and dialogue is bound to lead to the adoption of totalitarian and inhuman practices. More importantly, it entails the denial of the commonality of human experience. Interaction is inevitable; influences must occur. What need not be inevitable are exploitation and the movement toward a denial of one's own identity. As well, the kind of hierarchical structures that establish "superior" cultures as the ultimate goal of "inferior" cultures through the processes of so-called influence and change must be completely rejected as manifestations of genocidal tendencies. Cultural appropriation, understood in its most negative of manifestations, amounts to robbery. Coping with robbery and thievery is something that all societies have somehow had to do, and the principles inherent in such coping mechanisms could be applied to cultural appropriation. We abhor robbery. We resent when our things are taken from us without our permission and flaunted by the thief as trophies and as things that belong to that person. We resent it because in the process our achievements are denied and our enemy has managed to ride toward success on our backs. We also resent it when we give people permission to do something on our behalf and they completely misrepresent us. They make a mockery of our message and shamefully betray the trust that we had in them. Our instinct is to try and retrieve what was taken from us—the actual item that we gave in good faith to the bad messenger—and to reassert who we are and what is ours so that generations can see the truth and appreciate it. If we do not do this, our children's inheritance, that which was given to us, will no longer be there for them, and they will be very poor indeed.

It is time to ensure that such exploitation be arrested. More crucially, it is time to ensure that when our gift of culture is being displayed by those with whom we have been willing to share it, that it is presented in a manner that indicates that the artist feels accountable not only to one's financiers, but to us, the part-suppliers of this person's content.

Ultimately, then, it is possible to conceive of a situation in which artistic value operates side by side with cultural and political awareness in the judging and funding of projects within this society. We must accept that the criteria for what constitutes artistic quality are not only personally determined, but further determined by the cultural legacy of each of us, and that such legacies cannot be valued in terms of "good, better, best." While the pervasiveness of Western culture has supplied most cultural communities with shared criteria for artistic value, the same can be said about the impact of Eastern and Southern—that is, the Asian continent and the combined "Southern" worlds of Africa, Australia and South America[2]—values on what we understand to be modern universal artistic tastes. It is incumbent on the individual who seeks to value work to have a broad conception of what is of quality and value in a Canadian society, which is becoming increasingly complex in its cultural makeup. This is a wonderful challenge facing artists and art administrators across the country, and it must be seen as an opportunity for the enrichment of art within the country. To shy away from it through the protectionism of exclusionary and divisive legislative practices would be to deny this country of one of its greatest assets, the diversity of its cultural heritages. Further, to reinforce the division through ghettoized policies of funding and support will only deprive the community of a chance to enrich its cultural infrastructure through an equitable process of cross-fertilization.[3] Finally, to privilege one culture over another will simply ensure that a dominant and unequal trend of exploitation will

2. By using these terms, I am merely completing the global circuit in the illogical and geographically questionable Western political terms "East and West/North and South." In actuality, I am suggesting that the process of cultural influence is fairly universal and is usually reciprocal. What is often varied are the terms upon which such influence takes place.

3. I am acutely aware of the fact that I speak idealistically here and that the world I envisage is utopian. However, there is a lot that can be said about utopias which exist in our collective imaginations, as they provide us with useful paradigms: ideals upon which to test our actions and to base our interactions.

continue denying the identity and existence of a large segment of the population.

These were my contemplations after spending four days with a dynamic and motivated group of artists and facilitators at the "About Frame About Face" meeting of the Independent Film and Video Alliance in Banff, Alberta, in June 1992. Many of these artists have found themselves sometimes sacrificing time they would rather spend doing their own creative work, struggling to see that the systems that operate around the industry are so ameliorated to ensure that there exists a freedom to create in a climate of something that transcends mere tolerance[4]—one of deep interest and pride. Many are highly positioned in the structures-that-be and may function, through the alliance of ideas, visions, and strategies for change, and, importantly, through the support from fellow strugglers, as catalysts for fundamental change in a manner that will encourage a change in the system. At the end of the conference there was a sense of community, a shared vision about art and its incredible dynamic with society. Most significantly, there emerged a commitment to uphold and promote the values of respect, responsibility, accountability and equal opportunity in efforts that entailed the crossing of cultural lines and the sharing of multiple heritages. In this environment of trust and shared values, there was a kind of liberation from the prison of marginalization within marginalized and ghettoized communities, through a determination to work against the patterns of exploitation inherent in the many centuries of abusive cultural appropriation. Here, those who had felt what it meant to be robbed resisted the human urge to simply rob the next potential victim who seemed weaker (perpetuating the pattern of the colonizer), by seeking to assert a desire, instead, to share, to dialogue, and to work together in celebrating each other's culture. Each artist of color, each First Nations artist

4. When my mother said she wouldn't tolerate my behavior any longer, she meant that all this time she had hated my behavior and this would be the last straw. I don't understand how we have come to apply the term "tolerance" as a positive value in society. Tolerance is applicable only when two parties are so much against each other that grudging compromise is necessary. Tolerance is the last recourse before full-out war. Tolerance is not to be seen as the ideal. I hate to be tolerated: I would rather be accepted. If, of course, you really hate my guts, then please, by all means, tolerate me, but at least we will know exactly where we stand.

has the responsibility to act and speak out in defense of such liberating ideology. Non-white communities should force funding institutions and art centers to look at their policies and their track record over the past few years from the perspective of those who are most significantly affected. This examination will reveal the flaws in the systems and will then force the various agencies to listen to the directives given by these communities as to what must happen next.

Excitingly, the vision is founded upon the knowledge that there remain thousands of incredibly dynamic and appealing stories to be told by First Nations people and people of color and the country can only be enriched by the telling of these stories. These artists realize that they still have to sacrifice a great deal, but feel that things could be made better for those who are now emerging as film- and videomakers, poets, playwrights, artists, musicians, dancers and producers. The artists at this conference demonstrated what is becoming increasingly clear in the arts and cultural world of Canada, that art is inextricably linked to funding, and that funding is a deeply political issue which requires highly politicized artists to challenge it. One day we may be able to leave the artists to do their art, but this is not the day. Today we must define the parameters of our oppression and in doing so, evolve the mechanism of our liberation. It is we who must define what cultural appropriation really means and not allow it to be coopted into the strategies of exploitation and subjugation that mainstream society is so expert at creating and implementing. We must be watchful of those who, through what can only be described as cynical and twisted irony, choose to appropriate even the very weapons of our liberation. This is the challenge facing First Nations artists and artists of color today. Let us not be deceived: if we do not acknowledge our shared histories of oppression and instead choose to wage our wars in isolation, we will all lose. My language is, admittedly, adversarial, but this kind of rhetoric is sometimes necessary when we speak of something as critical as the fate of our cultures and heritages. The prospects are exciting and promise intriguing developments in the future.

1997

Sonia Sotomayor

b. 1954

Sonia Sotomayor gave this speech at the University of California, Berkeley, in 2002 at a symposium called "Raising the Bar: Latino and Latina Presence in the Judiciary and the Struggle for Representation," and it was published by La Raza Law Journal *that same year. As you will see from her opening remarks, Sotomayor imagines her audience to be largely made up of Latino and Latina legal professionals and students, and she spoke to this community as one of its members. At the time she was a judge on the prestigious federal court of the Southern District of New York. In 2010, President Barack Obama appointed her to the United States Supreme Court, and this speech became an issue of contention during the Senate's approval hearings. Newt Gingrich, then readying himself for a run for the Republican presidential nomination, called Sotomayor a "Latina racist" for the views she expressed here. The accusation indicates an inherent tension in dealing with ethnic and sexual identities in the United States. On one hand, generations of discrimination against various groups clearly violate constitutionally protected equality and demand some action to "level the playing field" (to use a familiar metaphor) that for a long time has been sloped against them. On the other hand, tilting the playing field—even to level it out—seems to require special treatment (often called "affirmative action"), and some conservatives consider any* special *treatment to be* unequal *treatment.*

Such issues are particularly acute in the courtroom, which is a rarified arena of rhetoric. For 2,000 years, the iconic image of "justice" has been a blindfolded woman holding scales. The judge should weigh one argument against another and, without prejudice or personal bias, evaluate their logic. Reason should prevail. No one should put their thumb on one side of the scale. Pathetic and ethical arguments should not be considered, especially in the Supreme Court. But Sotomayor calls this scenario an ideal. In reality, a judge can never be truly objective, and a court that includes no minority judges will almost certainly put its thumb upon the scale by reproducing the biases of society's dominant culture. Sotomayor insists that "bias" is a part of logical argument. As you learned in the introduction to this volume, even logos involves the audience's biases, developed through a lifetime of experience and culture. In deduction, whether or not you find premises to be truthful, and in induction, whether you find the data to be sufficient, relevant, representative, and accurate depends on your personal point of view. Sotomayor eloquently and humorously sketches the construction of her own particular identity, growing up as a girl and young woman in a Puerto Rican neighborhood of New York City. Can acknowledging one's own identity—and the biases that go along with that identity—make one a better judge of argument? Can the perspective inculcated by belonging to one cultural milieu be better than the perspective inculcated by growing up in another?

A Latina Judge's Voice

Judge Reynoso, thank you for that lovely introduction. I am humbled to be speaking behind a man who has contributed so much to the Hispanic community. I am also grateful to have such kind words said about me.

I am delighted to be here. It is nice to escape my hometown for just a little bit. It is also nice to say hello to old friends who are in the audience, to rekindle contact with old acquaintances and to make new friends among those of you in the audience. It is particularly heart warming to me to be attending a conference to which I was invited by a Latina law school friend, Rachel Moran, who is now an accomplished and widely respected legal scholar. I warn Latinos in this room: Latinas are making a lot of progress in the old-boy network.

I am also deeply honored to have been asked to deliver the annual Judge Mario G. Olmos lecture. I am joining a remarkable group of prior speakers who have given this lecture. I hope what I speak about today continues to promote the legacy of that man whose commitment to public service and abiding dedication to promoting equality and justice for all people inspired this memorial lecture and the conference that will follow. I thank Judge Olmos' widow Mary Louise's family, her son and the judge's many friends for hosting me. And for the privilege you have bestowed on me in honoring the memory of a very special person. If I and the many people of this conference can accomplish a fraction of what Judge Olmos did in his short but extraordinary life, we and our respective communities will be infinitely better.[1]

I intend tonight to touch upon the themes that this conference will be discussing this weekend and to talk to you about my Latina identity, where it came from, and the influence I perceive it has on my presence on the bench.

Who am I? I am a "Newyorkrican." For those of you on the West Coast who do not know what that term means: I am a born and bred New Yorker of Puerto Rican–born parents who came to the states during World War II.

Like many other immigrants to this great land, my parents came because of poverty and to attempt to find and secure a better life for themselves and the family that they hoped to have. They largely succeeded. For that, my brother and I are very grateful. The story of that success is what made me and what makes me the Latina that I am. The Latina side of my identity was forged and closely nurtured by my family through our shared experiences and traditions.

For me, a very special part of my being Latina is the *mucho platos de arroz, gandules y pernil*—rice, beans and pork—that I have eaten at countless family holidays and special events. My Latina identity also includes, because of my particularly adventurous taste buds, *morcilla* (pig intestines), *patitas de cerdo con garbanzo* (pigs' feet with beans) and *la lengua y orejas de cuchifrito* (pigs' tongue and ears). I bet the Mexican-Americans in this room are thinking that Puerto Ricans have unusual food tastes. Some of us, like me, do. Part of my Latina identity is the sound of merengue at all our family parties and the heart-wrenching Spanish love songs that we enjoy. It is the memory of Saturday afternoon at the movies with my aunt and cousins watching Cantinflas, who is not Puerto Rican, but who was an icon Spanish comedian on par with Abbott and Costello of my generation. My Latina soul was nourished as I visited and played at my grandmother's house with my cousins and extended family. They were my friends as I grew up. Being a Latina child was watching the adults playing dominos on Saturday night and us kids playing *lotería*

1. Judge Mario G. Olmos (1946–1990), born in Arizona to immigrant farm workers from Mexico, earned a law degree from the University of California, Berkeley, and eventually rose to the Fresno County Superior Court in California before he died in a car accident. [All notes are the editor's.]

(bingo), with my grandmother calling out the numbers which we marked on our cards with chickpeas.

Now, does any one of these things make me a Latina? Obviously not because each of our Caribbean and Latin American communities has their own unique food and different traditions at the holidays. I only learned about tacos in college from my Mexican-American roommate. Being a Latina in America also does not mean speaking Spanish. I happen to speak it fairly well. But my brother, only three years younger, like too many of us educated here, barely speaks it. Most of us born and bred here, speak it very poorly.

If I had pursued my career in my undergraduate history major, I would likely provide you with a very academic description of what being a Latino or Latina means. For example, I could define Latinos as those peoples and cultures populated or colonized by Spain who maintained or adopted Spanish or Spanish Creole as their language of communication. You can tell that I have been very well educated. That antiseptic description however, does not really explain the appeal of *morcilla*—pig's intestine—to an American-born child. It does not provide an adequate explanation of why individuals like us, many of whom are born in this completely different American culture, still identify so strongly with those communities in which our parents were born and raised.

America has a deeply confused image of itself that is in perpetual tension. We are a nation that takes pride in our ethnic diversity, recognizing its importance in shaping our society and in adding richness to its existence. Yet, we simultaneously insist that we can and must function and live in a race- and color-blind way that ignores these very differences that in other contexts we laud. That tension between "the melting pot and the salad bowl"—a recently popular metaphor used to describe New York's diversity—is being hotly debated today in national discussions about affirmative action.[2] Many of us struggle with this tension and attempt to maintain and promote our cultural

2. *affirmative action*: policies, such as hiring or admissions practices, designed to increase representation of certain populations, such as racial minorities or women. From one perspective, affirmative action evens scales that have been historically weighted against these groups; from another perspective, it violates the principle of unbiased judgments. The "salad bowl" metaphor suggests that ethnic identities should not be "melted" into one homogeneous cultural mix influenced by all and shared by all, but that they should retain their distinctions while mingling side by side.

and ethnic identities in a society that is often ambivalent about how to deal with its differences. In this time of great debate we must remember that it is not political struggles that create a Latino or Latina identity. I became a Latina by the way I love and the way I live my life. My family showed me by their example how wonderful and vibrant life is and how wonderful and magical it is to have a Latina soul. They taught me to love being a Puertorriqueña and to love America and value its lesson that great things could be achieved if one works hard for it. But achieving success here is no easy accomplishment for Latinos or Latinas, and although that struggle did not and does not create a Latina identity, it does inspire how I live my life.

I was born in the year 1954. That year was the fateful year in which *Brown v. Board of Education* was decided.[3] When I was eight, in 1961, the first Latino, the wonderful Judge Reynaldo Garza, was appointed to the federal bench, an event we are celebrating at this conference. When I finished law school in 1979, there were no women judges on the Supreme Court or on the highest court of my home state, New York. There was then only one Afro-American Supreme Court justice and then and now no Latino or Latina justices on our highest court. Now in the last twenty-plus years of my professional life, I have seen a quantum leap in the representation of women and Latinos in the legal profession and particularly in the judiciary. In addition to the appointment of the first female United States attorney general, Janet Reno, we have seen the appointment of two female justices to the Supreme Court and two female justices to the New York Court of Appeals, the highest court of my home state. One of those judges is the Chief Judge and the other is a Puertorriqueña like I am. As of today, women sit on the highest courts of almost all of the states and of the territories, including Puerto Rico. One Supreme Court, that of Minnesota, had a majority of women justices for a period of time.

As of September 1, 2001, the federal judiciary consisting of Supreme, circuit and district court judges was about 22 percent women. In 1992, nearly ten years ago, when I was first appointed a district court judge, the percentage of women in the total federal

3. *Brown v. Board of Education*: Supreme Court case that outlawed "separate but equal" public schools as inherently unequal and mandated racial integration.

judiciary was only 13 percent. Now, the growth of Latino representation is somewhat less favorable. As of today we have, as I noted earlier, no Supreme Court justices, and we have only 10 out of 147 active circuit court judges and 30 out of 587 active district court judges. Those numbers are grossly below our proportion of the population. As recently as 1965, however, the federal bench had only three women serving and only one Latino judge. So changes are happening, although in some areas, very slowly. These figures and appointments are heartwarming. Nevertheless, much still remains to happen.

Let us not forget that between the appointments of Justice Sandra Day O'Connor in 1981 and Justice Ginsburg in 1992, eleven years passed.[4] Similarly, between Justice Kaye's initial appointment as an Associate Judge to the New York Court of Appeals in 1983, and Justice Ciparick's appointment in 1993, ten years elapsed. Almost nine years later, we are waiting for a third appointment of a woman to both the Supreme Court and the New York Court of Appeals and of a second minority, male or female, preferably Hispanic, to the Supreme Court. In 1992 when I joined the bench, there were still two out of 13 circuit courts and about 53 out of 92 district courts in which no women sat. At the beginning of September of 2001, there are women sitting in all 13 circuit courts. The First, Fifth, Eighth and Federal Circuits each have only one female judge, however, out of a combined total number of 48 judges. There are still nearly 37 district courts with no women judges at all. For women of color the statistics are more sobering. As of September 20, 1998, of the then 195 circuit court judges only two were African-American women and two Hispanic women. Of the 641 district court judges only twelve were African-American women and eleven Hispanic women. African-American women comprise only 1.56 percent of the federal judiciary and Hispanic-American women comprise only 1 percent. No African-American, male or female, sits today on the Fourth or Federal Circuits. And no Hispanics, male or female, sit on the Fourth, Sixth, Seventh, Eighth, District of Columbia or Federal Circuits.

Sort of shocking, isn't it? This is the year 2002. We have a long way to go. Unfortunately, there are some very deep storm warnings

4. Sandra Day O'Connor (b. 1930) was the first woman appointed to the U. S. Supreme Court (by President Ronald Reagan); Ruth Bader Ginsburg (1933–2020) was the second, appointed by President Bill Clinton.

we must keep in mind. In at least the last five years the majority of nominated judges the Senate delayed more than one year before confirming or never confirming were women or minorities. I need not remind this audience that Judge Paez of your home circuit, the Ninth Circuit, has the dubious distinction of having had his confirmation delayed the longest in Senate history. These figures demonstrate that there is a real and continuing need for Latino and Latina organizations and community groups throughout the country to exist and to continue their efforts of promoting women and men of all colors in their pursuit for equality in the judicial system.

This weekend's conference, illustrated by its name, is bound to examine issues that I hope will identify the efforts and solutions that will assist our communities. The focus of my speech tonight, however, is not about the struggle to get us where we are and where we need to go but instead to discuss with you what it all will mean to have more women and people of color on the bench. The statistics I have been talking about provide a base from which to discuss a question which one of my former colleagues on the Southern District bench, Judge Miriam Cedarbaum, raised when speaking about women on the federal bench.[5] Her question was: What do the history and statistics mean? In her speech, Judge Cedarbaum expressed her belief that the number of women and, by direct inference, people of color on the bench was still statistically insignificant and that therefore we could not draw valid scientific conclusions from the acts of so few people over such a short period of time. Yet, we do have women and people of color in more significant numbers on the bench, and no one can or should ignore pondering what that will mean or not mean in the development of the law. Now, I cannot and do not claim this issue as personally my own. In recent years there has been an explosion of research and writing in this area. On one of the panels tomorrow, you will hear the Latino perspective in this debate.

For those of you interested in the gender perspective on this issue, I commend to you a wonderful compilation of articles published on the subject in Vol. 77 of the *Judicature*, the journal of the American Judicature Society of November–December 1993. It

5. Judge Miriam Cedarbaum (1929–2016), U.S. District Court Judge for the Southern District of New York, was appointed by President Ronald Reagan in 1986.

is on Westlaw/Lexis and I assume the students and academics in this room can find it.

Now Judge Cedarbaum expresses concern with any analysis of women and presumably again people of color on the bench, which begins and presumably ends with the conclusion that women or minorities are different from men generally. She sees danger in presuming that judging should be gender-, or anything else–based. She rightly points out that the perception of the differences between men and women is what led to many paternalistic laws and to the denial to women of the right to vote because we were described then "as not capable of reasoning or thinking logically" but instead of "acting intuitively." I am quoting adjectives that were bandied around famously during the suffragettes' movement.

While recognizing the potential effect of individual experiences on perception, Judge Cedarbaum nevertheless believes that judges must transcend their personal sympathies and prejudices and aspire to achieve a greater degree of fairness and integrity based on the reason of law. Although I agree with and attempt to work toward Judge Cedarbaum's aspiration, I wonder whether achieving that goal is possible in all or even in most cases: And I wonder whether by ignoring our differences as women or men of color we do a disservice both to the law and society: Whatever the reasons why we may have different perspectives, either as some theorists suggest because of our cultural experiences or as others postulate because we have basic differences in logic and reasoning, are in many respects a small part of a larger practical question we as women and minority judges in society in general must address. I accept the thesis of a law school classmate, Professor Steven Carter of Yale Law School, in his affirmative action book that in any group of human beings there is a diversity of opinion because there is both a diversity of experiences and of thought. Thus, as noted by another Yale Law School Professor—I did graduate from there and I am not really biased except that they seem to be doing a lot of writing in that area—Professor Judith Resnik says that there is not a single voice of feminism, not a feminist approach but many who are exploring the possible ways of being that are distinct from those structured in a world dominated by the power and words of men. Thus, feminist theories of judging are in the midst of creation and are not and perhaps will never aspire to be as solidified as the established legal doctrines of judging can sometimes appear to be.

That same point can be made with respect to people of color. No one person, judge or nominee will speak in a female or people of color voice. I need not remind you that Justice Clarence Thomas represents a part but not the whole of African-American thought on many subjects.[6] Yet, because I accept the proposition that, as Judge Resnik describes it, "to judge is an exercise of power" and because as, another former law school classmate, Professor Martha Minnow of Harvard Law School, states "there is no objective stance but only a series of perspectives—no neutrality, no escape from choice in judging," I further accept that our experiences as women and people of color affect our decisions. The aspiration to impartiality is just that—it's an aspiration because it denies the fact that we are by our experiences making different choices than others. Not all women or people of color, in all or some circumstances or indeed in any particular case or circumstance, but enough people of color in enough cases, will make a difference in the process of judging. The Minnesota Supreme Court has given an example of this. As reported by Judge Patricia Wald formerly of the DC Circuit Court, three women on the Minnesota Court with two men dissenting agreed to grant a protective order against a father's visitation rights when the father abused his child. The *Judicature* Journal has at least two excellent studies on how women on the courts of appeal and state supreme courts have tended to vote more often than their male counterparts to uphold women's claims in sex discrimination cases and criminal defendants' claims in search and seizure cases. As recognized by legal scholars, whatever the reason, not one woman or person of color in any one position but as a group we will have an effect on the development of the law and on judging.

In our private conversations, Judge Cedarbaum has pointed out to me that seminal decisions in race and sex discrimination cases have come from Supreme Courts composed exclusively of white males.

6. Justice Clarence Thomas (b. 1948), appointed to the U.S. Supreme Court in 1990 by President George H. W. Bush and confirmed by the Senate after contentious hearings that included Anita Hill's testimony that Thomas sexually harassed her. As a strong conservative, Thomas typically issues decisions that contradict the views of most African American public figures.

I agree that this is significant but I also choose to emphasize that the people who argued those cases before the Supreme Court which changed the legal landscape ultimately were largely people of color and women. I recall that Justice Thurgood Marshall, Judge Connie Baker Motley, the first black woman appointed to the federal bench, and others of the NAACP argued *Brown v. Board of Education*. Similarly, Justice Ginsburg, with other women attorneys, was instrumental in advocating and convincing the Court that equality of work required equality in terms and conditions of employment.[7]

Whether born from experience or inherent physiological or cultural differences, a possibility I abhor less or discount less than my colleague Judge Cedarbaum, our gender and national origins may and will make a difference in our judging. Justice O'Connor has often been cited as saying that a wise old man and wise old woman will reach the same conclusion in deciding cases. I am not so sure Justice O'Connor is the author of that line since Professor Resnik attributes that line to Supreme Court Justice Coyle. I am also not so sure that I agree with the statement. First, as Professor Martha Minnow has noted, there can never be a universal definition of wise. Second, I would hope that a wise Latina woman with the richness of her experiences would more often than not reach a better conclusion than a white male who hasn't lived that life.

Let us not forget that wise men like Oliver Wendell Holmes and Justice Cardozo voted on cases which upheld both sex and race discrimination in our society.[8] Until 1972, no Supreme Court case ever upheld the claim of a woman in a gender discrimination case. I, like Professor Carter, believe that we should not be so myopic as to believe that others of different experiences or backgrounds are

7. Before he was appointed the first African American U.S. Supreme Court justice, Thurgood Marshall (1908–1993) was a civil rights attorney who argued before the Supreme Court. Constance Baker Motley (1921–2005) was the first African American woman appointed to the federal bench, in 1966, by President Lyndon B. Johnson. Before Ruth Bader Ginsburg (1933–2020) was a Supreme Court justice, she was an attorney with the American Civil Liberties Union (ACLU). She often advocated for women's rights, including (for example) successfully persuading the Supreme Court in 1971 to extend the equal protection clause of the Fourteenth Amendment to women.

8. U.S. Supreme Court Justices Oliver Wendell Holmes Jr. (1841–1935) and Benjamin Cardozo (1870–1938) are remembered today for their liberal decisions on the Court.

incapable of understanding the values and needs of people from a different group. Many are so capable. As Judge Cedarbaum pointed out to me, nine white men on the Supreme Court in the past have done so on many occasions and on many issues including *Brown*.

However, to understand takes time and effort, something that not all people are willing to give. For others, their experiences limit their ability to understand the experiences of others. Others simply do not care. Hence, one must accept the proposition that a difference there will be by the presence of women and people of color on the bench. Personal experiences affect the facts that judges choose to see. My hope is that I will take the good from my experiences and extrapolate them further into areas with which I am unfamiliar. I simply do not know exactly what that difference will be in my judging. But I accept there will be some based on my gender and my Latina heritage.

I also hope that raising the question today of what difference having more Latinos and Latinas on the bench will make will start your own evaluation. For people of color and women lawyers, what does and should being an ethnic minority mean in your lawyering? For men lawyers, what areas in your experiences and attitudes do you need to work on to make you capable of reaching those great moments of enlightenment which other men in different circumstances have been able to reach? For all of us, how do we change the facts that in every task force study of gender and race bias in the courts, women and people of color, lawyers and judges alike, report in significantly higher percentages than white men that their gender and race has shaped their careers, from hiring, retention to promotion and that a statistically significant number of women and minority lawyers and judges, both alike, have experienced bias in the courtroom?

Each day on the bench I learn something new about the judicial process and about being a professional Latina woman in a world that sometimes looks at me with suspicion. I am reminded each day that I render decisions that affect people concretely and that I owe them constant and complete vigilance in checking my assumptions, presumptions and perspectives and ensuring that to the extent that my limited abilities and capabilities permit me, that I reevaluate them and change as circumstances and cases before me require. I can and do aspire to be greater than the sum total of my experiences but I accept my limitations. I willingly accept that we who judge must not deny the differences resulting from experience and heritage but attempt, as the Supreme Court suggests, continuously to judge when those opinions, sympathies and prejudices are appropriate.

There is always a danger embedded in relative morality, but since judging is a series of choices that we must make, that I am forced to make, I hope that I can make them by informing myself on the questions I must not avoid asking and continuously ponder. We—I mean all of us in this room—must continue individually and in voices united in organizations that have supported this conference, to think about these questions and to figure out how we go about creating the opportunity for there to be more women and people of color on the bench so we can finally have statistically significant numbers to measure the differences we will be and are making.

I am delighted to have been here tonight and extend once again my deepest gratitude to all of you for listening and letting me share my reflections on being a Latina voice on the bench. Thank you.

2002

CHAPTER 8

✶

Social Justice

Social Media

Angelina Grimké
1805–1879

Grimké, the daughter of a judge in Charleston, South Carolina, wrote a letter of support to the abolitionist paper The Liberator *in 1835. Without her permission the editor, William Garrison, published it, and Grimké found herself instantly notorious in both the South and the North for being an inflammatory radical. She was vilified and insulted; her own Quaker brethren ostracized her. In her hometown, her writings were publicly burned, and she was warned that if she returned to Charleston she would be jailed. But she relished the fight against slavery, dangerous as it was for a woman to write and speak publicly on this topic in the mid-nineteenth century. She delivered the speech that follows to members of the Anti-Slavery Convention of American Women and the Pennsylvania State Anti-Slavery Society, which met on May 16, 1837, in the brand-new Pennsylvania Hall for Free Discussion. The next day a mob burned the auditorium to the ground.*

Speech in Pennsylvania Hall

Men, brethren and fathers—mothers, daughters and sisters, what came ye out for to see? A reed shaken with the wind? Is it curiosity merely, or a deep sympathy with the perishing slave, that has brought this large audience together? Those voices without ought to awaken and call out our warmest sympathies. Deluded beings! "they know not what they do."[1] They know not that they are undermining their own rights and their own happiness, temporal and eternal. Do you ask, "what has the North to do with slavery?" Hear it—hear it. Those voices without tell us that the spirit of slavery is *here*, and has been roused to wrath by our abolition speeches and conventions: for surely liberty would not foam and tear herself with rage, because her friends are multiplied daily, and meetings are held in quick succession to set forth her virtues and extend her peaceful kingdom. This opposition shows

1. Luke 23.34. "Voices without": a mob outside the auditorium was shouting.

that slavery has done its deadliest work in the hearts of our citizens. Do you ask, then, "what has the North to do?" I answer, cast out first the spirit of slavery from your own hearts, and then lend your aid to convert the South. Each one present has a work to do, be his or her situation what it may, however limited their means, or insignificant their supposed influence. The great men of this country will not do this work; the church will never do it. A desire to please the world, to keep the favor of all parties and of all conditions, makes them dumb on this and every other unpopular subject. They have become worldly-wise, and therefore God, in his wisdom, employs them not to carry on his plans of reformation and salvation. He hath chosen the foolish things of the world to confound the wise, and the weak to overcome the mighty.

As a Southerner I feel that it is my duty to stand up here tonight and bear testimony against slavery. I have seen it—I have seen it. I know it has horrors that can never be described. I was brought up under its wing: I witnessed for many years its demoralizing influences, and its destructiveness to human happiness. It is admitted by some that the slave is not happy under the *worst* forms of slavery. But I have *never* seen a happy slave. I have seen him dance in his chains, it is true; but he was not happy. There is a wide difference between happiness and mirth. Man cannot enjoy the former while his manhood is destroyed, and that part of the being which is necessary to the making, and to the enjoyment of happiness, is completely blotted out. The slaves, however, may be, and sometimes are, mirthful. When hope is extinguished, they say, "let us eat and drink, for tomorrow we die."[2] What is a mob? What would the breaking of every window be?[3] What would the levelling of this Hall be? Any evidence that we are wrong, or that slavery is a good and wholesome institution? What if the mob should now burst in upon us, break up our meeting and commit violence upon our persons—would this be anything compared with what the slaves endure? No, no: and we do not remember them "as bound with them,"[4] if we shrink in the time of peril, or feel unwilling to sacrifice ourselves, if need be, for their sake. I thank the Lord that there is yet left life enough to feel the

2. Isaiah 22.13.

3. The mob had begun throwing stones at the windows of the hall.

4. Hebrews 13.3.

truth, even though it rages at it—that conscience is not so completely seared as to be unmoved by the truth of the living God.

Many persons go to the South for a season, and are hospitably entertained in the parlor and at the table of the slaveholder. They never enter the huts of the slaves; they know nothing of the dark side of the picture, and they return home with praises on their lips of the generous character of those with whom they had tarried. Or if they have witnessed the cruelties of slavery, by remaining silent spectators they have naturally become callous—an insensibility has ensued which prepares them to apologize even for barbarity. Nothing but the corrupting influence of slavery on the hearts of the Northern people can induce them to apologize for it; and much will have been done for the destruction of Southern slavery when we have so reformed the North that no one here will be willing to risk his reputation by advocating or even excusing the holding of men as property. The South know it, and acknowledge that as fast as our principles prevail, the hold of the master must be relaxed.

How wonderfully constituted is the human mind! How it resists, as long as it can, all efforts made to reclaim from error! I feel that all this disturbance[5] is but an evidence that our efforts are the best that could have been adopted, or else the friends of slavery, would not care for what we say and do. The South know what we do. I am thankful that they are reached by our efforts. Many times have I wept in the land of my birth over the system of slavery. I knew of none who sympathized in my feelings—I was unaware that any efforts were made to deliver the oppressed—no voice in the wilderness was heard calling on the people to repent and do works meet for repentance—and my heart sickened within me. Oh, how should I have rejoiced to know that such efforts as these were being made. I only wonder that I had such feelings. I wonder when I reflect under what influence I was brought up, that my heart is not harder than the nether millstone. But in the midst of temptation I was preserved, and my sympathy grew warmer, and my hatred of slavery more inveterate, until at last I have exiled myself from my native land because I could no longer endure to hear the wailing of the slave. I fled to the land of Penn;[6]

5. A reference to the continuing uproar of the mob outside the hall.

6. William Penn (1644–1718), founder of the state of Pennsylvania.

for here, thought I, sympathy for the slave will surely be found. But I found it not. The people were kind and hospitable, but the slave had no place in their thoughts. Whenever questions were put to me as to his condition, I felt that they were dictated by an idle curiosity, rather than by that deep feeling which would lead to effort for his rescue. I therefore shut up my grief in my own heart. I remembered that I was a Carolinian, from a state which framed this iniquity by law. I knew that throughout her territory was continued suffering, on the one part, and continual brutality and sin on the other. Every Southern breeze wafted to me the discordant tones of weeping and wailing, shrieks and groans, mingled with prayers and blasphemous curses. I thought there was no hope; that the wicked would go on in his wickedness, until he had destroyed both himself and his country. My heart sunk within me at the abominations in the midst of which I had been born and educated. What will it avail, cried I in bitterness of spirit, to expose to the gaze of strangers the horrors and pollutions of slavery, when there is no ear to hear nor heart to feel and pray for the slave. The language of my soul was, "Oh tell it not in Gath, publish it not in the streets of Askelon."[7] But how different do I feel now! Animated with hope, nay, with an assurance of the triumph of liberty and good will to man, I will lift up my voice like a trumpet, and show this people their transgression, their sins of omission towards the slave, and what they can do towards affecting Southern mind, and overthrowing Southern oppression.

We may talk of occupying neutral ground, but on this subject, in its present attitude, there is no such thing as neutral ground. He that is not for us is against us, and he that gathereth not with us, scattereth abroad. If you are on what you suppose to be neutral ground, the South look upon you as on the side of the oppressor. And is there one who loves his country willing to give his influence, even indirectly, in favor of slavery—that curse of nations? God swept Egypt with the besom of destruction, and punished Judea also with a sore punishment, because of slavery.[8] And have we any reason to believe that he is less just now?—or that he will be more favorable to us than to his own "peculiar people"?

7. 2 Samuel 1.20, meaning keep our adversaries from knowing of our plight.

8. See Exodus.

There is nothing to be feared from those who would stop our mouths, but they themselves should fear and tremble. The current is even now setting fast against them. If the arm of the North had not caused the Bastille[9] of slavery to totter to its foundation, you would not hear those cries. A few years ago, and the South felt secure, and with a contemptuous sneer asked, "Who are the abolitionists? The abolitionists are nothing?"—Ay, in one sense they were nothing, and they are nothing still. But in this we rejoice, that "God has chosen things that are not to bring to nought things that are."[1]

We often hear the question asked, "What shall we do?" Here is an opportunity for doing something now. Every man and every woman present may do something by showing that we fear not a mob, and, in the midst of threatenings and revilings, by opening our mouths for the dumb and pleading the cause of those who are ready to perish.

To work as we should in this cause, we must know what Slavery is. Let me urge you then to buy the books which have been written on this subject and read them, and then lend them to your neighbors. Give your money no longer for things which pander to pride and lust, but aid in scattering "the living coals of truth"[2] upon the naked heart of this nation,—in circulating appeals to the sympathies of Christians in behalf of the outraged and suffering slave. But, it is said by some, our "books and papers do not speak the truth." Why, then, do they not contradict what we say? They cannot. Moreover the South has entreated, nay commanded us to be silent; and what greater evidence of the truth of our publications could be desired?

Women of Philadelphia! allow me as a Southern woman with much attachment to the land of my birth, to entreat you to come up to this work. Especially let me urge you to petition. *Men* may settle this and other questions at the ballot box, but you have no such right; it is only through petition that you can reach the Legislature. It is therefore peculiarly *your* duty to petition. Do you say, "It does no good?" The South already turns pale at the number sent. They have read the reports of the proceedings of Congress, and there have seen

9. A Parisian prison, the storming of which marked the beginning of the French Revolution.

1. 1 Corinthians 26.31, meaning that everything is a part of God's plan.

2. From the poem "Our Countrymen in Chains" (1837) by abolitionist poet John Greenleaf Whittier (1807–1892).

that among other petitions were very many from the women of the North on the subject of slavery. This fact has called the attention of the South to the subject. How could we expect to have done more as yet? Men who hold the rod over slaves, rule in the councils of the nation: and they deny our right to petition and to remonstrate against abuses of our sex and of our kind. We have these rights, however, from our God. Only let us exercise them: and though often turned away unanswered, let us remember the influence of importunity upon the unjust judge, and act accordingly. The fact that the South look with jealousy upon our measures shows that they are effectual. There is, therefore, no cause for doubting or despair, but rather for rejoicing.

It was remarked in England that women did much to abolish Slavery in her colonies. Nor are they now idle. Numerous petitions from them have recently been presented to the Queen,[3] to abolish the apprenticeship with its cruelties nearly equal to those of the system whose place it supplies. One petition two miles and a quarter long has been presented. And do you think these labors will be in vain? Let the history of the past answer. When the women of these States send up to Congress such a petition, our legislators will arise as did those of England, and say, "When all the maids and matrons of the land are knocking at our doors we must legislate." Let the zeal and love, the faith and works of our English sisters quicken ours—that while the slaves continue to suffer, and when they shout deliverance, we may feel the satisfaction of *having done what we could.*

1837

Martin Luther King Jr.

1929–1968

In the early days of 1963, new orders from the federal courts were about to outlaw racial segregation in Alabama's schools and colleges. Local officials, including Commissioner of Public Safety Eugene "Bull" Connor and Governor George Wallace, publicly threatened to break these laws. On January 17, 1963, eleven

3. Queen Victoria (1819–1901), who ascended to the throne in 1837; slavery was abolished throughout the British Empire in 1833.

white clergymen criticized Connor and Wallace in a letter to the Birmingham News. *Connor's subsequent defeat in the mayoral election seemed to promise some lessening of the city's systematic oppression of Blacks, at least to moderate whites like these ministers. Nevertheless, on April 3, 1963, Black men and women, impatient for equality, opened a campaign to desegregate businesses in downtown Birmingham. For a week protestors openly defied segregation laws and, as a consequence, filled Bull Connor's jail cells beyond capacity. When the state courts of Alabama issued an injunction against such protests, King decided to defy the law and suffer the consequences. On Good Friday, he and about fifty other Blacks marched in the streets and were summarily arrested. Connor put King in solitary confinement and near-total darkness for three days, and only pressure from the U.S. attorney general, Robert Kennedy, softened the conditions of his imprisonment. (It would be eight days before bail money, raised by the singer Harry Belafonte, secured his release.) On the day King was arrested, eight of the eleven white clergymen—Catholic, Episcopal, Presbyterian, Baptist, Methodist, and Jewish—published a second letter in the* Birmingham News, *this one criticizing Dr. King. While ostensibly addressed to this group, King's response to their letter, composed on slips of paper sneaked into his cell by Black jailers, was really designed to address a national audience. A million copies of his "Letter from Birmingham Jail" were distributed in churches throughout the country, and published in various newspapers and magazines, including the* New York Post *and* Atlantic Monthly. *By inspiring weary, long-suffering Blacks and motivating sympathetic yet sluggish whites, this essay became, perhaps, the most influential document of the civil rights era.*

Letter from Birmingham Jail

My Dear Fellow Clergymen:

While confined here in the Birmingham city jail, I came across your recent statement calling my present activities "unwise and untimely." Seldom do I pause to answer criticism of my work and ideas. If I sought to answer all the criticisms that cross my desk, my secretaries would have little time for anything other than such correspondence in the course of the day, and I would have no time for constructive work. But since I feel that you are men of genuine good will and that your criticisms are sincerely set forth, I want to try to answer your statement in what I hope will be patient and reasonable terms.

I think I should indicate why I am here in Birmingham, since you have been influenced by the view which argues against "outsiders coming in." I have the honor of serving as president of the Southern Christian Leadership Conference, an organization operating in every southern state, with headquarters in Atlanta, Georgia. We have some eighty-five affiliated organizations across the South, and one of them is the Alabama Christian Movement for Human Rights. Frequently we share staff, educational, and financial resources with our affiliates. Several months ago the affiliate here in Birmingham asked us to be on call to engage in a nonviolent direct-action program if such were deemed necessary. We readily consented, and when the hour came we lived up to our promise. So I, along with several members of my staff, am here because I was invited here. I am here because I have organizational ties here.

But more basically, I am in Birmingham because injustice is here. Just as the prophets of the eighth century B.C. left their villages and carried their "thus saith the Lord" far beyond the boundaries of their home towns, and just as the Apostle Paul left his village of Tarsus and carried the gospel of Jesus Christ to the far corners of the Greco-Roman world, so am I compelled to carry the gospel of freedom beyond my own home town. Like Paul, I must constantly respond to the Macedonian call for aid.

Moreover, I am cognizant of the interrelatedness of all communities and states. I cannot sit idly by in Atlanta and not be concerned about what happens in Birmingham. Injustice anywhere is a threat to justice everywhere. We are caught in an inescapable network of mutuality, tied in a single garment of destiny. Whatever affects one directly, affects all indirectly. Never again can we afford to live with the narrow, provincial "outside agitator" idea. Anyone who lives inside the United States can never be considered an outsider anywhere within its bounds.

You deplore the demonstrations taking place in Birmingham. But your statement, I am sorry to say, fails to express a similar concern for the conditions that brought about the demonstrations. I am sure that none of you would want to rest content with the superficial kind of social analysis that deals merely with effects and does not grapple with underlying causes. It is unfortunate that demonstrations are taking place in Birmingham, but it is even more unfortunate that the city's white power structure left the Negro community with no alternative.

In any nonviolent campaign there are four basic steps: collection of the facts to determine whether injustices exist; negotiation; self-purification; and direct action. We have gone through all these steps in Birmingham. There can be no gainsaying the fact that racial injustice engulfs this community. Birmingham is probably the most thoroughly segregated city in the United States. Its ugly record of brutality is widely known. Negroes have experienced grossly unjust treatment in the courts. There have been more unsolved bombings of Negro homes and churches in Birmingham than in any other city in the nation. These are the hard, brutal facts of the case. On the basis of these conditions, Negro leaders sought to negotiate with the city fathers. But the latter consistently refused to engage in good-faith negotiation.

Then, last September, came the opportunity to talk with leaders of Birmingham's economic community. In the course of the negotiations, certain promises were made by the merchants—for example, to remove the stores' humiliating racial signs. On the basis of these promises, the Reverend Fred Shuttlesworth[1] and the leaders of the Alabama Christian Movement for Human Rights agreed to a moratorium on all demonstrations. As the weeks and months went by, we realized that we were the victims of a broken promise. A few signs, briefly removed, returned; the others remained.

As in so many past experiences, our hopes had been blasted, and the shadow of deep disappointment settled upon us. We had no alternative except to prepare for direct action, whereby we would present our very bodies as a means of laying our case before the conscience of the local and the national community. Mindful of the difficulties involved, we decided to undertake a process of self-purification. We began a series of workshops on nonviolence, and we repeatedly asked ourselves: "Are you able to accept blows without retaliating?" "Are you able to endure the ordeal of jail?" We decided to schedule our direct-action program

1. Frederick Lee Shuttlesworth (1922–2011), a Baptist minister in Birmingham. In 1957, he joined Martin Luther King Jr. in founding the civil rights group the Southern Christian Leadership Conference.

for the Easter season, realizing that except for Christmas, this is the main shopping period of the year. Knowing that a strong economic-withdrawal program would be the by-product of direct action, we felt that this would be the best time to bring pressure to bear on the merchants for the needed change.

Then it occurred to us that Birmingham's mayoral election was coming up in March, and we speedily decided to postpone action until after election day. When we discovered that the Commissioner of Public Safety, Eugene "Bull" Connor, had piled up enough votes to be in the run-off, we decided again to postpone action until the day after the run-off so that the demonstrations could not be used to cloud the issues. Like many others, we wanted to see Mr. Connor defeated, and to this end we endured postponement after postponement. Having aided in this community need, we felt that our direct-action program could be delayed no longer.

You may well ask, "Why direct action? Why sit-ins, marches, and so forth? Isn't negotiation a better path?" You are quite right in calling for negotiation. Indeed, this is the very purpose of direct action. Nonviolent direct action seeks to create such a crisis and foster such a tension that a community which has constantly refused to negotiate is forced to confront the issue. It seeks so to dramatize the issue that it can no longer be ignored. My citing the creation of tension as part of the work of the nonviolent-resister may sound rather shocking. But I must confess that I am not afraid of the word "tension." I have earnestly opposed violent tension, but there is a type of constructive, nonviolent tension which is necessary for growth. Just as Socrates felt that it was necessary to create a tension in the mind so that individuals could rise from the bondage of myths and half-truths to the unfettered realm of creative analysis and objective appraisal, so must we see the need for nonviolent gadflies to create the kind of tension in society that will help men rise from the dark depths of prejudice and racism to the majestic heights of understanding and brotherhood.

The purpose of our direct-action program is to create a situation so crisis-packed that it will inevitably open the door to negotiation. I therefore concur with you in your call for negotiation. Too long has our beloved Southland been bogged down in a tragic effort to live in monologue rather than dialogue.

One of the basic points in your statement is that the action that I and my associates have taken in Birmingham is untimely. Some have asked: "Why didn't you give the new city administration time to act?" The only answer that I can give to this query is that the new Birmingham administration must be prodded about as much as the outgoing one, before it will act. We are sadly mistaken if we feel that the election of Albert Boutwell as mayor will bring the millennium to Birmingham. While Mr. Boutwell is a much more gentle person than Mr. Connor, they are both segregationists, dedicated to maintenance of the status quo. I have hoped that Mr. Boutwell will be reasonable enough to see the futility of massive resistance to desegregation. But he will not see this without pressure from devotees of civil rights. My friends, I must say to you that we have not made a single gain in civil rights without determined legal and nonviolent pressure. Lamentably, it is an historical fact that privileged groups seldom give up their privileges voluntarily. Individuals may see the moral light and voluntarily give up their unjust posture; but, as Reinhold Niebuhr[2] has reminded us, groups tend to be more immoral than individuals.

We know through painful experience that freedom is never voluntarily given by the oppressor; it must be demanded by the oppressed. Frankly, I have yet to engage in a direct-action campaign that was "well timed" in the view of those who have not suffered unduly from the disease of segregation. For years now I have heard the word "Wait!" It rings in the ear of every Negro with piercing familiarity. This "Wait" has almost always meant "Never." We must come to see, with one of our distinguished jurists, that "justice too long delayed is justice denied."

We have waited for more than 340 years for our constitutional and God-given rights. The nations of Asia and Africa are moving with jet-like speed toward gaining political independence, but we still creep at horse-and-buggy pace toward gaining a cup of coffee at a lunch counter. Perhaps it is easy for those who have never felt the stinging darts of segregation to say, "Wait." But when you have seen vicious mobs lynch your mothers and fathers at will and drown your sisters and brothers at whim; when you have seen hate-filled policemen curse, kick, and even kill your black brothers and sisters; when you see the vast majority of your twenty million Negro brothers smothering in an airtight cage of poverty in the midst of an affluent society; when you suddenly

2. American Protestant theologian (1892–1971).

find your tongue twisted and your speech stammering as you seek to explain to your six-year-old daughter why she can't go to the public amusement park that has just been advertised on television, and see tears welling up in her eyes when she is told that Funtown is closed to colored children, and see ominous clouds of inferiority beginning to form in her little mental sky, and see her beginning to distort her personality by developing an unconscious bitterness toward white people; when you have to concoct an answer for a five-year-old son who is asking, "Daddy, why do white people treat colored people so mean?"; when you take a cross-country drive and find it necessary to sleep night after night in the uncomfortable corners of your automobile because no motel will accept you; when you are humiliated day in and day out by nagging signs reading "white" and "colored"; when your first name becomes "nigger," your middle name becomes "boy" (however old you are) and your last name becomes "John," and your wife and mother are never given the respected title "Mrs."; when you are harried by day and haunted by night by the fact that you are a Negro, living constantly at tiptoe stance, never quite knowing what to expect next, and are plagued with inner fears and outer resentments; when you are forever fighting a degenerating sense of "nobodiness"—then you will understand why we find it difficult to wait. There comes a time when the cup of endurance runs over, and men are no longer willing to be plunged into the abyss of despair. I hope, sirs, you can understand our legitimate and unavoidable impatience.

You express a great deal of anxiety over our willingness to break laws. This is certainly a legitimate concern. Since we so diligently urge people to obey the Supreme Court's decision of 1954 outlawing segregation in the public schools, at first glance it may seem rather paradoxical for us consciously to break laws.[3] One may well ask: "How can you advocate breaking some laws and obeying others?" The answer lies in the fact that there are two types of laws: just and unjust. I would be the first to advocate obeying just laws. One has not only a legal but a moral responsibility to obey just laws. Conversely, one has a moral responsibility to disobey unjust laws. I would agree with St. Augustine[4] that "an unjust law is no law at all."

3. *Brown v. Board of Education of Topeka*, which finally mandated the racial integration of public schools.

4. Early Christian theologian (354–430). The quotation comes from his *City of God.*

Now, what is the difference between the two? How does one determine whether a law is just or unjust? A just law is a man-made code that squares with the moral law or the law of God. An unjust law is a code that is out of harmony with the moral law. To put it in the terms of St. Thomas Aquinas:[5] An unjust law is a human law that is not rooted in eternal law and natural law. Any law that uplifts human personality is just. Any law that degrades human personality is unjust. All segregation statutes are unjust because segregation distorts the soul and damages the personality. It gives the segregator a false sense of superiority and the segregated a false sense of inferiority. Segregation, to use the terminology of the Jewish philosopher Martin Buber,[6] substitutes an "I-it" relationship for an "I-thou" relationship and ends up relegating persons to the status of things. Hence segregation is not only politically, economically, and sociologically unsound, it is morally wrong and sinful. Paul Tillich[7] has said that sin is separation. Is not segregation an existential expression of man's tragic separation, his awful estrangement, his terrible sinfulness? Thus it is that I can urge men to obey the 1954 decision of the Supreme Court, for it is morally right; and I can urge them to disobey segregation ordinances, for they are morally wrong.

Let us consider a more concrete example of just and unjust laws. An unjust law is a code that a numerical or power majority group compels a minority group to obey but does not make binding on itself. This is *difference* made legal. By the same token, a just law is a code that a majority compels a minority to follow and that it is willing to follow itself. This is *sameness* made legal.

Let me give another explanation. A law is unjust if it is inflicted on a minority that, as a result of being denied the right to vote, had no part in enacting or devising the law. Who can say that the legislature of Alabama which set up that state's segregation laws was democratically elected? Throughout Alabama all sorts of devious methods are used to prevent Negroes from becoming registered voters, and there are some counties in which, even though Negroes constitute a majority of the population, not a single Negro is registered. Can any law enacted under such circumstances be considered democratically structured?

5. Medieval Christian philosopher and theologian (1224–1274).

6. Austrian-born Israeli philosopher (1878–1965).

7. German-born American Protestant theologian (1886–1965). See his *History of Christian Thought* (1968).

Sometimes a law is just on its face and unjust in its application. For instance, I have been arrested on a charge of parading without a permit. Now, there is nothing wrong in having an ordinance which requires a permit for a parade. But such an ordinance becomes unjust when it is used to maintain segregation and to deny citizens the First-Amendment privilege of peaceful assembly and protest.

I hope you are able to see the distinction I am trying to point out. In no sense do I advocate evading or defying the law, as would the rabid segregationist. That would lead to anarchy. One who breaks an unjust law must do so openly, lovingly, and with a willingness to accept the penalty. I submit that an individual who breaks a law that conscience tells him is unjust, and who willingly accepts the penalty of imprisonment in order to arouse the conscience of the community over its injustice, is in reality expressing the highest respect for law.

Of course, there is nothing new about this kind of civil disobedience. It was evidenced sublimely in the refusal of Shadrach, Meshach, and Abednego to obey the laws of Nebuchadnezzar,[8] on the ground that a higher moral law was at stake. It was practiced superbly by the early Christians, who were willing to face hungry lions and the excruciating pain of chopping blocks rather than submit to certain unjust laws of the Roman Empire. To a degree, academic freedom is a reality today because Socrates[9] practiced civil disobedience. In our own nation, the Boston Tea Party represented a massive act of civil disobedience.

We should never forget that everything Adolf Hitler did in Germany was "legal" and everything the Hungarian freedom fighters[1] did in Hungary was "illegal." It was "illegal" to aid and comfort a Jew in Hitler's Germany. Even so, I am sure that, had I lived in Germany at the time, I would have aided and comforted my Jewish brothers. If today I lived in a Communist country where certain principles

8. See Daniel 3. Nebuchadnezzar, the king of Babylonia (c. 605–562 B.C.E.), commanded his people to worship a golden idol. When Shadrach, Meshach, and Abednego refused, they were thrown into a furnace but escaped unscathed. So Nebuchadnezzar forbade blasphemy against their god—Yahweh, the god of the Jews.

9. Ancient Greek philosopher who was tried for impiety and for corrupting Athenian youth through his skeptical, questioning teaching method; having refused to denounce his teachings, he was condemned to death and executed. See Plato's "Crito."

1. Anti-communists whose 1956 revolution was quickly put down by the Soviet army.

dear to the Christian faith are suppressed, I would openly advocate disobeying that country's anti-religious laws.

I must make two honest confessions to you, my Christian and Jewish brothers. First, I must confess that over the past few years I have been gravely disappointed with the white moderate. I have almost reached the regrettable conclusion that the Negro's great stumbling block in his stride toward freedom is not the White Citizen's Counciler[2] or the Ku Klux Klanner, but the white moderate, who is more devoted to "order" than to justice; who prefers a negative peace which is the absence of tension to a positive peace which is the presence of justice; who constantly says, "I agree with you in the goal you seek, but I cannot agree with your methods of direct action"; who paternalistically believes he can set the timetable for another man's freedom; who lives by a mythical concept of time and who constantly advises the Negro to wait for a "more convenient season."[3] Shallow understanding from people of good will is more frustrating than absolute misunderstanding from people of ill will. Lukewarm acceptance is much more bewildering than outright rejection.

I had hoped that the white moderate would understand that law and order exist for the purpose of establishing justice and that when they fail in this purpose they become the dangerously structured dams that block the flow of social progress. I had hoped that the white moderate would understand that the present tension in the South is a necessary phase of the transition from an obnoxious negative peace, in which the Negro passively accepted his unjust plight, to a substantive and positive peace, in which all men will respect the dignity and worth of human personality. Actually, we who engage in nonviolent direct action are not the creators of tension. We merely bring to the surface the hidden tension that is already alive. We bring it out in the open, where it can be seen and dealt with. Like a boil that can never be cured so long as it is covered up but must be opened with all its ugliness to the natural medicines of air and light, injustice must be exposed, with all the tension its exposure creates, to the light of human conscience and the air of national opinion, before it can be cured.

2. A group formed in Mississippi to maintain segregation after the Supreme Court's decision in *Brown v. Board of Education of Topeka, Kansas* (1954/55).

3. Acts 24.25.

In your statement you assert that our actions, even though peaceful, must be condemned because they precipitate violence. But is this a logical assertion? Isn't this like condemning a robbed man because his possession of money precipitated the evil act of robbery? Isn't this like condemning Socrates because his unswerving commitment to truth and his philosophical inquiries precipitated the act by the misguided populace in which they made him drink hemlock? Isn't this like condemning Jesus because his unique God-consciousness and never-ceasing devotion to God's will precipitated the evil act of crucifixion? We must come to see that, as the federal courts have consistently affirmed, it is wrong to urge an individual to cease his efforts to gain his basic constitutional rights because the quest may precipitate violence. Society must protect the robbed and punish the robber.

I had also hoped that the white moderate would reject the myth concerning time in relation to the struggle for freedom. I have just received a letter from a white brother in Texas. He writes: "All Christians know that the colored people will receive equal rights eventually, but it is possible that you are in too great a religious hurry. It has taken Christianity almost two thousand years to accomplish what it has. The teachings of Christ take time to come to earth." Such an attitude stems from a tragic misconception of time, from the strangely irrational notion that there is something in the very flow of time that will inevitably cure all ills. Actually, time itself is neutral; it can be used either destructively or constructively. More and more I feel that the people of ill will have used time much more effectively than have the people of good will. We will have to repent in this generation not merely for the hateful words and actions of the bad people, but for the appalling silence of the good people. Human progress never rolls in on wheels of inevitability; it comes through the tireless efforts of men willing to be co-workers with God, and without this hard work, time itself becomes an ally of the forces of social stagnation. We must use time creatively, in the knowledge that the time is always ripe to do right. Now is the time to make real the promise of democracy and transform our pending national elegy into a creative psalm of brotherhood. Now is the time to lift our national policy from the quicksand of racial injustice to the solid rock of human dignity.

You speak of our activity in Birmingham as extreme. At first I was rather disappointed that fellow clergymen would see my nonviolent efforts as those of an extremist. I began thinking about the fact that I stand in the middle of two opposing forces in the Negro community. One is a force of complacency, made up in part of Negroes who, as a result of long years of oppression, are so drained of self-respect and a sense of "somebodiness" that they have adjusted to segregation; and in part of a few middle-class Negroes who, because of a degree of academic and economic security and because in some ways they profit by segregation, have become insensitive to the problems of the masses. The other force is one of bitterness and hatred, and it comes perilously close to advocating violence. It is expressed in the various black nationalist groups that are springing up across the nation, the largest and best-known being Elijah Muhammad's[4] Muslim movement. Nourished by the Negro's frustration over the continued existence of racial discrimination, this movement is made up of people who have lost faith in America, who have absolutely repudiated Christianity, and who have concluded that the white man is an incorrigible "devil."

I have tried to stand between these two forces, saying that we need emulate neither the "do-nothingism" of the complacent nor the hatred and despair of the black nationalist. For there is the more excellent way of love and nonviolent protest. I am grateful to God that, through the influence of the Negro church, the way of nonviolence became an integral part of our struggle.

If this philosophy had not emerged, by now many streets of the South would, I am convinced, be flowing with blood. And I am further convinced that if our white brothers dismiss as "rabblerousers" and "outside agitators" those of us who employ nonviolent direct action, and if they refuse to support our nonviolent efforts, millions of Negroes will, out of frustration and despair, seek solace and security in black-nationalist ideologies—a development that would inevitably lead to a frightening racial nightmare.

Oppressed people cannot remain oppressed forever. The yearning for freedom eventually manifests itself, and that is what has happened to the American Negro. Something within has reminded him of his birthright of freedom, and something without has reminded him that it can be gained. Consciously or unconsciously, he has been caught

4. Leader of the Nation of Islam (1897–1975).

up by the *Zeitgeist*,[5] and with his black brothers of Africa and his brown and yellow brothers of Asia, South America, and the Caribbean, the United States Negro is moving with a sense of great urgency toward the promised land of racial justice. If one recognizes this vital urge that has engulfed the Negro community, one should readily understand why public demonstrations are taking place. The Negro has many pent-up resentments and latent frustrations, and he must release them. So let him march; let him make prayer pilgrimages to the city hall; let him go on freedom rides—and try to understand why he must do so. If his repressed emotions are not released in nonviolent ways, they will seek expression through violence; this is not a threat but a fact of history. So I have not said to my people, "Get rid of your discontent." Rather, I have tried to say that this normal and healthy discontent can be channeled into the creative outlet of nonviolent direct action. And now this approach is being termed extremist.

But though I was initially disappointed at being categorized as an extremist, as I continued to think about the matter I gradually gained a measure of satisfaction from the label. Was not Jesus an extremist for love: "Love your enemies, bless them that curse you, do good to them that hate you, and pray for them which despitefully use you, and persecute you."[6] Was not Amos an extremist for justice: "Let justice roll down like waters and righteousness like an ever-flowing stream."[7] Was not Paul an extremist for the Christian gospel: "I bear in my body the marks of the Lord Jesus."[8] Was not Martin Luther[9] an extremist: "Here I stand; I cannot do otherwise, so help me God." And John Bunyan:[1] "I will stay in jail to the end of my days before I make a butchery of my conscience." And Abraham Lincoln: "This nation cannot survive half slave and half free."[2] And Thomas Jefferson: "We hold these truths to be self-evident, that all men are created equal. . . ." So the question is not

5. The spirit of the times (German).

6. Matthew 5.44.

7. Amos 5.24. Amos was an Old Testament prophet.

8. Galatians 6.17. Paul, a great missionary of the early Christian church, often suffered for his teaching. He wrote some of his own biblical letters from prison.

9. German theologian and leader of the Reformation (1483–1546). The quote is from his defense of his teaching at the Trial of Worms, 1521.

1. English preacher (1628–1688) and author of *Pilgrim's Progress* (1678). The quote is a paraphrase of a passage in his *Confession of My Faith, and a Reason of My Practice.*

2. From a speech given June 16, 1858; the quotation is slightly inaccurate.

whether we will be extremists, but what kind of extremists we will be. Will we be extremists for hate or for love? Will we be extremists for the preservation of injustice or for the extension of justice? In that dramatic scene on Calvary's hill three men were crucified. We must never forget that all three were crucified for the same crime—the crime of extremism. Two were extremists for immorality, and thus fell below their environment. The other, Jesus Christ, was an extremist for love, truth, and goodness, and thereby rose above his environment. Perhaps the South, the nation, and the world are in dire need of creative extremists.

I had hoped that the white moderate would see this need. Perhaps I was too optimistic; perhaps I expected too much. I suppose I should have realized that few members of the oppressor race can understand the deep groans and passionate yearnings of the oppressed race, and still fewer have the vision to see that injustice must be rooted out by strong, persistent, and determined action. I am thankful, however, that some of our white brothers in the South have grasped the meaning of this social revolution and committed themselves to it. They are still all too few in quantity, but they are big in quality. Some—such as Ralph McGill, Lillian Smith, Harry Golden, James McBride Dabbs, Ann Braden, and Sarah Patton Boyle—have written about our struggle in eloquent and prophetic terms.[3] Others have marched with us down nameless streets of the South. They have languished in filthy, roach-infested jails, suffering the abuse and brutality of policemen who view them as "dirty-nigger-lovers." Unlike so many of their moderate brothers and sisters, they have recognized the urgency of the moment and sensed the need for powerful "action" antidotes to combat the disease of segregation.

Let me take note of my other major disappointment. I have been so greatly disappointed with the white church and its leadership. Of course, there are some notable exceptions. I am not unmindful of the fact that each of you has taken some significant stands on this issue.

3. Ralph McGill (1898–1969), editor of the newspaper *Atlanta Constitution*; Lillian Smith (1897–1966), liberal Southern writer best known for her 1944 anti–Jim Crow novel, *Strange Fruit*; Harry Golden (1902–1981), liberal writer for the newspaper the *Charlotte Observer*; James McBride Dabbs (1896–1970), anti-segregationist writer, professor, and Presbyterian churchman from South Carolina; Ann Braden (1924–2006), southern writer whose 1958 book *The Wall Between* dissected the psychology of white supremacy; Sarah Patton Boyle (1906–1994), author of the 1962 book *The Desegregated Heart: A Virginian's Stand in Time of Transition*.

I commend you, Reverend Stallings,[4] for your Christian stand on this past Sunday, in welcoming Negroes to your worship service on a nonsegregated basis. I commend the Catholic leaders of this state for integrating Spring Hill College several years ago.

But despite these notable exceptions, I must honestly reiterate that I have been disappointed with the church. I do not say this as one of those negative critics who can always find something wrong with the church. I say this as a minister of the gospel, who loves the church; who was nurtured in its bosom; who has been sustained by its spiritual blessings and who will remain true to it as long as the cord of life shall lengthen.

When I was suddenly catapulted into the leadership of the bus protest in Montgomery, Alabama, a few years ago,[5] I felt we would be supported by the white church. I felt that the white ministers, priests, and rabbis of the South would be among our strongest allies. Instead, some have been outright opponents, refusing to understand the freedom movement and misrepresenting its leaders; all too many others have been more cautious than courageous and have remained silent behind the anesthetizing security of stained-glass windows.

In spite of my shattered dreams, I came to Birmingham with the hope that the white religious leadership of this community would see the justice of our cause and, with deep moral concern, would serve as the channel through which our just grievances could reach the power structure. I had hoped that each of you would understand. But again I have been disappointed.

I have heard numerous southern religious leaders admonish their worshipers to comply with a desegregation decision because it is the law, but I have longed to hear white ministers declare: "Follow this decree because integration is morally right and because the Negro is your brother." In the midst of blatant injustices inflicted upon the Negro, I have watched white churchmen stand on the sideline and mouth pious irrelevancies and sanctimonious trivialities. In the midst of a mighty struggle to rid our nation of racial and economic injustice, I have heard many ministers say: "Those are social issues, with

4. One of the eight clergymen who criticized King's actions in their letter to the *Birmingham News.*

5. Inspired by the refusal of Rosa Parks (1913–2005) to move to the back of a bus in December 1955.

which the gospel has no real concern." And I have watched many churches commit themselves to a completely otherworldly religion which makes a strange, un-Biblical distinction between body and soul, between the sacred and the secular.

I have traveled the length and breadth of Alabama, Mississippi, and all the other southern states. On sweltering summer days and crisp autumn mornings I have looked at the South's beautiful churches with their lofty spires pointing heavenward. I have beheld the impressive outlines of her massive religious-education buildings. Over and over I have found myself asking: "What kind of people worship here? Who is their God? Where were their voices when the lips of Governor Barnett[6] dripped with words of interposition and nullification? Where were they when Governor Wallace gave a clarion call for defiance and hatred? Where were their voices of support when bruised and weary Negro men and women decided to rise from the dark dungeons of complacency to the bright hills of creative protest?"

Yes, these questions are still in my mind. In deep disappointment I have wept over the laxity of the church. But be assured that my tears have been tears of love. There can be no deep disappointment where there is not deep love. Yes, I love the church. How could I do otherwise? I am in the rather unique position of being the son, the grandson, and the great-grandson of preachers. Yes, I see the church as the body of Christ. But, oh! How we have blemished and scarred that body through social neglect and through fear of being nonconformists.

There was a time when the church was very powerful—in the time when the early Christians rejoiced at being deemed worthy to suffer for what they believed. In those days the church was not merely a thermometer that recorded the ideas and principles of popular opinion; it was a thermostat that transformed the mores of society. Whenever the early Christians entered a town, the people in power became disturbed and immediately sought to convict the Christians for being "disturbers of the peace" and "outside agitators." But the Christians pressed on, in the conviction that they were "a colony of heaven,"[7] called to obey God rather than man. Small in number, they were big

6. Ross Barnett (1898–1988), governor of Mississippi who opposed the integration of the University of Mississippi.

7. Philippians 3.20.

in commitment. They were too God-intoxicated to be "astronomically intimidated." By their effort and example they brought an end to such ancient evils as infanticide and gladiatorial contests.

Things are different now. So often the contemporary church is a weak, ineffectual voice with an uncertain sound. So often it is an archdefender of the status quo. Far from being disturbed by the presence of the church, the power structure of the average community is consoled by the church's silent—and often even vocal—sanction of things as they are.

But the judgment of God is upon the church as never before. If today's church does not recapture the sacrificial spirit of the early church, it will lose its authenticity, forfeit the loyalty of millions, and be dismissed as an irrelevant social club with no meaning for the twentieth century. Every day I meet young people whose disappointment with the church has turned into outright disgust.

Perhaps I have once again been too optimistic. Is organized religion too inextricably bound to the status quo to save our nation and the world? Perhaps I must turn my faith to the inner spiritual church, the church within the church, as the true *ekklesia*[8] and the hope of the world. But again I am thankful to God that some noble souls from the ranks of organized religion have broken loose from the paralyzing chains of conformity and joined us as active partners in the struggle for freedom. They have left their secure congregations and walked the streets of Albany, Georgia, with us. They have gone down the highways of the South on tortuous rides for freedom. Yes, they have gone to jail with us. Some have been dismissed from their churches, have lost the support of their bishops and fellow ministers. But they have acted in the faith that right defeated is stronger than evil triumphant. Their witness has been the spiritual salt that has preserved the true meaning of the gospel in these troubled times. They have carved a tunnel of hope through the dark mountain of disappointment.

I hope the church as a whole will meet the challenge of this decisive hour. But even if the church does not come to the aid of justice, I have no despair about the future. I have no fear about the outcome of our struggle in Birmingham, even if our motives are at present misunderstood. We will reach the goal of freedom in Birmingham and all

8. Greek word for the early Christian church.

over the nation, because the goal of America is freedom. Abused and scorned though we may be, our destiny is tied up with America's destiny. Before the pilgrims landed at Plymouth, we were here. Before the pen of Jefferson etched the majestic words of the Declaration of Independence across the pages of history, we were here. For more than two centuries our forebears labored in this country without wages; they made cotton king; they built the homes of their masters while suffering gross injustice and shameful humiliation—and yet out of a bottomless vitality they continued to thrive and develop. If the inexpressible cruelties of slavery could not stop us, the opposition we now face will surely fail. We will win our freedom because the sacred heritage of our nation and the eternal will of God are embodied in our echoing demands.

Before closing I feel impelled to mention one other point in your statement that has troubled me profoundly. You warmly commended the Birmingham police force for keeping "order" and "preventing violence." I doubt that you would have so warmly commended the police force if you had seen its dogs sinking their teeth into unarmed, nonviolent Negroes. I doubt that you would so quickly commend the policemen if you were to observe their ugly and inhumane treatment of Negroes here in the city jail; if you were to watch them push and curse old Negro women and young Negro girls; if you were to see them slap and kick old Negro men and young boys; if you were to observe them, as they did on two occasions, refuse to give us food because we wanted to sing our grace together. I cannot join you in your praise of the Birmingham police department.

It is true that the police have exercised a degree of discipline in handling the demonstrators. In this sense they have conducted themselves rather "nonviolently" in public. But for what purpose? To preserve the evil system of segregation. Over the past few years I have consistently preached that nonviolence demands that the means we use must be as pure as the ends we seek. I have tried to make clear that it is wrong to use immoral means to attain moral ends. But now I must affirm that it is just as wrong, or perhaps even more so, to use moral means to preserve immoral ends. Perhaps Mr. Connor and his policemen have been rather nonviolent in public, as was Chief Pritchett[9] in Albany, Georgia, but they have used the moral means of

9. Chief of police who, in an effort to prevent violence, prosecuted anyone who violated segregation laws; he was a hero to those who valued peace over social justice.

nonviolence to maintain the immoral end of racial injustice. As T. S. Eliot[1] has said, "The last temptation is the greatest treason: To do the right deed for the wrong reason."

I wish you had commended the Negro sit-inners and demonstrators of Birmingham for their sublime courage, their willingness to suffer, and their amazing discipline in the midst of great provocation. One day the South will recognize its real heroes. They will be the James Merediths,[2] with the noble sense of purpose that enables them to face jeering and hostile mobs, and with the agonizing loneliness that characterizes the life of the pioneer. They will be old, oppressed, battered Negro women, symbolized in a seventy-two-year-old woman in Montgomery, Alabama, who rose up with a sense of dignity and with her people decided not to ride segregated buses, and who responded with ungrammatical profundity to one who inquired about her weariness: "My feets is tired, but my soul is at rest."[3] They will be the young high school and college students, the young ministers of the gospel and a host of their elders, courageously and nonviolently sitting in at lunch counters and willingly going to jail for conscience's sake. One day the South will know that when these disinherited children of God sat down at lunch counters, they were in reality standing up for what is best in the American dream and for the most sacred values in our Judaeo-Christian heritage, thereby bringing our nation back to those great wells of democracy which were dug deep by the founding fathers in their formulation of the Constitution and the Declaration of Independence.

Never before have I written so long a letter. I'm afraid it is much too long to take your precious time. I can assure you that it would have been much shorter if I had been writing from a comfortable desk, but what else can one do when he is alone in a narrow jail cell, other than write long letters, think long thoughts, and pray long prayers?

If I have said anything in this letter that overstates the truth and indicates an unreasonable impatience, I beg you to forgive me. If I have said anything that understates the truth and indicates my having a patience that allows me to settle for anything less than brotherhood, I beg God to forgive me.

1. American-born Modernist poet (1888–1965). The quotation is from his *Murder in the Cathedral* (1935).

2. Meredith was the first Black student to enroll at the University of Mississippi.

3. Mother Pollard, an elderly supporter of King.

I hope this letter finds you strong in the faith. I also hope that circumstances will soon make it possible for me to meet each of you, not as an integrationist or a civil-rights leader but as a fellow clergyman and a Christian brother. Let us all hope that the dark clouds of racial prejudice will soon pass away and the deep fog of misunderstanding will be lifted from our fear-drenched communities, and in some not too distant tomorrow the radiant stars of love and brotherhood will shine over our great nation with all their scintillating beauty.

Yours for the cause of Peace and Brotherhood,
Martin Luther King, Jr.

1963

Chief Seattle

c. 1790–1866

This work has a curious history. Although it and similar versions are attributed to Chief Seattle (as here), he didn't actually write it. When Isaac Stevens, commissioner of Indian Affairs for the Washington Territory, offered a treaty to various tribes of the Northwest in 1854, Seattle did, indeed, rise and deliver a powerful speech, which was translated into English by another Native American. But it was Henry Smith, a witness to the event, who took notes and, thirty-three years later, in 1887, used them to reconstruct the speech for his column, a series of ten "Early Reminiscences," published in the Seattle Sunday Star. *And that was only the beginning. In 1969, William Arrowsmith, a professor of classics at the University of Texas, "translated" Smith's account from its Victorian idiom into contemporary English. Based on Arrowsmith's translation, Ted Perry wrote a script for a television special that aired on ABC in 1972. Modifications of Perry's script found their way into various popular venues, from Joseph Campbell's television series* The Power of Myth, *to children's books, political pamphlets, and even monuments and essay anthologies—all purporting to be the authentic words of Chief Seattle. These modern versions are only vaguely similar to Smith's 1887 account, which itself is highly suspect. In fact, the speech no longer has anything to do with relations between whites and Native Americans. And in some places the modern versions say the opposite of what appeared in Smith's account, and so they represent neither the words nor the sentiments of Chief Seattle. Instead, they express the sentiments of environmentalists in the 1970s, who romanticized and stereotyped Native Americans in their fight against pollution. You should think of the speech's audience, then, as citizens of industrialized nations in the 1970s (European environmentalists distributed the letter widely, especially in Germany) and its authors as white Americans from the same era. The version here comes from the first edition of a 1978 anthology of Native American speeches and writing; it was dropped from the 1991 edition of the anthology, presumably because the editors discovered its inauthenticity. I include the "Letter to President Pierce" here to provide an interesting example of ethical arguments, the effectiveness of which depends, obviously, on the reader's mistaken belief that these are Chief Seattle's words.*

Letter to President Pierce

We know that the white man does not understand our ways. One portion of the land is the same to him as the next, for he is a stranger who comes in the night and takes from the land whatever he needs. The earth is not his brother, but his enemy, and when he has conquered it, he moves on. He leaves his fathers' graves, and his children's birthright is forgotten. The sight of your cities pains the eyes of the red man. But perhaps it is because the red man is a savage and does not understand.

There is no quiet place in the white man's cities. No place to hear the leaves of spring or the rustle of insect's wings. But perhaps because I am a savage and do not understand, the clatter only seems to insult the ears. The Indian prefers the soft sound of the wind darting over the face of the pond, the smell of the wind itself cleansed by a mid-day rain, or scented with the piñon pine. The air is precious to the red man. For all things share the same breath—the beasts, the trees, the man. Like a man dying for many days, he is numb to the stench.

What is man without the beasts? If all the beasts were gone, men would die from great loneliness of spirit, for whatever happens to the beasts also happens to man. All things are connected. Whatever befalls the earth befalls the sons of the earth.

It matters little where we pass the rest of our days; they are not many. A few more hours, a few more winters, and none of the children of the great tribes that once lived on this earth, or that roamed in small bands in the woods, will be left to mourn the graves of a people once as powerful and hopeful as yours.

The whites, too, shall pass—perhaps sooner than other tribes. Continue to contaminate your bed, and you will one night suffocate in your own waste. When the buffalo are all slaughtered, the wild horses all tamed, the secret corners of the forest heavy with the scent of many men, and the view of the ripe hills blotted by talking wires,[1] where is the thicket? Gone. Where is the eagle? Gone. And what is it to say goodbye to the swift and the hunt, the end of living and the beginning of survival? We might understand if we knew what it was that the white man dreams, what he describes to his children on the long winter nights, what visions he burns into their minds, so they will wish for tomorrow. But we are savages. The white man's dreams are hidden from us.

c. 1972

Hillary Rodham Clinton
b. 1947

The United Nations' first World Conference on Women was held in 1975 in Mexico City, a convention repeated in 1980 in Copenhagen and again in 1985 in Nairobi. The Fourth World Conference on Women met ten years later in Beijing, China, and is widely regarded as a turning point in the advancement of women's rights around the world. In particular, it produced a "Platform of Action" that would achieve the goals and principles of women's social, economic, and political empowerment articulated since the beginning of the United Nations in 1946. This speech, delivered when Clinton was the First Lady of the United States, was the "galvanizing moment of the conference," according to the president of the American Bar Association. With the recent collapse of the

1. Telegraph wires.

Soviet Union, the United States was then the unrivaled leader in world affairs, and Clinton's appearance lent credibility, prestige, and urgency to the proceedings. It was particularly noteworthy that her remarks were made in China, which she identified as a violator of women's rights. The New York Times *reported that the speech was "a devastating litany of abuse that has afflicted women around the world today," and it was widely praised for its forthright revelation of crimes against women and the toleration of such crimes by many societies. The speech itself had an empowering effect and is credited with emboldening women in many nations to speak openly about their experiences.*

Speech to the Fourth World Conference on Women

Thank you very much, Gertrude Mongella,[1] for your dedicated work that has brought us to this point, distinguished delegates, and guests:

I would like to thank the Secretary General for inviting me to be part of this important United Nations Fourth World Conference on Women. This is truly a celebration, a celebration of the contributions women make in every aspect of life: in the home, on the job, in the community, as mothers, wives, sisters, daughters, learners, workers, citizens, and leaders.

It is also a coming together, much the way women come together every day in every country. We come together in fields and factories, in village markets and supermarkets, in living rooms and board rooms. Whether it is while playing with our children in the park, or washing clothes in a river, or taking a break at the office water cooler, we come together and talk about our aspirations and concerns. And time and again, our talk turns to our children and our families. However different we may appear, there is far more that unites us than divides us. We share a common future, and we are here to find common ground so that we may help bring new dignity

1. Gertrude Mongella (b. 1945), Tanzanian stateswoman; she was an Assistant Secretary General to the United Nations and the Secretary General of the Fourth World Conference on Women when Clinton delivered this speech.

and respect to women and girls all over the world, and in so doing bring new strength and stability to families as well.

By gathering in Beijing, we are focusing world attention on issues that matter most in our lives—the lives of women and their families: access to education, health care, jobs and credit, the chance to enjoy basic legal and human rights and to participate fully in the political life of our countries.

There are some who question the reason for this conference. Let them listen to the voices of women in their homes, neighborhoods, and workplaces. There are some who wonder whether the lives of women and girls matter to economic and political progress around the globe. Let them look at the women gathered here and at Huairou—the homemakers and nurses, the teachers and lawyers, the policymakers and women who run their own businesses.[2] It is conferences like this that compel governments and peoples everywhere to listen, look, and face the world's most pressing problems. Wasn't it after all—after the women's conference in Nairobi ten years ago that the world focused for the first time on the crisis of domestic violence?[3]

Earlier today, I participated in a World Health Organization forum. In that forum, we talked about ways that government officials, NGOs[4], and individual citizens are working to address the health problems of women and girls. Tomorrow, I will attend a gathering of the United Nations Development Fund for Women. There, the discussion will focus on local—and highly successful—programs that give hard-working women access to credit so they can improve their own lives and the lives of their families.

What we are learning around the world is that if women are healthy and educated, their families will flourish. If women are free from violence, their families will flourish. If women have a chance to work

2. Several grassroots, nongovernmental organizations concerned with the issues facing ordinary women around the globe were excluded from the main proceedings of the conference in Beijing. They met in tents in Huairou, a suburb of the Chinese capital, and together formed the Huairou Commission, which assures that women's perspective will be represented in several United Nations initiatives.

3. The Third World Conference on Women met in Nairobi, Kenya, in 1985.

4. Nongovernmental organizations; according to the United Nations, an NGO "is a not-for-profit group, principally independent from government, which is organized on a local, national or international level to address issues in support of the public good."

and earn as full and equal partners in society, their families will flourish. And when families flourish, communities and nations do as well. That is why every woman, every man, every child, every family, and every nation on this planet does have a stake in the discussion that takes place here.

Over the past 25 years, I have worked persistently on issues relating to women, children, and families. Over the past two and a half years, I've had the opportunity to learn more about the challenges facing women in my own country and around the world.

I have met new mothers in Indonesia, who come together regularly in their village to discuss nutrition, family planning, and baby care. I have met working parents in Denmark who talk about the comfort they feel in knowing that their children can be cared for in creative, safe, and nurturing after-school centers. I have met women in South Africa who helped lead the struggle to end apartheid and are now helping to build a new democracy.[5] I have met with the leading women of my own hemisphere who are working every day to promote literacy and better health care for children in their countries. I have met women in India and Bangladesh who are taking out small loans to buy milk cows, or rickshaws, or thread in order to create a livelihood for themselves and their families. I have met the doctors and nurses in Belarus and Ukraine who are trying to keep children alive in the aftermath of Chernobyl.[6]

The great challenge of this conference is to give voice to women everywhere whose experiences go unnoticed, whose words go unheard. Women comprise more than half the world's population, 70 percent of the world's poor, and two-thirds of those who are not taught to read and write. We are the primary caretakers for most of the world's children and elderly. Yet much of the work we do is not valued—not by economists, not by historians, not by popular culture, not by government leaders.

At this very moment, as we sit here, women around the world are giving birth, raising children, cooking meals, washing clothes, cleaning

5. The white-supremacist government of South Africa, a legacy of Dutch and British colonization, ended in 1994.

6. The worst nuclear power plant disaster in history was a meltdown in 1986 at Chernobyl, a Ukrainian city then part of the Soviet Union. Fatality estimates run as high as 20,000.

houses, planting crops, working on assembly lines, running companies, and running countries. Women also are dying from diseases that should have been prevented or treated. They are watching their children succumb to malnutrition caused by poverty and economic deprivation. They are being denied the right to go to school by their own fathers and brothers. They are being forced into prostitution, and they are being barred from the bank lending offices and banned from the ballot box.

Those of us who have the opportunity to be here have the responsibility to speak for those who could not. As an American, I want to speak for those women in my own country, women who are raising children on the minimum wage, women who can't afford health care or child care, women whose lives are threatened by violence, including violence in their own homes.

I want to speak up for mothers who are fighting for good schools, safe neighborhoods, clean air, and clean airwaves; for older women, some of them widows, who find that, after raising their families, their skills and life experiences are not valued in the marketplace; for women who are working all night as nurses, hotel clerks, or fast food chefs so that they can be at home during the day with their children; and for women everywhere who simply don't have time to do everything they are called upon to do each and every day.

Speaking to you today, I speak for them, just as each of us speaks for women around the world who are denied the chance to go to school, or see a doctor, or own property, or have a say about the direction of their lives, simply because they are women. The truth is that most women around the world work both inside and outside the home, usually by necessity.

We need to understand there is no one formula for how women should lead our lives. That is why we must respect the choices that each woman makes for herself and her family. Every woman deserves the chance to realize her own God-given potential. But we must recognize that women will never gain full dignity until their human rights are respected and protected.

Our goals for this conference, to strengthen families and societies by empowering women to take greater control over their own destinies, cannot be fully achieved unless all governments—here and around the world—accept their responsibility to protect and promote internationally recognized human rights. The international community has long acknowledged and recently reaffirmed at Vienna that both women and men are entitled to a range of protections and personal freedoms, from the right of personal security to the right to determine freely the number and spacing of the children they bear. No one—No one should be forced to remain silent for fear of religious or political persecution, arrest, abuse, or torture.

Tragically, women are most often the ones whose human rights are violated. Even now, in the late 20th century, the rape of women continues to be used as an instrument of armed conflict. Women and children make up a large majority of the world's refugees. And when women are excluded from the political process, they become even more vulnerable to abuse. I believe that now, on the eve of a new millennium, it is time to break the silence. It is time for us to say here in Beijing, and for the world to hear, that it is no longer acceptable to discuss women's rights as separate from human rights.

These abuses have continued because, for too long, the history of women has been a history of silence. Even today, there are those who are trying to silence our words. But the voices of this conference and of the women at Huairou must be heard loudly and clearly:

> It is a violation of human rights when babies are denied food, or drowned, or suffocated, or their spines broken, simply because they are born girls.
>
> It is a violation of human rights when women and girls are sold into the slavery of prostitution for human greed—and the kinds of reasons that are used to justify this practice should no longer be tolerated.
>
> It is a violation of human rights when women are doused with gasoline, set on fire, and burned to death because their marriage dowries are deemed too small.
>
> It is a violation of human rights when individual women are raped in their own communities and when thousands of women are subjected to rape as a tactic or prize of war.
>
> It is a violation of human rights when a leading cause of death worldwide among women ages 14 to 44 is the violence they are subjected to in their own homes by their own relatives.

> It is a violation of human rights when young girls are brutalized by the painful and degrading practice of genital mutilation.
>
> It is a violation of human rights when women are denied the right to plan their own families, and that includes being forced to have abortions or being sterilized against their will.

If there is one message that echoes forth from this conference, let it be that human rights are women's rights and women's rights are human rights once and for all. Let us not forget that among those rights are the right to speak freely—and the right to be heard.

Women must enjoy the rights to participate fully in the social and political lives of their countries, if we want freedom and democracy to thrive and endure. It is indefensible that many women in nongovernmental organizations who wished to participate in this conference have not been able to attend—or have been prohibited from fully taking part.

Let me be clear. Freedom means the right of people to assemble, organize, and debate openly. It means respecting the views of those who may disagree with the views of their governments. It means not taking citizens away from their loved ones and jailing them, mistreating them, or denying them their freedom or dignity because of the peaceful expression of their ideas and opinions.

In my country, we recently celebrated the 75th anniversary of women's suffrage.[7] It took 150 years after the signing of our Declaration of Independence for women to win the right to vote. It took 72 years of organized struggle, before that happened, on the part of many courageous women and men. It was one of America's most divisive philosophical wars. But it was a bloodless war. Suffrage was achieved without a shot being fired.

But we have also been reminded, in V-J Day observances last weekend, of the good that comes when men and women join together to combat the forces of tyranny and to build a better world. We have seen peace prevail in most places for a half century. We have avoided another world war. But we have not solved older, deeply rooted problems that continue to diminish the potential of half the world's population.

7. The Nineteenth Amendment to the U.S. Constitution, which asserted women's right to vote, was ratified in 1919.

Now it is the time to act on behalf of women everywhere. If we take bold steps to better the lives of women, we will be taking bold steps to better the lives of children and families too. Families rely on mothers and wives for emotional support and care. Families rely on women for labor in the home. And increasingly, everywhere, families rely on women for income needed to raise healthy children and care for other relatives.

As long as discrimination and inequities remain so commonplace everywhere in the world, as long as girls and women are valued less, fed less, fed last, overworked, underpaid, not schooled, subjected to violence in and outside their homes—the potential of the human family to create a peaceful, prosperous world will not be realized.

Let this conference be our—and the world's—call to action. Let us heed that call so we can create a world in which every woman is treated with respect and dignity, every boy and girl is loved and cared for equally, and every family has the hope of a strong and stable future. That is the work before you. That is the work before all of us who have a vision of the world we want to see—for our children and our grandchildren.

The time is now. We must move beyond rhetoric. We must move beyond recognition of problems to working together, to have the common efforts to build that common ground we hope to see.

God's blessing on you, your work, and all who will benefit from it. Godspeed and thank you very much.

1995

Barbara Ehrenreich

b. 1941

Reforming public welfare was one of the highest priorities of the Republican Party when it became the majority in both houses of Congress in 1994 for the first time in forty-five years. It criticized what it called a bloated social safety net for encouraging the poor to avoid work, and the moral character of poor Americans became the heart of the public debate about welfare. People on welfare were often described as more content to play the system and maximize government handouts than to work for a living, and many pathetic, racially charged arguments paraded the image of an urban, African American "welfare queen" living her life of comfort on the backs of hardworking white taxpayers.

Reform wasn't championed just by Republicans. Though he rejected the rhetorical trope of the welfare queen, Democratic president Bill Clinton thought the system trapped people in a "cycle of dependency" that "exil[ed] them from the world of work." Clinton vetoed the first two reform bills that Congress passed because he felt they eliminated important protections, but he and the Republicans negotiated and passed into law the third bill, which became the Personal Responsibility and Work Opportunity Reconciliation Act of 1996. In the coming years, millions of Americans moved off of welfare and into the low-wage work force, where the federally mandated minimum wage was $5.15 per hour.

In the spring of 1998, Barbara Ehrenreich, a writer for Harper's Magazine, *set out to discover whether someone could actually make a living in the low-wage sector of the American economy. As she says near the end of this essay, the working poor are generally invisible not only to her readers, the "newspaper-reading professional middle class," but to herself as well. Ehrenreich decided to find out for herself what their life was like, whether or not those portraits of people refusing to shoulder "personal responsibility" were accurate. So Ehrenreich abandoned her comfortable upper-middle-class life in Key West, closed the door on her comfortable house, took a job as a waitress, and moved into an efficiency apartment. For more than a year she lived the life of the low-wage American worker, and she took notes.*

The notes became an article in Harper's *and then a full-length book,* Nickel and Dimed: On (Not) Getting By in America. *Essentially, Ehrenreich was gathering anecdotal evidence in an inductive argument proving that, in the United States, it's nearly impossible to make a living in a menial job. Ehrenreich felt that waiting tables in the Florida Keys would not be very representative, so she took five other jobs in two other states—Maine and Minnesota—to widen her experience. The essay below is the conclusion to the book, which sums up her findings. Ehrenreich presents her anecdotes in an engaging way, and she uses those particular experiences to illustrate statistical data from several scientific studies of poverty, the economy, etc. Pay careful attention to these mixes of anecdote and scholarly research, because they are excellent models for how to construct strong inductive arguments. Note also how the conclusions of several of these inductive arguments in turn provide premises in deductive arguments. For instance, a major premise of many arguments about economic policy assumes that, in a free market, supply and demand ought to determine cost. That seems to be true when it comes to the price of housing: a scarce supply in the late 1990s drove up rents. But Ehrenreich's experience and the data she found through research show that this fundamental economic "law" does not seem to apply to wages. In 1998, the nation was near full-employment, but the scarcity of labor did not lead to a commensurate increase in workers' pay. Based on her experience in various workplaces, Ehrenreich walks us through several reasons the labor market might not be as "free" as the housing market.*

"Evaluation" from *Nickel and Dimed*

How did I do as a low-wage worker? If I may begin with a brief round of applause: I didn't do half bad at the work itself, and I claim this as a considerable achievement. You might think that unskilled jobs would be a snap for someone who holds a PhD and whose normal line of work requires learning entirely new things every couple of weeks. Not so. The first thing I discovered is that no job, no matter how lowly, is truly "unskilled." Every one of the six jobs I entered into in the course of this project required concentration, and most demanded that I master new terms, new tools, and new skills—from placing orders on restaurant computers to wielding the backpack vacuum cleaner. None of these things came as easily to me as I would have liked; no one ever said, "Wow, you're fast!" or "Can you believe she just started?" Whatever my accomplishments in the rest of my life, in the low-wage work world I was a person of average ability—capable of learning the job and also capable of screwing up.

* * *

. . . So all in all, with some demerits for screwups and gold stars for effort, I think it's fair to say that as a worker, a jobholder, I deserve a B or maybe B+.

But the real question is not how well I did at work but how well I did at life in general, which includes eating and having a place to stay. The fact that these are two separate questions needs to be underscored right away. In the rhetorical buildup to welfare reform, it was uniformly assumed that a job was the ticket out of poverty and that the only thing holding back welfare recipients was their reluctance to get out and get one. I got one and sometimes more than one, but my track record in the survival department is far less admirable than my performance as a jobholder. On small things I was thrifty enough; no expenditures on "carousing," flashy clothes, or any of the other indulgences that are often smugly believed to undermine the budgets of the poor. True, the $30 slacks in Key West and the $20 belt in Minneapolis were extravagances; I now know I could have done better at the Salvation Army or even at Wal-Mart. Food, though, I pretty much got down to a science: lots of chopped meat, beans, cheese, and noodles when I had a kitchen to cook in; otherwise, fast food, which I was able to keep down to about $9 a day. But let's look at the record.

In Key West, I earned $1,039 in one month and spent $517 on food, gas, toiletries, laundry, phone, and utilities. Rent was the deal breaker. If I had remained in my $500 efficiency, I would have been able to pay the rent and have $22 left over (which is still $78 less than the cash I had in my pocket at the start of the month). This in itself would have been a dicey situation if I had attempted to continue for a few more months, because sooner or later I would have had to spend something on medical and dental care or drugs other than ibuprofen. But my move to the trailer park—for the purpose, you will recall, of taking a second job—made me responsible for $625 a month in rent alone, utilities not included. Here I might have economized by giving up the car and buying a used bike (for about $50) or walking to work. Still, two jobs, or at least a job and a half, would be a necessity, and I had learned that I could not do two physically demanding jobs in the same day, at least not at any acceptable standard of performance.

In Portland, Maine, I came closest to achieving a decent fit between income and expenses, but only because I worked seven days a week. Between my two jobs, I was earning approximately $300 a week after taxes and paying $480 a month in rent, or a manageable 40 percent of my earnings. It helped, too, that gas and electricity were included in my rent and that I got two or three free meals each weekend at the nursing home. But I was there at the beginning of the off-season. If I had stayed until June 2000 I would have faced the Blue Haven's summer rent of $390 a week, which would of course have been out of the question. So to survive year-round, I would have had to save enough, in the months between August 1999 and May 2000, to accumulate the first month's rent and deposit on an actual apartment. I think I could have done this—saved $800 to $1,000—at least if no car trouble or illness interfered with my budget. I am not sure, however, that I could have maintained the seven-day-a-week regimen month after month or eluded the kinds of injuries that afflicted my fellow workers in the housecleaning business.

In Minneapolis—well, here we are left with a lot of speculation. If I had been able to find an apartment for $400 a month or less, my pay at Wal-Mart—$1,120 a month before taxes—might have been sufficient, although the cost of living in a motel while I searched for such an apartment might have made it impossible for me to save enough for the first month's rent and deposit. A weekend job, such as the one I almost landed at a supermarket for about $7.75 an hour, would have helped, but I had no guarantee that I could arrange my schedule at Wal-Mart to reliably exclude weekends. If I had taken the job at Menards and the pay was in fact $10 an hour for eleven hours a day, I would have made about $440 a week after taxes—enough to pay for a motel room and still have something left over to save up for the initial costs of an apartment. But were they really offering $10 an hour? And could I have stayed on my feet eleven hours a day, five days a week? So yes, with some different choices, I probably could have survived in Minneapolis. But I'm not going back for a rematch.

All right, I made mistakes, especially in Minneapolis, and these mistakes were at the time an occasion for feelings of failure and shame. I should have pulled myself together and taken the better-paying job; I should have moved into the dormitory I finally found (although at $19 a night, even a dorm bed would have been a luxury on Wal-Mart wages). But it must be said in my defense that plenty of other people were making the same mistakes: working at Wal-Mart rather than at one of the better-paying jobs available (often, I assume, because of transportation problems); living in residential motels at $200 to $300 a week. So the problem goes beyond my personal failings and miscalculations. Something is wrong, very wrong, when a single person in good health, a person who in addition possesses a working car, can barely support herself by the sweat of her brow. You don't need a degree in economics to see that wages are too low and rents too high.

The problem of rents is easy for a noneconomist, even a sparsely educated low-wage worker, to grasp: it's the market, stupid.[1] When the rich and the poor compete for housing on the open market, the poor don't stand a chance. The rich can always outbid them, buy up their tenements or trailer parks, and replace them with condos, McMansions, golf courses, or whatever they like. Since the rich have become more numerous, thanks largely to rising stock prices and executive salaries, the poor have necessarily been forced into housing that is more expensive, more dilapidated, or more distant from their places of work. Recall that in Key West, the trailer park convenient to hotel jobs was charging $625 a month for a half-size trailer, forcing low-wage workers to search for housing farther and farther away in less fashionable keys. But rents were also skyrocketing in the touristically challenged city of Minneapolis, where the last bits of near-affordable housing lie deep in the city, while job growth has occurred on the city's periphery, next to distinctly unaffordable suburbs. Insofar as the poor have to work near the dwellings of the rich—as in the case of so many service and retail jobs—they are stuck with lengthy commutes or dauntingly expensive housing.

If there seems to be general complacency about the low-income housing crisis, this is partly because it is in no way reflected in the official poverty rate, which has remained for the past several years at a soothingly low 13 percent or so. The reason for the disconnect between the actual housing nightmare of the poor and "poverty," as officially defined, is simple: the official poverty level is still calculated by the archaic method of taking the bare-bones cost of food

1. "It's the market, stupid" echoes a very successful phrase made famous in Bill Clinton's bid to unseat the incumbent president George W. Bush in the 1992 election. "The economy, stupid" or "It's the economy, stupid" was used to remind Clinton's campaign staff to stay on message: if elected, President Clinton would lead the nation out of the 1991 recession [editor's note].

for a family of a given size and multiplying this number by three. Yet food is relatively inflation-proof, at least compared with rent. In the early 1960s, when this method of calculating poverty was devised, food accounted for 24 percent of the average family budget (not 33 percent even then, it should be noted) and housing 29 percent. In 1999, food took up only 16 percent of the family budget, while housing had soared to 37 percent.[2] So the choice of food as the basis for calculating family budgets seems fairly arbitrary today; we might as well abolish poverty altogether, at least on paper, by defining a subsistence budget as some multiple of average expenditures on comic books or dental floss.

When the market fails to distribute some vital commodity, such as housing, to all who require it, the usual liberal-to-moderate expectation is that the government will step in and help. We accept this principle—at least in a halfhearted and faltering way—in the case of health care, where government offers Medicare to the elderly, Medicaid to the desperately poor, and various state programs to the children of the merely very poor. But in the case of housing, the extreme upward skewing of the market has been accompanied by a cowardly public sector retreat from responsibility. Expenditures on public housing have fallen since the 1980s, and the expansion of public rental subsidies came to a halt in the mid-1990s. At the same time, housing subsidies for homeowners—who tend to be far more affluent than renters—have remained at their usual munificent levels. It did not escape my attention, as a temporarily low-income person, that the housing subsidy I normally receive in my real life—over $20,000 a year in the form of a mortgage-interest deduction—would have allowed a truly low-income family to live in relative splendor. Had this amount been available to me in monthly installments in Minneapolis, I could have moved into one of those "executive" condos with sauna, health club, and pool.

But if rents are exquisitely sensitive to market forces, wages clearly are not. Every city where I worked in the course of this project was experiencing what local businesspeople defined as a "labor shortage"—commented on in the local press and revealed by the ubiquitous signs

2. Jared Bernstein, Chauna Brocht, and Maggie Spade-Aguilar, "How Much Is Enough? Basic Family Budgets for Working Families," Economic Policy Institute, Washington, D.C., 2000, p. 14.

saying "Now Hiring" or, more imperiously, "We Are Now Accepting Applications." Yet wages for people near the bottom of the labor market remain fairly flat, even "stagnant." "Certainly," the *New York Times* reported in March 2000, "inflationary wage gains are not evident in national wage statistics."[3] Federal Reserve chief Alan Greenspan, who spends much of his time anxiously scanning the horizon for the slightest hint of such "inflationary" gains, was pleased to inform Congress in July 2000 that the forecast seemed largely trouble-free. He went so far as to suggest that the economic laws linking low unemployment to wage increases may no longer be operative, which is a little like saying that the law of supply and demand has been repealed.[4] Some economists argue that the apparent paradox rests on an illusion: there is no real "labor shortage," only a shortage of people willing to work at the wages currently being offered.[5] You might as well talk about a "Lexus shortage"—which there is, in a sense, for anyone unwilling to pay $40,000 for a car.

In fact, wages *have* risen, or did rise, anyway, between 1996 and 1999. When I called around to various economists in the summer of 2000 and complained about the inadequacy of the wages available to entry-level workers, this was their first response: "But wages are going up!" According to the Economic Policy Institute, the poorest 10 percent of American workers saw their wages rise from $5.49 an hour (in 1999 dollars) in 1996 to $6.05 in 1999. Moving up the socioeconomic ladder, the next 10 percent–sized slice of Americans—which is roughly where I found myself as a low-wage worker—went from $6.80 an hour in 1996 to $7.35 in 1999.[6]

Obviously we have one of those debates over whether the glass is half empty or half full; the increases that seem to have mollified many economists do not seem so impressive to me. To put the wage gains of the past four years in somewhat dismal perspective: they have not been sufficient to bring low-wage workers up to the amounts they

3. "Companies Try Dipping Deeper into Labor Pool," *New York Times*, March 26, 2000.

4. "An Epitaph for a Rule That Just Won't Die," *New York Times*, July 30, 2000.

5. "Fact or Fallacy: Labor Shortage May Really Be Wage Stagnation," *Chicago Tribune*, July 2, 2000; "It's a Wage Shortage, Not a Labor Shortage," *Minneapolis Star Tribune*, March 25, 2000.

6. I thank John Schmidt at the Economic Policy Institute in Washington, D.C., for preparing the wage data for me.

were earning twenty-seven years ago, in 1973. In the first quarter of 2000, the poorest 10 percent of workers were earning only 91 percent of what they earned in the distant era of Watergate and disco music. Furthermore, of all workers, the poorest have made the least progress back to their 1973 wage levels. Relatively well-off workers in the eighth decile, or 10 percent–sized slice, where earnings are about $20 an hour, are now making 106.6 percent of what they earned in 1973. When I persisted in my carping to the economists, they generally backed down a bit, conceding that while wages at the bottom are going up, they're not going up very briskly. Lawrence Michel at the Economic Policy Institute, who had at the beginning of our conversation taken the half-full perspective, heightened the mystery when he observed that productivity—to which wages are theoretically tied—has been rising at such a healthy clip that "workers should be getting much more."[7]

The most obvious reason why they're not is that employers resist wage increases with every trick they can think of and every ounce of strength they can summon. I had an opportunity to query one of my own employers on this subject in Maine. [There was a time] when Ted, my boss at The Maids, drove me about forty minutes to a house where I was needed to reinforce a shorthanded team. In the course of complaining about his hard lot in life, he avowed that he could double his business overnight if only he could find enough reliable workers. As politely as possible, I asked him why he didn't just raise the pay. The question seemed to slide right off him. We offer "mothers' hours," he told me, meaning that the workday was supposedly over at three—as if to say, "With a benefit like that, how could anybody complain about wages?"

In fact, I suspect that the free breakfast he provided us represented the only concession to the labor shortage that he was prepared to make. Similarly, the Wal-Mart where I worked was offering free doughnuts once a week to any employees who could arrange to take their breaks while the supply lasted. As Louis Uchitelle has reported in the *New York Times*, many employers will offer almost anything—free meals, subsidized transportation, store discounts—rather than raise wages. The reason for this, in the words of one employer, is

7. Interview, July 18, 2000.

that such extras "can be shed more easily" than wage increases when changes in the market seem to make them unnecessary.[8] In the same spirit, automobile manufacturers would rather offer their customers cash rebates than reduced prices; the advantage of the rebate is that it seems like a gift and can be withdrawn without explanation.

But the resistance of employers only raises a second and ultimately more intractable question: Why isn't this resistance met by more effective counterpressure from the workers themselves? In evading and warding off wage increases, employers are of course behaving in an economically rational fashion; their business isn't to make their employees more comfortable and secure but to maximize the bottom line. So why don't employees behave in an equally rational fashion, demanding higher wages of their employers or seeking out better-paying jobs? The assumption behind the law of supply and demand, as it applies to labor, is that workers will sort themselves out as effectively as marbles on an inclined plane—gravitating to the better-paying jobs and either leaving the recalcitrant employers behind or forcing them to up the pay. "Economic man," that great abstraction of economic science, is supposed to do whatever it takes, within certain limits, to maximize his economic advantage.

I was baffled, initially, by what seemed like a certain lack of get-up-and-go on the part of my fellow workers. Why didn't they just leave for a better-paying job, as I did when I moved from the Hearthside to Jerry's? Part of the answer is that actual humans experience a little more "friction" than marbles do, and the poorer they are, the more constrained their mobility usually is. Low-wage people who don't have cars are often dependent on a relative who is willing to drop them off and pick them up again each day, sometimes on a route that includes the babysitter's house or the child care center. Change your place of work and you may be confronted with an impossible topographical problem to solve, or at least a reluctant driver to persuade. Some of my coworkers, in Minneapolis as well as Key West, rode bikes to work, and this clearly limited their geographical range. For those who do possess cars, there is still the problem of gas prices, not to mention the general hassle, which is of course far more onerous for the carless, of getting around to fill out

8. "Companies Try Dipping Deeper into Labor Pool," *New York Times*, March 26, 2000.

applications, to be interviewed, to take drug tests. I have mentioned, too, the general reluctance to exchange the devil you know for one that you don't know, even when the latter is tempting you with a better wage-benefit package. At each new job, you have to start all over, clueless and friendless.

There is another way that low-income workers differ from "economic man." For the laws of economics to work, the "players" need to be well informed about their options. The ideal case—and I've read that the technology for this is just around the corner—would be the consumer whose Palm Pilot displays the menu and prices for every restaurant or store he or she passes. Even without such technological assistance, affluent job hunters expect to study the salary-benefit packages offered by their potential employers, watch the financial news to find out if these packages are in line with those being offered in other regions or fields, and probably do a little bargaining before taking a job.

But there are no Palm Pilots, cable channels, or websites to advise the low-wage job seeker. She has only the help-wanted signs and the want ads to go on, and most of these coyly refrain from mentioning numbers. So information about who earns what and where has to travel by word of mouth, and for inexplicable cultural reasons, this is a very slow and unreliable route. Twin Cities job market analyst Kristine Jacobs pinpoints what she calls the "money taboo" as a major factor preventing workers from optimizing their earnings. "There's a code of silence surrounding issues related to individuals' earnings," she told me. "We confess everything else in our society—sex, crime, illness. But no one wants to reveal what they earn or how they got it. The money taboo is the one thing that employers can always count on."[9] I suspect that this "taboo" operates most effectively among the lowest-paid people, because, in a society that endlessly celebrates its dot-com billionaires and centimillionaire athletes, $7 or even $10 an hour can feel like a mark of innate inferiority. So you may or may not find out that, say, the Target down the road is paying better than Wal-Mart, even if you have a sister-in-law working there.

Employers, of course, do little to encourage the economic literacy of their workers. They may exhort potential customers to "Compare

9. Personal communication, July 24, 2000.

Our Prices!" but they're not eager to have workers do the same with wages. I have mentioned the way the hiring process seems designed, in some cases, to prevent any discussion or even disclosure of wages—whisking the applicant from interview to orientation before the crass subject of money can be raised. Some employers go further; instead of relying on the informal "money taboo" to keep workers from discussing and comparing wages, they specifically enjoin workers from doing so. The *New York Times* recently reported on several lawsuits brought by employees who had allegedly been fired for breaking this rule—a woman, for example, who asked for higher pay after learning from her male coworkers that she was being paid considerably less than they were for the very same work. The National Labor Relations Act of 1935 makes it illegal to punish people for revealing their wages to one another, but the practice is likely to persist until rooted out by lawsuits, company by company.[1]

But if it's hard for workers to obey the laws of economics by examining their options and moving on to better jobs, why don't more of them take a stand where they are—demanding better wages and work conditions, either individually or as a group? This is a huge question, probably the subject of many a dissertation in the field of industrial psychology, and here I can only comment on the things I observed. One of these was the co-optative power of management, illustrated by such euphemisms as *associate* and *team member.* At The Maids, the boss—who, as the only male in our midst, exerted a creepy, paternalistic kind of power—had managed to convince some of my coworkers that he was struggling against difficult odds and deserving of their unstinting forbearance. Wal-Mart has a number of more impersonal and probably more effective ways of getting its workers to feel like "associates." There was the profit-sharing plan, with Wal-Mart's stock price posted daily in a prominent spot near the break room. There was the company's much-heralded patriotism, evidenced in the banners over the shopping floor urging workers and customers to contribute to the construction of a World War II veterans' memorial (Sam Walton having been one of them). There

1. "The Biggest Company Secret: Workers Challenge Employer Practices on Pay Confidentiality," *New York Times*, July 28, 2000.

were "associate" meetings that served as pep rallies, complete with the Wal-Mart cheer: "Gimme a 'W,'" etc.

The chance to identify with a powerful and wealthy entity—the company or the boss—is only the carrot. There is also a stick. What surprised and offended me most about the low-wage workplace (and yes, here all my middle-class privilege is on full display) was the extent to which one is required to surrender one's basic civil rights and—what boils down to the same thing—self-respect. I learned this at the very beginning of my stint as a waitress, when I was warned that my purse could be searched by management at any time. I wasn't carrying stolen salt shakers or anything else of a compromising nature, but still, there's something about the prospect of a purse search that makes a woman feel a few buttons short of fully dressed. After work, I called around and found that this practice is entirely legal: if the purse is on the boss's property—which of course it was—the boss has the right to examine its contents.

Drug testing is another routine indignity. Civil libertarians see it as a violation of our Fourth Amendment freedom from "unreasonable search"; most jobholders and applicants find it simply embarrassing. In some testing protocols, the employee has to strip to her underwear and pee into a cup in the presence of an aide or technician. Mercifully, I got to keep my clothes on and shut the toilet stall door behind me, but even so, urination is a private act and it is degrading to have to perform it at the command of some powerful other. I would add pre-employment personality tests to the list of demeaning intrusions, or at least much of their usual content. Maybe the hypothetical types of questions can be justified—whether you would steal if an opportunity arose or turn in a thieving coworker and so on—but not questions about your "moods of self-pity," whether you are a loner or believe you are usually misunderstood. It is unsettling, at the very least, to give a stranger access to things, like your self-doubts and your urine, that are otherwise shared only in medical or therapeutic situations.

There are other, more direct ways of keeping low-wage employees in their place. Rules against "gossip," or even "talking," make it hard to air your grievances to peers or—should you be so daring—to enlist other workers in a group effort to bring about change, through a union organizing drive, for example. Those who do step out of line

often face little unexplained punishments, such as having their schedules or their work assignments unilaterally changed. Or you may be fired; those low-wage workers who work without union contracts, which is the great majority of them, work "at will," meaning at the will of the employer, and are subject to dismissal without explanation. The AFL-CIO estimates that ten thousand workers a year are fired for participating in union organizing drives, and since it is illegal to fire people for union activity, I suspect that these firings are usually justified in terms of unrelated minor infractions. Wal-Mart employees who have bucked the company—by getting involved in a unionization drive or by suing the company for failing to pay overtime—have been fired for breaking the company rule against using profanity.[2]

So if low-wage workers do not always behave in an economically rational way, that is, as free agents within a capitalist democracy, it is because they dwell in a place that is neither free nor in any way democratic. When you enter the low-wage workplace—and many of the medium-wage workplaces as well—you check your civil liberties at the door, leave America and all it supposedly stands for behind, and learn to zip your lips for the duration of the shift. The consequences of this routine surrender go beyond the issues of wages and poverty. We can hardly pride ourselves on being the world's preeminent democracy, after all, if large numbers of citizens spend half their waking hours in what amounts, in plain terms, to a dictatorship.

Any dictatorship takes a psychological toll on its subjects. If you are treated as an untrustworthy person—a potential slacker, drug addict, or thief—you may begin to feel less trustworthy yourself. If you are constantly reminded of your lowly position in the social hierarchy, whether by individual managers or by a plethora of impersonal rules, you begin to accept that unfortunate status. To draw for a moment from an entirely different corner of my life, that part of me still attached to the biological sciences,[3] there is ample evidence that animals—rats and monkeys, for example—that are forced into a subordinate status within their social systems adapt their brain chemistry accordingly, becoming "depressed" in humanlike ways.

2. Bob Ortega. *In Sam We Trust*, p. 356; "Former Wal-Mart Workers File Overtime Suit in Harrison County," *Charleston Gazette*, January 24, 1999.

3. Before turning first to advocacy of women's health and then to journalism, Ehrenreich earned a doctorate in cellular immunology [editor's note].

Their behavior is anxious and withdrawn; the level of serotonin (the neurotransmitter boosted by some antidepressants) declines in their brains. And—what is especially relevant here—they avoid fighting even in self-defense.[4]

Humans are, of course, vastly more complicated; even in situations of extreme subordination, we can pump up our self-esteem with thoughts of our families, our religion, our hopes for the future. But as much as any other social animal, and more so than many, we depend for our self-image on the humans immediately around us—to the point of altering our perceptions of the world so as to fit in with theirs.[5] My guess is that the indignities imposed on so many low-wage workers—the drug tests, the constant surveillance, being "reamed out" by managers—are part of what keeps wages low. If you're made to feel unworthy enough, you may come to think that what you're paid is what you are actually worth.

It is hard to imagine any other function for workplace authoritarianism. Managers may truly believe that, without their unremitting efforts, all work would quickly grind to a halt. That is not my impression. While I encountered some cynics and plenty of people who had learned to budget their energy, I never met an actual slacker or, for that matter, a drug addict or thief. On the contrary, I was amazed and sometimes saddened by the pride people took in jobs that rewarded them so meagerly, either in wages or in recognition. Often, in fact, these people experienced management as an obstacle to getting the job done as it should be done. Waitresses chafed at managers' stinginess toward the customers; housecleaners resented the time constraints that sometimes made them cut corners; retail workers wanted the floor to be beautiful, not cluttered with excess stock as management required. Left to themselves, they devised systems of cooperation and work sharing; when there was a crisis, they rose to it. In fact, it was often hard to see what the function of management was, other than to exact obeisance.

4. See, for example, C. A. Shively, K. Laber-Laird, and R. F. Anton, "Behavior and Physiology of Social Stress and Depression in Female Cynomolgous Monkeys," *Biological Psychiatry* 41:8 (1997), pp. 871–82, and D. C. Blanchard et al., "Visible Burrow System as a Model of Chronic Social Stress: Behavioral and Neuroendocrine Correlates," *Psychoneuroendocrinology* 20:2 (1995), pp. 117–34.

5. See, for example, chapter 7, "Conformity," in David G. Myers, *Social Psychology* (McGraw-Hill, 1987).

There seems to be a vicious cycle at work here, making ours not just an economy but a culture of extreme inequality. Corporate decision makers, and even some two-bit entrepreneurs like my boss at The Maids, occupy an economic position miles above that of the underpaid people whose labor they depend on. For reasons that have more to do with class—and often racial—prejudice than with actual experience, they tend to fear and distrust the category of people from which they recruit their workers. Hence the perceived need for repressive management and intrusive measures like drug and personality testing. But these things cost money—$20,000 or more a year for a manager, $100 a pop for a drug test, and so on—and the high cost of repression results in ever more pressure to hold wages down. The larger society seems to be caught up in a similar cycle: cutting public services for the poor, which are sometimes referred to collectively as the "social wage," while investing ever more heavily in prisons and cops. And in the larger society, too, the cost of repression becomes another factor weighing against the expansion or restoration of needed services. It is a tragic cycle, condemning us to ever deeper inequality, and in the long run, almost no one benefits but the agents of repression themselves.

But whatever keeps wages low—and I'm sure my comments have barely scratched the surface—the result is that many people earn far less than they need to live on. How much is that? The Economic Policy Institute recently reviewed dozens of studies of what constitutes a "living wage" and came up with an average figure of $30,000 a year for a family of one adult and two children, which amounts to a wage of $14 an hour. This is not the very minimum such a family could live on; the budget includes health insurance, a telephone, and child care at a licensed center, for example, which are well beyond the reach of millions. But it does not include restaurant meals, video rentals, Internet access, wine and liquor, cigarettes and lottery tickets, or even very much meat. The shocking thing is that the majority of American workers, about 60 percent, earn less than $14 an hour. Many of them get by by teaming up with another wage earner, a spouse or grown child. Some draw on government help in the form of food stamps, housing vouchers, the earned income tax credit, or—for those coming off welfare in relatively generous states—subsidized child care. But others—single mothers for example—have nothing but their own wages to live on, no matter how many mouths there are to feed.

Employers will look at that $30,000 figure, which is over twice what they currently pay entry-level workers, and see nothing but bankruptcy ahead. Indeed, it is probably impossible for the private sector to provide everyone with an adequate standard of living through wages, or even wages plus benefits, alone: too much of what we need, such as reliable child care, is just too expensive, even for middle-class families. Most civilized nations compensate for the inadequacy of wages by providing relatively generous public services such as health insurance, free or subsidized child care, subsidized housing, and effective public transportation. But the United States, for all its wealth, leaves its citizens to fend for themselves—facing market-based rents, for example, on their wages alone. For millions of Americans, that $10—or even $8 or $6—hourly wage is all there is.

It is common, among the nonpoor, to think of poverty as a sustainable condition—austere, perhaps, but they get by somehow, don't they? They are "always with us." What is harder for the nonpoor to see is poverty as acute distress: the lunch that consists of Doritos or hot dog rolls, leading to faintness before the end of the shift. The "home" that is also a car or a van. The illness or injury that must be "worked through," with gritted teeth, because there's no sick pay or health insurance and the loss of one day's pay will mean no groceries for the next. These experiences are not part of a sustainable lifestyle, even a lifestyle of chronic deprivation and relentless low-level punishment. They are, by almost any standard of subsistence, emergency situations. And that is how we should see the poverty of so many millions of low-wage Americans—as a state of emergency.

In the summer of 2000 I returned—permanently, I have every reason to hope—to my customary place in the socioeconomic spectrum. I go to restaurants, often far finer ones than the places where I worked, and sit down at a table. I sleep in hotel rooms that someone else has cleaned and shop in stores that others will tidy when I leave. To go from the bottom 20 percent to the top 20 percent is to enter a magical world where needs are met, problems are solved, almost without any intermediate effort. If you want to get somewhere fast, you hail a cab. If your aged parents have grown tiresome or

incontinent, you put them away where others will deal with their dirty diapers and dementia. If you are part of the upper-middle-class majority that employs a maid or maid service, you return from work to find the house miraculously restored to order—the toilet bowls shit-free and gleaming, the socks that you left on the floor levitated back to their normal dwelling place. Here, sweat is a metaphor for hard work, but seldom its consequence. Hundreds of little things get done, reliably and routinely every day, without anyone's seeming to do them.

The top 20 percent routinely exercises other, far more consequential forms of power in the world. This stratum, which contains what I have termed in an earlier book the "professional-managerial class," is the home of our decision makers, opinion shapers, culture creators—our professors, lawyers, executives, entertainers, politicians, judges, writers, producers, and editors.[6] When they speak, they are listened to. When they complain, someone usually scurries to correct the problem and apologize for it. If they complain often enough, someone far below them in wealth and influence may be chastised or even fired. Political power, too, is concentrated within the top 20 percent, since its members are far more likely than the poor—or even the middle class—to discern the all-too-tiny distinctions between candidates that can make it seem worthwhile to contribute, participate, and vote. In all these ways, the affluent exert inordinate power over the lives of the less affluent, and especially over the lives of the poor, determining what public services will be available, if any, what minimum wage, what laws governing the treatment of labor.

So it is alarming, upon returning to the upper middle class from a sojourn, however artificial and temporary, among the poor, to find the rabbit hole close so suddenly and completely behind me. You were *where*, doing *what*? Some odd optical property of our highly polarized and unequal society makes the poor almost invisible to their economic superiors. The poor can see the affluent easily enough—on television, for example, or on the covers of magazines. But the affluent rarely see the poor or, if they do catch sight of them in some public space, rarely know what they're seeing, since—thanks to consignment stores and, yes, Wal-Mart—the poor are usually able

6. *Fear of Falling: The Inner Life of the Middle Class* (Pantheon, 1989).

to disguise themselves as members of the more comfortable classes. Forty years ago the hot journalistic topic was the "discovery of the poor" in their inner-city and Appalachian "pockets of poverty." Today you are more likely to find commentary on their "disappearance," either as a supposed demographic reality or as a shortcoming of the middle-class imagination.

In a 2000 article on the "disappearing poor," journalist James Fallows reports that, from the vantage point of the Internet's nouveaux riches, it is "hard to understand people for whom a million dollars would be a fortune . . . not to mention those for whom $246 is a full week's earnings."[7] Among the reasons he and others have cited for the blindness of the affluent is the fact that they are less and less likely to share spaces and services with the poor. As public schools and other public services deteriorate, those who can afford to do so send their children to private schools and spend their off-hours in private spaces—health clubs, for example, instead of the local park. They don't ride on public buses and subways. They withdraw from mixed neighborhoods into distant suburbs, gated communities, or guarded apartment towers; they shop in stores that, in line with the prevailing "market segmentation," are designed to appeal to the affluent alone. Even the affluent young are increasingly unlikely to spend their summers learning how the "other half" lives, as lifeguards, waitresses, or housekeepers at resort hotels. The *New York Times* reports that they now prefer career-relevant activities like summer school or interning in an appropriate professional setting to the "sweaty, low-paid and mind-numbing slots that have long been their lot."[8]

Then, too, the particular political moment favors what almost looks like a "conspiracy of silence" on the subject of poverty and the poor. The Democrats are not eager to find flaws in the period of "unprecedented prosperity" they take credit for; the Republicans have lost interest in the poor now that "welfare-as-we-know-it" has ended. Welfare reform itself is a factor weighing against any close investigation of the conditions of the poor. Both parties heartily endorsed it, and to acknowledge that low-wage work doesn't lift people out of poverty would be to admit that it may have been, in human terms,

7. "The Invisible Poor," *New York Times Magazine*, March 19, 2000.

8. "Summer Work Is Out of Favor with the Young," *New York Times*, June 18, 2000.

a catastrophic mistake. In fact, very little is known about the fate of former welfare recipients because the 1996 welfare reform legislation blithely failed to include any provision for monitoring their post-welfare economic condition. Media accounts persistently bright-side the situation, highlighting the occasional success stories and down-playing the acknowledged increase in hunger.[9] And sometimes there seems to be almost deliberate deception. In June 2000, the press rushed to hail a study supposedly showing that Minnesota's welfare-to-work program had sharply reduced poverty and was, as *Time* magazine put it, a "winner."[1] Overlooked in these reports was the fact that the program in question was a pilot project that offered far more generous child care and other subsidies than Minnesota's actual welfare reform program. Perhaps the error can be forgiven—the pilot project, which ended in 1997, had the same name, Minnesota Family Investment Program, as Minnesota's much larger, ongoing welfare reform program.[2]

You would have to read a great many newspapers very carefully, cover to cover, to see the signs of distress. You would find, for example, that in 1999 Massachusetts food pantries reported a 72 percent increase in the demand for their services over the previous year, that Texas food banks were "scrounging" for food, despite donations at or above 1998 levels, as were those in Atlanta.[3] You might learn that in San Diego the Catholic Church could no longer, as of January 2000, accept homeless families at its shelter, which happens to be the city's largest, because it was already operating at twice its normal capacity.[4] You would come across news of a study showing that the percentage of Wisconsin food-stamp families in "extreme poverty"—defined as less than 50 percent of the federal poverty line—has tripled in the

9. The *National Journal* reports that the "good news" is that almost 6 million people have left the welfare rolls since 1996, while the "rest of the story" includes the problem that "these people sometimes don't have enough to eat" ("Welfare Reform, Act 2," June 24, 2000, pp. 1, 978–93).

1. "Minnesota's Welfare Reform Proves a Winner," *Time*, June 12, 2000.

2. Center for Law and Social Policy, "Update," Washington, D.C., June 2000.

3. "Study: More Go Hungry since Welfare Reform," *Boston Herald*, January 21, 2000; "Charity Can't Feed All while Welfare Reforms Implemented," *Houston Chronicle*, January 10, 2000; "Hunger Grows as Food Banks Try to Keep Pace," *Atlanta Journal and Constitution*, November 26, 1999.

4. "Rise in Homeless Families Strains San Diego Aid," *Los Angeles Times*, January 24, 2000.

last decade to more than 30 percent.[5] You might discover that, nationwide, America's food banks are experiencing "a torrent of need which [they] cannot meet" and that, according to a survey conducted by the U.S. Conference of Mayors, 67 percent of the adults requesting emergency food aid are people with jobs.[6]

One reason nobody bothers to pull all these stories together and announce a widespread state of emergency may be that Americans of the newspaper-reading professional middle class are used to thinking of poverty as a consequence of unemployment. During the heyday of downsizing in the Reagan years, it very often was, and it still is for many inner-city residents who have no way of getting to the proliferating entry-level jobs on urban peripheries. When unemployment causes poverty, we know how to state the problem—typically, "the economy isn't growing fast enough"—and we know what the traditional liberal solution is—"full employment." But when we have full or nearly full employment, when jobs are available to any job seeker who can get to them, then the problem goes deeper and begins to cut into that web of expectations that make up the "social contract." According to a recent poll conducted by Jobs for the Future, a Boston-based employment research firm, 94 percent of Americans agree that "people who work full-time should be able to earn enough to keep their families out of poverty."[7] I grew up hearing over and over, to the point of tedium, that "hard work" was the secret of success: "Work hard and you'll get ahead" or "It's hard work that got us where we are." No one ever said that you could work hard—harder even than you ever thought possible—and still find yourself sinking ever deeper into poverty and debt.

When poor single mothers had the option of remaining out of the labor force on welfare, the middle and upper middle class tended to view them with a certain impatience, if not disgust. The welfare poor were excoriated for their laziness, their persistence in reproducing in unfavorable circumstances, their presumed addictions, and above all

5. "Hunger Problems Said to Be Getting Worse," *Milwaukee Journal Sentinel*, December 15, 1999.

6. Deborah Leff, the president and CEO of the hunger-relief organization America's Second Harvest, quoted in the *National Journal*, op. cit.; "Hunger Persists in U.S. despite the Good Times," *Detroit News*, June 15, 2000.

7. "A National Survey of American Attitudes toward Low-Wage Workers and Welfare Reform," Jobs for the Future, Boston, May 24, 2000.

for their "dependency." Here they were, content to live off "government handouts" instead of seeking "self-sufficiency," like everyone else, through a job. They needed to get their act together, learn how to wind an alarm clock, get out there and get to work. But now that government has largely withdrawn its "handouts," now that the overwhelming majority of the poor are out there toiling in Wal-Mart or Wendy's—well, what are we to think of them? Disapproval and condescension no longer apply, so what outlook makes sense?

Guilt, you may be thinking warily. Isn't that what we're supposed to feel? But guilt doesn't go anywhere near far enough; the appropriate emotion is shame—shame at our *own* dependency, in this case, on the underpaid labor of others. When someone works for less pay than she can live on—when, for example, she goes hungry so that you can eat more cheaply and conveniently—then she has made a great sacrifice for you, she has made you a gift of some part of her abilities, her health, and her life. The "working poor," as they are approvingly termed, are in fact the major philanthropists of our society. They neglect their own children so that the children of others will be cared for; they live in substandard housing so that other homes will be shiny and perfect; they endure privation so that inflation will be low and stock prices high. To be a member of the working poor is to be an anonymous donor, a nameless benefactor, to everyone else. As Gail, one of my restaurant coworkers put it, "you give and you give."

Someday, of course—and I will make no predictions as to exactly when—they are bound to tire of getting so little in return and to demand to be paid what they're worth. There'll be a lot of anger when that day comes, and strikes and disruption. But the sky will not fall, and we will all be better off for it in the end.

2001

Carla R. Monroe

This essay was first published in The Clearing House: A Journal of Educational Strategies, Issues, and Ideas. *It's the best example in this volume of a scholarly, peer-reviewed article. Before the editors of the* Clearing House *accepted it for publication, they sent it to other education experts, probably college professors, who approved it either outright or pending certain revisions. Monroe, a professor at Wheelock College when she researched and wrote this article, knew her main audience would be other social scientists, especially scholars who study the American system of K–12 education and administrators who influence school policies. So you'll see several of the rhetorical conventions that are common when experts talk to each other. Monroe writes in a largely impersonal, scientific style. After the opening anecdote, she does little to engage the readers' attention, trusting that their professional interest will sustain them throughout. The focus is on logical argument, and because Monroe is a social scientist, she reasons inductively, drawing her conclusions from data gathered by other social scientists. Her extensive bibliography allows readers not only to check her sources but also to continue their own investigation by looking into the relevant literature.*

Why Are "Bad Boys" Always Black?

Causes of Disproportionality in School Discipline and Recommendations for Change

Curiosity about the crowd forming on the next block attracted me to the scene in time to witness Kevin's[1] arrest. I watched him struggle futilely against the police officer's determined hold of his upper body. Kevin's winced expression was briefly visible as the handcuffs were placed around his restrained wrists. His body seemed limp and defeated as he was moved from the grassy plot into the back of the police car, sobbing. As the climax of the arrest slowly subsided, clipped thoughts and questions flooded my mind. Kevin was an eighth grade kid from my school. I had never seen a 13-year-old in the back of a police car; definitely never anyone that young in police custody. Why? What happened? What now? Unfortunately, I had arrived too late to know how the arrest had been set in motion. Some of the other onlookers said that Kevin had tried to rob someone, others commented that the incident was drug related. As strands of truth and speculation shaped Kevin's story, I turned

1. "Kevin" is a pseudonym.

and walked back to the school campus. He was in my second period class. I knew that I would learn the details of the story at work.

The form of notification soon arrived from the district office. Beside Kevin's name were the expected words. *Status: Suspended, Location: Juvenile detention.* The document provided a crisp and matter-of-fact conclusion to the story. Yet, my own experiences with Kevin, coupled with observations by students and colleagues, raised complicated questions about the situation. Already struggling academically, what effect would Kevin's incarceration have on his intellectual development? How would he readjust to mainstream society and school following his release? What life implications did juvenile detainment hold for a young adolescent, particularly a black male? Unfortunately, such questions surround the lives of many African American youths as crime continues to be a familiar component of the nation's urban landscape.

I was a middle-school teacher employed in a large urban school district when the events related to Kevin's arrest unfolded. I taught in a predominately African American institution in which some of my students were middle- and working-class and others were from decidedly low-income backgrounds. Improving student outcomes, both inside and outside school walls, was a shared institutional concern. Yet, young people such as Kevin symbolized the ways in which articulated goals frequently failed to become reality.

At first glance, Kevin's predicament may appear to reside beyond the boundaries of the public education enterprise. However, numerous social scientists have identified compelling connections between students' schooling experiences and negative outcomes such as delinquency (Noguera 2003; Voelkl, Welte, and Wieczorek 1999). Examinations of low-income communities further suggest that antisocial behaviors surfacing during adolescence often become a trenchant component of youths' experiences across the lifespan, thereby heightening their likelihood of entering the juvenile and criminal justice systems (Simon and Burns 1997). Notably, studies conducted with middle-school learners have linked school disciplinary patterns with trends in delinquency and recidivism (Gottfredson, Gottfredson, and Hybl 1993; Skiba, Peterson, and Williams 1997). The present overrepresentation of African American males in the U.S. justice system (Wacquant 2000), combined with racial disproportionality on measures of school discipline (Applied Research Center 2002), provide compelling reasons for continued scrutiny of connections between the two areas.

Although previous studies have revealed powerful insights about the salience of culture, particularly race, in schools and society, few scholars have explored how culturally-based constructs relate to school discipline. In this article I expand on current research by examining factors that contribute to the discipline gap, or the over-representation of black, male, and low-income students on indices of school discipline. Whereas researchers commonly agree that cultural mismatches create conditions for systematic school failure, less is known about how societal forces may inform teachers' perceptions of African American student behaviors. There is a particular need to understand how and why teachers' views of these students, particularly males, mediate their disciplinary actions in the classroom. Specifically, how do images of African American men and boys in society at large relate to teachers' notions about effective disciplinary strategies based on student race and gender? Moreover, how do prevailing norms and practices in society at large influence the shape of disciplinary problems in schools? This article is grounded in a consideration of the criminalization of black males, race and class privilege, and zero tolerance policies as key forces in the genesis and evolution of the discipline gap. The article concludes with recommendations for how educators and policymakers should approach disciplinary concerns for middle-school learners.

Why the Discipline Gap? A Synopsis of Research Findings

Nationally, African American students are targeted for disciplinary action in the greatest numbers (Johnston 2000). According to quantitative reports, black pupils are statistically two to five times more likely to be suspended than their white counterparts (Irvine 1990). Qualitative findings simultaneously indicate that teachers confine reprimands and punitive consequences to black children even when youths of other races engage in the same unsanctioned behaviors (McCadden 1998), Skiba et al.'s (2000) research further reveals that African Americans receive harsher punishments than their peers, often for subjectively defined offenses. Inequities in school discipline are most pronounced among boys (Ferguson 2000).

Because school trends reflect currents of the national contexts in which they exist, core causes of the discipline gap are both internal and external to schools. In this section, I discuss three conditions that contribute to current disparities. They are (*a*) the criminalization of black males, (*b*) race and class privilege, and (*c*) zero tolerance polices. Each is discussed at length.

Criminalizing African American Males

Popular views of African American life are connected to threatening images with predictable regularity. Both media and scholarly portrayals of contemporary black life often highlight cultures of violence, drugs, antiauthoritarianism, and other social deficiencies. When confining attention to urban black males, threatening and criminal archetypes frequently ground their perceived existence, particularly in low-income environments (Canada 1996). Notably, unflattering prototypes tend to emerge from youths' efforts to assert their identities and protect themselves in disenfranchised communities (Anderson 1999). For example, in analyzing the relationship between self-presentation and power, West writes that

> for most young black men, power is acquired by stylizing their bodies over space and time in such a way that their bodies reflect their uniqueness and provoke fear in others. To be "bad" is good not simply because it subverts the language of the dominant white culture but also because it imposes a unique kind of order for young black men on their own distinctive chaos and solicits an attention that makes others pull back with some trepidation. This young black male style is a form of self-identification and resistance in a hostile culture; it also is an instance of machismo identity ready for violent encounters. (1994, 128).

West's analysis captures a fundamental dilemma facing many young black males. Although attempting to assert self-affirming identities in adverse environments, behaviors among African American youths often fuel pejorative stereotypes that distinguish black males as troublesome and threatening. Grant (1988), Noguera (2002a, 2002b), and others have argued that negative views of black males largely emanate from environmental dynamics that circumscribe how young African American boys' identities are perceived both inside and outside their communities.

When examining research literature on school discipline, the criminalization of black males appears to provide a powerful context for the discipline gap. On one level, researchers widely recognize that teachers frequently approach classes populated by low-income and African American youths with a strong emphasis on controlling student behaviors. Custodial tendencies tend to be most pronounced with low-ability level and male students (Gouldner 1978). On a second level, practitioner responses to incidents of perceived misbehavior tend to reside at either extreme of the disciplinary continuum. That is, when disciplining African American students, teachers are likely to demonstrate reactions that appear to be more severe than required. Additionally, there is evidence that practitioners may devote little effort to addressing behavioral concerns in their infancy when nonpunitive techniques are likely to be effective (Emihovich 1983). Such tendencies are less likely to be true with white students.

Although many factors influence teachers' work, previous research has marked practitioner perceptions and accompanying expectations of youths as key mediating influences in their decisions concerning discipline (Bennett and Harris 1982). Many teachers may not explicitly connect their disciplinary reactions to negative perceptions of black males, yet systematic trends in disproportionality suggest that teachers may be implicitly guided by stereotypical perceptions that African American boys require greater control than their peers and are unlikely to respond to nonpunitive measures. Although movements to address diversity in teacher education programs are useful means of heightening teachers' awareness of racial issues, the trenchancy of the discipline gap suggests that education professionals insufficiently interrogate connections between generic perceptions of black males and their treatment in the classroom.

Race and Class Privilege

Educational expectations, practices, and policies reflect the values of the individuals who create them. As a consequence, judgments about student disruption are imbued with cultural norms. Because white and middle-class individuals occupy most positions of power in educational settings, decisions concerning behavioral expectations and infractions are set forth by a culturally-specific bloc, juxtaposing the leading reasons for disciplinary referrals with qualitative research findings make the culturally-influenced nature of school discipline clear. For instance, Skiba et al.'s (1997) analysis of nineteen Midwestern middle schools revealed that disobedience, conduct, disrespect, and fighting were the most common reasons for teachers to write disciplinary referrals. Yet, empirical comparisons of cultural interaction styles indicate that teachers regularly interpret African American behaviors as inappropriate when the actions are not intended to be so (Hanna 1988; Weinstein, Curran, and Tomlinson-Clarke 2004; Weinstein, Tomlinson-Clarke, and Curran 2003). Examples include viewing overlapping speech as disrespect, play fighting as authentic aggression, and ritualized humor as valid insults.

Limited racial and socioeconomic diversity in educational circles of power has inhibited professionals' recognition of school disciplinary practices as socially defined constructs. Because prevailing beliefs and practices often proceed unchallenged, the culturally based nature of school discipline has remained an unquestioned component of school life. Moreover, structural oversights have facilitated explanations for disciplinary action that assign culpability to the children involved. Altering present disciplinary trends demands improved cross-cultural competency among classroom practitioners regarding behavioral norms in African American communities. Unfortunately, teacher preparation programs often fail to encourage candidates to expand their vision of culturally responsive pedagogy beyond academic material to include classroom management and student discipline. Teacher preparation and professional development programs that remain innocent community-based practices for African American students risk perpetuating approaches that have little relevance for pupils who are most at risk for disciplinary action.

Zero Tolerance Initiatives

Convictions that a stern approach to school discipline would curb inappropriate—particularly criminal—behavior have speeded the national growth and implementation of zero tolerance policies. In fact, a reported 94 percent of U.S. public schools have adopted such initiatives (Johnson, Boydon, and Pittz 2001). Yet, analyses of zero tolerance efforts indicate that the policies may be yielding unintended consequences to a greater extent than they eradicate inappropriate behaviors. The exacerbation of racial discrepancies currently ranks among the most serious concerns. Educators' unwillingness to draw distinctions between severe and minor offenses and the breadth with which zero tolerance approaches are applied appear to be primary sources of the problem (Skiba and Peterson 1999).

What appears to be a more significant challenge, however, is educators' general inattention to the value of working cooperatively with parents and communities to construct schools where disruption is minimized overall. Rather, by most accounts, institutional decisions concerning student behavior are reached in isolation of input from other relevant stakeholders. Even parental efforts to legally challenge punishments have failed to make an incision in rigid interpretations of the policies (Dohrn 2001). Although teachers lack the institutional authority to alter principals' and policymakers' decisions, practitioners should appreciate the power that falls within their purview: whether to write a disciplinary referral at all. Encouraging teachers to address behavioral concerns in their classes would be a significant stride toward lowering suspension and expulsion rates.

Recommendations for Middle School Professionals

Closing the discipline gap requires reshaping individual and institutional orientations and practices. This section contains four broad recommendations designed to guide middle-school educators' efforts to address disproportionality.

1. *Provide opportunities for teachers to interrogate their beliefs about African American students.* Racial and gender stereotypes often undergird teachers' interactions with students. As a result, many teachers, consciously or unconsciously, believe that boys present more disciplinary problems than girls, and that black students are more likely to misbehave than youths of other races. Because school structures seldom provide opportunities for practitioners to interact and observe alternative classroom environments, teachers' perceptions

frequently proceed unquestioned and may be crystallized by incidents that affirm preexisting stereotypes.

In-service professional development efforts focused on discipline should be designed to identify and critique teachers' perceptions of students of color, particularly African American boys. Such workshops should be designed to attract a wide-ranging cadre of teachers from alternative school environments, and conducted by racially diverse facilitators. Enabling teachers to share their views and experiences in a multiracial environment provides opportunities for teachers to be exposed to experiences and approaches that may challenge marginalizing beliefs about African American youths. Moreover, these efforts are powerful means of encouraging teachers to recognize culturally-based behaviors that are not intended to be disruptive.

2. *Incorporate and value culturally responsive disciplinary strategies.* The field of education is replete with programs and approaches designed to elicit desirable student behavior, yet the disproportionate percentage of disciplinary action targeting African American students raises twin questions. With whom are these models successful? And why have they failed to reverse negative trends among culturally diverse students from high poverty backgrounds?

Many classroom and institutional disciplinary approaches suffer from a basic inattention to cultural context. Because common techniques and expectations are moored in middle class, white norms, numerous approaches fail to prove useful with students of color. In fact, many prevailing techniques are at odds with the very disciplinary practices to which many African American students are exposed, particularly low-income youths. Eradicating the discipline gap requires theorists, researchers, and practitioners to familiarize themselves with culturally specific behavioral norms, and incorporate culturally familiar behavior management strategies into their practice. For example, successful teachers of African American students tend to incorporate demonstrations of affect and emotion, as well as culturally based humor, into their interactions with students (Irvine 2003). Empirical findings further suggest that culturally responsive teachers are more comfortable in their roles as disciplinarians, less likely to write disciplinary referrals, and have stronger relationships with students and parents than their counterparts (Cooper 2002; Monroe and Obidah 2004).

3. *Broaden the discourse around school disciplinary decisions.* Despite provisions that permit school officials to address disciplinary concerns on a case-by-case basis, there is significant evidence that most organizational leaders elect not to do so. Rather, many administrators uphold narrow applications of disciplinary consequences. Consider a few of the following examples:

- In Ohio a fourteen-year-old student was suspended for giving Midol tablets to a classmate. The recipient of the pills was suspended as well and required to complete a drug awareness class.
- A Georgia middle-school student was suspended for bringing a Tweety Bird key chain to school on the basis that the trinket violated policies concerning weapons.

Concentrating decisions about expulsions and suspensions in the hands of a few has restricted opportunities to raise concerns about troubling disciplinary procedures. Stated more plainly, the closed nature of school discipline precludes important stakeholders from questioning dubious reasons for suspensions and expulsions in addition to disturbing racial and gender patterns that accompany sanctions.

Flattening the organizational hierarchy by creating advisory boards for school discipline would be a useful means of closing the discipline gap on several levels. First, the board may serve as a means for monitoring demographic trends in referrals and highlighting discriminatory patterns that emerge. Identifying problems early in the school year would be a strong step toward preventing recurrent problems across the year. Secondarily, schools would structurally enable well-qualified individuals to provide important feedback on how to serve students' and teachers' needs most effectively. Urban institutions would be well served to select advisory members from well-regarded teachers as well as parent and community volunteers who are familiar with the school and its constituents.

4. *Maintain learners' interest through engaging instruction.* A clear and logical correlation exists between student discipline and academic achievement. Throughout the nation, there is evidence that students who are disproportionately targeted for disciplinary action are the same pupils who perform poorly on most measures of achievement. For example, Skiba and Rausch (2004) analyzed the relationship

between standardized tests scores and suspension and expulsion rates for students in the state of Indiana and found that schools with high out-of-school suspension rates had a lower percent of students passing the math and English/Language Arts section of the Indiana State Test of Educational Progress (ISTEP). The correlation held true even after the researchers controlled for poverty and the percentage of African American students enrolled. Correlations between discipline and achievement were strongest at the secondary level.

Student behavior is intimately connected to the quality of instruction in the classroom. When students are intellectually immersed in learning tasks they are less likely to engage in behaviors that detract from the instruction at hand. Ladson-Billings' (1994) seminal study of effective teachers of African American students cited several pedagogical tools that teachers may use to guide their efforts. Among other findings, she noted that academic material drawn from students' home environments anchors teachers' instruction and sets the stage for inviting lessons that students found relevant, meaningful, and affirming. Although not focused on classroom discipline specifically, Ladson-Billings' research holds particular relevance for the discipline gap.

When students perceive that their lives and experiences are valued, they are less likely to engage in behaviors that express resistance against alienating school forces. Moreover, youths are provided opportunities to appreciate benefits gleaned from sharpening their scholastic skills and broadening their knowledge base. Additionally, relying on students' intellectual capacity as a means of addressing discipline draws on intrinsic behavioral motivations—an approach that tends to be effective with low-income students of color (Noguera 2001).

Conclusion

Educators across the nation share a common dilemma. Research inquiries completed since the 1970s provide evidence that black males are disciplined with greater frequency and severity than their peers. The glaring persistence of such patterns challenges educators to approach their work with African American youth in new ways. Although many problems are connected to cultural mismatches between teachers and students, there remains a broader conversation to explore with regard to societal factors that provide fertile ground for the discipline gap. Based on prior scholarship, I assert that disproportionality in school discipline is in large part a function of macro-level problems such as the criminalization of black males and race and class privilege. At the school level, zero tolerance policies provide a conduit by which a significant percent of students are systematically removed from school for subjectively defined offenses. Unfortunately, few policymakers and school officials appear to weigh decisions to expel or suspend students against research evidence regarding the culturally influenced nature of school discipline or harmful outcomes associated with removing students from school, such as delinquency. Rather, most accounts suggest that school officials uphold rigid interpretations of zero tolerance initiatives.

Ending racial disparities in school discipline is a formidable responsibility. Yet, encouragingly, some school systems are taking strides to eliminate the discipline gap (Denn 2002). Growing evidence supports the view that school inequities involving African Americans are best addressed through race-conscious approaches at the teacher preparation and professional development levels. Providing opportunities for teachers to interrogate their own beliefs about student groups as well as culturally based expectations concerning discipline are powerful means of shifting present trends in disproportionality. To date, there is mounting evidence that culturally responsive teachers, particularly African American practitioners, play pivotal roles in promoting transformative outcomes among students. School systems would be well served to employ such individuals in leadership roles that enable them to mentor practicing colleagues as well as to have a voice in decisions concerning discipline.

2005

Michelle Alexander

b. 1967

For a brief time after the Civil War, newly freed African Americans enjoyed a remarkable measure of civil rights, enacted in law and protected by federal troops. But when the troops withdrew in the 1870s, Southern states began removing those right systematically, and by the turn of the twentieth century "Jim Crow" reigned. Laws all over the United States but especially in the South made African Americans second-class citizens. This legal caste system was largely ended with a wave of Supreme Court decisions and civil rights legislation in the 1950s and 1960s (see, for example, Doris Kearns Goodwin's essay, "Visionary Leadership: Lyndon Johnson and Civil Rights").

Then around 1970, President Richard Nixon announced a new "War on Drugs," which focused federal policy and funding on what he called "public enemy number one": drug abuse. President Ronald Reagan in the 1980s and President Bill Clinton in the 1990s ramped up those policies. Alexander argues in her book, The New Jim Crow: Mass Incarceration in the Age of Colorblindness, *that, just as Jim Crow rolled back newly acquired civil rights after Reconstruction, the War on Drugs has, for the last fifty years, been rolling back the civil rights supposedly secured in the 1960s.*

Alexander's book was published two years into the administration of the first Black president, Barack Obama, which seemingly ushered America into a "post-racial" age. In fact, the book did not sell particularly well at first. But, as Alexander pointed out in a 2020 interview, several notorious deaths, such as those of Trayvon Martin (2012), Michael Brown (2014), Kalief Browder (2015), and Sandra Bland (2015), demonstrate that reform of the system comes slow. Gradually, Alexander's book became a national bestseller, as the whole country took up the debate about criminal justice. The Black Lives Matter movement, Colin Kaepernick's protest during the national anthem, and arguments about "stop-and-frisk" policing are all part of the same public debate. "The election of President Trump" in 2016, Alexander asserts, "has completely decimated any fantasies we had that we are living in a post-racial America."

What was particularly striking about Alexander's argument was not the evidence she cites. The statistical data about incarceration and criminalization during the War on Drugs has long been available, fairly well known, and generally accepted. What was astonishing to many readers, conservatives and liberals alike, were the conclusions she drew about the motives of these public policies. This selection, the introduction to her book, shows us that inductive data is never inert or straightforward: to be meaningful at all, data requires the rhetorician to interpret *what the facts mean. Alexander admits that "[s]kepticism about the claims made here are warranted." Of course that's true of* every *essay in this anthology. You might recall that in the first chapter of this anthology I advised you, as a reader of essays, to be skeptical. All essay writers ought to presume that their readers are skeptical. But Alexander takes that one step further with a very effective ethical argument. She tells us that she herself was skeptical at first, and much of the essay becomes the story of her slow conversion to a new opinion—a new interpretation of the facts. The expectation is that her readers will take that same journey, vicariously, from skepticism to belief, by following along.*

Even so, you should bear in mind that this selection is an introduction to a book. Introductions are intended to get skeptical readers not necessarily to change their minds, but to open up their minds, to make them willing to hear arguments that contradict their own opinions. If an introduction is successful, it will get you to read the rest of the book. So introductions often feature the chapter-by-chapter summary you see at the end of this essay: a road map of the book's entire, long, complex argument.

Introduction to *The New Jim Crow*

Jarvious Cotton cannot vote. Like his father, grandfather, great-grandfather, and great-great-grandfather, he has been denied the right to participate in our electoral democracy. Cotton's family tree tells the story of several generations of black men who were born in the United States but who were denied the most basic freedom that democracy promises—the freedom to vote for those who will make the rules and laws that govern one's life. Cotton's great-great-grandfather could not vote as a slave. His great-grandfather was beaten to death by the Ku Klux Klan for attempting to vote. His grandfather was prevented from voting by Klan intimidation. His father was barred from voting by poll taxes and literacy tests. Today, Jarvious Cotton cannot vote because he, like many black men in the United States, has been labeled a felon and is currently on parole.[1]

1. Jarvious Cotton was a plaintiff in *Cotton v. Fordice*, 157 F.3d 388 (5th Cir. 1998), which held that Mississippi's felon disenfranchisement provision had lost its racially discriminatory taint. The information regarding Cotton's family tree was obtained by Emily Bolton on March 29, 1999, when she interviewed Cotton at Mississippi State Prison. Jarvious Cotton was released on parole in Mississippi, a state that denies voting rights to parolees.

Cotton's story illustrates, in many respects, the old adage "The more things change, the more they remain the same." In each generation, new tactics have been used for achieving the same goals—goals shared by the Founding Fathers. Denying African Americans citizenship was deemed essential to the formation of the original union. Hundreds of years later, America is still not an egalitarian democracy. The arguments and rationalizations that have been trotted out in support of racial exclusion and discrimination in its various forms have changed and evolved, but the outcome has remained largely the same. An extraordinary percentage of black men in the United States are legally barred from voting today, just as they have been throughout most of American history. They are also subject to legalized discrimination in employment, housing, education, public benefits, and jury service, just as their parents, grandparents, and great-grandparents once were.

What has changed since the collapse of Jim Crow has less to do with the basic structure of our society than with the language we use to justify it. In the era of colorblindness, it is no longer socially permissible to use race, explicitly, as a justification for discrimination, exclusion, and social contempt. So we don't. Rather than rely on race, we use our criminal justice system to label people of color "criminals" and then engage in all the practices we supposedly left behind. Today it is perfectly legal to discriminate against criminals in nearly all the ways that it was once legal to discriminate against African Americans. Once you're labeled a felon, the old forms of discrimination—employment discrimination, housing discrimination, denial of the right to vote, denial of educational opportunity, denial of food stamps and other public benefits, and exclusion from jury service—are suddenly legal. As a criminal, you have scarcely more rights, and arguably less respect, than a black man living in Alabama at the height of Jim Crow. We have not ended racial caste in America; we have merely redesigned it.

I reached the conclusions presented in this book reluctantly. Ten years ago, I would have argued strenuously against the central claim made here—namely, that something akin to a racial caste system currently exists in the United States. Indeed, if Barack Obama had been elected president back then, I would have argued that his election marked the nation's triumph over racial caste—the final nail in the coffin of Jim Crow. My elation would have been tempered by the distance yet to be traveled to reach the promised land of racial justice in America, but my conviction that nothing remotely similar to Jim Crow exists in this country would have been steadfast.

Today my elation over Obama's election is tempered by a far more sobering awareness. As an African American woman, with three young children who will never know a world in which a black man could not be president of the United States, I was beyond thrilled on election night. Yet when I walked out of the election night party, full of hope and enthusiasm, I was immediately reminded of the harsh realities of the New Jim Crow. A black man was on his knees in the gutter, hands cuffed behind his back, as several police officers stood around him talking, joking, and ignoring his human existence. People poured out of the building: many stared for a moment at the black man cowering in the street, and then averted their gaze. What did the election of Barack Obama mean for him?

Like many civil rights lawyers, I was inspired to attend law school by the civil rights victories of the 1950s and 1960s. Even in the face of growing social and political opposition to remedial policies such as affirmative action, I clung to the notion that the evils of Jim Crow are behind us and that, while we have a long way to go to fulfill the dream of an egalitarian, multiracial democracy, we have made real progress and are now struggling to hold on to the gains of the past. I thought my job as a civil rights lawyer was to join with the allies of racial progress to resist attacks on affirmative action and to eliminate the vestiges of Jim Crow segregation, including our still separate and unequal system of education. I understood the problems plaguing poor communities of color, including problems associated with crime and rising incarceration rates, to be a function of poverty and lack of access to quality education—the continuing legacy of slavery and Jim Crow. Never did I seriously consider the possibility that a new racial caste system was operating in this country. The new system had been developed and implemented swiftly, and it was largely invisible, even to people, like me, who spent most of their waking hours fighting for justice.

I first encountered the idea of a new racial caste system more than a decade ago, when a bright orange poster caught my eye. I was rushing to catch the bus, and I noticed a sign stapled to a telephone pole that screamed in large bold print: THE DRUG WAR IS THE NEW JIM CROW. I paused for a moment and skimmed the text of the flyer. Some radical group was holding a community meeting about police brutality, the new three-strikes law in California, and the expansion of America's prison system. The meeting was being held at a small community church a few blocks away; it had seating capacity for no more than fifty people. I sighed, and muttered to myself something like, "Yeah, the criminal justice system is racist in many ways, but it really doesn't help to make such an absurd comparison. People will just think you're crazy." I then crossed the street and hopped on the bus. I was headed to my new job, director of the Racial Justice Project of the American Civil Liberties Union (ACLU) in Northern California.

When I began my work at the ACLU, I assumed that the criminal justice system had problems of racial bias, much in the same way that all major institutions in our society are plagued with problems associated with conscious and unconscious bias. As a lawyer who had litigated numerous class-action employment-discrimination cases, I understood well the many ways in which racial stereotyping can permeate subjective decision-making processes at all levels of an organization, with devastating consequences. I was familiar with the challenges associated with reforming institutions in which racial stratification is thought to be normal—the natural consequence of differences in education, culture, motivation, and, some still believe, innate ability. While at the ACLU, I shifted my focus from employment discrimination to criminal justice reform and dedicated myself to the task of working with others to identify and eliminate racial bias whenever and wherever it reared its ugly head.

By the time I left the ACLU, I had come to suspect that I was wrong about the criminal justice system. It was not just another institution infected with racial bias but rather a different beast entirely. The activists who posted the sign on the telephone pole were not crazy; nor were the smattering of lawyers and advocates around the country who were beginning to connect the dots between our current system of mass incarceration and earlier forms of social control. Quite belatedly, I came to see that mass incarceration in the

United States had, in fact, emerged as a stunningly comprehensive and well-disguised system of racialized social control that functions in a manner strikingly similar to Jim Crow.

In my experience, people who have been incarcerated rarely have difficulty identifying the parallels between these systems of social control. Once they are released, they are often denied the right to vote, excluded from juries, and relegated to a racially segregated and subordinated existence. Through a web of laws, regulations, and informal rules, all of which are powerfully reinforced by social stigma, they are confined to the margins of mainstream society and denied access to the mainstream economy. They are legally denied the ability to obtain employment, housing, and public benefits—much as African Americans were once forced into a segregated, second-class citizenship in the Jim Crow era.

Those of us who have viewed that world from a comfortable distance—yet sympathize with the plight of the so-called underclass—tend to interpret the experience of those caught up in the criminal justice system primarily through the lens of popularized social science, attributing the staggering increase in incarceration rates in communities of color to the predictable, though unfortunate, consequences of poverty, racial segregation, unequal educational opportunities, and the presumed realities of the drug market, including the mistaken belief that most drug dealers are black or brown. Occasionally, in the course of my work, someone would make a remark suggesting that perhaps the War on Drugs is a racist conspiracy to put blacks back in their place. This type of remark was invariably accompanied by nervous laughter, intended to convey the impression that although the idea had crossed their minds, it was not an idea a reasonable person would take seriously.

Most people assume the War on Drugs was launched in response to the crisis caused by crack cocaine in inner-city neighborhoods. This view holds that the racial disparities in drug convictions and sentences, as well as the rapid explosion of the prison population, reflect nothing more than the government's zealous—but benign—efforts to address rampant drug crime in poor, minority neighborhoods. This view, while understandable, given the sensational media coverage of crack in the 1980s and 1990s, is simply wrong.

While it is true that the publicity surrounding crack cocaine led to a dramatic increase in funding for the drug war (as well as to sentencing policies that greatly exacerbated racial disparities in incarceration rates), there is no truth to the notion that the War on Drugs was launched in response to crack cocaine. President Ronald Reagan officially announced the current drug war in 1982, before crack became an issue in the media or a crisis in poor black neighborhoods. A few years after the drug war was declared, crack began to spread rapidly in the poor black neighborhoods of Los Angeles and later emerged in cities across the country.[2] The Reagan administration hired staff to publicize the emergence of crack cocaine in 1985 as part of a strategic effort to build public and legislative support for the war.[3] The media campaign was an extraordinary success. Almost overnight, the media was saturated with images of black "crack whores," "crack dealers," and "crack babies"—images that seemed to confirm the worst negative racial stereotypes about impoverished inner-city residents. The media bonanza surrounding the "new demon drug" helped to catapult the War on Drugs from an ambitious federal policy to an actual war.

The timing of the crack crisis helped to fuel conspiracy theories and general speculation in poor black communities that the War on Drugs was part of a genocidal plan by the government to destroy black people in the United States. From the outset, stories circulated on the street that crack and other drugs were being brought into black neighborhoods by the CIA. Eventually, even the Urban League came to take the claims of genocide seriously. In its 1990 report "The State of Black America," it stated: "There is at least one concept that must be recognized if one is to see the pervasive and insidious nature of the drug problem for the African American community. Though difficult to accept, that is the concept of genocide."[4] While the conspiracy theories were initially dismissed as far-fetched, if not

2. The *New York Times* made the national media's first specific reference to crack in a story published in late 1985. Crack became known in a few impoverished neighborhoods in Los Angeles, New York, and Miami in early 1986. See Craig Reinarman and Harry Levine, "The Crack Attack: America's Latest Drug Scare, 1986–1992," in *Images of Issues: Typifying Contemporary Social Problems* (New York: Aldine De Gruyter, 1995), 152.

3. The Reagan administration's decision to publicize crack "horror stories" is discussed in more depth in chapter 1.

4. Clarence Page, "'The Plan': A Paranoid View of Black Problems," *Dover* (Delaware) *Herald*, Feb. 23, 1990. See also Manning Marable, *Race, Reform, and Rebellion: The Second Reconstruction in Black America, 1945–1990* (Jackson: University Press of Mississippi, 1991), 212–13.

downright loony, the word on the street turned out to be right, at least to a point. The CIA admitted in 1998 that guerrilla armies it actively supported in Nicaragua were smuggling illegal drugs into the United States—drugs that were making their way onto the streets of inner-city black neighborhoods in the form of crack cocaine. The CIA also admitted that, in the midst of the War on Drugs, it blocked law enforcement efforts to investigate illegal drug networks that were helping to fund its covert war in Nicaragua.[5]

It bears emphasis that the CIA never admitted (nor has any evidence been revealed to support the claim) that it intentionally sought the destruction of the black community by allowing illegal drugs to be smuggled into the United States. Nonetheless, conspiracy theorists surely must be forgiven for their bold accusation of genocide, in light of the devastation wrought by crack cocaine and the drug war, and the odd coincidence that an illegal drug crisis suddenly appeared in the black community after—not before—a drug war had been declared. In fact, the War on Drugs began at a time when illegal drug use was on the decline.[6] During this same time period, however, a war was declared, causing arrests and convictions for drug offenses to skyrocket, especially among people of color.

The impact of the drug war has been astounding. In less than thirty years, the U.S penal population exploded from around 300,000 to more than 2 million, with drug convictions accounting for the majority of the increase.[7] The United States now has the highest rate of incarceration in the world, dwarfing the rates of nearly every developed country, even surpassing those in highly repressive regimes like Russia, China, and Iran. In Germany, 93 people are in prison for every 100,000 adults and children. In the United States, the rate is roughly eight times that, or 750 per 100,000.[8]

5. See Alexander Cockburn and Jeffrey St. Clair, *Whiteout: The CIA, Drugs, and the Press* (New York: Verso, 1999). See also Nick Shou, "The Truth in 'Dark Alliance,'" *Los Angeles Times*, Aug. 18, 2006; Peter Kornbluh, "CIA's Challenge in South Central," *Los Angeles Times* (Washington edition), Nov. 15, 1996; and Alexander Cockburn, "Why They Hated Gary Webb," *The Nation*, Dec. 16, 2004.

6. Katherine Beckett and Theodore Sasson, *The Politics of Injustice: Crime and Punishment in America* (Thousand Oaks, CA: Sage Publications, 2004), 163.

7. Marc Mauer, *Race to Incarcerate*, rev. ed. (New York: The New Press, 2006), 33.

8. PEW Center on the States, *One in 100: Behind Bars in America 2008* (Washington, DC: PEW Charitable Trusts, 2008), 5.

The racial dimension of mass incarceration is its most striking feature. No other country in the world imprisons so many of its racial or ethnic minorities. The United States imprisons a larger percentage of its black population than South Africa did at the height of apartheid. In Washington, D.C., our nation's capital, it is estimated that three out of four young black men (and nearly all those in the poorest neighborhoods) can expect to serve time in prison.[9] Similar rates of incarceration can be found in black communities across America.

These stark racial disparities cannot be explained by rates of drug crime. Studies show that people of all colors *use and sell* illegal drugs at remarkably similar rates.[1] If there are significant differences in the surveys to be found, they frequently suggest that whites, particularly white youth, are more likely to engage in drug crime than people of color.[2]

9. Donald Braman, *Doing Time on the Outside: Incarceration and Family Life in Urban America* (Ann Arbor: University of Michigan Press, 2004), 3, citing D.C. Department of Corrections data for 2000.

1. See, e.g., U.S. Department of Health and Human Services, Substance Abuse and Mental Health Services Administration, *Summary of Findings from the 2000 National Household Survey on Drug Abuse*, NHSDA series H-13, DHHS pub. no. SMA 01-3549 (Rockville, MD: 2001), reporting that 6.4 percent of whites, 6.4 percent of blacks, and 5.3 percent of Hispanics were current users of illegal drugs in 2000; *Results from the 2002 National Survey on Drug Use and Health: National Findings*, NHSDA series H-22, DHHS pub. no. SMA 03-3836 (2003), revealing nearly identical rates of illegal drug use among whites and blacks, only a single percentage point between them; and *Results from the 2007 National Survey on Drug Use and Health: National Findings*, NSDUH series 11-34, DHHS pub. no. SMA 08-4343 (2007), showing essentially the same finding. See also Marc Mauer and Ryan S. King, *A 25-Year Quagmire: The "War on Drugs" and Its Impact on American Society* (Washington, DC: Sentencing Project, 2007), 19, citing a study suggesting that African Americans have slightly higher rates of illegal drug use than whites.

2. See, e.g., Howard N. Snyder and Melissa Sickman, *Juvenile Offenders and Victims: 2006 National Report*, U.S. Department of Justice, Office of Justice Programs, Office of Juvenile Justice and Delinquency Prevention (Washington, DC: U.S. Department of Justice, 2006), reporting that white youth are more likely than black youth to engage in illegal drug sales. See also Lloyd D. Johnson, Patrick M. O'Malley, Jerald G. Bachman, and John E. Schulenberg, *Monitoring the Future, National Survey Results on Drug Use, 1975–2006*, vol. 1, *Secondary School Students*, U.S. Department of Health and Human Services, National Institute on Drug Abuse, NIH pub. no. 07-6205 (Bethesda, MD: 2007), 32, "African American 12th graders have consistently shown lower usage rates than White 12th graders for most drugs, both licit and illicit"; and Lloyd D. Johnston, Patrick M. O'Malley, and Jerald G. Bachman, *Monitoring the Future: National Results on Adolescent Drug Use: Overview of Key Findings 2002*, U.S. Department of Health and Human Services, National Institute on Drug Abuse, NIH pub. no. 03-5374 (Bethesda, MD: 2003), presenting data showing that African American adolescents have slightly lower rates of illicit drug use than their white counterparts.

That is not what one would guess, however, when entering our nation's prisons and jails, which are overflowing with black and brown drug offenders. In some states, black men have been admitted to prison on drug charges at rates twenty to fifty times greater than those of white men.[3] And in major cities wracked by the drug war, as many as 80 percent of young African American men now have criminal records and are thus subject to legalized discrimination for the rest of their lives.[4] These young men are part of a growing undercaste, permanently locked up and locked out of mainstream society.

It may be surprising to some that drug crime was declining, not rising, when a drug war was declared. From a historical perspective, however, the lack of correlation between crime and punishment is nothing new. Sociologists have frequently observed that governments use punishment primarily as a tool of social control, and thus the extent or severity of punishment is often unrelated to actual crime patterns. Michael Tonry explains in *Thinking About Crime*: "Governments decide how much punishment they want, and these decisions are in no simple way related to crime rates."[5] This fact, he points out, can be seen most clearly by putting crime and punishment in comparative perspective. Although crime rates in the United States have not been markedly higher than those of other Western countries, the rate of incarceration has soared in the United States while it has remained stable or declined in other countries. Between 1960 and 1990, for example, official crime rates in Finland, Germany, and the United States were close to identical. Yet the U.S. incarceration rate quadrupled, the Finnish rate fell by 60 percent, and the German rate was stable in that period.[6] Despite similar crime rates, each government chose to impose different levels of punishment.

Today, due to recent declines, U.S. crime rates have dipped below the international norm. Nevertheless, the United States now boasts an incarceration rate that is six to ten times greater than that of other

3. Human Rights Watch, *Punishment and Prejudice: Racial Disparities in the War on Drugs*, HRW Reports, vol. 12, no. 2 (New York, 2000).

4. See, e.g., Paul Street, *The Vicious Circle: Race, Prison, Jobs, and Community in Chicago, Illinois, and the Nation* (Chicago: Chicago Urban League, Department of Research and Planning, 2002).

5. Michael Tonry, *Thinking About Crime: Sense and Sensibility in American Penal Culture* (New York: Oxford University Press, 2004), 14.

6. Ibid.

industrialized nations[7]—a development directly traceable to the drug war. The only country in the world that even comes close to the American rate of incarceration is Russia, and no other country in the world incarcerates such an astonishing percentage of its racial or ethnic minorities.

The stark and sobering reality is that, for reasons largely unrelated to actual crime trends, the American penal system has emerged as a system of social control unparalleled in world history. And while the size of the system alone might suggest that it would touch the lives of most Americans, the primary targets of its control can be defined largely by race. This is an astonishing development, especially given that as recently as the mid-1970s, the most well-respected criminologists were predicting that the prison system would soon fade away. Prison did not deter crime significantly, many experts concluded. Those who had meaningful economic and social opportunities were unlikely to commit crimes regardless of the penalty, while those who went to prison were far more likely to commit crimes again in the future. The growing consensus among experts was perhaps best reflected by the National Advisory Commission on Criminal Justice Standards and Goals, which issued a recommendation in 1973 that "no new institutions for adults should be built and existing institutions for juveniles should be closed."[8] This recommendation was based on their finding that "the prison, the reformatory and the jail have achieved only a shocking record of failure. There is overwhelming evidence that these institutions create crime rather than prevent it."[9]

These days, activists who advocate "a world without prisons" are often dismissed as quacks, but only a few decades ago, the notion that our society would be much better off without prisons—and that the end of prisons was more or less inevitable—not only dominated mainstream academic discourse in the field of criminology but also inspired a national campaign by reformers demanding a moratorium on prison construction. Marc Mauer, the executive director of the Sentencing Project, notes that what is most remarkable about the moratorium campaign in retrospect is the context of imprisonment at the time. In 1972, fewer than 350,000 people were being held in prisons and jails nationwide, compared with more than 2 million

7. Ibid., 20.

8. National Advisory Commission on Criminal Justice Standards and Goals, *Task Force Report on Corrections* (Washington, DC: Government Printing Office, 1973), 358.

9. Ibid., 597.

people today. The rate of incarceration in 1972 was at a level so low that it no longer seems in the realm of possibility, but for moratorium supporters, that magnitude of imprisonment was egregiously high. "Supporters of the moratorium effort can be forgiven for being so naïve," Mauer suggests, "since the prison expansion that was about to take place was unprecedented in human history."[1] No one imagined that the prison population would more than quintuple in their lifetime. It seemed far more likely that prisons would fade away.

Far from fading away, it appears that prisons are here to stay. And despite the unprecedented levels of incarceration in the African American community, the civil rights community is oddly quiet. One in three young African American men will serve time in prison if current trends continue, and in some cities more than half of all young adult black men are currently under correctional control—in prison or jail, on probation or parole.[2] Yet mass incarceration tends to be categorized as a criminal justice issue as opposed to a racial justice or civil rights issue (or crisis).

The attention of civil rights advocates has been largely devoted to other issues, such as affirmative action. During the past twenty years, virtually every progressive, national civil rights organization in the country has mobilized and rallied in defense of affirmative action. The struggle to preserve affirmative action in higher education, and thus maintain diversity in the nation's most elite colleges and universities, has consumed much of the attention and resources of the civil rights community and dominated racial justice discourse in the mainstream media, leading the general public to believe that affirmative action is the main battlefront in U.S. race relations—even as our prisons fill with black and brown men.

My own experience reflects this dynamic. When I first joined the ACLU, no one imagined that the Racial Justice Project would focus

1. Mauer, *Race to Incarcerate*, 17–18.

2. The estimate that one in three black men will go to prison during their lifetime is drawn from Thomas P. Bonczar, "Prevalence of Imprisonment in the U.S. Population, 1974–2001," U.S. Department of Justice, Bureau of Justice Statistics, August 2003. In Baltimore, like many large urban areas, the majority of young African American men are currently under correctional supervision. See Eric Lotke and Jason Ziedenberg, "Tipping Point: Maryland's Overuse of Incarceration and the Impact on Community Safety," Justice Policy Institute, March 2005, 3.

its attention on criminal justice reform. The ACLU was engaged in important criminal justice reform work, but no one suspected that work would eventually become central to the agenda of the Racial Justice Project. The assumption was that the project would concentrate its efforts on defending affirmative action. Shortly after leaving the ACLU, I joined the board of directors of the Lawyers' Committee for Civil Rights of the San Francisco Bay Area. Although the organization included racial justice among its core priorities, reform of the criminal justice system was not a major part of its racial justice work. It was not alone.

In January 2008, the Leadership Conference on Civil Rights—an organization composed of the leadership of more than 180 civil rights organizations—sent a letter to its allies and supporters informing them of a major initiative to document the voting record of members of Congress. The letter explained that its forthcoming report would show "how each representative and senator cast his or her vote on some of the most important civil rights issues of 2007, including voting rights, affirmative action, immigration, nominations, education, hate crimes, employment, health, housing, and poverty." Criminal justice issues did not make the list. That same broad-based coalition organized a major conference in October 2007, entitled Why We Can't Wait: Reversing the Retreat on Civil Rights, which included panels discussing school integration, employment discrimination, housing and lending discrimination, economic justice, environmental justice, disability rights, age discrimination, and immigrants' rights. Not a single panel was devoted to criminal justice reform.

The elected leaders of the African American community have a much broader mandate than civil rights groups, but they, too, frequently overlook criminal justice. In January 2009, for example, the Congressional Black Caucus sent a letter to hundreds of community and organization leaders who have worked with the caucus over the years, soliciting general information about them and requesting that they identify their priorities. More than thirty-five topics were listed as areas of potential special interest, including taxes, defense, immigration, agriculture, housing, banking, higher education, multimedia, transportation and infrastructure, women, seniors, nutrition, faith initiatives, civil rights, census, economic security, and emerging leaders. No mention was made of criminal justice. "Re-entry" was listed, but a community leader who was interested in criminal justice reform had to check the box labeled "other."

This is not to say that important criminal justice reform work has not been done. Civil rights advocates have organized vigorous challenges to specific aspects of the new caste system. One notable example is the successful challenge led by the NAACP Legal Defense Fund to a racist drug sting operation in Tulia, Texas. The 1999 drug bust incarcerated almost 15 percent of the black population of the town, based on the uncorroborated false testimony of a single informant hired by the sheriff of Tulia. More recently, civil rights groups around the country have helped to launch legal attacks and vibrant grassroots campaigns against felon disenfranchisement laws and have strenuously opposed discriminatory crack sentencing laws and guidelines, as well as "zero tolerance" policies that effectively funnel youth of color from schools to jails. The national ACLU recently developed a racial justice program that includes criminal justice issues among its core priorities and has created a promising Drug Law Reform Project. And thanks to the aggressive advocacy of the ACLU, NAACP, and other civil rights organizations around the country, racial profiling is widely condemned, even by members of law enforcement who once openly embraced the practice.

Still, despite these significant developments, there seems to be a lack of appreciation for the enormity of the crisis at hand. There is no broad-based movement brewing to end mass incarceration and no advocacy effort that approaches in scale the fight to preserve affirmative action. There also remains a persistent tendency in the civil rights community to treat the criminal justice system as just another institution infected with lingering racial bias. The NAACP's website offers one example. As recently as May 2008, one could find a brief introduction to the organization's criminal justice work in the section entitled Legal Department. The introduction explained that "despite the civil rights victories of our past, racial prejudice still pervades the criminal justice system." Visitors to the website were urged to join the NAACP in order to "protect the hard-earned civil rights gains of the past three decades." No one visiting the website would learn that the mass incarceration of African Americans had already eviscerated many of the hard-earned gains it urged its members to protect.

Imagine if civil rights organizations and African American leaders in the 1940s had not placed Jim Crow segregation at the forefront of their racial justice agenda. It would have seemed absurd, given that racial segregation was the primary vehicle of racialized social control in the United States during that period. This book argues that mass incarceration is, metaphorically, the New Jim Crow and that all those who care about social justice should fully commit themselves to dismantling this new racial caste system. Mass incarceration—not attacks on affirmative action or lax civil rights enforcement—is the most damaging manifestation of the backlash against the Civil Rights Movement. The popular narrative that emphasizes the death of slavery and Jim Crow and celebrates the nation's "triumph over race" with the election of Barack Obama, is dangerously misguided. The colorblind public consensus that prevails in America today—i.e., the widespread belief that race no longer matters—has blinded us to the realities of race in our society and facilitated the emergence of a new caste system.

Clearly, much has changed in my thinking about the criminal justice system since I passed that bright orange poster stapled to a telephone pole ten years ago. For me, the new caste system is now as obvious as my own face in the mirror. Like an optical illusion—one in which the embedded image is impossible to see until its outline is identified—the new caste system lurks invisibly within the maze of rationalizations we have developed for persistent racial inequality. It is possible—quite easy, in fact—never to see the embedded reality. Only after years of working on criminal justice reform did my own focus finally shift, and then the rigid caste system slowly came into view. Eventually it became obvious. Now it seems odd that I could not see it before.

Knowing as I do the difficulty of seeing what most everyone insists does not exist, I anticipate that this book will be met with skepticism or something worse. For some, the characterization of mass incarceration as a "racial caste system" may seem like a gross exaggeration, if not hyperbole. Yes. we may have "classes" in the United States—

vaguely defined upper, middle, and lower classes—and we may even have an "underclass" (a group so estranged from mainstream society that it is no longer in reach of the mythical ladder of opportunity), but we do not, many will insist, have anything in this country that resembles a "caste."

The aim of this book is not to venture into the long-running, vigorous debate in the scholarly literature regarding what does and does not constitute a caste system. I use the term *racial caste* in this book the way it is used in common parlance to denote a stigmatized racial group locked into an inferior position by law and custom. Jim Crow and slavery were caste systems. So is our current system of mass incarceration.

It may be helpful, in attempting to understand the basic nature of the new caste system, to think of the criminal justice system—the entire collection of institutions and practices that comprise it—not as an independent system but rather as a *gateway* into a much larger system of racial stigmatization and permanent marginalization. This larger system, referred to here as mass incarceration, is a system that locks people not only behind actual bars in actual prisons, but also behind virtual bars and virtual walls—walls that are invisible to the naked eye but function nearly as effectively as Jim Crow laws once did at locking people of color into a permanent second-class citizenship. The term *mass incarceration* refers not only to the criminal justice system but also to the larger web of laws, rules, policies, and customs that control those labeled criminals both in and out of prison. Once released, former prisoners enter a hidden underworld of legalized discrimination and permanent social exclusion. They are members of America's new undercaste.

The language of caste may well seem foreign or unfamiliar to some. Public discussions about racial caste in America are relatively rare. We avoid talking about caste in our society because we are ashamed of our racial history. We also avoid talking about race. We even avoid talking about class. Conversations about class are resisted in part because there is a tendency to imagine that one's class reflects upon one's character. What is key to America's understanding of class is the persistent belief—despite all evidence to the contrary—that anyone, with the proper discipline and drive, can move from a lower class to a higher class. We recognize that mobility may be difficult, but the key to our collective self-image is the assumption that mobility is always possible, so failure to move up reflects on one's character. By extension, the failure of a race or ethnic group to move up reflects very poorly on the group as a whole.

What is completely missed in the rare public debates today about the plight of African Americans is that a huge percentage of them are not free to move up at all. It is not just that they lack opportunity, attend poor schools, or are plagued by poverty. They are barred by law from doing so. And the major institutions with which they come into contact are designed to prevent their mobility. To put the matter starkly: The current system of control permanently locks a huge percentage of the African American community out of the mainstream society and economy. The system operates through our criminal justice institutions, but it functions more like a caste system than a system of crime control. Viewed from this perspective, the so-called underclass is better understood as an *undercaste*—a lower caste of individuals who are permanently barred by law and custom from mainstream society. Although this new system of racialized social control purports to be colorblind, it creates and maintains racial hierarchy much as earlier systems of control did. Like Jim Crow (and slavery), mass incarceration operates as a tightly networked system of laws, policies, customs, and institutions that operate collectively to ensure the subordinate status of a group defined largely by race.

This argument may be particularly hard to swallow given the election of Barack Obama. Many will wonder how a nation that just elected its first black president could possibly have a racial caste system. It's a fair question. But as discussed in Chapter 6, there is no inconsistency whatsoever between the election of Barack Obama to the highest office in the land and the existence of a racial caste system in the era of colorblindness. The current system of control depends on black exceptionalism; it is not disproved or undermined by it. Others may wonder how a racial caste system could exist when most Americans—of all colors—oppose race discrimination and endorse colorblindness. Yet as we shall see in the pages that follow, racial caste systems do not require racial hostility or overt bigotry to thrive. They need only racial indifference, as Martin Luther King Jr. warned more than forty-five years ago.

The recent decisions by some state legislatures, most notably New York's, to repeal or reduce mandatory drug sentencing laws have led some to believe that the system of racial control described in this book is already fading away. Such a conclusion, I believe, is a serious mistake. Many of the states that have reconsidered their harsh sentencing schemes have done so not out of concern for the lives and families that have been destroyed by these laws or the racial dimensions of the drug war, but out of concern for bursting state budgets in a time of economic recession. In other words, the racial ideology that gave rise to these laws remains largely undisturbed. Changing economic conditions or rising crime rates could easily result in a reversal of fortunes for those who commit drug crimes, particularly if the drug criminals are perceived to be black and brown. Equally important to understand is this: Merely reducing sentence length, by itself, does not disturb the basic architecture of the New Jim Crow. So long as large numbers of African Americans continue to be arrested and labeled drug criminals, they will continue to be relegated to a permanent second-class status upon their release, no matter how much (or how little) time they spend behind bars. The system of mass incarceration is based on the prison label, not prison time.

Skepticism about the claims made here is warranted. There are important differences, to be sure, among mass incarceration, Jim Crow, and slavery—the three major racialized systems of control adopted in the United States to date. Failure to acknowledge the relevant differences, as well as their implications, would be a disservice to racial justice discourse. Many of the differences are not as dramatic as they initially appear, however; others serve to illustrate the ways in which systems of racialized social control have managed to morph, evolve, and adapt to changes in the political, social, and legal context over time. Ultimately, I believe that the similarities between these systems of control overwhelm the differences and that mass incarceration, like its predecessors, has been largely immunized from legal challenge. If this claim is substantially correct, the implications for racial justice advocacy are profound.

With the benefit of hindsight, surely we can see that piecemeal policy reform or litigation alone would have been a futile approach to dismantling Jim Crow segregation. While those strategies certainly had their place, the Civil Rights Act of 1964 and the concomitant cultural shift would never have occurred without the cultivation of a critical political consciousness in the African American community and the widespread, strategic activism that flowed from it. Likewise, the notion that the *New* Jim Crow can ever be dismantled through traditional litigation and policy-reform strategies that are wholly disconnected from a major social movement seems fundamentally misguided.

Such a movement is impossible, though, if those most committed to abolishing racial hierarchy continue to talk and behave as if a state-sponsored racial caste system no longer exists. If we continue to tell ourselves the popular myths about racial progress or, worse yet, if we say to ourselves that the problem of mass incarceration is just too big, too daunting for us to do anything about and that we should instead direct our energies to battles that might be more easily won, history will judge us harshly. A human rights nightmare is occurring on our watch.

A new social consensus must be forged about race and the role of race in defining the basic structure of our society, if we hope ever to abolish the New Jim Crow. This new consensus must begin with dialogue, a conversation that fosters a critical consciousness, a key prerequisite to effective social action. This book is an attempt to ensure that the conversation does not end with nervous laughter.

It is not possible to write a relatively short book that explores all aspects of the phenomenon of mass incarceration and its implications for racial justice. No attempt has been made to do so here. This book paints with a broad brush, and as a result, many important issues have not received the attention they deserve. For example, relatively little is said here about the unique experience of women, Latinos, and immigrants in the criminal justice system, though these groups are particularly vulnerable to the worst abuses and suffer in ways that are important and distinct. This book focuses on the experience of African American men in the new caste system. I hope other scholars and advocates will pick up where the book leaves off and develop the critique more fully or apply the themes sketched here to other groups and other contexts.

What this book is intended to do—the only thing it is intended to do—is to stimulate a much-needed conversation about the role of the criminal justice system in creating and perpetuating racial hierarchy in the United States. The fate of millions of people—indeed the future of the black community itself—may depend on the willingness of those who care about racial justice to re-examine their basic assumptions about the role of the criminal justice system in our society. The fact that more than half of the young black men in many large American cities are currently under the control of the criminal justice system (or saddled with criminal records) is not—as many argue—just a symptom of poverty or poor choices, but rather evidence of a new racial caste system at work.

Chapter 1 begins our journey. It briefly reviews the history of racialized social control in the United States, answering the basic question: How did we get here? The chapter describes the control of African Americans through racial caste systems, such as slavery and Jim Crow, which appear to die but then are reborn in new form, tailored to the needs and constraints of the time. As we shall see, there is a certain pattern to the births and deaths of racial caste in America. Time and again, the most ardent proponents of racial hierarchy have succeeded in creating new caste systems by triggering a collapse of resistance across the political spectrum. This feat has been achieved largely by appealing to the racism and vulnerability of lower-class whites, a group of people who are understandably eager to ensure that they never find themselves trapped at the bottom of the American totem pole. This pattern, dating back to slavery, has birthed yet another racial caste system in the United States: mass incarceration.

The structure of mass incarceration is described in some detail in Chapter 2, with a focus on the War on Drugs. Few legal rules meaningfully constrain the police in the drug war, and enormous financial incentives have been granted to law enforcement to engage in mass drug arrests through military-style tactics. Once swept into the system, one's chances of ever being truly free are slim, often to the vanishing point. Defendants are typically denied meaningful legal representation, pressured by the threat of lengthy sentences into a plea bargain, and then placed under formal control—in prison or jail, on probation or parole. Upon release, ex-offenders are discriminated against, legally, for the rest of their lives, and most will eventually return to prison. They are members of America's new undercaste.

Chapter 3 turns our attention to the role of race in the U.S. criminal justice system. It describes the method to the madness—how a formally race-neutral criminal justice system can manage to round up, arrest, and imprison an extraordinary number of black and brown men, when people of color are actually no more likely to be guilty of drug crimes and many other offenses than whites. This chapter debunks the notion that rates of black imprisonment can be explained by crime rates and identifies the huge racial disparities at every stage of the criminal justice process—from the initial stop, search, and arrest to the plea bargaining and sentencing phases. In short, the chapter explains how the legal rules that structure the system guarantee discriminatory results. These legal rules ensure that the undercaste is overwhelmingly black and brown.

Chapter 4 considers how the caste system operates once people are released from prison. In many respects, release from prison does not represent the beginning of freedom but instead a cruel new phase of stigmatization and control. Myriad laws, rules, and regulations discriminate against ex-offenders and effectively prevent their meaningful re-integration into the mainstream economy and society. I argue that the shame and stigma of the "prison label" is, in many respects, more damaging to the African American community than the shame and stigma associated with Jim Crow. The criminalization and demonization of black men has turned the black community against itself, unraveling community and family relationships, decimating networks of mutual support, and intensifying the shame and self-hate experienced by the current pariah caste.

The many parallels between mass incarceration and Jim Crow are explored in Chapter 5. The most obvious parallel is legalized discrimination. Like Jim Crow, mass incarceration marginalizes large segments of the African American community, segregates them physically (in prisons, jails, and ghettos), and then authorizes discrimination against them in voting, employment, housing, education, public benefits, and jury service. The federal court system has effectively immunized the current system from challenges on the grounds of racial bias, much as earlier systems of control were protected and endorsed by the U.S. Supreme Court. The parallels do not end there, however. Mass incarceration, like Jim Crow, helps to define the meaning and significance of race in America. Indeed, the stigma of criminality functions in much the same way that the stigma of race once did. It justifies a legal, social, and economic boundary between "us" and "them." Chapter 5 also explores some of the differences among slavery, Jim Crow, and mass incarceration, most significantly the fact that mass incarceration is designed to warehouse a population deemed disposable—unnecessary to the functioning of the new global economy—while earlier systems of control were designed to exploit and control black labor. In addition, the chapter discusses the experience of white people in this new caste system; although they have not been the primary targets of the drug war, they have been harmed by it—a powerful illustration of how a racial state can harm people of all colors. Finally, this chapter responds to skeptics who claim that mass incarceration cannot be understood as a racial caste system because many "get tough on crime" policies are supported by African Americans. Many of these claims, I note, are no more persuasive today than arguments made a hundred years ago by blacks and whites who claimed that racial segregation simply reflected "reality," not racial animus, and that African Americans would be better off not challenging the Jim Crow system but should focus instead on improving themselves within it. Throughout our history, there have been African Americans who, for a variety of reasons, have defended or been complicit with the prevailing system of control.

Chapter 6 reflects on what acknowledging the presence of the New Jim Crow means for the future of civil rights advocacy. I argue that nothing short of a major social movement can successfully dismantle the new caste system. Meaningful reforms can be achieved without such a movement, but unless the public consensus supporting the current system is completely overturned, the basic structure of the new caste system will remain intact. Building a broad-based social movement, however, is not enough. It is not nearly enough to persuade mainstream voters that we have relied too heavily on incarceration or that drug abuse is a public health problem, not a crime. If the movement that emerges to challenge mass incarceration fails to confront squarely the critical role of race in the basic structure of our society, and if it fails to cultivate an ethic of genuine care, compassion, and concern for every human being—of every class, race, and nationality—within our nation's borders (including poor whites, who are often pitted against poor people of color), the collapse of mass incarceration will not mean the death of racial caste in America. Inevitably a new system of racialized social control will emerge—one that we cannot foresee, just as the current system of mass incarceration was not predicted by anyone thirty years ago. No task is more urgent for racial justice advocates today than ensuring that America's current racial caste system is its last.

2010

Zoë Heller

b. 1965

If you are studying this textbook in a college class, probably one of your classmates has been sexually assaulted. And there's a high likelihood that the person who assaulted them is still enrolled at your college. Nevertheless, as this provocative essay indicates, attempts to remedy such conditions involve several competing rights and interests. Before the modern feminist movement, laws purportedly enacted to protect women often simultaneously subjugated them. For example, until 1971 employers could require pregnant women to take unpaid leave, ostensibly to protect them from the dangers of work. But advocates of equal rights opposed the law and got it repealed because it imposed a severe disadvantage on working women. Add to these issues the special status that college campuses have often enjoyed in American society. Up until the 1960s, colleges regularly suspended the civil rights of undergraduates, especially behaviors that were legal but regarded by administrators as immoral and the exercise of rights that disrupted campuses, such as free speech. These powers were based on a principle of in loco parentis, *suggesting that the college administration was acting as the student's parent, and have largely disappeared. But colleges today are often empowered to regulate students' illegal and even criminal behavior through their own judicial systems, such as honor boards. This essay provides an excellent example of everyone agreeing on a goal (the elimination of sexual assaults on college campuses) but disagreeing about how to achieve that goal.*

Rape on the Campus

According to the most commonly cited estimate, 20 percent of women are sexually assaulted during their time at college and as few as 5 percent of these assaults are ever reported to the police.[1] College authorities are required by law to investigate and adjudicate sexual assault complaints from their students, but they have repeatedly proven unwilling or incompetent to do so. (Some colleges stand accused of ignoring or downplaying sexual assault allegations in the interests of protecting themselves from bad publicity, others of conducting inept investigations and of handing out inadequate punishments to those found guilty.) The Department of Education currently has eighty-four US schools under investigation for mishandling cases of sexual assault.

Few would disagree that the systems for preventing and prosecuting sexual assault on US campuses are in need of change. But the efficacy and fairness of recent reforms that focus on making college grievance procedures more favorable to complainants and on codifying strict new definitions of sexual consent remain highly questionable. Advocates of these reforms tend to dismiss their opponents as reactionaries and "rape apologists"—a characterization that is probably accurate in some cases—but feminists, too, have cause to view these measures and the protectionist principles on which they are based with alarm.

1. This estimate is derived from the Campus Sexual Assault Study of 2007, and, like most of the statistics related to campus sexual assault, it requires some parsing. The CSA study, which found that 19 percent of the senior women students it surveyed had suffered some sort of sexual assault during their college years, relied on a self-selecting sample of college students from two public universities and, as its authors have pointed out, its findings cannot be regarded as nationally representative. The study also used a definition of sexual assault that encompassed a very wide range of incidents, from violent rape to "forced kissing," and it made the decision to classify incidents as assault, even when the respondents themselves took issue with that classification. These caveats do not justify the conclusion of some conservative pundits that concerns about campus rape are merely "hysterical," but they are significant nevertheless.

The Obama administration first signaled its determination to tackle the issue of campus sexual assault in 2011, when the Department of Education's Office for Civil Rights (OCR) wrote a letter to every college in the country, pointedly reminding them that failure to adopt appropriate policies for dealing with sexual misconduct was a violation of Title IX, the section of the Education Amendments of 1972 that forbids discrimination on the basis of gender. The letter, which announced itself as a "significant guidance document," offered detailed recommendations on what such appropriate policies would include. Since institutions found in violation of Title IX risk having their federal funding withdrawn, these recommendations were effectively government directives and schools responded accordingly.

Some of the recommendations related to "proactive measures" that schools were to take in order to prevent sexual harassment and violence. These included publishing a notice of nondiscrimination, publishing grievance procedures, training employees in how to identify and report sexual misconduct, and designating a specific employee to coordinate compliance with Title IX. There were also recommendations on what Valerie Jarrett, senior adviser to the president, has called "more victim-centered incident-intake and justice response policies."

Schools were advised to ensure that "steps taken to accord due process rights to the alleged perpetrator do not restrict or unnecessarily delay the Title IX protections for the complainant." This ambiguous instruction seemed to advocate some due process for the accused, but not too much. Schools were also told that if they granted the right of appeal to students found guilty of sexual misconduct, the same right should be granted to complainants. (Thus a student found innocent of sexual assault charges by a college grievance panel could be tried again on the same charges.) Most notably, the letter instructed schools to use a "preponderance of the evidence" standard when judging the innocence or guilt of an accused student:

> In order for a school's grievance procedures to be consistent with Title IX standards, the school must use a preponderance of the evidence standard (i.e., it is more likely than not that sexual harassment

> or violence occurred). The "clear and convincing" standard (i.e., it is highly probable or reasonably certain that the sexual harassment or violence occurred), currently used by some schools, is a higher standard of proof. Grievance procedures that use this higher standard are inconsistent with the standard of proof established for violations of the civil rights laws, and are thus not equitable under Title IX.

In other words, a college grievance panel has now only to establish that it is 50.1 percent likely that a student committed sexual assault in order to find him guilty.

Part of the OCR's honorable intention, it would seem, is to ensure that complaints of sexual assault are not dismissed or minimized by college authorities as they have been in the past. Yet as the troubling phrase "victim-centered" suggests, the new rules go beyond insisting on fair and equal treatment for sexual assault complainants. They effectively cancel the presumption of a defendant's innocence, and replace it with the presumption of a complainant's victimhood.

For some, this is a salutary development, a necessary antidote to the unfair disadvantages that rape victims have traditionally suffered when seeking redress in college tribunals. According to Colby Bruno, senior counsel at the Victim Rights Law Center, the preponderance of evidence standard "helps counterbalance so much of the bias and rape culture that permeates these cases." But the proper remedy for bias is surely not more bias in the opposite direction. And while there is certainly a long history of rape victims being demeaned and automatically disbelieved, not *all* of the difficulties associated with prosecuting rape are attributable to sexist prejudice. Rape cases, which often boil down to the relative credibility of two conflicting narratives, are inherently difficult to prove. No fair adjudication process can get around this fact by assuming a posture of reflexive credulity toward a victim's testimony.

Last October, twenty-eight current and retired Harvard law professors wrote a public letter to the *Boston Globe* expressing concern about the university's Sexual Harassment Policy and Procedures that had recently been revised to comply with OCR directives. The procedures, they wrote, "lack the most basic elements of fairness and due process" and "are overwhelmingly stacked against the accused." They also argued that these procedures did not reflect the university's legal obligations but rather a dubious interpretation of those obligations as provided by OCR bureaucrats:

> The goal must not be simply to go as far as possible in the direction of preventing anything that some might characterize as sexual harassment. The goal must instead be to fully address sexual harassment while at the same time protecting students against unfair and inappropriate discipline, honoring individual relationship autonomy, and maintaining the values of academic freedom. The law that the Supreme Court and lower federal courts have developed under Title IX and Title VII attempts to balance all these important interests. The university's sexual harassment policy departs dramatically from these legal principles, jettisoning balance and fairness in the rush to appease certain federal administrative officials.
>
> We recognize that large amounts of federal funding may ultimately be at stake. But Harvard University is positioned as well as any academic institution in the country to stand up for principle in the face of funding threats. The issues at stake are vitally important to our students, faculties, and entire community.[2]

Some supporters of the new rules believe that the imperative to address the sexual assault crisis on campuses overrides any footling concerns about due process. Since women are not generally inclined to lie about rape, they argue, the chances of false convictions under the new evidentiary standards are low.[3] And if, in the end, a few men are found guilty of rapes they didn't commit, this is an acceptable price to pay for ensuring that hundreds of assault victims receive justice. "We should believe, as a matter of default, what an accuser says," Zerlina Maxwell asserted recently in *The Washington Post*. "Ultimately, the costs of wrongly disbelieving a survivor far outweigh the

2. On December 30, 2014, after a four-year investigation of Harvard Law School, the OCR announced that the school's "current and prior" sexual harassment policies had been found in violation of Title IX. Harvard has now entered a resolution agreement with the OCR, under which it must again revise its policies.

3. The statistics on false rape allegations are murky. Law enforcement data show that, on average, between 8 and 10 percent of all rape reports are judged to be "unfounded" at the investigative stage. But not all of the reports in the "unfounded" category are necessarily false, and conversely, not all false reports make it into the "unfounded" statistics.

costs of calling someone a rapist." The *Guardian* columnist Jessica Valenti sums up the argument thus: "On the one side, there are the 20 percent of college women who can expect to be victimized by rapists and would-be rapists; on the other side is a bunch of adult men (and a few women) worrying themselves to death that a few college-aged men might have to find a new college to attend."

The perils of this ends-justifies-the-means calculus (variants of which have been used in recent years to defend racial profiling, the mass government surveillance of US citizens, and the torture of terrorism suspects) ought to be self-evident. It is a moral and strategic error for feminism—or any movement that purports to care about social justice—to argue for undermining or suspending legitimate rights, even in the interests of combating egregious crimes. If the chance of an unfounded assault allegation is "only" eight in a hundred, that is reason enough to avoid basing standards of evidence on the assumed good faith of complainants.

Even less plausible is the claim that miscarriages of justice are tolerable because the punishments inflicted by college disciplinary panels are relatively minor. Last summer *The New York Times* editorial board noted that the new evidentiary standards "seem justified" since they apply only to "administrative proceedings in which the accused student might be facing expulsion, not a loss of liberty."

This argument displays a startling complacency not only about the prospect of expelling innocent men, but equally about the prospect of letting genuine offenders go free. To be branded as a rapist and expelled from university would seem to be a very terrible outcome for an innocent student, and not really terrible enough for a guilty one. Indeed, the fact that college rapists only face expulsion would seem to be a good reason why colleges ought not to be trying rape cases at all. If the aim is to address sexual assault with the seriousness it deserves, why leave it to panels made up of minimally trained professors, administrators, and in some instances students to deal with such cases? Why treat rape as a Title IX issue, rather than as a felony?

When Title IX was passed by Congress in 1972, its intended purpose was to ensure that women had equal access to educational institutions, both as students and as professors. The crucial passage of the amendment reads: "No person in the United States shall, on the basis of sex, be excluded from participation in, be denied the benefits of, or be subjected to discrimination under any education program or activity receiving federal financial assistance." In 1977, a group of female undergraduates at Yale University, using an argument developed by Catharine MacKinnon, brought a suit against the school, proposing that the sexual harassment they had experienced on campus—professors offering to give them better grades in exchange for sexual favors—was a form of sex discrimination. The case of *Alexander v. Yale* was eventually thrown out on technical grounds, but the judge upheld the plaintiffs' legal argument and in the years since then the OCR has officially recognized sexual harassment as a Title IX violation.

Since much of what is commonly understood by the term "sexual harassment" does not amount to criminal behavior, but may nonetheless be capable of creating a hostile environment for female students, it would seem to make sense to have such conduct fall within the remit of Title IX. (If, for example, fraternity pledges march through a campus chanting "No means yes, yes means anal," as they did at Yale a few years ago, it is appropriate that the university authorities, rather than the police, discipline their behavior.)

But sexual harassment, as defined by the OCR, includes not only "unwelcome sexual advances" and "requests for sexual favors" but also sexual assault and rape. The result is a preposterous situation wherein rape is characterized—and punished—by college authorities principally as an infringement of a student's right to equal educational opportunity. This is rather like having a group of train conductors prosecute the rape of a female commuter, on the basis that the crime violates her equal right to use public transport.

A number of organizations, including the Rape, Abuse and Incest National Network (RAINN), have expressed their opposition to having rape cases adjudicated by college tribunals.[4] But most anti-rape campus activists remain strongly in favor of keeping rape allegations an internal college matter. Students, they point out, are usually reluctant to go to the police (whose willingness to take sexual assault claims seriously they have good reason to mistrust), and because of this any attempt to institutionalize partnerships between campus

4. In an open letter to the White House in February 2014, RAINN wrote, "It would never occur to anyone to leave the adjudication process of a murder in the hands of a school's internal judicial process. Why, then, is it not only common, but expected, for them to do so when it comes to sexual assault?"

security and law enforcement will only result in even fewer assaults being reported. Danielle Dirks, a sociology professor at Occidental College, and one of a group of women who have filed Title IX complaints against the university, recently told *The Nation*:

> I say this as a criminologist. I've given up on the criminal justice system. College campuses, which are supposed to be the bastions of cutting-edge knowledge and a chance to shape the rest of the country, actually can do right.

There is no doubt that the police and the courts are guilty of all manner of negligence, insensitivity, and rank stupidity in handling cases of sexual assault, but the wisdom of "giving up" on criminal justice—of retreating from the fight for fair treatment under the law—and taking refuge in a system of ersatz college justice remains highly questionable. In addition to the fear of not being believed, the chief reason that students cite for not reporting their assaults to law enforcement is their uncertainty about whether the incidents constitute sufficiently grave crimes.[5] Asking those students to take their allegations to campus tribunals—to have their claims adjudicated in essentially the same manner as plagiarism charges—does nothing to clear up their confusion about the seriousness of sexual assault. On the contrary, it actively encourages the trivialization of sexual violence.

"Giving up" on criminal justice also suggests a rather cavalier attitude to the majority of American women who do not have recourse to college grievance panels. Even if, like Professor Dirks, one is persuaded that Title IX procedures represent the frontier of enlightened jurisprudence, the proper aim of feminism is surely to make prosecuting sexual assault fairer and safer for *all* women.

Much the same dubious desire to create privileged enclaves of protection unavailable to the general female population is apparent in the widespread support for a new "affirmative" standard of consent on college campuses. Bill 967, passed in California this year, requires all colleges that receive state funding to use an

5. In a study commissioned by the National Institute of Justice in 2000, 42.1 percent of surveyed assault victims said they did not report their assault to the police because they were "not sure a crime or harm was intended."

"affirmative consent" standard in arbitrating cases of sexual misconduct. According to the statute, commonly referred to as the "Yes Means Yes" law, sex is deemed to be consensual only when both partners have provided, verbally or nonverbally, an "affirmative, conscious, and voluntary agreement to engage in sexual activity." (Such consent, which is rendered invalid if the party is unconscious or "incapacitated" by alcohol or drugs, must be "ongoing throughout a sexual activity.")

Significantly, the Department of Education has deliberately refrained from specifying a "national standard for what it means to consent to sexual activity" because, as it noted last summer in a set of draft amendments to the Violence Against Women Act, a definition would create ambiguity and confusion for institutional officials, students, employees, and the public, particularly in jurisdictions which either do not define consent or have a definition that differed from the one that would be in the regulations. This argument has not, however, deterred colleges and states from going ahead and codifying consent standards of their own. "Yes Means Yes" bills have now been introduced in the state legislatures of New York, New Hampshire, and New Jersey. And according to the National Center for Higher Education Risk Management, more than eight hundred US colleges and universities are already using some sort of affirmative consent standard in their sexual assault policies.

The putative merit of affirmative consent is that it removes from a rape victim any obligation to prove that she physically or verbally resisted her assailant. This is a crucial matter because there are clearly many circumstances in which a victim's lack of struggle or protest does not indicate willingness or complacency, but rather fear and the desire to avoid injury. However, the laws in California, New York, and many other states already explicitly exempt rape victims from having to prove that they resisted their assaults, verbally or otherwise. And there are good reasons for sticking with this simple proviso. To acknowledge that the absence of "no" does not necessarily mean "yes" responds to something observably true about the way in which humans conduct themselves in stressful or threatening circumstances. It adds nuance to the law. To insist, instead, that the absence of "yes" *always* indicates assault makes the law a considerably blunter instrument. It ignores the fact that many—perhaps most—consensual sexual encounters take place without unambiguous permission being granted, and in doing so it dangerously broadens the category of sexual behavior that may be deemed assault.

Defenders of affirmative consent insist that this is alarmist nonsense. Since the law allows for "nonverbal" expressions of consent, all that is really required of men is that they ascertain the willingness of their sexual partners. "You don't need an advanced degree to determine whether the person you're being amorous with is into it or not," Jessica Valenti contends in *The Guardian.* "Grabbing you closer: *Into it.* Lying there silently staring at the ceiling: *Not into it.*" Nor is it difficult, she writes, to establish whether a person is compos mentis or only semiconscious:

> We're all adults here, and it's not difficult to tell when someone is too drunk to make a decision. A half muttered and barely coherent "yes" by a half-passed out person? No. A buzzy, happy, "rip my clothes off"! Yes. Let's not pretend we don't know the difference.

In the general run of things, Valenti may be right: gauging the enthusiasm and inebriation of a person is not an unduly challenging task. But the emotions with which people—particularly young, sexually inexperienced people—enter into sexual encounters are often more complicated and ambivalent than the simple categories of "into it" and "not into it" will allow. And college standards for what constitutes acceptable levels of drunkenness—levels, that is, at which consent is considered valid—are often more stringent than Valenti suggests.

Lena Dunham's account of an unhappy sexual episode that she experienced as a freshman at Oberlin College is a case in point. The recollection, which appears in her recent book, *Not That Kind of Girl*, describes the confused and fundamentally equivocal spirit in which she took a man home from a party and ended up having sex with him. She was drunk and high, and although the man did not coerce her in any explicit way, she did not feel fully in control. The fact that she responded to his sexual advances by asking him if he would like "to make me come" was less an expression of genuine desire, she writes, than an attempt to convince herself that she was pursuing a grown-up sexual adventure of her own choosing. Only when she discovered that he was not wearing a condom did she call a halt to the proceedings and kick him out.

Dunham, who was initially inclined to look upon this experience as a miserable but educational mistake, has since come to regard it as rape. "I feel like there are fifty ways it's my fault. . . . But I also know that at no moment did I consent to being handled that way." Given that her verbal and nonverbal cues seem to have strongly suggested consent, and given that she was intoxicated but not incapacitated at the time, one might think that, even under affirmative consent rules, a college tribunal would be hard pressed to find in her favor. But according to Oberlin College's current sexual offense policy, consent is not consent when given by a person whose "judgment is substantially impaired by drugs or alcohol."[6] Even though the man in this case was equally drunk (and could conceivably have regretted the incident himself), only the impaired judgment of his accuser would be considered relevant in establishing whether an assault took place.

Ezra Klein has observed, in an article titled "Yes Means Yes Is a Terrible Law, and I Completely Support It," that branding men rapists for their roles in "genuinely ambiguous situations" is a likely and necessary outcome of affirmative consent law:

> To work, "Yes Means Yes" needs to create a world where men are afraid. . . . It's those cases—particularly the ones that feel genuinely unclear and maybe even unfair, the ones that become lore in frats and cautionary tales that fathers e-mail to their sons—that will convince men that they better Be Pretty Damn Sure.

Leaving aside for a moment whether this is a just or reasonable way of treating men, one has to wonder whether such a policy is ultimately good for women.

6. KC Johnson at the Manhattan Institute's Minding the Campus blog has surveyed the consent policies of fifty-five top-ranked American universities and found that roughly a third of them—including those at Brown, Stanford, Duke, and Columbia—state or imply that consent is invalid when the consenting party is intoxicated.

Elsewhere on the website *Vox*, Amanda Taub argues that

> by exempting sexual aggressors from the responsibility of figuring out whether their partners are "eager and ready to sleep with them," we're asking their targets to either give in to sexual activity they don't want, or to run the risk that a firm, assertive, continued rejection will end in violence.

But to exempt women from the responsibility of stating their own sexual wishes without prompting—to insist that it is the man's job to "figure out" those wishes—comes dangerously close to infantilizing women.

Since affirmative consent law is officially gender neutral, it seems possible—in fact, likely—that at some point a man will use it to bring a sexual assault charge against a female student. He will attest that he was drunk when the woman made sexual advances toward him, that he felt too intimidated or confused to demur, that he never actually said "yes." This will strike many people as a ludicrous misappropriation of a law that was designed to protect women. But it will be impossible to deny the legitimacy of such a complaint without acknowledging the retrograde premise on which affirmative consent is based: that men and women differ fundamentally in their ability to assert their sexual wishes; that even in the absence of violence, or overt threat of violence, the looming fact of men's superior physical strength always acts as an implicit constraint on women's expression of their sexual free will.

Laws that offer special protections to women based on their difference from men have a habit of redounding to women's disadvantage. In the case of affirmative consent, the payback is readily apparent: women are deemed to have limited agency in their sexual relations with men, so men are designated as their sexual guardians—tenderly coaxing from them what it is they want or don't want and occasionally overruling their stated wishes when they've had too much to drink. What a pity it will be if a campaign against sexual violence ends by undermining the very idea of female sexual autonomy that it seeks to defend.

2014

Valeria Luiselli
b. 1983

In 2014, when Luiselli first began her research, an alarming number of children were apprehended migrating across the Mexico-Texas border—nearly 70,000. Almost the same number of families with children were arrested that same year, which was nearly three times as many as the year before. Most of these migrants were fleeing spikes in criminal violence in Central American countries like Guatemala, Honduras, and El Salvador. This influx overwhelmed the existing processes, which were designed to deal with numbers closer to 10,000 per year. The Obama administration hastily erected facilities and procedures, and by October 2014, nearly four-fifths of the families that were apprehended illegally crossing the border were released to relatives in the United States, either having secured asylum or having scheduled a later date before an immigration judge; similarly, about half the unaccompanied children attained some legal status in the United States.

By 2019, when the New Yorker *published this article, a new crisis was triggered by President Donald Trump, who, elected in 2016 on an anti-immigration platform, considered these practices too lenient and introduced a new "zero-tolerance" policy. Henceforth, when Immigration and Customs Enforcement agents apprehended families crossing the border illegally, they took children from their parents, incarcerated them in different locations, and imposed "the full prosecutorial powers of the Department of Justice," according to directions from Attorney General Jeff Sessions. This policy was so obviously inhumane that it sparked widespread outrage among Americans, even among such notable conservatives as former-First Lady Laura Bush, and President Trump disavowed blame for the change in policy. But that crisis was only one manifestation of a larger system of violence—both legal and illegal—continually plaguing the U.S.-Mexico border.*

The New Yorker *is a fairly liberal magazine, and Luiselli can assume that the people she describes in Tombstone, Arizona, are not the type who will read her work. In fact, most people who subscribe to the* New Yorker *deplored Trump's immigration policies, including the border wall, and they disliked the attitudes exhibited by the white people Luiselli interviewed for this piece. Luiselli did not need to persuade her readers that the vigilantes patrolling the deserts of Arizona and New Mexico were inhumane. You might then ponder what is the rhetorical purpose of this essay? What is Luiselli trying to get her readers to believe or do? That purpose is less overt than it would be in, say, an op-ed piece or in an academic article. The "literary" essay (to use Luiselli's own term for this genre) submerges what we might call its thesis in its emotional appeals as much as in logical argument. Look to the end of the essay, not to its introduction, for the clearest articulation of Luiselli's purpose.*

The Wild West Meets the Southern Border

Shakespeare is in New Mexico. Tombstone, in Arizona. Both are old mining towns near the U.S.-Mexico border. They came into existence in the 1870s, during the silver strike, but soon suffered the same fate as most of the other mining towns in the region: boom, depression, abandonment, and then a strange kind of afterlife.

Some years ago, I spent a summer in the Southwest with my then husband, our daughter, and my two stepsons, and we visited both places. It was 2014, the immigration crisis was very much in the news—unaccompanied children from Central America were arriving at the border in unprecedented numbers, seeking asylum—and I was beginning to do research on the situation. My husband and I were obsessively meeting deadlines, and the kids were getting impatient with us, feeling that we had scammed them into a vacation with no vacation plan. So we looked online and found that Shakespeare and Tombstone offered family-friendly activities: stagecoaches, historamas, and Wild West reenactments.

Apparently, some of the biggest legends of the Wild West had passed through Shakespeare. Dangerous Dan had been there. Curly Bill, too. And Bean Belly Smith. To be honest, I had no idea who these men were. But, reading their names out loud to the kids, I showed enthusiasm. At least I had heard of Billy the Kid, who, it was claimed, had washed dishes at Shakespeare's only hotel—the Stratford, on Avon Avenue—after escaping from jail in 1875.[1]

Tombstone had a world-famous reenactment show, "The O.K. Corral," which was staged four times a day. It had museums, theatres, and another form of entertainment: "While you are enjoying the festivities you can be hung or have someone hung by the Tombstone Vigilantes at the hanging scaffold."

We took a vote. Two adults versus three offspring. Shakespeare was closer. Shakespeare was called Shakespeare. Shakespeare won.

When we got there, it turned out that we hadn't done our research well: the town was privately owned and open only by appointment, and only for guided tours. At some point, Shakespeare had ceased staging reenactments and had become a rehearsal space for reenactment groups from other parts of the country, a place to practice gunfights and hangings. Now it no longer served that role, either.

So we continued on to Tombstone, which, to our relief, was everything the kids could have hoped for. It was like walking onto the set of an old Western. The streets were lined with haunted brothels and restored saloons, little museums and souvenir shops. On corners, frugal cowboys smoked cigarettes down to the butt, and announced the next gunfight in loud, hoarse voices. Horse-drawn stagecoaches passed by, their mostly senior passengers gazing abstractly out the window toward an invisible but vivid past.

"The O.K. Corral" re-created a dispute that led to a thirty-second shoot-out between outlaw cowboys (the Clanton brothers, the McLaury brothers, et al.) and Tombstone's lawmen Doc Holliday and the brothers Virgil, Morgan, and Wyatt Earp, in the course of which lawlessness was defeated by lawfulness—or, at least, by a different kind of law.[2]

While the kids watched another reenactment, I waited outside. I wanted quiet and solitude. But horse-drawn carriages kept passing

1. Born Henry McCarty in 1859, Billy the Kid was a young outlaw in the New Mexico and Arizona territories. He was convicted of killing a sheriff and sentenced to hang but escaped jail. Sheriff Pat Garrett shot him dead in 1881, when McCarty was just twenty-one years old. Newspaper and magazine stories turned him into a legend of the Old West. [All notes are the editor's.]

2. The shoot-out in 1881 between the figures mentioned here was immortalized first in a 1931 biography of Wyatt Earp, then in John Ford's 1946 film, *My Darling Clementine* (starring Henry Ford). The mythologized incident has helped define white culture's version of American identity.

by, and a man dressed as a kind of harlequin-cowboy occupied a shady corner nearby and began singing country songs. I was asked for a light, and then a cigarette, and ended up smoking with a mildly depressed and very talkative Doc Holliday. At some point, he was greeted by another Doc Holliday, who also asked for a cigarette. The town, it seemed, existed not only in a loop of embodied repetitions of odd historical moments but also in a kind of cut-and-paste of the same people. It is entirely possible that, at any given moment in Tombstone, Wyatt Earp is having a beer with Wyatt Earp.

What were these towns? Shakespeare, as we had seen, had never quite recovered from the post-boom depression, and was now a ghost of a ghost town. Tombstone had recovered, and was a tourist destination visited by almost half a million people a year, though in many ways it was also a ghost town, a kind of Hades, ruled by the law of eternal return. It was a space where the past had been replaced by a peculiar, repetitive, and selective representation of the past.

Before leaving, the kids insisted on having a family portrait taken—one of those kitsch, sepia, barrels-in-the-background, rifles, and hats kinds of portrait. We were given a menu of costumes to choose from. We could be Doc Holliday, Wyatt Earp, or one of the Clantons—or an "Outlaw Mexican" or a "Native American." We had our portrait taken, and that was that for our visit. But I was, of course, left with questions and thoughts about why some people get to have a name in history while others remain a generic category, why some identities are mapped into history and others are mapped out.

I returned to Shakespeare and Tombstone again this year—with my friend Pejk Malinovski, a writer and audio documentarian with whom I'd collaborated before—looking for answers. Or maybe I was looking for better questions. Since my last trip to Arizona, the national fixation on "the border crisis" had reached a fever pitch, and the treatment of undocumented migrants at the border had hit record lows. It was a good moment to return to these places which, although they are near the U.S.-Mexico border and along the most common migration corridors in the United States, seemed, at least at first glance, oblivious both of history and of the current political reality.

It's late April, and Pejk and I meet in Tucson. We visit two local friends, Francisco Cantú and Karima Walker, to get their perspective on the towns by the border and on immigration. (Cantú worked for some years for the U.S. Border Patrol, and later wrote a book about the experience, called *The Line Becomes a River*.) Walker asks if we're going to interview Chris Simcox, who was a founder of the Minuteman Civil Defense Corps (MCDC), a Tombstone-based civilian border militia group. After working as a reenactor in one of the gunfights performed in Tombstone, Simcox bought and began editing the now defunct Tombstone *Tumbleweed*. And, in 2002, using the newspaper as his platform, he issued a call to arms, inviting volunteers to take part in a new citizens' border militia: "Join together and protect your country in a time of war!" The MCDC, which was connected to the deaths of multiple migrants, disbanded in 2010, but Walker's question reinforces my sense that there may be a connection between these places which glorify and commodify a violent frontier past and the violence that is so frequently directed toward undocumented immigrants in the area. That night, I Google Simcox and discover that he is now in prison, for reasons unrelated to his Minuteman activities. (He was found guilty of child molestation in 2016 and is serving a nineteen-year sentence.)

Vigilante and civilian patrol groups like the MCDC have existed for as long as the frontier has existed; the difference is that the perceived enemy is no longer Native Americans but undocumented immigrants, most of whom are also, by the way, indigenous Americans (from America the continent). Indeed, the nineteenth-century narrative of the "savage Indian" is not so different from that of the "illegal immigrant" today. Most of the current discourse that condemns immigration across the southern border, from the White House on down, has to do with the supposed savagery, criminality, and illegality of the "invaders." The MCDC no longer exists, but there are other groups. Most of them have Facebook and Web pages, some of which you need to be approved for before joining. In Arizona, there is Arizona Border Recon. In New Mexico, there's the United Constitutional Patriots (UCP), founded in 2014 and led by Larry Mitchell Hopkins, who also goes by Johnny Horton Jr. Videos posted on the Facebook page of the UCP's spokesman, Jim Benvie, show civilian militiamen in military-style uniforms driving down dark roads at night, following and then detaining migrants, and forcing them to sit or kneel on the ground to await the arrival of Border

Patrol agents. Two weeks before our trip, the group posted a live video showing its members detaining two hundred migrants, among them children, at gunpoint. Hopkins was arrested and charged with illegal weapons possession soon afterward, and, in early May, after Paypal and GoFundMe shut down the group's donations page, the UCP rebranded itself as Guardian Patriots.

The next morning, Pejk, Cantú, and I head for Tombstone. I've been reading a book titled *Tombstone's Most Haunted*, by Joshua Hawley, who is the director of reenactments at the O.K. Corral, and also the director of Tombstone's paranormal investigations. In the book, Hawley lists the instruments that ghost hunters commonly use: "Video cameras with infrared night vision, still cameras, analog and digital audio recorders, motion detectors, and thermal-imaging cameras." Cantú tells us that most of the same equipment is used by the Border Patrol (and probably also by civilian militias) to detect border crossers. He views this as another manifestation of the way in which migrants are dehumanized, seen as ghosts—or as targets in a high-tech video game.

As we distance ourselves from Tucson, the desert stretches endlessly before us, the saguaros, creosote, and mesquite becoming more frequent. Soon, the soft undulations of the hills are interrupted by the jagged peaks of the Dragoon Mountains, their contours sharp in the clear morning light. As we park in Tombstone, we notice a young man in nineteenth-century cowboy gear walking toward us. Spaghetti-bodied, he moves with a joyful kind of skip. He's on his way to work at the O.K. Corral, it turns out, and the first show of the day starts in less than an hour. He tells us that he's originally from Connecticut but now lives in Tombstone. Today, he's playing the outlaw Frank McLaury, and when we ask him if he likes his job he furrows his brow, looks romantically toward the horizon, then back at us, and says, "Well, there's nothin' quite like getting to shoot guns at your friends all day, and then getting up and going to have a beer when you're done." He also sees it as a stepping stone toward some other acting job, maybe in the film industry, and, as he says this, his mouth opens in a wide, boyish smile. When we ask him what he doesn't like about his job, he points to his gun and says that working with real guns onstage can be a safety hazard. He smiles again, but, with his hand on his gun, his boyishness seems a little less endearing.

He is the first person we talk to, and the first to readily show us his gun. Everyone else we talk to in the days that follow will do the same, always unprompted, at some point in our conversation. Outside the O.K. Corral, a monumental Virgil Earp with a full, graying mustache and a degree in history talks to us about his fascination with the Old West—and then shows us his guns. The cowboy Billy Claiborne tells us about his acting career, and then shows us his gun. A Wyatt Earp (or maybe it was a Morgan) follows suit. And then an Ike Clanton tells us that, in addition to acting in "The O. K. Corral," he's in charge of "making the ammo"—blanks—for all the reenactors: "You clean the shells, we use .45 shells, prime them, pack them with gun powder and vermiculite, to keep the powder inside the shell . . . and make it *boom*."

"Boom?" I say.

"Yeah, *boom*!"

Going to Tombstone can feel like stepping into someone's psychotic episode—one fuelled by testosterone and paranoia. At the same time, it's clear that the O.K. Corral reenactors are just actors, people trying to pay the bills, or kind of; when I was in Tombstone the first time, the two Doc Hollidays I talked to told me that the pay was so bad that another Doc Holliday spent half the year being Mickey Mouse at Disneyland to supplement it.

I want to talk to a reenactor who plays Big Nose Kate, who was at some point married to Doc Holliday and supposedly witnessed the gunfight from the boarding house next door. But there are no Kates to be seen. When I ask the elderly woman who sells T-shirts in the shop next to the O.K. Corral why she thinks women are mostly absent from the reenactment scene, she tells me that women do appear, but only on special weekends, and explains that, in the Old West, "women were either housewives or prostitutes. Not visible."

I also ask her about one of the T-shirts on display. It has a picture of two guns, with the caption "The Original Homeland Security." She looks at me with a smile and says, "Well, guns!"

The show is about to start, so we step into the O. K. Corral and find seats in the metal bleachers, among twenty or thirty spectators. The show itself goes over my head—Clantons, Earps, Clantons, Earps—but every single one of the many gunshots in the short performance makes me jump. Perhaps because I didn't grow up in the United States, Wild West reenactments evoke no nostalgia in me. When I ask American friends what they know about the reenactment world, most mumble something about the Civil War. Some were dragged as kids to a reenactment of the Battle of Gettysburg, which for the past twenty-five years has taken place annually at the site where the real battles were fought. Few people I come across know that there are more than fifty thousand Civil War reenactors in the country, members of a guild with strict hierarchies and distinctions. Tony Horwitz, in his book *Confederates in the Attic*, analyzes what he calls "a period rush," the particular adrenaline-fuelled energy that comes with being fully immersed in an authentic re-creation. Authenticity is the yardstick in reenactment culture. A "farb" is a reenactor who doesn't spend enough time or money on props and costumes. The most committed call themselves "living historians," and the "hardcores" among them sometimes go on spartanlike diets in order to resemble underfed nineteenth-century soldiers; others soak the buttons that they sew on their uniforms in urine, to generate just the right amount of rust.

Towns like Tombstone began staging reenactments in the late 1920s. Military forts around the country were being converted into tourist attractions, landmarks commemorating wars and battles dotted the landscape, and some ghost towns were repurposed as life-size stages.

America was mythologizing, via tourism and pop culture, its still recent past, and there was plenty of material to work with. In the latter half of the nineteenth century, nickelodeons and dime novels[3] had featured the "lawless towns" of the West, and stories of cowboys, saloons, gunfights, and outlaws had become part of the collective imagination. Then came television and Hollywood, to further consolidate the myths of the Wild West.

Frontier towns, the mining booms decades behind them, had to choose between extinction and transforming themselves into caricatures of their glory days for public consumption. Adapting involved mapping that collective imagination back into real space, capitalizing

3. Nickelodeons: Precursors to movie theaters, these crude, storefront auditoriums usually featured series of short films, for which patrons paid five cents. Dime novels: cheap paperbacks catering to popular rather than literary taste.

on and commodifying the myths—along with whatever deep currents those myths activated in people. In 1929, a group of residents in Tombstone, which was approaching its fiftieth anniversary and already almost a ghost town, decided to organize a celebration of the town's heritage, with reenactments of its epic moments. They called it the Helldorado. A success, it was repeated for a few subsequent years, and then revived, by a group called the Tombstone Vigilantes, after the Second World War; in the 1950s, the group established year-round shows celebrating the town's frontier days.

From the O.K. Corral, we wander into a cluttered, dark store, where books, magazines, and files are stacked in columns. In a corner of the shop, we find an old man with a snowy mustache and some strands of white hair, combed and gelled back. He is Ben Traywick, the ninety-one-year-old, now retired official historian of Tombstone. He was born in Tennessee and worked in nuclear fission, before being transferred to a missile project, Polaris, in California. He later owned an explosives factory near Tombstone, where he relocated in the '60s.

Traywick is full of stories, a kind of Wizard of Oz of Tombstone, and the author of countless reenactment skits. He wrote the original O.K. Corral scene (and played Wyatt Earp for twenty years).

I ask him what he thinks draws so many people to the Tombstone reenactments.

"When I came here, in 1968, I saw that Tombstone was not being advertised," he says. "That's the key, right there, advertisement. So I wrote a script for all those big acts that happened here. We decided to do historical acts that really happened. We were very careful to have proper costumes, proper attitudes. . . . We re-created history. . . . Nobody got it right till I came along!"

An interesting paradox of the reenactment scene's obsession with authenticity and historical accuracy, this "getting it right," is that accuracy is measured in terms of the minute details of a particular event, which does not necessarily amount to historical accuracy in the broader sense. Old West history buffs may endlessly dispute whether Wyatt Earp was wearing a specific kind of bow tie during the O.K. Corral shoot-out in 1881, but may be oblivious of much of what was happening in the region during those years.

When the original shoot-out at the O.K. Corral took place, one of the United States' genocidal campaigns against Native Americans, known more widely and conveniently as the Apache Wars, was underway. Chief Cochise died in 1874, but Geronimo defended the Apacheria until 1886, before being driven, with thirty of his people, onto the Fort Sill Reservation, in Oklahoma. By 1848, Mexico had lost California, Nevada, Utah, and parts of present-day Arizona, New Mexico, Colorado, Oklahoma, Kansas, and Wyoming, after a war that is known here as the Mexican War and in Mexico, more objectively but somehow also more courteously, as the United States Intervention. Then, in 1853, in a maneuver to insure the construction of the Pacific Railroad, the southern portion of a transcontinental railroad, the United States negotiated the Gadsden Purchase, and Mexico lost southern Arizona and southern New Mexico.[4] Tombstone lies within that portion of the country, and in the 1880s there were still many Mexicans living there. In 1882, according to a framed document in Traywick's bookstore, there were 400 Mexicans and 2,800 Americans living in Tombstone. Native Americans were (and are, of course) also present in the region, as were small numbers of African-Americans and Asians. When I went to Tombstone for the first time, with my family—all of us born in Mexico—we quickly noticed that there were no Mexicans being portrayed in the reenactments. No Native Americans, either. Non-whites seemed to have been completely erased from the popular narratives.

I ask Traywick why Mexicans and Native Americans don't appear, even as enemies or adversaries, in borderland reenactments.

He stumbles a little, searching for the right words: "Mexicans were an accepted part of the problem here. They were part of the population here. Part of the civilization we had here."

"Yes, but you know how we have Doc Holliday, Wyatt Earp, the Clantons—are there any reenactments in town where there is a Mexican character?"

"Well, we had Mexican characters in our show."

"Like who?"

4. The transfer of territory in 1848 was stipulated in the Treaty of Guadalupe Hidalgo, which ended the Mexican-American War. The Gadsden Purchase (negotiated in 1853 and signed in 1854) settled the border between the two countries along the line that exists today.

"Hard to say. You have to take them as a whole. They were in our group."

"Can you remember any Mexican characters?"

"Well, there was a Mexican here in town. He cooked the best beef in the world."

Traywick tells Pejk and Cantú a long story about beheadings in China and shows them pictures of decapitated men, while I browse in the bookstore. There's a Confederate flag in the back, some Mayan masks and relics behind Traywick's desk, a few dusty mariachi hats, many framed pictures of admirals and generals—among them Nathan Bedford Forrest, a Confederate Army general and the first Grand Wizard of the Ku Klux Klan—and a poster of Donald Trump dressed as a cowboy, with a gun under his belt, and the slogan "Keeping America Safe Again."[5]

I ask Traywick his opinion on current border issues.

"Let me tell you something I would like to see, and that will answer your question," he says. "I think that the U.S. made a big mistake. When they had Santa Anna, and had a chance to, they should have annexed Mexico. That would solidify the whole continent of North America."

"Including Central America?"

"Yeah, get them, too!"

"That said, do you think there should be a wall between Mexico and the U.S.?"

"Yeah, I do, I do, because we have gotten so many criminals, and so many people with diseases. We need to protect ourselves. We still oughta take immigrants, but we oughta be choosy about taking them. Not take the people that have AIDS, and whatever."

When we ask if there are many undocumented immigrants in Tombstone, he says, "When people come to town, illegals, they leave quickly. . . . They know that everybody here owns a gun. No trouble."

And yet Traywick denies that there is any connection between Tombstone's obsession with nineteenth-century vigilante justice and the civilian militia groups currently in the area. That is, he sees no

5. A play on Donald Trump's campaign slogan in 2016: Make America Great Again. The attitudes expressed by Traywick in the subsequent paragraphs are themes Trump promoted before and after his election.

connection between reenactments that celebrate hangings and gunfights as the "original homeland security" and contemporary forms of extrajudicial justice in which civilians deputize themselves to perform the tasks normally reserved for law enforcement.

I ask Traywick if he's familiar with Chris Simcox and the Minuteman Civil Defense Corps. "He had nothing to do with the rest of the people. That was his own project," he replies starkly. "Well, when he started that it looked like a good thing, but he let it take over his life. It got all out of bounds. I think he finally went to jail, didn't he?"

I wonder what Traywick means by "he let it take over his life"—what that "it" means. Hatred? guns? vigilante justice? According to an article published by the Southern Poverty Law Center in 2006, Simcox was arrested in 2003 for illegally carrying a semi-automatic weapon in a national park along the border: "Also in Simcox's possession at the time of that arrest . . . were a document entitled 'Mission Plan,' a police scanner, two walkie-talkies, and a toy figure of Wyatt Earp on horseback." It seems plausible that, just as fictions about the Wild West have spilled over into real spaces like Tombstone, the fiction, repeated endlessly in reenactments, could somehow spill back into reality, be performed back into existence.

Before we say goodbye to Traywick, he takes us to the back of his shop and pulls out a long, curved black metal sword. He holds it up, looking proud and solemn, like a boy showing off his *Star Wars* lightsabre. He tells us that he had it shipped from China. "It's a beheading sword!" he says.

On our way to an appointment with Dave Ochsenbine, the owner of Shakespeare, I read an advisory on the town's webpage: "There is an abundance of rattle snakes [SIC], animals, mine borings and shafts that can cause you injury or death. There is also the current danger of drug mules walking from the Southern Border into the Lordsburg area. You do not want to come across or stop any person walking on the range." "Drug mules" are one of the first things I bring up with Rod Linkous, a cowboy reenactor from El Paso, who gives us a tour of Shakespeare. He says that there is, indeed, evidence of drug mules passing through town, especially down by the arroyo, where they leave tracks.

"But they could just be people migrating, right?"

"There's both: the coyotes and the mules."

He doesn't acknowledge the idea of "people," just repeats the words "coyotes" and "mules," terms that fit in well with the other creatures on the Shakespeare advisory list—rattlesnakes and animals. I ask Linkous if there are also civilian militias in the area. He says that they are definitely out here, too, but, he adds, "they've been kicked out because of . . . politics, basically. But they never threaten anybody. All they can do, under U.S. law, is effect a citizen's arrest, detain illegals until the Border Patrol gets there. They're doing the job. I figured it out one day: any one day there's 4,000 Border Patrol agents to cover 6,000 miles of territory, Canadian and Mexican borders. That's not a whole lot. So I can see the militia trying to help in some way."

Shakespeare consists of nine or ten abandoned buildings, two inhabitants, and a spindly aluminum windmill. Our visit doesn't last long, but Linkous is well versed in history, and we discuss the murky distinction between lawfulness and lawlessness in the nineteenth century. We're talking about the history of vigilante groups in the Southwest when Ochsenbine joins us. His father-in-law's family, the Hills, bought the abandoned town in 1935, and he and his wife, Gina, moved here from Ohio just last year. They plan to do everything they can to keep the place alive and to preserve its history. He tells us about the Shakespeare Guard, which was formed in 1879, by a group of about seventy men, to protect the town from Apaches (the original inhabitants of the land).

When we ask the two men what they like about nineteenth-century history, Linkous explains, "Well, there's people moving West, fighting Indians, the Mexicans, the elements themselves, and somehow producing the country that we have today."

"Aren't people who are coming here now the same as those independent settlers who were simply looking for a better life?" I ask.

Ochsenbine answers, "Whether they're coming from Central America or China, they're looking for a better life. I get that. But there's a right way to go about it and a wrong way to go about it. And just coming over the border illegally is the wrong way."

The mythos of the Wild West celebrates the spirit of those who sought to settle in a new land, domesticate its difficulties, and thrive. Why, I ask, is that spirit admired in some cases and condemned in others? Our Shakespeare guides protest that I'm conflating two different things. One case is "historical" and the other is . . . not.

Driving south, toward the border, we see no signs of crisis, no migrants, and few cars. We see a Border Patrol cam truck—a pickup with a surveillance camera mounted on a tall mast—and many commercial trucks, probably transporting commodities in and out of the country. The great paradox of the North American Free Trade Agreement (NAFTA) is that it has allowed for freer trade of merchandise across the border, and less freedom of movement for people.[6]

In Douglas, Arizona, we reach the wall—or part of the wall that was constructed during the Obama Administration. There are two walls, in fact—one painted creamy white, on the American side; the other copper-colored, on the Mexican side—with a strip of land the width of about ten long strides between the two. Being there makes me feel slightly nauseated—as though my body wanted to cry, but from the belly, not the chest.

We drive west along the wall until we see a sign for an RV park called Twin Buttes, and decide to go in. When we knock on the door of the main office, a woman in her sixties named Beverly greets us with a neighborly smile. Pejk tells her, holding his microphone in her direction, that we are there to talk about immigration, and she says, "I can, but maybe my husband might like to talk to you, too. Oh, we know a lot about the border." She tells us that her husband is just around the back, with some other RV residents. "It's happy hour!" she adds.

Out back, there are four men and one woman sitting at a long wooden picnic table, sipping beers. They look a little surprised as we approach. Beverly's husband, Roger Kercher, greets us, and when he hears our accents he says, "You guys aren't from America."

Pejk says that he's originally Danish but is now a U.S. citizen, and Roger replies, "Okay, the accent, I recognized it right off!"

He laughs with an expansive roar. He's obviously the alpha man of the bunch, and he's happy to talk at length about his views on the southern border. Between 2002 and 2008, before Obama put up

6. NAFTA: The North American Free Trade Agreement (1994) established a virtual free-trade zone between Mexico, Canada, and the United States.

this section of the wall, he tells us, he and Beverly sometimes had twenty people at their front door at two in the morning, looking for help, water, food. Beverly chimes in, "And especially for a ride to Phoenix—everybody wanted a ride to Phoenix."

"What would you do?" I ask.

"Well, we would call the Border Patrol!" Roger answers. "And then we, well, *she* would give them water, bananas, bread, peanut butter, 'cause there'd be all sorts of little kids."

Since the wall went up, he says, they mostly "get" young people, fewer kids, fewer old people. He refers to the men as "males." He adds that all the twenty-one-year-olds who come are carrying fifty pounds of drugs on their back and have a sniper with them. So, if you see "illegals with backpacks," you have to ignore them: "Because someone is watching you watching them."

He tells a story about a Guatemalan who recently showed up, asking for a cell-phone charger and a ride to Phoenix, and boasts that he himself sent the man back to Mexico. It was the fourth time that the man had been deported. He points to one of the trailers in the park and says, "I have a Border Patrol agent who lives in that trailer, and a very good friend that's a customs agent." His Border Patrol friend tells him that, these days, there are Guatemalans, Chinese, and Cubans, and that "everybody is coming over now because they know they can sneak over with the other illegals."

One of the men at the table, who has been silent until now, finishes his sentence: "And be released!"

The others, in a chorus, repeat, "And be released!"

The rule in the RV park, they say, is "You see one, you call one," meaning that you call Border Patrol. When we ask Roger if he belongs to a civilian patrol group, he chuckles, and says not formally, but he surely drives out to the desert to help and support his fellow-patriots.

The main complaint in the RV park is that "illegals" cost money. That they are given free services everywhere, in the ER and in Social Security offices, where they ask for pensions, and that Americans have to pay for this. (This is, of course, not the reality of an undocumented immigrant.) Roger says that part of the problem is "bleeding-heart societies," like the Catholic Charities, that have become an "incentive" for migrants. He suggests that all the illegals should just go to Minnesota. The others smile.

Pejk asks them what the solution might be.

Roger turns to him and holds his hand as if it were a pistol, aimed at Pejk's chest. "I can't shoot you, unless you're robbing me, because then I broke the law, it's illegal to shoot you," he says. "But you can't come into somebody's country without legal documentation."

"What would your solution be?"

"First off is, I'd go ahead and put the wall up, because it does regulate the young people and the old people, and vehicles."

"So a solid wall, all the way?"

"Would be a good start," Roger says, but he has more ideas: "Like the Guatemalan guy I sent back the fourth time, he's gotta go to prison, and he's gonna spend some time. . . . All right, well, let's put 'em on a chain gang and let 'em cut the road ditches, and teach 'em a lesson!"

The RV park has thirty RV stations, a recreational area, and marked walking paths. Roger heads off down one of them, but says he'll be back and instructs us to wait for him. The sky above is vast and cloudless.

When Roger returns, he is driving a golf cart. It has a blue siren light stuck to the top and a bumper sticker that says "Tombstone, Arizona: Justice Is Coming." As he steps out of the golf cart, he explains that the other residents say he's like the sheriff around there, so, as a joke, they gave him the siren light and the bumper sticker. As we thank him for his time and begin to say goodbye, he reaches into the glove box of the golf cart and says, "By the way, wait, just to show you what the truth is . . ." He takes out a pistol. "I never leave home without one! We live in a dangerous area. One in my car, one in my golf cart."

"Are you folks ready for a gunfight?"

"Yeah!" we answer.

Firing his gun into the air, Doc Holliday repeats, "I said, Are you folks ready for a gunfight?"

"Yeah!" we say again.

"All right! Now, before we get started, I do have to talk to you about a couple of things. First things first, these are not toys—these are real firearms."

He aims at a soda can and fires. The can explodes.

We all go, "Ahhhh!"

And then there's another gunshot, and the O.K. Corral reenactment officially begins.

The history of frontier towns like Shakespeare and Tombstone is one in which primarily white populations moved West, claiming territory and forcibly ejecting or killing those who were already there, then defending that territory against "invaders," who were often the previous inhabitants—that is, Native Americans and, later, Mexicans—and, finally, establishing law. This last stage of frontier history is what is most often mined for reenactments: a Manichean representation of good (white) lawmen vs. bad (white) cowboys, which is ultimately a celebration of the founding of white America.[7] The rest—the part about killing or banishing non-white others in order to defend claimed land—is conveniently elided. But the practice lives on, in a kind of reenactment with very real consequences, in which the protagonists are civilian border patrollers—people who feel they have a right to do whatever they can to keep others, and especially non-white others, out of this land. This vigilantism rests on the myth of the frontier, or on the idea of a place at the very edge of civilization that needs to be conquered and tamed and then guarded—with guns or with walls—against potential invaders, or *bandidos*. Like two mirrors facing each other, Wild West reenactments and the myths that fuel them shed light on the emotions driving the response to "the border crisis," and, conversely, thinking about civilian border militias unveils some of the myths behind reenactment culture. The knot of intuitions I came with on this trip is finally unravelling. But, of course, there are new questions.

There are many ways of engaging politically with the world, of interacting with and establishing an emotional and intellectual connection with the communities to which we belong, as well as with communities that we don't recognize as our own. There are rallies, classrooms, social networks, publishing spaces, sweat lodges, churches, bars, theatres, dinner parties. There are reenactments. But we're living in a time when most forms of political engagement seem highly curated, cut sharply around the edges so as to include only

7. Manichaeism, named after the third-century philosopher Mani, posits a dualistic worldview where forces of good (light) and evil (darkness) compete in human history.

that and those with whom we have a perceived affinity. I returned to Tombstone and Shakespeare in an effort to change the angle from which I approach immigration issues, to step outside my usual dynamics. In effect, I wanted to reenact my own past, in a different persona. I returned to the borderlands to look hatred in the face. But what I saw was not quite hatred. It was something more hollow, circular, repetitive. Something more like a reenactment of hate.

2019

✶

Biographical Sketches

Michelle Alexander (*b. 1967*) After earning her bachelor's degree from Vanderbilt University, Alexander completed her education at Stanford Law School. She clerked for Justice Harry Blackmun of the U.S. Supreme Court; directed the American Civil Liberties Union's Racial Justice Project in Northern California; taught at Stanford Law School; and, in 2005, took a joint position at the Ohio State University's Moritz College of Law and the Kirwan Institute for the Study of Race and Ethnicity. She has been a public advocate for reform in the criminal justice system, most visibly in her national campaign to eradicate racial profiling by police. In 2010, Alexander published *The New Jim Crow*, which solidified her reputation as one of the leading experts on racial justice in the United States. She contributes regularly to the *New York Times*.

Maya Angelou (*1928–2014*) Poet, playwright, director, actress, dancer, Angelou was born Marguerite Johnson and grew up in Stamps, Arkansas, and San Francisco. When she moved to New York in the late 1950s, she joined the Harlem Writers Guild. In 1961 she moved to Cairo, Egypt, to work for the *Arab Observer*, and later to Ghana, to work for the *African Review*. She returned to the United States in 1966 to write for television and work for the Southern Christian Leadership Conference. Her autobiographical

I Know Why the Caged Bird Sings (1970) was on the *New York Times* best-seller list for two years. Before her death Angelou was Reynolds Professor of American Studies at Wake Forest University in North Carolina and was one of the few U.S. poets to have written and delivered a poem at a presidential inauguration.

Kwame Anthony Appiah (*b. 1954*) Appiah's mother is a British art historian and his father a Ghanaian politician and lawyer. His maternal grandfather was a leader in the British House of Lords. He was raised in Ghana but studied at Cambridge University in England, where he earned a doctorate in philosophy. His peripatetic teaching career, which includes the University of Ghana, has followed an Ivy League trail—Cornell, Yale, Harvard, Princeton—before settling at New York University. His writing explores the ethics of race, identity, nationalism, and cosmopolitanism. In 2006, he published *Cosmopolitanism: Ethics in a World of Strangers*, and he has also written several novels.

Anne Applebaum (*b. 1964*) Applebaum graduated from Yale University before she took a job in 1988 as a correspondent for the London *Economist*, reporting from Warsaw, Poland. She filed stories on the fall of communism for a number of periodicals and, in 1992, became foreign editor of the London *Spectator* magazine. Her first book was the acclaimed *Between East and West: Across the Borderlands of Europe*. She was a columnist and editor at the *Washington Post* until 2006. She lives in Poland with her family and continues to write on international affairs in Eastern Europe.

James Baldwin (*1924–1987*) Baldwin was born in poverty in Harlem, the eldest of nine children. At seventeen, he left home and began writing seriously, ultimately publishing reviews and essays in magazines like *The Nation* and *The Partisan Review* and winning the Rosenwald Fellowship (1948). Baldwin moved to Europe in 1948 and lived largely in Paris for the next ten years. In 1957, he returned to the United States to take part in the civil rights movement. In 1983, Baldwin became Five College Professor of Afro-American Studies at the University of Massachusetts. His most successful novel, *Go Tell It on the Mountain* (1953), treats his early experience as an evangelical preacher. His later works often deal with issues of racism and homosexuality.

Deborah Brandt *(b. 1951)* Brandt earned her undergraduate degree from Rutgers University and a PhD in 1983 from Indiana University, Bloomington. Her scholarship is in writing studies, especially on the acquisition of "literacies"—that is, the skills needed to successfully read and write in our society. She practices interdisciplinary research involving sociology, economics, and biography: she is especially known for collecting literacy narratives, which are autobiographical accounts of how the narratives' authors acquired their reading and writing skills. Much of Brandt's influence on the study of literacies comes from her award-winning 2001 book, *Literacy in American Lives*, which popularized the term *literacy sponsors*.

David Brooks (*b. 1961*) Brooks writes opinion columns for the *New York Times* and regularly interprets current events from a conservative perspective on National Public Radio. He succeeds with the generally liberal-leaning audiences of these venues because he is never doctrinaire, pays no attention to the Republican Party's official talking points, and listens to the arguments of liberal thinkers with openness and respect. He found success as a political pundit through the usual channels: his father was a professor at New York University; he attended prestigious prep schools; he earned an internship at the *National Review* within a couple years of graduating college, which connected him with important conservative intellectuals. He paid his dues as a crime reporter, movie critic, and book review editor with various newspapers, eventually landing a job as a European correspondent for the *Wall Street Journal*. In 2000, he published *Bobos in Paradise: The New Upper Class and How They Got There*. The term "bobos" combines *bourgeoisie* (mostly upper-middle-class professionals and executives) and *bohemian* (counterculture, anti-materialist hipsters). Brooks has become a chief spokesperson for moderate conservatives. His principled opposition to President Donald Trump and commitment to civil discourse has earned him fans across the political divide.

Rachel Carson (*1907–1964*) Born in Springdale, Pennsylvania, Carson studied at Woods Hole Marine Biological Laboratory and received her master's degree in zoology from Johns Hopkins (1932). In 1936, she became the first woman to pass the civil service test and joined the Bureau of Fisheries as a junior biologist. Over the next fifteen years she rose to become editor in chief of all publications for the U.S. Fish and Wildlife Service. In her free time, Carson wrote lyrical prose about marine life, publishing two prize-winning books, *The Sea Around Us* and *The Edge of the Sea.* In 1952 Carson resigned from government service to devote herself to her writing. Her most famous work is *Silent Spring* (1962), which exposed the dangers of pesticides, particularly DDT.

Emily Chamlee-Wright (*b. 1966*) A seasoned academic, Chamlee-Wright taught economics at Beloit College for nearly two decades and later served as provost at Washington College in Maryland. She researches the intersection of culture and economics, focusing on urban economics in sub-Saharan African nations, such as Ghana and Zimbabwe. She also studied the economic recovery in American gulf coast communities in the aftermath of Hurricane Katrina. Since 2016, she has been the president and CEO of the Institute for Humane Studies, a conservative educational nonprofit that supports research, conferences, and teaching that promote classical liberalism. The institute draws its funding from a range of donors, most notably the billionaire Koch brothers, Charles and David.

Amy Chua (*b. 1962*) Born in the Midwest, Chua moved to California in 1970 when her father took a job as a professor at UC Berkeley. She graduated from Harvard University in 1984 and three years later from Harvard Law School. After a clerkship with a federal judge and four years in private practice, Chua began teaching, first at Duke University and then Yale University, where she earned a "Best Teaching" award. Her first book, *The World on Fire: How Exporting Free Market Democracy Breeds Ethnic Hatred and Global Instability* (2003), was a *New York Times* best seller. In 2011, she published the controversial memoir *Battle Hymn of the Tiger Mother,* which was an international best seller. Chua has written three other books, all provocative cultural analyses, including 2019's *Political Tribes: Group Instinct and the Fate of Nations.*

Hillary Rodham Clinton (*b. 1947*) Clinton rose to national prominence when her husband, William Jefferson Clinton, was elected president in 1992. The first First Lady to hold a post-graduate degree and the first to have her own career independent of her husband (she was a lawyer), Clinton immediately assumed a prominence in public affairs similar to that of Eleanor Roosevelt in the 1930s. She headed the Task Force on National Health Care Reform, which resulted in a proposal for universal health insurance coverage, defeated in Congress but similar in many ways to the Affordable Care Act eventually enacted during the Obama administration. In 2000, New York elected Clinton to the U.S. Senate, and President Obama appointed her U.S. secretary of state in 2009. She directed the State Department for the next four years. In 2016, she lost the presidential election to Donald Trump.

Ta-Nehisi Coates (*b. 1975*) Coates was born and raised in West Baltimore, the son of a former member of the activist group the Black Panthers. His father operated Black Classic Press, which brought him into contact with leading Black writers such as Amiri Baraka and Walter Mosley. He attended Howard University until he left the school for opportunities as a journalist. Eventually, he landed at *The Atlantic*, a premier national monthly, where he served as senior editor. He has published articles in venues as diverse as *The Village Voice* and *O*. His most famous article is a feature in *The Atlantic*, "The Case for Reparations," which argues that the United States ought to pay reparations to African Americans to compensate for land and property stolen by whites in the last century. He has also published four books, including *The Beautiful Struggle: A Father, Two Sons, and an Unlikely Road to Manhood* (2009), and *We Were Eight Years in Power* (2018). His popular blog at *The Atlantic* has done much to raise that genre to a level on par with more traditional forms of essay writing and publishing.

The Dalai Lama (*b. 1935*) *Dalai Lama* is a title designating the spiritual and political leader of Tibet. Monks identified two-year-old Lhamo Thondup, who was born to an obscure peasant family, as the reincarnation of the thirteenth Dalai Lama, who had recently died. The boy was then raised and educated by monks, and the title was bestowed on him at age fifteen. That same year, 1950, acting on historical claims of sovereignty, the newly established People's Republic of China invaded Tibet, forcing the Dalai Lama to flee to India, where he established a government in exile which still today advocates for Tibet's independence. In 1950, Tibet was a relic of older centuries, with a theocratic government and a feudal economy. The Dalai Lama has democratized the Tibetan government in exile, won the Nobel Peace Prize, and earned an international reputation for probity and justice.

Kwame Dawes (*b. 1962*) Dawes was born in Ghana, and his family moved to Jamaica when he was nine years old. He earned an undergraduate degree at the University of the West Indies and a doctorate in comparative literature at the University of New Brunswick in Canada. It is tempting to say that he is primarily a poet, because his poems fill twenty volumes, and he taught poetry at the University of South Carolina for twenty years before moving to the University of Nebraska–Lincoln, where he edits the prestigious literary journal *Prairie Schooner.* But he is amazingly productive in several fields: he has written plays and the definitive study of the lyrics of Bob Marley, a fellow Jamaican; he's edited more than a dozen books; and he's written several works of fiction and three books of nonfiction, including the memoir *A Far Cry from Plymouth Rock.*

Frederick Douglass (*c. 1817–1895*) Douglass, the son of an unknown white man and Sarah Bailey (a slave of African and Native American ancestry), was born Frederick Augustus Washington Bailey near Easton, Maryland, and spent his childhood and early adult years as a slave. He unsuccessfully tried to escape, was jailed, worked as a ship's calker, and finally, on September 3, 1838, succeeded in fleeing the South. He assumed the name Douglass to elude recapture. Impressed by his speaking skills, William Garrison, the great abolitionist, hired Douglass as an agent of the Massachusetts Anti-Slavery Society. Douglass published his autobiography in 1845 and shortly thereafter left America for England and Ireland to avoid claims made upon him by his former master. When he returned in 1847 he bought his freedom legally and started his own abolitionist paper, *North Star.* He fled to Canada when his association with the militant abolitionist John Brown became known but returned to the United States after the Civil War started. He helped raise Black regiments in Massachusetts and advised Lincoln during the war. After the war, he worked for the rights of freed slaves. He was a longtime supporter of women's rights, and he died while attending a conference on women's suffrage.

Barbara Ehrenreich (*b. 1941*) Ehrenreich, a feminist and socialist, received her PhD in biology and published initially on inequities in health care; she now frequently writes on the politics of class and gender. She has published many books, including the *New York Times* best-seller *Nickel and Dimed*, and writes regularly for *Harper's* magazine, *Time*, and *The Nation*. She has served as an honorary co-chair of the Democratic Socialists of America.

Tavi Gevinson (*b. 1996*) Growing up in Chicago as the child of an English teacher and a weaver, Gevinson started writing about fashion when she was eleven years old, posting her thoughts on a blog she titled *Style Rookie*. Her work caught on, and very quickly designers were consulting her about what girls want to buy and wear. At the age of fifteen she branched out into all aspects of teen-aged life when she launched the online magazine *Rookie*. Admiring figures like Kanye West and Beyoncé, Gevinson has turned herself into a new kind of multimedia celebrity. Though her roots are in fashion and she has already succeeded as a writer and editor of a popular magazine, Gevinson is now acting and has aspirations to be a singer. In 2014, when Gevinson was seventeen, *Forbes* magazine recognized her as one of its "30 under 30" highly influential people in the category of "Media."

Doris Kearns Goodwin (*b. 1943*) Goodwin graduated from Colby College and then earned a PhD in government from Harvard University; as a graduate student, she met and was recruited by President Lyndon Johnson to work in the White House, which launched her career as a presidential historian. She's written seven best-selling and award-winning histories (not biographies) of presidents and their administrations, including volumes on Abraham

Lincoln, Theodore Roosevelt, Franklin D. and Eleanor Roosevelt (which won the Pulitzer Prize in 1995), the Kennedys, and Lyndon Johnson. Steven Spielberg's blockbuster film *Lincoln*, about the passage of the Thirteenth Amendment to the U.S. Constitution (which outlawed slavery) and starring Daniel Day Lewis, who won an Academy Award, was based on Goodwin's book *Team of Rivals.*

Angelina Grimké (*1805–1879*) Although born to a wealthy slaveholding family in Charleston, South Carolina, Grimké abhorred slavery and moved to Philadelphia in 1829, where she wrote a number of pamphlets urging Southerners to abolish the institution. Through the American Anti-Slavery Society, she began meeting with small groups of women and eventually giving lectures on abolition to large audiences. A persuasive speaker, Grimké was one of the first American women to speak publicly on the issues of slavery and women's rights. In 1838, she married a fellow abolitionist and retired from public life.

Komysha Hassan (*b. 1988*) Hassan graduated cum laude in writing and rhetoric and political science from the University of Central Florida and holds a certificate in teaching English as a foreign language. She is the recipient of the Bledsoe-Young award for outstanding writing in political science and received an Outstanding Thesis Scholarship for her honors thesis on the evolving literacies of the digital interface. Currently, she is an English-language editor for academic publications and is pursuing a juris doctorate. She has published in both research and literary contexts.

Zöe Heller (*b. 1965*) Born in London and educated at Oxford University, Heller earned a master's degree from Columbia University in New York. Her mother, a German Jewish immigrant to England, was an outspoken activist for leftist causes. Her father was a successful screenwriter. Heller herself is a journalist, having written articles for such magazines as *Vanity Fair* and the *New Yorker* and opinion columns for British newspapers. But she is best known as a novelist. Her 2003 *What Was She Thinking? Notes on a Scandal,* a novel that turns on a schoolteacher's affair with a fifteen-year-old student, was short-listed for the prestigious Booker Prize in the UK and was adapted into a successful film in 2006.

Debra Humphreys Humphreys earned her undergraduate degree from Williams College and her doctorate from Rutgers. She has worked at the American Association of Colleges and Universities for the better part of two decades, first directing programs promoting women and diversity on college campuses, later in public affairs, and now as a vice president for policy and public engagement. She regularly contributes her views on higher education policies in the United States to such venues as *The Chronicle of Higher Education*, Fox and NBC news programs, PBS, and *USA Today*.

Zora Neale Hurston (*1903–1960*) Hurston was raised in the all-Black town of Eatonville, Florida. At sixteen, she joined a traveling theater company and made her way to New York City. She graduated from Barnard College (1928), where she studied anthropology with Franz Boaz, and then pursued a graduate degree at Columbia and did fieldwork on African American folklore in the South. After collaborating with Langston Hughes on a play that was never finished, she published her first novel, *Jonah's Gourd Vine* (1934), which offered an unsentimental treatment of life among Black Americans. She continued to write fiction (including *Their Eyes Were Watching God*, 1937) and anthropological studies. Hurston's work was neglected for many years (she died in obscurity in Florida), but since the late 1970s there has been a resurgence of interest in and a renewed appreciation of her contribution to literature and her role in the Harlem Renaissance.

Noel Ignatiev (*1940–2019*) Ignatiev grew up in a Philadelphia working-class family with Jewish Russian roots. He attended three years of college (though did not finish his degree) and joined various communist and socialist organizations in the turbulent 1960s, including Students for a Democratic Society. He worked for twenty years in a steel mill in Indiana, all the while organizing labor groups and advocating socialist policies. In 1985, he started graduate work at Harvard University, ultimately earning a PhD in history. His research brought him into race as well as class studies, and he helped edit a journal called *Race Traitor*, which aimed to abolish the privileges and penalties that society assigns to people of certain skin tones.

Thomas Jefferson (*1743–1826*) In 1776, Thomas Jefferson, Virginia's delegate to the Second Continental Congress, drafted the Declaration of Independence. He was elected governor of Virginia in 1779 and in 1784 was appointed minister to France. He became George Washington's secretary of state on his return (1790–1793), served as vice president under John Adams (1797–1801), and was elected president in 1800, after a rancorous campaign against his rival, Aaron Burr. His greatest act as president (1801–1809) was probably the successful conclusion of the Louisiana Purchase (1803), which doubled the size of the nation. After two terms as president, he retired to Monticello, the home he had designed in Virginia, where he made continual improvements to his estate, entertained widely, and kept up a voluminous correspondence. His extravagant habits led him to incur enormous debt, and on his death his belongings were all absorbed by creditors, except for his extensive library, which was purchased by the federal government and forms the foundation for the collection of the Library of Congress. Jefferson's legacy is contradictory. He vigorously opposed the national debt but was responsible for a huge increase through the Louisiana Purchase and was himself personally profligate; and while enlightened for his time on the issue of slavery, he himself owned and enslaved people and eventually freed only a few of them: his chidlren with Sally Hemings, one of the women he enslaved.

Patrick Kelly Patrick Kelly earned an undergraduate degree from the University of Alabama, Birmingham, before going on to the University of Louisville, where he studied sociology and graduated with a PhD in urban and public affairs. For six years he worked for the Kentucky Council on Postsecondary Education, the agency that supervises several aspects of the state's colleges. Since 2002 he has worked for the nonprofit National Center for Higher Education Management Systems, an organization that provides research and recommendations to those state officials who determine policies for public colleges and universities.

Robert F. Kennedy (*1925–1968*) Born into the wealthy and powerful Kennedy family in Massachusetts, Robert was the seventh of nine children, the younger brother of the promising Joe and John Kennedy, and older brother of Ted Kennedy, a U.S. senator for almost four decades until his death in 2009. He left Harvard to join the navy in 1944 during World War II, eventually graduating from Harvard and then the University of Virginia Law School in 1951. He worked first for the Department of Justice and then for the Senate, a position he resigned in protest of Senator Joseph McCarthy's notorious methods of pursuing communists. Again working for the Senate, he prosecuted leaders of the Teamsters Union, including Jimmy Hoffa, in 1957. He chaired John F. Kennedy's presidential campaign and was appointed attorney general by his brother when he was elected. A year after John F. Kennedy was assassinated in 1963, Robert was elected to the Senate by the State of New York. He ran for president himself in 1968 and was assassinated shortly after winning the California Democratic primary.

Martin Luther King Jr. (*1929–1968*) King, leader of the civil rights movement in the 1950s and 1960s, was born in Atlanta, Georgia, the son and grandson of Baptist ministers. He entered Morehouse College at fifteen and studied theology at Crozer Theological Seminary, where he became acquainted with Mohandas Gandhi's philosophy of nonviolent protest. He was ordained for the ministry and earned a PhD in theology at Boston University. In 1954, he moved to his wife Coretta Scott's home state of Alabama, where he became pastor of the Dexter Avenue Baptist Church in Montgomery. With Rosa Parks's 1955 arrest for refusing to give up her seat on a bus to a white rider and the bus boycott that followed, King was catapulted to the forefront of the civil rights movement. He founded the Southern Christian Leadership Conference; worked for the passage of the 1964 Civil Rights Act, the 1965 Voting Rights Act, and the 1968 Open Housing Act; and was awarded the Nobel Peace Prize in 1964 for his civil rights work. On April 4, 1968, he was assassinated in Memphis, Tennessee.

Maxine Hong Kingston (*b. 1940*) Born in Stockton, California, the daughter of Chinese immigrants, Kingston spoke Cantonese before she spoke English, but by the age of nine she was writing poems and stories in her adopted tongue. At the University of California, Berkeley, Kingston first studied engineering but soon switched to English literature. In 1964 she married Earl Kingston, an aspiring actor, and they moved to Hawaii, where Kingston held a series of teaching jobs. In 1976, while teaching creative writing at the Mid-Pacific Institute, Kingston published her first book, *The Woman Warrior*, which won the 1976 National Book Critics Circle Award for nonfiction. Her next book, *China Men* (1980), won the American Book Award for nonfiction. Kingston has published seven other books and was awarded the National Medal of Arts in 2013.

Michael Kinsley (*b. 1951*) A native of Detroit, Kinsley graduated from Harvard College before winning a Rhodes scholarship to Oxford University. While in Harvard Law School, he discovered his true calling as editor at *The New Republic*, an ideologically ambiguous political magazine closely associated with officials in the Reagan administration in the 1980s. Kinsley himself tends toward liberal opinions, but his openness to opposing points of view helped win him a spot on the popular "talking head" television show *Crossfire*, where he represented liberalism, sitting opposite Pat Buchanan, the show's resident conservative. Microsoft hired Kinsley to launch its pioneering online magazine, *Slate*, which he piloted from 1995 to 2002. Since then, he has been a ubiquitous political commentator, appearing on television, in newspapers, and in magazines such as *Time* and *Politico.*

Elizabeth Kolbert (*b. 1961*) Kolbert was born in New York, earned her undergraduate degree in literature at Yale University, and, in 1983, became a Fulbright scholar studying in Hamburg, Germany. She began her journalism career by reporting from Germany for the *New York Times.* She worked her way up to bureau chief in Albany, New York, before moving to the *New Yorker* in 1999, where she has established herself as one of the foremost science journalists in the United States and won several awards, including the National Magazine Award for Public Interest in 2006. Her book *The Sixth Extinction*, which won the Pulitzer Prize for nonfiction in 2015, argued that human activity is producing a global event similar to other mass extinctions triggered by catastrophic climate changes, like the asteroid collision that killed off the dinosaurs.

Paul Krugman (*b. 1953*) Krugman grew up in New York, the third generation of a family that immigrated to the United States shortly after World War II. He went to Yale University and earned a PhD in economics at the Massachusetts Institute of Technology, before embarking on a career as a professor that ultimately led, via Princeton University, to the Graduate Center of the City University of New York. He has published extensively in the field of international trade, theorizing a new economic model appropriate to the age of globalization, and he has cowritten a popular undergraduate economics textbook. In 2008, he won the Nobel Memorial Prize in Economic Sciences. He has been interpreting economic indicators and policy for the general public since 1999, when he joined the *New York Times* as a regular columnist on its op-ed page.

Abraham Lincoln (*1809–1865*) Lincoln was born to barely literate parents in Kentucky, which was then the frontier. He attended school only sporadically but studied on his own and developed a passion for reading. He passed the Illinois bar in 1836 and served in the Illinois state legislature for four terms, before being elected in 1846 to one term in the U.S. House of Representatives. Lincoln became the candidate for the U.S. Senate in Illinois's newly formed Republican Party, and although he lost that campaign, he gained national recognition for his oratory in the Lincoln-Douglas debates. He was elected president in 1860, and by the time he took office, seven southern states had seceded from the Union. As president, he waged the Civil War to reunite the nation and issued the Emancipation Proclamation (1863), which freed all people enslaved in the Confederacy. He was assassinated on April 15, 1865, by John Wilkes Booth, a fanatical advocate of slavery.

Valeria Luiselli (*b. 1983*) Luiselli is a cosmopolitan. The daughter of a diplomat, Luiselli has lived in more than half a dozen countries, including the United States, South Africa, South Korea, and Costa Rica. Though she's a citizen of Mexico, she once said that the country "feel[s] particularly foreign" to her, and she spent more years in New York than in Mexico. Nevertheless, her writing is part of the Mexican tradition of letters, more experimental and genre-bending than American fiction tends to be. Her second novel, *The Story of My Teeth*, was crowdsourced with the workers in a Mexican juice factory, who contributed plot suggestions as the novel evolved. Luiselli is an interpreter for the young asylum-seeking Central Americans caught up in the American justice system, and several of her literary works derive from this labor, notably, the novel *Lost Children Archive* (2019) and *Tell Me How It Ends: An Essay in 40 Questions* (2017). That book began as an essay written in English; Luiselli expanded it to book-length in Spanish, and the Spanish parts were translated back into English for the American edition. Luiselli has received several prestigious writing awards, including the MacArthur "Genius Grant" in 2019.

Malcolm X (*1925–1965*) Born Malcolm Little in Lansing, Michigan, Malcolm X was the son of an outspoken critic of racism whose house was burned down by the Ku Klux Klan and who was likely murdered for his views. After his mother was institutionalized for mental illness, Malcolm spent time in detention homes and in 1946 moved to Boston to live with his sister. In Boston, he was arrested for burglary and sent to prison, where he embarked upon a campaign of self-education and joined the Nation of Islam. On his release in 1952, he became a key figure in the Nation of Islam, lecturing widely on white exploitation of Black people and calling for Black self-dependence, Black separatism, and Black pride. He left the Nation of Islam in 1964, after making disparaging comments about Martin Luther King Jr. A pilgrimage to Mecca in 1964 inspired him to convert to orthodox Islam and to recant his more virulent antiwhite positions. He was assassinated at a rally in Harlem by three Black Muslims, members of a rival group.

Louis Menand (*b. 1952*) Menand received his PhD in English from Columbia University in 1980 and has enjoyed a distinguished teaching and research career as a professor at Princeton University, City University of New York (CUNY), and Harvard University. For a brief time in the 1980s he was an editor at *The New Republic* magazine, but he's better known as a contributing editor to the

New York Review of Books, a position he held from 1994 to 2001, and as a staff writer for the *New Yorker* magazine since 2001. In 2001, he published his book about American pragmatism, *The Metaphysical Club*, which won the Pulitzer Prize for nonfiction.

N. Scott Momaday (*b. 1934*) Navarre Scott Momaday, of the Kiowa tribe, was born in Oklahoma but was raised on reservations in Arizona. His parents were teachers and, after earning his BA from the University of New Mexico, he followed them into that profession. Eventually, he returned to school to earn a PhD in literature from Stanford University. In 1969, his first novel, *House Made of Dawn*, won the Pulitzer Prize, and led to an appointment teaching Native American literature at the University of California, Berkeley. He followed his initial novel with books of essays, Kiowa tales, poetry, and memoirs. He is also a painter and printmaker. In 2007 he received the National Medal of Arts.

Carla R. Monroe Monroe graduated with honors from Meredith College, where she completed her BA degree. She also holds MA and PhD degrees from Emory University where she was a recipient of the prestigious Dean's Teaching Fellowship. She has served as a faculty member at Wheelock College and also worked as a research scientist at the University of Georgia. Her research broadly addresses issues of race, gender, social class, and immigration, particularly as related to the field of education, and her scholarship has appeared in outlets such as the *Atlanta Journal-Constitution*, the *Journal of Teacher Education*, and *Urban Education.*

Susan Moller Okin (*1946–2004*) Born and raised in New Zealand, Okin did her graduate studies first at Oxford University and then at Harvard. She held several teaching posts at a succession of universities, ultimately at Stanford, where she was working when she died mysteriously at the age of fifty-seven. Much of Okin's work challenged the presumptions of standard political theorists, like John Rawls, insisting that any theory of justice must account for the sexism institutionalized in the structure of families in nearly every culture. She published several philosophical, feminist correctives, often dealing with thorny issues of equality in law, such as *Women in*

Western Political Thought (1979) and *Justice, Gender, and the Family* (1989). Near the end of her life these interests led her to criticize the tendency of multiculturalism to gloss over the sexism cemented into certain cultures.

George Orwell (*1903–1950*) Orwell was born Eric Arthur Blair, the son of a minor British official in the India service. After being educated at Eton as a scholarship pupil, Orwell went out to Myanmar (1922) as a policeman. That experience informs his first novel, *Burmese Days* (1934), and one of his most famous essays, "Shooting an Elephant" (1936). Disgusted by British imperialism, he returned to England, where he resigned his commission and dropped out, living with poor people in cheap lodgings and on the road, from which experience he produced *Down and Out in Paris and London* (1933). Like many in the 1930s, Orwell embraced socialism, which he advocated for the rest of his life. But his experiences during the Spanish Civil War—he went to report on the war and remained to fight on the side of the Republicans—left him disenchanted with the Communists, who had attempted to squeeze out their rivals in the Republican forces. His disgust with Soviet communism informs his two most popular works, the novels *Animal Farm* (1945) and *1984* (1949). He died of tuberculosis shortly after the publication of *1984*.

Malloy Owen (*b. 1996*) Owen recently graduated from the University of Chicago, where he studied philosophy and for several years contributed to the school's undergraduate political blog *The Gate.* He interned at *The American Conservative* magazine. Owen taught high school in Arizona for two years before becoming a research assistant at the Institute for Advanced Studies in Culture in June 2020.

Leonard Pitts (*b. 1957*) Pitts grew up in South Central Los Angeles. He entered the University of Southern California at the age of fifteen and graduated in 1977 with a degree in English. He embarked on a career as a freelance writer, often writing music criticism for a variety of periodicals, and even wrote for Casey Kasem's popular radio show *American Top 40*. In 1991, he went to work as music critic for the *Miami Herald*, winning numerous awards, until, in 1995, he was promoted to columnist. A series of columns he wrote from his own experience was published as a book, *Becoming Dad: Black Men and the Journey to Fatherhood*, in 1999. His column was syndicated by Knight-Ridder, and he rocketed to national prominence because of his widely acclaimed essay the day after 9/11. Today, his column is circulated in 150 newspapers throughout the country. He won the Pulitzer Prize for Commentary in 2004.

Ronald Reagan (*1911–2004*) Born in Tampico, Illinois, and raised in nearby Dixon, Reagan grew up in near poverty, the son of an unsuccessful and alcoholic shoe salesman. He attended Eureka College and after graduation (in 1932) worked as a radio announcer and sportscaster. In 1937, he had a successful screen test and was thereafter cast in a series of movies as a wholesome, genial fellow. During World War II, Reagan served at an army film unit in California and never saw active duty. He was president of the Screen Actors Guild from 1947 to 1952. Initially a Democrat, he supported the California senatorial campaign of Richard Nixon (1950) and the presidential candidacies of Dwight Eisenhower (1952, 1956) and Richard Nixon (1960) before registering as a Republican in 1962. He was elected governor of California (1966, 1970) on a promise to make government more efficient and accountable and was elected president (1980, 1984) on a platform both fiscally and socially conservative. In 1994, Reagan announced that he had been diagnosed with Alzheimer's disease and withdrew from public life.

Chief Seattle (*c. 1790–1866*) Chief of several Puget Sound tribes, Seattle ceded Indian lands to white settlers by signing the Port Elliott treaty (1855) and moved his people to a reservation. Grateful for the chief's protection during a period of Indian uprisings (1855–1858), local residents named their town after him.

Margaret Chase Smith (*1897–1995*) Margaret Chase was born in Maine to working-class parents (barber, waitress). After graduating high school, she went to work for a small-town newspaper. Always involved in women's and professional organizations, Smith entered politics in 1930 and was elected to the U.S. House of Representatives in 1936, where she served until she was elected to the U.S. Senate in 1948. In 1964, she ran for the Republican nomination for president, which she lost to Barry Goldwater. Considered a moderate, Smith is best remembered today for being the first member of Congress of either party to condemn her fellow Republican senator Joseph McCarthy and his witch hunt for communists.

Sonia Sotomayor (*b. 1954*) Sotomayor's parents, who are both Puerto Rican, immigrated to New York and settled in the Bronx. She grew up in working-class neighborhoods, including, for a time, a public housing project. Sotomayor attended Catholic schools before earning her undergraduate degree from Princeton and her law degree from Yale University in 1979. She started her career in the district attorney's office in New York before moving into private practice, focusing on international trade. By the late 1980s, she was accepting appointments to public agencies and boards, which increased her profile. With bipartisan support, in 1991 she was appointed by President George H. W. Bush to the federal bench for the Southern District of New York, one of the more prominent federal courts. In 1997 she was elevated to the U.S. Court of Appeals for the Second District, and in 2009, President Barack Obama nominated her to the U.S. Supreme Court. Sotomayor is the first Latina U.S. Supreme Court justice.

Elizabeth Cady Stanton (*1815–1902*) Born to affluent parents in Johnstown, New York, Stanton was educated at Johnstown Academy and the rigorous Troy Female Seminary before studying law at her father's office, where she learned of legal discrimination against women. She married the abolitionist Henry Stanton in 1840 and that same year met Lucretia Mott at the World Anti-Slavery Convention in London, where several women abolitionists were refused recognition. Her experience in her father's office and in London prompted her to begin speaking publicly about women's rights. Stanton's activism was instrumental in the passage of New York's 1848 Married Women's Property Act. Together with Mott, she organized the first women's rights convention (1848), and she worked closely with Susan B. Anthony (from 1851 on) to liberalize divorce laws, give women greater control over their earnings and their children, and extend the vote to women. She helped found the National Woman Suffrage Association (later the National American Women's Suffrage Association) and was its president from 1869 to 1892. She also wrote the amendment extending the vote to women that was presented to Congress at every session from 1878 until women finally won the franchise in 1920.

Dana Stevens (*b. 1966*) Stevens's background is in comparative literature—she earned a PhD in that field from the University of California, Berkeley, in 2001, writing her dissertation on the Portuguese poet Fernando Pessoa. Since 2003, she has been a movie and television critic for *Slate* magazine. Stevens wrote a popular blog, *High Sign*, using the pen name Liz Penn. In addition to articles for various media, including the *New York Times* and *The Atlantic* magazine, she has written a book on the silent film actor Buster Keaton, soon to be released by Simon and Schuster.

Jonathan Swift (*1667–1745*) Born in Dublin, Ireland, to English parents, Swift attended Trinity College in Dublin, but fled to England following the Revolution of 1688, the abdication of James II, and the subsequent upheaval in Ireland. From 1689 to 1699, he was secretary to Sir William Temple (a distant relative), took religious orders, and wrote *The Tale of a Tub*, one of his most successful satires. After Sir William's death, Swift returned to Ireland as secretary to the Earl of Berkeley but visited England on extended trips and gained renown for his satiric writings and personal charm. On his visits to England he was drawn into politics, and by 1710 he was the Tories' chief pamphleteer. In 1713, his services were rewarded with the deanship of Saint Patrick's Cathedral in Dublin. When George I took the throne in 1714, however, the Whigs gained ascendance, and Swift returned permanently to Ireland. In this period Swift wrote extensively about the social and economic problems of Ireland, publishing the "Drapier's Letters" (1724–25) and "A Modest Proposal" (anonymously in 1729). His greatest work, *Gulliver's Travels*, was published in 1726.

Amy Tan (*b. 1952*) Tan was born in Oakland, California, and raised in the Bay Area. Her father, educated in Beijing, emigrated to the United States in 1947; her mother emigrated shortly before the Communists came to power in 1949, leaving behind three daughters from a previous marriage. When Tan was fourteen, both her father and her brother died of brain tumors, and her mother moved the family to Europe briefly. She attended a number of colleges before getting her BA and MA in linguistics from San Jose State University. In 1985, Tan wrote a short story titled "Rules of the Game" for a writing workshop; that story later became part of her extremely successful first book, *The Joy Luck Club* (1989). Tan often writes about the awkward position in which second-generation Americans find themselves, poised between the world of their parents and that of their peers.

Deborah Tannen (*b. 1945*) Partially deaf from a childhood illness, Tannen, a Brooklyn native, took an early interest in nonverbal signs, which she began to study formally as a student of linguistics. She got her PhD in linguistics from the University of California, Berkeley, and has studied and taught this subject ever since as a fellow at the Center for Advanced Study in the Behavioral Sciences in Stanford, California, at the Institute for Advanced Study at Princeton, and in her current position as University Professor and professor of linguistics at Georgetown University. Her books *You Just Don't Understand! Women and Men in Conversation* (1990) and *You're Wearing That? Understanding Mothers and Daughters in Conversation* (2006) were best-sellers. Tannen also writes poetry, fiction, and personal essays.

Henry David Thoreau (*1817–1862*) A native of Concord, Massachusetts, Thoreau attended Harvard College and in 1838 founded a progressive school with his brother John. But the death of his brother in 1842 and his friendship with Ralph Waldo Emerson, founder of the Transcendentalist movement, led him to poetry and nature writing, so in 1842 Thoreau moved to New York to cultivate literary society. His failure there, however, pushed him back to Concord in 1843. In 1845 he embarked on a two-year quest for self-sufficiency and a bond with nature that he described in *Walden* (1854). On his return from Walden Pond, he took up surveying and running his family's pencil-making business, and he committed himself to the abolition of slavery. He worked on the Underground Railroad, wrote and lectured on the evils of slavery, and adopted John Brown as his ideal. With the failure of Brown's raid on Harpers Ferry in 1859, Thoreau broke down. He died three years later, probably of tuberculosis. While little appreciated in his own lifetime, Thoreau is now recognized as one of the most important members of the Transcendentalist movement and the forerunner of nature writers like Edward Abbey.

Greta Thunberg (*b. 2003*) Thunberg's mother is an opera singer and her father an actor in Sweden, where she has lived her whole life. Thunberg rocketed to prominence in 2018 when she began a one-person school strike to raise awareness about climate change and induce Swedish officials to impose public policy reducing carbon emissions. Her protest went viral on social media, and she became an international spokesperson for her generation: for instance, she was invited to speak at the 2018 United Nations Climate Change Conference. Thunberg has also spoken publicly about being diagnosed with Asperger's syndrome, obsessive compulsive disorder, and selective mutism. She credits these conditions with giving her moral clarity on sustainability: "we autistic are the normal ones, and the rest of the people are pretty strange."

Elizabeth Warren (*b. 1949*) Warren grew up in Oklahoma on the lower edge of the middle class: her parents both worked in department stores, and she started waitressing when she was thirteen years old. She dropped out of college and got married, but she later earned a bachelor's degree (University of Houston). She earned her law degree (Rutgers University) while raising a young daughter. She taught in a succession of law schools (Rutgers, University of Houston, University of Texas, University of Pennsylvania, and finally Harvard University), where she developed her expertise in bankruptcy and commercial law. She began her public service as an advisor to various congressional commissions, which culminated with her crucial contributions to the creation of the Consumer Financial Protection Bureau in 2010. As a progressive, Warren was elected in 2013 to the U.S. Senate, where she continues to represent Massachusetts. Warren unsuccessfully ran for the Democratic nomination to the presidency in 2020.

*

Glossary

abstract brief summary of a scholarly article, usually in one paragraph; abstracts are often included in database entries for articles, or as preliminary material at the head of an article.

accuracy the quality ascribed to evidence in an inductive argument when it is free from error. See *induction.*

ad hominem the fallacy in ethical argument of attempting to discredit a logical argument by attacking the character of its author. For example:

> We can't expect this policy to work; the congressman sponsoring it doesn't even have a college degree.

Logical arguments should be evaluated on their own merits, not on the basis of their author's background or character.

analysis/analyze to break an argument down into its parts. Inductive arguments have two parts: evidence and conclusion. Deductive arguments have three parts: major premise(s), minor premise(s), and conclusion.

anecdote/anecdotal evidence the testimony of a single person or a few individuals, usually conveyed in a brief story. When used in an inductive argument, anecdotal evidence should fairly represent other cases.

bandwagon appeal a fallacy of pathetic argument in which readers are persuaded to adopt a position because that position is popular.

cherry-pick to exclude on purpose evidence that does not support the conclusion in an inductive argument.

common ground principles shared by the writer and the reader of an argument; the writer should use common ground for the major premises of a deductive argument

conclusion see *deduction, induction.*

deduction/deductive reasoning "top-down" reasoning in which one begins with a statement of general applicability (the major premise) and a statement concerning a particular case (the minor premise), and from these draws a conclusion. For example:

> *Major premise:* Cats are smarter than dogs.
> *Minor premises:* Felix is a cat, and Goofy is a dog.
> *Conclusion:* Felix is smarter than Goofy.

(Note that deductive arguments can have many premises.) You consider an argument to be true if you agree with its premises. You consider an argument to be valid if you think the conclusion logically follows from the premises. To be considered sound, an argument must be both true and valid.

discourse a network of verbal communication; for example, academic discourse is the network of communication shared by scholars, including journal articles, conference presentations, textbooks, administrative reports, etc.

discourse community a group of people who, because they share similar goals, have developed a way of communicating effectively with each other and a set of conventions that determines for them which arguments are and which are not persuasive.

either/or fallacy the fallacy in logical reasoning of excluding all but two choices. For example:

> If this city wants to balance its budget, it's got to raise taxes. The only alternative is to cut services to the bone.

Such arguments are seductive, but they typically depend on oversimplifying the situation.

enthymeme a deductive argument that suppresses one of its premises. For example:

The United States had the best women's soccer team in the world in 2019 because it won the World Cup.

Major premise (unstated): The World Cup is a contest between the best soccer teams in the world.

Minor premise: The United States won the women's World Cup in 2019.

Conclusion: The United States had the best women's soccer team in the world in 2019.

ethical argument/ethos the methods of self-presentation by which a writer establishes their character, and the use of those methods to persuade.

exigence the particular circumstances that summon a piece of rhetoric; the urgency that sparks the writer/speaker to persuade the reader/audience.

fallacies ways in which arguments can go wrong. See *ad hominem, bandwagon appeal, either/or fallacy, false analogy, hasty generalization,* and *straw man argument.*

false analogy a fallacy in logical reasoning in which the writer draws conclusions about one case by comparing it to another, dissimilar case. For example:

Puerto Rico is bound to become a state eventually. After all, Alaska did.

Alaska and Puerto Rico are too dissimilar for the history of one to give much insight into the future of the other.

falsity the quality ascribed to a deductive argument when one or more of its premises are untrue or to an inductive argument when some or all of the evidence it offers is inaccurate. See *deduction, induction.*

genre a form of writing specific to a discourse community. Literacy narratives, arguments, and even social media posts constitute genres.

hasty generalization a fallacy in logical reasoning in which an inductive conclusion is drawn from insufficient evidence.

induction/inductive reasoning "bottom-up" reasoning in which one begins by examining a number of individual cases and from these draws a conclusion—some assertion of general applicability—that governs all similar cases. For example:

> The air war against Germany could not win World War II, the air war against North Vietnam could not win the Vietnam War, and the air war against Iraq could not win the Gulf War. In all of these wars, ground troops were required for victory. Therefore, bombing the enemy will never by itself win a war.

The evidence in an inductive argument must be accurate, relevant, sufficient, and representative. The evidence is inaccurate if any of the cases cited are false. It is irrelevant if it does not support the stated conclusion. It is insufficient if the conclusion is drawn from too small a sample of cases. It is unrepresentative if the cases cited belong to a narrow subgroup of all the cases. Because the example above ignores an important recent case—the war in Kosovo—the argument is faulty because the evidence is unrepresentative.

logical argument/logos the methods by which we reason; the two types of logical arguments are deductive and inductive.

major premise see *deduction*.

minor premise see *deduction*.

paraphrase putting someone else's words into your own words; paraphrase is a common way to present one's research, and it must be documented with citation as if it were quotation.

pathetic argument/pathos the methods by which a writer manipulates the emotions of the audience in order to persuade.

peer review the editorial process through which most manuscripts published in scholarly journals and books must pass; the "peers" are experts in the appropriate academic field, and they scrutinize the manuscript for errors in fact, method, and logic, often asking authors to address certain deficiencies before resubmitting their manuscripts for eventual publication.

persuade/persuasion to get the readers/audience to change their mind about something or to do something they would not otherwise have done.

plagiarism using someone else's ideas, arguments, evidence, etc. in a piece of writing without giving that person appropriate credit.

quotation using someone else's exact words in a piece of your own writing.

recursive literally "circling back"; the repetition of stages in the process of writing a paper.

refutation the part of an essay that demonstrates the flaws in one's opponent's argument.

relevance the quality ascribed to evidence in an inductive argument if that evidence supports the conclusion.

representative in an inductive argument, a quality ascribed to evidence that considers both cases that support the conclusion and those that do not support it. See *induction.*

review of literature a standard section of most academic writing that summarizes what previous scholars have written about a subject.

rhetoric the art of persuasion, using logical, ethical, and pathetic arguments.

skeptical the attitude of a reader who disagrees with the writer's position before reading the writer's argument.

sound argument a deductive argument that has true premises and valid reasoning.

straw man argument a fallacy in which one refutes an argument never offered by your disputant; usually the argument refuted is an absurd exaggeration or falsification of what the disputant actually asserted.

strong argument an inductive argument with persuasive evidence.

sufficiency the quality ascribed to evidence in an inductive argument in which a large enough number of cases has been cited to support the conclusion. See *induction.*

thesis the assertion that expresses what a writer is trying to persuade a reader to believe; the main point of an essay.

truth the quality ascribed to a deductive argument when its premises are factually correct. See *deduction.*

unsound argument a deductive argument that is either invalid (the premises do not logically support the conclusion) or false (one or more premises is disbelieved by the reader/audience).

validity the quality ascribed to a deductive argument when the conclusion follows logically from the premises. See *deduction.*

weak argument an inductive argument with inadequate evidence; that is, the reader/audience considers the evidence to be irrelevant to the conclusion, or inaccurate, or insufficient, or unrepresentative, or some combination of those flaws.

✶

Permissions Acknowledgments

Photos

Page 36: Courtesy of the U.S. National Library of Medicine; **p. 243:** Panther Media GmbH/Alamy Stock Photo; **p. 244:** Murat Baysan/Shutterstock; **p. 245 (top):** Goncalo Diniz/ Alamy Stock Photo; **p. 245 (bottom):** Jim Williams, NASA GSFC Scientific Visualization Studio, and the Landsat 7 Science Team; **p. 246 (top):** NASA/JPL-Caltech; **p. 246 (bottom):** Chumash Maxim/ Shutterstock; **p. 247 (top):** NASA/Goddard Space Flight Center Scientific Visualization Studio, The Blue Marble data is courtesy of Reto Stockli (NASA/GSFC); **p. 247 (bottom):** FotoKina/Shutterstock; **p. 248:** Ilsa Kuffner/USGS.

Text

ACLU: "Speech on Campus," ACLU, May 17, 2017; https://www.aclu.org/other/speech-campus. Reprinted with permission.

Michelle Alexander: Excerpt from *The New Jim Crow* – Copyright © 2010, 2012 by Michelle Alexander. Reprinted by permission of The New Press. www.thenewpress.com.

Maya Angelou: "Chapter 23 (Graduation)" from *I Know Why the Caged Bird Sings* by Maya Angelou, copyright © 1969 and renewed 1997 by Maya Angelou. Used by permission of Random House, an imprint and division of Penguin Random House LLC. All rights reserved.

APA: Copyright 2015 by the American Psychological Association. Reprinted with permission. The official citation that should be used in referencing this material is American Psychological Association. (2015). Resolution on Violent Video Games. http://www.apa.org/about/policy/violentvideo-games.aspx. No further reproduction or distribution is permitted without written permission from the American Psychological Association.

Kwame Appiah: From *Cosmopolitanism: Ethics in a World of Strangers* by Kwame Anthony Appiah. Copyright © 2006 by Kwame Anthony Appiah. Used by permission of W. W. Norton & Company, Inc.

Anne Applebaum: "The Torture Myth," *The Washington Post*, January 12, 2005. Copyright © 2005. Reprinted by permission of Anne Applebaum.

James Baldwin: From "Notes of a Native Son" by James Baldwin. Copyright © 1955, renewed 1983, by James Baldwin. Reprinted by permission of Beacon Press, Boston.

Deborah Brandt: "Sponsors of Literacy." *College Composition and Communication*, 49.2 (1998): 165–185. Copyright 1998 by the National Council of Teachers of English. Reprinted with permission.

David Brooks: "Harvard's False Path to Wisdom." From *The New York Times*, June 17, 2019. © 2019 The New York Times. All rights reserved. Used under license. NYTimes.com.

Rachel Carson: "A Fable for Tomorrow" from *Silent Spring* by Rachel Carson. Copyright © 1962 by Rachel L. Carson, renewed 1990 by Roger Christie. Reprinted by permission of Houghton Mifflin Harcourt Publishing Company. All rights reserved. And by permission of Francis Collin, Trustee. All copying, including electronic, or redistribution of this text, is expressly forbidden.

Emily Chamlee-Wright: "The Need to Presume Good Faith in Campus Conversations and Debates," by Emily Chamlee-Wright. Originally published in *Inside Higher Ed*, August 13, 2019. Reprinted by permission of Emily Chamlee-Wright.

Amy Chua: "The Chinese Mother," from *Battle Hymn of the Tiger Mother* by Amy Chua, copyright © 2011 by Amy Chua. Used by permission of Penguin Press, an imprint of Penguin Publishing Group, a division of Penguin Random House LLC. All rights reserved.

Ta-Nehisi Coates: "In Defense of a Loaded Word." From *The New York Times*, November 23, 2013 © 2013 *The New York Times*. All rights reserved. Used under license. NYTimes.com.

Kwame Dawes: "Re-appropriating Cultural Appropriation," by Kwame Dawes. First published in *Fuse Magazine* (Summer 1993), 7–15. Reprinted by permission of the author.

Barbara Ehrenreich: Excerpt from "Evaluation" from the book *Nickel and Dimed: On (Not) Getting By in America* by Barbara Ehrenreich. Copyright © 2001 by Barbara Ehrenreich. Used by permission of Henry Holt and Company, LLC.

Tavi Gevinson: "Editor's Letter" from *Rookie Magazine* Issue 61: Infinity by Tavi Gevinson. Copyright © 2016 by Tavi Gevinson, used by permission of The Wylie Agency LLC.

Doris Kearns Goodwin: *From Leadership in Turbulent Times* by Doris Kearns Goodwin. Copyright © 2018 by Blithedale Productions, Inc. Reprinted with the permission of Simon & Schuster, Inc. All rights reserved.

Komysha Hassan: "Righting History," by Komysha Hassan. Reprinted by permission of the author.

Zoë Heller: "Rape on the Campus." This essay first appeared in the *New York Review of Books* in February 2015. Reprinted by permission of the author.

Debra Humphreys and Patrick Kelly: Excerpted with permission from *How Liberal Arts and Science Majors Fare in Employment*, by Debra Humphreys and Patrick Kelly. Copyright 2014 by the Association of American Colleges and Universities. Contains figures from Georgetown Center of Education and the Workforce, "The College Advantage: Weathering the Economic Storm." Reprinted with permission.

Noel Ignatiev: Excerpt from *How the Irish Became White* Copyright © 1995, 2009 Noel Ignatiev, reprinted by permission of the publisher (Taylor & Francis Group).

Martin Luther King Jr.: "Letter from Birmingham Jail." Reprinted by arrangement with The Heirs to the Estate of Martin Luther King Jr., c/o Writers House as agent for the proprietor New York, NY. Copyright © 1963 Dr. Martin Luther King Jr., © renewed 1991 Coretta Scott King.

Maxine Hong Kingston: "No Name Woman" from *The Woman Warrior: Memoirs of a Girlhood Among Ghosts* by Maxine Hong Kingston, copyright © 1975, 1976 by Maxine Hong Kingston. Used by permission of Alfred A. Knopf, an imprint of the Knopf Doubleday Publishing Group, a division of Penguin Random House LLC. All rights reserved.

Michael Kinsley: "The Intellectual Free Lunch." © 1995 by Michael Kinsley. First Printed in *The New Yorker*. Reprinted by permission of ICM Partners.

Elizabeth Kolbert: "Can Carbon-dioxide Removal Save the World?" *The New Yorker*, November 13, 2017. © Conde Nast. Reprinted with permission.

Paul Krugman: "Why We're in a New Gilded Age," by Paul Krugman. Originally published in *The New York Review of Books*, May 8, 2014. Reprinted with permission. Includes figure: "After Tax Rate of Return vs. Growth Rate at the World Level, from Antiquity until 2100" by Thomas Piketty. http://piketty.pse.ens.fr/fr/capital21c. Reprinted with permission.

The Dalai Lama, with Rasmas Hougaard: "The Dalai Lama on Why Leaders Should be Mindful, Selfless and Compassionate," *Harvard Business Review*, February 20, 2019. Reprinted by permission of Harvard Business Publishing.

Valeria Luiselli: "The Wild West Meets the Southern Border" was first published in *The New Yorker* © 2019. Reprinted by permission of Valeria Luiselli and Aragi Inc. All rights reserved.

Louis Menand: From *The Marketplace of Ideas: Reform and Resistance in the American University* by Louis Menand. Copyright © 2010 by Louis Menand. Used by permission of W. W. Norton & Company, Inc.

N. Scott Momaday: "An American Land Ethic" from *The Man Made of Words*. Copyright © 1997 by N. Scott Momaday. Reprinted by permission of the author.

Carla R. Monroe: "Why Are 'Bad Boys' Always Black?: Causes of Disproportionality in School Discipline and Recommendations for Change," *The Clearing House: A Journal of Educational Strategies, Issues and Ideas*, Vol. 79, No. 1, Sept. 1, 2005, pp. 45–50. Copyright © 2005 Routledge, reprinted by permission of the publisher (Taylor & Francis Ltd, http://www.tandfonline.com).

Susan Moller Okin: "Part I" from *Is Multiculturalism Bad for Women?* Edited by Joshua Cohen, Matthew Howard, and Martha C. Nussbaum (Princeton: Princeton University Press, 1999). © 1999 by Princeton University Press. Reprinted by permission of Princeton University Press.

George Orwell: "Politics and the English Language from *A Collection of Essays* by George Orwell. Copyright © 1946, renewed 1974 by Sonia Brownell Orwell. Reprinted by permission of Houghton Mifflin Harcourt Publishing Company. All rights reserved.

Mallow Owen: "Funding the Humanities," by Malloy Owen, from *The American Conservative*, March 28, 2017. © The American Conservative. Reprinted with permission.

Leonard Pitts Jr.: "Fox Faux News Forces Rare Apology," from *The Miami Herald*, January 24, 2015 © 2015 McClatchy. All rights reserved. Used under license. https://www.miamiherald.com

William D. Ruckelshaus, Lee M. Thomas, William K. Reilly and Christine Todd Whitman: "A Republican Case for Climate Action," *The New York Times*, August 1, 2013. Reprinted with permission.

Sonia Sotomayor: "Raising the Bar: Latino and Latina Presence in the Judiciary and the Struggle for Representation 'A Latina Judge's Voice.'" © 2002 by the Regents of the University of California. Reprinted from the La Raza Law Journal 13 Berkeley La Raza L.J.87 (2002). By permission of the Regents of the University of California.

Dana Stevens: "Waiting for Thanos." From *Slate*, April 24, 2019. © 2019 The Slate Group. All rights reserved. Used under license. Slate.com

Amy Tan: "Mother Tongue." Copyright © 1990 by Amy Tan. First appeared in *The Threepenny Review*. Reprinted by permission of the author and the Sandra Dijkstra Literary Agency.

Deborah Tannen: "The Triumph of the Yell." *The New York Times*, January 14, 1994. Copyright Deborah Tannen. Reprinted with permission.

Greta Thunberg: "The World is Waking Up (UN General Assembly, NYC 9/23/19)" from *No One is Too Small to Make a Difference* by Greta Thunberg, copyright © 2018, 2019 by Greta Thunberg. Used by permission of Penguin Books, an imprint of Penguin Publishing Group, a division of Penguin Random House LLC. All rights reserved.

Elizabeth Warren: "A New Farm Economy," by Elizabeth Warren. Originally published on Medium.com, August 7, 2019. Reprinted with permission.

Malcolm X: Excerpt from *Malcolm X Speaks*, by Malcolm X, published by Pathfinder Press in 1989. Copyright © 1965, 1989 by Betty Shabazz and Pathfinder Press. Reprinted by permission.